The Business of Fashion

DESIGNING, MANUFACTURING, AND MARKETING

2nd Edition

Leslie Davis Burns
Nancy O. Bryant
Oregon State University

Fairchild Publications, Inc.
NEW YORK

Executive Editor: Olga Kontzias
Editor: Sylvia L. Weber
Assistant Editor: Beth Applebome
Copyeditor: Betsy Feist
Art Director: Nataliya Gurshman
Production Manager: Priscilla Taguer

Cover and Interior Design: Howard Levy Design

Second Printing 2005

Copyright © 2002
Fairchild Publications, Inc.

First Edition, Copyright © 1997 Fairchild Publications

Library of Congress Catalog Card Number: 2001087114

ISBN: 1-56367-182-4

GST R 133004424

Printed in the United States of America

Contents

Extended Contents

Preface

Since the publication of the first edition of *The Business of Fashion: Designing, Manufacturing, and Marketing*, the textile, apparel, accessories, home fashions, and retailing industries have continued to undergo tremendous change. Quick Response strategies have evolved into supply chain management; Web-based business-to-business and business-to-consumer communications and commerce have grown; mass customization is now a reality; and retailing venues continue to expand. As such, the second edition of this book attempts to capture the dynamics of the fashion industry by emphasizing the technological changes, organizational changes, and changes in the global dimensions of its various components.

The Business of Fashion focuses on the organization and operation of the U.S. fashion industry—how fashion apparel and accessories and home fashions are designed, manufactured, marketed, and distributed. As we investigate this ever-changing industry, it is important to set current strategies within their historical context. Thus, Chapter 1 begins with a history of the U.S. textile and apparel industry, from its inception in the late 1700s to the development and implementation of

Quick Response and supply chain management strategies. Once this historical context is set, we turn to current organization structures of and forms of competition among companies within the fashion industry. Chapter 2 discusses types of company ownership within the fashion business, including sole proprietorships, partnerships, and corporations. Because of the prevalence of licensing, licensing contracts, and the advantages and disadvantages of licensing are discussed. Marketing channels within the industry (i.e., direct, limited, and extended) as well as marketing channel integration also are outlined and explained. The chapter ends with an overview of the laws affecting the textile and apparel industries, including laws protecting inventions and designs and laws related to business practices.

Chapter 3 outlines the organization and operation of the U.S. textile industry—that is, the designing, manufacturing, and marketing of fabrics used in the production of apparel and home fashions. We follow textile production from color forecasting and fiber processing through the marketing of seasonal lines of fabrics. Recent developments and issues within the industry, including textile trade, supply chain management strategies, and environmental issues, provide a basis for our understanding of future trends in the textile industry.

Chapter 4 focuses on the general classifications and organizational structures of apparel companies that produce men's, women's, and children's apparel. Comparisons between ready-to-wear and couture, among types of producers, among classifications of apparel brand names, and among wholesale price zones reinforce an appreciation of the complexities of the apparel industry. The major divisions within apparel organizations (merchandising, design development, operations, sales/marketing, advertising/sales promotion, and finance and information technology) are introduced. Trade associations and trade publications also are introduced in this chapter.

Chapter 5 begins a four-chapter sequence on the creation and marketing of fashion apparel. This sequence follows an apparel line/collection through the various stages of research, design development and style selection, and marketing. Chapter 5 focuses on the various forms of research conducted prior to the development of the line/collection: consumer research, product research, market analysis, and fashion research. The chapter explains the importance of accurately profiling the company's target customer. Chapter 6 highlights the design stage—design inspirations, designing for the market niche, planning the line, design sketches, and writing garment specification sheets. The creation of an apparel line continues in Chapter 7, which discusses design development and style selection, including the development of first patterns, sewing of prototypes, initial cost estimates, and selection of styles for the final line. This chapter also describes product development for two growing segments of the industry: private label and store brand merchandise. The discussion concludes at the stage when the final line is marketed to retail buyers. Chapter 8 describes locations of and roles played by marts and trade shows in facilitating the marketing of apparel. Next, it discusses how apparel is sold through corporate selling and through sales representatives. The chapter ends with an overview of marketing strategies used by apparel companies in the distribution and promotion of their lines. Throughout this sequence of events in the creation and marketing of an apparel line, the chapters highlight new technological developments including computer-aided design, business-to-business Web-based communications, global perspectives, and organizational changes within the industry.

Chapter 9 begins a four-chapter sequence on the production and distribution of apparel. Preproduction processes, including determining production orders, factoring, ordering production fabrics, pattern finalization, pattern grading, making the production marker, and production cutting are described. Chapter 10 outlines the sourcing options for apparel production and the criteria used by apparel companies in making sourcing decisions. Issues surrounding domestic and foreign production of apparel, such as sweatshops and human rights, are also discussed. Chapter 11 explores the various methods by which apparel is produced, focusing on new technological advancement in these methods. Manufacturing environments including mass production, short-cycle production, and mass customization are explained. Next, production sewing systems and technological developments in production equipment are described. The chapter ends with a summary of product finishing and the creation of floor ready merchandise. Once produced, the apparel is distributed (often through distribution centers) to retailers. Chapter 12 summarizes distribution strategies and processes used by apparel companies. A description of the various types of store and nonstore retailers ends this chapter. Quick Response and supply chain management strategies are also highlighted throughout this discussion of production and distribution.

Our focus turns to accessories and home fashions in Chapters 13 and 14. A strong relationship exists between these industries and the textile and apparel industries. Thus an overview of the organization and operation of the primary accessories industries is included in Chapter 13. Chapter 14 introduces the various facets of the home fashion industry with specific focus on the use of textiles in the production of home fashions such as sheets, towels, and draperies.

In introducing students to this dynamic, multifaceted business, the book incorporates real-world examples from its component industries. Career profiles are also included at the end of each chapter to give readers a sampling of the many career opportunities throughout the fashion industry. Other end-of-chapter features that help students prepare for their own entry into the fashion business include chapter summaries, lists of key terms, discussion question, and references.

Many people have assisted with the development of this book, and we would like to thank them for their time, effort, and support. Leslie Burns would like to thank her students, former students, and colleagues at Oregon State University, who have shared ideas and resources in the development of the book. She would also like to thank her husband, Chris, for his patience and infinite support through the project. Leslie particularly appreciates her coauthor, Nancy Bryant, who brought extensive technical expertise and knowledge of the apparel industry to this work and was a true collaborator throughout the writing process.

Nancy Bryant would like to express her appreciation first to her coauthor, Leslie Burns, whose initial concept and direction for this text brought it into existence. Her knowledge of marketing and merchandising provided this text with the breadth necessary to reflect the industry as it operates now and will operate in the future. Her leadership through the publication process was invaluable. Nancy would also like to thank her former students for their continual sharing of information about the apparel industry and especially Tammy Wilson Sutter for her comments. Many other professional contacts in the apparel industry have also most willingly shared their expertise. The support of her colleagues at Oregon State University, her family, and most especially her husband, Dick, is deeply appreciated.

We wish to thank the following readers and reviewers on the two editions of the book: Ardis Koester, Cheryl Jordan, Carol Caughey, and Elaine Pedersen, Oregon State University; and Pamela Ulrich, Auburn University. Readers selected by the publisher were also very helpful. They include Cindi Baker, Berkeley College; Martha Baker, University of Massachusetts-Amherst; Mary Boni, Kwantlen University College; and Robert L. Woods, Berkeley College.

Leslie Davis Burns
Nancy O. Bryant
Oregon State University

Credits for Figures

Chapter 1

P.2 Courtesy of [TC]², Textile/Clothing Technology Corporation, Cary, NC. **1.1-1.11:** Bettman/Corbis. **1.12:** Courtesy of Fairchild Publications, Inc. **1.13:** Courtesy of VF Playwear, Inc. **1.14:** Courtesy of [TC]², Textile/Clothing Technology Corporation, Cary, NC. **1.16:** Crafted with Pride in USA Council. **1.17:** © Sandia National Laboratories.

Chapter 2

2.1: Courtesy of Federated Department Stores, Inc.; Celanese Acetate; DuPont; Milliken & Company; and Levi Strauss & Co. **2.4 (left):** Courtesy of Franco Apparel Group. Logo: Kid Athlete. **2.5:** Courtesy of Tencel Inc.; Lacoste; Guess? © 2001; and Nike, Inc. **2.6:** Courtesy of Levi Strauss & Co. **2.8:** GARFIELD © Paws, Inc., Reprinted with permission of UNIVERSAL PRESS SYNDICATE. All rights reserved.

Chapter 3

3.1: *Apparel Manufacturing* by Glock/Kunz © 2000, Reprinted by permission of Pearson Education, Inc., Upper Saddle River, NJ 07458. **3.5:** The Seal of Cotton is a Registered Service Mark/Trademark of Cotton Incorporated. **3.6:** The Woolmark Company. **3.7:** Mohair Council of America. **3.8:** The Seal of Cotton is a Registered Service Mark/Trademark of Cotton Incorporated. **3.9:** Courtesy of DuPont. **3.10:** © Courtesy of the Color Association of the US, New York. **3.11:** Pendleton Woolen Mills. **3.14:** Courtesy of Fairchild Publications, Inc. **3.15:** American Textile Manufacturers Institute. **3.16:** Lectra. **3.17:** American Textile Manufacturers Institute.

3.19: Life Cycle of Fortrel® EcoSpun® is the property of Wellman, Inc.

Chapter 4

4.1: Courtesy of Fairchild Publications, Inc. **4.2 and 4.7:** Jantzen Inc. **4.8:** Gerber Technology, Inc. **4.10:** Courtesy of Bobbin Group. **4.12:** Courtesy of Fairchild Publications, Inc.

Chapter 5

5.2: Pendleton Woolen Mills. **5.5:** Courtesy of Fairchild Publications, Inc.; **(left)**, © J. Aquino; **(center)**, © George Chinsee; **(right)**, © Tom Iannaccone. **5.7:** Courtesy of Promostyl.

Chapter 6

6.3 (top left): National Museum of American History, Smithsonian Institution. **6.3 (bottom left):** Bettman/Corbis. **6.3 (bottom right):** Courtesy of Fairchild Publications, Inc. **6.4 (left):** Courtesy of the Staten Island Historical Society. **6.4 (center):** Fine Arts Museum of San Francisco, Gift of Mrs. Eloise Heidland, 1982.18.1, Hat gift of Mr. E.J. Larson, Photograph by Kaz Tsuruta. **6.4 (right):** Courtesy of Fairchild Publications, Inc.; Photographer: Robert Mitra. **6.5 (left):** The Royal Collection © 2000, Her Majesty Queen Elizabeth II. **6.5 (right):** Courtesy of Fairchild Publications, Inc. **6.6 (left):** Courtesy of Fairchild Publications, Inc. **6.6 (right):** Murray Warner Collection of Oriental Art, University of Oregon Museum of Art. **6.7:** Jantzen Inc. **6.9:** Jantzen Inc. **6.11:** Courtesy of Fairchild Publications, Inc. **6.13-6.15:** KaratCAD Inc. **6.16:** Gerber Technology, Inc.

6.17: Lectra. **6.19:** Bettman/Corbis. **6.20:** Jantzen Inc.

Chapter 7
7.2: Pendleton Woolen Mills—Sandra S. Arditi/Designer. **7.3:** Kristen Kasper, Akimbo. **7.4 and 7.7:** Gerber Technology, Inc. **7.8 and 7.9:** Jantzen Inc. **7.11 and 7.12:** Jantzen Inc. **7.13:** The Gerry Group. **7.14:** Courtesy of Macy's East.

Chapter 8
8.1: Courtesy of the Bobbin Group. **8.3, 8.4, and 8.8:** Courtesy of Fairchild Publications, Inc. **8.9:** Spitfire Studios.

Chapter 9
9.1: Gerber Technology, Inc. **9.2:** Jantzen Inc. **9.3:** Spring Industries/Dairy Kingdom. **9.4:** Kristen Sandberg. **9.5:** Apparel Business Systems, Inc. **9.6:** Union Special Corporation. **9.7:** Gerber Technology, Inc. **9.8:** Sporthill. **9.9:** Gerber Technology, Inc. **9.10-9.13:** Lectra. **9.14-9.15:** Gerber Technology, Inc.

Chapter 10
10.3: Maurizio Pracella. **10.5:** Courtesy of Nike, Inc. **10.6:** Courtesy of Levi Strauss & Co. **10.7 (left):** Cindy Karp/NYT Pictures. **10.7 (right):** Courtesy of David Wilson. **10.8:** Edward Keating/NYT Pictures.

Chapter 11
11.1: Copyright © 1994 by The New York Times Company. Reprinted by permission. **11.2:** Courtesy of [TC]², Textile/Clothing Technology Corporation, Cary, NC. **11.3:** Lectra. **11.5 and 11.6:** Gerber Technology, Inc. **11.7:** Lectra. **11.8:** Courtesy of [TC]², Textile/Clothing Technology Corporation, Cary, NC.

11.9: Ellis Corporation. **11.10:** AP/Wide World Photos.

Chapter 12
12.1, 12.2, and 12.4: Courtesy of Fairchild Publications, Inc. **12.5:** Reprinted with special permission, North America Syndicate. **12.6-12.9:** Courtesy of Fairchild Publications, Inc. **12.11:** Courtesy of Fashionmall.com. **12.12:** QVC, Inc.

Chapter 13
13.3: © John Cole/Stock, Boston Inc./PictureQuest. **13.5:** Courtesy of Nike, Inc. **13.7:** Bettman/Corbis. **13.8:** Courtesy of DuPont. **13.10:** Courtesy of Fairchild Publications, Inc.; Photographer: D. Maitre. **13.14:** Art Director: Paul Marciano, Photographer: Dean Isidro, Guess? © 2001.

Chapter 14
14.2: Virgil Smithers/Fieldcrest Cannon. **14.4:** Image from Vision Carpet Studio™ by NedGraphics BV. **14.6:** The Seal of Cotton is a Registered Service Mark/Trademark of Cotton Incorporated. **14.7 (left):** Norman Y. Lono/NYT Pictures. **14.10:** Courtesy of Milliken & Company. **14.19:** Courtesy, Park B. Smith, Ltd.

Color Plates
1: Pendleton Woolen Mills—Sandra S. Arditi/Designer. **2:** The Seal of Cotton is a Registered Service Mark/Trademark of Cotton Incorporated. **4:** Courtesy of Ecom Partners. **5:** The Gerry Group. **6:** Courtesy of Monarch Design Systems and Chopak Mills. **8:** The Gerry Group. **9:** Jantzen Inc. **10 and 11:** Gerber Technology, Inc. **12:** Courtesy of Nike, Inc. **13:** © Lands' End, Inc. and My Virtual Model, Inc. Used with permission.

Organization of the U.S. Textile and Apparel Industries

PART 1

CHAPTER 1

Spinning Machine
From to
Supply Chain
Management

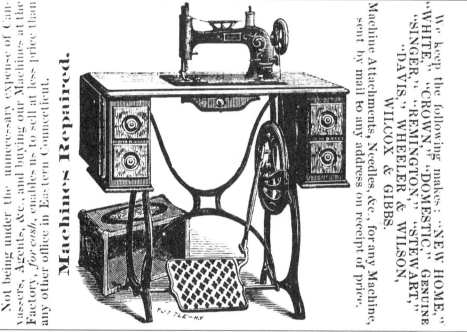

Not being under the unnecessary expense of Canvassers, Agents, &c., and buying our Machines at the Factory, *for cash*, enables us to sell at less price than any other office in Eastern Connecticut.

Machines Repaired.

We keep the following makes: "NEW HOME," "WHITE," "CROWN," "DOMESTIC," GENUINE "SINGER," "REMINGTON," "STEWART," "DAVIS," WHEELER & WILSON, WILCOX & GIBBS.

Machine Attachments, Needles, &c., for any Machine, sent by mail to any address on receipt of price.

IN THIS CHAPTER YOU WILL LEARN:

- The technological developments in the textile and apparel industries.
- The history of the transition of the apparel industry from a craft industry to a factory-based industry.
- The historical basis for the emergence of the Quick Response philosophy.
- The forms of interindustry cooperation needed for the success of Quick Response strategies, including supply chain management.

The U.S. textile and apparel industries consist of companies that produce fibers, textiles, and apparel and home fashion products for consumers in the United States as well as around the world. These industries are among the largest and most productive in the world. Textile and apparel companies can be found in every state, employing one and a quarter million people. When apparel distribution through retailers is included, these industries contribute to the economy of virtually every town in the nation. But how did it all begin? How did these industries develop and grow into the dynamic industries they are today? To understand fully the modern textile and apparel industries, a brief review of how they began, grew, and changed over the past two hundred-plus years is important.

1789–1890: Mechanization of Spinning, Weaving, and Sewing

For thousands of years, the spinning and weaving of fabrics were labor-intensive hand processes. Then, in England, in the mid-1700s, the spinning of yarn and weaving of cloth began to be mechanized. At this time, England's cotton and wool textile industries were the most technologically developed in the western world. In response to a growing demand for textiles both in England and abroad, a series of advances in the spinning and weaving of fabrics by such English inventors as John Kay (1733, invention of the flying shuttle loom), James Hargreaves (1764, invention of the spinning jenny), Sir Richard Arkwright (1769, invention of a water-powered spinning machine), and Edmund Cartwright (1785–1787, invention of the mechanized power loom) brought the British industry to world prominence. In addition, the process for printing fabrics was also being mechanized. England was protective of its technological developments, and severe penalties existed for attempting to take blueprints and/or machines or their parts out of the country. Even the mechanics themselves were restricted from leaving the country.

In the United States, a fledgling cotton industry was taking root, but America lacked England's advanced technology for spinning and weaving cotton fibers. Then, in 1789, Samuel Slater, a skilled mechanic, brought English textile technology to the United States by memorizing the blueprints of the Arkwright water-powered spinning machine. He declared himself a farmer (farmers were permitted to leave England) and came to the United States, settling in New England where a ready supply of water existed. Hired by Moses Brown, a merchant, Slater set up a **spinning mill** similar to the one shown in Figure 1.1. Who would have thought that this small spinning mill in Pawtucket, Rhode Island, would prove that cotton yarn could be

Figure 1.1: Early spinning mill, including carding, drawing, roving, and spinning, as introduced by Samuel Slater.

spun profitably in the United States? This mill, which opened in 1791, sparked the textile industry in the United States. Within a few years, spinning mills had sprung up all over New England. By the mid-1800s, towns such as Waltham, Lowell, Lawrence, and New Bedford, Massachusetts, and Biddeford, Maine, became centers of the newly emerging textile industry. A reliance on British inventions still existed; any technological changes were based on reproducing and improving textile machinery used in England.

Although the spinning process was becoming mechanized, the weaving process continued to be contracted out to individual handweavers. Then, in 1813, Francis Cabot Lowell originated a functional **power loom**. He set the stage for vertical integration within the industry; his factory was the first in the United States to perform mechanically all processes from spinning yarn to producing finished cloth under one roof. As early as 1817, power looms were being installed in textile mills all over New England. However, despite the technological developments in weaving, the contracting out of the weaving process to handweavers for complex fabrics continued until the late 1800s.

The mechanization of spinning and weaving made these processes so much faster that fiber producers were pressured to supply a greater amount of cotton and wool. Cotton growers in the South were limited, however, by the time needed to hand pick seeds from cotton. Then, in 1794, Eli Whitney patented the **cotton gin** (*gin* for *engine*), which could clean as much cotton in one day as 50 men (see Figure 1.2). As a result of this invention, the cotton growers soon were able to supply New England's spinning and weaving mills with the needed amount of fiber. To be closer to this very important source of cotton, manufacturers built textile mills in the southern states. By 1847, more people were employed in textile mills than in any other industry in the United States.

Figure 1.2: The Whitney Cotton Gin, constructed by Eli Whitney, increased the speed of the cotton-cleaning process.

The **ready-to-wear** (RTW) industry had its beginnings in the early eighteenth century. To meet the demand for ready-made clothing, tailors would make less-expensive clothes from scrap material left over from sewing custom-made suits. Sailors, miners, and slaves were the primary target market for these early ready-made clothes, which were cut in "slop shops" and sewn by women at home. The term *slops* later became a standard term for cheap ready-made clothing.

In the early nineteenth century, the demand for ready-to-wear clothing grew. The expanding number of middle-class consumers wanted good-quality apparel but did not want to pay the high prices associated with custom-made clothing. It was not until the sewing process of apparel production became mechanized, however, that ready-to-wear apparel became available to the majority of consumers. **Sewing machine** inventions by Walter Hunt (1832), Elias Howe (1845), and Isaac Singer (1846) made it possible for apparel to be produced by machine, thereby speeding the process by which it could be made. From 1842 to 1895, 7,339 patents for sewing machines and accessories were issued in the United States. The ad in Figure 1.3, shows how competitive the business had become. The sewing machine allowed relatively unskilled immigrant workers to sew garments in their homes. In addition, sewing factories were established, with some of the first men's clothing factories appearing as early as 1831. Singer's sewing machine, patented in 1851, was, in fact, designed for factory use.

Men's RTW developed first in the United States, then children's (boys' apparel before girls' apparel), and finally women's. One reason for this is that men's size standards existed for apparel producers to use. The development of men's wear size standards and their use in sewing uniforms during the Civil War allowed further advances in the industry. The term **size standards** refers to the proportional increase or decrease in garment measurements for each size produced. Patterns could be made for a range of men's sizes. Thus, multiple sizes could be cut and sewn using mass production methods. In addition, in the late nineteenth century, the styling of men's apparel was less complicated than that of women's.

By 1860, a variety of ready-made men's clothing was available. Indeed, between 1822 and 1860, the ready-to-wear segment of the men's wear tailoring industry grew larger than the custom-made segment. Because of this increased demand, sewing factories also grew.

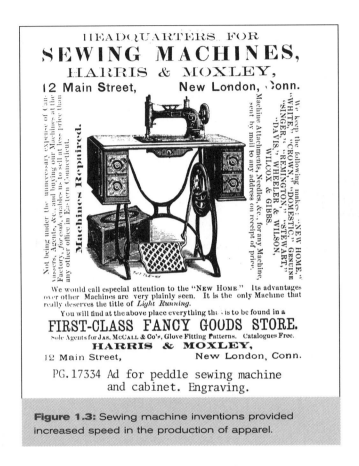

Figure 1.3: Sewing machine inventions provided increased speed in the production of apparel.

A number of other advances contributed to the growth of the industry at this time. During the late 1800s, motorized cutting knives and pressing equipment were developed. Mass production of apparel was also facilitated by the invention of paper patterns. Ebenezer Butterick started a pattern business in 1863; James McCall started a similar one in 1870. Thus, by the end of the nineteenth century, mechanization of the textile and apparel production processes resulted in a growing number of companies.

With the availability of ready-made clothing, distribution outlets to consumers in cities increased. Brooks Brothers, the first men's apparel store, opened in New York City in 1818 and catered primarily to sailors and working-class men who could not afford custom-tailored clothing. The mid-1800s saw the development of dry goods stores, which later became department stores, in cities. In New York City's Greenwich

Figure 1.4: Distribution of ready-to-wear apparel and accessories was facilitated by retail stores, such as R.H. Macy's Dry Goods in New York City (left) and Rike's Department Store in Dayton, Ohio (right).

Village, Lord & Taylor opened in 1826 (and in 1903 moved to Fifth Avenue); in Haverhill, Massachusetts, Macy's Wholesale and Retail Dry Goods House (Figure 1.4, left) opened in 1857; in Chicago, Marshall Field's opened in 1852 and Carson Pirie Scott & Co. in 1854; and in Philadelphia, John Wanamaker and Co. opened in 1869. Although these stores initially offered a limited range of products, by the end of the Civil War, the range of merchandise expanded and included apparel.

To those consumers unable to shop in the cities, illustrated catalogs offered a wide variety of goods by the latter part of the nineteenth century. With the expansion of the U.S. postal service (parcel post was introduced in 1913), railroads, and rural free delivery (RFD, introduced in 1893), a growing mail-order business for ready-made clothing was created by such companies as Montgomery Ward (established in 1872) and Sears, Roebuck & Co. (established in 1886). Table 1.1 summarizes these supply and demand needs for the emergence and growth of the textile and apparel industries in the United States.

TABLE 1.1

Supply and Demand Needs for the Emergence and Growth of Textile and Apparel Industries in the United States

SUPPLY

■ Need plenty of inexpensive fabric and means to sew it quickly
   spinning machine (1764)
   power loom (1785–87)
   cotton gin (1794)
   sewing machine (1832, 1845, 1846)

■ Need supply of labor
   immigrant workers began production sewing in their homes

DEMAND

■ Need customers, a demand for mass-produced apparel
   sailors, miners, and slaves needed cheap, ready-made clothing (slops)
   an expanding number of middle-class consumers wanted good quality apparel at "reasonable" prices

■ Need distribution system
   mail order catalogs
   department stores (mid-1800s)

1890–1950: Growth of the Ready-to-Wear Industry

Although most men's apparel was available ready made by the mid-nineteenth century, the women's RTW industry did not expand until the late nineteenth century (see Figures 1.5, 1.6, and 1.7). The first types of RTW apparel produced for women were outerwear capes, cloaks, and coats. Because these garments fit more loosely than fashionable dresses, sizing was not a critical problem. Manufactured corsets, petticoats, and other underwear items were also accepted by consumers, perhaps because these clothing items were hidden from public view. By the beginning of the twentieth century, RTW skirts and shirtwaists (blouses) were offered for sale. The popularity of the shirtwaist, made fashionable by Charles Dana Gibson's "Gibson girl," shifted women's apparel production away from a craft industry to a factory-based industry. It was the shirtwaist and the popularity of *separates,* that is, coat, blouse (shirtwaist), and skirt worn by young working women in the cities, that provided the basis for the development of the women's RTW industry.

The production of RTW apparel was labor intensive. A ready supply of immigrant workers spurred the growth of the **mass production** of apparel. By 1900, approximately 500 shops in New York City were producing shirtwaists. The contracting system of production grew in popularity, as it was estimated that a $50 investment was all that was necessary to start a business with a few workers and a bundle of cut garments obtained from a manufacturer or wholesaler. Production was divided into two segments: (1) a large number of sewing operations located in the homes of immigrants producing lower-priced garments, and (2) a relatively small number of large, modern

Figure 1.5: The popularity of separates for women, epitomized by the "Gibson girl," led to a growth in RTW production.

sewing factories engaged in the production of better-quality garments. These sewing factories, primarily on the Lower East Side of New York City, were notorious for their poor working conditions. The term *sweatshop* originally referred to the system of contractors and subcontractors whereby work was "sweated off." Later, the term became associated with the dismal conditions of *home factories*, where contract workers sewed clothing, and with the long hours, unclean and unsafe working conditions, and low pay of contract sewing factories. In an effort to improve working conditions for the employees in the industry, most of whom were young immigrant women, the **International Ladies' Garment Workers' Union** (ILGWU) was formed in 1900 at a convention in New York City. The tragic fire in the Triangle Shirtwaist Co. factory on March 25, 1911, in which 146 young women died, brought public attention to the horrid working conditions and increased support for the ILGWU (now part of the Union of Needletrades, Industrial, and Textile Employees, UNITE).

12   **PART 1**
**Organization of the U.S. Textile
and Apparel Industries**

Figure 1.6: By the 1890s, most men's apparel and some women's apparel was available as RTW.

In the 1920s, the women's fashion industry in New York moved from the Lower East Side to Seventh Avenue. This area of midtown Manhattan became known as New York's *garment district* and has remained the hub of women's fashions. The manufacturing of men's wear was less centralized, with Chicago, Baltimore, and New York emerging as manufacturing centers.

At the beginning of the twentieth century, the majority of RTW clothing was made from cotton and wool. Silk fabric, imported from France and Italy, was highly desired for its luxurious qualities. However, it was very expensive and the supply was limited. Therefore, when synthetic substitutes for natural fibers were initially explored, "artificial silk" (rayon, made from wood pulp) was the first to be developed and patented in the United States. The first American rayon plant was opened

Figure 1.7: Boy's apparel was also available as RTW by the 1890s.

in 1910. Synthetic dyestuffs for textile dyeing were developed and available by the beginning of the twentieth century.

Other inventions made during this time became staples in the RTW industry. An invention called the *locker* was demonstrated at the Chicago World's Fair in 1893. Named the *zipper* in 1926, it was to have a major impact on the apparel industry. First used to fasten boots, the zipper was not generally used in fashion apparel until the 1930s.

Fashion magazines, such as *Vogue*, first published in 1892, provided consumers with up-to-date fashion information and helped spur the desire for new fashions. Between 1910 and 1920, a variety of communication channels helped unite the fledgling RTW industry. Trade publications, such as the *Daily Trade Record* (men's wear), established in 1892, and *Women's Wear Daily*, established in 1910, provided a great impetus to the RTW industry.

Another step in the developmental progress of the RTW industry was the result of wartime manufacturing. World War I spurred the need for the manufacture of military uniforms, and, in turn, helped streamline apparel production methods. Also important to the U.S. textile and apparel industries was the closing of French and British fashion houses during the war, which allowed American fashion to develop from 1914 to 1918.

Although most items of women's clothing were available ready made by the early 1900s, growth in the garment industry came about with the simplification of garment styles in the 1920s (see Figure 1.8). Who knows which came first? The simpler styles may have spurred the growth of the industry, but industry methods also affected the styles of apparel that could be produced for, and thus adopted by, consumers. By the 1920s mass-produced clothing was available to the majority of individuals. The era of inexpensive fashion had begun. New styles and variety became more valued than costly one-of-a-kind apparel by the majority of consumers. Retail

Figure 1.8: The loose-fitting styles of the 1920s were ideal for mass production.

stores increased their inventory ratio of moderately priced clothing in proportion to more expensive goods. A new development in retailing during this decade was the country's first outdoor shopping mall. The Country Club Plaza was built in 1922 in Kansas City, Kansas. It remains a gem among shopping malls, with its Spanish style architecture and fountains reminiscent of Seville, Spain.

The boyish chemise-style dresses of the 1920s were easy to manufacture because there were few contours to shape and fit. This loose, boxy style also fit a wider variety of figures than did previous styles. However, this style was not favored by the textile manufacturers because it utilized approximately one-third less yardage per garment than the styles of the previous decade. With the growing popularity of movies, movie stars began to influence the fashion preferences of consumers. Fashion news also became available over a new invention—radio. Fortunately for the textile manufacturers, the women's garment styles of the 1930s used more fabric than those of the 1920s.

New York City remained the center of the women's fashion industry, and Seventh Avenue was becoming synonymous with women's fashion. By 1923 New York City was producing nearly 80 percent of U.S. women's apparel in the city's growing garment district. Also during the 1920s, specialized sewing machines, such as over-lockers (sergers) and power-driven cutting equipment were developed.

As mass communications expanded in the 1920s, so did the flow of fashion information. France dominated the fashion scene, where a new generation of high-fashion designers, including Patou, Chanel, Vionnet, and Schiaparelli, was rising. Covering the fashion shows in Paris and bringing this news to American consumers was a huge undertaking. In 1926, more than one hundred reporters covered the Paris couture openings for newspapers and magazines. When the stock market crashed in 1929, it devastated all aspects of the American economy. Repercussions were felt in Paris, as retail stores and private clients canceled orders overnight.

The Great Depression of the 1930s, which resulted from the 1929 stock market crash, caused a severe blow to the textile and apparel industries. These and other industries did not recover until the start of World War II. In 1929, it was estimated that New York had 3,500 dress companies; by 1933 there were only 2,300. However, the 1930s brought about the development of the first "synthetic" fibers synthesized entirely from chemicals. Because most manufactured fibers were developed as substitutes for natural fibers, their properties were intended to emulate those of silk, wool, and cotton. Nylon, the first synthetic fiber, was first conceptualized by E. I. duPont de Nemours & Co. in 1928, successfully synthesized in 1935, marketed in 1938, and introduced in nylon stockings in 1939. However, nylon production for consumer use was interrupted by World War II, so that its widespread use for consumer products did not come until after the war.

It also became more common for manufacturers to contract and subcontract some of the sewing operations. Some contractors specialized in specific processes, such as fabric pleating. For example, the manufacturer would ship the needed quantity of yard goods to the contractor for pleating. The contractor would return the pleated goods to the apparel manufacturer, which would proceed with cutting and sewing operations.

During the 1930s, a number of large dress and sportswear companies emerged and grew in New York. In addition, the sportswear industry in California and other western states began to expand. The California sportswear industry actually began in the 1850s, when Levi Strauss & Co. began production of work trousers. It was not until the 1930s that sportswear made by other companies, such as White Stag, Jantzen, Cole of California, Pendleton Woolen Mills, and Catalina, became popular. The sportswear trend was further legitimized by American designers such as Claire McCardell and Vera Maxwell who, in the late 1930s, introduced informal, casual "designer" clothing.

A number of fashion magazines also debuted in the 1930s, each catering to a particular segment of consumers. *Mademoiselle,* established in 1935, and *Glamour*, first published in 1939 as *Glamour of Hollywood*, catered to fashionable college coeds and young working women. *Esquire*, first published in 1933, was designed to enlighten men about the world of fashion and elegance. Movies of the era also served as a source of fashion information for consumers, and movie stars became the fashion leaders of the day (See Figure 1.9.).

Brand names of manufacturers gained strong consumer recognition during the 1930s. One of the first to gain national recognition was the Arrow shirt. Launched in 1905, the Arrow shirt advertising campaign continued for many years. The ads featured color fashion illustrations of a very sophisticated male, wearing an Arrow shirt, of course, engaged in a variety of activities suitable to a man of taste and leisure. These ads remain a classic example of lifestyle advertising. By the 1930s, the college student and young working woman were clearly identified as target customers for the fashion industry; special markets included junior and large-size customers. Size standards were widely adopted by the industry after the U.S. Department of Agriculture published size measurements in 1941. The demand for good-quality RTW was strong, and fashion news spread quickly.

A number of changes in the 1940s had profound influences on the U.S. apparel industry. Although World War II devastated the fashion industry in France, Paris emerged once again after the war as a prominent player in the international fashion industry. However, the war did allow American designers, such as Claire McCardell, to become

Figure 1.9: The 1930s brought a growth in the sportswear industry and the influence of California (particularly Hollywood) on fashion.

well known among consumers. The United States became known as the sportswear capital and held on to this title even after the Paris fashion houses reopened.

The U.S. fashion industry founded several organizations during the 1930s and 1940s, including The Fashion Group International, the New York Couture Group, and the California Fashion Creators, to strengthen and promote the industry. The Coty American Fashion Critics Award was founded in 1942 to recognize outstanding American fashion designers.

By the 1940s, the production of ready-to-wear clothing was located primarily in modern factories. Because of rising costs in New York City, factories had been built in New Jersey, Connecticut, and upstate New York. Apparel manufacturing factories also were springing up in other parts of the country. The apparel industry in California, centered in Los Angeles, emerged as the hub for the growing active and casual sportswear industry in the West. Dallas, Texas, also gained prominence in apparel manufacturing.

1950–1980: Diversification and Incorporation

The 1950s saw not only a general growth in consumer demand for apparel, but also a shift in the product mix demanded by consumers. Because of lifestyle changes, casual clothing and sportswear were an expanding segment of the fashion industry. In fact, between 1947 and 1961, wholesale shipments of casual apparel and sportswear increased approximately 160 percent. During the same period, suit sales decreased by approximately 40 percent. Teenage fashion, which developed as a special category during the 1950s (see Figure 1.10), reached its peak during the youth explosion of the 1960s, when "mass fashion" became affordable to the majority of the population. In 1965, half the U.S. population was under 25, and teenagers spent $3.5 million annually on apparel.

Figure 1.10: Ozzie and Harriet Nelson, with sons David and Ricky. Spurred by the popularity of television and pop music, teenage fashion becomes a separate category in the 1950s.

Spurred by increased orders from the military in the early 1950s, the textile indus-try also grew. In 1950, Burlington ranked as the largest Fortune 500 textile manufac-turer, with annual sales just over $1 billion. Developed in the 1940s, acrylic and poly-ester were available to the U.S. market by the early 1950s. Triacetate, introduced in 1954, provided a less heat sensitive alternative to acetate, a previously developed syn-thetic fiber. The use of synthetic fibers in apparel provided consumers with easy-care, wrinkle-free, and "drip-dry" clothing that freed them from the high demands of car-ing for cotton and woolen clothing. These new fibers provided lower-cost and lighter-weight alternatives. Textile mills developed new texturizing processes, that made pos-sible such innovations as stretch yarn. Nylon stretch socks became available in 1952. Later in the decade, nylon stretch pants became a fashion sensation. In the 1960s, manufactured fibers began to overtake natural fibers in popularity. Apparel designers such as Pierre Cardin experimented with space-age materials. Plastic was used exten-sively, and heat fusing techniques were developed. The natural fiber industry fought back with strong organizations, such as the Cotton Council and the International Wool Secretariat. Eventually, natural fibers would again gain public favor, but not until after the decade of Amer-ica's love affair with polyester—the 1970s.

After World War II came Christian Dior's New Look, and consumer atten-tion turned again to Paris. During the 1950s and 1960s, Parisian haute cou-ture continued to set fashion trends worldwide. However, increased pro-ductivity in mass-produced clothing now made it possible for designer fashions to be copied and reproduced at a fraction of the cost of haute cou-ture (see Figure 1.11). During this peri-od, ready-to-wear fashions became the standard worldwide; and "Chanel"

Figure 1.11: Mass-produced apparel, such as the clothing worn by these UCLA students in 1958, copied the couture designers of the time.

suits (less expensive copies of the originals), were available to everyone. Since the 1970s, haute couture has been overshadowed by mass-market apparel. In fact, currently all haute couture designers also create ready-to-wear collections.

One of the most apparent changes in the apparel industry during the late 1950s and throughout the 1960s was the increase in large, publicly owned apparel corporations. In 1959, only 22 public apparel companies existed, but by the end of the 1960s more than 100 apparel companies had become public corporations. Some companies that "went public" early on were Jonathan Logan, Bobbie Brooks, and Leslie Fay.

Because of the growth of suburbia in the United States, fewer people lived in cities, and consumers wanted shopping outlets closer to their new homes. Thus emerged the shopping mall. In 1956, Southdale Center, the first enclosed shopping mall was built in a suburb of Minneapolis. During the 1960s, shopping malls appeared in virtually every suburb, typically with regional or national department stores as anchors.

During the 1960s and 1970s, the American designer name saw increased prominence. Although American designers were first promoted by the Lord & Taylor department store in New York in the 1930s, it was not until the late 1960s that stores such as Saks Fifth Avenue featured specific American designers. Aware of the broad appeal of their names, designers such as Halston and Bill Blass ventured into licensing their names for a variety of products.

However, rising labor costs in the United States led to increased prices for consumers. In an attempt to keep costs down, retailers explored the idea of low overhead, self-service, and high-volume stores for apparel and other products. The strategy was successful, and retailers such as Kmart (Figure 1.12), Target, Wal-Mart, and Woolco, known as *discounters*, flourished. In addition, as labor costs continued to rise, companies searched for a cheaper workforce, first within the United States (particularly in the South) and then outside the United States (particularly in Hong Kong and Southeast Asia). Textile technology, once the domain of American companies, was increasingly imported from abroad. In 1967, for the first time in its history, the United States ran a trade deficit in textile machinery.

The 1970s saw the beginning of trends in which companies became vertically integrated and large, publicly owned conglomerates bought apparel companies. For example, during this time, General Mills acquired Izod, David Crystal, and Monet

Figure 1.12: Discount retailers, such as Kmart, grew out of the attempt to keep merchandise costs down for consumers.

jewelers; Consolidated Foods purchased Hanes hosiery and Aris gloves; and Gulf & Western bought Kayser-Roth.

Technological advances in the textile industry included a new generation of photographic printing and dyeing processes. Computer technology entered the textile and apparel manufacturing areas. The popularity of polyester double knit and denim fabrics sparked sales in the textile industry. However, increased competition from textile companies outside the United States cut into profits, and textile imports rose 581 percent between 1961 and 1976.

1980–Present: Quick Response and Beyond

In the 1970s and early 1980s, the U.S. textile and apparel industries saw a decline in consumer demand for their products and an increase in labor, energy, and materials costs. Consumer demands for lower prices, quality merchandise, and better service were reflected in business strategies. During the 1980s, several of the largest department store groups were leveraged by management or as part of aquisitions and takeovers. Among the largest of these deals included May Department Stores' acquisition of Associated Dry Goods in 1986; Robert Campeau's purchase of Allied Stores in 1986 and Federated in 1988; and Macy's purchase of Bullock's and I. Magnin in 1988. Store acquisitions continued through the 1990s as evidenced by Federated's acquisition of Macy's in 1994 and Broadway Stores in 1995 and Profitt's purchase of Saks Fifth Avenue and of smaller regional stores in 1998. Not all retailers were able to adapt, however. By 1990 many well-known New York retailers were out of business, including B. Altman & Co., Bonwit Teller, E. J. Korvette, and Peck & Peck. At the same time, stores such as Nordstrom, The Limited, Gap, and Wal-Mart were thriving.

The 1980s and 1990s also saw an increase in verticalization among manufacturing and retailers. Strategies included manufacturers (e.g., NIKE, Tommy Hilfiger, Liz Claiborne) opening or expanding retail store operations, department and specialty stores entering into partnerships with manufacturers and contractors to produce private label merchandise for their stores, and retail stores (e.g., The Limited, Gap, Banana Republic, Old Navy, Eddie Bauer) adopting a store-is-brand concept. In the *store-is-brand strategy*, the store offers only merchandise with the store name as its brand. With the introduction of e-commerce in the mid-1990s, many companies began experimenting with on-line business. While e-commerce accounts for only a small percentage of overall retail sales for apparel and accessories, continued growth in its use is likely to be seen.

During the early 1980s, certain segments of the industry were affected by the continued growth of textile and apparel imports. Companies such as Liz Claiborne, founded in 1976, were producing apparel worldwide in order to obtain the best labor price for production. Concern about rising labor costs in the United States and the continued surge of imports led industry executives to join forces in examining ways to improve the productivity of the U.S. textile and apparel industries. Analyses indicated that apparel manufacturers and retailers were working with a 66-week ($1^1/_4$ years) cycle to go from raw fiber to a garment on the retail selling floor. It was estimated that for 55 weeks (83 percent of the cycle) of this cycle, products were in inventory. Thus, products were actually being processed for only 11 weeks (*Quick Response*, 1988). Industry executives recognized that this represented a huge inefficiency.

In 1984–1985, the Crafted with Pride in U.S.A. Council engaged Kurt Salmon Associates, textile and apparel industry analysts, to analyze industry inefficiencies.

This project developed the idea of **Quick Response (QR)** to describe a philosophy that promoted potential ways to increase efficiencies. The following year, the Crafted with Pride in U.S.A. Council sponsored pilot projects linking fabric producers, apparel manufacturers, and retailers to determine if QR was feasible and to identify obstacles and difficulties in implementing QR strategies. Results from these pilot projects, in terms of increases in sales, *stock turnover* (the number of times during a specific period that the average inventory on hand has been sold), and *return on investment* (relationship between company profits and investment in capital items), were positive, and a few mass merchants and department stores as well as top name-branded manufacturers ventured to implement new technologies (Hasty, 1994). Because investments in technology led to higher productivity, companies found their investments paid off quickly. Pioneers in QR included textile companies such as Milliken and Burlington; apparel manufacturers such as Haggar, Levi Strauss, and Arrow; and retailers such as Dillard's, JCPenney, and Belk, among others.

WHAT IS QUICK RESPONSE?

The phrase *Quick Response* is an umbrella term used to identify various management systems and business strategies in the textile and apparel industries that reduce the time between fiber production and sale to the ultimate consumer. Specific definitions of QR vary, depending on the industry division. For textile producers, QR focuses on connections among fiber producers, fabric producers, and apparel manufacturers; for apparel manufacturers, QR focuses on increased use of technology and connections among fabric producers, apparel producers, and retailers. As defined by the Quick Response Leadership Committee of the American Leadership Committee (AAMA, 1995), Quick Response is:

> A comprehensive business strategy to continually meet changing requirements of a competitive marketplace which promotes responsiveness to consumer demand, encourages business partnerships, makes effective use of resources and shortens the business cycle throughout the chain from raw materials to the consumer.

In general, these strategies include increasing the speed of design and production through the use of computers, increasing the efficiency with which companies communicate and conduct business with one another, reducing the amount of time goods are in warehouses or in transit, and decreasing the amount of time needed to replenish stock on the retail floor. Quick Response is a change from the *push system* of the past, in which supply-side strategies were used to push the products produced on the consumer. In contrast, QR is a *pull system* of demand-side strategies that are based on the flow of timely and accurate information about consumers' wants and needs from consumers to the manufacturers.

Quick Response strategies are implemented at all stages of the textile and apparel manufacturing and distribution marketing channel or pipeline, from fiber production to retail sale to the ultimate consumer. As such, QR strategies will be discussed throughout this text. Business strategies that fall under the QR umbrella include the use of computer-aided design and manufacturing systems, the use of the most efficient fabric and apparel production systems, the use of bar codes on merchandise and shipping cartons, the receiving and sharing of product information, and the sending of orders and other forms electronically. In other words, any business strategy that improves accuracy and/or quality and reduces the amount of time used in the production and distribution of fabric and apparel can be considered part of QR.

It soon became apparent that the key barrier in the implementation of QR was the use of a variety of computer systems by manufacturers and retailers and the lack of standards within the industry. Thus, in the mid-1980s, interindustry councils were formed to establish voluntary communications standards. Once these standards were instituted and adopted, companies that had embraced QR saw growth in sales and market share. By the late 1990s virtually all successful firms had implemented some QR strategies. Even though the phrase Quick Response is used in conjunction with the slogans *Made in U.S.A.* and *Crafted with Pride in U.S.A.*, QR strategies have also been adopted by overseas apparel manufacturers, especially those manufacturers that work with large retailers in the United States (Douglas-David, 1989).

INDUSTRY COOPERATION AND PARTNERSHIPS

For Quick Response strategies to be successful, cooperation among the various components of the textile, apparel, and retailing industries is essential (see Figure 1.13). A level of trust also must exist between companies for many of the strategies to be effective. For example, with QR, because fabric is inspected for flaws at the mill, apparel producers do not have to rein-spect it at the apparel plant. However, the apparel producers must trust that the fabric producers, in fact, adequately inspected the fabric. A number of the partnerships have been formalized to focus on ways in which companies within the various industries could best cooperate in achieving increased productivity. These partnerships include Textile/Clothing Technology Corporation [TC]², industry linkage councils, the Crafted with Pride in U.S.A. Council, and the American Textile Partnership.

Figure 1.13: The Internet and World Wide Web are being used to enhance communications among companies in the textile, apparel, and retailing industries.

Textile/Clothing Technology Corporation

In the late 1970s, Harvard professors John T. Dunlop and Frederick H. Abernathy assessed the productivity of the U.S. apparel industry within the global economy. They argued that new approaches were needed to reduce labor costs if the apparel industry was to maintain its market share. This study led to a two-day conference of industry, union, government, and university representatives to plan a joint research and development program. This 1979 conference led to much industry speculation about the viability of a joint research and development program. In 1981, the Tailored Clothing Technology Corporation, commonly known as [TC]², was established by the Amalgamated Clothing and Textile Workers Union (ACTWU), three men's suits manufacturers (Hartmarx, Palm Beach, and Greif), and the men's wear division of fabric producer Burlington Industries (Kazis, 1989). In 1985, the name was changed to the **Textile/Clothing Technology Corporation** to better reflect its broader focus (see Figure 1.14, left). Currently, [TC]² remains a nonprofit consortium of over two hundred textile, apparel, retail, labor, and government organizations with the mission of being the "premier source of assistance to the sewn products industry for improving business systems and manufacturing resource" ([TC]², 2001). Although the focus of [TC]² has been to reduce labor costs by increasing computer automation within the industry, ACTWU (now part of UNITE) has been an active

Figure 1.14: Left: Established in 1980, [TC]² conducts research and development for the apparel industry. Right: An example of the technology provided is the engineered design of this blouse with pattern-matching across seams and darts.

participant from its beginning. According to Murray Finley, former president of the ACTWU:

> By improving the technology, you reduce the labor content and thereby you reduce the advantage that low-wage areas around the world have. You involve fewer person-hours in the manufacturing, of course, but our idea is that we can be more competitive, and that means more consistency of employment in the domestic industry. (Fortess, 1988, p. 104)

Since its beginning, [TC]² has focused on developing, testing, and teaching advanced apparel technology that could contribute to the reduction of direct labor costs involved in the production of apparel made in the United States (see Figure 1.14 left). Initially, its work focused on automating the men's tailored clothing industry, but the group's current work is much broader in nature and represents needs throughout the entire fiber-textile-apparel industry (Kazis, 1989).

One of the biggest challenges for [TC]² was to gain the support of small and mid-size apparel companies through technology transfer. Therefore, in 1988, a "teaching factory"—the National Apparel Technology Center was opened. Located in Cary, North Carolina, the purpose of the center is to demonstrate, educate, and carry out short-term development of state-of-the-art equipment for apparel production. The mission statement for the National Apparel Technology Center states three objectives:

■ To *demonstrate* in a credible manner the latest state-of-the-art machinery, computer systems, and methodology for apparel manufacturing.

■ To foster the utilization of these systems by *educating* apparel manufacturing management, engineers, and technicians on the benefits, capabilities, operations, and financial ramifications of these systems.

■ To carry out *short-term development* activities that will enhance the performance and product quality of existing production equipment (Fortess, 1988, p. 108).

These objectives are carried out in the following ways:

■ The operation of a manufacturing and teaching facility/factory that applies state-of-the-art equipment, software, and production methods.

■ Educational services that include seminars and workshops; on-site training; hands-on learning opportunities; faculty and student internships; interactive video training tools; and Value-Added Coaching services, whereby employees are coached in implementing new processes.

■ Simulation services that promote the use of computer simulation modeling systems for design and manufacturing modification analysis.

■ Research and development projects, funded by the U.S. Department of Commerce, including the apparel-on-demand project focusing on body measurement scanners for use in mass producing garments on a made-to-order basis (mass customization), knitwear automation, real-time automation of markers, and digital printing.

The Textile/Clothing Technology Corporation has also developed partnerships with the American Apparel Manufacturers Association (AAMA), the Association of Manufacturing Excellence (AME), the American Textile Partnership (AMTEX), the National Coalition for Advanced Manufacturing (NACFAM), and the National Center for Manufacturing Sciences (NCMS) to facilitate the communication of industry needs to researchers and the transfer of technology and research from the center to the apparel industry (Fortess, 1988).

Interindustry Linkage Councils

In the mid-1980s a number of councils were formed to develop and encourage the use of voluntary standards to facilitate faster, more accurate information flow between producers and suppliers (see Figure 1.15). The **Voluntary Interindustry Communications Standards Committee (VICS)** was formed in 1986 by a group of industry executives who wanted to "take a global leadership role in the ongoing improvement of the flow of product and information about the product throughout the entire supply chain in the retail industry" (VICS Mission Statement). Initial efforts of VICS focused on gaining agreement among retailers and producers on the use of the Universal Product Code (UPC) system to identify products and to acquire information accurately on consumers' purchases on an individual stock keeping unit (SKU) basis; encourage the creation of common item-identification standards for yarn and fabric products used in the production of consumer apparel and textile items; gain agreement on a single set of communication formats and electronic data interchange (EDI); and encourage the development of equipment to record and make available to producers information concerning consumer purchases of these products.

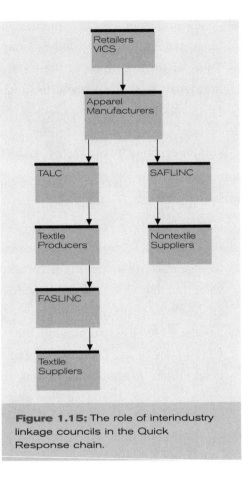

Figure 1.15: The role of interindustry linkage councils in the Quick Response chain.

VICS was very successful in meeting these objectives. In 1987, the UPC-A bar code was recommended for branded general merchandise, including apparel. This voluntary standard was later endorsed by the National Retail Merchants Association (now called the National Retail Federation) and the International Mass Retailer Association. Shipping container marking (SCM) standards were also established. These marking standards support the flow of merchandise through distribution centers. In terms of EDI, a retail-specific version of the ANSI X.12 standard was published and made available through the Uniform Code Council. This standard was developed by the American National Standards Institute (ANSI), a national voluntary organization of companies and individuals who develop standardized business practices. The retail-specific version of the ANSI X.12 standard focuses on electronic transmission of data for business transactions, such as purchase orders and invoices.

Once these standards were put in place, VICS refocused its work on conducting cost/benefit analyses of using VICS' voluntary standards for UPC marking, EDI, and shipping container marking. Under a new name, **Voluntary Interindustry Commerce Standards Association,** this organization recently published reports on recommended floor-ready merchandise standards and recommended technologies for Internet commerce.

The **Textile/Apparel Linkage Council (TALC)** and **Sundries and Apparel Findings Linkage Council (SAFLINC)** were originally formed (in 1986 and 1987, respectively) to establish voluntary EDI standards between apparel manufacturers and their suppliers. Since that time, the councils have completed and published all of the required standards. In 1992 they merged to form TALC/SAFLINC, and in 1994 they were integrated into the Quick Response Committee of the American Apparel Manufacturers Association (now part of the American Apparel and Footwear Association). The **Fabric and Suppliers Linkage Council (FASLINC),** also organized in 1987, focused on communications standards between textile manufacturers and their suppliers. After completing its goals, the FASLINC disbanded in 1991, leaving the implementation of future programs to the American Textile Manufacturers Institute.

Crafted with Pride in U.S.A. Council

The **Crafted with Pride in U.S.A. Council** is a "one-industry" approach to marketing textiles and apparel made in the United States. As indicated in its mission statement, "The Crafted with Pride in U.S.A. Council, Inc. is a committed force of U.S. cotton growers and shippers, labor organizations, fabric distributors and manufacturers of man-made fibers, fabric, apparel and home fashion whose mission is to convince consumers, retailers and apparel manufacturers of the value of purchasing and promoting U.S.-made products" (Crafted with Pride in U.S.A. mission statement). From its conception in 1984, the Crafted with Pride in U.S.A. Council has played a major role in coordinating unified efforts among the various segments of the industry to communicate to consumers that "buying American" matters, for them and for the U.S. economy. This has been accomplished by the use of TV spots, magazine supplements, syndicated columns and newsletters, labels and hangtags, in-store displays, and other promotions (see Figure 1.16).

Figure 1.16: Crafted with Pride in U.S.A. logo.

American Textile Partnership

A number of other partnership groups have been formed to build cooperative efforts. The American Textile Partnership (AMTEX) strives to "enhance the competitiveness of the U.S. Textile Industry, from fibers through fabricated products and retail, by implementing technolgies developed in collaborative R&D programs that link the scientific and engineering resources of government, universities, and industry" (AMTEX Mission Statement). Currently, AMTEX links eight Department of Energy laboratories operated by the U.S. government with nonprofit technical organizations such as [TC][2]. The Demand Activated Manufacturing Automation (DAMA) project is part of AMTEX (see Figure 1.17). DAMA, created in 1993, is assessing and analyzing infrastructure needs and methods to improve collaboration across the supply chain.

BEYOND QR: SUPPLY CHAIN MANAGEMENT

By the late 1990s, QR strategies had been adopted by large and small companies alike. By this time, three types of apparel companies made up the supply chain for soft goods (Parnell, 1998):

- Companies that performed almost all of their own manufacturing, from yarn or fabric to finished garments or other textile products.
- Companies that had a particular niche within the industry, performing specific manufacturing operations, such as manufacturing yarns or fabrics, finishing fabrics, or performing sewing operations.

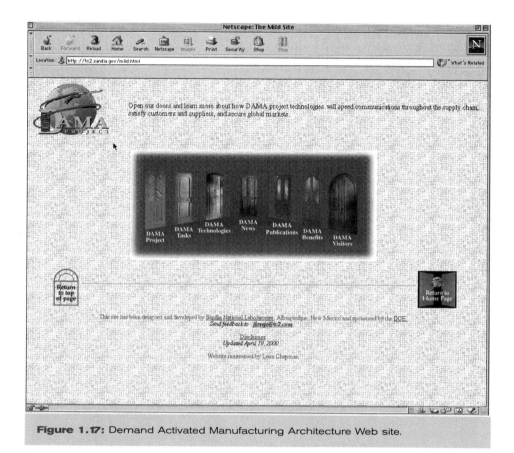

Figure 1.17: Demand Activated Manufacturing Architecture Web site.

■ Companies that were involved in the design, marketing, and distribution of apparel but contracted sewing operations to other companies, either domestically or in other countries.

For each type of company, QR highlighted the importance of and need for additional partnerships among companies throughout the soft goods pipeline. With advances in information technology, the ways companies design, manufacture, and distribute soft goods were affected. This philosophy of sharing and coordinating information across all segments of the soft goods industry was termed **supply chain management**. Supply chain management (SCM) comprises the "collection of actions required to coordinate and manage all activities necessary to bring a product to market,

TABLE 1.2

A Brief History of the U.S. Textile, Apparel, and Retailing Industries

1789–1890: Mechanization of Spinning, Weaving, and Sewing

1791	Samuel Slater, who came to the United States in 1788, opens the first U.S. spinning mill.
1793	Hannah Slater, Samuel's wife, invents the 2-ply cotton sewing thread.
1794	Eli Whitney's cotton gin is patented.
1818	Brooks Brothers opens in New York City.
1853	Levi Strauss joins the family business founded by his brother-in-law, David Stern, which will come to be known as Levi Strauss & Co.
Mid-1880s:	Peddlers open dry goods stores (forerunners of today's department stores):
	1826 - Lord & Taylor
	1842 - Gimbel's
	1849 - Famous-Barr
	1851 - Jordan Marsh
	1852 - Marshall Field's
	1854 - Carson Pirie Scott & Co.
	1857 - Macy's
	1862 - Stewart's
	1867 - Rich's
	1869 - John Wanamaker and Co.
1854	The first U.S. trade association, Hampden County Cotton Manufacturers Association, starts in Hampden County, Massachusetts.
1860	Census data on the women's clothing industry indicated 96 manufacturers producing apparel worth $2,261,546 annually.
1865	William Carter begins knitting cardigan jackets in the kitchen of his house in Needham Heights, Massachusetts. The William Carter Co. will grow to be one of the nation's largest children's underwear companies.

1890–1950: Growth of the Ready-to-Wear Industry

1892	American *Vogue* magazine begins publication.
1892	*Daily Trade Record*, the trade newspaper for the RTW men's wear industry begins publication; became *Daily News Record* in 1916.
1900	The International Ladies' Garment Workers' Union (ILGWU) is founded.
1901	Walin & Nordstrom Shoe Store opens in downtown Seattle.
1902	James Cash Penney, age 26, opens a dry goods and clothing store in Kemmerer, Wyoming. Opening day receipts totaled $466.59.

TABLE 1.2 (continued)

1904	New York seamstress Lena Bryant introduces ready-to-wear maternity wear. Her company, named Lane Bryant, becomes the first large size ready-to-wear producer.
1907	Herbert Marcus, Sr., his sister Carrie, and brother-in-law, A. L. Neiman, start Neiman Marcus department store in Dallas.
1908	Filene's opens its "automatic bargain basement" in Boston. Merchandise in the upstairs store is automatically marked down 25% every week for 3 weeks, then sent to the basement. This practice marks the beginnings of the off-price store.
1909	In November, 20,000 New York shirtwaist makers stage the largest strike by American women to that time.
1910	***Women's Wear Daily***, trade newspaper for the women's wear industry, begins publication.
1911	146 garment workers die in a fire at the Triangle Shirtwaist Co. factory in New York's garment district. The tragedy stimulates a movement to end sweatshop conditions.
1914	The Amalgamated Clothing Workers of America Union is formed as the primary union for the men's wear industry.
1920	Membership in the ILGWU grows to 200,000.
1922	Country Club Plaza, the country's first outdoor shopping mall opens in Kansas City, Kansas.
1923	Pushed by the growing demand among women for ready-to-wear clothing, New York leads the growing industry, manufacturing 80 percent of all women's apparel.
1925	The first Sears Roebuck & Co store opens in Chicago.
1926	J. M. Haggar starts his own men's wear company in Dallas, Texas, using assembly lines to manufacture mens' trousers.
1927	The average price for women's full-fashioned silk stockings is $11.50 per dozen; by 1933 the price plummets to a low of $5.10 per dozen.
1928	Sanford Cluett develops a process to compress fabric under tension to reduce shrinkage, and the "Sanforized" trademark is licensed to cotton finishers.
1932	Sales at Sears, Roebuck & Co retail stores surpass catalog sales.
1934	Membership in the ILGWU grows to 217,000.
1939	Textile Workers Union is founded.
1939	Nylon stockings are introduced.
1941	Congress fixes Thanksgiving, which previously had been a floating holiday in November, at the fourth Thursday in November. Fred Lazarus, Jr., is credited with the idea as a way to expand the Christmas shopping season.
1941	Employment in the textile industry peaks at approximately 1.4 million.

(continued)

TABLE 1.2 (continued)

1944	The Fashion Institute of Technology is founded to support New York's fashion industry.
1947	Leslie Fay is established—and becomes one of the largest women's apparel companies.
1949	Bloomingdale's opens its first branch store in Fresh Meadows, New York.

1950–1980: Diversification and Incorporation

1951	Employment in the apparel and knitwear industries in New York City peaks at 380,000.
1952	Stiletto heels, introduced by Christian Dior.
1952	Orlon® acrylic is introduced; and by 1956, over 70 million Orlon sweaters are sold.
1955	Mary Quant opens her boutique, Bazaar, in London.
1956	Southdale Center, the first enclosed shopping mall, is built in a Minneapolis suburb to serve shoppers.
1957	***Gentlemen's Quarterly*** is first published and distributed through men's wear stores.
1957	Christian Dior dies and Yves Saint Laurent takes over as head designer of the House of Dior.
1958	Supp-hose, a 100 percent nylon stocking designed for women suffering from leg fatigue is patented by the Chester H. Roth Co.
1958-59	To the benefit of intimate apparel, hosiery, and swimwear companies, DuPont introduces its first spandex fiber.
1960	Hanes-Millis Sales Corp. becomes the first national sock manufacturer to distribute its products through wholesalers.
1960	The first Bobbin Show takes place in Columbia, South Carolina, with 12 exhibitors.
1960	American Apparel Manufacturers Association (AAMA) is founded.
1964	John Weitz becomes the first American designer to put his name on a men's wear collection.
1967	Pierre Cardin and Bill Blass boutiques open in Bonwit Teller's New York store.
1968	Calvin Klein Ltd. is established.
1968	Polo Ralph Lauren is created.
1968	Minimum wage is increased to $1.60 per hour.
1969	The Gap opens in San Francisco, selling records, cassettes, and Levi's. The store drew its name from the "generation gap."
1970	L'eggs Products introduces egg-shaped packaging and self-service distribution for hosiery.
1970	First introduced in Europe, hot pants are a short-lived fad in America.
1971	Diane Von Furstenberg introduces her jersey wrap dress, which is an immediate success.

TABLE 1.2 (continued)	
1972	The Care Labeling of Textile Wearing Apparel and Certain Piece Goods Act goes into effect.
1973	No nonsense hosiery is first distributed by Kayser Roth.
1975	Giorgio Armani Co. is founded, and Armani launches his first menswear line.
1975	Geoffrey Beene becomes the first American designer to show his collections during fashion openings in Milan, Italy.
1975	John T. Malloy's *Dress for Success* is published.
1976	Liz Claiborne, Inc., is created and later grows to be the largest U.S. women's apparel company.
1976	The nation's first major warehouse retailer, Price Club, opens in San Diego.
1976	The Amalgamated Clothing Workers of America Union merges with the Textile Workers of America and the United Shoe Workers of America unions to form the Amalgamated Clothing and Textile Workers Union (ACTWU).
1977	Ralph Lauren designs the costumes for the movie *Annie Hall*.
1978	Calvin Klein introduces his first men's wear collection.

1980–Present: Quick Response and Beyond

1980	[TC]^2 begins operation to research and demonstrate new computer technology in the textile and apparel industries.
1984	Donna Karan New York is founded by Donna Karan and her husband Stephan Weiss.
1984	Crafted With Pride in U.S.A. Council is formed.
1986	The Voluntary Interindustry Communications Standards Committee (VICS) is formed.
1986	May Department Stores acquires Associated Dry Goods.
1987	Christian Lacroix opens a new couture house in Paris.
1991	Donna Karan launches her men's wear line.
1994	The North American Free Trade Agreement (NAFTA) goes into effect.
1994	Federated Stores acquires Macy's.
1995	The two primary labor unions in the textile and apparel industries, the Amalgamated Clothing and Textile Workers Union and the International Ladies Garment Workers Union merge to become the Union of Needletrades, Industrial, and Textile Employees (UNITE).
1995	Federated Stores acquires Broadway Stores.
1997	Designer superstar, Gianni Versace, is murdered.
1998	[TC]^2 makes a 3-D body measurement system commercially available.
2005	Quotas on textiles and apparel imported from World Trade Organization (WTO) members are phased out.

including procuring raw materials, producing goods, transporting and distributing those goods and managing the selling process" (Abend, 1998, p. 48).

Similar to QR, the goals of SCM are to reduce inventory, shorten the time for raw material to become a finished product in the hands of a consumer, and provide better service to the consumer. Collaboration, trust, and dependability are the cornerstones to making both the QR and the SCM processes effective. However, some analysts view SCM as what enables the QR philosophy to be successful. SCM goes beyond QR in that SCM companies share forecasting, point-of-sale data, inventory information, and information about unforeseen changes in supply or demand for materials or products. Currently, large companies such as VF Corporation have invested in the information technology infrastructure to make SCM a reality. Smaller companies are exploring Web-based technology for information sharing (Abend, 1998; Butenhoff, 1999; Parnell, 1998).

Summary

Since their beginnings in the Industrial Revolution of the eighteenth century, the textile and apparel industries have maintained an important place in the American economy. Spurred by mechanization of spinning, weaving, and sewing processes, the textile and apparel industries moved from craft industries to factory-based industries. Immigrants provided the necessary labor force for these growing industries.

By the 1920s, ready-made apparel was available to most consumers. Two types of apparel production were developed—modern, large factories and small contractors who sewed piecework at home. The textile and apparel industries emerged from the Great Depression of the 1930s with the need to address growing and changing demands from consumers. Technological advancements in synthetic fibers provided a new source of materials for apparel. However, it was not until after World War II that these easy-care fibers hit the American market.

The 1950s saw growth and expansion of apparel companies, many becoming large, publicly owned corporations. This growth continued through the 1960s. However, as labor costs in the United States increased and consumer demand for lower-cost clothing also increased, companies began moving production outside the United States. As imports of textiles and apparel surged, the American industry examined how it could increase productivity and global competitiveness. The result of this analysis was the development of the Quick Response system, an industrywide program made up of a number of strategies to shorten the production time from raw fiber to the sale of a finished product to the ultimate consumer. Quick Response strategies are seen in all segments of the textile, apparel, and retailing industries. Interindustry cooperation through joint research ventures, [TC]², interindustry linkage councils, the Crafted with Pride in U.S.A. Council, and the American Textile Partnership have increased the effectiveness of Quick Response strategies. Enhanced information technology has allowed for increased partnerships throughout the soft goods pipeline. Supply chain management encompasses these information-sharing processes to improve the efficiency and effectiveness of the textile and apparel industries.

Key Terms

cotton gin

Crafted with Pride in U.S.A. Council

Fabric and Suppliers Linkage Council (FASLINC)

International Ladies' Garment Workers' Union (ILGWU)

mass production

power loom

Quick Response (QR)

ready-to-wear (RTW)

sewing machine

size standards

spinning mill

Sundries and Apparel Findings Linkage Council (SAFLINC)

supply chain management

Textile/Apparel Linkage Council (TALC)

Textile/Clothing Technology Corporation [TC]²

Voluntary Interindustry Commerce Standards Association (VICS)

Discussion Questions

1. What technological developments were imperative for the development and growth of the textile and apparel industries in the United States?

2. Look in a historic costume book and select a fashion from at least 15 years ago. What social and technological developments were necessary for the production and distribution of the fashion?

3. In your own words, define *Quick Response*. Why would a textile or apparel manufacturer want to adopt QR strategies? What technology developments have led to supply chain management?

References

Abend, Jules. (1995, October). Textiles making all the right moves. *Bobbin*, pp. 40–45.

Abend, Jules. (1998, May). SCM is putting a buzz in industry ears. *Bobbin*, pp. 48–54.

American Apparel Manufacturing Association. (1995, January). *Quick Response Handout* [online]. Available: http://www.tc2.com/qrlc/qrhand.htm [December 6, 1995].

American Textile Manufacturers Institute. (1978). *Textiles: Our First Great Industry*. Charlotte, NC: Author.

Bedell, Thomas. (1994, March). Innocents lost: The great Triangle fire. *Destination Discovery*, pp. 24–31.

Bicentennial of U.S. Textiles. (1990, October). *Textile World*.

Brill, Eileen B. (1985). From immigrants to imports. In *WWD/75 Years in Fashion, 1910–1985*. Supplement to *WWD*, pp. 10–14. New York: Fairchild Publications.

Butenhoff, Peter. (1999, May). Future perfect: Will past tensions dissolve with SCM? *Apparel Industry Magazine*, pp. SCM-2–SCM-4.

Davis-Meyers, Mary L. (1992). The development of American menswear pattern drafting technology, 1822 to 1860. *Clothing and Textiles Research Journal*, 10 (3), 12–20.

Douglas-David, Lynn. (1989, October). EDI: Fiction or reality? *Bobbin*, pp. 86–90.

Ewing, Elizabeth. (1992). *History of Twentieth Century Fashion*. (3rd ed.). Lanham, MD: Barnes & Noble Books.

Fortess, Fred. (1988, May). Squaring off with the competition. *Bobbin*, pp. 104–110.

Fraser, Steven. (1983). Combined and uneven development in the men's clothing industry. *Business History Review*, 57, 522–547.

Hasty, Susan E. (Ed.). (1994, March). *The Quick Response Handbook*. Supplement to *Apparel Industry Magazine*.

Hohanty, Gail F. (1990). From craft to industry: Textile production in the United States. *Material History Bulletin*, 31, 23–31.

Hosiery and Underwear. (1976, July). Issue devoted to the history of hosiery and underwear. NY: Harcourt Brace Jovanovich.

Kazis, Richard. (1989, August/September). Rags to riches? *Technology Review*, pp. 42–53.

Kidwell, Claudia B., and Christman, Margaret C. (1974). *Suiting Everyone: The Democratization of Clothing in America*. Washington, DC: Smithsonian Institution.

Kramer, William M., and Stern, Norton B. (1987). Levi Strauss: The man behind the myth. *Western States Jewish Historical Quarterly*, 19 (3), 257–263.

Melinkoff, Ellen. (1984). *What We Wore*. New York: Quill.

Parnell, Clay. (1998, June). Supply chain management in the soft goods industry. *Apparel Industry Magazine*, pp. 60–61.

Quick Response: America's Competitive Advantage [slide set program guide]. (1988). Washington, DC: American Textile Manufacturer's Institute.

Richards, Florence S. (1951). *The Ready-to-Wear Industry* 1900–1950. New York: Fairchild Publications.

Smarr, Susan L. (1988, December). [TC]²'s call to action. *Bobbin*, pp. 127–135.

Steele, Valerie. (1988). *Paris Fashion: A Cultural History*. New York: Oxford University Press.

Stegemeyer, Anne. (1996). *Who's Who in Fashion*. (3rd ed.). New York: Fairchild Publications.

[TC]² Mission (2001). [TC]² Home Page [online]. Available: http://www.tc2.com [February 1, 2001].

"I Hate Copycats"

and **Legal Framework** Business of Textile and
Apparel Companies

MILLIKEN

IN THIS CHAPTER YOU WILL LEARN:

- the ways in which a business can be owned and operated—sole proprietorships, partnerships, and corporations.

- Terminology related to business organization.

- the ways in which businesses within the textile and apparel complex compete.

- What licensing is and how textile and apparel companies use licensing agreements.

- the primary marketing channels used by textile and apparel companies.

- the federal laws that can affect textile and apparel companies.

Business Organization and Company Ownership

Textile and Apparel Companies come in all sizes and types. Some are large corporations that employ thousands of people; others are small companies with one or two employees. Regardless of size and organizational structure, every company in the textile and apparel pipeline is in business to make a profit while providing consumers with the products and services they desire. Because many people planning careers in the textile and apparel industries hope to own their own businesses someday, an understanding of the variety of business organizations among textile and apparel companies in the United States is an important starting point for our further examination of the operation of these companies. In addition, information about business organizations is important for planning careers and assessing companies in terms of employment and advancement opportunities. Depending on their objectives, needs, and size, textile and apparel companies can be owned and organized in a number of ways. The three most common legal forms of business ownership are sole proprietorships, partnerships, and corporations. The three types of business ownership are compared in Table 2.1. Each form of business can be found among textile and apparel companies.

SOLE PROPRIETORSHIPS

The **sole proprietorship** is a very common form of business ownership in which an individual, the "sole proprietor," owns the business and its property. The sole proprietor typically runs the day-to-day operations of the company but may have employees to help in running the business. Any profit from the business is considered personal income and taxed accordingly; the owner is personally liable for any debt the business may incur.

TABLE 2.1

Comparisons Among Sole Proprietorships, Partnerships, and Corporations

Business Organization Form	Sole Proprietorship	Partnership	Corporation
Ease of formation	Easy to form Business licenses required	Easy to form Business licenses required Written contract advisable	Difficult to form Charter required Registration with the SEC required for publicly held corporations
Operational Strategies	Owner also runs the business	Partners can bring range of expertise to running the business	Board hires individuals with specific expertise to run the business
Liability	Unlimited personal liability	Unlimited personal liability for each partner	Limited liability; stockholders not personally liable for corporate debt
Tax Considerations	Sole proprietor's income taxed as personal income	Partners' income taxed as personal income	Double taxation (corporation's income taxed and dividends taxed as personal income)
Potential for employee advancement	Limited, depending upon size of company	Some incentive for employees to become partners	Employees can move up through the ranks
Examples	Small companies Freelance designer Independent sales representative	Small- or medium-size companies Designer and marketer who join forces to form an apparel company	Large companies May be private or publicly held (e.g., Liz Claiborne, Monsanto, VF Corporation) Some may be multinational

Advantages of Sole Proprietorships

This type of business ownership has a number of advantages. For one thing, only a few business licenses are needed. For example, in Los Angeles the following licenses are needed to open an apparel manufacturing business: (1) City of Los Angeles business license, (2) garment license, (3) resale license, (4) public health license, (5) federal employer identification number (if there are employees), (6) state employer identification number (if there are employees), and (7) registration number (for labeling purposes; in lieu of putting the company name on labels). Sole proprietorships are also easy to dissolve. When the sole proprietor decides to stop doing business, the sole proprietorship is essentially ended.

Another advantage of a sole proprietorship is the control and flexibility given the sole proprietor, who often finds personal satisfaction in being the boss and making the decisions regarding the direction the business will take. This personal satisfaction is the characteristic of this form of business ownership that individuals most often desire.

Disadvantages of Sole Proprietorships

This type of business ownership also has a number of disadvantages. The biggest disadvantage is that sole proprietors are personally liable for any business debts. This means that if the business owes money, creditors can take all business and personal assets (such as the owner's home) to pay the debts of the business. This **unlimited liability** is one of the largest risks a sole proprietor takes in starting the business.

Another disadvantage of sole proprietorships is that because there are no partners, the sole proprietor needs to have expertise in all areas of running the business. For example, an apparel designer who wants to start his or her own business not only must handle the design aspect of the business, but may also need to work with fabric suppliers, contractors, and retailers; deal with accounting; manage personnel; and market the product. The difficulty in running all aspects of the business is often overwhelming for new sole proprietors. In some cases, sole proprietors will hire employees who have expertise in specific areas in which the owner is not expert.

In a sole proprietorship, raising capital (funds or resources) for business initiation or expansion can be difficult. Capital needed to start or expand the business may be obtained by tapping the owner's personal funds, by purchasing goods and services on credit, or by the sole proprietor personally borrowing money. As with other forms of business ownership, sole proprietorships must keep books of account for federal, state, and municipal income tax and other regulatory purposes. Profits are taxed as personal income.

Examples of Sole Proprietorships

Sole proprietorships tend to be small companies, the resources and complexities or which can be handled by one owner. Individuals may start companies as sole proprietorships and then, as the company grows, change the form of ownership to a partnership or corporation. Examples of sole proprietorships within textile and apparel industries might include a freelance textile or apparel designer who sells his or her work to larger textile or apparel companies, an independent sales representative who sells apparel lines to retailers, or an apparel retailer who owns a small specialty store.

PARTNERSHIPS

There are times when two or more people want to join forces in owning a business. In these cases a **partnership** may be formed. According to the Uniform Partnership Act (UPA), a partnership is an "association of two or more persons to carry on as co-owners of a business for profit." A partnership may be formed between two individuals or among three or more individuals through written contracts called *articles of partnership*. Although contracts will vary, they typically include:

1. The partnership's name.

2. The partners' and officers' names.

3. The intentions or purpose of the partnership.

4. The amount and form of contributions (money and real estate, for example) from each partner.

5. The length of the partnership.

6. Procedures to add and eliminate partners.

7. The way profit or losses will be divided among the partners.

8. The degree of management authority each partner will have.

9. The designation of which partners, if any, are entitled to salaries.

10. How partnership affairs will be handled if a partner dies or is disabled.

Profits are shared among the partners, known as **general partners**, according to the conditions laid out in the partnership contract. Profit from a partnership is taxed as part of each partner's personal income. Like sole proprietors, partners have unlimited liability in that they are together liable for the entire debt of the partnership as outlined in the partnership contract. Dissolution of a partnership can result from a partner's withdrawal, the entry of new partners, a partner's death, a partner's bankruptcy, a partner's incapacity or misconduct, or the goals of the business becoming obsolete.

Limited Partnerships.

Sometimes individuals want to join or invest in a partnership, but do not want to have the unlimited liability for partnership dept that may be larger than their investment. This can be achieved through a **limited partnership.** In this type of partnership, a limited partner has **limited liability;** that is, he or she is liable only for the amount of capital he or she invested in the business, and any profits are shared according to the conditions of the limited partnership contract. Establishing limited partnerships can be an attractive way for general partners to raise capital to initiate or expand their business. Typically the limited partner does not take an active role in managing the business, which is handled by the general partners.

Advantages of Partnerships

Partnerships have some advantages over sole proprietorships. Like sole proprietorships, partnerships are relatively easy to establish; the same business licenses are required to start a partnership as a sole proprietorship. Unlike sole proprietorships, however, where only one person owns the business, partners can pool their range of expertise and resources to run the company. For example, one partner in an apparel company may have expertise in design and another partner may have expertise in business and accounting. Raising capital for partnerships is also somewhat easier than for sole proprietors because the resources of more than one person can be tapped and the combined resources of partners can be used as collateral when borrowing money. Through the use of limited partnerships, resources can also be raised for business initiation or expansion.

Another advantage of partnerships over sole proprietorships is that advancement opportunities for employees are greater: employees may be given the opportunity to become partners in the business. This can be a valuable incentive when recruiting and hiring employees.

Disadvantages of Partnerships

Partnerships also have a number of disadvantages. As with sole proprietorships, the primary disadvantage of partnerships is liability exposure. This means that each partner is personally liable for any debt of the partnership, regardless of which partner was responsible for incurring the debt. In addition to books of account, the UPA also requires that partnerships keep minutes of meetings and business records.

Another disadvantage of a partnership is the potential for disagreement among partners in running the business or setting the future direction of the business. Partnerships often dissolve because of such disagreements. As with sole proprietorships, a partnership is dependent on its owners, and dissolution is presumed when a partner leaves the partnership. Although ease of dissolution of a partnership can be viewed as an advantage, it can also lead to a lack of continuity in the organization.

Examples of Partnerships

Partnerships are typically small-to-medium-size companies that require a combination of specialized skills to be successful. For example, two or more individuals may start an apparel company, each bringing unique skills (e.g., design, marketing, operations, etc.) to the business. A number of large apparel manufacturers, such as Calvin Klein, Esprit de Corp., and Liz Claiborne, started as partnerships. For example, Calvin Klein borrowed money from his friend Barry Schwartz to start his design company, and the two have remained partners in the business (now a private corporation). In the 1960s and 1970s, Doug Tompkins, Susie Tompkins, and Jane Tise owned an apparel company called Plain Jane. In 1979, the Tompkins bought out Tise and renamed the company Esprit de Corp. Since the Tompkins divorced in the early 1990s, Susie Tompkins runs Esprit (now a private corporation). Elisabeth "Liz" Claiborne started her business in 1976 with her husband, Arthur Ortenberg, and a manufacturing expert, Leonard Boxer, as partners. Later, Jerome Chazen joined as a partner. Within a year the company was making a profit, and in 1981 it became a publicly held corporation.

CORPORATIONS

The **corporation** is the most complex form of business ownership because corporations are considered legal entities that exist regardless of who owns them. Although assets owned by the corporation, such as buildings or equipment, are tangible, the corporation itself is considered intangible. Unlike a sole proprietorship or partnership, ownership of a corporation is held by **stockholders** (or *shareholders*), who own shares of stock in the corporation. Each share of stock represents a percentage of the company, so that if someone owns 50 percent of the stock in a company, he or she owns 50 percent of the company. Stockholders in a corporation are only liable for the amount they paid for their stock. Thus, if the company fails, stockholders are not liable for the corporation's debts beyond their initial investment.

The **board of directors** of the corporation is elected by the stockholders. Each stockholder has a percentage of votes in electing the board that reflects the percentage of stock he or she owns. The board of directors is the chief governing body of the corporation. It plans the direction the company will take and sets policy for the corporation. The board also hires the officers of the corporation (e.g., the president, chief executive officer, chief financial officer, etc.) who run the business. Stockholders may participate in the management of the business, but many stockholders in corporations have very little or no participation in day-to-day operations. Profit is paid out to stockholders in the form of **dividends** which are taxed as personal income. Stockholders may also receive dividends in the form of additional stock in the company. Figure 2.1 shows some examples of corporations in the textile, apparel, and retailing industries.

Figure 2.1: Examples of corporations in the textile, apparel, and retailing industries.

Types of Corporations

The two basic types of corporations are publicly held corporations and private corporations. Differences between publicly held and private corporations are primarily
in terms of the ownership and transferability of shares of stock. In **publicly held
corporations**, at least some of the shares of stock are owned by the general public.
Publicly held corporations usually have a large number of stockholders who buy and
sell their stock on the public market, either through an exchange (New York Stock
Exchange, American Stock Exchange, or National Association of Securities Dealers
Automatic Quotation System [NASDAQ]) or through brokers "over the counter." Publicly held corporations must submit financial information to the Securities and
Exchange Commission (SEC), which regulates the securities markets. Table 2.2 lists
top publicly held corporations in the textile industry; Table 2.3 lists top publicly
held corporations in the apparel industry.

Private corporations are those in which the shares are owned by a small number of individuals; that is, the stock is not available in public markets and has not been
issued for public purchase. Typically, the stockholders of a private corporation are
highly involved in the operations of the company. Calvin Klein Inc. and Pendleton

---

TABLE 2.2

Top U.S. Publicly Held Fiber and Textile Corporations

Monsanto
Hoechst Celanese
DuPont (fibers division)
Owens-Corning
Springs Industries
Collins & Aikman
West Point-Pepperell
Dominion Textile
Fieldcrest Cannon
Unifi
Delta Woodside
Guilford Mills
Dixie Yarns
DWG (textiles division)
Galey & Lord
Thomaston
United Merchants & Mfrs.
Fab
Dyersburg

TABLE 2.3

U.S. Public Apparel Corporations

Sara Lee Branded Apparel
VF Corporation
Reebok International
NIKE
Liz Claiborne
Fruit of the Loom
Warnaco Group
Kellwood
Jones Apparel Group
Polo Ralph Lauren
Tommy Hilfiger
Phillips-Van Heusen
Russell Corporation
Oxford Industries
Hartmarx
Donna Karan International
Nautica
Angelica
Guess?
Columbia Sportswear
OshKosh B'Gosh
Haggar
Tarrant Apparel Group
Authentic Fitness
McNaughton Apparel Group

Source: DesMarteau, Kathleen; Kalman, Jordan; and Meadows, Shawn. (1999, June). The Bobbin Top 40. **Bobbin**, pp. 46–62.

Woolen Mills are examples of private corporations in the apparel industry. **Multinational corporations** are either private or publicly held corporations that operate in several countries. With increased world production and trade of apparel, accessories, and home fashions, multinational corporations have grown in number and importance.

Advantages of Corporations

Corporations have a number of advantages over other forms of business ownership. For publicly held corporations, the act of going public (becoming a publicly held corporation) itself can be a benefit to businesses in raising capital to expand or diversify. When a corporation goes public, investors buy shares of stock based upon how well they believe the company will perform in the future. These investments can then be used to expand or improve the company. For example, Liz Claiborne went public in 1981 and grew to become one of the largest apparel companies in the world.

For both publicly held and private corporations, the main advantage of incorporation is the **limited liability** of the owners (stockholders). If the corporation fails, creditors cannot seize the personal assets of the stockholders to pay the corporate debt. This is the primary reason why two or more individuals may decide to create a private corporation rather than a partnership when beginning a business. Another advantage corporations have is the flexibility and ease with which ownership can be transferred. Unlike a sole proprietorship or partnership, a corporation does not cease to exist if one of its owners withdraws or dies. Shares are simply transferred to heirs or sold. In most cases, stockholders are free to sell their stock at any time. Thus, because of this ease of transferring ownership, corporations seldom dissolve because of ownership issues.

Unlike the management of a sole proprietorship or partnership, management of a corporation is not dependent on ownership. The management group runs the day-to-day operations of the company regardless of who owns the business that day. This allows the board of directors to hire the best-qualified individuals to manage the specialized areas of the company.

In addition, in large corporations there is a great potential for employee advancement within the organization. Employees may work in specialized areas of the company and advance through the ranks. Such potential for advancement can serve as an incentive for employees within the organization.

Disadvantages of Corporations.

With all of these advantages, why are not all businesses corporations? Despite the apparent advantages, a number of disadvantages exist. It is much more complicated to establish a corporation than a sole proprietorship or partnership. A corporation is organized around a legal charter that outlines its scope and activity. Because of this, legal fees and other costs involved in incorporation are higher than for other forms of business ownership. This is especially true if a company wants to go public. It is estimated that out-of-pocket expenses for going public can exceed $250,000 (Alterbaum, 1987). The corporation's formal charter also restricts the type of business performed by the corporation. In other words, the board of directors or officers of a publicly held apparel company cannot shift from producing apparel to producing automobiles without filing a new charter. Corporations are organized under the laws of specific states, and each state has statutes that governs corporations. There are also federal laws (i.e., Securities Act of 1933, Securities Exchange Act of 1934) that regulate publicly held corporations in the issuing and selling of their shares of stock. Other federal laws that govern businesses, including corporations, are described later in this chapter.

Another disadvantage to corporations are corporate taxes. Because they are legal entities, corporations are taxed on their income at a tax rate higher than that on personal income. In addition, dividends paid to stockholders are considered personal income and therefore subject to personal income tax.

Corporations are often large companies that can have thousands of employees. Because of this, employees sometimes view corporations as impersonal and bureaucratic. In addition, unlike other forms of business ownership, owners of corporations (especially publicly held corporations) might not be involved in the day-to-day operations of the business; employees who are not stockholders are not likely to have the same commitment to the corporation as owners of sole proprietorships or partnerships may have.

Despite these disadvantages, the limited liability associated with corporations and ease of transferring ownership make them very attractive for investors who want to own part of specific companies. Thus, private and publicly held corporations are the most powerful forms of business in the textile and apparel industries. In fact, some categories within the industry, such as intimate apparel, are dominated by large corporations. Within the intimate apparel category, corporations including Warnaco Group (with brands including Warner's, Olga, and Calvin Klein), Sara Lee (with brands including Playtex, Bali, Wonderbra, Hanes, and Polo Ralph Lauren), and VF Corporation (with brands including Vanity Fair and Vassarette) control most of the production and distribution.

TERMS ASSOCIATED WITH COMPANY EXPANSION AND DIVERSIFICATION

As one reads trade and consumer literature about companies' organizations and operations, one comes across a number of terms (e.g., *merger, consolidation, takeover, leveraged buyout,* and *conglomerate*) related to the company's organization. In order to interpret the literature, it is important to have a basic understanding of these terms. A **merger** is the blending of one company into another company. For example, if company A and company B merge, the result will be a larger company A, which will assume ownership of company B's assets and liability for all company B's debts. On the other hand, a **consolidation** is the combining of two companies, with the result being a new company. For example, if company A and company B consolidate, the result is company C. A **takeover** results when one company or individual gains control of another company by buying a large enough portion of its shares. Takeovers can be either mergers or consolidations; *friendly,* in that the company that is taken over agrees to the association, or *hostile,* in that the company that is taken over does not agree to the association. Being informed about possible mergers and consolidations within the industry is important for management-level textile and apparel executives in their strategic decision making.

In a **leveraged buyout (LBO),** a publicly held corporation's stock is purchased by a group of investors who borrow money from an investment firm using the corporation's assets as collateral. A leveraged buyout is often used in changing a publicly held corporation into a private corporation. For example, in 1985 Levi Strauss & Co. went through a $1.6 billion leveraged buyout led by its chief executive officer, Robert D. Haas, that resulted in the then publicly held corporation becoming a private corporation.

Conglomerates are diversified companies (typically corporations) that are involved with significantly different lines of business. For example, Sara Lee is considered a conglomerate because it not only produces food products, but is also the parent company for a number of businesses that produce other products, including hosiery (e.g., Hanes, L'eggs), intimate apparel (e.g., Bali), sportswear (e.g., Champion), and accessories and small leather goods (e.g., Coach).

Forms of Competition

The goal of every sole proprietorship, partnership, and corporation in the textile and apparel industries is to provide products or services that are desired by the ultimate consumer. However, many companies are vying for the consumer's dollar. Thus companies, whether they be sole proprietorships, partnerships, or corporations, compete with one another. Companies that successfully compete will make a profit that will either be reinvested in the company or paid to the company's owners or stockholders.

COMPETITIVE STRATEGIES

Companies compete in a number of ways that in part determine their business strategies. Companies typically compete on any of the following bases:

- The price of the merchandise to the retailer or consumer.
- The quality of the design, fabrics, and construction.
- Innovation—how unique or fashionable the merchandise is.
- Services offered to the retailer or consumer.
- A combination of these factors.

For example, one company that produces children's wear may have lower prices than its competition; another may provide better-quality merchandise; another may produce children's wear that is more fashionable; and still another may provide consumers with catalogs or other services. Thus a company's business practices are based on competitive strategies. For example, Hanna Andersson, a children's apparel manufacturer headquartered in Portland, Oregon, is known for its socially responsible business practices (see Figure 2.2). As part of this corporate philosophy, Hanna Andersson offers its customers the opportunity to recycle their Hanna Andersson clothing through the "Hannadowns" program. Used Hanna Andersson children's clothing can be returned to the company, which donates the clothing to charities across the country. In return, the customers receive a credit of 20 percent of the purchase price on their Hanna Andersson accounts. Such services are one way Hanna Andersson separates itself from its competition and appeals to the company's customers.

COMPETITIVE SITUATIONS

Within American society, four primary competitive situations can exist: monopoly, oligopoly, pure competition, and monopolistic competition. In a **monopoly,** one company typically dominates the market and can thus price its goods and/or services at whatever level it wishes. Because a monopoly essentially eliminates or drastically reduces competition, federal laws prohibit companies from buying out their competition and, in effect, becoming a monopoly. Only essential services, such as utilities, can legally operate as monopolies in today's market, and the prices they charge are heavily regulated by the government. In an **oligopoly,** a few companies dominate and essentially have control of the market, thereby making it very diffi-

Figure 2.2: Hanna Andersson's competitive strategies focus on quality of merchandise, service, and social responsibility.

cult for other companies to enter. The dominant companies compete among themselves through product and service differentiation and advertising. Although oligopolies are not illegal, it is illegal for the dominant companies to set artificial prices among themselves. In many ways, the athletic shoe industry can be considered an oligopoly because it is dominated by a few companies (e.g., NIKE, Adidas, Reebok). Thus the companies have some control over the price they charge for their goods.

In **pure competition,** there are many producers and consumers of similar products, so price is determined by market demand. The market for agricultural commodities, such as cotton or wool, is the closest to pure competition that can be found in the textile and apparel industries. In these cases the price for the product—raw cotton or wool—is determined by supply and demand of the commodity. For example, in the early 1990s the price for raw cotton skyrocketed because of high consumer demand and worldwide shortages (low supply).

The most common form of competition in the textile and apparel industries is **monopolistic competition,** in which many companies compete in terms of product type, but the specific products of any one company are perceived as unique by consumers. For example, many companies produce denim jeans, including Levi Strauss & Co., Lee, Wrangler, Guess?, Girbaud, Chic by H.I.S., Liz Claiborne, Gap, Old Navy, and Calvin Klein. However, through product differentiation, advertising, distribution strategy and pricing, each company has created a unique image. By creating this unique image in consumers' minds, each has, in some respect, a monopoly in terms of its specific product and therefore has some control over price. A consumer who wants only Calvin Klein jeans and seeks out that particular brand may be willing to pay a premium for that brand.

Within monopolistic competition, each company must create a perceived difference between its product and the competitions' products. This can be achieved in a number of ways:

- The product is differentiated by design characteristics.
- The company uses advertising to create public awareness of its brand name or trademark (see Figure 2.3).
- The company buys the use of a well-established brand name, trademark, or other image through licensing programs.
- A retailer creates **private label** or **store brand** merchandise that is unique to its store or catalog. Some private labels are Arizona (JCPenney), Classiques Entier (Nordstrom), Cascade Blues (Mervyn's), Gap, Eddie Bauer, and L.L.Bean.
- A manufacturer may expand its services to consumers, as when it opens retail stores (e.g., Polo Ralph Lauren, Liz Claiborne, Tommy Hilfiger) or offers goods through catalogs and other home shopping venues.

Figure 2.3: Apparel companies strive to create unique images to gain competitive advantage.

In these ways, consumers associate a company's goods with a particular unique image.

Licensing

One of the methods used by textile and apparel companies to create a perceived difference in their product is **licensing.** Because of the widespread use of licensing within the textile and apparel industries, an understanding of the role it plays in textile and apparel production is important. Licensing is the selling by the owner (*licensor*) of the right to use a particular name, image, or design to another party (*licensee*), typically a manufacturer for payment of royalties. The licensee buys the right to use the name, image, or design, referred to as the *property,* on merchandise to add value to the merchandise. Examples of licensed products include sunglasses manufactured by Bausch & Lomb with the Donna Karan label on them; hosiery manufactured by Pennaco, Inc., a subsidiary of Danskin, as the Ralph Lauren Collection; sweatshirts manufactured by Champion with the San Francisco 49ers football team logo on the front; infant and toddler apparel produced by Franco Apparel under the name Starter Baby and Starter Kids; athletic activewear produced by Fruit of the Loom under the Wilson label; jackets manufactured by Haddad Apparel under the name Harley-Davidson; or sheets and pillowcases manufactured by Dundee Mills with Disney Babies characters printed on the fabric.

According to Murray Altchuler, executive director of the Licensing Industry Merchandisers' Association, "licensed merchandise well marketed creates excitement and uniqueness by adding an extra dimension to a product line" (1988, p. 5). This extra dimension is the image of the property transferred to the product. Some companies are entirely licensed (e.g., J. G. Hook, Hang Ten) in that all of their products are licensed; other companies license certain product lines (e.g., Liz Claiborne fragrance, Donna Karan sunglasses, Polo by Ralph Lauren boy's wear).

TYPES OF LICENSED NAMES, IMAGES, AND DESIGNS

The types of names, images, and designs that are licensed vary widely, although the majority fall into the following categories:

- *Character and entertainment licensing.* Such images as cartoon characters, movie or television characters, and fictional characters are often lisensed to appear on a range of goods. Examples include Disney characters; Peanuts cartoon characters; Barbie dolls; Lion King characters; Star Wars characters; and likenesses of Indiana Jones or Superman. In recent years, licensed merchandise relating to movies and movie characters has been extremely popular, particularly for infant and children's clothing and other children's merchandise (see Figure 2.4a).

- *Corporate licensing.* The licensing of brand names and trademarks of corporations such as IBM, Harley-Davidson, or Coca-Cola is also common. Brand extension licensing extends a brand well-know in a particular product area to a different product area such as Porsche sunglasses, Coca-Cola stuffed toy polar bears, Pillsbury Doughboy potholders, or Harley-Davidson armchairs.

- *Designer name licensing.* Designers including Pierre Cardin, Chanel, Yves Saint Laurent, Ralph Lauren, Calvin Klein, Donna Karan, and many others license their names as brand names for products including scarves, jewelry, fragrances, cosmetics, home fashions, and shoes (see Figure 2.4b).

- *Celebrity name licensing.* Celebrities also license their names and brands. Examples include Stephanie Powers, who has licensed her name to Sears for a line of women's apparel; Jaclyn Smith and Martha Stewart, who have licensed their names to Kmart for apparel and home fashions, respectively; and Kathie Lee Gifford, who has licensed her name to Wal-Mart for lines of private label apparel.

- *Nostalgia licensing.* Manufacturers license the names and images of legends such as Marilyn Monroe, James Dean, or Babe Ruth, as well as old-time movies and radio and TV shows, such as *The Lone Ranger* and *King Kong.*

- *Sports and collegiate licensing.* Professional sports team and university logos are licensed to appear on sport-related merchandise, such as sweatshirts with the Green Bay Packers logo or caps with the University of Tennessee logo.

- *Event and festival licensing.* The names or logos of such events as the Kentucky Derby, the Indianapolis 500, Wimbledon, and the U.S. Open golf tournament are also licensed for use on products.

- *Art licensing.* Manufacturers license great works of art for merchandise featuring reproductions of them.

The success of licensing depends on consumers' desire for goods with a perceived difference based on brand name, trademark, or image. The diversity of types of licensed goods attests to its effectiveness in creating a favorable perceived difference in the eyes of consumers.

THE DEVELOPMENT OF LICENSED PRODUCTS

A well-established image-oriented property is a must for the success of any licensed product. When such a property exists, the development of licensed products based on it involves a number of steps. The stages of development of licensed products are as follows (Altchuler, 1988):

1. The image or design, commonly referred to as the property, is created. For example, the red, white, and blue logo of Tommy Hilfiger is created.

2. Consumers are exposed to the property through the media. The Tommy Hilfiger name and trademark are used in advertising, hangtags, publications, and so on.

3. The property is marketed by the licensor to build name or image recognition. Tommy Hilfiger builds a reputation among consumers for trendy fashion, quality, and value. The name and trademark are associated with these characteristics in consumers' minds.

4. Merchandise with the property added is produced by a variety of manufacturers. Tommy Hilfiger licenses the name and trademark to several manufacturers of apparel, accessories, and fragrances.

5. Merchandise is distributed by retailers. Retailers who have been successful with Tommy Hilfiger sportswear also will want to carry licensed Tommy Hilfiger merchandise, such as accessories and fragrances.

6. Merchandise is demanded by consumers. Consumers identify with the Tommy Hilfiger name and perceive the licensed products as having an added value because the Tommy Hilfiger name and trademark are attached to the merchandise.

THE LICENSING CONTRACT

The terms of the agreement between the licensee and licensor is outlined in a contract. Typically a licensing agreement will include the following elements:

■ *Time limit.* For many licensed products timing is everything. For example, the contract for the image of a currently popular movie character may be for a shorter contract than for a classic designer name.

- *Royalty payment.* Typically royalties of 7 to 14 percent of the wholesale price of the goods sold are paid by the licensee to the licensor.
- *Image.* Contract clauses specify how the image will appear, giving the licensor control over graphics, colors, and other design details. For example, Ocean Pacific (OP) controls the design of all graphics on its licensed merchandise.
- *Marketing and distribution.* Licensors often want to control the consistency of the marketing of their licensed merchandise. Also many designers do not want their licensed merchandise distributed through discount or off-price retailers, and put clauses in their contracts to prevent it.
- *Quality.* Clauses about the materials and manufacture of merchandise and the submission of samples of merchandise for approval by the licensor give the licensor control over the quality of the product.
- *Advances.* Contract clauses set the amount of the advance money that will be paid up front and then deducted from the royalty payments.
- *Guarantees.* Contracts often guarantee that minimum dollar amount will be paid to the licensee, even if royalties fall below this amount.
- *Notification of agreements to customs department.* If goods are being manufactured offshore (outside the United States), this notification is needed so the goods will clear customs, and not be confiscated as counterfeit goods. Contract clauses assure licensees that the licensor will provide notification if it is needed.

ADVANTAGES OF LICENSING

Licensing agreements have a number of advantages for both the licensee and licensor. For the licensee, the value added to the merchandise by a licensed name, image, or design comes in many interrelated forms. The licensee gets automatic brand identification (see Figure 2.4). For example, a children's T-shirt with a picture of Queen Amidala, from the 1999 movie *Star Wars: The Phantom Menace*, received automatic recognition from children and parent-consumers. In many instances, the licensed product is trusted for qualities that stem from the licensor. For example, a designer name attached to a silk scarf adds fashion credibility to the scarf. For manufacturers, a licensed product can also be a marketing shortcut for launching new products. For example, by purchasing the rights to a designer or celebrity name, a fragrance company can launch a new fragrance with immediate brand name recognition (Henricks, 1998).

Figure 2.4: Character licensing (left) is an important competitive strategy among infant and children's apparel companies. Designer name licensing of accessories (right) adds immediate fashion image to the product.

The licensor also gains from licensing agreements. Licensing allows for brand extension into other categories of merchandise without revealing to consumers that the licensor is not manufacturing the merchandise. Such arrangements allow companies to expand their product lines by taking advantage of the manufacturing and distribution expertise and facilities of other companies. For example, when NIKE decided to expand its product line into women's swimwear, rather than spending the resources to develop the expertise in this area, it licensed its name to Jantzen, one of the world's largest women's swimwear manufacturers. By such an agreement, NIKE was able to take advantage of the expertise at Jantzen, and Jantzen had the opportunity to expand its business by producing a new line of women's swimwear for a new target market. As another example of this cooperation between corporations in licensing, Hartmarx, a well-known and well-respected producer of men's tailored clothing, is one of Tommy Hilfiger's licensees, handling all tailored clothing and slacks for Tommy Hilfiger. Hilfiger controls the design, distribution, and visual presentation of the products, and Hartmarx handles the production. Designer-manufacturer licensing collaborations are common in intimate apparel. Tommy Hilfiger Corporation has a licensing agreement with VF Corporation's Bestform division, which produces and distributes intimate apparel with the Hilfiger label; Sara Lee Personal Products produces a line of intimate apparel under the label Ralph Lauren Collection; and Warnaco Group produces Calvin Klein women's underwear. For well-established names or images, licensing arrangements can also be very lucrative. It is estimated that designers such as Pierre Cardin, Calvin Klein, and Ralph Lauren make millions of dollars each year in royalties from licensed merchandise.

DISADVANTAGES OF LICENSING

There are also a number of disadvantages for the licensor and licensee. For the licensor, overuse of licensing arrangements may result in a saturation of the property in the marketplace. This can lead to consumers who do not perceive a distinct image with the property. For example, with hundreds of licensing agreements, Pierre Cardin's name can be seen on everything from luggage to cookware to children's apparel. Because of this, in recent years, the name has lost some of its prestige. When a licensed product sells well, the licensor must rely on the licensee's ability to react by producing goods quickly. Depending on the licensing contract, licensors also risk a loss of control over quality or distribution of licensed merchandise. To assure consistent quality, the licensor must provide constant monitoring of production quality by inspecting samples or production facilities. A tragic example of the risk involved with losing control of a licensed name is that of the designer Halston. In the 1960s and 1970s, Halston became a well-known designer of expensive apparel worn by celebrities. This status was lost in 1973, when he sold the use of his name to JCPenney for a line of affordable mass-merchandised clothing. With this arrangement he also lost control over the use of his name. Although he received some royalties until his death in 1990, he never regained control over the use of the Halston name, which changed ownership six times during the 1980s. The Halston name continues to gain prestige with new management.

The major disadvantage of licensing for the licensee, is the risk associated with predicting the popularity of the licensed name or image. Timing is extremely important for the success of many licensed products, and licensees must be experts in understanding and predicting consumer demand. Sometimes, however, the license does not turn out as anticipated. For example, sales of licensed products from the 1998 movie *Godzilla* did not reach expected levels. Licensees also incur the expense of controlling channels of distribution and trying to prevent the counterfeiting of the licensed goods. They are also responsible for additional costs related to the manufacture of the licensed products according to the licensor's rules and regulations. For example, many licensors have rules governing where a product may be manufactured, which may make producing more expensive than it otherwise might be (Henricks, 1998). However, despite these disadvantages, licensing will continue to be an important business strategy for many companies.

Marketing Channels

In addition to understanding the different forms of business ownership and competitive strategies of companies in the textile and apparel industries, it is important to differentiate among the various **marketing channels** within the industry. Marketing channels are routes products follow to get to the ultimate user. They consist of businesses that perform manufacturing, wholesaling, and retailing functions in order to get merchandise to the consumer. Marketing channels have several structural systems including the following (see also Table 2.4):

■ Direct marketing channel
■ Limited marketing channel
■ Extended marketing channel

With the **direct marketing channel,** apparel manufacturers sell directly to consumers. For example, consumers may purchase goods directly from the manufacturer

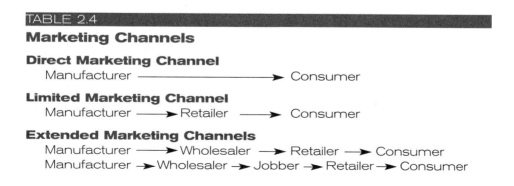

TABLE 2.4
Marketing Channels

Direct Marketing Channel
Manufacturer ⟶ Consumer

Limited Marketing Channel
Manufacturer ⟶ Retailer ⟶ Consumer

Extended Marketing Channels
Manufacturer ⟶ Wholesaler ⟶ Retailer ⟶ Consumer
Manufacturer ⟶ Wholesaler ⟶ Jobber ⟶ Retailer ⟶ Consumer

through catalogs or over the Internet. Although some apparel products are available to consumers through this channel, consumers do not have the resources to deal directly with manufacturers for all of their apparel purchases (nor do manufacturers have the resources to deal directly with individual consumers). Therefore, consumers must rely on retailers to search for and screen manufacturers and products for them.

In a **limited marketing channel,** retailers survey the various manufacturers and select (that is, buy) merchandise they believe their customers will want. Retailers also serve as a gatekeeper by narrowing the choices for consumers and providing them with access (through retail outlets) to the merchandise, thus performing an important service to consumers. Retailers may also arrange for the production of specific goods (private label merchandise) that they then make available to their customers. In some cases, apparel manufacturers sell merchandise through their own retail stores (Ralph Lauren, NIKE, Jantzen). Because of the use of a retail store in the process, this form of distribution is considered a limited marketing channel, rather than a direct marketing channel, even though the product is sold by the manufacturer. The limited marketing channel is the most typical marketing channel for apparel products.

Extended marketing channels involve the use of either wholesalers, which acquire products from manufacturers and make them readily available to buyers— usually retailers, or intermediaries that buy products from wholesalers at special rates and make them available to retailers (sometimes referred to as *jobbers* in this segment of the industry). Extended marketing channels are used in the distribution of many basic items, such as T-shirts, underwear, and hosiery. For example, a company may produce white T-shirt "blanks" and sell them to wholesalers. The wholesalers will sell the T-shirts to manufacturers that will have designs screen printed on the shirts (using a textile converter for the screen printing process). The shirts are then sold to retailers. However, because of the increased time involved in this marketing channel, it is seldom used for fashion goods that companies want to get to the consumer as quickly as possible.

MARKETING CHANNEL INTEGRATION

Marketing channel integration is the process of connecting the various levels of the marketing channel so that they work together to provide the right products to consumers in the right quantities, in the right place, and at the right time. Integration can be created through conventional marketing channels or through vertical marketing channels.

Conventional marketing channels consist of independent companies that separately perform the manufacturing, distribution, and retailing functions. **Vertical marketing channels** (also called *vertical integration*) consist of companies that work as a united group. For example, when a manufacturer sells merchandise only through its own (or franchised) retail stores, it is using a vertical marketing channel. Private label (e.g., JCPenney's Arizona brand, Kmart's Jaclyn Smith brand) and store brand merchandise (e.g., The Limited, Gap, Old Navy) produced specifically for a retailer are also types of vertical marketing. In some cases, manufacturers will sell their merchandise through their own stores as well as through other retailers. This distribution strategy is known as **dual distribution** or **multichannel distribution**. Many manufacturers, such as Tommy Hilfiger, Liz Claiborne, Ralph Lauren, Pendleton, and NIKE distribute merchandise through both their own stores and other retailers. Thus, they are engaged in dual distribution.

MARKETING CHANNEL FLOWS

A marketing channel connects the companies in it in several streams, including ones for physical flow, ownership flow, information flow, payment flow, and promotion flow. Each stream relates to specific functions that companies perform throughout the marketing channel.

- **Physical flow** involves the tracking of merchandise from the manufacturer to the retailer or ultimate consumer. It includes warehousing (or storing), handling, and transporting merchandise so that it is available to consumers at the right time and at the right place, and in the right quantity.

- **Ownership flow** or **title flow** involves the transfer of ownership or title from one company to the next. For example, does the retailer own the merchandise when it leaves the manufacturer's distribution center or when the retailer actually receives the merchandise? The point at which the title is transferred is negotiated between the manufacturer and retailer.

- **Information flow** involves communication among companies within the marketing channel pipeline. Increased information flow between manufacturers and retailers has resulted from many QR and supply chain management strategies.

- **Payment flow** involves the transfer of monies among companies as payment for merchandise or services rendered. This includes both the methods used for payment and to whom payments are made.

■ **Promotion flow** involves the flow of communications designed to promote the merchandise either to other companies (*trade promotions*) or to consumers (*consumer promotions*) in order to influence sales.

Laws Affecting the Textile and Apparel Industries

This section briefly reviews a number of federal laws and international treaties that affect the textile and apparel industries. Obviously, not all of these laws will affect all companies, but it is important to note the variety of areas that are covered by federal laws and international treaties—everything from protecting personal property to protecting consumers to protecting fair trade. In addition to these federal laws, a number of state and municipal laws may apply to companies. Professionals in the industries must be aware of and abide by these laws, the details of which can be found in federal, state, and municipal government documents.

LAWS PROTECTING TEXTILE AND APPAREL INVENTIONS AND DESIGNS

Many companies in the textile and apparel industries are involved in creating, inventing, or designing new processes and products. Laws related to patents, trademarks, and copyrights were established to protect such inventions and creations. Laws protecting original garment designs vary from one country to another. Unlike designs created in European countries, in the United States, apparel designs, in and of themselves, are not protected. The United States has generally held a philosophy that laws protecting industrial design (including apparel) would impede design innovation. Whereas inventions, textile print designs, and logos are protected under patent, trademark, and copyright laws, respectively, apparel designs are not protected by U.S. law. Some believe this lack of design protection in the United States inhibits apparel design innovation in the United States and has resulted in many U.S. designers working instead in Europe (Keyder, 1999).

The laws in Europe do provide more design protection than do current U.S. laws. As noted by Virginia Brown Keyder (1999), an attorney who specializes in design law, "European design law, though widely divergent in terms of detail at the national level, continues to afford stronger protection to the designer and is fast becoming harmonized across Europe. In addition, EU [European Union] design law is increasingly being used as a model of legal reform throughout the world." An example of how a designer in France used French laws to protect his work occurred in 1994 when French designer Yves Saint Laurent took Ralph Lauren to court in a dispute over the copying of a tuxedo dress ("Tuxedo Junction," 1994).

Patents

A **patent** is a "publicly given, exclusive right to an idea, product, or process" (Fisher & Jennings, 1991, p. 595). A patent allows the inventor or producer the exclusive right to use, make, or sell a product for a period of 17 years. For processes, patents can run for $3^1/_2$ to 14 years. From a legal perspective, products must be new inventions or technological advancements in product design. In the textile and apparel industries, patents can be acquired for technological advancements in textile processing, apparel production, or in products themselves. For example, NIKE recently acquired a patent (#5,396,675) for a "method of manufacturing a midsole for a shoe and construction therefor." If someone else uses a patented product or process, the owner of the patent has the right to sue the party for patent infringement. For example, in the early 1990s, NIKE sued L.A. Gear and Etonic for patent infringement. NIKE claimed that these companies' athletic shoes infringed on NIKE's patents for shoe technology. Patents cannot be acquired for garment designs per se.

Trademarks

A **trademark** is a "distinctive name, word, mark, design, or picture used by a company to identify its product" (Fisher & Jennings, 1991, p. 595). The Lanham Act (Federal Trademark Act) provides for federal registration and protection of trademarks. Trademarks and trade names can be registered for a period of 10 years and can be renewed as long as the trademark or trade name remains in use. Once it has been registered, others cannot use a trademark or trade name without permission. If they do, they can be sued for trademark infringement. Trademark and patent searches are conducted by attorneys who specialize in ensuring that a trademark, trade name, patent, or business name is available for use. Trademarks and trade names may not be generic terms such as *wonderful* or *exciting,* or, in the apparel industry, such generic terms as *trouser* or *dress.* In the early 1990s, Fruit of the Loom claimed to have ownership of the word *fruit* and sued another company for trademark infringement for using the word *fruit* as a trademark on apparel goods. Fruit of the Loom did not win the case.

Sometimes even similar names can be considered trademark infringement. For example in the 1980s, when a northern California company, Blue Puma, wanted to expand its distribution nationally, the athletic shoe company, Puma, protested. The courts upheld Puma's protest and required Blue Puma to change its name because of trademark infringement.

In the textile and apparel industry, registered trademarks and trade names are widespread and include trade names of manufactured fibers (e.g., Dacron polyester), apparel manufacturers' trade names (e.g., Levi's Dockers), trademarks of trade associations (e.g., the Woolmark of the Wool Bureau), and trademarks of apparel manufacturers (e.g., NIKE's swoosh, the stitching on the back pocket of Levi's jeans). Well-known and well-respected trade names and trademarks take years to establish through concentrated efforts in designing goods that meet the needs of consumers, quality control, and advertising. Consumers become confident that goods with a well-known trade name or trademark will meet certain standards in terms of quality and/or image, and thus desire these goods. Figure 2.5 shows some well-known trademarks and trade names.

Consumers' desire for apparel with well-known and visible trade names and trademarks has led to numerous trademark infringements and a proliferation of **counterfeit goods** (those goods that have unauthorized registered trade names or trademarks on them). Typically, counterfeit goods are of much lower quality than the authentic merchandise and are sold at a fraction of the genuine merchandise's price. Counterfeiters exploit the consumer awareness and trust of a brand image by producing low-quality merchandise, and they do not pay royalties to the companies

Figure 2.5: Trade names and trademarks provide immediate consumer recognition of products.

that may have spent millions creating that awareness and trust. The International Anti-Counterfeiting Coalition estimates that more than $250 billion worth of counterfeit goods are sold every year to knowing or unknowing consumers; and the International Trademark Association estimates that 22 percent of all apparel and footwear sold worldwide is counterfeit.

The Trademark Counterfeiting Act of 1984 created criminal sanctions against the domestic manufacture of counterfeit goods. Retailers who knowingly traffic in counterfeit goods can also be criminally liable (see Figure 2.6). Companies also discourage trademark infringement by monitoring the production of their goods, using fabric codes and coded labels (see Figure 2.7) to identify authentic goods from imitations, and working with the U.S. Customs Service to stop the flow of imported counterfeit goods into the United States. To establish trademark infringement in court, the plaintiff must prove all of the following: (1) its trademark has achieved a secondary meaning (that is the consumer associates the trademark with the company or product), (2) the trademark is nonfunctional (that is the trademark is ornamental or does not contribute to the function of the product), and (3) there would be a likelihood of public confusion if the trademark were copied (Gerber, 1984).

Recently, trade dress infringement has been tested in the courts with mixed rulings. **Trade dress** is, "a subset of trademark law, only instead of protecting the identifying words or logos, the law of trade dress protects the overall look or image of a product itself or the packaging of a product, provided that the overall look or combination of features has come to identify the manufacturer of the product." (Welt, 1999) A classic example of trade dress is the distinctive shape of a Coca-Cola bottle. Although it is more

THESE YOU CAN BORROW.

THESE YOU CAN'T.

Only Levi Strauss & Co. is entitled by the U.S. Patent and Trademark office to use the Arcuate Stitching Design®, Tab Device® or the Two Horse Design® trademarks. Our lawyers agressively pursue every legal means at their disposal to protect our trademarks. So if you're thinking of borrowing something, it's probably best to stick with tools and stuff.

Figure 2.6: Trademark infringement—the unauthorized use of a registered trademark—is illegal.

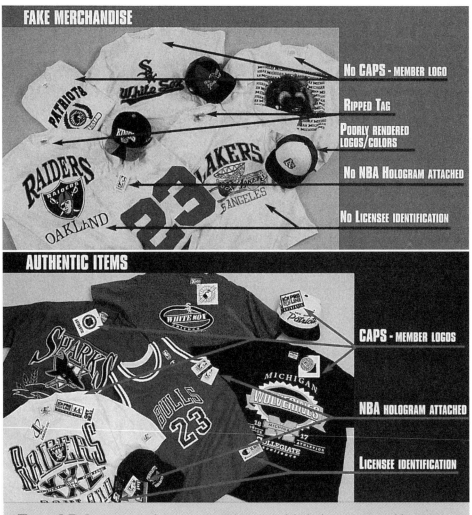

Figure 2.7: Companies often use special sewn-in labels, hangtags, and logos on authentic licensed goods.

difficult to prove trade dress infringement than trademark infringement and courts generally do not want to interfere with competition, recently a federal court of appeals upheld a jury award against Wal-Mart stores for selling, under its own Small Steps label, almost identical copies of children's seersucker jumpers made by the apparel manufacturer, Samara Brothers. Columbia Sportswear Co. also settled a trade dress infringement against the Orvis Company, which agreed to remove from its product line a pullover windbreaker that Columbia described as a "substantial copy" of Columbia's Gizzmo parka (Bosworth, 1999). In both cases, the plaintiffs had to prove product configuration; that is, that the shape and combination of features of the product are not only distinctive, but also identify the source of the product.

Copyrights

Copyrights protect a number of written, pictorial, and performed work including literature, music, films, television shows, artworks, dramatic works, and advertisements. Under the Copyright Act of 1947 (amended in 1976), the copyright holder has the exclusive right to use, perform, or reproduce the material. Under the *fair use* doctrine, works protected by copyright can be used on a limited basis for educational or research purposes. Reproduction of material protected by copyright without permission is considered infringement. In the U.S. textile and apparel industries, although garment style is not protected by copyright, original textile prints and graphic designs (even when incorpo-

rated into a garment) are. In order to be able to collect damages when a copyright is infringed, the copyright must be registered with the Copyright Office of the U.S. Library of Congress. A textile designer may also put a copyright notice (©) in the selvage of the fabric, although this notice is not necessary (Hughes, 1991). A designer owns the copyright unless the designer is a salaried employee of a company; then the copyright is held by the employer. Any unauthorized reproduction of the textile print or design protected by copyright is considered copyright infringement, and once the copyright is registered, the copyright holder can take the infringer to court. Examples of copyright infringement in the textile indus-

"I Hate Copycats"

Figure 2.8: The U.S. Customs Service can provide information to companies about obtaining copyright, trademark, and patent protection.

try include dishonest textile converters who buy apparel at retail in order to then copy the textile print, unscrupulous apparel manufacturers that work with one converter to develop new prints and then take the samples to another converter to have them reproduced more cheaply, or fraudulent retailers that copy textile prints for use in their private label merchandise (Ellis, 1995). U.S. copyrights are partially protected in the international market under the Berne Convention, an international treaty designed to help fight infringement across national borders.

FEDERAL LAWS RELATED TO BUSINESS PRACTICES

Many federal laws relate to how a company must run its business, including requirements concerning fair competition, international trade, environmental practices, consumer protection, and employment practices.

Fair Competition

A number of federal laws have been established to assure fair competition. Table 2.5 reviews the primary laws that prohibit monopolies and unfair or deceptive practices in interstate commerce. Any textile and apparel company that distributes products

---

TABLE 2.5

Federal Laws Related to Competition

- Sherman Antitrust Act (1890): outlaws monopolies and attempts to form monopolies.
- Clayton Act (1914): amends the Sherman Antitrust Act by forbidding a seller from discriminating in price between and among different purchases of the same commodity, outlawing exclusive dealing and tie-in arrangements, forbidding corporate asset or stock mergers where the effect may be to create a monopoly, and forbidding persons from serving on boards of directors of competing corporations.
- Federal Trade Commission Act (1914): declares unlawful unfair methods of competition in or affecting commerce and unfair or deceptive acts or practices in interstate commerce.
- Robinson-Patman Act (1936): amends the Clayton Act by preventing large firms from exerting excessive economic power to drive out small competitors in local markets.
- Cellar-Kefauver Act (1950): makes it illegal to create a monopoly by eliminating competition through company mergers and acquisitions.
- Wheeler-Lea Act (1938): amends the Federal Trade Commission Act by allowing the FTC to stop unfair competition even if a competitor is not shown to be harmed by a business practice when a consumer is injured by deceptive acts or practices.

or services across state lines is governed by these laws. These laws are all adminis-tered by the Federal Trade Commission (FTC).

International Trade

Federal regulations and international treaties also exist concerning the internation-al trade of products, including textiles and apparel (see Table 2.6). The primary objective of these laws and treaties is to establish fair trade among countries. Because of shifts in international relations, these laws and treaties are regularly reviewed and amended. Any textile or apparel company that imports goods into or exports goods from the United States is affected by these laws and treaties. Except for the Export Trade Act, which is administered by the FTC, these laws are administered by the U.S. Customs Service of the Treasury Department.

Environmental Practices

Federal environmental laws regulate business practices related to environmental pollution. The goal of these laws is to protect the environment from toxic pollu-tants. In the fashion industries, these laws particularly affect chemical companies that manufacture fibers. These companies' processes often produce or require the use of toxic substances, and their factories may emit toxic substances considered pollutants. Table 2.7 lists the primary environmental laws. These laws are adminis-tered by the Environmental Protection Agency (EPA).

Consumer Protection

Beginning in the 1930s and 1940s a number of laws were enacted to protect the health and safety of consumers (see Table 2.8). Over the years since then, many additional protections have been added. These laws require companies to label truthfully the fiber content and care procedures of products and prohibit companies from selling flammable products. They are administered by either the Federal Trade Commission or the Consumer Product Safety Commission.

Employment Practices

To assure fair hiring and employment practices among companies, a number of laws have been enacted to regulate child labor and homework (piecework contracted to individuals who do the work in their homes) and to prohibit discrimination based on such characteristics as race, sex, age, or physical disability. Any company with employees is regulated by these laws (see Table 2.9).

TABLE 2.6

Laws Related to International Trade Practices

■ General Agreement on Tariffs and Trade (GATT, 1947): a multinational agreement regarding global trade policies. In international trade of textiles and apparel, GATT allows for the use of tariffs (taxes on imports) to protect domestic industries and for quantitative limits (quotas) of certain textile and apparel merchandise to enter the United States from specified countries during a specified period of time. By 2005, GATT will reduce tariffs and eliminate quotas on imports in most countries. Under GATT, country-of-origin marking on apparel must include where the garment was sewn.

■ Multifiber Arrangement (MFA I: 1947–1977, MFA II: 1977–1981, MFA III: 1981–1986, MFA IV: 1986–1991, extensions to MFA IV: 1991, 1992, 1993): a general framework for international textile trade that operates under the authority of GATT and allows for the establishment of bilateral agreements between trading partners. The MFA will be phased out by 2005 and will bring the textile and apparel industry under the jurisdiction of the World Trade Organization. At that time, quotas on textiles and apparel will be phased out and tariffs reduced.

■ Customs and Trade Act of 1990: makes permanent the Caribbean Basin Initiative giving duty-free treatment to most goods produced in the Caribbean region.

■ North American Free Trade Agreement (NAFTA, 1994): authorizes duty-free trade among the United States, Canada, and Mexico for goods manufactured in these three countries.

■ Export Trade Act: authorizes FTC supervision of the registration and operation of associations of U.S. exporters.

■ World Trade Organization (WTO, 1995): According to the Office of Textiles and Apparel, "The World Trade Organization (WTO) Agreement on Textiles and Clothing (the Agreement) provides for the phased liberalization and elimination over the transition period of quotas on textiles and apparel imported from WTO member countries." The Agreement was approved as part of the Uruguay Round Agreements Act by the U.S. Congress in December 1994. The Agreement went into effect on January 1, 1995. Article 2 of the Agreement states that "product integration, including the phase out of Multifiber Arrangement (MFA) quotas and acceleration of quota growth rates for products not yet integrated into the WTO, is to occur over 10 years [to 2005], in three stages."

TABLE 2.7

Federal Laws Related to Practices to Protect the Environment

- Clean Air Act (1970): controls air pollution through air-quality standards to protect public health.
- Resource Conservation and Recovery Act of 1976: controls the management of solid waste products and encourages resource conservation and recovery.
- Toxic Substances Control Act (1976): allows regulation of the manufacturing, use, and disposal of toxic substances.
- Clean Water Act (1977): controls water pollution by keeping pollutants out of lakes, rivers, and streams.

TABLE 2.8

Federal Laws Associated with Practices for Consumer Protection

- Wool Products Labeling Act (1939), Fur Products Labeling Act (1952), the Textile Fiber Products Identification Act (1958, effective 1960): require specified information be on textile and fur product labels; require the advertising of country of origin in mail order catalogs and promotional materials. Administered by the FTC.
- Flammable Fabrics Act (1954, amended 1971): prohibits interstate commerce of wearing apparel and fabrics that are so highly flammable as to be dangerous when worn. Sets standards of flammability and test methods. Sets standards for flammability of children's sleepwear. Administered by the CPSC.
- Care Labeling of Textile Wearing Apparel and Certain Piece Goods Act (effective 1972): requires that care labels be affixed to most apparel and be attached to retail piece goods. Administered by the FTC.
- Federal Hazardous Substance Act: addresses issue of choking, ingestion, aspiration of small items by children and hazards from sharp points or edges on articles intended for use by children by requiring that decorative buttons or other decorative items on children's clothing pass use and abuse testing procedures. Prohibits the use of lead paint to be used on children's articles including clothing. Administered by the CPSC.

TABLE 2.9

Federal Laws Related to Employment Practices

- Fair Labor Standards Act (1938): guarantees fair employment status by establishing minimum wage standards, child labor restrictions, and other employment regulations.
- Equal Pay Act of 1963: amends the Fair Labor Standards Act by requiring employers to provide equal pay to men and women for doing equal work.
- Age Discrimination in Employment Act (1967): prohibits an employer from discriminating in hiring or other aspects of employment because of age. Administered by Equal Employment Opportunity Commission (EEOC).
- Occupational Safety and Health Act (OSHA) of 1970: assures safe and healthful working conditions for employees by setting general occupational safety and health standards and requiring that employers prepare and maintain records of occupational injuries and illnesses. Administered by the Department of Labor.
- Equal Employment Opportunity Act of 1972: prohibits discrimination by employers in hiring, promotions, discharge, and conditions of employment if such discrimination is based on race, color, religion, sex, or national origin.
- Worker Adjustment and Retraining Notification Act (1988): provides protection to workers, their families, and communities by requiring employers to notify workers 60 calendar days in advance of plant closings and mass layoffs. Administered by the Department of Labor.
- Americans with Disabilities Act (ADA) of 1990: prohibits discrimination against qualified individuals with disabilities in all aspects of employment; prohibits discrimination on the basis of disability by requiring public accommodations and commercial facilities be designed, constructed, and altered in compliance with accessibility standards. Administered by the Office on the ADA, Department of Justice.

Summary

Depending on the objectives, needs, and size of textile and apparel companies, they are owned as sole proprietorships, partnerships, or corporations. The advantages and disadvantages of each form of business ownership are related to the ease of formation and dissolution (advantage of sole proprietorship and partnership and disadvantage of corporations), the degree of liability owners have for business debts (advantage of corporations and disadvantage for sole proprietorship and partnerships), and operational strategies (some advantages or disadvantages for each form of ownership).

Each company, whether a sole proprietorship, partnership, or corporation, competes with other companies on the basis of price, quality, innovation, service, or a combination of these factors. Within the textile and apparel industries the competitive strategies include pure competition (e.g., textile commodities), oligopolies (e.g., athletic shoe industry), and monopolistic competition, the most common of the three. In monopolistic competition, although companies compete in terms of product type (denim jeans), the specific product attributes of any one company (Levi's jeans) are perceived as different from the product attributes of other companies (Guess? jeans, Calvin Klein jeans).

Companies create this perceived difference through product differentiation, advertising, licensing programs, private label merchandise, or services offered. In licensing programs, the owner (licensor) of a particular name, image, or design (property) sells the right to use the name, image, or design to another party, typically a manufacturer (licensee), for payment of royalties. For example Hartmarx pays Tommy Hilfiger royalties for the use of the Tommy Hilfiger name on a line of men's tailored clothing. Tommy Hilfiger controls the design, distribution, and presentation of the products; Hartmarx controls the production. A licensing contract outlines the terms of the licensing agreement. Licensing programs can be advantageous to both licensors and licensees in terms of expanding product lines and exposure. Possible disadvantages include market saturation and problems in timing of the release of the product.

To get merchandise to the consumer, direct, limited, and extended marketing channels are used by businesses that perform manufacturing, wholesaling, and retailing functions. In conventional marketing channels, separate companies perform these functions; in vertical marketing channels, a single company performs multiple functions.

A number of federal laws affect businesses in the textile and apparel industries. Laws related to patents, trademarks, and copyrights protect the identity, inventions, and designs of designers and companies. For example, a textile designer's fabric design is protected by the copyright law so that others cannot legally copy it. Laws have also been established that relate to how companies must run their businesses, including requirements regarding competition, international trade, protecting consumers, protecting the environment, and employment practices.

CAREER PROFILES

Individuals who have careers in the apparel, accessories, and home fashions industries may be part of companies that are sole proprietorships, partnerships, or corporations.

Owner, Sole Proprietor
WOMEN'S SPECIALTY STORE

Position Description
Responsible for all of the purchasing (buying), advertising, supervising of personnel, special events (in-store and community), in-store selling, and visual merchandising.

Typical Tasks and Responsibilities
- Write orders for merchandise
- Handle special orders
- Organize and implement store promotions
- Determine pricing policies
- Determine policies regarding merchandise returns
- In-store customer service
- Ongoing merchandising of the store to create a "fresh" look
- Hire, train, schedule, and motivate sales associates

Corporate Executive Officer, Chairman of the Board
PRIVATELY OWNED CHILDREN'S APPAREL MANUFACTURER AND RETAILER

Position Description
Ultimately responsible for everything from financial decisions to store maintenance. Conceive and create all new products sold wholesale by the company. Run the retail stores. Work with all management, direct reports, as well as with 300 employees. Motivate and supervise employees at all levels. Sell all products to customers at wholesale and retail.

Typical Tasks and Responsibilities
- Set the vision of the organization
- Model the values of the company with regard to professionalism, integrity, and community involvement
- Apply knowledge of latest trends and ideas in the market to the design and sale of new products
- Oversee the overall management of the organization
- Make sure everyone remembers that the customer is always right

Key Terms

board of directors

conglomerate

consolidation

conventional marketing channel

copyright

corporation

counterfeit goods

direct marketing channel

dividends

dual distribution

extended marketing channel

general partner

leveraged buyout (LBO)

licensing

limited liability

limited marketing channel

limited partnership

marketing channel

merger

monopolistic competition

monopoly

multichannel distribution

multinational corporation

oligopoly

ownership flow

partnership

patent

payment flow

physical flow

private corporation

private label

promotion flow

publicly held corporation

pure competition

sole proprietorship

stockholder

store brand

takeover

title flow

trade dress

trademark

unlimited liability

vertical marketing channel

Discussion Questions

1. Interview a small business owner in your community. Find out whether the business is a sole proprietorship, partnership, or corporation. Ask the owner why this form of business ownership was chosen and what he or she views as the primary advantages and disadvantages to the ownership form. Find out what business licenses were required of the owner to start the company. Compare this information with information others in class received.

2. Suppose you wanted to invest (buy stock) in a publicly held corporation. Where can you find information about the corporation? Select a publicly held corporation in the textile and apparel industry and find information about the company.

3. What are some examples of licensed textile and apparel products that you own? Which category of licensed goods does each fall into? What characteristic of the property or product was appealing to you as a consumer? Why?

4. Currently textile designs and prints are protected by copyright from illegal copying, but apparel designs (designs of the garment itself) are not protected in the United States. Do you think that apparel designs should also be covered under copyright law? Why or why not? Justify your response.

References

Altchuler, Murray. (1988). Welcome to your share of $13 million an hour! In F. Ash (Ed.) *The International Licensing Directory*, p. 5. East Sussex, England: A4 Publications Ltd.

Alterbaum, James. (1987, January). What to look for in going public. *Apparel Industry Magazine*, pp. 30–31.

American Apparel Manufacturers Association. (1992). *Federal Standards and Regulations for the Apparel Industry.* Arlington, VA: Author.

Bosworth, Mike. (1999, April). Gavels pound on knockoff vendors. *Apparel Industry Magazine*, pp. 86–90.

Cohen, Gordon S. (1995, April). Hartmarx and Hilfiger team up for success. *Bobbin*, pp. 54–62.

Dickerson, Kitty G. (1999). *Textiles and Apparel in the Global Economy* (3rd ed.). Englewood Cliffs, NJ: Prentice-Hall.

Ellis, Kristi. (1995, June 2–8). Imitation has its price. *California Apparel News*, pp. 18, 20.

Fisher, Bruce D., and Jennings, Marianne M. (1991). *Law for Business* (2nd ed.). St. Paul, MN: West Publishing Co.

Gerber, David A. (1984, September 14). Protecting apparel designs: Tough, but there are ways. *California Apparel News*, p. 24.

Henricks, Mark. (1998, June). The licensing explosion. *Apparel Industry Magazine*, pp. 50–57.

Hughes, John. (1991, January 4–10). Getting it in writing. *California Apparel News*, pp. 16–17.

Keyder, Virginia Brown. (November 12, 1999). *Design Law in Europe and the U.S.* Presentation at the Annual Meeting of the International Textile and Apparel Association, Santa Fe, NM.

Office of Textiles and Apparel, U.S. Department of Commerce. *WTO (World Trade Organization)* [online]. Available HTTP: http://www.ita.cod.gov/industry/textiles/ wto/html [February 29, 1996].

Tuxedo Junction: YSL, Ralph square off. (1994, April 28). *Women's Wear Daily*, pp. 1, 15.

Welt, Henry. (1999, April). Trade dress: Another look at the Samara case. *Apparel Industry Magazine*, p. 88.

CHAPTER 3

Structure of the U.S. Textile Industry

IN THIS CHAPTER YOU WILL LEARN:

■ The importance of textile knowledge for the successful design, production, and marketing of apparel and home fashions.

■ Terms used in describing textiles and textile manufacturing.

■ The organization and operation of the domestic textile industry.

■ Procedures followed in the processing and marketing of natural and manu-factured fibers, yarns, and fabrics.

■ Current developments in the textile industry including textile-trade, Quick Response, and supply chain management strategies and industry responses to environmental issues.

Consider the Following scenarios: an apparel designer is starting a new line of apparel, but before she begins she examines the newest textiles shown by textile companies; or, a retail buyer decides to attend a textile trade show in order to become familiar with the newest trends in colors and fabrics. These scenarios highlight the integrated nature of the textile, apparel, home fashions, and retailing industries. As textiles are the foundation of the soft goods industries, an understanding of the organization and operation of the textile industry is important for all professionals. Therefore, this chapter describes the organization and operation of the U.S. textile industry and the marketing of fibers and fabrics and gives an overview of new developments in the field.

What Are Textiles?

Before we review the organization and operation of the U.S. textile industry, let us first reexamine the basic terminology used to describe textiles. This terminology forms the basis for an understanding of the fabrics used in apparel and home fashions. First, what are textiles? The term **textile** is used to describe "any product made from fibers" (Joseph, 1988, p. 347). The four basic components of textile production are:

- Fiber processing
- Yarn spinning
- Fabric production
- Fabric finishing

Fibers are the basic unit used in making textile yarns and fabrics. Fibers are classified into **generic families** according to their chemical composition and can be divided into two primary divisions: natural fibers and manufactured (man-made) fibers. Natural fibers include those made from natural protein fibers of animal origin (e.g., wool, cashmere, camel, mohair, angora, and silk) and natural cellulose fibers of plant origin (e.g., cotton, flax, jute, ramie, and sisal). Leather and fur are considered natural fiber products created from the pelts, skins, and hides of various animals. Leather and fur are unique textiles in that the fibers are not spun into yarns and then constructed into fabrics. Instead the pelts are tawned or tanned to create supple and durable "fabrics."

Whereas natural fibers have been used in making textiles for thousands of years, manufactured fibers have been around for just over one hundred years. In the mid-1800s scientists became interested in duplicating natural fibers. In 1891 "artificial silk," made from a solution of cellulose, was commercially produced in France. In 1924, the name of this fiber was changed to rayon. In 1939, nylon, the first fiber to be synthesized entirely from chemicals (synthetic), was introduced by E. I. DuPont de Nemours & Co. Since then many more manufactured fibers have been developed, including ones that are cellulose-based (e.g., lyocell, acetate), synthetic (e.g., acrylic, aramid, modacrylic, olefin, polyester, and spandex), and mineral-based (e.g., glass, metallic).

Until the 1930s, fiber production in the United States focused entirely on natural fibers. By the end of the 1940s, natural fiber production accounted for 85 percent of the nation's textile mill fiber consumption and manufactured fiber production accounted for only 15 percent. By 1965, manufactured fibers accounted for more than 42 percent of total fiber consumption by U.S. textile mills. In 1998, 16.7 billion pounds of fibers were consumed by textile mills, with manufactured fibers accounting for 68 percent, cotton accounting for 31 percent, and wool accounting for 1 percent.

The word **yarns** refers to the collection of fibers or filaments laid or twisted together to form a continuous strand strong enough for use in fabrics. Yarns are classified as **spun yarns** made from shorter staple fibers or **filament yarns** made from long continuous fibers. Filament yarns can be either plain or textured. The type of yarn selected will affect the performance, tactile qualities, and appearance of the fabric.

Fabric construction processes include methods used to make fabrics from solutions (e.g., films, foam), directly from fibers (e.g., felt, nonwoven fabrics), and from yarns (e.g., braid, knitted fabrics, woven fabrics, and lace). The fabric construction process used often determines the name of the fabric (e.g., satin, jersey, lace, felt).

Dyeing and finishing the fabric complete the textile production process. **Finishing** refers to "anything that is done to fiber, yarn, or fabric either before or after weaving or knitting to change the *appearance* (what you see), the *hand* (what you feel), and the *performance* (what the fabric does)" (Hollen, Sadler, Langford & Kadolph, 1988, p. 300). **Greige goods** (also referred to as *grey, gray,* or *loom state goods*) are fabrics that have not received finishing treatments such as bleaching, shearing, brushing, embossing, or dyeing. Once finished, the fabrics are then referred to as **converted** or **finished goods**. Finishes can be classified as *general* or *functional*, *mechanical* or *chemical*, and *durable* (permanent) or *renewable* (impermanent). Both greige goods and finished fabrics are used in a variety of end uses.

Organization of the Textile Industry

OVERVIEW OF THE INDUSTRY

The textile industry is one of the oldest manufacturing industries in the United States. With its beginnings during the Industrial Revolution, the textile industry has been an important part of the U.S. manufacturing base for over 200 years. A $61 billion industry, the U.S. textile industry encompasses approximately 5000 companies. In 1999, the textile industry employed, on average, 560,000 workers, down from 760,000 employees and a high of 1.3 million employees in 1951. In the United States, the majority (75 percent) of textiles are produced in eight southeastern states (Virginia, North Carolina, South Carolina, Tennessee, Georgia, Mississippi, Alabama, and Louisiana). In 1999, North Carolina had the largest number of workers (149,000) in the textile industry (including employment in textile mills and manufactured fiber processing, wool growing, and cotton growing), followed by Georgia (105,100), South Carolina (70,400), Alabama (38,200), Virginia (28,900), and California (27,100).

STRUCTURE OF THE INDUSTRY

Companies within the textile industry take part in one or more of the four basic components of textile production: fiber processing, yarn spinning, fabric production, and fabric finishing. The structure of the textile industry is diagrammed in Figure 3.1. Some companies specialize in certain aspects of textile production. For example, **throwsters** modify filament yarns for specific end uses, such as increasing luster or texture through altering the yarn. **Textile mills** concentrate on the fabric construction stage of production (e.g., weaving, knitting, nonwoven fabric, lace). Companies that specialize in finishing fabrics are called **textile converters**. Finished fabrics are sold to apparel and home fashions manufacturers, to retailers that sell fabrics, or to jobbers that sell surplus goods. Retailers that sell private label merchandise may also work directly with converters and/or textile mills.

Within the textile industry are a number of large corporations that operate through a vertically integrated marketing channel; handling all four steps—from processing the fiber to finishing the fabric—within its own organization. Some vertically integrated companies are also involved in the production of end-use products such as towels, sheets, or hosiery. Vertically integrated companies include companies that produce textile products made from both natural and manufactured fibers. Although vertically integrated companies may process fibers, they might not actually produce their own fibers. For example, a vertically integrated company that produces cotton knit fabrics might not be involved in growing the cotton, but might purchase raw cotton from cotton growers instead. Some companies are partially integrated, in that they focus on several steps of production. For example, some knitting operations (e.g., hosiery, sweaters) not only knit, dye, and cut the fabrics but also construct the knitted garments to be sold to retailers.

One of the oldest vertically integrated textile companies in the United States is Pendleton Woolen Mills, headquartered in Portland, Oregon. Pendleton was started by Clarence and Roy Bishop in Pendleton, Oregon, in 1909. Led by a fourth generation of Bishops, the company now manufactures woolen men's wear, women's wear, and blankets; nonwoolen apparel; and over-the-counter fabrics. It is involved with the selection and processing of wool; the designing and weaving of fabrics; the development of garments; and the shipment and sale of garments, over-the-counter

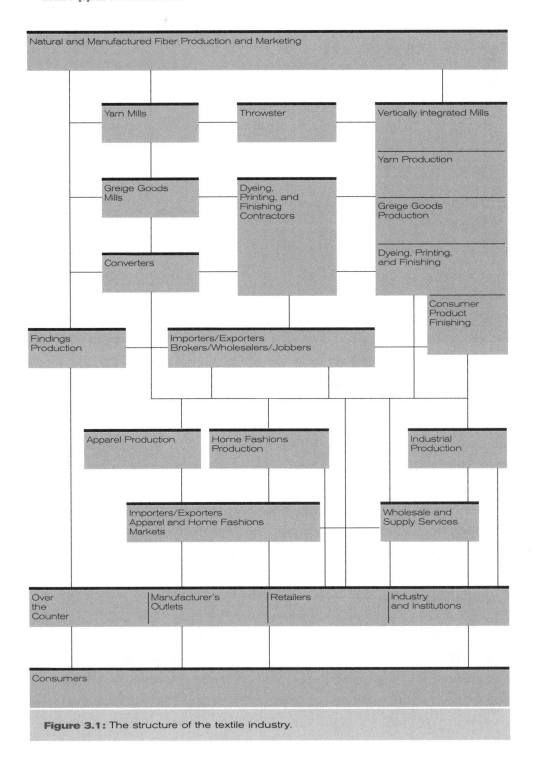

Figure 3.1: The structure of the textile industry.

piece goods, and blankets. Such vertical integration allows for coordination among all production steps and increased control of quality throughout the production of the textiles and end-use products. For example, Pendleton textile designers work closely with the apparel designers in engineering the plaid fabrics that will work best for pleated skirt designs.

A number of trade publications cater to the textile industry by providing timely information about trends in the industry, new products, company success stories, and technological advancements. Table 3.1 lists selected trade publications in the textile industry.

END USES OF TEXTILES

Although apparel and home fashions are the primary end uses for textiles made in the United States, it is important to note the variety of other goods made from natural and manufactured fibers. According to the American Textile Manufacturers Institute, end uses for U.S. textiles vary widely:

- Thirty-six percent of the total pounds of textiles produced in the United States goes into apparel, such as fabrics for men's, women's, and children's apparel and hosiery; over-the-counter retail piece goods; and craft fabric.
- Twenty-five percent goes into floor coverings, such as carpets, rugs, and paddings.
- Twenty-three percent goes into industrial and other products, such as tires, ropes and cordage, tents, belting, bags, shoes and slippers, and medical and surgical supplies.
- Sixteen percent goes into home fashions products, such as drapery and upholstery fabrics; sheets, pillowcases, and mattresses; blankets; bedspreads; tablecloths; and towels.

According to the American Fiber Manufacturers Association, of the manufactured fibers produced in the United States:

- Forty-five percent is used in home fashions (providing 80 percent of U.S. carpets, sheets, drapery fabric, and upholstery).
- Thirty percent is used in apparel.
- Twenty-five percent is used in industrial products.

TABLE 3.1

Selected Trade Publications in the Textile Industry

America's Textiles International (www.billian.com/textile/): published monthly; for managers in the textile industry; includes information regarding textile business, finances, and manufacturing/technology.

American Dyestuff Reporter: published monthly; for plant and mill executives, owners, managers, dyers, finishers, and processors; covers textile wet-processing.

Daily News Record (www.dailynewsrecord.com/): news and in-depth features on menswear retailing, apparel, fibers, and fabrics every Monday, Wednesday, and Friday.

Fiber Organon (www.fibersource.com/feb/feb3c.thm): published monthly; statistical journal summarizing producer information on the natural and manufactured fiber markets including monthly production and shipments, quarterly trends and analyses, and trade information.

Fiber World: published quarterly; provides information for fiber producers.

Knitting Times (www.apparelex.com/nksa/): published monthly by the National Knitwear and Sportswear Association; covers business conditions, technical developments and forecasts for knitted fabrics and apparel.

Nonwovens Industry: published monthly; for manufacturers, converters, distributors, and suppliers of nonwoven soft goods; covers manufacturing processes, distribution, and end-use applications of nonwoven textile products.

Textile HiLights (www.atmi.org/graphic/hilights.html): published quarterly by the American Textile Manufacturers Institute; reports statistical and trade information on the American manufacturing and textile industries.

Textile Technology Digest (www.philacol.edu/library/lib4dtex.html): index covering over 450 journals and reports devoted to textile technology and the textile industry.

Textile World (www.intertec.com/pubs/tw.htm): published monthly; for textile executives in their dual role as technologists and managers; covers technical developments in the textile industry.

Fiber Processing and Yarn Spinning

The development and marketing of natural and manufactured fibers vary greatly. In general, natural fibers, as part of the larger agricultural industry, are the product of a crop that is grown and harvested or of an animal that is raised. Manufactured fibers, on the other hand, are created by large nonagricultural corporations through research and development efforts.

NATURAL FIBER PROCESSING

Of the natural fibers produced in the United States, cotton has the largest production and wool the second largest production. In 1998, 5.23 billion pounds of cotton (increasing steadily from 2.49 billion pounds in 1982) and 114.8 million pounds of wool (down from a high of 156.8 million pounds in 1993) were used by textile mills. On a much smaller level, specialty fibers, such as mohair and cashmere, are also produced. Almost all linen and silk are imported into the United States.

Figure 3.2: Textiles are used for a variety of end-use products, including apparel, hosiery, and home fashions.

Cotton is obtained from the fibers surrounding the seeds of the cotton plant. The plant is grown most satisfactorily in warm climates where irrigation water is available. Although cotton production has steadily increased over the years, employment by cotton growers in the United States has decreased from 183,221 employees in 1987 to 31,493 in 1997. In 1997, Texas had the largest number of cotton growers in the United States (10,971), followed by Georgia (4,188) and North Carolina (2,320). In conventionally grown cotton, synthetic fertilizers, insecticides, herbicides, fungicides, and defoliants are used. The significant amounts of chemical pesticides and fertilizers—as well as of water—has led to criticism of the industry. However, efforts to reduce the environmental impact of cotton production, such as by the production of organic cotton, are being studied and implemented. These recent developments will be discussed later in this chapter.

In traditional cotton production, after the cotton is picked, a cotton gin is used to separate the fiber, called *cotton lint*, from the seeds. (The seeds are a valuable by-product of the cotton industry that are used to produce cattle feed and cottonseed oil.) The cotton lint is then packed into large bales and shipped to yarn and textile mills. The spinning process of cotton yarns is highly automated; cotton fibers are cleaned, carded, combed, and drawn and spun to create yarns. For blended yarns, other fibers such as polyester, nylon, or wool are blended with the cotton during the spinning process. Figure 3.3 shows a cotton processing plant.

Wool fibers are derived from the fleece of sheep, goats, alpacas, and llamas. In the United States, most wool comes from a number of specific breeds of sheep, including Delaine-Merino, Rambouillet, Hampshire, and Suffolk. Wool production is often a secondary industry for sheep producers, who raise sheep primarily for food. Sheep production occurs in every state, with the largest number of wool producers found in Texas (7,600), Iowa (6,500), Ohio (5,200), and California (5,000). Some breeds of sheep can graze in areas of the country with extreme climates that are unsuitable for other livestock. Farm flock production (animals raised in a more confined area) is best suited for other breeds of sheep.

Figure 3.3: Cotton fiber production includes multiple steps of carding and combing the cotton fibers.

The first step in wool processing is shearing the sheep. Shearing usually takes place once a year in the spring, just before lambing. Using electric clippers, a skilled shearer can remove the fleece from a sheep in five minutes. Some shearers can shear more than one hundred sheep per day. A chemical shearing process is also used on a limited basis. Bags of wool fleece are inspected, graded, and sorted according to the diameter and length of the wool fibers. Then, the fibers are scoured to remove grease (unrefined lanolin) and impurities. The lanolin is separated from the wash water, purified, and used in soaps, creams, cosmetics, and other products. Next, clean wool fibers from different batches are blended to achieve uniform color and quality. Fibers are then carded, a process that straightens the fibers and removes any remaining vegetable matter. Wool to be used in worsted fabrics undergoes a combing process in which the fibers are further straightened. The fibers are then drawn and spun into yarns.

Wool fibers and fabrics are often finished by the same company that processes the fiber. Wool, like other fibers, can be dyed at several stages in the production process: immediately after it is washed and blended (*stock dyed*), after it has been spun into yarns (*yarn dyed*), or after it has been woven or knitted into fabric (*piece dyed*). Wool absorbs uniformly many different dyes. Some wool producers market wools that, rather than being dyed, are sorted and sold in natural sheep colors, ranging from cream to a broad spectrum of browns and grays.

Mohair comes from the wool of the Angora goat. The United States accounts for 45 percent of world mohair production. There are more than ten thousand growers of Angora goats in 47 states, although approximately 90 percent of U.S. production is in southwest Texas. More than 90 percent of the raw mohair fiber produced is exported for processing because most U.S. textile mills have equipment designed to process cotton and wool—which are much larger industries in the United States than is mohair. Cotton and wool fibers measure 2 inches or less; whereas mohair fibers are often 4 to 6 inches long. Therefore, machinery designed to process cotton and wool cannot be used for mohair.

LEATHER PRODUCTION

Leather is obtained from the skins and hides of cattle, goats, and sheep, as well as from a variety of reptiles, fish, and birds. Most skins and hides are a by-product of animals raised primarily for their meat or fiber. Thus, "the leather industry is a bridge between production of the hide, a by-product of the meat industry, and man-ufacture of basic raw material into non-durable goods, such as shoes and wearing apparel" (Eberspacher, 1993, p. 26). The term **skins** refers to pelts weighing 15 pounds or less when shipped to the tannery; the term **kips** refers to pelts weighing from 15 to 25 pounds; and the term **hides** refers to pelts weighing more than 25 pounds. Animal pelts go through a number of processes that transform them into leather. They are first cleaned to remove hair and are then tanned, colored or dyed, and finished (e.g., glazed, embossed, napped, or buffed).

Tanning is the process used to make skins and hides pliable and water resistant. The tanning process can use a number of agents, including vegetable materials, oils, chemicals, and minerals, or a combination of more than one type of agent. With vegetable tanning, natural tannic acids found in extracts from tree bark are used. Because vegetable tanning is extremely slow and labor intensive, it is seldom used in commercial tanning. Oil tanning uses a fish oil (usually codfish) as a tanning agent. Oil tanning is used to make chamois, doeskin, and buckskin. One of the quickest tanning methods is through the use of chemicals, typically formaldehyde.

Two tanning methods use minerals—alum tanning and chrome tanning. Alum tanning is rarely used today. Chrome tanning, the least expensive and most com-monly used method, requires the use of heavy metals and acids, which are toxic. The chrome tanning process also produces acidic waste water with a pH of 4.5 to 5.0 (acidic). This explains why there are few leather tanneries remaining in the United States (approximately two hundred) and a proliferation of them in countries where environmental standards are not as strict.

The few U.S. tanneries remaining are typically small companies. **Regular tan-neries**, the most common type of tannery, buy skins and hides and sell finished leather. Leather **converters** buy skins and hides, contract with a tannery to tan them according to specifications, and then sell the finished leather. The number of tanneries with 20 or more employees declined by 82 percent between 1968 and 1988 (Eberspacher, 1993).

Compared to other textiles, leather production is a relatively slow process. Because of the longer lead time needed in the production from hide to finished product, leather producers often must make styling and color decisions before other textile producers. Therefore, they are keenly involved with trend forecasting and market research. Footwear accounts for approximately half of all U.S. leather production. Leather is also used for such products as apparel (e.g., jackets, coats) and handbags (see Figure 3.4).

FUR PRODUCTION

Fur fibers are considered luxury products that come from animals, such as mink, rabbit, beaver, and muskrat, valued for their pelts. **Pelts** are the unshorn skins of these and other animals. The United States is the largest consumer market for fur products in the world and the third largest producer of raw fur.

Figure 3.4: End uses for leather include footwear, apparel, handbags, and other leather accessories.

Fur is divided into two categories—farm-raised and wild fur. Farm-raised fur is derived from reproducing, rearing, and harvesting domestic fur-bearing animals in captivity. Mink comprises 80 percent of farm-raised, fur-bearing animals. The United States has approximately two thousand mink and fox farms and produces approximately 10 percent of the world's mink supply. Wild fur is derived from the selective and regulated harvesting of surplus fur-bearing animals that are not endangered or threatened species and that do not live in captivity. Fur pelts are sold at fur auctions to fur processors. Most fur processors are located in New York City.

The raising and processing of mink, sable, and fox are promoted by the industries as more "environmentally responsible" than the processing of other textiles. According to fur industry literature, environmentally responsible aspects of fur processing include the animals' consumption of waste by-products from the food industry that are not suitable for or graded for human consumption by government agencies; the animals' low water consumption; the fact that manure produced by fur-bearing animals is organically natural and is used as fertilizer for crops; and the fact that all of the animal is used. (The carcass is rendered for its fats and oils, then cooled to create meal and fertilizer. The oils are processed and sold as leather protectors.)

The tanning process for fur, known as **tawning**, differs from the tanning of hides for leather. To tan fur pelts, salt, water, alum, soda ash, sawdust, cornstarch, and lanolin are used. Each ingredient is natural and nontoxic, and the tanning process produces neutral waste water with a pH of 7 (neutral—neither acidic nor alkaline). Many furs are also bleached or dyed to improve their natural color or to give them a nonnatural color (e.g., blue, green). Pelts are also glazed to add beauty and luster to the fur.

In recent years, animal rights organizations have organized antifur campaigns, creating an intense and widespread debate over the humane treatment of animals used for fur production. According to the Fur Farm Animal Welfare Coalition, "North American mink and fox farmers are strongly committed to the ethic of humane care." Euthanasia techniques, recommended by the Fur Farm Animal Welfare Coalition, and practiced in fur farms, are recognized as humane. In its "Statement of Environmental Principles," the coalition resolved to support the international treaties that prohibit the trade of pelts of endangered species, to adhere to standards for the humane care of animals in fur farms, to use safe and efficient systems for harvesting animals in the wild that minimize injury and/or stress to the animal, to endorse principles regarding proper natural resource conservation, and to support efforts to ensure clean air and water. However, even with such assurances, antifur activists continue to campaign against the killing of animals for the production of luxury goods.

MANUFACTURED FIBER PROCESSING

The U.S. manufactured fiber industry is the largest in the world, employing approximately 42,000 people, primarily in North Carolina, South Carolina, Alabama, Georgia, Virginia, and Tennessee. In 1998, 11.38 billion pounds of manufactured fibers were used by textile mills (up steadily from 6.78 billion pounds in 1982). The most widely produced manufactured fibers in the United States are polyester, nylon, olefin, and acrylic. Because of the high capital investment needed, manufactured fiber producers are typically owned by or are part of large chemical companies, such as E. I. du Pont de Nemours & Co. (DuPont), Hoechst Celanese, BASF Corporation, Monsanto Chemical Co., Allied Signal, and Courtaulds North America. Table 3.2

TABLE 3.2

Selected U.S. Manufactured Fiber Producers

Allied Signal
Key fibers: nylon, polyester

BASF Corporation, a subsidiary of
BASF AG
Key fibers: nylon, bicomponent
BASF also makes polyester chip

Courtaulds Fibers
(includes chemicals)
Key fibers: rayon and Tencel
lyocell

Cytec Industries
Key fiber: acrylic

DuPont
Key fibers: Dacron polyester, Lycra
spandex, nylon

Globe Manufacturing Co.
Key fiber: spandex

Hoechst Celanese
Key fibers: ESP stretch polyester,
Polar Guard and Trevira polyester,
Microsafe AM and Celebrate!
acetate fibers

Lenzing Fibers
Key fiber: rayon

Martin Color-Fi
Key fibers: nylon, polyester (both
virgin and recycled), polypropylene

Miles
Key fibers: Dralon acrylic, Dorlas-
tan spandex, type 6 nylon, type
6.6 nylon

Monsanto Co.
Key fibers: Acrilan acrylic, nylon

Nan Ya Plastics
Key fiber: polyester

Wellman
Key fibers: Fortrel polyester
(virgin fiber), Fortrel EcoSpun
(recycled polyester fiber), nylon,
wool processing

lists selected U.S. manufactured fiber producers. These companies are said to be **horizontally integrated**, in that they produce several fibers or variations of fibers that are at the same stages in the process (i.e., fiber processing). For example, Hoechst Celanese is involved in the production of several manufactured fibers including acrylic and polyester.

New manufactured fibers are developed through research efforts that take up to five years before the fiber is available on the market. According to the Textile Products Identification Act, when a fiber belonging to a new generic family is invented, the U.S. Federal Trade Commission assigns it a new generic name. Currently there are more than 20 generic fiber names.

The first step of manufactured fiber production is the conversion of the raw material into a group of related chemical compounds that are treated with intense steam heat, chemicals, and pressure. During this process, which is called *polymerization*, the molecules become long-chain synthetic polymers. The molten resin is then converted into flakes or chips.

Next the flakes or chips are melted and extruded to form filaments. Variations in the appearance of the filaments may be obtained at this stage by changing the shape of the fiber or adding chemicals to modify the fiber characteristics. In the last step, the cold-drawing process winds and stretches the filaments from one rotating wheel to a second faster-rotating one. This straightens the molecules and permanently introduces strength, elasticity, flexibility, and pliability to the yarn. Manufactured fibers can be modified in terms of shape (cross section), molecular structure, chemical additives, or spinning procedures to create better quality or more versatile fibers and yarns. Generic fibers are also combined within a single fiber or yarn to take advantage of specific fiber characteristics. Yarn variations include monofilament and multifilament yarns, stretch yarns, textured yarns, and spun yarns. Companies continue to invest in research to create fiber and yarn innovations to meet consumer demand. Innovations such as microfiber yarns and Tencel lyocell have met with favorable consumer response. Table 3.3 lists selected U.S. yarn producers of both natural and manufactured fibers.

Fiber Marketing and Distribution

MARKETING NATURAL FIBERS

Natural fibers are considered commodities; they are bought and sold on global markets, with prices based upon market demand. For example, in the mid-1990s, cotton prices soared as consumer demand went up and cotton supplies dwindled because of devastating weather and insect-related crop failures in China (the world's largest producer of cotton) and other major producing countries such as India and Pakistan. The largest commodity markets for cotton in the United States are Dallas, Houston, Memphis, and New Orleans; for wool, Boston; and for mohair, a warehouse system throughout Texas. These natural fibers are sold to mills for yarn spinning and fabric production. Furs are sold at public auction. In the United States, the largest fur markets (where furs are auctioned) are St. Louis and New York.

TABLE 3.3

Selected U.S. Yarn Producers

Company	Key Products
Amicale Industries	acrylic, angora, camel hair, cashmere, lambswool, various blends of natural and manufactured fibers
Amital Spinning	acrylic high-bulk yarns and acrylic open-end yarns, in both dyed and natural form
Burlington Madison Yarn Co., a division of Burlington Industries	textured polyester, air-texture and spun rayon yarns, rayon blends, polyester, polyester blends, acrylic; ring-spun and open-end yarns, plied yarns
Commonwealth Yarn Sales	acrylic and acrylic blends, cotton, polyester, wool and worsted
Dixie Yarns	cotton, nylon, rayon, acrylic, polyester, various blends of manufactured and natural fibers
Dominion Yarn Group	aramid; blended, carded, combed cotton; knitting; manufactured; novelty; open-end spun; roving
Doran Textiles	ring-spun and open-end cotton heathers, package-dyed yarns including linen, wool, polyester/cotton heather blends
Glen Raven Mills	open-end spinner acrylic yarns, rayon and acrylic blends, ring-spun and package-dyed acrylic yarns, textured nylon yarns, microdeniers
National Spinning Co.	acrylic, polyester, rayon, wool blends, acrylic, polyester, rayon blends, microdeniers, various specialty yarns
Pharr Yarns	dyed-cotton, acrylic, polyester, rayon, worsted wool
SCT Yarns	mercerized, thread yarns, package-dyed yarns, ring spun, combed spandex, cotton
Spectrum Dyed Yarns	cotton, filament polyester, polyester/cotton blends, spun polyester, rayon, acrylic, various novelty yarns
Unifi	dyed, hosiery, industrial, knitting, textured and weaving nylon, polyester

Not until the late 1940s and early 1950s, when the popularity of manufactured fibers was growing, were marketing efforts for natural fibers initiated by each trade association that represents a specific fiber. These **trade associations**, such as Cotton Incorporated, the Wool Bureau, the American Wool Council, the Mohair Council of America, and the Cashmere and Camel Hair Manufacturers Institute (CCMI) are supported by natural fiber producers and promote the use of the natural fibers through activities such as research, educational programs, and advertising on television and in trade and consumer publications. Through these activities, natural fiber trade associations have become an important support arm for the apparel and home fashions industries, and strong relationships have developed between the trade associations and the apparel and home fashions companies that use the natural fibers.

Founded in 1961, Cotton Incorporated is a research and promotional organization supported by U.S. cotton growers. Cotton Incorporated's members receive technical services, color and trend forecasting services, and promotional services. In 2000, Cotton Incorporated opened a new research and development headquarters in Cary, N.C. The research facility includes textile testing, product care, and color labs. Cotton Incorporated's "Cotton Seal" registered trademark (see Figure 3.5) is used on hangtags and in advertisements along with the association's slogan "The Fabric of Our Lives." In recent years, Cotton Incorporated has sponsored collections of new designers during the spring fashion shows in New York City. Cotton Incorporated is also involved in market research such

Figure 3.5: Cotton Incorporated's registered trademark for products made of 100 percent (U.S. upland) cotton.

as its ongoing Lifestyle Monitor program designed to "monitor America's attitudes and behaviors toward apparel and home furnishings." Research results are published as print and Web reports in the *Lifestyle Monitor*. It includes consumer segment profiles, retail patronage profiles, summaries of consumers' attitudes, and forecasts.

Trade associations focusing on wool fall into two categories: (1) those that focus on wool production (e.g., California Wool Growers Association, Montana Wool Growers Association) and (2) those that focus on product development, marketing, and education (e.g., American Wool Council and The Woolmark Company). Established in 1955, the American Wool Council is a division of the American Sheep Industry Association. Its programs are involved in all aspects of wool marketing, from raw wool marketing and product development to registered trademark programs, advertising, and publicity. The American Wool Council has been involved in standardizing quality levels of wool and promoting wool applications with spinners, weavers, knitters, designers, manufacturers, and retailers. The Wool-

PURE NEW WOOL

WOOLMARK

Figure 3.6: The Woolmark, a registered trademark of the Woolmark Company, is used on hangtags and in advertising.

mark Company was established in 1937 as the International Wool Secretariat (IWS) with a goal of expanding the use of wool throughout the world. In 1964, the Woolmark program, with its well-known Woolmark symbol, was created to identify quality products made from new wool. The Woolmark Blend symbol was introduced in 1971 to identify products made from at least 50% new wool and the Wool Blend symbol was introduced in 1999 to identify products containing between 30% and 50% new wool. These symbols are currently registered in more than 140 countries. The IWS officially changed its name to the Woolmark Company in 1997 and has 18 offices throughout the world.

Established in 1966, the Mohair Council of America is "dedicated to promoting the general welfare of the mohair industry" (Mohair Council of America). The council has offices in San Angelo, Texas, and New York. The council's programs focus on market surveys, research, and development activities including advertising, workshops, and seminars. Because 90 percent of the mohair produced in the United States is exported, the council conducts foreign as well as domestic market research and promotion. The council's trademark in shown in Figure 3.7.

The Cashmere and Camel Hair Manufacturers Institute (CCMI) is "an international trade association representing the interests of producers and manufacturers of camel hair and cashmere fiber, yarn, fabric and garments throughout the world." Established in 1984, the goal of the institute is to "promote and protect the image and integrity of camel hair and cashmere textile products. This is accomplished through government relations, product testing, media relations, and industry relations (CCMI, 2001)." Other trade associations focusing on natural fibers include the International Linen Promotion Commission, National Cotton Council, and International Silk Association.

Trade associations also play an important part in marketing leather and fur. Associations, such as the Leather Industries of America and the American Fur Information and Industry Council, are involved with promotion, including advertising (see Figure 3.8) and consumer education programs. The mink industry also has a number of breeder associations, such as the Eastern Mink Breeders Association (EMBA) and the Great Lakes Mink Association (GLMA), involved in promotion efforts.

The trade associations discussed above concentrate their efforts on specific segments of the natural fiber industry. The American Textile Manufacturers Institute (ATMI) has a broader mission. Covering both natural and manufactured fibers, ATMI "is the national trade association representing the domestic mill products industry. ATMI members operate in 30 states and use in their production about 75 percent of all textile fibers consumed in

Figure 3.7: Registered trademark of the Mohair Council of America.

Figure 3.8: Natural fiber trade associations promote the use of natural fibers through advertising.

the United States. ATMI provides international trade, government relations, economic information, communications and product services in support of the U.S. textile industry." Among other activities, ATMI publishes a quarterly periodical, *Textile HiLights*, which covers economic developments in textiles, textile markets, international trade, mill consumption, production, financial information, end use markets, and employment information. Table 3.4 lists selected trade associations in the textile industry.

TABLE 3.4

Textile Trade Associations

Acrylic Council
1285 Avenue of the Americas
New York, NY 10016
(212) 554-4040
Fax: (212) 554-4042
www.fashiondex.com/acrylic.council/

American Association of Textile
Chemists and Colorists
One Davis Drive
P.O. Box 12215
Research Triangle Park, NC
27709
(919) 549-8141
Fax: (919) 549-8933
www.aatc.org

American Fiber Manufacturers
Association
1150 17th Street NW
Washington, DC 20036
(202) 296-6508
Fax: (202) 296-3052
www.fibersource.com/afma/
afma.htm

American Printed Fabrics Council
469 7th Avenue
New York, NY 10018
(212) 744-4111
Fax: (212) 744-0413

American Textile Machinery
Association
111 Park Place
Falls Church, VA 22042
(703) 538-1789
Fax: (703) 241-5603
www.webmasters.net/atma

American Textile Manufacturers
Institute
1130 Connecticut Avenue, NW
Suite 1200
Washington, DC 20036
(202) 862-0500
Fax: (202) 862-0537
www.atmi.org

American Wool Council
c/o American Sheep Industry
Association
6911 Yosemite Street
Englewood, CO 80112
50 Rockefeller Plaza, Suite 830
New York, NY 10020
(212) 245-6710
Fax: (212) 333-5609
www.americanwool.org

American Yarn Spinners
Association, Inc.
P.O. Box 99
Gastonia, NC 28053
2500 Lowell Road
Ranlo, NC 28054
(704) 824-3522
(704) 824-0630

Carpet and Rug institute
310 S. Holiday Avenue
P.O. Box 2048
Dalton, GA 30722
(706) 278-3176
Fax: (706) 278-8835
www.carpet-rug.co,

(continued)

TABLE 3.4 (continued)

Textile Trade Associations

Cashmere and Camel Hair Manufacturers Institute
230 Congress Street
Boston, MA 02110
(617) 542-7481
Fax: (617) 542-2199
www.cashmere.org

Cotton Council International
1521 New Hampshire Avenue NW
Washington, DC 20036
(202) 745-7805
Fax: (202) 483-4040
www.cottonusa.org

Cotton Incorporated
1370 Avenue of the Americas
34th Floor
New York, NY 10019
(212) 586-1070
Fax: (212) 265-5386
www.cottoninc.com

Fur Farm Animal Welfare
Coalition, Ltd.
225 6th Street East
St. Paul, MN 55101
(612) 222-1080

Fur Information Council of
America
224 W. 30th Street
New York, NY 10001
(212) 564-5133
Fax: (212) 643-9124
www.fur.org

International Linen Promotion
Commission
200 Lexington Avenue, #225
New York, NY 10016
(212) 685-0424
Fax: (212) 725-0438

International Silk Association
c/o Gerli & Co. Inc.
41 Madison Avenue
New York, NY 10010
(212) 213-1919
Fax: (212) 683-2370

Knitted Textile Association
386 Park Avenue South
New York, NY 10016
(212) 689-3807
Fax: (212) 889-6160
www.kta-usa.org

Leather Industries of America
1000 Thomas Jefferson Street NW
Suite 515
Washington, DC 20007-3805
(202) 342-8086
Fax: (202) 342-9063

Mohair Council of America
516 Norwest Bank Building
P.O. Box 5337
San Angelo, TX 76903
(915) 655-3161
Fax: (915) 655-4761
499 7th Avenue
New York, NY 10018
(212) 736-1898
Fax: (212) 629-6373
www.mohairusa.com/mohairco.htm

National Cotton Council of America
1918 N. Parkway
P.O. Box 12285
Memphis, TN 38182
(901) 274-9030
Fax: (901) 725-0510

Polyester Council of America
1675 Broadway
33rd Floor
New York, NY 10019
(212) 527-8941
Fax: (212) 527-8989

The Woolmark Company
1633 Broadway, 23rd Floor
New York, NY 10019-6708
(646) 756-2534
www.woolmark.com

MARKETING MANUFACTURED FIBERS

Manufactured fibers are most often produced by vertically integrated companies. Prices are set primarily by the cost of developing and producing the fiber. Manufactured fibers are sold either as commodity fibers or brand name fibers. *Commodity fibers* are generic manufactured fibers (parent fibers) sold without a brand name attached. For example, a carpet labeled "100 percent" nylon is probably manufactured with commodity nylon fibers. Manufactured fibers are also sold under **brand names** or **trade names**) given to the fibers by manufacturers. Brand names distinguish one fiber from another in the same generic family. Modified manufactured fibers with special characteristics are typically sold under brand names. Examples include Lycra spandex fiber (DuPont), Dacron polyester fiber (DuPont), Fortrel polyester fiber (Hoechst Celanese), Acrilan acrylic fiber (Monsanto), and Antron nylon fiber (DuPont). To establish consumer recognition of brand name fibers, promotion activities focus on the company, the brand name, and the specific qualities of the fiber (see Figure 3.9). Chemical companies spend a great deal of money establishing brand name identification among consumers, and brand name fibers are generally higher in price than commodity fibers. Advertisements also connect brand name fibers with specific end uses. Therefore, cooperative advertising between manufactured fiber companies and apparel manufacturers is common.

Licensed or **controlled brand name programs** set minimum standards of fabric performance for the trademarked fibers. Determined through regular textile testing, these standards are established as a form of quality assurance and relate to a specific end use. For example, the Trevira

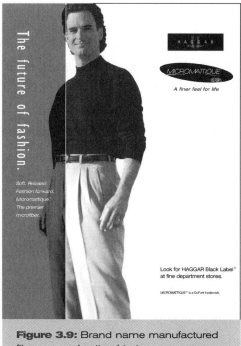

Figure 3.9: Brand name manufactured fibers are advertised to increase name recognition among customers.

polyester program (Hoechst Celanese) establishes minimum standards for fabric quality, and the Zepel program (DuPont) establishes standards for the fabric's water and stain repellency quality. These standards can be especially beneficial to apparel and home fashions manufacturers in quality assurance and marketing end-use products.

Fiber producers also design and create **concept garments** to promote their new fibers to textile mills. For example, when DuPont has a new product to show textile mills, it will often show the new product in garment form. When creating concept garments, fiber companies will either create fabrics and the garment on their own machinery or work with a textile mill that will produce small runs of the concept garment. For example, "when DuPont's yarn developers projected that the next logical use for Cool-Max was in woven fabrics, they approached Russell Fabrics, which collaborated with them on a crisp Tactel blend. The result was a technological innovation: Russell Athletic's golf pant that combines both stretch and wicking" (Musselman, 1998, p. 48).

Trade associations are also important to the manufactured fiber industry. The American Fiber Manufacturers Association (AFMA) began in 1933, first as the Rayon Institute and then as the Man-Made Fiber Producers Association. The current name was adopted in 1988. AFMA members include companies such as BASF Corporation, E.I. du Pont de Nemours & Co., Hoechst Celanese, Monsanto Chemical Company, and Wellman. The AFMA focuses on domestic production of synthetic and cellulosic manufactured fibers. Programs include government relations, international trade policy, the environment, technical issues, and education services. AFMA's subsidiary, the Fiber Economics Bureau, collects and publishes data on production and trade of manufactured fibers. In 1982, AFMA established the Polyester Council of America to "inform the trade and consumers about the fashionability and performance benefits of today's polyester." The Polyester Council of America, supported by U.S. polyester producers and suppliers, promotes the use of polyester in the apparel and home fashions industries through activities such as issuing press releases, co-sponsoring fashion shows, and staging promotional events with retailers.

Color Forecasting in the Textile Industry

Color is an important criterion used by consumers in the selection of textile products, including apparel and home fashions. Therefore an understanding of color preferences by consumers is crucial to successfully marketing a particular textile product. Whereas some classic colors remain popular over many years, fashion colors have a shorter fashion life cycle. Because color is typically applied at the textile production stage, textile companies are often involved in determining which colors are to be used in the end-use products. Through the process of **color forecasting**, color palettes or **color stories** are selected and translated into fabrics produced by a company for a specific fashion season. Color forecasting is also conducted by apparel manufacturers (see Chapter 5).

The Color Association of the United States (CAUS) is a nonprofit service organization that has been involved in color forecasting since 1915. More than seven hundred companies, including fiber producers, textile companies, apparel manufacturers, and home fashions producers, belong to CAUS. A committee of volunteers from these companies determines general color palettes for the coming 18 to 24 months. Twice a year (in March and September), swatch cards (see Figure 3.10) are sent to member companies for their use in determining color palettes for their own products.

Intercolor and the International Color Authority are two international color-forecasting services. Representatives from member companies meet biannually to determine general color palettes approximately 24 months before the products they produce would be available to the consumer. Forecasts are then sent to member companies for their use.

A number of color-forecasting services also sell color forecasts to companies. These forecasts may be specific to a particular target market and product (e.g., women's apparel, children's apparel). Often the services will also include style and fabrication forecasting. For example, Promostyl is an international color-, fabric-, and style-forecasting service that provides trend analyses for men's, women's, and children's apparel 12 to 18 months ahead of the fashion season. Color forecasts may also be conducted by trade associations for their member companies. For example, Cotton Incorporated provides color forecasting services to its members.

Companies also conduct their own color forecasting, which is more specific to their product and target market than the information provided by color-forecasting services. This type of color forecasting is accomplished by

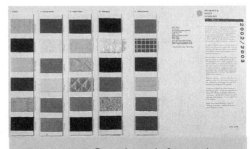

Figure 3.10: Swatch cards from color-forecasting services assist textile companies in their color decisions.

reviewing color predictions from color forecasting services, tracking color trends by examining the colors that were the best and worst selling from previous seasons, observing general trends that may affect color preferences of the target market, and looking at what colors have been missing from the color palettes in order to select colors that may be viewed as "new."

Fabric Production

TEXTILE MILLS

Textile mills focus on the fabric construction stage of textiles. The two most common of fabric construction methods are weaving and knitting. Except for vertically integrated companies that produce both woven and knitted goods, textile mills typically specialize in the production of one type of fabric. In addition to fabric production, woven textile mills often spin their own yarn (see Figure 3.11), whereas knitters typically purchase their yarn. All textile mills sell greige goods. Greige goods may be used "as is" or bought by converters who finish the goods. In addition to selling greige goods, vertically integrated companies also finish the goods themselves and may produce end-use products, such as home textiles (e.g., sheets and towels). Some large vertically integrated textile mills include Burlington Industries, Cone Mills, Dan River, Milliken and Co., Springs Industries, and Swift Denim (see Table 3.5).

Figure 3.11: Fabric production is highly automated. These machines are used at Pendleton Woolen Mills for carding, or straightening the tangled wool fibers (top); spinning the wool into yarn (center); and weaving woolen fabric (bottom).

TABLE 3.5

Selected U.S. Apparel Fabric Weaving Mills

Alice Mills
Headquarters: Easley, SC
Marketing headquarters: New York, NY
Ownership: private
Key fabrics: gray polyester/cotton print cloths, broadcloths and sheetings, gray 100% cotton print cloths and sheetings

Avondale Mills
Headquarters: Monroe, GA
Marketing headquarters: Sylacauga, AL
Ownership: subsidiary of Avondale, a privately held company
Trade names and trademarks: Fast Times, Bermuda Blue, Bermuda Triangle, Ancient Age Colors, Homebrew, Oldye Tymes, Pioneer, Ranch Denim, Green Card Collection (eco-products), Avonspun yarns, Softspun yarns, Nature's Collection (organically grown, naturally colored cotton)
Key fabrics: yarn, indigo-dyed denim, multicolored sports denim, and piece-dyed fabrics for sportwear and activewear markets

Burlington Industries
Headquarters: Greensboro, NC
Marketing headquarters: New York, NY
Ownership: public
Trade names and trademarks: Plateau, Pyramid Ultra, Resillia, Esenzia, Ultrex, Versatech, Durepel, UltraWeaves, Fluid Attitudes, M.C.S., Washable Weaves, Reused, Stonefree, Crystal, Black Nova, Profile, Goldrush, Tenderskin, Iron Horse
Key fabrics: wool worsted and wool/worsted blends, denim, polyester and poly-blend sportswear fabrics, 100% nylon, nylon and polyester blends, and waterproof, breathable fabrics for activewear

Cone Mills
Headquarters: Greensboro, NC
Ownership: public
Trade names and trademarks: Cone Deeptone Denim, Conesport, Cone XX Denim, Cone North Pointe Specialty Sportswear Fabrics, Splashdown, Brawny, Cone XXX Denim
Key fabrics: apparel fabrics for jeans and casual sportswear; manufactures, dyes, prints, and finishes fabrics for home furnishing and retail markets

Dan River
Headquarters: Danville, VA
Marketing Headquarters: New York, NY
Ownership: private
Trade names and trademarks: Dan River, Criterion,, Bed-in-Bag
Key fabrics: yarn-dyed and piece dyed fabrics of cotton and cotton blends; velour and fashion circular knits; sheets, pillowcases, pillow shams, comforters, drapes and other bedroom accessories

Delta Mills Marketing Co.
Headquarters: Greenville, SC
Sales headquarters: New York, NY
Ownership: public—Delta Woodside Industries
Trade names and trademarks: Suncatcher, Trinidad-Twister, Triblend, Irish Linen
Key fabrics: polyester and rayon linens, polyester and wool blends, polyester, rayon, acrylic, 100% cotton

(continued)

TABLE 3.5 (continued)

Selected U.S. Apparel Fabric Weaving Mills

Galey & Lord
Headquarters: New York, NY
Ownership: public
Key fabrics: Woven cotton and polyester/cotton sportswear fabrics, corduroy, printed fabrics, home furnishings fabrics

Greenwood Mills
Headquarters: Greenwood, SC
Sales office: New York, NY
Ownership: private
Trade names and trademarks: Clipper, Winchester, Silverdust, Elite Denim
Key fabrics: denim and chambray, gray goods in print cloth, batiste, broadcloth, twill, poplin

Hamrick Mills
Headquarters: Gaffney, SC
Marketing Headquarters: New York, NY
Ownership: private
Key fabrics: gray fabrics, polyester/cotton blended, textured-fill print cloths, 48–135 inches

Inman Mills
Headquarters: Inman, SC
Marketing headquarters: New York, NY
Ownership: private
Key fabrics: all-cotton twills, oxfords, sailcloths; polyester/cotton poplins, broadcloths, twills, sailcloths sheetings; dobbies and other specialty weaves; all fabrics are sold in loom/gray state

JPS Textile Group
Headquarters: Greenville, SC
Marketing headquarters: New York, NY
Ownership: private
Key fabrics: high-twist filament and spun novelties, satins, crepes, linens, challis, acetate linings

Mayfair Mills
Headquarters: Arcadia, SC
Marketing headquarters: Hoboken, NJ
Ownership: private
Trade names and trademarks: American Premium Quality
Key fabrics: wide print cloth, broadcloth, sheetings, twills, medium and bottom-weight fabrics, poplins, chamois cloth

Milliken & Co.
Headquarters: Spartanburg, SC
Marketing headquarters: New York, NY
Ownership: private
Trade names and trademarks: Visa, Capture, Millitorn, Blazon, Agilon, Worsterlon, Virtuoso, Weathermark, Soft-Trek, Barrier
Key fabrics: cotton, cotton blend, manufactured fiber fabrics for apparel, industrial, home furnishings, and automotive use

Mount Vernon Mills
Headquarters: Greenville, SC
Ownership: private
Trade names and trademarks: Mount Vernon, Riegel, LaFrance, Brentex
Key fabrics: velvet, denim, print cloth, piece-dyed bottom weights, infant bedding, napery

RAMTEX
Headquarters: Ramseur, NC
Marketing headquarters: New York, NY
Ownership: private
Key fabrics: yarns and greige woven goods including broadwoven and sheeting fabrics, basket weave, dobby weaves, oxfords, and sateens

TABLE 3.5 (continued)

Selected U.S. Apparel Fabric Weaving Mills

Texfi Industries

Headquarters: Raleigh, NC
Marketing headquarters: New York, NY
Ownership: public
Trade names and trademarks: Texfi Blends, Special T., Kingstree,

Fashion Knits, Texfi Elastics
Key fabrics: rayon, polyester; plains, novelties, piece-dyed fancies; 100% filament polyester, polyester/wool blends; flame retardant fabrics; woven and knitted elastics

Mills sell staple and/or specialty (novelty) fabrics. Staple fabrics, such as denim or tricot, are produced continually each year with little change in construction or finish. Novelty fabrics have special design features (e.g., surface texture, specialty weave) that are fashion-based and therefore change with fashion cycles. Because of this, fashion fabrics require shorter production runs and greater flexibility.

The knitting industry has two main divisions: (1) the knitted products industry, which manufactures end-use products such as T-shirts, hosiery, and sweaters, and (2) the knitted fabrics industry, which manufactures knitted yard goods sold to apparel and home fashions manufacturers and retailers.

TEXTILE DESIGN

Textile design involves the interrelationships among color (e.g., dyeing, printing), fabric structure (e.g., woven or knitted fabric), and finishes (e.g., napping, embossing). In addition to knowing about color and fabric structure, textile designers must have expertise in computer-aided design and an understanding of the technology used in producing textiles. The use of computer-aided design allows the textile designer to experiment with color and fabric construction, and then to print and prepare exact instructions to replicate the fabric design (see Figure 3.12). Textile designers specialize according to printing method and fabric structure; they may be freelance designers or work for textile design studios, textile mills, or converters. For example, one textile designer may work for a textile mill and specialize in direct roller-printing processes; another may be a freelance designer of graphics for T-shirts and specialize in screen printing processes. The term **textile stylist** is currently used to designate individuals who have expertise in the design and manufacturing of textiles as well as an understanding of the textile market. The stylist's combination of

Figure 3.12: Computer-aided design facilitates the work of textile designers in creating new fabrics.

design, technical, and consumer/business expertise is particularly important in reflecting consumer preferences in the textiles being designed. Designers and stylists may work directly with apparel and home fashions manufacturers to create special prints or with retailers to create prints to be used for private label merchandise.

TEXTILE CONVERTERS

Textile converters buy greige goods from mills, have the fabrics dyed, printed, or finished, and then sell the finished fabrics. Textile converters focus on aesthetic finishes (e.g., glazing, crinkling), performance finishes (e.g., colorfast, stain resistant, water resistant, durable pressed), and dyeing or printing fabrics. Most textile converters are headquartered in New York City, although they can also be found in other major apparel markets (e.g., Los Angeles, Dallas, Atlanta). Textile converters are experts in color forecasting and understand consumer preferences in fiber content, fabric construction, and various aesthetic and performance fabric finishes. Often textile converters will contract with dyers, printers, and finishers to create fabrics that they market to apparel and home fashions manufacturers, jobbers, and retailers. Some converters specialize in a certain type of fabric; others may design several types of fabrics. Most converters that print fabrics use rotary printing presses. However, some are now exploring digital printing with ink jet printers. Because the fabric is finished close to the time when consumers will be purchasing the end-use product, converters play an important role in analyzing and responding to changing consumer preferences.

Although most fabric finishing is done by converters, not all finishing operations are handled by them. For example, apparel and home fashions manufacturers and retailers fulfill the converter's functions to some extent when they specify to a textile mill the color they want a fabric dyed. Woolen and worsted wool fabrics are seldom sold through converters, but rather are generally sold finished by mills. In addition, industrial fabrics are typically sold directly from mills because they are made to meet buyer specifications and may require special performance tests. Also converters are seldom used in the manufacturing of sweaters and other knitwear, which is typically knitted and then constructed into garments by the same company.

OTHER FABRIC RESOURCES

Textile jobbers and fabric retail stores buy and sell fabric without any involvement in producing or finishing the fabric. Textile jobbers buy from textile mills, converters, and large manufacturers, and then sell to smaller manufacturers and retailers. Typically jobbers will buy mill overruns (fabrics the textile mill produces beyond what was ordered) or discontinued fabric colors or prints. For example, a textile jobber may buy extra or discontinued fabric from a textile mill and sell it to a small apparel manufacturer who does not need a large volume of fabric. Retail fabric stores sell over-the-counter piece goods primarily to home sewers. Fabric stores may purchase their bolt yardage from fabric wholesalers that have purchased large rolls from textile mills. Textile brokers serve as a liaison between textile sellers and textile buyers. For example, a broker may connect a small textile mill wanting to sell greige goods to a small converter that wants to buy them. Textile brokers differ from jobbers in that brokers never own the fabric.

TEXTILE TESTING AND QUALITY ASSURANCE

The textile industry is highly involved in quality assurance programs and **textile testing**. "Textile testing is the process of inspecting, measuring and evaluating characteristics and properties of textile materials" (Cohen, 1989, p. 165). Standard test methods developed by the American Society for Testing and Materials (ASTM) and the American Association of Textile Chemists and Colorists (AATCC) are used by companies in testing the quality and specific performance requirements of the textile materials they use. Although the terms *quality control* and *quality assurance* are sometimes used interchangeably, they have different meanings. **Quality control** involves inspecting finished textiles to make sure they adhere to specific quality standards as measured by a variety of textile testing methods (see Figure 3.13). **Quality assurance** is a broader concept, covering not only the fabric's general functional performance (quality), but also how well it satisfies consumer needs for a specific end use. For example, a textile to be used in children's apparel must not

Figure 3.13: Fabrics are inspected by trained experts to ensure that they meet quality standards.

only meet minimum standards of functional performance, but must also meet specifications such as color fastness that are important to the consumer of children's apparel. Whereas a textile mill may test for general functional performance of the fabric, often the apparel or home fashions manufacturer or retailer must determine if the fabric meets the specifications of importance to their consumers. This is why the testing of fabrics is often conducted by apparel and home fashions manufacturers (e.g., NIKE, Jantzen), by retailers (e.g., JCPenney, Target) of these goods, or by independent textile testing companies contracted by manufacturers or retailers.

Marketing and Distribution of Fabrics

MARKETING SEASONAL LINES

Fiber producers, textile mills, and converters take part in the marketing of textile fabrics. Most manufactured fiber producers have showrooms that exhibit fabrics and end-use products made from their fibers. Textile showrooms are located in most major U.S. cities (e.g., Los Angeles, Dallas, Atlanta, Chicago), although New York is the primary market center for textile mills, converters, and textile product manufacturers. Showrooms house the fabric samples to be marketed by textile mills or converters to designers and apparel or home fashions manufacturers.

Textile mills and converters market their textile fabrics as fall/winter and spring/summer seasonal lines. Each fabric line includes a grouping of fabrics with a similar theme or *color story*. It is the responsibility of the merchandising or marketing staff of textile companies to show fabric samples to prospective buyers in their showrooms or at textile trade shows. Samples of fall/winter lines of fabrics are shown to prospective fabric buyers in October or November, approximately six to nine months before the end-use product (e.g., apparel) hits the stores. Spring/summer lines of fabrics are shown in March or April. During these shows, apparel and home fashions companies will purchase yardage for their samples. Some large manufacturers may order their end-use fabrics at this time, but most will wait until their own orders from retailers are known. For large accounts, fabric samples can be *confined,* which means that the textile company will not sell the fabric to other end-use companies.

Fabric companies also promote their lines through sites on the Internet and through other on-line services. Such on-line marketing of fabrics offers an efficient method for companies to advertise their products to prospective fabric buyers (Greco, 1996). On-line buying and selling of wholesale fabrics/textiles has emerged as a growing segment of the industry. A number of dot-com companies focus on connecting fabric/textile sellers with fabric/textile buyers in the apparel industry. This type of business-to-business (B2B) e-commerce benefits fabric/textile sellers by linking them to prospective buyers throughout the world. It also benefits fabric/textile buyers by creating a faster and more efficient process for finding and selecting fabrics for their next lines (Maycumber, 2000).

TEXTILE TRADE SHOWS

Textile **trade shows** exhibit textile mills' newest fabrics for the coming fashion seasons. Typically held twice per year, in spring (March) and fall (October/November), textile trade shows offer visitors a look at general trends in color, textures, prints, and fabrications (see Figure 3.14). For example, a textile trade show held in March 2002 would exhibit spring/summer 2003 fabrics. Because every apparel line or collection begins with fabrics, textile shows provide designers and manufacturers with inspirations for their next line or collection. "A designer's creativity is limited by what a fabric can be made to do, so in a sense a collection doesn't really start with the [apparel] designer but with the fabric mill" (Schiro, 1995, p. L16).

Interstoff Europe is considered one of the most important and one of the largest international textile trade shows. It features more than 1,000 exhibitors from over 40 countries and attracts more than 25,000 visitors. Interstoff is attended by designers, manufacturers, and retailers from around the world who wish to purchase fabrics or become familiar with

Figure 3.14: Textile trade shows provide opportunities for textile companies to promote their lines to manufacturers.

fabric trends. Since 1996, Interstoff has consisted of six textile fairs held each year, three per fashion season—Take Off, Interstoff World, and Interstoff Season—each catering to a slightly different group of buyers.

Another important European textile trade show is Première Vision, held twice a year in Villepinte, near Paris, with more than 800 European textile mills exhibiting their textiles. The show has attracted more than 44,000 attendees from around the world including designers, apparel manufacturers, retailers, and representatives from cosmetic companies (Schiro, 1995). Designers often get inspirations for apparel designs from the textiles shown at Première Vision. Cosmetic companies are also interested in general color trends and textures in fabrics.

Other textile trade shows are Ideacomo held in Como, Italy (near Milan); Texitalia held in Milan, Italy, and New York City; Interstoff/Asia in Hong Kong; the International Fashion Fabric Exhibition (with more than 450 exhibitors held in conjunction with the Boutique Show) in New York City; the L.A. International Textile Show; and Textile Association of Los Angeles (TALA) Show. Leather producers also use trade shows to market their products. Two of the best known are Semaine du Cuir, held in Paris in September, and the Tanner's Apparel and Garment (TAG) Show, held in New York City in October.

Developments in the Textile Industry

TEXTILE TRADE AND QUICK RESPONSE

As part of a global economy, textiles are traded among countries throughout the world. Until 1981, the United States exported more textiles than it imported. Since that time, however, a trade deficit has existed. This means that the United States imports more textiles than it exports. In recent years, increased productivity in the industry because of capital investments has resulted in an increase of textile exports. According to U.S. Department of Commerce data, textile exports have risen every year since 1986. In 2000, textile exports reached an all-time high of $10.5 billion. The largest market for U.S. textiles is Mexico; Canada is the second largest, the United Kingdom is third, and Japan is fourth. Even with this growth in exports, however, the trade deficit still exists because textile imports have risen steadily over the past 15 years; they set a record in 2000 at $14.46 billion. This is primarily the result of a number of factors including the North American Free Trade Agreement (NAFTA), the Caribbean Basin Initiative, and lower labor costs in other countries.

In order to compete successfully in a global economy, the U.S. textile industry has invested in new technology to increase productivity in textile mills and improve communication among textile mills, their suppliers, and their customers. These investments in technology are part of the soft goods industry **Quick Response** philosophies and supply chain management. As discussed in Chapter 1, Quick Response is an umbrella term that refers to any strategy that shortens the time from fiber production to sale to the ultimate consumer. In the textile industry, Quick Response strategies include such technological advance as computer-aided textile design, computerized knitting machines, and computer-controlled robots (see Figure 3.15). Enhanced communication links between textile companies, their suppliers, and their customers have also contributed to effective supply chain management strategies. The textile industry has also played an important role in the research, development, and implementation of new strategies to increase productivity and competitiveness. During the past decade, the textile industry has spent on average $2 billion per year (3 to 4 percent of sales of the entire industry) on capital expenditures (plants and equipment). For example, in the woven fabric industry, companies have invested in shuttleless looms (e.g., rapier, projectile, air-jet, and water-jet looms) that have the capability to weave more than twice as many yards per hour as shuttle looms. Digital textile printing (see Figure 3.16) is also reshaping the way in which fabric designs are created (IT strategies, 1997). Digital textile

Figure 3.15: Computer-controlled robots are used to transport packages in textile mills. Such investments in technology have increased the textile industry's productivity.

Figure 3.16: Digital printing allows companies to send fabric designs from computers directly to fabric printing machinery.

printing is "the process of creating printable designs for fabric on a computer, which can be sent directly from the computer to fabric printing machinery without the use of screens and color separation" (Campbell & Kim, 1999, p. 113). In addition, greater flexibility and a willingness to manufacture shorter runs of fabrics have also increased the competitiveness of U.S. textile mills. Mills also have become more specialized, building on areas of strength (Abend, 1994).

ENVIRONMENTAL ISSUES

According to some analysts, the demand for environmentally responsible products, particularly among younger consumers and consumers who have a sense of social responsibility, appears significant. In an effort to improve environmental conditions and to show they are environmentally conscious, companies (including textile producers) are manufacturing and making available to consumers products that include organic or recycled materials, are produced with less-toxic materials such as low-impact dyes, use less water in production, or have incorporated other environmentally responsible processes (see Figure 3.17). Apparel manufacturers are also pressuring textile producers to supply environmentally responsible textiles. Some companies, such as L.L.Bean, have indicated that they will not work with suppliers that are not environmentally sound. L.L.Bean has, for example, pressured denim companies to eliminate the use of pumice stone (it becomes sand and grit) in the manufacture of stonewashed products (Maycumber, 1994). Therefore, in the last few years a number of environmentally responsible textile manufacturing processes have been introduced, including organically grown cotton, cleaner dyeing and finishing processes, and waste reduction.

Each year textile companies spend billions of dollars to ensure that their processes are environmentally responsible through efforts in conserving water, energy, and electricity and in recycling products (i.e., paper and plastic) and natural resources (i.e., water or energy). Plants are built or adapted with environmental impact in mind.

Figure 3.17: Fabrics made with environmentally responsible processes are targeted at consumers who share environmental concerns.

For example, Malden Mills' (producer of Polartec and Polarfleece fleece fabric) new plant in Lawrence, Massachusetts, has built in environmental systems that reduce water use, reuse heat, and treat wastewater. Burlington Industries removes the water from sludge at a dyeing and finishing plant so it can be used by local farmers as fertilizer (Bonner, 1997).

Trade associations have played an important role in research and implementation of environmentally safe processes. In 1992, ATMI launched its Encouraging Environmental Excellence (E3) program (see Figure 3.18). According to ATMI, "the E3 program calls for textile companies to implement a 10-point plan that starts with a corporate environmental policy and includes a detailed environmental audit of facilities, an outreach program to suppliers and customers that encourages recycling,

establishment of corporate environmental goals and the development of
employee education, and community
awareness programs." In 2000, 36
members of ATMI had qualified for
membership in the E3 program (see
Table 3.6). Success stories from this
program abound, citing companies'
recycling wastewater, reducing the use
of dyes that contain chromium, recycling manufacturing waste such as
fibers or carpet trim, reducing air
emissions, and lowering energy costs.

Figure 3.18: Membership in ATMI's
Encouraging Environmental Excellence
(E3) program requires textile companies
to implement environmental processes
that take them beyond compliance with
federal and state laws and regulations.

A number of "environmentally
cleaner" processes have been tried in
the cotton industry. These include
naturally colored cotton, organic cotton, "cleaner" dyeing methods, and reduced
water use. For example, one cotton producer, Sally Fox, grows naturally colored cotton in various shades of green and brown. Natural colors had been bred out of modern cotton because the colored fibers were too short and weak for automated textile
manufacturing. Fox began crossing the longer, stronger white cotton fibers with colored cotton to create Foxfibre cotton, the first naturally colored cotton that can be
processed with modern textile equipment (Robbins, 1994). The natural colors do
more than eliminate the need for dyeing the cotton; instead of fading, naturally colored cotton actually deepens in color when washed. In addition, Foxfibre cotton has
a silky feel and a wool-like elasticity.

Fox is also committed to organic cotton production, in which synthetic chemical fertilizers and pesticides are used minimally or not used at all. Fox is not the only
cotton producer interested in organic cotton. According to the Organic Fiber Council, organic cotton is grown in five states (Arizona, California, Missouri, New Mexico, and Texas) and seventeen countries around the world. Rather than using synthetic chemical fertilizers and pesticides, with organic techniques, natural fertilizers
(e.g., manure, which biodegrades) are used, fields are weeded by hand or cover crops

TABLE 3.6

Encouraging Environmental Excellence (E3) Program Criteria

An E3 Company

1. Has a formal, written environmental policy that articulates its commitment to the environment.
2. Ensures that senior management is committed to and involved in the company's environmental program.
3. Adopts and carries out a formal environmental regulatory compliance audit process.
4. Works with suppliers and customers to address environmental concerns.
5. Establishes annual specific, measurable environmental goals that relate to the E3 criteria and sets targeted achievement dates.
6. Has an employee environmental education and awareness program.
7. Adopts and maintains necessary and required emergency response plans.
8. Communicates its environmental interests and concerns to the community and its residents.
9. Offers its environmental assistance and insights to others within the community.
10. Interacts with federal, state and local policymakers regarding environmental interests and concerns.

are planted to control weeds, crops are rotated for disease control, and beneficial insects that consume destructive insects are introduced. Once harvested, certified organic cotton is stored without the use of chemical rodenticides and fungicides. Mission Valley Textiles was the first woven apparel and home furnishings fabrics mill in the United States to receive the government's organic fiber processing certification (Rudie, 1994). This certification is used in advertising end-use products to the consumer.

A few apparel companies are using organic cotton for at least some of their production. In 1996, Patagonia (the Ventura, California, manufacturer of sportswear and outdoor clothing), shifted its entire line of cotton apparel to organic cotton fabrics. Although the goods cost slightly more than if regular cotton fabrics were used, its customers have responded positively to the more innovative fabrics. NIKE blends 3% organic fiber into fabrics for its T-shirts and socks. It has set a goal of including

3% organic fiber into all their cotton products by 2003. Levi Strauss & Co. also blends organic cotton into the denim for its jeans.

Because the majority of textiles are colored using chemical dyes to create bright, colorfast characteristics, some manufacturers are attempting to lessen the environmental impact of cotton production through the use of "cleaner" dyeing processes, including new forms of synthetic "low-impact" dyes, natural dyes, and undyed, unbleached cottons. In an effort to reduce the amount of effluence during denim laundering, Burlington Industries has developed Stone Free, a dyeing process that allows indigo shades to break down 50 percent faster in the laundering cycle, without the use of stones or chemicals. However, using a cleaner dyeing process does not necessarily mean that the entire manufacturing process is totally clean.

Natural dyes are extracted from a variety of leaves, barks, flowers, berries, lichens, mushrooms, roots, wood, peels, nutshells, minerals, shellfish, and insects. However, many of these sources do not produce stable dyes for textiles. The most common natural dyes currently used are cochineal (red), which is derived from the body of an insect; osage orange (yellow), which is extracted from the osage orange tree; madder root (red), which is extracted from the woody root of the madder plant; and indigo (blue), which is extracted from a number of plants. It is estimated, however, that in current production, natural dyes add 10 to 40 percent to the cost of the goods. This is primarily the result of the cost of the dyestuffs themselves, since most natural dye producers are small operations (McManus & Wipplinger, 1994).

A number of manufactured fiber companies have explored the use of recycling as a means of creating more environmentally responsible processes. Tencel lyocell is Courtaulds Fibers' cellulosic fiber made from harvested wood pulp that is processed with recycled chemicals. In its production, virtually all the dissolving agent is recycled. The resulting fiber is machine washable and is stronger than cotton or wool— as well as having a silkier touch. Fabrics can be made from 100 percent Tencel or in a variety of blends. Often companies will combine the use of Tencel with other environmentally friendly processes. For example, Esprit's ecollection uses Tencel, organically grown cotton and linen, natural and low-impact dyes, and buttons of reconstituted glass.

Currently, polyester staple fibers are also being recycled from plastic soda bottles, which are made of polyethylene teraphthalate, or PET. In the process of making recycled polyester fibers, all caps, labels, and bases made of other materials are removed from the bottles. The bottles are sorted by color (clear and green), then chopped, and the pieces are washed and dried. Next, the pieces are heated, purified, and formed into pellets. The purified polyester is extruded as fine fibers that can be spun into thread, yarn, or other materials. It takes an average of 25 plastic soda bottles to make 1 garment. Wellman's fibers division produces Fortrel EcoSpun, a polyester that contains 100 percent recycled fiber used by dozens of apparel companies (see Figure 3.19). It is estimated that 2.4 billion bottles are kept out of landfills per year through the manufacturing of Fortrel EcoSpun fibers. Hoechst Celanese's recycled polyester fiber is marketed under the name Trevira II. It is a blend of 50 percent postconsumer waste (plastic bottles) and 50 percent virgin polyester. Malden Mills is promoting Trevira II for its collections of lightweight outerwear fabrics.

Several companies are also recycling scrap yarns and fabric. Dixie Yarns manufactures recycled 100 percent cotton or cotton/polyester blend yarn made from

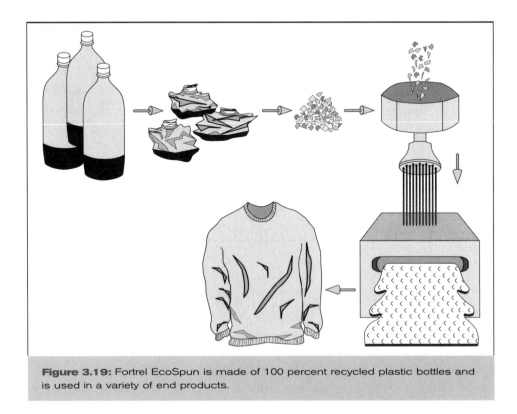

Figure 3.19: Fortrel EcoSpun is made of 100 percent recycled plastic bottles and is used in a variety of end products.

waste fibers that were collected during the yarn-spinning process, baled, and sold in bulk as a waste product. Joma International is producing sweaters from recycled cotton for their Waste Knot line. The process combines waste fabric from new cotton garments with virgin cotton yarn, creating an 85 percent recycled and 15 percent virgin cotton fabric. At Burlington Industries, denim scraps left over after garment pieces have been cut are broken down into fibers and then respun and woven back into denim. The reclaimed denim is made from 50 percent virgin cotton and 50 percent recycled denim (Bonner, 1997; Scrap denim, 1995).

Although consumers say that environmental aspects of textiles are important to them, some retailers are finding it more difficult to sell organic and recycled textile products because of their higher prices. Many companies are asking the question, "How much can we afford to do for the environment and still be competitive?" For example, Dixie Yarns introduced Earthwise, a collection of naturally dyed cotton yarns in 1992. Although initially well received, colorfastness problems forced Dixie to take them off the market in 1994. Some analysts note that environmentally responsible products are best suited to a niche market of environmentally aware consumers.

Summary

The textile industry includes companies that contribute to the four basic stages of textile production: fiber processing, yarn spinning, fabric production, and fabric finishing. Some companies specialize in one or more of the production processes; vertically integrated companies handle all four. Both natural and manufactured fibers are processed in the United States. Natural fibers produced in the United States include cotton, wool, and mohair and other specialty fibers. Leather and fur, also produced in the United States, are considered natural fiber products. Natural fibers are commodities bought and sold on international markets and are generally promoted by trade associations that focus on specific fibers. These trade associations encourage the use of the various natural fibers through such activities as market research, advertising, and consumer education programs.

Manufactured fibers are typically produced by large chemical companies. They are marketed either as commodity fibers or brand name (trademarked) fibers, such as Lycra spandex fiber or Dacron polyester fiber. Brand name fibers are advertised by companies in order to create consumer awareness and preference for the specific fibers. Trade associations are also involved in promoting manufactured fibers.

Textile companies are often involved in determining the colors to be used in end-use products. Through the process of color forecasting, color palettes are selected and translated into fabrics produced by a company for a specific fashion season. Color forecasts are available from nonprofit service organizations, such as the Color Association of the United States, or from color-forecasting services. Companies may also conduct their own color forecasting.

Textile mills focus on fabric production and sell greige goods; some textile mills will finish the fabric as well. Textile design involves the interrelationships among color (e.g., dyeing, printing), fabric structure (e.g., woven, knitted), and finishes (e.g., napping, embossing). Textile converters specialize in fabric finishing. They buy greige goods and finish the fabric according to textile mills', apparel manufacturers', or retailers' specifications. Other fabric resources include textile jobbers, textile brokers, and fabric retail stores. Through quality assurance programs, textile mills, apparel manufacturers, and retailers test textiles according to standards for end-use products. Textile mills and converters market their textile fabrics as fall/winter and spring/summer seasonal lines in showrooms and at textile trade shows held throughout the world.

In order to compete successfully in a global economy, the U.S. textile industry has invested in new technology to increase the productivity of textile mills and improve communication among textile mills, their suppliers, and their customers. These investments in technology are part of the soft goods industry's Quick Response and supply chain management strategies, designed to shorten the time from fiber to finished product.

The textile industry is addressing environmental concerns through manufacturing and by making available to consumers products that include organic or recycled materials, are produced with less-toxic materials such as low-impact dyes, use less water in production, or have incorporated other environmentally responsible processes.

Careers in the textile industry are as varied as the industry itself. Textile chemist, textile designer, textile production supervisor, and textile marketer are just a few of the many careers available in this industry.

Textile Designer
PRODUCT DEVELOPMENT DEPARTMENT, PUBLICLY HELD RETAILER

Position Description
Part of a dynamic product development team responsible for creating private label merchandise for a major publicly held retail corporation. Work with textile mills in designing fabrics to be used in private label merchandise.

Typical Tasks and Responsibilities
- Create color artwork for prints, stripes, and yarn dyes using CAD
- Approve lab dips for production use
- Track lab dip status
- Prepare presentation boards
- Travel overseas

Independent Sales Representative
FABRICS AND TRIMS

Position Description
Show lines of fabrics and trims to designers and merchandisers, send samples, help design products, follow up with vendors to see that goods are delivered through production, negotiate prices, make presentation books and boards.

Typical Tasks and Responsibilities
- Drive to accounts in several states and Canada—traveling 2 to 3 days per week minimum
- Show lines to designers and merchandisers
- Pack and unpack sample bags
- Keep price lists organized
- Manage office and finances; purchase supplies and office equipment
- Work with purchasing agents
- Write orders, follow-up letters, price quotes
- File, update files and materials, keep office clean

CAREER PROFILES

Key Terms

brand name

color forecasting

color stories

concept garment

converted goods

cotton

fabric construction

fiber

filament yarns

finished goods

finishing

generic family

greige goods

hide

horizontally integrated

kip

licensed (or controlled)
  brand name program

mohair

pelt

quality assurance

quality control

regular tannery

skin

spun yarns

tanning

tawning

textile

textile converter

textile jobber

textile mills

textile stylist

textile testing

throwsters

trade association

trade name

trade show

vertically integrated

wool

yarns

Discussion Questions

1. What are the advantages and disadvantages to a textile company of being horizontally integrated? Vertically integrated? How are the advantages and disadvantages of each type of integration related to the types of textile companies that are horizontally and vertically integrated?

2. Follow a cotton/polyester blend woven fabric from the fiber production to the marketing of the fabric to apparel manufacturers. What are the primary stages of production and marketing? Give the approximate time frame for this process.

3. What are the differences between the production and marketing of natural fibers and manufactured fibers? Why do these differences exist?

4. What roles do trade associations play in the promotion of natural and manufactured fibers? Give examples of the activities performed by trade associations. Bring in examples of cooperative advertising between trade associations and end-use producers.

5. What are greige goods? Why are converters important in creating the end-use products that can best meet the needs of consumers?

References

Abend, Jules. (1994, November). The green wave swells. *Bobbin*, pp. 92–98.

American Fiber Manufacturers Association. *The American Manufactured Fiber Industry*. Washington, DC: Author.

American Textile Manufacturers Institute. (1999, June). *Textile HiLights*. Washington, DC: Author.

American Textile Manufacturers Institute. *America's Textiles*. Washington, DC: Author.

Bonner, Staci. (1997, February). It's not easy being green: Strategies and challenges. *Apparel Industry Magazine*, pp. 52–68.

Campbell, J. R. and Eundeok, Kim. (1999, November). Concepts in Digital Textile Printing That Affect the Approach to Textile Design. Proceedings Annual Meeting of the Textile and Apparel Association. Santa Fe, NM, pp. 113–114.

Cashmere and Camel Hair Manufacturers Institute. (2001). CCMI Home Page [online]. Available: http://www.cashmere.org [March 14, 2001].

Cohen, Allen C. (1989). *Marketing Textiles: From Fiber to Retail*. New York: Fairchild Publications.

Eberspacher, Jinger J. (1993). The declining domestic leather industry: Implications and opportunities. *Clothing and Textiles Research Journal*, 12 (1), 26–30.

Greco, M. (1996, February). Is on-line fabric sourcing next? *Apparel Industry Magazine*, pp. 32–34.

Hollen, Norma; Sadler, Jane; Langford, Anna L.; and Kadolph, Sara J. (1988). *Textiles*. (6th ed.). New York: Macmillan.

IT Strategies. (1997, February). Getting a grip on digitial printing. [online] Available: http://www.bobbin.com/media/97feb/digital.htm

Joseph, Marjory L. (1988). *Essentials of Textiles* (4th ed.). New York: Holt, Rinehart and Winston.

Maycumber, S. Gray. (1994, April 26). L.L.Bean to ATMI: Environment key factor. *Women's Wear Daily*, p. 14.

Maycumber, S. Gray. (2000, May 12). Online sourcing/selling: textiles' biggest revolution is coming. *Daily News Record*, pp. 4–5.

McManus, Fred, and Wipplinger, Michele. (1994, February/March). Nature shows her true colors. *Green Alternatives*, pp. 26–31.

McNamara, Michael. (1995, February 9). Cotton Inc. lifestyle monitor to survey consumer attitude. *Women's Wear Daily*, p. 11.

Musselman, Faye. (1998, March). Clear on the concept. *Apparel Industry Magazine*, pp. 46–50.

Patagonia switches to organic cotton. (1995, October). *Bobbin*, p. 24.

Robbins, Jim. (1994, December). Undying devotion. *Destination Discovery*, pp. 18–21.

Rudie, Raye. (1994, February). How green is the future? *Bobbin*, pp. 16–20.

Schiro, Anne-Marie. (1995, May 7). Mills weave trends in fabric of fashion. *The Oregonian*, p. L16.

Scrap denim spun into "Green" jeans. (1995, February). *Apparel Industry Magazine*, p. 16.

Yates, Dorian. (1994, February/March). Organic cotton. *Green Alternatives*, pp. 33–36.

Merchandising

- merchandise managers
- merchandise coordinators

Design Development

- designers
- stylists
- pattern makers
- sample sewers

Sales/Marketing

- sales
- marketing
- market research
- sales representatives

Production, Planning, and Control

- fabric buying
- production
- shipping
- outside contractors
- quality control/assurance

Advertising and Sales Promotion

- national media (with agency)
- retail promotions
- public relations

CHAPTER 4

Ready-to-Wear: Company Organization

IN THIS CHAPTER YOU WILL LEARN:

- The difference between the ready-to-wear industry and haute couture.
- The various types of ready-to-wear companies.
- The organizational structure of apparel companies.
- The merchandising philosophies of apparel companies.
- The primary trade associations and trade publications in the apparel industry.

Tommy Hilfiger, Donna Karan International, Russell Athletic, Osh-Kosh B'Gosh, Authentic Fitness, Polo Ralph Lauren—all are examples of successful U.S. apparel companies. Although each of these companies creates merchandise recognized by consumers around the world, they vary in the way they are organized and in the way they operate. This chapter focuses on the general organization and operation of companies that produce men's, women's, and children's apparel. Apparel companies are classified by the categories of apparel products they produce, such as size range, styling, price zone, type of product (suits, active sportswear), as well as the age and gender of the target marker customer. These classifications, in turn, relate to the organizational structure of the producers and retailers of fashion goods.

Ready-to-Wear: What Does It Mean?

The majority of apparel produced and sold is called **ready-to-wear (RTW)**. As the term implies, the apparel is completely made and ready to be worn (except for finishing details such as pant hemming in tailored clothing) at the time it is purchased. In England, this merchandise is called *off-the-peg*, in France it is called *prêt-à-porter*, and in Italy it is called *moda pronto*. RTW apparel is made in large quantities using mass manufacturing processes that require little or no hand sewing.

Apparel companies produce seasonal **lines** or **collections** of merchandise. Lines or collections are groups of styles designed for a particular **fashion season**. The primary difference between a line and a collection is the cost of the merchandise—the term collection typically refers to more expensive merchandise. Often "name designers" will create and offer *collections*; other apparel companies will offer *lines*.

Apparel companies typically produce four to six new collections or lines per year, corresponding to the fashion seasons: spring, summer, fall I, fall II, holiday, and resort. These fashion seasons coincide with the times consumers would most likely wear the merchandise, not to when companies design or manufacture the merchandise or when the merchandise is delivered to stores. For example, a company may start to design a fall season line in September, market the line in March, actually manufacture it from March through April, and deliver the merchandise to the stores in June. Color Plate 3 shows the calendar for four seasonal lines, each line represented by a color. An 18-month time span is used to illustrate the overlaps among seasons from design to delivery.

Not all companies will produce lines for all six fashion seasons. The number of lines a company will produce depends on both the product category and the target market (the group of customers the line is designed for). For example, a company that produces men's tailored suits may create only two lines per year (fall and spring), whereas a men's sportswear company may create five lines per year (fall I, fall II, holiday, spring, and summer). Some companies produce more than six lines per year.

As discussed in Chapter 1, the standardization of sizing was necessary for the development of the ready-to-wear industry. Sizes in RTW are based on a combination of standardized body dimensions, company size standards, and wearing and design ease. Clothing sizes were developed by grouping computed average circumference measurements of a large group of people (of average height) into specific size categories. For example, the men's size 42 relates to an "average height" (5 feet 10 inches) male with a chest circumference of 42 inches, waist of 37 inches, and hip measurement of 43 inches. These body measurements or dimensions are what are referred to as the standardized size. Standardized tables of body dimensions are available from the American Society for Testing and Materials (ASTM) for various figure types. The standardized tables are revised periodically.

However, the apparel industry does not adhere strictly to the "set" standardized sizes. A company may develop its "company size" based on a target customer with a smaller waist in comparision to the hip circumference, or a larger chest in comparision to the waist circumference. The term, *athletic fit* is used to refer to a men's suit built to fit the male body with a larger chest-to-waist ratio than the standard-ized size. This is why many consumers find that one brand of apparel fits them bet-ter than other brands. As catalog sales of apparel have increased, direct marketing apparel companies have worked to develop consistent body measurements and related size measurements for all styles produced. A fit that can be determined accu-rately from body measurement charts can reduce returns and thus increase customer satisfaction with the product and the company.

Wearing ease and design ease allowances are added to the body measurements to create the garment measurements. Each company decides how much wearing and design ease to add to create the "look" for the company. Some styles are designed to fit more loosely than other styles. The company sizing will reflect these style aspects. Each company's size range is based on its predetermined body measurements, plus ease. The size measurements increase and decrease in specified increments from the base or sample size to create the size range. The size increments used to create the various sizes will be discussed in more detail in Chapter 9.

The Difference Between Ready-to-Wear and Couture

Designer names, such as Coco Chanel, Christian Dior, and Yves Saint Laurent, first became famous in the realm of French *haute couture* (high fashion) and later became associated with expensive ready-to-wear. Because of the continued prominence and importance of these designer labels, it is important to understand the distinction and the relationship between couture and ready-to-wear. *Couture* is a French term that literally means "sewing." In general, **couture** apparel is produced in smaller quantities, utilizes considerable hand-sewing techniques, and is sized to fit an individual's body measure-ments. Generally, more expensive fabrics are used in couture apparel than in RTW.

The term *couture* is derived from **haute couture** (pronounced oat coo-tur), which literally means *high sewing*. As discussed in Chapter 1, the haute couture industry developed in Paris during the nineteenth century. At that time, apparel was produced by dressmakers and tailors who custom fit each garment to the client. The garment's style and fabric were selected for or by each client, the client's body mea-surements were taken, and the garment was completed after one or more fittings during the construction process. For persons who did not have personal dressmakers or tailors, apparel was produced in the home, by whoever had the necessary skills.

Selecting a fabric and creating a garment prior to an order from a client was a new concept, attributed to Charles Frederick Worth, the founder of the haute couture business. He created several gowns which were modeled by his wife. Clients came into his shop and selected a style to be copied for them, custom fit to their body measurements. Soon he had a clientele of wealthy and noble patrons. He used exquisite fabrics and trims and employed a bevy of seamstresses to complete the intricate handwork. In time other designers followed Worth's lead, and the haute couture business was formed. These designers "created" new fashions, while the rest of the western fashion world followed their lead.

During the early twentieth century, the *Chambre Syndicale de la Couture Parisienne* was formed to provide an organizational structure and to offer protection for designers against their designs being copied. Currently, the *Chambre Syndicale* arranges the calendar for the showings of the collections twice per year, organizes accreditation for press and buyers who want to attend the showings, and assists the couture houses so each gains the maximum press coverage possible. Today, there are fewer than thirty haute couture designers in Paris. To be a member of the Paris haute couture requires specific qualifications, including the use of one's own "house" seamstresses, the presentation of fall and spring collections each year, adherence to the dates of showings set by the *Chambre Syndicale*, and registration of the original designs to protect against copying designs.

Each designer's business is called a *house*. Thus, there is the House of Dior, the House of Saint Laurent, and the House of Chanel. The haute couture designer is called the **couturier** (or **couturière**) or the "head of the house." Whereas some couturiers control their own businesses, many couture houses are owned by corporations that finance the house. In recent years, some financial backers have been known to hire and fire head designers.

A Paris haute couture designer typically has a *boutique* (store) located on one of several "fashion avenues" in Paris. The boutique sells the designer's licensed products, such as perfume, scarfs, jewelry, and other accessories, and home fashions. Some boutiques sell boutique collections of apparel and shoes as well.

The **salon de couture** is the showroom of the couture designer. The salon is typically located on the second floor of the building that houses the designer's boutique. Entry to the second level, the salon, is limited to those with invitations to a collection show. The **atelier de couture** (pronounced ah-tal´-lee-aye), or workrooms, may be on the floors above the salon or in a separate building.

The twice-per-year Paris haute couture collection openings continue to be huge events in the fashion world and are covered in detail by the fashion press (see Figure 4.1). Fall fashion season haute couture collections are typically shown in July, and spring fashion season haute couture collections are typically shown in January. The press, buyers, other designers, celebrities, and wealthy clients are in attendance. While the fashion influence of the couturiers waxes and wanes, the designs presented are considered to represent "a laboratory of design creativity." Paris haute couture houses also produce RTW (*prêt-à-porter*) collections. These RTW collections may be sold in the house boutique, in freestanding boutiques (e.g., Yves Saint Laurent's *Rive Gauche* boutiques), or in upscale department or specialty stores. Currently all haute couture houses offer *prêt-à-porter* collections.

Figure 4.1: The shows at couture houses—such as the Karl Lagerfeld for Chanel, Fall 2001 show—are huge events in the fashion world and are covered in detail by the press.

In addition to the couturiers who are members of the *Chambre Syndicale*, other designers consider themselves to be couture designers. Generally, a couture designer uses elegant fabrics, creates original designs (as opposed to copying another's designs); uses high-quality, hand-finishing details; and custom fits the garment to a client's body measurements. Couture designers may produce all custom work (ordered by a specific client), or they may present a seasonal collection and then take custom orders for the collection. There are couture designers in New York, Los Angeles, and other cities around the world.

The term *couture* is sometimes used in the apparel industry to impart an elite ambience to an apparel collection. For example, an apparel company might produce a high-priced RTW collection and call it a *couture collection*. Indeed, some stores even have what they call *couture* departments. However, if mass-production techniques are used in producing the apparel, and if garments are not custom fit to the client, the line should be called RTW and *not* couture.

Types of RTW Apparel Producers

From large corporations to small companies, from those that produce innovative, trendy merchandise to those that produce classics, RTW companies come in all types and sizes and vary tremendously in their organization. Because of the diversity found in RTW apparel company organization, any attempt to classify types of apparel producers is difficult. However, according to industry analysts, the major types of apparel suppliers can be grouped into the categories that follow (Kurt Salmon Associates, 1989).

Conventional manufacturers perform all functions of creating, marketing, and distributing an apparel line on a continual basis. These companies typically make products in their own plant(s) or factories, but might also use outside companies (*contractors*) to make their products. Manufacturers include multidivision companies that produce several product lines of nationally advertised merchandise (e.g., Levi Strauss & Co., VF Corporation) as well as companies that specialize in one or more product categories, such as infants' and children's wear (e.g., Carter's) or fleece wear (e.g., Russell Athletic). Manufacturers may produce brands of merchandise distributed nationally or regionally, licensed products, or private label merchandise for a specific store. Retail distribution of products will vary depending on the manufacturer.

Jobber is the traditional term for companies that buy fabrics and acquire styles from independent designers or by copying or designing lines themselves, but use contractors to make their products. This type of company became popular in the early 1900s, with New York (Seventh Avenue) men's and women's apparel companies serving as intermediaries. They carried huge inventories of merchandise and could make prompt deliveries to retailers. As retailers started sending their own buyers to New York and as resident buyers became more popular, the need for jobbers declined. Today, because so many apparel producers contract out the manufacturing functions, the use of the term *jobber* is not as widespread as it used to be. Instead, most apparel producers are referred to as *manufacturers* regardless of whether or not they use contractors. In fact, this recent definition of *manufacturer* offered by industry analysts suggests a broader perspective: "Manufacturers in the apparel industry are the main contractors of apparel production. Some have internal production capabilities, but most contract out a substantial portion of actual production to contractors" (Southern California Edison Company, 1995, Appendix A).

Contractors are companies that specialize in the sewing and finishing of goods. Contractors are used by full-function manufacturers that lack sufficient capacity in their own plants, by jobbers, and by retailers for private label merchandise. According to the industry definition, "contractors in the apparel industry are the many, usually small factories in which most apparel production actually takes place. Several different types of industry entities source apparel goods from contractors, including manufacturers, retailers, buyers, importers, and trading companies" (Southern California Edison Company, 1995, Appendix A). Most contractors specialize in a product category (e.g., knit tops) or have specialized equipment (e.g., embroidery machines) and skilled workers. The term **item house** is used to describe contractors that specialize in the production of one product. For example, item houses are used in the production of baseball caps. Contractors offer their customers fast turnarounds. Some contractors, in working with retailers, also offer fabric procurement and apparel design services that were traditionally part of the manufacturers' role.

Some manufacturers and contractors produce goods for the sole use of a particular retailer as a private label brand or **retail/store/direct market brand** merchandise. Some retailers offer a combination of national brands and private label merchandise (e.g., Nordstrom, Lord & Taylor, Macy's), whereas other retailers will offer only store brand merchandise (e.g., Gap, The Limited, Eddie Bauer, Talbot's). Some manufacturers and contractors will produce merchandise for both national brands and private label or store brands; other manufacturers and contractors will produce merchandise for one national or private label/store brand only.

Licensors are companies that have developed a well-known designer name (e.g., Calvin Klein, Donna Karan, Ralph Lauren), brand name (e.g., Guess?, Hang Ten), or character (e.g., Mickey Mouse, Barbie, Star Wars) and sell the use of these names or characters to companies to put on merchandise. As discussed in Chapter 2, successful licensing depends on a well-known name or image (property).

It should be noted that these categories are not mutually exclusive. For example, a manufacturer may use a contractor when its own plant's capacity is exceeded, or may license its brand name to a company that produces product categories different from its own. The details of these various types of apparel production will be discussed in later chapters.

Classifying Apparel Organizations

Apparel producers are classified in a number of ways; by the type of merchandise they produce, by the wholesale prices of the products or brands, and by an industry classification system for governmental tracking. An examination of these classification systems is in order to better understand the diversity of apparel organizations.

GENDER/AGE, SIZE RANGE, PRODUCT CATEGORY

The apparel industry is divided into the primary categories of men's, women's and children's apparel manufacturers. Some companies produce apparel in only one of these categories; others produce apparel for more than one. In some cases, companies began as producers of one category of apparel, then branched out into one or more other categories as the company grew. For example, Levi Strauss & Co. began as a producer of men's apparel and later expanded into women's and children's wear; Liz Claiborne began as a producer of women's apparel and then developed a men's division.

The separate gender/age categories have their roots in the early history of the U.S. apparel industry. Apparel producers specialized in one category because of a variety of factors. The types of machinery used for producing men's apparel were often different from the types needed for women's apparel. The sizing standards developed differently for men's, women's and children's apparel. The number of seasonal lines produced per year differs for each category; therefore the production cycle varies.

The organizational structure of retail stores is related to these categories of apparel, which is another reason why the apparel industry remains divided into the three primary categories. Retail buyers are often assigned responsibilities in one of the three categories of apparel. For example, a men's wear buyer buys apparel for the retail store from men's apparel producers. This allows for the producers and retailer to establish and maintain profitable working relationships.

Within each of the three primary categories, apparel producers are subdivided into additional categories. Apparel producers generally specialize in one or several subcategories. These subcategories relate to the **classification** of apparel. Apparel classifications are by type of garment produced (product type). Traditional classifications by product type for women's apparel include the following:

▉ Outerwear (coats, jackets, and rainwear)

▉ Dresses

▉ Blouses

▉ Career wear (suits, separates, and career wear dresses)

▉ Sportswear and active sportswear (separates such as pants, sweaters, and skirts; and active sportswear such as swimwear and tennis wear)

▉ Evening wear

▉ Bridal and bridesmaid dresses

▉ Maternity wear

▉ Uniforms

▉ Furs

▉ Accessories

▉ Intimate apparel

Intimate apparel is further classified into the following categories:

▉ Foundations (girdles or body shapers, bras, and other shape wear)

▉ Lingerie (petticoats, slips, panties, camisoles, nightgowns, and pajamas)

▉ Loungewear (robes, bed jackets, and housecoats)

Foundations and lingerie worn under other clothing are sometimes referred to as *innerwear*. In addition, lingerie and loungewear are sometimes divided into day wear and night wear.

From four to six seasonal lines per year are typically produced in the women's apparel category. A number of apparel companies produce smaller lines shipped to retailers more frequently; the frequent infusion of new merchandise appeals to customers.

The various subcategories are organized by size range and clothing classification (see Table 4.1). For example, some apparel companies manufacture apparel only in missy or only in junior sizes. Some companies produce apparel in missy and women's (large) sizes, while other companies manufacture missy, women's, petite,

TABLE 4.1

Men's, Women's and Children's Wear Categories

Men's Wear:
Subcategories (organized by classification of apparel):
Tailored clothing
> suits, sport coats, evening wear (tuxedos), overcoats
> sizes: 36 to 50 (chest circumference) and portly sizes 46 to 50, regular, short, long
> separate trousers, sizes: waist/hemmed at retailer's
> Examples: Hartmarx, Christian Dior, private label (e.g., Worthington for JC Penney)

Sportswear
> sport shirts (S-M-L-XL sizes), pants (waist/inseam or S-M-L sizes), casual jackets (36 to 50 or S-M-L-XL sizes)
> Examples: Levi's, Dockers, Liz Claiborne, private/store label (e.g., Gap, Old Navy)

Furnishings
> shirts (neck/sleeve length or S-M-L-XL sizes), neckwear, sweaters, underwear (waist size), socks, robes, pajamas
> Examples: John Henry, Arrow, Pendleton

Active sportswear
> swimwear, athletic wear, windbreakers
> sizes: S-M-L-XL-XXL
> Examples: NIKE, Speedo, Authentic Fitness

Uniforms and work wear
> overalls, work pants (waist/inseam or S-M-L-XL sizes), work shirts (S-M-L-XL)
> Examples: Levi's, OshKosh B'Gosh

Women's Wear:
Subcategories (organized by size, then by product type classification):
Not all companies produce the entire size range.
Missy—sizes 4 to 18 or S-M-L
Women's (large size, queen, custom)—sizes 16W to 26W or 1X to 4X or Plus sizes 1X, 2X, 3X
Petite—sizes 2P to 16P, under 5'4"
Tall—sizes 10T to 18T, over 5'9"
Junior—sizes 1 to 15
Classifications: outerwear, dresses, career wear, blouses, sportswear and active sportswear, evening/bridal, maternity, uniforms, furs, intimate apparel, accessories

Children's Wear:
Subcategories (organized by gender and size):
Infants—sizes by weight/height or 3 month, 6 month 12 month, 18 month
Toddler—sizes 2T to 4T
Boys—sizes 4 to 7 and 8 to 20 and Husky or Chubby
Girls—sizes 4 to 6X and 7 to 16
Preteen (girls)—sizes 6 to 16
Young junior—sizes 3 to 13

and tall sizes. Figure 4.2 shows how the measurements in different size categories vary. Within one size range, an apparel producer may manufacture clothing in one or more of the product classifications previously listed.

In addition to the difference between size range categories of missy and junior apparel, there are styling differences as well (see Figure 4.3). The junior size range is designed for a customer who is approximately 16 to 22 years old, whereas the missy size range is designed for a target customer who is approximately 22 years old and older. The styling, fabrics, and trims of missy apparel have a more mature fashion look than that of junior apparel.

SWIM BODY SIZES

MISSES SWIM

SIZE	6	8	10**	12	14	16	18
BUST	34½	35½	36½	38	39½	41	43
RIBCAGE	28	29	30	31½	33	34½	36½
WAIST	25½	26½	27½	29	30½	32	34
HIP	36½	37½	38½	40	42	44	46
TORSO	59	60½	62	62½	65	66½	71
LONG TORSO	62	63½	65	66½	68	69½	71

JUNIOR SWIM

SIZE	3	5	7	9**	11	13
BUST	32½	33½	34½	35½	36¾	38¼
RIBCAGE	26½	27½	28½	29½	30¾	32¼
WAIST	23½	24½	25½	26½	27¾	29¼
HIP	34½	35½	36½	37½	38¾	40¼
TORSO	57	58½	60	61½	63	64½

WOMEN SWIM

SIZE	16W	18W**	20W	22W	24W	26W	28W
BUST	40	42	44	46	48	50	52
RIBCAGE	33½	35½	37½	39½	41½	43½	45½
WAIST	32	34	36	38	40	42	44
HIP	41½	43½	45½	47½	49½	51½	53½
TORSO	65	66½	68	69½	69½	69½	69½

** = BASE SIZE (sample size)

Figure 4.2: Women's apparel includes size ranges such as misses (missy), junior, and women's. The base size for each size range is indicated with **.

Traditional men's wear classifications include the following:

- ▇ Tailored clothing (structured or semi-
  structured suits, coats, and separates,
  such as sportsjackets and dress slacks)
- ▇ Sportswear (casual pants, including jeans)
- ▇ Furnishings (dress shirts and casual shirts; sweaters; neckties, handkerchiefs, and other accessory
  items; underwear and night wear;
  hosiery; and hats and caps)
- ▇ Active sportswear (athletic clothing,
  golf wear, tennis wear, swimwear)
- ▇ Uniforms and work wear (work
  shirts and pants, overalls)

Figure 4.3: Both sizing and styling
differences differentiate junior apparel
from missy apparel.

Table 4.1 lists these classifications, typical sizes offered, and examples of men's
wear producers. The number of season-
al lines produced per year in men's wear varies with the classification of apparel. Tailored clothing producers tend to develop a large fall line and a somewhat smaller
spring line, while sportswear producers develop four to six seasonal lines per year.

In children's wear, the subcategories are organized by age-related size ranges and
by gender (see Table 4.1). Many children's wear manufacturers produce apparel in
both infant and toddler sizes. In the older size ranges, apparel companies usually specialize in either boys' wear or girls' wear. Seasonal lines produced in children's wear
typically include back-to-school (the largest line), holiday, spring, and summer lines.

WHOLESALE PRICE ZONES

Ready-to-wear apparel companies typically specialize in one or more **wholesale
price zones**, which are categories based on the approximate wholesale cost of the
merchandise. The price zone categories include the following:

■ **Designer.** The designer price zone is the most expensive of the wholesale price zones. It includes collections of name designers such as Calvin Klein, Donna Karan, Yves Saint Laurent, Bill Blass, Giorgio Armani, and Chanel, as well as collections of brands such as St. John Knits. Although this category is sometimes referred to as *couture*, it should not be confused with couture apparel that is custom made to the body measurements of an individual.

■ **Bridge.** Bridge lines traditionally fall between designer and better price zones. These may include designers' less expensive lines, sometimes called **diffusion lines** (e.g., Emporio, Donna Karan Signature), or those brands that are situated between designer and better price zones (e.g., Ellen Tracy, Dana Buchman, Adrienne Vittadini).

■ **Better.** Lines in the better wholesale price zone are generally nationally known brand names, such as DKNY in women's wear, or Nautica, and Re-union in men's wear. Store brands (e.g., Banana Republic—see Figure 4.4) and private label merchandise (goods that carry the retailer's name) are sometimes in this price zone as well (e.g., Nordstrom's Classiques Entier brand).

■ **Moderate.** Lines in the moderate wholesale price zone include nationally known sportswear brand names (e.g., Dockers, Guess, Jones New York Sport) or store brands (e.g., Gap) and other reasonably priced lines (e.g., Kasper suits). Moderate lines also include less-expensive lines of companies that also produce better merchandise (e.g., Lizwear). Private label and store brand merchandise may also be in this price zone (e.g., JCPenney's Arizona brand, and Federated's Charter Club brand.

■ **Budget or mass.** Found primarily at mass merchandisers and discount stores, budget lines are the

Figure 4.4: Store brand apparel such as Banana Republic might be priced in the better wholesale price zone.

least expensive of the wholesale price zones. These may include store brands of retailers with low prices as a competitive strategy (e.g., Old Navy). Private label merchandise for discount stores is also considered to be in the budget price zone category (e.g., Kmart's Jaclyn Smith brand).

It is important to note that the wholesale price zones can be considered a continuum for classification purposes. For example, some lines may be considered to be between budget and moderate, while others may be considered between moderate and better. Also, a brand may be offered in the bridge price zone as direct-mail merchandise while the same brand may be offered in the designer price zone at retail stores. Some companies produce labels in several price zones, or **brand tiers**. Giorgio Armani includes the Giorgio Armani label, the Emporio label, and the Armani A/X label, each targeted for a different price zone.

BRAND NAME CLASSIFICATIONS

Companies also vary in the brands they produce. Brand names fall into one of the following categories (Lewis, 1995, p. 3):

- **National/designer brands.** A **National/designer brand** is "a label that is distributed nationally, to which consumers attach a specific meaning. Typically a national brand represents a certain image, quality level and price-point range to consumers." Examples include Hanes, Fruit of the Loom, Calvin Klein, Wrangler, NIKE, and Victoria's Secret (see Figure 4.5).

- **Private label brands.** A private label brand is "a label that is owned and marketed by a specific retailer for use in their stores." Examples include JCPenney's Worthington label and Target's Mossimo label.

Figure 4.5: Victoria's Secret is one of the 25 most recognizable brands of women's apparel and accessories.

■ **Retail store/direct market brands.** A retail store/direct market brand is "a name of a retail chain that is, in most cases, used as the exclusive label on the items in the store." These are sometimes referred to as *store brand*. Examples include Gap, Eddie Bauer, Banana Republic, The Limited, Victoria's Secret, and L.L.Bean.

■ **All other brands.** In addition to these brands there are "miscellaneous labels that are not included in the categories above. Includes licensed brands." Examples include Wilson, Mickey & Co, and Looney Tunes/Warner Bros.

■ **Nonbrands.** In addition, a product may have "a label to which consumers attach no significant identity, awareness, or meaning."

See Table 4.2 for a listing of the 25 most recognizable brands in women's apparel and accessories.

NORTH AMERICAN INDUSTRY CLASSIFICATION SYSTEM

The U.S. Department of Commerce categorizes companies based on their chief industrial activity. Industry data are often compiled and reported according to these categories. In the past, *Standard Industrial Classification (SIC)* numbers were used. With the phasing out of the SIC system, a new system, the **North American Industry Classification System (NAICS)**, was created. In this classification system, industry sectors in the United States, Mexico, and Canada can be compared. The primary NAICS groups are:

■ NAICS 313: Textile Mills
■ NAICS 314: Textile Product Mills (produce nonapparel textile products)
■ NAICS 315: Apparel Manufacturing
■ NAICS 316: Leather and Allied Product Manufacturing

Within these major groups, additional numbers are used to designate more specific products (e.g., 31521 refers to cut and sew apparel contractors). Table 4.3 lists the NAICS categories for textiles and apparel.

Organizational Structure of Apparel Companies

Figure 4.6 outlines the organizational structure of a typical apparel company. Although companies will vary in terms of their exact organizational structure, the following activities are often included: merchandising; design development; sales

TABLE 4.2

The 25 Most Recognizable Brands in Women's Apparel and Accessories

1. **Timex**
   Product: watches
   Volume: $600 million
   Owner: Timex Corp.,
   Middlebury, CT

2. **L'eggs**
   Product: legwear
   Volume: $388 million
   Owner: Sara Lee Corp.,
   Chicago

3. **Hanes**
   Products: hosiery, innerwear
   Volume: $200 million
   Owner: Sara Lee Corp.,
   Chicago

4. **Hanes Her Way**
   Products: underwear, daywear, bras, at-home wear,
   bodywear, baby wear, kid's
   wear, casual wear, socks,
   casual shoes
   Volume: Over $800 million
   Owner: Sara Lee Corp.,
   Chicago

5. **Levi Strauss**
   Products: jeans, licensing
   Volume: $6 billion (includes
   Dockers and Slates brands)
   Owner: Levi Strauss & Co.,
   San Francisco

6. **NIKE**
   Products: activewear, athletic
   footwear, accessories, sport-
   ing goods
   Volume: $8.7 billion
   Owner: NIKE Inc.,
   Beaverton, OR

7. **Liz Claiborne**
   Products: sportswear, dresses,
   licenses
   Volume: $2.5 billion
   Owner: Liz Claiborne Inc.,
   New York

8. **Lee**
   Product: jeans
   Volume: $900 million
   Owner: VF Corp.,
   Greensboro, NC

9. **No nonsense**
   Product: legwear
   Volume: $240 million
   Owner: Golden Lady SpA,
   Castiglione della Stiviere, Italy

10. **London Fog**
    Products: outerwear, rain-
    wear
    Volume: $300 million
    Owner: London Fog Indus-
    tries, New York

11. **Seiko**
    Product: watches
    Volume: $400 million (U.S.
    estimate)
    Owner: Seiko Corp., Tokyo

12. **Playtex**
    Products: bras, shapewear
    Volume: $800 million
    Owner: Sara Lee Corp.,
    Chicago

13. **Victoria's Secret**
    Products: bras, panties, day-
    wear, hosiery, sleepwear,
    robes, swimwear, casual-
    wear; beauty, bath, and body
    products
    Volume: $3.9 billion
    Owner: Intimate Brands Inc.,
    Columbus, OH

14. **Reebok**
    Products: activewear, athletic
    footwear, accessories
    Volume: $3.4 billion
    Owner: Reebok International
    Ltd., Stoughton, MA

(continued)

TABLE 4.2 (continued)

The 25 Most Recognizable Brands in Women's Apparel and Accessories

15. Gap
Products: retailer of jeans and sportswear
Volume: Approximately $4.5 billion, Gap stores only
Owner: Gap Inc., San Francisco

16. Fruit of the Loom
Products: underwear, daywear, activewear
Volume: $2.17 billion (corporate), $120–$125 million (women's FTL innerwear)
Owner: Fruit of the Loom Inc., Chicago

17. Wrangler
Products: jeans, licensing
Volume: $1.5 billion
Owner: VF Corp., Greensboro, NC

18. Disney
Products: sportswear, footwear, activewear, sleepwear, accessories, retail
Volume: $3.03 billion in consumer products
Owner: The Walt Disney Co., Burbank, CA

19. Calvin Klein
Products: designer apparel, jeans, fragrance, licensing, retail
Volume: $2.55 billion
Owner: Calvin Klein Inc., New York

20. Ralph Lauren
Products: sportswear, licensing
Volume: $3.55 billion worldwide
Owner: Polo Ralph Lauren Corp., New York

21. Adidas
Products: active wear, athletic footwear, accessories, sporting goods
Volume: $6 billion
Owner: Adidas AG-Solomon, Herzogonaurach, Germany

22. Bali
Products: bras, shape wear, daywear, panties
Volume: $550 million
Owner: Sara Lee Corp., Chicago

23. Nine West
Products: footwear, accessories
Volume: $950 million at retail for Nine West brand alone, includes licensing royalties
Owner: Jones Apparel Group, New York

24. Tommy Hilfiger
Products: sportswear, accessories, swimwear, fragrance
Volume: $1.7 billion, overall; women's $405.7 million
Owner: Tommy Hilfiger Inc., New York

25. Jantzen
Products: swimwear, sportswear
Volume: $130 million (swimwear, $100 million; sportswear, $30 million)
Owner: VF Corp., Greensboro, NC

Source: Nardoza, Edward. (2000, January 24). The Fairchild 100. **Women's Wear Daily: WWD Special Report.** New York: Fairchild.

TABLE 4.3

North American Industry Classification System

313 Textile Mills	Industries in the Textile Mills subsector include establishments that transfrom a basic fiber (natural or synthetic) into a product, such as yarn or fabric, that is further manufacturerd into usable items, such as apparel, sheets, towels, and textile bags for individual or industrial consumption. There are 19 classifications such as yarn spinning, fabric mills, and textile and fabric finishing mills in this subsector.
314 Textile Product Mills	Industries in the Textile Product Mills subsector include establishments that produce nonapparel textile products. There are 13 classifications such as carpet and rug mills, textile furnishings mills, and canvas and related product mills in this subsetor.
315 Apparel Manufacturing	Industries in the Apparel Manufacturing subsector include establishments that produce apparel textile and apparel sewn products. There are 34 classifications such as apparel knitting mills, hosiery and sock mills, underwear and nightwear knitting mills, cut and sew apparel contractors and cut and sew manufacturing classified by garment type, and gender.
316 Leather and Allied Product Manufacturing	This subsector includes 15 classifications such as leather and hide tanning and finishing as well as footwear, personal leather goods, luggage manufacturing, and other leather goods manufacturing.

Source: U.S. Census Bureau (www.census.gov/epcd/naics/NAICS31B.HTM)

and marketing; operations including production, planning, distribution, and control; advertising and sales promotion; and finance and information technology. Very large companies may have separate departments or divisions with dozens of employees who handle each of these activities. On the other hand, in very small companies a few employees may handle several of these activities.

150   PART 1
**Organization of the U.S. Textile
and Apparel Industries**

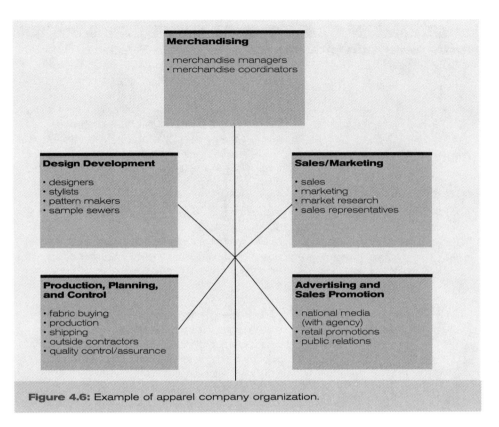

Figure 4.6: Example of apparel company organization.

In reviewing Figure 4.6, it is important to note the connections among all of the areas or divisions. Communication among the various activities is imperative for the success of the company. Merchandisers must communicate with designers; designers must communicate with production management and marketers; those in information technology must understand the computer needs of all areas. This can be a challenge for large companies.

MERCHANDISING

The term **merchandising** generally refers to "a management process of collecting and assimilating information from a variety of sources and drawing conclusions from that information regarding the product offering" (Brown & Brauth, 1989, p. 78). This process includes developing strategies to get the right merchandise, at the right price, at the right time, in the right amount, to the right locations to meet the wants and needs of the target customer. The merchandising area of apparel companies may include merchandise managers, merchandise coordinators, and fashion directors. These individuals research and forecast fashion trends and trends in consumer purchasing behavior in order to develop color, fabric, and garment silhouette directions for the company's merchandise. When making these forecasts, merchandisers interpret these trends for the company's target market, which is determined by their customer's age, sex, income, and lifestyle. The role of merchandisers in apparel companies can vary. In some companies they facilitate the creation of lines; in other companies they oversee the fashion direction of the company. The merchandising function of the apparel company will be discussed in greater detail later in this chapter and in Chapter 5.

DESIGN DEVELOPMENT

The merchandisers work closely with those in the **design development** area, who will interpret the trend forecasts and create designs to be manufactured by the company. Those in the design development area include designers, product developers, stylists, pattern makers, and sample sewers. For companies that own their own factories, the design development area may also include the management and operation of the company-owned factories, including the employment and training of sewing operators. Chapters 5 through 7 focus on the design development activities of an apparel company.

SALES AND MARKETING

The sales and marketing area of the apparel company works to sell the company's merchandise to the retail buyers. Sales and marketing includes regional sales managers and sales representatives, as well as those who conduct marketing research for the company. The sales and marketing staff show the company's merchandise to retail buyers in the company's showrooms during market weeks and at trade shows (see Figure 4.7). Some companies will employ their own sales staff, others will contract with independent sales representatives to handle their merchandise. Chapter 8 discusses the marketing and sales activities of an apparel company.

Figure 4.7: A sales representative sells the apparel manufacturer's merchandise to retail store buyers.

OPERATIONS: PRODUCTION, PLANNING, CONTROL, AND DISTRIBUTION

The preproduction, production, planning, and control area of the apparel company includes those people involved with the material buying, production (Figure 4.8), quality assurance, and shipping of the merchandise. It also includes those who work with domestic and foreign contractors to sew the garments, if the company contracts out these services. Some companies refer to these activities as product engineering. Chapters 9 through 11 focus on production, planning, and control. Chapter 12 focuses on distribution strategies of apparel companies.

ADVERTISING AND SALES PROMOTION

Working with the design development staff and the sales and marketing staff, those in the advertising and sales promotion area focus on creating promotional and advertising strategies and tools to sell the merchandise to the retail buyers and to the ultimate consumer (see Figure 4.9). Often these services are contracted to an outside advertising agency that specializes in these activities.

FINANCE AND INFORMATION TECHNOLOGY

Because all companies are in business to make a profit, effective financial management of companies is imperative to their success. More than simply "churning out numbers," those in the finance area of an apparel company are responsible for the overall finan-

Figure 4.8: The production, planning, and control area includes the management of production facilities.

cial health of companies and work closely with all other areas.

With the increased importance of computer systems in the design and production of products and in the supply chain management of companies, information technology (IT) areas of companies play important roles in overseeing companies' computer operations. Those who work within IT not only must have technical expertise, but also must understand the operation of the apparel industry. Some companies have chosen to outsource their information technology area. For example, NIKE's corporate information systems, including desktop computers, the data center and network infrastructure were outsourced to Lockheed Martin Integrated Business Solutions in order to enhance their focus on product development and customer service.

Merchandising Philosophies of Apparel Companies

According to industry analysts, the overall goal of the merchandising area is to "make a profit by developing an assortment of products that reflects the company's market strategy and that can be delivered and sold on time" (Brauth & Brown, 1989,

Figure 4.9: Advertising and sales promotion departments create promotion and advertising strategies and tools to sell the merchandise to retail buyers and to the ultimate consumer.

p. 110). To meet this goal, apparel merchandisers set the overall direction for the merchandise assortment and work closely with the other areas of the apparel company that carry out the design, production, marketing, and distribution of the goods. Effective merchandising and product development depends on the company's product category (e.g., men's sportswear, women's dresses, children's outerwear), the wholesale price zone, and its marketing strategy. Companies can be classified according to their merchandising philosophy on the following continuum (Brown & Brauth, 1989)—from a truly design-driven company at one end to a real-time merchandiser at the other end (see Figure 4.10).

A truly *design-driven company* depends upon its innovative designs to attract its target market, which is generally composed of fashion innovators (see Figure 4.11). Because their target market represents a very small number of customers, competition among design-driven companies is intense and the odds of a company succeeding are probably less than one in one hundred. Designers for design-driven companies rely on their skill, reputation, and advertising to attract customers. Examples of design-driven companies are Calvin Klein, Donna Karan, and Anna Sui.

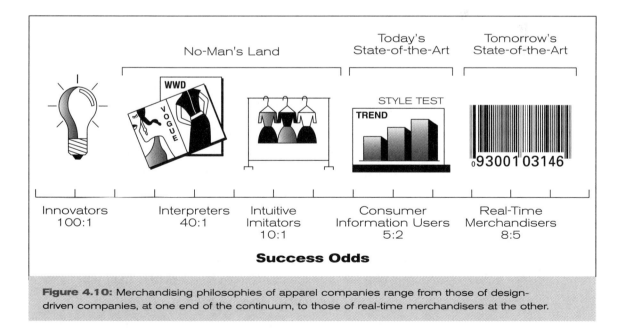

Figure 4.10: Merchandising philosophies of apparel companies range from those of design-driven companies, at one end of the continuum, to those of real-time merchandisers at the other.

Rather than creating their own design innovations, a number of companies interpret successful innovative trends of design-driven companies for their own target market. Although design skills and reputation are often key factors in the success of these interpreters, the risk of creating unsuccessful innovations is reduced.

Next along the continuum are the imitators who develop their product lines based on unsystematic "research," including trade information, observations as to what is selling at market and in the stores, and gut-level feelings about what will sell. The success of *imitators* often depends on their ability to produce affordable knockoffs. Timing is crucial for the imitators, who must react immediately to new trends in the market.

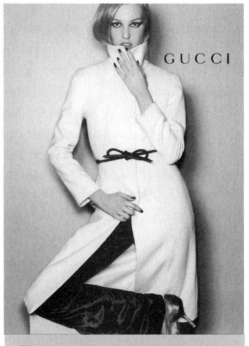

Figure 4.11: A truly design-driven company depends on its innovative designs to attract its target market.

Beyond interpreters and imitators, are companies that base their merchandising decisions on systematic research. *Consumer information users* conduct market research and obtain direct feedback from consumers on the product line through style testing. Although they may interpret and imitate, they often research and conduct their own fashion forecasts and therefore tend to be more accurate in their predictions.

At the far end of the continuum, opposite the design-driven companies, are the *real-time merchandisers*. These companies assess consumer preferences based on style testing and analyses of trends in retail sales. Real-time merchandisers get sales information directly from retailers and can produce and ship goods within weeks. Their focus is on producing only the merchandise wanted by consumers and assuring retailers that they will have the appropriate stock on hand at all times. These companies are highly involved with Quick Response strategies.

Trade Associations and Trade Publications in the Apparel Industry

A number of trade associations in the apparel industry promote their industry segments, conduct market research, sponsor trade shows, and develop and distribute educational materials related to various segments of the apparel industry. The largest of these associations is the American Apparel & Footwear Association (AAFA), which serves as an umbrella trade association for apparel companies. Representatives of member companies and other professionals in the industry are active in many committees. Activities of the AAFA include the compilation of statistical information related to apparel manufacturing, industry forecasts, and trend forecasts; publication of educational materials and information for use by industry analysts and company executives; and is one of the sponsors of the Bobbin Show. Started in 1960, the Bobbin Show is currently the largest annual trade show for the apparel/sewn products industry. Every third year, the show expands to an international scope and is called Bobbin World. Other trade associations focus their efforts on specific divisions of the RTW industry, such as intimate apparel, men's sportswear, or knitwear, to name just a few (see Table 4.4).

TABLE 4.4

Selected Trade Associations in the Apparel Industry

American Apparel & Footwear
Association
1601 N. Kent Street, Suite 1200
Arlington, VA 22209
(800) 520-2262
www.apparelandfootwear.org

Associated Corset & Brassiere Manufacturers Inc.
1430 Broadway, Suite 1603
New York, NY 10018
(212) 354-0707

California Fashion Association
515 South Flower Street, 32nd Floor
Los Angeles, CA 90071
(213) 688-6288
www.californiafashion.org

Canadian Apparel Federation
130 Slater Street, Suite 1050
Ottawa, Ontario K1P 6E2
(613) 231-3220
www.apparel.ca

Children's Apparel Manufacturers'
Association
6900 Decane Blvd.
Montreal, QC 4X32T8
Canada
(514) 731-7774
www.cama-apparel.org

Clothing Manufacturers Association
730 Broadway
New York, NY 10003
(212) 529-0823

(continued)

TABLE 4.4 (continued)

Selected Trade Associations in the Apparel Industry

Council of Fashion Designers of America
1412 Broadway
New York, NY 10018
(212) 302-1821

The Fashion Group International Inc.
597 Fifth Avenue, 8th Floor
New York, NY 10017
(212) 593-1715
www.fgi.org

International Association of Clothing
Designers and Executives
475 Park Avenue South
New York, NY 10016
(212) 685-6602
www.iacde.com

International Swimwear & Activewear
Market and the Swim Association
110 East 9th Street, A-727
Los Angeles, CA 99079
(213) 630-3610
www.apparel.net/isam/

The Intimate Apparel Council
c/o The Bromley Group
150 Fifth Avenue, Suite 510
New York, NY 10011
(212) 807-0978
www.apparel.net/iac/

Men's Apparel Guild in California
(MAGIC International)
6200 Canoga Ave., Suite 303
Woodland Hills, CA 91367
(818) 593-5000
www.magiconline.com

The Hosiery Association
3623 Latrobe Drive, Suite 130
Charlotte, NC 28211
(704) 365-0913
www.nahm.com

National Association of Men's Sportswear Buyers (NAMSB)
60 East 42 Street
New York, NY 10165
(212) 856-9644
www.namsb.com

National Knitwear & Sportswear
Association
386 Park Avenue South
New York, NY 10016
(212) 683-7520
www.asktmag.com

National Retail Federation
325 7th Street, NW, Suite 1100
Washington, DC 20004
(202) 783-7971
www.nrf.com

Neckwear Association of America
151 Lexington Ave., #2F
New York, NY 10016
(212) 683-8454
www.apparel.net/naa/

Underfashion Club Inc.
347 Fifth Avenue, Suite 1406
New York, NY 10016
(212) 481-7792
www.underfashionclub.org

United Infants & Children's Wear
Association
1430 Broadway
New York, NY 10018-3308
(212) 244-2953

A number of trade publications focus on the apparel industry and are of use to professionals in the RTW industry. These publications (see Table 4.5 for a listing of selected trade publications in the apparel industry) range from daily newspapers to monthly magazines (see Figure 4.12).

TABLE 4.5

Selected Trade Publications in the Apparel Industry

Newspapers

California Apparel News (CAN): Published weekly, every Friday. Covers fashion industry news with an emphasis on regional companies and markets on the West Coast. Includes classified advertisements.

DNR: Published weekly by Fairchild Publications. Covers national and international news in men's wear retailing, apparel, fiber and fabric. Includes classified advertisements.

Women's Wear Daily (WWD): Published Monday through Friday by Fairchild Publications. Covers national and international news in the women's and children's fashion industry for retailers and manufac-turers. Covers textiles, accessories and fragrances in addition to apparel. Includes classified advertisements.

Magazines

Bobbin (www.bobbin.com): Published monthly by Miller Freeman Co. Contains technical, managerial, and production information for all segments of apparel/sewn products manufacturing.

Children's Business (CB): Published monthly by Fairchild Publications. Targeted to retailers. Provides news and fashion coverage of appar-el, footwear, toys, entertainment, and juvenile products for infants through preteens.

Earnshaw's Infants, Girls, and Boys Wear Review: Published monthly by Earnshaw Publications. Targeted to retailers of fashion and acces-sories, from newborns to young children.

Stores (www.stores.org): Published monthly by the National Retail Federation. Targeted to retailers. Provides information of general interest as well as reports on electronic commerce, loss prevention, and computer software and hardware.

International Magazines

Collezioni: Published in Italy by Zanfi Editori. Issues with focused con-tents include haute couture, prêt-à-porter, men's wear, children's wear, bridal, shoes, bags and accessories, sport and street, and trends in fabrics and yarns.

Book Moda: Published in Italy by Publifashion. Issues with focused content include haute couture, prêt-à-porter and bridal.

L'Officiel de la Couture et de la Mode de Paris: Published in Paris by Les Editions Jalou. Ten issues per year focus on haute couture and prêt-à-porter.

Collections Haute Couture: Published in Japan by Gap Press. Two issues per year highlight the Paris fall-winter and spring-summer haute couture collections.

Styling News: Published in Germany by mode . . . information Heinz Kramer GmbH. Two issues per year focus on color, fabric and fashion trends.

Figure 4.12: Trade publications provide important information for people employed in the apparel industry.

Summary

Most of the apparel produced and sold today is considered ready-to-wear (RTW); that is, it is completely made and ready to be worn at the time of purchase. RTW apparel is possible because of standardized sizing and mass production techniques used in the apparel industry. Apparel companies typically produce four to six lines or collections corresponding to the fashion seasons: spring, summer, fall I, fall II, holiday, and resort. It is important to note the distinctions between RTW and couture. In couture, garments are made to the specific body measurements of an individual rather than to standardized sizes found in RTW. In addition, couture garments are generally made with some hand techniques and from more expensive materials than RTW. Haute couture collections are shown twice per year (in July and January) to the press, others in the fashion industry, and wealthy clients.

Based on their organization and operations, RTW apparel companies fall into the following categories: conventional manufacturers, jobbers, contractors, and licensors. Apparel companies are also classified according to the type of merchandise they produce, the wholesale price zones of their products or brands, and by the North American Industry Classification System (NAICS) established by the government.

A typical apparel company includes areas or divisions that focus on the following activities: merchandising; design development; sales and marketing; production, planning, control, and distribution; advertising and sales promotion; and finance and information technology. Apparel merchandisers set the overall direction for the merchandise assortment and work closely with the other divisions of the company that carry out the design, production, marketing, and distribution of the goods. Companies vary in their merchandising philosophies from those of design-driven companies to those of real-time merchandisers.

A number of trade associations in the apparel industry promote, conduct market research, sponsor trade shows, and develop and distribute education materials related to various segments of the apparel industry. Examples include the American Apparel & Footwear Association (AAFA), Men's Apparel Guild in California (MAGIC International), and the Underfashion Club. A number of trade publications focus on the apparel industry and are of use by professionals in the RTW industry. Examples include *Women's Wear Daily*, *DNR*, and *Bobbin Magazine*.

Careers within apparel companies include positions in merchandising; product/fashion development; sales and marketing; preproduction; production, control, and quality assurance; and advertising and promotion.

Women's Merchandise Manager
BETTER MEN'S AND WOMEN'S APPAREL COMPANY

Position Description
Manage and control the development of merchandise from color, fabric and style selection to presentation and sales marketing. Work with the development team, which consists of a designer, pattern maker, sample sewer and product engineer. The Merchandise Manager is ultimately responsible for the line.

Typical Tasks and Responsibilities
- Analyze wholesale and retail performance of the product
- Read trade and fashion publications to keep current on market direction
- Communicate with retail accounts to gain sales information
- Estimate units per style/color for the designated season. Design development team produces patterns; merchandising decides in which fabrics each style will be available
- Write and deliver presentations to sales representatives, attend sales meetings held throughout the year
- Travel domestically to meet with sales reps and retail accounts three to four times per year
- Travel to New York twice a year for major development trips
- Work with Fabric Design Department to develop fabrics and patterns for future seasons
- Work with contractors to develop garments not produced by the company's factories
- Work with quality control on production problems
- Work with design to develop a style plan, design follows up with prototype development. Merchandise Manager attends fitting sessions, signs off on all pieces to be included in the line

Key Terms

atelier de couture

brand tiers

classification

collection

contractor

conventional manufacturer

couture

couturier(ière)

design development

diffusion line

fashion season

haute couture

item house

jobber

licensor

line

merchandising

national/designer brand

North American Industry
  Classification System (NAICS)

ready-to-wear (RTW)

retail store/direct market brand

salon de couture

wholesale price zone

Discussion Questions

1. Name your three favorite apparel brands. What companies manufacture these brands? How would you classify these brands in terms of product category, wholesale price zone, and type of brand name?

2. Examine copies of trade publications in the apparel industry. To whom does each of the trade publications cater (i.e., what are the publications' target markets)? What types of information are included in the trade publications? How might this information be used by professionals in the industry?

References

Brown, Peter, and Brauth, Bonnie. (1989, August). Merchandising methods. *Apparel Industry Magazine*, pp. 78–82.

Brauth, Bonnie, and Brown, Peter. (1989, June). Merchandising malpractice. *Apparel Industry Magazine*, pp. 108–110.

Kurt Salmon Associates. (1989, January). The changing lineup. *Bobbin*, pp. 56–57.

Lewis, Robin. (1995, November). What's in a Name? *DNR Infotracs: Supplement to DNR*. New York: Fairchild Publications.

Southern California Edison Company. (1995, February). *Southern California's Apparel Industry: Building a Path to Prosperity*. Rosemead, CA: Author.

Creating and Marketing an Apparel Line

PART 2

Step 1: Research

Market Research:	Fashion Research:
Consumer Research	Fashion Trend Research
Product Research	Color Research
Market Analysis	Fabric and Trim Research
Target Customer	
Profile	

Step 2: Design

Design Inspiration
↓
Plan the Line
↓
Sketch Design and Select
Fabrics and Trims
↓
Design Team Reviews Line
↓
Write Garment Specification Sheet

Step 3: Design Development and Style Selection

Make First Pattern
↓
Cut and Sew Prototype
↓
Approve Prototype Fit,
Revise Style or Drop Style
↓
Estimate Initial Cost
↓
Present and Review the Line
↓
Select Styles for Final Line (Final Adoption)
↓
Determine the Final Cost
↓
Order Fabric for Sales Samples
↓
Order Sales Samples

Step 4: Marketing an Apparel Line

Sales Representatives Show Line at Market
and Through Other Promotion Strategies
↓
Retail Buyers Place Orders

Step 5: Preproduction

Order Production Fabrics, Trims, and Sundries
↓
Finalize Production Pattern and
Written Documents
↓
Grade Production Pattern into Size Range
↓
Make Production Marker
↓
Inspect Fabric
↓
Production Spreading, Cutting, Bundling
and Dye Lot Control

Step 6: Sourcing

Select Production Facility

Step 7: Apparel Production Process and
 Quality Assurance

Sew Production Order (May Include Approval
of First Size Run by Contractor)
↓
Finish, Inspect, Press, Tag, and Bag Order

Step 8: Distribution and Retailing

Send Order to Manufacturer's
Distribution Center or Retailer's DC
or Directly to Retailer
↓
Quality Assurance Check
↓
Pick Orders and Send to Retail Store
Distribution Center
↓
Review Season's Sales Figures

CHAPTER 5

Creating a Line: Research

Pendleton Originals/Oregon Country · Fall 1999
(May 25-June 30) (June 25-July 31) (July 25-Aug 31) (Aug 25-Sept 30)

IN THIS CHAPTER YOU WILL LEARN:

- the concept of an apparel line.

- the various types of market research used to understand target customers' characteristics and preferences.

- the scope of the job responsibilities of the apparel designer and merchandiser in conducting and interpreting market research.

- resources for fashion trend, color trend, and fabric trend forecasting.

Creating an Apparel Line

The creation of a group of apparel items into a collection or a line involves a series of steps. Each step is closely related to and influenced by all the other steps in the process. The next several chapters will discuss these steps sequentially. The flowchart at the beginning of this chapter will help acquaint you with the "big picture" before each stage in the design process is explored in greater detail. The first step, research, is discussed in this chapter. The flowchart in Figure 5.1 shows the research step in detail. It is important to keep in mind that the flowchart is a generic one. Some apparel companies deviate from this sequence for a variety of reasons. The industry is constantly changing in areas such as computer integration, speed of production, geographic location for production, regulations on goods manufactured outside the United States, number of new lines introduced each year, and distribution channels. These changes affect the sequence of events. A company may also follow one sequence for some lines and use a modified sequence for other lines. In addition, several activities may occur simultaneously during the progress of a line's development.

The terms *line, group,* and *collection* are used to designate a combination of apparel items presented together to the buying public for a particular season. The term *collection* is used generally to refer to the apparel presented through runway shows each fall and spring by the high-fashion designers in Paris, Milan, New York, London, and other locations. The runway shows of designer collections often include a wide range of apparel, including swimwear, dresses, suits, sportswear, evening wear,

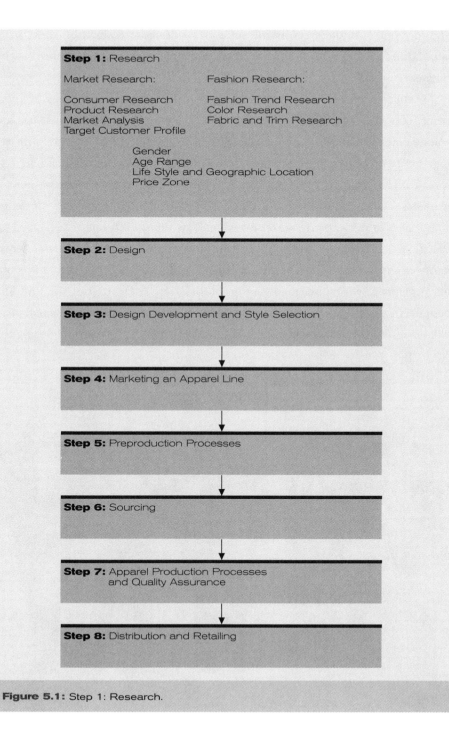

Figure 5.1: Step 1: Research.

and, of course, bridal wear as the finale. The designer collections may include approximately 100 to 150 apparel items. Collections are typically inspired by a theme.

An apparel *line* consists of one large group or several small groups of apparel items, or *styles*, developed around a theme that may be based on such factors as color, fabric, design details, or a purpose (such as golf or tennis) that links the items together (see Figure 5.2). For example, NIKE develops a line for each of a variety of sports, including men's cycling, men's running, men's tennis, women's aerobics, women's tennis, and women's running. A line is composed of a variety of items or styles, such as shirts, pants, jackets, vests, and sweaters. Each line is developed for a specific target customer and could consist of as many as 50 or 60 apparel items. A designer, often with a team of several others, such as a design assistant and a product developer, will be assigned responsibilities for the creation of the line; some designers will have responsibility for several lines. Sometimes, several small groups will be developed within a line, each with its own theme. A **group** might use three

Pendleton Originals/Oregon Country · Fall 1999
(May 25-June 30) (June 25-July 31) (July 25-Aug 31) (Aug 25-Sept 30)

Figure 5.2: A group of products is developed around a theme.

to five fabrics in varying combinations and include approximately a dozen apparel items, all carefully coordinated.

Just as fashion, in general, follows an evolutionary pattern, apparel designers who work for companies generally create new seasonal lines in an ongoing, evolutionary manner. New lines tend to develop from previous lines, with some repetition or modification of successful styles. Styles repeated from one seasonal line to the next are called **carryovers**. The target customer, general market trends, fashion trends, color trends, fabric trends, and retailer's needs are all taken into careful consideration in the planning and development of an apparel line.

The stereotypical image of a fashion **designer** is that he or she sits at a drawing table, sketching garment idea after garment idea. The sketches are handed to a staff who turn them into garments. Is this what really happens in the apparel industry? In actuality, the creation of an apparel line is a carefully orchestrated series of processes—a team effort, involving many people. The designer's job includes a variety of responsibilities, such as researching the market; selecting the colors, fabrics, and garment styling for the line based on fashion direction from merchandisers; consulting with product engineers on costing factors; preparing the preliminary specification sheets; presenting technical drawings; providing suggestions for linings, interfacings, trims, buttons, and other components; and releasing the approved styles for pattern making.

A designer typically works with a **merchandiser** to plan the overall look of an apparel line, the color story, the fabrics, the price, and the number of styles for each line (see Chapter 6). The merchandiser's role is to see that all the company's needs for the line are met. This might include coordinating several lines presented by the company. The merchandiser conducts market research, develops and maintains the line estimate and price targets to meet budget objectives, reviews the designer's proposed line, and approves the line. Years of experience in design or retailing provide the perspective needed for the apparel company's merchandiser.

The creation stage of one line overlaps with the production stage of the previous line and the selling stage of the line presented prior to that one (see Color Plate 3). Thus, at any given time, designers and merchandisers are handling at least three lines, each in a different stage of the product cycle. Developing a line would be much easier if one had the final sales statistics from the previous line before beginning to work on the creation stage of the new line. Unfortunately, this is not possible in the fast-paced world of fashion. Ever increasing numbers of shopping malls, factory outlet malls, direct mail, and electronic shopping have provided increased opportunities for purchasing apparel and accessories. To help meet consumers' wishes, the timeline in today's apparel industry calls for creating more lines, more quickly than even five years ago. Some companies create new apparel groups to be shipped to retail stores at frequent intervals so that fresh merchandise awaits shoppers on a continuing basis.

Market Research: Understanding Consumer Market Trends

The most important concept for success in the apparel industry is that the company should know its customer and provide the merchandise assortment desired by that customer when the customer wants it, and where he or she will purchase it. In other words, consumer demand is the driving force in the apparel industry. The industry expression, "You can make it only if it sells," relates to the concept of the consumer-driven market. Thus, the success of any apparel or textile company depends on determining the needs and wants of the consumer. To determine what the customer will need and want and when and where the customer will want it, a variety of types of research must be conducted. This process is called **market research**.

Market research can be defined as "the systematic and objective approach to the development and provision of information for the marketing management decision-making process" (Kinnear & Taylor, 1983, p. 16). Market research is divided into two general categories: (1) basic research that deals with extending knowledge about the marketing system, and (2) applied research that helps managers make better decisions (Kinnear & Taylor, p. 17). Company executives, merchandisers, and designers conduct applied market research as a part of the planning process.

Applied market research includes the following three types of research:

- **Consumer research**, which provides information about consumer characteristics and consumer behavior.
- **Product research**, which provides information about preferred product design and characteristics.
- **Market analysis,** which provides information about general market trends.

All three types of market research will be discussed in this chapter.

Each form of applied market research provides valuable information to company executives, merchandisers, and designers about the wants and needs of their target market customers. Some forms of market research take considerable time to conduct, analyze, and interpret. Because of the fast-paced nature of the fashion business, fashion products require a short research-and-development stage. Timing is crucial to the fashion item's successful sale in the marketplace. Therefore, companies generally conduct market research on an ongoing basis.

Trade associations, such as the American Apparel & Footwear Association and Cotton Incorporated also conduct market research, providing information that can be very beneficial to apparel manufacturers and retailers. (Selected trade associations are discussed in Chapters 3 and 4.) Examples of other sources of information to assist with conducting research will be discussed in this chapter.

CONSUMER RESEARCH

Consumer research provides information about consumer characteristics and consumer behavior. Some forms of consumer research study broad trends in the marketplace. Research on **demographics** focuses on understanding characteristics of consumer groups such as age, sex, marital status, income, occupation, ethnicity, and geographic location. Consumer research may also focus on **psychographics**. Psychographic characteristics of consumer groups include buying habits, attitudes, values, motives, preferences, personality, and leisure activities. Demographic information helps describe who the customer is, while psychographic information helps explain why the customer makes the choices he or she makes. Some of these demographic and psychographic characteristics will be discussed further in the market analysis section of this chapter.

Consumer research is conducted and interpreted in a variety of ways. To understand broad consumer trends, companies may review various sources of information available in print form and online. Examples are *American Demographics* (available on-line at www.demographics.com), and Spectra, a Chicago-based company that provides demographic analysis. Marketing research companies also conduct general consumer research. For example, Teenage Research Unlimited, a marketing research company that tracks teenage trends, found that, in 1998, the "coolest" brands among teenagers were NIKE, Adidas, and Tommy Hilfiger (Stoughton, 1999).

Companies may also conduct and interpret their own consumer research. This often happens when a company is considering expanding into a new target market. For example, Mackey McDonald, chairman, president and CEO of VF Corporation "noticed that the Lee Brand did not have a strong franchise among 12- to 14-year-old boys. After extensive consumer research, Lee introduced its Lee Pipes and Lee BMX brands, with styles inspired by board sports and mountain biking" ("Execution is the key to selling," 1999, p. 4). In 1999, that new segment of the business was worth several hundred million dollars.

Similarly, Jerell, a moderately priced women's wear manufacturer based in Dallas, Texas, conducted consumer research when it ventured into a new demographic market, the Hispanic customer. "Marketing to different demographic groups is another path along Jerell's road of diversification. Interested in exploring the possibility, Jerell set to work conducting focus groups and identifying the needs of the Hispanic consumer" (Rabon, 1998, p. 44). Focus groups are composed of potential customers of the new market. A small group of these potential consumers is interviewed to learn more about their needs, wants, and whether they anticipate a market for a new product.

Consumer research is also conducted by companies expanding their markets beyond U.S. consumers to better understand the preferences of these new consumer groups. For example, some women's activewear companies in the United States are expanding into the European market. To market a U. S. company's activewear apparel in France, it is important to research the French activewear consumer if the product is to succeed in this marketplace. It is essential to learn, among other things, that the styles of activewear preferred by French women are not the same as those currently most popular in the United States. *Women's Wear Daily* reported as follows on the French market for activewear: "Unlike American women, who have increased their participation in sports instead of doing formal aerobics, French women continue to take fitness classes. France is a country where women dress up, even when they are dressed down. Unlike the U.S., where sneakers are common weekend wear, in France women will not wear activewear when not exercising" (Weisman, 1996, p. 11).

Often color preferences in foreign markets are different from the trends seen in the United States. These preferences might be related to the country's climate, personal skin tones of the residents, or cultural heritage. When expanding into a new foreign market, consumer research dealing with color preferences of the intended new market would be important for the success of the line.

Conducting consumer research related to fashion items can be a challenge. Apparel purchase decisions are based on a number of factors (including psychological, social, and financial considerations) of which consumers are often not consciously aware. Therefore, results of market research indicate that consumers often do not actually purchase what they indicate they would purchase when queried in advance.

PRODUCT RESEARCH

Product research provides information about preferred product design and product characteristics. When new products are developed, or existing products are modified, it is advantageous to assess how well a new or revised product will fare in the marketplace. To try to find out, one could survey potential consumers orally, send a questionnaire, or offer a free trial of a product in exchange for feedback. Sometimes an apparel company will conduct substantial market research before introducing a new line, especially if the company is interested in developing a new product type. For example, Sears conducted focus group research before it ventured into a new suit market. Some large apparel manufacturers, such as JCPenney (for their private label merchandise) and VF Corporation, have been testing style preferences for years.

Is it possible to predict how apparel consumers will react to a style? Style testing techniques, refined by some of the most respected names in apparel manufacturing, show that one can predict what consumers will want to buy. Some companies use outlet stores to gather data on how consumers react to various styles and prices. JCPenney surveys mall shoppers and uses in-house video testing to guide the decisions of its buyers as well as its manufacturing operations. Focus groups guide VF Corporation's style decisions (Henricks, 1991).

Some companies survey a target group to determine potential improvements in their products. "Quiksilver CEO Robert McKnight said his firm keeps close tabs on some 300 avid surfers, snowboarders and skateboarders to tweak designs that will be more appealing to their consumers. For example, by talking to surfers in Hawaii, McKnight developed board shorts with a special pocket for a bottle of sunscreen" ("Execution is the key to selling," 1999, p. 4).

VF Corporation's Lee brand has established Lee's Trend Leaders Panel, a group "comprised of thirty-five young men and women who are peer-group fashion leaders who share their views with the product development staff" (Hill, 1998, p. AS-6). The Internet is another source for consumer product input. Lee's Web site receives product input from about 1,000 kids per day.

Listening to comments from sales representatives, retailers, and customers about the success of a line provides another part of the feedback necessary for continued success. Designer John Galliano stated that "he plans to communicate regularly with Bergdorf [Goodman] sales staff to find out what's happening on the floor, including reactions to the cut, fit and finishing of the clothes, right down to the durability of a button. That kind of information is a gold mine for the designer, he explained" (Socha, 1997, p. 12).

MARKET ANALYSIS

Market analysis provides information about general market trends. Planning ahead to meet the future needs of the consumer is a critical part of continued success in the apparel industry. In the apparel industry, market analysis can be subdivided into long-range forecasting (or research) and short-range forecasting. **Long-range forecasting** projects market trends one to five years in advance while **short-range forecasting** focuses on market trends one year or less in advance. Both long-range forecasting and short-range forecasting strategies are used for market analysis. Long-range forecasting includes researching economic trends related to consumer spending patterns and the business climate that affects the apparel industry. For example, will interest rates be increasing on money borrowed by an apparel manufacturer to purchase fabric? Will corporate taxes for the apparel company be increasing? Will cost-of-living expenses rise because of inflation, resulting in fewer apparel purchases by consumers? Will rising labor costs result in noticeable increases in the purchase price for apparel? All of these trends can influence the company's plans and the consumer's future purchases.

Long-range forecasting also includes sociological, psychological, political, and global trends. For example, changes in international trade policies will affect long-range forecasting. Political fluctuations among countries can affect sourcing options when planning offshore production. Currency devaluations, economic decline, and financial turmoil around the world have an impact on the U.S. apparel industry.

Other long-range forecasting deals with ongoing changes in the apparel industry. Publications directed specifically toward market analysis in the apparel industry include *The Apparel Strategist* (www.apparelstrategist.com). Kurt Salmon Associates (KSA) is an example of a business that specializes in conducting and publishing soft goods market analysis such as *Consumer Outlook*. Cotton Incorporated, a textile trade organization discussed in Chapter 3, publishes *Lifestyle Monitor*. The publication's focus is to "monitor America's attitudes and behavior toward apparel and home furnishings." Eight barometers cover topics from natural fiber preference to external influences.

The apparel marketplace is in a constant state of flux. Changes in a company's target market, market shifts, or new markets all need to be considered. Recent trends in the market have included increased interest in the Big & Tall business in men's sportswear. As a result of market analysis, Polo Ralph Lauren, Tommy Hilfiger, and Nautica expanded their apparel lines and entered the Big & Tall market in 1999 (see Figure 5.3). Another target market receiving increased interest is the teen market. Market analysis indicated that demographic changes will affect the youth market: "The U.S. population of teen boys, aged 13–19, is projected to grow from 14.2 million in 2000 to 15.4 million by 2010, or an 8.3 percent increase over the decade. The Hispanic and Asian markets will experience the most increases of any ethnic markets" (Schneiderman, 1999, p. 42). Another market currently of interest to the apparel industry is the aging boomers market. Market research on apparel spending patterns suggests consumers over age 55 will spend less

Figure 5.3: Market analysis provides the data needed for apparel companies to expand their markets by offering new size ranges, such as Big & Tall sizes.

on apparel than this group spent before reaching 55. As the fashion conscious baby boomers reach age 55, their apparel spending patterns may well change. "The aging of America is slowly sneaking up on the apparel industry, and the purse strings are beginning to tighten as the boomers age" (Behling, 1999, p. 53). Table 5.1 provides expenditures on apparel and apparel services by age group between 1988 and 2000 (estimated).

Environmental concerns and quality-of-life factors are other examples of long-range trends that affect apparel companies. Some companies have made the commitment to use fabrics made from recycled products, such as aluminum cans or plastic bottles. For example, Patagonia uses a postconsumer recycled (PCR) material, Synchilla, that incorporates Wellman's EcoSpun fiber (see Figure 5.4). This fabric is often made from recycled soda bottles. The use of PCR material in its product line reflects Patagonia's decision to offer products consistent with its company's and customers' values. Patagonia's environmental assessment coordinator, Eric Wilmanns stated, "From a lifecycle analysis approach, we look not only at the materials and energy we use, but also what goes into sustaining our products, how they are used and what eventually happens to them when consumers are finished using them" (Welling, 1999, p. AS26). Consistent with Patagonia's environmental philosophy, in 1996, the company switched to using 100 percent organic cotton in their apparel products. Earth friendly choices often cost more to the company, and sometimes a part of this cost must be absorbed by the customer. Each company makes a philosophical choice about whether these decisions will, in fact, gain customers who respect the company philosophy and are willing to pay more for a product if needed, or whether price is so important that customers might be lost if the product's price is increased. Patagonia's company philosophy regarding environmental concerns

TABLE 5.1

Total U.S. Expenditures on Apparel and Apparel Services by Age Group (in millions of dollars)

Age	25–34	35–44	45–54	55–64	65–74	75–
1988	$33,072	$40,124	$28,727	$17,001	$11,056	$3,735
1995	$29,976	$48,195	$38,092	$16,577	$11,727	$4,452
2000	$27,083	$51,063	$45,628	$18,840	$11,249	$5,016

Source: Behling, Dorothy U. (1999, January). Aging boomers may shift the apparel empire. **Bobbin**, p. 53.

Figure 5.4: Patagonia's Synchilla vest is made from fiber that contains recycled plastic bottles.

extends to all aspects of its business. "Currently, polyurethane-free fabric coatings, recycling alternatives from scraps left over from cutting and sewing, green packaging methods and reducing the content of metals in dyestuffs are all issues topping Wilmanns' environmental apparel hit list" (Welling, 1999, p. AS28).

Jantzen Inc., a major swimwear manufacturer, developed the "Clean Water" campaign. It focused on showing the company's commitment to social responsibility by sponsoring beach cleanups and joining forces with environmental groups to effect change. Jantzen linked forces with retailers to bring the message to customers through a donation-with-purchase program. Another type of environmental concern focuses on waste products resulting from the manufacture of textiles and apparel. Wrangler advertised its EarthWash process as an alternative to dyes and finishing processes that pollute the water supply. Advertising campaigns are structured to let the retailer and consumer know about the company's activist stance on environmental issues.

What about forecasting long-range fashion trends? Is it possible to forecast fashion trends several years in advance of a season? Long-range forecasting can reap benefits. For example, *The Popcorn Report* (Popcorn, 1991) predicted a trend toward "cocooning," in which people would want to stay home more in the evenings, enjoying leisure time spent in quiet rather than in restaurants, movies, or sports events surrounded by others. Evenings spent at home could signal increased consumer interest in loungewear. Thus the loungewear industry was wise to prepare for this trend.

The trend toward more casual office attire, which began with casual Fridays and now often lasts all week, has implications for the long-range planning of some apparel companies. The casual dress trend has spread to apparel markets beyond the United States. "In London's financial district, professional bankers can be spotted in turtlenecks and blazers, a move triggered in part by the expansion of U.S. branches of investment banks overseas, which have exported their casual dress policies" (Casual Fridays, 1995, p. 8).

Short-range forecasting is critical to an apparel company's success. Planning meetings are held with designers, merchandisers, planners, and sales personnel to discuss the company's short-range forecasts and strategic planning. This planning includes such components as determining the desired percentage of increased sales growth for a company. For example, perhaps the company managers have determined that a 5 percent growth in sales should be planned. The designer for each apparel line that the company produces may be asked to increase the line with a 5 percent sales growth factor in mind. Using sales figures from the current selling season, the designer (and merchandiser) may select one or several styles that are selling particularly well, and add one or several similar styles to the upcoming line.

Short-range forecasting also includes the careful study of what the competition is doing. If a competitor seem to be expanding one of its lines, for example, the water sports category of apparel, then perhaps it would be wise to study whether this growth area would be feasible for your company. Short-range forecasting also includes predicting changes in retailing. A retailer may be in the process of expansion, with a number of new stores ready to open in the forthcoming year. If this retailer has been a strong client of an apparel manufacturer in the past, the expansion can signal increased orders for the apparel company. As retailers file for bankruptcy, merge, and divide, it is important for the apparel company to be wary of shipping goods to retailers who may be in the process of disruption.

TARGET CUSTOMER PROFILE

Each apparel company's goal is to position its apparel lines to be different from the competition and to be enticing to potential customers. The merchandising and design staff's objective is to develop the right product for the company's **target customer**. This is called its **brand position**. Eddie Bauer describes its brand position as follows: "Inspired by the Northwest since 1920, Eddie Bauer is the authority for your active casual lifestyle offering physical and emotional comfort with unsurpassed quality" (Lewis, 1999). Within the company's position in the marketplace, each apparel line produced by the apparel company requires a clearly defined target customer.

The profile, or description, of the target customer usually includes demographic and psychographic characteristics such as the gender, age range, lifestyle, and geographic location and the price zone (see Figure 5.5) determined for the majority of customers. A swimwear company may produce several lines, each based on a specific target customer profile. One line may be designed for very conservative missy customers, while other lines may range from appealing to less-conservative customers to appealing to updated missy customers and to fashion forward junior customers. Developing a well-defined target customer profile helps the designers and merchandisers focus the line to the specific audience, or market niche. For example, Eddie Bauer outlines its target customer for its classic Eddie Bauer line as follows:

- 42–46 years old.
- College educated.

Figure 5.5: The target customer for Donna Karan's DKNY lines (left) is similar to the target customer for the more expensive Donna Karan designer lines for men (center) and women (right). The main difference between the two markets is the price zone.

- Average income $70,000.
- Young families and empty nesters, currently working.
- Quality and value are a priority.
- Prefer an active, casual lifestyle.

Some companies develop a very detailed target customer profile. A photograph of the "typical" customer might be included with the target customer profile statement to help merchandisers, designers, product developers, and sales representatives visualize the customer. The models used for product advertisements are also selected to portray the image of the target customer. The design team relies on the target customer profile to identify market trends, to develop the initial direction for the line, and to develop style sketches (concept sketches) and color concepts.

VF Corporation uses a variety of strategies to develop the products that consumers want and need. According to VF Corporation's president and CEO, a company must recognize that it will constantly be changing its business to respond to the continuous changes going on with consumers.

VF's new Consumer Response System (CRS) creates an active, continuous link between consumer research and new product development. "We focus on specific target consumer segments, defined by differences in key attitudes, lifestyles and needs. The discovery part is learning everything we can about each brand's specific target consumer—who she is, how she thinks, how her life is changing and what she really needs." (Hill, 1998, p. AS-5)

Gender

Whereas some companies produce lines of unisex clothing (for example a T-shirt company), most lines are focused on men's, women's, or children's apparel. Many companies produce both men's and women's apparel, but will have separate lines specifically designed for each gender.

Age Range

Companies tend to focus on a specific age range as defined in their target customer profile statement for each of their lines. For a line of junior apparel, a company might profile its customers as ages 15 to 25. This does not mean that a woman over the age of 25 would not wear the apparel in this line. Rather, the design team visualizes the majority of customers as falling within the age range of 15 to 25 and keeps this age range firmly in mind while creating the line. A company may decide to adjust the targeted age of its customer. Raising the age range of the target customer might be a logical adjustment as the average age of the population increases. Or, perhaps the company wants to retain an established customer by broadening the age range at the older end to continue to include the established customer in its target market. After acquiring a loyal customer who likes a company's brand, it could be very cost effective to adjust the styling slightly over time to continue to appeal to this customer as he or she ages.

Lifestyle and Geographic Location

A study of the target customer's lifestyle might include information such as type of career, stage in career, geographic location and its population size, social or political direction, education, attitudes, values, interest in fashion (for example, prefers classic looks or is a fashion trendsetter), and price consciousness. Lifestyle preference descriptions could suggest that the target customer is focused on entertainment or is comfortable with technology. Lifestyle research is conducted to help define the various target groups.

The term *lifestyle merchandising* was coined to recognize the importance of appealing to the target customer's lifestyle choices. The proliferation of popular lifestyle magazines, direct mail catalogs, and Web sites indicates the importance in appealing to customers' lifestyles. For example, the fitness market has a myriad of lifestyle magazines. Some apparel companies design clothing to appeal to a specific lifestyle preference. Some direct mail catalogs offer apparel as well as home accessories ranging from candles to furniture as a lifestyle approach to merchandising products.

Some companies may focus a line on a specific geographic location. For example, the resort market in Florida might be a location for a targeted customer. There is a special fashion "look" to resort apparel in Florida that may not sell well in other geographic locations.

Price zone

The target customer profile also typically includes a targeted price zone, such as moderate, better, or bridge price, as discussed in Chapter 4. Each line will be planned to fall within the specified price zone, based on the target customer profile. Within the line, not every style of shirt will sell for the same price. There will be a range of prices, based on differences in styling and fabric variations. However, the overall prices for the line will fall within expected ranges for the determined price zone. If a company is known to produce goods in the moderate price zone, a jacket style in its line priced in a better price zone will look overpriced in comparison to the rest of the line. A customer would question why the price is higher than expected and might not purchase the jacket due only to its price.

The design team always keeps the target customer profile in mind in order to create a line that will appeal to the customer. It is important for a company to review and update its target customer profile from time to time. The target customer profile is an important component of an apparel line's marketing campaign, both to the retail "customer" and to the ultimate customer.

Fashion Research

In addition to market research, fashion research is also conducted. Fashion research focuses on trends in silhouettes, design details, colors, fabrics, and trims. Similar to market research, fashion research may be conducted and interpreted by fashion research or forecasting firms or by companies themselves.

FASHION TREND RESEARCH

Fashion trend research tends to be a daily activity for the designer and the merchandiser. **Trend research** activities include reading or scanning appropriate **trade publications**. Each segment of the apparel industry has specific trade newspapers and magazines directed toward fashion trends in that industry segment. Examples include *Earnshaw's Infant, Girls, and Boys Wear Review*, focusing on children's wear industry fashion trends, *Footwear News* for the footwear industry, and *Body Fashions Intimate Apparel* for the intimate apparel industry. These trade publications require subscriptions, so they are not available for individual purchase at specialty magazine stores. Trade newspapers include *Women's Wear Daily, California Apparel News*, and *DNR* (men's wear and textiles). *Women's Wear Daily* covers fabrics, fashion ready-to-wear, sportswear, furs, and financial news daily. In addition, each day of the week is targeted to specific market segments (for example, accessories, innerwear, and legwear are covered on Mondays). A few newspaper and magazine sellers offer these publications over the counter, but for the most part, they are available by subscription only. Several trade publications are available on-line, as on Fairchild Publications Web site, www.fashioncentral.com.

European **fashion magazines**—such as *French Vogue, Italian Vogue, Elegance*, and *Book Moda Alta Moda* (women's wear); *Book Moda Uomo* and *Vogue Homme* (men's wear); and *Vogue Bambini* (children's wear)—are important sources for fashion trends. Subscriptions to many of the specific fashion magazines are provided to the design team by the apparel company. For design students, these fashion magazines are available for purchase at specialty magazine stores in larger cities. Other specialized publications are available by subscription from fashion publication subscription services in New York and Los Angeles. A magazine that features high fashion designs, *Book Moda Alta Moda* (see Chapter 4), is available by subscription for about $145 per year.

Popular fashion magazines read by the target customer are sources for fashion trend information and provide an insight into the preferences of the customer. Designers and merchandisers peruse the appropriate publications, depending on their target market. Examples of popular fashion magazines include *Vogue, Elle, Jane, Harper's Bazaar, W, Glamour, Allure, Cosmopolitan, Self, Vanity Fair, Town & Country, Essence, InStyle, Lucky, Savvy, YM, Seventeen, Jump, Teen, Teen People, Details, Maxim*, and *GQ* (see Figure 5.6). These magazines are readily available to the public at news

Figure 5.6: Popular fashion magazines are a source of fashion trend information.

and magazine stands and bookstores. Some of these magazines such as *Elle, Jane, Seventeen, Teen, Teen People*, and *Cosmopolitan* have joined the electronic highway with editorial Web sites on the Internet. Other magazines such as *Vogue, Harper's Bazaar, Mademoiselle,* and *Glamour* have developed Web sites for marketing purposes (Lockwood, 1999). A convenient and fast way to search for fashion trend information related to a specific target customer is by using online access from one's computer.

Apparel companies and retailers often subscribe to **fashion forecasting services**. Some of these forecasting services cover a broad range of fashion trends, some specialize in color trends, while others provide both fashion trend and color trend analysis. D3 (Doneger Design Direction), a division of The Doneger Group based in New York, provides fashion trend and color forecasts for the apparel and accessories markets. The Doneger Group publishes *The Weir/Wolfe Report*, a monthly newsletter that focuses on fashion trends. Reports such as these help merchandisers and designers analyze upcoming fashion trends. An annual subscription to a fashion trend newsletter might cost about $200. Bureau de Style is a fashion trend, fabric, and color trend forecasting service that conducts fashion and fabric trend seminars in locations such as New York, Seattle, San Francisco, and Los Angeles several times a year. (See Chapter 3 for examples of color forecasting companies.)

Fashion videos of recent runway shows are another source of fashion trend information. Several resources provide runway videos of recent designs shown in Milan, Paris, London, and New York. Fashion information is available online as well. There are many Web sites that show the latest styles as seen on the runways of Milan, Paris, London, and New York. These sources provide examples of current fashions rather than forecasting future trends. However, many of the new styles shown are those that set new trends and provide a sense of fashion direction for many moderate and mass priced manufacturers. Some sources are accessible without a fee, whereas other sources require an online subscription. Often a free introductory preview is available to assess their usefulness before subscribing. A big advantage of these online sources, like online magazines, is their ease of accessibility.

The design team often attends textile and apparel trade shows geared to a specific segment of the market. The trade shows are held in various locations from Las Vegas to Beijing. Attendance at trade shows might be for a variety of purposes. Often the attendee's company is represented at the trade show. Fashion trend and color forecasting seminars geared for a specific product market are conducted at trade shows. Some of these trade shows, such as the Men's Apparel Guild in California (MAGIC) and The Super Show, sponsored by Sporting Goods Manufacturers Association (SGMA) are discussed in Chapter 8.

Computer software programs have been developed to assist with consumer-driven fashion forecasting. One program, Consumer Outlook!, works with point-of-sale (POS) data. The software "interprets the company's POS data and uses it to spot trends that otherwise would be overlooked" (Bonner, 1996, p. 32). Consumer Outlook! does more than give total sales figures—it enables an apparel company to determine specifically who is buying what, and where, taking into account factors such as weather, special events in the area, and store promotions.

Fashion trend research also involves **shopping the market**. Although this sounds like fun, it actually requires considerable concentration and constant vigilance. Merchandisers and designers look for new trends that may influence the direction of an upcoming line. Bodice design details in evening wear may inspire a similar feature in a swimsuit, for example. One aspect of shopping the market involves visiting retail stores that carry the company's line. Talking with retailers about how the line is selling at retail provides helpful information for predicting fashion trends. Watching retail store customers' reactions to the line provides helpful feedback. Studying the competitors' lines in retail stores is also important for predicting trends.

The "fantasy" aspect of trend research involves viewing the high-fashion couture and ready-to-wear collections in Paris, Milan, London, Tokyo and New York. Designers and merchandisers for some apparel companies are given the assignment to view these twice-yearly collections. The high-fashion collections are often filled with avant-garde styles probably not worn by the target customer. However, important fashion trends can be extracted and then modified for a line in the moderate price zone.

Some designers and merchandisers also study customers "on the street," or, if the line is an active sportswear line, they watch potential customers on the ski slopes or at the beach. Fashion is a reflection of the time and the lifestyle of the society from which and for which it is created. Therefore, trend research involves the collection of information from multiple sources on a continuing basis. The design team does not create in a vacuum, but is influenced by everything on a daily basis. It is important to visit art museums, concerts, and movies and to participate in other activities that expose the design team to fashion-related trends.

COLOR RESEARCH AND RESOURCES

When color trends in apparel, accessories, or home fashions are reviewed over time, it becomes clear that certain staple colors appear frequently in the fashion cycle. In apparel, black, navy, white, and beige are considered **staple colors** and are seen almost continuously season after season. One or more staple colors is included in each line. Pendleton Woolen Mills is known for maintaining a group of staple colors in its classic apparel lines. Pendleton's tartan navy and tartan green are examples of colors that are color matched season after season. If a customer had purchased a navy Pendleton jacket from its classic line, a pair of navy slacks purchased two years later will match the color of the jacket (unless it had faded because of improper care or excessive wear). Pendleton tracks the sales, ranked by dollar volume and color, to ensure that long-term, high-selling colors are represented in each line.

Some companies vary the specific staple color to reflect fashion influences. One season, a navy may be a violet-navy while another season the navy may be a black-navy. This lends an up-dated, fashion look to staple colors. If a print fabric in the line contained navy, then it is necessary to match the navy in the print fabric to the solid navy.

Other colors, called **fashion colors**, appear less frequently over time than the staple colors do. These colors often follow cycles, reappearing in a different shade, value, or intensity from one fashion season to the next. For example, an orange-red may evolve into a blue-red, which may evolve into a blue-magenta. It is interesting to follow the trend of a fashion color over a period of years. A color such as aubergine (eggplant) will recur every few years. It may be slightly redder one season, slightly bluer another. For those who have tried to match the color of an item purchased in a previous season or year, it becomes painfully obvious that the life cycle of some fashion colors is very short. Some customers have learned to purchase all color-matched pieces of a line at one time to avoid disappointment later, when they might be unable to match the color of a shirt they would like to purchase to wear with the pants purchased a year earlier.

Some fashion colors sell more readily, and therefore tend to reappear more frequently, than others. In the United States, dark reds and wine tones tend to recur often. Orange is a color that flatters fewer people's personal coloring than some other colors, such as blue. Thus, orange does not occur as frequently in the color cycle as some other colors.

Some colors tend to suit the personal coloring of Europeans or Asians or North Americans. For example, loden, an olive green, is more frequently seen in European apparel lines than in North American lines. Apparel designers and merchandisers keep in mind the ethnic coloring of their target customers as they look at color trends.

The **color-forecasting services** used by textile producers (see Chapter 3) are also used by apparel companies. These services study color trends in textiles, apparel, home fashions, and related fields. Some color-forecasting services predict color trends 18 months or 24 months in advance of when the product is available to consumers, while others, for a higher subscription fee, predict farther ahead. An apparel company subscribes to the color-forecasting service based on the field, such as men's apparel, as well as the length in advance for which forecasts are provided. Most services publish color forecasts twice a year for men's, women's, and children's apparel (see Figure 5.7).

Resources for color-forecasting services based in the United States include the Color Association of the United States (CAUS). It produces seasonal predictions with 36 fabric swatches twice a year. The annual subscription for 2 seasonal forecasts costs about $650. Pantone publishes color trends and forecasts, provides a source for color chips (see Chapter 6 for more information about color), and offers consulting services. International Colour Authority, a European color trend service, is based in Amsterdam. Promostyl is based in Paris, with subsidiary offices in New York, London, and Tokyo.

Many people wonder how color trends are determined. Does "someone" predict that ruby red will be *the* color of the fall season, and that all designers will then include ruby red in their lines? Although this is not the case, color-forecasting services do conduct color research to assist the fashion industry in the assessment of the color trends. Many U.S. forecasters rely on the color directions of fabric producers in Europe. They might watch to see whether these colors are adopted by fashion forward designers and consumer fashion innovators in the United States. Other color-

THE EVOLUTION OF COLORS

LES ROUGES THE REDS

LES VERTS THE GREEN TONES

LES BLEUS THE BLUE TONES

La suite des rouges éclatants, rouge vermillon et le retour de l'orange, rouge carmin et les fuchsias d'hiver.
The continuation of brilliant reds, vermilion red and the return of orange, carmine red and winter fuchsia.

Les verts restent très présents et correspondent à tous les marchés du plus chic au plus sport. Ce sont des basiques
The greens remain very present and correspond to all the markets - from the most chic to the most sport. They are true basics.

Très importants les bleus de cet hiver : d'une part les bleus canard et pétrole, d'autre part, la suite du marine pour l'hiver.
Highly important this winter the blues : on one hand, the duck and petrol blues, and on the other, the continuation of navy for winter.

Confirmation des rouges Couture, des rouges entre-deux, rosés ou orangés et le violet.
The confirmation of Couture reds, in-between reds, pinkish or orange touched reds and purple.

Encore les verts pour des tonalités de kakis toupés pour un marché plus sophistiqué.
The greens remain important, but here with taupe touched khaki shades for a more sophisticated market.

La suite du pétrole avec des bleus grisés et le retour du turquoise en accent tonique.
The follow-up of teal blue with grayish-blues and the return of turquoise for energetic accents.

Les vrais rouges classiques et éclatants, le rouge cramoisi et le violet fuchsia à continuer et à suivre.
Real reds are classical and brilliant wine red and fuchsia purple to continue and follow.

Les verts deviennent turquoises et canard en fusionnant avec les bleus.
Greens take on blue overtones for various shades of turquoise and teal.

Le retour des bleus authentiques, bleu dur et électrique, ciel et marine.
The return of authentic shades : royal blue, electric blue, sky blue and navy blue.

⊙⊙⊙ **07** evolution

Figure 5.7: Color trend reports are issued by color forecasting services.

forecasting services will focus on analyzing trends in consumer color preferences through sales data.

From the wide variety of possible colors, a palette of certain hues, values, and intensities that reflect upcoming color trends will be identified by the color-forecasting service. Many apparel companies subscribe to several color-forecasting services. It is interesting to compare the similarities and differences of several color-fore-casting services' predictions for the same season.

The color palettes presented by the forecasting services are represented by a grouping of paint chips, fabric swatches, or yarn pompoms, arranged attractively in a spiral bound notebook or magazine format. These charts may include up to several dozen colors. The colors selected tend to span a range of darks and lights, neutrals and fashion colors. Thus, one color service will not predict all dark colors while another service shows all light colors. Designers and merchandisers will be able to identify certain overall trends recurring among the various color-forecasting services. After studying the color trends, designers and merchandisers will select a color palette for the upcoming season, taking into consideration the many factors important to the success of that line. A designer may note that varying shades of purple have appeared in many of the color forecasts, indicating a purple trend. Some services provide fashion names for the color chips. The various shades of purple might be named *violet, plum, dahlia, wisteria, African violet*, and *lavender*. The specific name may be transferred to the color name used by the apparel company for that color, or a new name may be created by the apparel company to identify their company's seasonal color. The theme of a line might be linked to the color names used. For example, color names such as *adobe, cactus, sage*, and *sandstone* might be selected to correlate with a southwestern theme for a line.

FABRIC AND TRIM RESEARCH AND RESOURCES

Fashion trend research is focused on general garment silhouettes, lengths (such as jacket lengths, skirt lengths), widths (such as pant leg width, lapel and necktie widths), and design detail trends (such as shawl collars, circular ruffled collars, two-button suit jackets). The designer and merchandiser research the fabric and trim market in addition to studying fashion and color trends. The designer undertakes fabric research, beginning with such broad fabric trends as the trend toward the use of spandex blended with wool for career apparel, or the use of microfibers for men's suits and raincoats. This research might include such trends as the use of metallic fibers in fabrics, or the use of chenille yarns in suitings. Resources for this type of fabric research include the same trade publications that designers and merchandisers use for fashion trends, as well as textile trade publications such as *International Textiles*.

For more specific fabric trends, textile mills, textile trade associations, and textile manufacturers are eager to acquaint designers with the latest fibers, fabrics, and textures. Fabric manufacturers employ sales representatives who supply designers with fabric swatch cards, usually in response to a phone call by the design team member to the textile sales representative. Sample yardage can also be ordered from the sales representative. Many fabric manufacturers have showrooms in New York and other cities that display the latest fabrics. The textile trade associations' headquarters are excellent resources as well. For example, a designer might visit the New York office of Cotton Incorporated to research a wide range of woven and knit cotton fabrications.

A very effective way to research fabric resources is to visit one of the textile trade shows (see Chapter 3 for a discussion of these trade shows). The shows are usually held twice a year, in the fall and the spring. The American fabric manufacturers hold their textile trade shows in New York and Los Angeles. Here, many fabric manufacturers have booths displaying the latest and most enticing fabrics.

Some of the international fabric manufacturers bring their fabric lines to New York and Los Angeles to show to the American designers not able to travel to Europe. Exhibitors at the British Woolen Show, Texitalia (Italian fabrics), International Fashion Fabric Fair, as well as Asian fabric manufacturers, are eager to attract clients who visit the textile trade shows held in New York.

Some designers also travel to the European textile trade shows held twice a year to see the latest goods produced by fabric manufacturers in Europe (see Chapter 3 for detailed information). Première Vision, showcasing Europe's fabric manufacturers, is held in Paris (see Figure 5.8). Italian fabrics are shown at Ideacomo, near Milan. British fabrics are shown at Fabrex. Interstoff, held in Frankfurt, Germany, is known especially for displaying German, Austrian, and Swiss fabrics. Some designers purchase sample cuts from European fabric manufacturers. For many designers, though, these textile shows serve a similar purpose as the couture design shows—as an inspiration and a means to sift through the multitude of ideas for trends appropriate to their company's target customers.

Designers can place orders for **sample cuts**. Each cut is usually a three-to-five-yard length, enough yardage to produce a prototype garment in order to evaluate the possible use of the fabric. The sample cuts are sent to the apparel company after the order is placed at a trade show. Sample cuts also can be ordered directly from the sales representative after the trade show.

Figure 5.8: Designers attend textile trade shows for fabric research and inspiration.

Some apparel designers and product developers work with fabric manufacturers to produce custom fabrics to meet a specific need. For example, after Gore-Tex's success as a woven fabrication, active wear apparel designers longed for a knit version of the waterproof, breathable fabric. The fabric's manufacturer was able to meet this need. W. L. Gore & Associates and NIKE employees work together to create special technical performance fabrics. StormFIT, is an example of "a breathable, lightweight fabric, designed to handle any combination of extreme weather, including rain, snow, sleet, ice or heat ("Nike braves the elements," 1995, p. 10). Fabrics that have been developed by a textile producer for a specific apparel company can be restricted for use solely by that apparel company for a specified period. This adds exclusivity to the product, which in turn can enhance sales. Such a fabric is *proprietary*; that is, it is the property of the private owner (the apparel company).

Some types of apparel, for example, outdoor activewear, are especially suited to the use of specialty trims and fasteners. A new design idea might be sparked by a novelty trim or fastener. Trims as a source of design inspiration will be discussed in Chapter 6. Research regarding new products is an important aspect for these designers and merchandisers. Product trade shows, trade publications, and specialty trim sales representatives are sources of information about new products.

Armed with information from market research, fashion and color trend research, and fabric and trim research, the designer is ready to bring everything together in the creation of a new line.

Summary

Creating an apparel line begins with research. Sales figures from the current selling season are taken into consideration as the designer and merchandiser plan the upcoming line. A fashion apparel company cannot survive long if it only repeats what has sold well in the past. Market research is often conducted to help predict what specific items or general trends will appeal to customers in the upcoming season. The merchandiser's and designer's job responsibilities include long-range forecasting of major social, economic, retail, apparel manufacturing, and customer trends. Short-range forecasting is also tied to the economy, political climate, availability of resources, and customer needs. The target customer profile, describing the age, lifestyle, and price zone, requires constant updating and careful consideration in the creation of an apparel line.

The merchandiser and designer conduct fashion trend research on a daily basis by reading fashion publications, attending fashion events, and developing the ability to sense the fashion mood of the times. They translate this information into styles for the target customer. Color-forecasting services provide information for color trend research, another important component of the creation stage. The apparel company may subscribe to one or more of these services. Fabric trend research is another aspect of the designer's responsibility. This may include scrutinizing fashion and textile industry publications or attending textile trade shows in New York and European or Asian fashion centers. While research is being conducted on the upcoming line, it is important to remember that the designer may also be working on fabric and style development for a subsequent line, is involved with production of the current line, and is watching the sales figures on the line selling currently in retail stores.

CAREER PROFILE

If you are particularly interested in fashion-related research or the analysis of market trends, color, or fashion trends, additional coursework in consumer behavior, market analysis, and statistics, and some related job experience may be helpful.

Fashion Trend Forecaster
PUBLISHER OF TREND FORECASTING REPORT

Position Description
Scan stores in trend setting locales to identify key fashion trends, analyze shopping behavior, advise retail store buyers, and write trend forecasts.

Typical Tasks and Responsibilities
- Travel extensively to determine trends
- Gauge shifting trend patterns, public interest in product innovation
- Scan merchandise in trend setting stores
- Talk with sales associates to discuss trends
- Confer with retail store buyers about significant trends affecting their businesses
- Observe and analyze shopping behavior
- Write trend forecasts for trend reports

Key Terms

brand position	market research
carryover	merchandiser
color-forecasting services	popular fashion magazines
consumer research	product research
demographics	psychographics
designer	sample cut
fashion colors	shopping the market
fashion forecasting services	short-range forecasting
fashion magazines	staple colors
group	target customer
long-range forecasting	trade publications
market analysis	trend research

Discussion Questions

1. What are some examples of trends (perhaps five years from now) that can be predicted by long-range forecasting? How might these trends affect the apparel industry?

2. What are some examples of short-range trend forecasting (perhaps six months from now) in men's apparel, women's apparel, and children's apparel? How might these trends be reflected in an apparel line?

3. Describe what you perceive as the target customer profile of a national brand such as the Tommy Hilfiger sportswear line.

4. What are some current color trends in women's wear? In men's wear? What color or colors do you predict will be popular next season in women's wear? In men's wear? Why do you think these colors will be popular?

5. What are some fabric trends that are on the upswing in the fashion cycle?

6. What are some examples of specific sources of research information for designers and merchandisers? How would you locate examples of these?

References

Behling, Dorothy U. (1999, January). Aging boomers may shift the apparel empire. *Bobbin*, pp. 53–54.

Bonner, Staci. (1996, March). Forecasting fashion. *Apparel Industry Magazine*, pp. 32–34.

Casual Fridays: A global warming. (1995, December 13). *Women's Wear Daily*, pp. 8–9.

Execution is the key to selling. (1999, May 24). *Daily News Record*, p. 4.

Henricks, Mark. (1991, February). Testing consumer tastes. *Apparel Industry Magazine*, pp. 50–54.

Hill, Suzette. (1998, December). VF's consumerization: a "right stuff" strategy. *Apparel Industry Magazine*, pp. AS-4-12.

Kinnear, Thomas C., and Taylor, James R. (1983). *Marketing Research: An Applied Approach.* New York: McGraw-Hill Book Company, pp. 16–17.

Lewis, Tim. (1999, June 29). Personal communication, Redmond, WA.

Lockwood, Lisa. (1999, April 9). Mags online: different strokes. *Women's Wear Daily*, p. 14.

Nike braves the elements. (1995, May 18). *Women's Wear Daily*, p. 10.

Popcorn, Faith. (1991). *The Popcorn Report.* New York: Doubleday.

Rabon, Lisa C. (1998, December). Master of the mix. *Bobbin*, pp. 42–46.

Schneiderman, Ira P. (1999, September 27). Target marketing to teens should increase in next decade. *Daily News Record*, p. 42.

Socha, Mike. (1997, December 7). Romancing the store. *Women's Wear Daily*, p. 12.

Stoughton, Stephanie. (1999, January 25). Teens burning out on team-logo clothes. *The Oregonian*, p. E3.

Weisman, Katherine. (1996, February 29). France's finicky market. *Women's Wear Daily*, p. 11.

Welling, Holly. (1999, December). Patagonia: Small world view of big business. *Apparel Industry Magazine*, pp. AS26–32.

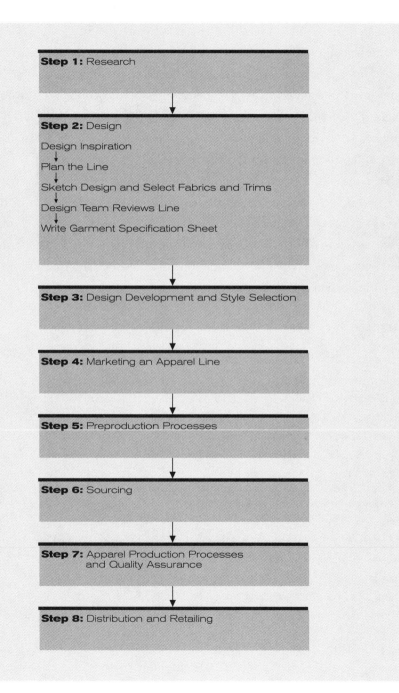

Step 1: Research

Step 2: Design

Design Inspiration
↓
Plan the Line
↓
Sketch Design and Select Fabrics and Trims
↓
Design Team Reviews Line
↓
Write Garment Specification Sheet

Step 3: Design Development and Style Selection

Step 4: Marketing an Apparel Line

Step 5: Preproduction Processes

Step 6: Sourcing

Step 7: Apparel Production Processes
and Quality Assurance

Step 8: Distribution and Retailing

Creating
a Line:
Design

ner Style Book

Chapter	Page

at sample ▼   Demo ▼   Demo

mbols

Edit

front_body	02front_Sleeves	03_front_collar	03a_Rnd_collar	04back_body

Symbol
Info
Zoom
Creat
Revis
Erase

back_sleeves	06_back_collar	07_pocket	07a_Round_pkt	07b_square_pkt

IN THIS CHAPTER YOU WILL LEARN:

■ The various sources of design inspiration.

■ The market forces that direct the company's design focus.

■ The scope of the job responsibilities of the apparel design and merchandising team in designing a line.

■ The interrelationship between design and merchandising in developing a new season's line.

■ The ways computer-aided design systems are used in the design process.

Design Inspiration

The design stage of creating a line combines the designer's and merchandiser's interpretation of market and fashion trends, their understanding of the target customer, and new design inspirations appropriately interpreted for the target customer. But where do designers come up with the multitude of new designs each season? Designers' inspirations for a new line can come from a variety of sources that may have been part of the market and fashion research conducted. All the research information discussed in the previous chapter sifts through the designer's mind during this phase of the design process. For example, designers may be inspired by studying pictures of design ideas from fashion trend sources, collecting swatches of interesting fabric textures and trims, developing some innovative design details, conducting research about an historical period or another culture, or searching the marketplace for a "lightning bolt" idea. Designers may visit historical costume and textile collections such as the Fashion Institute of Technology's collection or the Metropolitan Museum of Art's Costume Institute, both in New York City. When designers live in close proximity to one of the extensive costume and/or textile resources, the apparel company may pay an annual fee to the resource center to provide the designer with continual access to the costume and textile collections. These sources of design inspirations are then interpreted for the particular company's target customer.

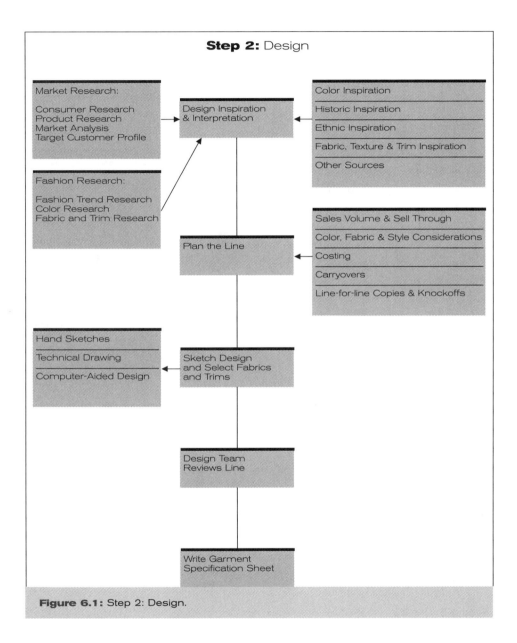

Figure 6.1: Step 2: Design.

A THEME FOR THE NEW LINE

Based on market research, design inspirations, and discussions among the designers and merchandisers who are coordinating the various lines for the company, a theme for the line might be developed. Not every group or line will have a theme, but a theme can help sell a group or a line to retailers and consumers. In some cases, an advertising campaign may be developed around a chosen theme. For example, a company producing an outdoor fishing group might use the theme of bass, a popular sport fish, familiar to fishing enthusiasts (see Figure 6.2). The theme might be carried through in the graphic art used on T-shirts in the group.

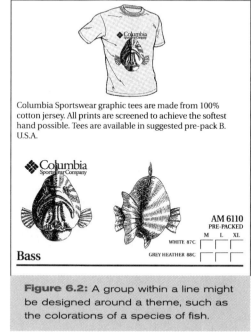

Columbia Sportswear graphic tees are made from 100% cotton jersey. All prints are screened to achieve the softest hand possible. Tees are available in suggested pre-pack B. U.S.A.

Figure 6.2: A group within a line might be designed around a theme, such as the colorations of a species of fish.

COLOR INSPIRATION

The design team studies color trend reports gathered during the research phase and discusses possible groups of colors (also referred to as *color stories*) for the new line while thinking about a color theme. The theme might be reflected in the colors chosen for some of the new styles. For example, the colorations seen on a golden trout might be an inspiration for a group of fishing apparel. Colors for fabrics used in the group might include various hues, tones, and values of the fish. A graphic design of a golden trout leaping up to catch a fishing fly could be created for a T-shirt in the line. A small version of the leaping trout could be used as a motif on other pieces in the group. As another example, an Americana theme might be chosen for a group of missy pieces in a spring collection with a "country flavor" that features fabrics in ruby red, navy blue, and bisque colors in solids, small prints, and plaids.

HISTORIC INSPIRATION

The high-fashion "name" designers typically develop a theme for a collection and invest heavily in marketing that theme to retailers and the public. Often the designer's theme is based on an historical or an ethnic inspiration. Fashion silhouettes or garment details popular during historical periods provide a source of design inspiration. For example, the **Empire** silhouette was fashionable during the early 1800s.

The Empire style was named for Napoleon's empire and was worn by Empress Josephine in France. The long, tubular dress included a raised waistline located just under the bustline. Some fashion historians believe that Napoleon was inspired by the ancient Greek silhouette for this new fashion look. This style, known as *neo-classical*, became a fashion trend that spread throughout western Europe and the United States. The Empire silhouette reappeared in the early 1900s in the fashions of French designer Paul Poiret, seen in his Directoire Revival dress (Mackrell, 1990). Once again, other designers copied this style as the fashion look spread throughout Europe and the United States. In the 1960s, the raised waistline of the Empire silhouette appeared again, this time in an above-the-knee minidress version as well as a long version. In the early 1990s, the Empire style again made fashion headlines. Figure 6.3 shows how the Empire style was adapted for different eras. As another example of historical inspiration, American designer Adrian and French designer Balenciaga both were inspired by the bustle silhouette of the 1880s for their designs created in the 1940s and 1950s (see Figure 6.4).

A return to the fashion look of more recent decades is called a **Retro** *fashion* or *Retro look*. During the early 1990s, fashion looks reminiscent of the decades of the 1930s, 1940s, 1950s, 1960s, and 1970s were evident in mass fashion as well as designer collections. Retro fashions tend not to be exact replicas of the previous fashion look, but to include a "new" fashion twist. For example, a Retro look design may be made from a currently popular fabric or include updated style details that are different from the original.

Garment details of an historic era serve as another source of inspiration for designers. French designer Karl Lagerfeld used Renaissance fashion details as inspiration for a Chanel design in the 1988–1989 collection (Martin & Koda, 1989). Figure 6.5 shows how Lagerfeld incorporated period details in an imaginative way. The ruff collar popular on Renaissance clothing may inspire a group, a line, or a collection. A sleeve detail from the Renaissance period could be an inspiration for a young girl's party dress.

ETHNIC INSPIRATION

Designers may be inspired by the clothing styles of other cultures. The global environment has increased interest in products from the far reaches of the world. Designers seek inspiration from "exotic" cultures with clothing styles, fabrics, and acces-

Figure 6.3: The Empire style recurs periodically throughout fashion history. Shown here are examples from: (top left) early nineteenth century (neoclassical), (top right) early twentieth century (Directoire Revival), (bottom left) the 1960s, and (bottom right) the 1990s.

Figure 6.4: Historical fashion silhouettes often serve as a source of inspiration: (left) the bustle silhouette of the 1880s, as interpreted (center) by Balenciaga in the 1940s, and by Richard Tyler (right) in 2000.

Figure 6.5: Karl Lagerfeld was inspired by a sixteenth-century fashion look (left) for an outfit in his 1988–1989 collection (right).

sories that are unique. Some designers travel to other locales to seek inspiration for a new line. Purchasing and wearing apparel inspired by other cultures may provide a sense of adventure and vicarious enjoyment of that culture for the consumer.

Asian clothing styles have been a source of inspiration historically as well as currently. *Chinoiserie* is a French term for a style that incorporates Chinese motifs. The fabrics of China were used to create Western high-fashion apparel during the 1850s. The Chinese influence on Western fashion grew during the last decades of the 1800s. In the United States, Chinese motifs became fashionable in home fashions, chinaware, house style details, and such clothing styles as the kimono sleeve, Mandarin collar, and frog closures. Chinese clothing and fabrics continue to inspire apparel designers today. The film *The Last Emperor* spurred a new interest in Chinese culture. After the film's release, numerous designers' collections included Chinese-inspired clothing styles.

In 1995, the Costume Institute of the Metropolitan Museum of Art in New York presented *Orientalism: Visions of the East in Western Dress*. This exhibition and the catalog (Martin & Koda, 1994) featured apparel inspired by Asian cultures from various decades. Included in the exhibit were several examples of Asian-inspired garments from recent collections of American designers Ralph Lauren, Oscar de la Renta, and Todd Oldham. Donna Karan also has been inspired by the culture and philosophy of Asia for several of her collections (Knight, 1999, p. 14). The dress in Figure 6.6 (left) from a recent Dior collection shows an Asian influence.

Yves Saint Laurent, a French couture designer, is renowned for his use of various national and ethnic groups and cultures as inspirations for his collections. He has created collections inspired by such regions as Russia, Africa, China, and Spain (Saint Laurent, Vreeland, et al., 1983). American designer Mary McFadden created collections inspired by Africa and Persia, among others. In the early 1970s, British designer Zandra Rhodes traveled to the United States to study the art and culture of American Indians. Her collection featured fabric designs filled with motifs of feathers, cactus, and other images inspired by American Indian cultures.

New York designer Gene Meyer's visit to St. Petersburg, Russia, "sparked the theme for his fall 1999 collection called 'In the Shadow of the Winter Palace.' '. . . St. Petersburg was just amazing. It was a combination of the way the city basked in sunlight, the bright pearly sky and the snow everywhere that inspired me'" (Knight,

Figure 6.6: This 1999 design for Christian Dior (left) reflects a Chinese inspiration such as this Chinese Qing dynasty embroidered yellow silk satin chi-fu, 1740–1760 (right), remade and over embroidered in the early 20th century.

1999, p. 16). Meyer based his spring 2000 collection on the theme of the south of France.

FABRIC, TEXTURE, AND TRIM INSPIRATION

Whereas some designers who create apparel for the higher price zones research a specific period or ethnic culture for inspiration, designers often rely on studying new fabric and texture trends. The previous chapter discussed the sources of information and inspiration used for fabric research. An intriguing fabric texture or interesting print might serve as the design foundation for a group. Several fabrics in prints, plaids, and solid colors, and with smooth as well as textured surfaces, might be combined to create an interesting group. During this design stage of creation, some designers work with specific fabric ideas gathered at textile shows or directly from textile manufacturers as they begin to sketch garment design ideas. Less frequently, designers might develop a design sketch, then seek the perfect fabric for it. Another option for designers at some companies is to develop, or work with others to develop, a textile print for the new line. This will be discussed in more detail later in this chapter.

Special trims and **findings** (also known as notions or sundries) are important features of some garment designs. A unique trim can transform an ordinary or classic garment into a new look. Trims inspired by other cultures were a popular design addition to denim jeans, vests, and jackets for the junior market in the late 1990s. For children's apparel, special ribbons, trims, and appliqués frequently "make" the design. A unique clasp or closure on a swimsuit design can increase its appeal (see Figure 6.7), or a special button on a classic jacket may create a fresh look. Designers constantly seek interesting trims and findings as a source of inspiration.

OTHER SOURCES OF INSPIRATION

The inspiration for a garment within a line or for an entire line can come from an infinite variety of sources. Sources of inspiration are often linked to the social "spirit of the times," also called the **zeitgeist**. Events and the general spirit of the popular culture might be reflected in new apparel lines. "Tommy Hilfiger, who travels

Figure 6.7: Findings such as the metal ring on this Jantzen swimsuit provide innovative design details.

extensively, said he's most inspired by the younger generations in cities across the globe. The most influential factor in every major city is the kids on the streets who set the trends" (Knight, 1999, p. 16).

Ask designers what inspired them to create a particular line. You may be surprised to learn that Japanese kites were the inspiration for a line of swimsuits or that graffiti was the inspiration for a line of sportswear.

The Market Niche

Successful designers and merchandisers are able to interpret their design inspirations appropriately for their target customer. As noted in Chapters 4 and 5, most apparel companies specialize in a certain type of product, such as casual clothes, swimwear, or evening wear. The apparel company's **product type** or product line is the basis for the development of its line. For example, Steve Madden is known for a look in shoes that appeals to young adults. If you are familiar with this company, a certain type of product comes to mind when the name of the company is mentioned (see

Figure 6.8). Consistency in a company's product type helps the customer develop company brand recognition, build product loyalty, and encourage repeat customers. Thus the design team, which consists of designers, product developers, and merchandisers, will develop the line for the new season with the product type as its foundation.

The importance of keeping the target customer profile in mind when creating a line was discussed in the previous chapter. A strong connection exists between the type of product included in the line and the company's target customer. The blend of product type with target customer is

Figure 6.8: Consumers associate the name of a company such as Steve Madden with a specific fashion image.

referred to as the **market niche**. Developing and maintaining a line based on the market niche is important to the success of the apparel line. The line for the new season will include some variation of styles to appeal to the variety of customers' needs and tastes within the market niche. For example, a missy swimwear manu-facturer will include some very conservative swimsuit styles, as well as some styles that have an updated look (see Figure 6.9). The missy swimwear line might be divid-ed into several groups to appeal to a variety of missy customers.

Based on the changing needs and preferences of the target customer, a company's product line may change over time. If the product line does not change at all, cus-tomers might become bored with the same look and decide that they do not need to purchase another item so similar to items they already own. Perhaps a company wants to change the direction of its product from a focus on career suits to a focus on coordinated separates after sensing that women are no longer interested in the look of a matched suit. Or a sportswear company may decide to add a golf apparel

Figure 6.9: Jantzen's missy swimwear line includes styles ranging from conser-vative (left) to updated (right) looks.

group to its product line because of the growth in popularity of golf among its target customers.

Sometimes new designers and/or merchandisers are hired by a company to help revamp the product type. However, if a new look for a product is too radical, or if the product type is changed too quickly, it can cause problems for the retailer and the customer. Retaining the loyal customer is important, just as it is important to attract new customers for company growth. The customer who is familiar with and enjoys wearing the company's product may not understand the new look. Balancing the relationship among the current product look, changes that need to occur in the product to maintain interest and provide fashion change, and keeping the target customer happy is one of the responsibilities of the design team.

Planning the Line

Although the research and design inspiration stages of the design process—consisting of market research, as well as trend, color, and fabric and trim research—continues throughout the year, at a specified time in the year the design team must begin to develop concrete ideas for the new season's line. Based on the number of lines a company produces each year, each apparel company maintains a master calendar with target due dates for completion of the remaining stages of the creation and production of each line (see the flowchart at the opening of Chapter 5 and Color Plate 3). The design team looks at the due date for the finalization of a line, and works backward to determine what date to move from the research stage to the design stage.

THE DESIGN TEAM

The creation of each line relies on a team of people. Designers typically work with merchandisers and product developers on the creation of each new style in the line (see Figure 6.10). As discussed in Chapter 5, many larger apparel companies employ a merchandiser whose responsibility it is to oversee and guide the designer or design team to determine what, when, and how much apparel to produce. A merchandiser often works with designers of several lines to oversee the coordination among the lines. In some companies, especially smaller ones, the designer also performs the job responsibilities of the merchandiser. Some companies employ both designers and

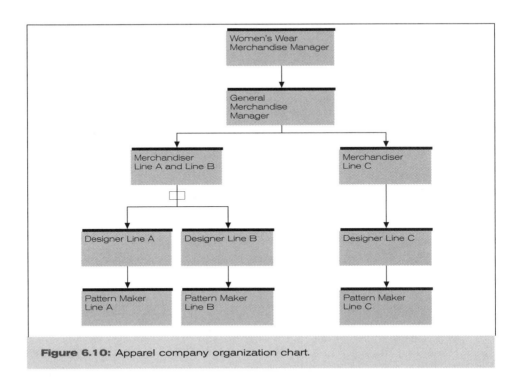

Figure 6.10: Apparel company organization chart.

product developers. A product developer takes the designer's idea and is responsible for developing the product. The product developer researches possible fabrics and trims, works with vendors in securing all components for the style, and coordinates all aspects of style creation. At some smaller companies, the designer also handles the product development responsibilities.

The designer(s) and merchandiser(s) attend planning meetings during the research and design stages. At planning meetings, the sales figures (including sales volume and sell through) for the previous season are reviewed, the sales projections for the new season are considered, and the overall plan and schedule for the upcoming season's line are discussed. This might include decisions about the target number of styles to include in the line, the ratio of jackets compared to vests or the ratio of skirts compared to pants, the styles that will be repeated from the previous season (carryovers), the types of silhouettes for various styles, or a decision to try something new to be added to the line. In addition to style considerations, fabric, color, and cost are also considered.

SALES VOLUME AND SELL THROUGH

There is an expression in the fashion business—"you're only as good as your last line"—that means a company's success is measured by how well the previous season's line sold. Success of a line is measured by sales volume and also by sell through at the retail level. **Sales volume** is the actual level of sales in terms of either the total number of units of each style sold or the total number of dollars consumers spent on the style (dollar volume). Manufacturers tend to measure the success of a line by the total number of units sold while retailers tend to measure the success of a line by the dollar volume. The designer and merchandiser have to hit the targeted sales volume with a mix of repeated styles, revised styles, and new styles. Because of the number of lines typically produced per year, the sales volume figures are not usually available in time to rely on the number of units sold during the previous season in order to predict accurately the strategy for the line under development. Therefore, one's intuition also becomes a part of planning the line.

A line may sell well at market to the retailer, but a delay in delivery to the retailer could reduce the dollar volume at the retail store. This is one reason why another measurement tool, the line's sell through, is considered a good indicator of the line's success. **Sell through** denotes the percentage of items sold at retail compared to the number of items in the line the retailer purchased from the manufacturer. A strong sell through is the goal for both the manufacturer and the retailer. The sales figures from the current and previous selling seasons are an important guideline in planning how many and what type of apparel to include in the new line.

COLOR, FABRIC, AND STYLE CONSIDERATIONS

During planning meetings, colors and fabrics for the new season's line are discussed. A color story will be developed based on the color research conducted before the planning meetings. Lines need a balance between some staple colors and some fashion colors (see Chapter 5). The line needs to have a cohesive look, so a great deal of time is spent deciding on the correct balance of colors. The group of colors selected may need to include a color that the design team does not expect to sell well (for example, white used in a group of warmups) because they know that buyers expect to see this color for a balanced look in the color group.

Most garment styles will be produced in more than one color. A specific style may be available in three of four different solid colors, or in three or four color variations of the same print. The varieties of colors available for a style are called **colorways**. Producing the same style in several colorways is efficient in terms of development cost since fewer patterns, spec sheets, prototypes, and cost estimates need to be prepared than if each style were produced in only one colorway. This variety also offers more options to retailers who might want to buy part of a line but not duplicate the same colorways as competing local retailers will offer in their stores.

As discussed earlier, designers typically attend textile trade shows and are aware of the new colors and fabrics available. Therefore, their decisions regarding the colors and fabrics are frequently made before the garment styles are determined. The new line needs to provide a balance among the colors, styles, and prices offered.

COSTING

The production cost of each style in a line is an important factor for designers to consider throughout the design stage. Thus, many companies include cost personnel as a part of the team during the planning meetings for a new line. Their role is to provide cost estimates on the new styles in the line as it develops.

There are many factors to keep in mind related to costing. Even prior to providing an initial cost estimate, each company has pricing strategies that guide costing. For example, it is important that two garments in the same line do not compete against each other for sales. Some apparel manufacturers follow a pricing strategy that specifies that the prices of two different shirt styles should not be the same—and style differences in the two styles need to support the price difference. Also, a shirt made from a more expensive fabric might have fewer garment details while a shirt made from a less expensive fabric could have more details to be sold at similar (but not identical) prices. Pricing strategies need to make sense to the customer. Comparing two shirts in a line with different prices, the higher price of a shirt made from the more expensive fabric or more complex style details needs to be apparent to the customer.

Other manufacturers follow another pricing strategy called **price averaging**. With this strategy, a shirt manufactured from a more expensive fabric is priced to equalize a shirt manufactured from a less expensive fabric. The manufacturer averages the costs of the two shirts to keep the price of both styles similar. Thus, the shirt made from the more expensive fabric is priced slightly low while the shirt made from the less expensive fabric is priced slightly high. If both styles sell equally, the company breaks even. If more of the shirts priced slightly high sell, the company comes out ahead; while if more of the shirts prices slightly low sell, the company loses some profit.

In recent years, the apparel industry has made a significant change in the design-produce-sell cycle. The process had been to create a new style, then calculate its cost based on materials and labor. Now, price tends to drive the style decisions, especially in the moderate and mass wholesale price zones. The term, **target costing** is used to signify this pricing strategy. The style and fabric components are manipulated by setting a cost first, then determining how many yards of fabric and at what price, estimating the cost of other components such as zipper or buttons, and estimating how many minutes of labor are available based on a per-hour labor price. The design team might know from previous seasons' costs that it takes 60 minutes to sew a basic jacket, and that one and one-half yards of fabric are required. After estimating a cost per yard of a typical fabric and other components, the design team can calculate how many minutes of sewing labor and/or yards of additional fabric are available to enhance the style to meet the target cost.

The target costing process has been used for some time for certain types of goods, such as styles produced for a specific retail chain (sometimes called *special makeups*) and private label goods. The design of private label goods and store brand merchnadise will be discussed in more detail later. One of the driving forces behind target costing is that in today's market (with the exception of the couture and some designer price zones), the upper limit of price is based on what the target customer will buy.

CARRYOVERS

A line of apparel typically does not consist of only new styles. In a new line, some styles will be carryovers, some styles will be modifications of good sellers, and some styles will be new designs. A **carryover** will repeat the same garment style as a successful garment style from a previous season, but often in a new fabric. Thus, carryovers provide a less expensive route to add a fresh look to a line. If the new fabric has identical textile characteristics as the previous fabric, the development cost will be minimal because the production patterns can be reused. However, if the new fabric is different—for example, it has a different shrinkage factor—a new pattern and prototype will need to be made.

Companies vary regarding the number of new items compared with the number of carryovers for each line. For an idea of the approximate ratio for a company that produces apparel in the moderate wholesale price zone, some companies target about one-third of the line to be carryovers, one-third as revisions of previous styles, and one-third as new designs. The percentage of new styles could be as low as 10 percent at some mass to moderate wholesale price zone companies, whereas a bridge or designer label might produce mostly new styles.

LINE-FOR-LINE COPIES AND KNOCKOFFS

Rather than starting with a designer's drawing for a new design, a "new" style might be added to a line in another way. Sometimes while shopping the market or looking through fashion magazines, a designer or merchandiser will find a garment that seems ideal for the company's upcoming line. Thus, the designer and merchandiser may decide to create a copy of an existing garment. Copying a garment may be done in several ways. Sometimes the uniqueness of a design, for example a shirt with innovative design details, seems perfect for the upcoming line. The designer might request that a **line-for-line copy** of the shirt be made by the pattern development department and produced in a similar fabric. The new shirt would be an exact replica of the original; thus the term *line-for-line copy* is used.

Taking a garment that exists in a higher price zone and copying it to be sold at a lower price can also be done in several ways. By selecting a less expensive fabric, a copy of the original garment could be sold at a lower price. Another way to reduce cost is to eliminate or modify some of the design detail. These two methods are used to create **knockoffs**, designs that are similar to the original but not exact replicas.

Is it legal to copy an existing garment design? The United States has laws to protect against copyright and trademark infringement (see Chapter 2). A specific "invention" in a garment (for example, a unique molding process to create a seamless panty) can be patented in the United States. However, in some countries (including the U.S.) the actual garment design is considered to be in the public domain. Therefore, it is quite common to see line-for-line copies and knockoffs in the U.S. apparel business. For example, the apparel company, ABS, is well known for its adaptations of the dresses worn by stars to the Academy Awards ceremony. An article in *Women's Wear Daily* stated that creating knockoffs "is a practice so commonplace, and one not clearly prohibited by law, that most designers who have been copied have felt helpless to stop it" (Wilson, 1999, p. 8). Design laws are much more strict in Europe, as evidenced by the 1994 case in which French designer, Yves Saint Laurent, took Ralph Lauren to court in France in a dispute over the design copy of a tuxedo dress (see Figure 6.11) ("Tuxedo Junction," 1994).

Figure 6.11: The tuxedo dress as presented by Yves Saint Laurent (left) and the tuxedo dress as presented by Ralph Lauren (right)

218   **PART 2**
Creating and Marketing an
Apparel Line

Several court cases in the United States regarding trade dress law, a part of trademark law (see Chapter 2), have brought the issue of copying into the headlines. As reported by *Women's Wear Daily*, "there have been several recent legal challenges, and now that the Supreme Court has taken up a case with the potential to define what constitutes a violation of existing trade dress law, the practice of knockoffs is under the spotlight, raising questions among manufacturers of what the ramifications of such a decision could be" (Wilson, 1999, p. 8).

In summary, many factors need to be considered during the planning of the line. Among them is the overall number of styles to be included in the line. Some of these styles will be carryover styles from the previous line, some styles will be revisions of previous styles, and some styles will be new designs. Decisions are made about the balance of tops and bottoms, styling variety (such as single-breasted and double-breasted jackets), color and fabric offerings for each style, cost to produce each style, and overall pricing balance of the line.

The Design Sketch and Selection of Fabrics and Trims

At some point in the design stage (usually determined by the master calendar due date), the designer will begin to transform interpretations of design inspirations into garment idea sketches. A designer might develop some garment sketches early in this stage and then face a pressing deadline for sketching the remaining pieces. Is it difficult to create twenty new sweater or swimsuit designs each season? By constantly seeking inspiration from a variety of sources, most designers have plenty of new ideas.

HAND SKETCHES

Some designers rely on hand sketches of their garment ideas. The designer's sketches do not look like finished artwork of a fashion illustration. In fact, some designers state that they are not good at drawing. Partially because of time constraints, some designers use a body silhouette called a **croquis**, or **lay figure**, to develop their garment design sketches. A swimwear designer may have numerous copies of a croquis available onto which the swimsuit design idea will be drawn in pencil or marker. Other designers begin with a sheet of drawing paper and sketch the garment idea portrayed on a body silhouette (see Figure 6.12). Some designers add color to their sketches by using colored pencils or markers. Often a back view sketch is shown as well as the front view.

TECHNICAL DRAWING

Some garment design sketches do not include the body silhouette. If only the garment design is drawn, without an indication of the body, the sketch is called a *technical drawing*, or **tech drawing**. The garment is drawn as it would appear lying flat, as on a table, so sometimes the term **flat** or *flat sketch* is used to indicate this type of drawing. Tech drawings are used by some companies in place of design sketches, especially in the active sportswear industry. Activewear garments might have many details. Tech

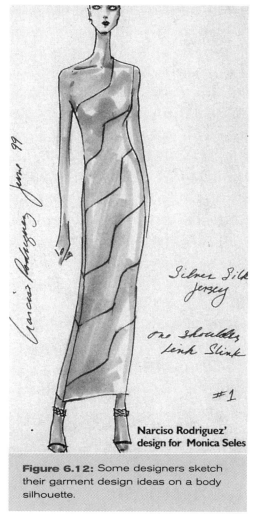

Silver Silk Jersey

one shoulder
tink Slink

#1

Narciso Rodriguez'
design for Monica Seles

Figure 6.12: Some designers sketch their garment design ideas on a body silhouette.

drawings might include a close-up sketch of a detail such as a pocket, cuff, or collar, as well as the back view. Tech drawings are especially useful and often necessary for pattern making and production needs. Sometimes specific dimensions, such as the size and/or placement of a patch pocket, are indicated on the tech drawing. Tech drawings can be drawn quickly with **computer-aided design (CAD)** or graphics software programs (see Figure 6.13). A previous season's similar technical garment drawing from a computer file can be used as the starting point to make modifications for the new design's tech drawing.

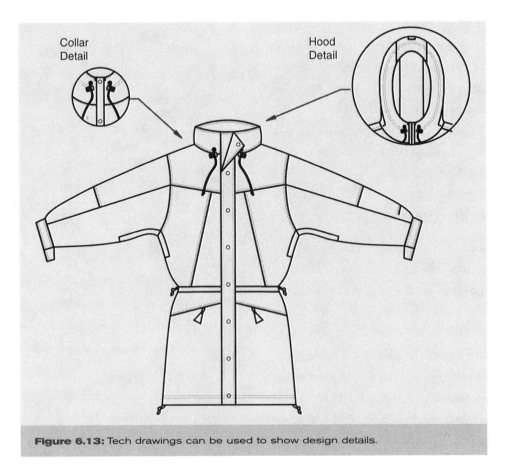

Collar
Detail

Hood
Detail

Figure 6.13: Tech drawings can be used to show design details.

COMPUTER-AIDED DESIGN

Apparel Design

Computer workstations that include computer-aided design software programs or graphics software have become common in many apparel design studios. Many software programs are designed specifically for creating drawings and design sketches. In the past, the cost of CAD and graphics systems was a hurdle for some companies. The price for computer systems has dropped substantially, making CAD and graphics systems affordable to even small apparel companies. In addition, newer software uses the Windows environment and runs on mainstream industry hardware, whereas earlier systems required specialized hard drives and printers. The integration of mainstream printers provides better pricing as well as multiuse capabilities within a company. Trade shows provide an opportunity to compare CAD systems and to learn about upgrades and new technology. They are an excellent resource for assisting in the selection of CAD software and hardware for the apparel industry. CAD systems used for pattern making, for pattern grading (sizing), and for marker making (developing the master cutting plan) will be discussed in other chapters.

Two major advantages of using a CAD system to create design sketches are the time-saving potential and the capability to try out numerous design ideas quickly. The designer may select a garment sketch from the previous season's line and simply modify design details for the new design for the upcoming line. This procedure greatly speeds up this phase of the design process.

Some designers may think it stifles their creativity to sketch on a computer. They prefer to "think" with pencil in hand. To assist the artist, there are graphics computer programs that allow the designer to use a pencil-like stylus to simulate the act of drawing. After becoming familiar with the process of sketching by CAD, most designers find that the speed with which a design can be modified is such an advantage that they have no desire to revert to drawing by hand. However, for the high-end designer price zones, hand sketching design ideas may still be the preferred process. This is due, in part, to the differences in the creation process involved, which will be discussed later.

The computer can store a croquis (see Figure 6.14), or a series of croquis in various poses. The designer selects a desired pose that then appears on the computer screen. The desired garment sketch can be drawn onto the croquis. KaratCAD is an example of a software program used by designers for creating garment sketches. It provides a library of garment bodies and basic garment silhouettes such as shirts and pants as well as garment components such as collar and pocket styles. The designer sketches the new style by bringing the desired components together (see Figure 6.15). Other alternatives are to draw new garment designs by using true proportions from a croquis stored in the system, or by drawing one's own garment by specifying exact measurements.

To visualize what the garment style might look like in a specific color, the garment sketch can be colored. Computer graphics programs can be used to simulate the color of a specific fabric swatch. With some software programs, it is necessary to

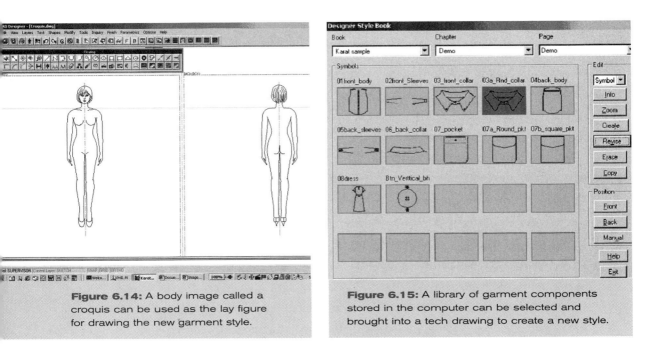

Figure 6.14: A body image called a croquis can be used as the lay figure for drawing the new garment style.

Figure 6.15: A library of garment components stored in the computer can be selected and brought into a tech drawing to create a new style.

blend colors on the computer monitor to create an accurate color match, then print the sketch of the new style in order to compare the printed color on paper to the actual color of the fabric swatch. The computer industry is hard at work perfecting the ink technology to match the color on paper to the color as seen on the computer screen. One system, the "Sophis Smart Colour calibration tool enables designers to create color standards for different fabrics and ink sets to help ensure that the desired color is printed" ("ITMA unveils advances," 1999, p. 10).

Some of the grahpics software programs are integrated with the same color system used by textile producers so an exact match can be produced very quickly by keying in the color number. The Pantone color system is supported by a number of graphics software programs and is used by textile producers to match the printed visual version of the garment with the actual fabrics. These integrated systems can be used to produce accurate color matching of the line catalog used later to sell the line at market.

A scanner can be used to input an existing fabric print into the computer system. A facsimile of the fabric will appear on the computer screen. The scale of the print or plaid fabric motif can be adjusted to approximate the correct size of the motif for the scale of the drawing. This is much faster than hand drawing and coloring fabric motifs. Some of the more complex software programs can simulate the drape of the fabric on the designer's computer sketch (see Figure 6.16). The computer technology of simulating the three-dimensional drape of fabric is called **virtual draping**.

Using CAD at the design stage helps to integrate later steps in the design process. The designer's CAD sketch will be the basis for garment technical drawings used in product

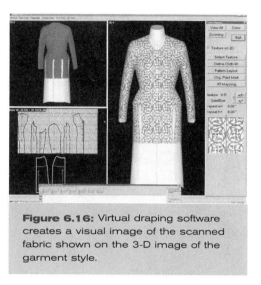

Figure 6.16: Virtual draping software creates a visual image of the scanned fabric shown on the 3-D image of the garment style.

development and production. The integration of computers in the entire design process will be discussed at each step in the design process.

Advances in computer technology will allow the designer's sketch to be translated from a three-dimensional image to a two-dimensional pattern. Other advances include the technology to compute the cost difference (in material usage and time to sew) between slightly different versions of a design.

The concept of designing entirely on the computer may seem far off, but the reality is that not only will we create the image of the garment style with replica fabric on the computer screen, but retail buyers will write their orders from the garments viewed on the screen. No prototype samples will be sewn. The cost savings compared to today's process of design development will be substantial. In fact, some companies such as Liz Claiborne currently use CAD to create a virtual collection. The "style and design teams create simulated fabric and knit swatches for each apparel line directly on screen. They can show all their collections in virtual form. They 'map' sketches and even photos of models with the different materials, including aspects such as shadow and fabric distortion" ("U4ia contributing to creativity," 1999, p. 9). Other aspects of CAD systems will be discussed in Chapter 7.

It has become increasingly important for designers to be proficient with CAD and graphics software systems, and design students will increase their opportunities for future employment by developing the ability to use a computer system to sketch their design ideas. If the advantages of using a CAD system are many, why aren't all apparel companies currently using CAD? Of course, expense is a factor, but perhaps even more daunting is the time required to train designers, developers, pattern makers, and other personnel and to implement the use of a CAD system. "Apparel manufacturers are constantly driven to shorten production cycle, making one of the main reasons for buying a CAD system a crippling factor in the implementation process. Short-term focus on getting products out the door limits time for both training on and experimentation with the systems" (Weldon, 1999, p. 42). As computer software programs become more user friendly, the length of training and cost to the company may be greatly reduced.

Textile Design

Computer-aided design and graphics software programs are also an important tool for textile design. Since textile design is such an integral part of the garment design, it is important for apparel designers and merchandisers to know as much as possible about the textile design process. Textile designers often work for textile producers or freelance. More frequently today than in the past, apparel designers find textile design and/or graphic design assignments a part of their responsibilities, as when they design a graphics logo to coordinate with a print fabric used in a line or perhaps redesign an existing textile print.

At other companies, textile designers work side by side with the apparel design team. For example, at Pendleton Woolen Mills, the design of the textile is integrated with the garment design. The textile designers calculate the spacing of the plaid repeat to coincide with the pleat widths of the skirt pattern, or vice versa depending on the specific style process. The Anne Klein textiles department "defines the color trends, the materials and the prints for each of the three annual collections. . . One of the major strengths of our company is that we have our own textiles department. We are independent and the fabrics we design are a reflection of our image" ("Anne Klein," 1999, p. 5). The Anne Klein textiles department uses CAD software to design its prints. The head of the textiles office stated, "we can combine several ideas or go back to previous collections. We have also considerably improved our organization as we keep all our styles in our computer database" ("Anne Klein," 1999, p. 5).

CAD and graphics software systems provide numerous advantages for textile design. Some of the new computer textile design systems can print the newly created print design directly onto a piece of fabric. Several repeats of the printed fabric pieces can be joined together to simulate a large piece of the printed textile. Viewing a large section of the print design helps the textile designer visualize the scale, repeat, and color combination (see Figure 6.17). Changes can be made immediately. This is much faster and less expensive than sending a printed paper sample to a textile mill to make a length of sample yardage of the print, called a **strike off**.

It took years to develop processes to print directly onto fabric without backing the fabric with paper to stabilize the fabric. Now, fabric can

Figure 6.17: Textile designers experiment with various color combinations while designing prints.

be printed digitally in sufficient yardage to create entire garments. This technology opens the field to cost savings, time savings, and totally new customization possibilities. With digital printing, the textile design moves from the designer's computer screen to fabric without the textile producer having to make a strike off and perfect the sample fabric ("ITMA unveils advances," 1999). Not only is there a cost savings, but a time savings as well. Sometimes it takes weeks for a textile print developed by traditional processes to reach final approval. The ability to perfect the print design quickly and inexpensively using digital printing adds flexibility to the design process. According to the J. Crew director of CAD, "more work can be shown, in a shorter time, than was possible before. This helps everyone in getting a real sense of what something's going to really look like before we ever get involved with the mill" (Weldon, 1999, p. 40). Additional benefits of digital printing are the capability to produce very small runs for limited production or to create custom prints.

Some companies use CAD to develop textile prints that can be electronically communicated to textile mills. The textile print computer file can be delivered electronically to the textile mill. This process allows "direct communication with textile mills—or direct printing on greige goods. Eliminating the labor spent re-creating these designs in strike offs and samples shortens production cycles and significantly reduces mis-communication and simple human errors" (Weldon, 1999, p. 40).

Where will digital printing technology lead us next? A designer specializing in digital printing at [TC]² "is breaking industry paradigms by creating and applying custom prints to individual pattern pieces and producing them on a digital printer" (Weldon, 1999, p. 40). This technology merges the textile print and the fit and style options of the pattern to exact customization for the customer.

SELECTION OF FABRICS AND TRIMS

The fabrics and trims are usually selected before a design is approved for inclusion in a line. Each design sketch or tech drawing includes a small sample of the intended fabric, called a **swatch** that is attached to the sketch or drawing. It is essential that the fabric be chosen before a design is reviewed by the merchandiser, designer, and cost personnel for possible inclusion in the final line. Sometimes the actual fabric intended for the design is not yet available from the textile manufacturer. In these cases a facsimile fabric will be used temporarily for the design development stage. The design sketch will also include any trim swatches that will be used and may indicate specific findings as well.

DESIGNERS WHO CREATE BY DRAPING

Some designers create a design idea three dimensionally using actual fabric as a starting point instead of beginning with a sketch of a garment (see Figure 6.18). For this design process, a mannequin or dress form in the sample size is used. Fabrics vary in their **hand** (tactile qualities) and ability to drape around the body. Working with the actual fabric can be a source of design inspiration, especially for fabrics with special draping qualities, such as charmeuse or permanently pleated fabric. Fabrics that are plaid or striped or that have a large print motif are suited to creating the initial design by the **draping** process. Couture designers and some ready-to-wear designers creating lines in the designer price zone frequently use draping to create the initial design.

Some ready-to-wear designers and sometimes couture designers might develop the design from the designer's sketch by draping in **muslin**. Muslin is an inexpensive trial fabric, similar to cotton broadcloth. It helps the designer determine silhouette, proportion, and design details, but does not have the drape of many fashion fabrics. For many fabric types and garment styles, muslin serves the purpose adequately. The muslin trial garment is sometimes referred to as the **toile**, from a French word whose literal translation is *cloth*.

French designer Madeleine Vionnet created innovative bias cut garments during the 1920s and 1930s. She always draped, rather than sketched, her design ideas. She worked out the design in fabric on a small-size wooden mannequin (see Figure 6.19). Her design team then draped a full-size

Figure 6.18: Some designers, such as Jacques Fath, create three dimensionally by draping designs in fashion fabric on a live model.

replica in muslin. A prototype in fashion fabric was then cut using the pattern pieces developed from the muslin toile. Donna Karan is an example of a contemporary designer who creates designs by draping.

There are advantages to developing the design idea by draping, especially if fashion fabric is used. Seeing the design develop, sensing the drape of the fabric, molding the fabric into a three-dimensional shape, and evolving the design during the process bring a great deal of creativity to the design process. However, draping a design may take more time than preparing a design sketch or tech drawing, and draping requires more fabric than first making a pattern and then cutting fabric from the pattern. Therefore, many designers rely on drawings for the design phase of the process.

Design Team Reviews Line

Typically, many more design ideas are sketched than will appear in the final line. At a line review meeting (also called a **first adoption meeting**), the designer presents the design sketches to the review team (for example, the merchandiser, fit or production engineer, and head of sample sewing) according to the timeline on the master calendar (see Figure 6.20). Some designers present the new line as a formal presentation with beautifully rendered drawings, fabric swatches, and perhaps an indication of the design theme or inspiration shown on presentation boards or storyboards. The designer might make an oral presentation to the design team, upper management, or private label managers to "sell" the line. This first adop-

Figure 6.19: French designer Madeleine Vionnet developed her design ideas by draping on a small-scale wooden mannequin and perfecting them later on a full-size mannequin.

tion meeting is the first of several review processes the line must undergo. There will be several subsequent line reviews before the final adoption. The review team discusses and evaluates each of the designs. The team will have determined during previous planning meetings how many items of each type of apparel item it will be possible to include in the line. Out of 60 design ideas presented for review, perhaps only 30 or 40 sketches will be selected to continue into the design development stage. Some of these designs will be dropped at later stages as well. At other companies, the merchandisers may request that all or most of the designs be developed as prototypes to visualize better the product.

Guided by the total number of pieces previously determined for the line, other factors enter into the decision to accept or drop designs from the line. The balance of the line is an important factor in deciding which designs should be included. For

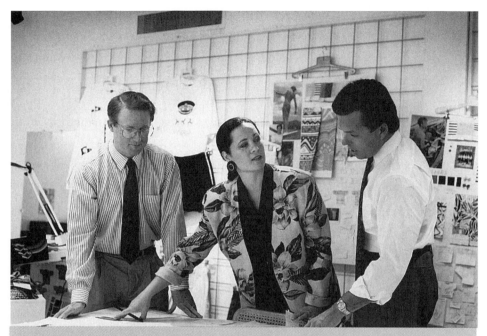

Figure 6.20: At review meetings, the designer, merchandiser, and production engineer discuss the feasibility of each style in the line.

a missy career line, jacket style variations are considered so that there will be a range of styles to suit a variety of customers. For example, it is important to include a balance of the number of short versus long, boxy versus fitted, single- versus double-breasted, and collar versus collarless jackets. The ratio of solid to plaid or print fabrics is another consideration. Skirt style variations must be balanced—short versus long, fitted versus flared, full versus pleated. The skirts need to coordinate with as many of the jacket styles as possible. The mix of classic and fashion-forward styles needs to be considered.

Anticipated cost is an important factor in the review process. The anticipated prices need to be similar to the previous season's prices unless a new market niche is sought. Some cost considerations were discussed earlier in this chapter. It is important that style features need to match price—a customer expects to pay more for a longer, double-breasted jacket than for a short, single-breasted style, for example. The team discusses cost estimates and possible style, design details, findings, and fabric changes than might reduce cost.

Other factors to consider include ease of adjusting the style to fit varied body types. For example, elastic added at the sides of the skirt waistband can enhance the adaptability of a garment to fit more figure shapes, especially in the missy and larger-size markets. However, for the junior market, elastic in the waistband may be considered a negative feature and could adversely affect sales. Ease in alterations is another consideration. A wrap skirt with a curved, faced hemline is not easily shortened and cannot be lengthened.

There is a constant struggle among production personnel who want new styles to be similar to previous styles and as simple as possible; merchandisers who want the line to "sell itself" in the marketplace with great prices and high quality; and designers who want highly creative, complex styles. This may explain why some companies call the conference room where design reviews are conducted the *war room*. It is important for the designer to be prolific with design ideas and to develop an impersonal attitude about the designs that need to be modified or are dropped from the line.

In summary, the merits of each styles as it fits in the big picture of the overall line will be discussed at the design review meeting. Sometimes design details will need to be modified to lower the expected cost or to coordinate better with other styles. The team is guided in their review process by the following aims:

■ To create a cohesive theme.
■ To include an appropriate number of items and a balance of styles.
■ To fit the overall merchandising orientation of the company for the season (e.g., fit the price and lifestyle of the target customer).

Writing the Garment Specification Sheet

The designer often has some specific design details in mind that need to be conveyed to the pattern maker and sample sewer in order to create the sample or prototype garment at the next stage of the design process. These details, as well as other vital information, are conveyed on a **garment specification sheet**, also called a *garment spec sheet*, or shortened still more to *spec sheet*. Examples of types of design details that need to be specified include the number, size, and style of buttons, any edge stitching or top stitching, the spacing between pleats or tucks, and the size of a patch pocket. Pocketing, lining fabric, and interfacings are also specified. Any information not specified will be decided by the pattern maker. Thus, it is the designer's responsibility to specify all garment aspects that are important to the look of the design. A drawing of the garment design is included on the spec sheet along with fabric swatches. The spec sheet may also include the measurement specifications and construction specifications (see Chapter 9).

A **style number** is assigned to each new style in the line. This number (which might include a letter code as well) is coded to indicate the season and year in which the line will be presented to buyers, plus other information desired by the apparel company. The code may include a category indicator, such as swimwear or sportswear. The size category of junior, missy, petite or tall might be another item included in the code. The style number is used as the style's reference throughout development, marketing, and production.

Summary

In creating an apparel line, the design process follows the research process. The design team works with planning and production personnel to plan the calendar of due dates in order to provide garments to the retailer at the season's outset. The line is planned to provide the right product type for the target customer at the right time and at the right price. The sales volume and sell through of a line at the retail level are important indicators used to plan the next line. The balance between carryover styles, revisions of popular styles from the previous season, and new styles is a critical decision to the success of the line.

The merchandiser may work with the designer to develop a theme for a new line. A theme for a line can help sell the products. An example of a color theme for a sport fishing group is one based on the colors of a sport fish. This theme can be enhanced by the use of the fish image as a graphic design on a T-shirt in the collection. Historical and ethnic clothing are sources of design inspiration, as are new fabrics, textures, trims, and fasteners.

Some designers hand sketch their garment design ideas, some use a computer-aided design or graphics program, some prepare technical drawings, and some create the design idea three dimensionally in fabric by draping. The designer is responsible for creating far more design ideas than will be selected for the line. The designer is also responsible for selecting fabrics, trims, and linings for each design and specifying details such as buttons and top stitching. The garment specification sheet includes all the pertinent information required to complete a pattern and prototype of the design.

If you are considering a career as a designer or merchandiser for an apparel company, you need to have a creative flair, good technical knowledge, and confidence.

Assistant Designer
PRIVATELY OWNED SPORTSWEAR COMPANY

Position Description
Assist the design director and merchandise manager

Typical Tasks and Responsibilities
- Create a catalog of the season's prototype garments including computer illustrations and colorways of all garments
- Create and weave yarn dyes on the computer and scan in prints
- Prepare all of the information necessary for the textile mills to do strike offs and handlooms
- Update and change CAD/CAM data when changes in colors are made
- Design garments from initial sketches through fit sessions
- Prepare special computer projects for sales reps—drawing and coloring garments and creating mini catalogs
- Work with all fit models
- Work with overseas correspondence in the absence of the designer

Designer
PUBLICLY HELD SPORTSWEAR AND ATHLETIC SHOE COMPANY

Position Description
Work with merchandisers and marketers to design lines. Work with graphic designer and textile designer in creating the line.

Typical Tasks and Responsibilities
- Provide ideas, direction, images, and concept(s) for the season's line
- Research fabric vendor resources
- Select fabrics for the garments in the line
- Work with pattern makers in creating patterns for the garments in the line
- Provide follow-through to production of all garments in the line
- Give presentations of the line to various groups for feedback

Key Terms

carryover	first adoption meeting	market niche	style number
colorway	flat or flat sketch	muslin	swatch
computer-aided	garment	price averaging	target costing
design (CAD)	specification sheet	product type	tech drawing
croquis	hand	Retro	toile
draping	knockoff	sales volume	virtual draping
Empire	lay figure	sell through	zeitgeist
findings	line-for-line copy	strike off	

Discussion Questions

1. What are some possible themes for a junior sportswear line?

2. What are some current societal trends (zeitgeist) that might provide an inspiration for a group or line of apparel?

3. What might be an example of an *unconventional* source of design inspiration?

4. What are some of the job responsibilities of a merchandiser and a designer in the design stage of the design process? What are some activities that might be helpful for you to complete as students to help prepare you for these job responsibilities? Examples include a target customer collage for a specific company, a trend board for a jacket line for a year in advance, or an inspiration board for a children's wear beach group.

References

Anne Klein. (1999, Vol. 1). *Lectra Mag*, p. 5.

ITMA unveils advances in digital printing. (1999, September). *Bobbin*, pp. 8–11.

Knight, Molly. (1999, September 24). Globetrotting for inspiration. *DNR*, pp. 14–16.

Mackrell, Alice. (1990). *Paul Poiret*. New York: Holmes & Meier.

Martin, Richard, and Koda, Harold. (1989). *The Historical Mode*. New York: Rizzoli International Publications.

Martin, Richard, and Koda, Harold. (1994). *Orientalism: Visions of the East in Western Dress*. New York: Metropolitan Museum of Art. Distributed by Harry N. Abrams, Inc.

Saint Laurent, Yves, Vreeland, Diana, et al. (1983). *Yves Saint Laurent*. New York: Metropolitan Museum of Art.

Tuxedo Junction: YSL, Ralph square off. (1994, April 28). *Women's Wear Daily*, pp. 1, 15.

U4ia contributing to creativity. (1999, Vol. 2). *Lectra Mag*, pp. 8–9.

Weldon, Kristi. Identifying expert CAD users. (1999, October). *Apparel Industry Magazine*, pp. 38–44.

Wilson, Eric. (1999, November 2) The culture of copycats. *Women's Wear Daily*, pp. 8–9.

Step 1: Research

↓

Step 2: Design

↓

Step 3: Design Development and Style Selection

Make First Pattern
↓
Cut and Sew Prototype
↓
Approve Prototype Fit, Revise Style or Drop Style
↓
Estimate Initial Cost
↓
Present and Review Line
↓
Select Styles for Final Line (Final Adoption)
↓
Determine the Final Cost
↓
Order Fabric for Sales Samples
↓
Order Sales Samples

↓

Step 4: Marketing an Apparel Line

↓

Step 5: Preproduction Processes

↓

Step 6: Sourcing

↓

Step 7: Apparel Production Processes
and Quality Assurance

↓

Step 8: Distribution and Retailing

CHAPTER 7

Design
Development and
Style
Selection

IN THIS CHAPTER YOU WILL LEARN:

- The steps required to develop a sketch into a prototype garment and to prepare the garment for design team review.

- The advantages and disadvantages of using a computer pattern design system for pattern making.

- Reasons why a style might be eliminated from the line during the review process.

- Style factors that influence the estimated cost of a new garment style.

- The relationships among traditional design development and private label and store brand product development.

At this point in the design process, the line for the new season consists of a group of sketches with fabric swatches that have made it through the design team's preliminary selection process. This chapter discusses the next stages in the process (see Figure 7.1). The first pattern is developed from the designer's sketch, swatch, and garment specification sheet, and the prototype garment is cut and sewn from the first pattern. The prototype is then tried on a fit model whose body measurements match the company's size standard. The designer, merchandiser, pattern maker, and production engineer analyze the fit and design and discuss cost factors. An initial cost estimate is calculated. The cost estimate is an important factor in deciding the feasibility of producing the style. At this point, changes may be made to the prototype, or perhaps the pattern will be modified and a new prototype will be cut and sewn. This process continues with all the styles for the line. The styles in the line are reviewed, and final decisions are made to determine which styles will be included in the final line. Seeing the development of a new style from its sketch (or the first drape) to a finished prototype is an exciting part of the design process. On the other hand, it can be a difficult decision to cut some styles from the line after seeing the prototypes and liking all of them.

This chapter focuses on the development process typically used by apparel companies that manufacture brand merchandise. This is apparel whose brand labels are well recognized by the public, including Levi Strauss & Co., Liz Claiborne, Calvin Klein, NIKE, and Jantzen. Later in the chapter, private label and store brand product

Step 3: Design Development and Style Selection

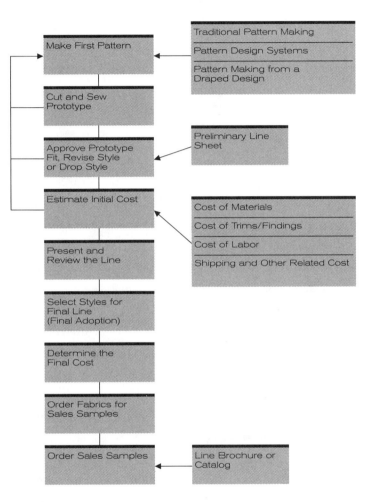

Figure 7.1: Step 3: Design Development and Style Selection

development processes are discussed. Increased vertical integration and changes in the design-retail relationship during the 1980s led to the growth and expansion of this alternative product development process. With private label and store brand product development, retailers are a part of the design team and/or are in charge of the manufacturing process. Such changing roles and relationships among design, production, and retail will continue in our complex economic market.

Design Development

The design development stage of creating a line occurs within the design development department of an apparel company. Other names for this department include *design department* and *product development department*. Design development teams in this department include designers, assistant designers (also called *design assistants*) and *product developers* (also called *technical designers*). Merchandisers may also be part of the design department. At some companies, the pattern makers and production engineers (also called *cost engineers* or *product technicians*) are a part of the design development team. If the apparel company also has production pattern makers, they may be a part of the design development department. At other companies, a pattern development department may be separate from the design development department.

As discussed in Chapter 6, designers sketch, by hand or by using a CAD or graphics system, an idea for a new style as the preliminary design step (see Figure 7.2). After the design team has approved the style for development, the designer's sketch, fabric swatch, and garment specification sheet are delivered to the design development department to begin the pattern making process. In the case of apparel manufacturers that use contractors, the first pattern may be developed by the contractor, or the pattern may be developed by the apparel manufacturer. The responsibility for developing the first pattern is fairly common for contractors who provide full-package (FP) contractor services.

Other designers prefer to drape the preliminary design idea using either muslin or a fashion fabric on a mannequin or dress form (see Chapter 6). After careful markings have been made, the fabric pieces of the draped design are removed from the mannequin. The "drape" is then ready for pattern making.

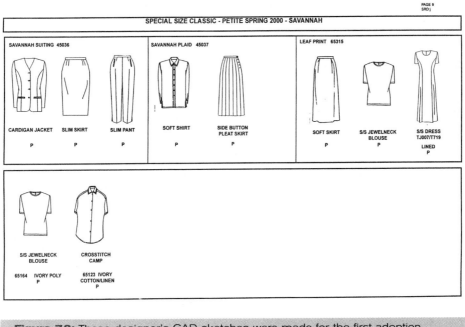

PAGE 9
SRD j

| SPECIAL SIZE CLASSIC - PETITE SPRING 2000 - SAVANNAH |

SAVANNAH SUITING 45036

CARDIGAN JACKET   SLIM SKIRT   SLIM PANT

P   P   P

SAVANNAH PLAID 45037

SOFT SHIRT   SIDE BUTTON
                   PLEAT SKIRT

P   P

LEAF PRINT 65315

SOFT SKIRT   S/S JEWELNECK   S/S DRESS
              BLOUSE   TJ007/T719

P   P   LINED
                               P

S/S JEWELNECK   CROSSTITCH
BLOUSE   CAMP

65164   IVORY POLY   65123 IVORY
        P   COTTON/LINEN
                      P

Figure 7.2: These designer's CAD sketches were made for the first adoption meeting.

MAKING THE FIRST PATTERN

As noted earlier, some apparel manufacturers develop the line, create the design sketches with accompanying fabric swatches, and write the garment specification sheet. They then use either domestic or off-shore contractors to manufacture the garments. (These firms are called *CMT contractors* because they cut, make, and trim the garments.) The steps between, those involving the making of the pattern and cutting and sewing the **prototype** or sample, may be performed by either the apparel company or the contractor.

It may be advantageous for those apparel companies that use contractors to retain the capability to develop the pattern and prototype in-house because schedule delays and communication and visual interpretation problems are possible when a contractor develops the pattern and prototype. A number of factors must be considered by each apparel manufacturer regarding the pattern making, grading, and marker-making responsibilities. One of the potential problem areas when using contractors for pattern making has to do with the base pattern used. Two contractors producing different styles for the same line might not use identical base patterns for pattern making. This can cause differences in the fit of the finished stylized garments between a style produced by one contractor and another style produced by another contractor. More offshore contractors now have computer pattern making systems that eliminate many of the problems apparel companies previously encountered when they had contractors perform the pattern making functions.

At some companies, the designer is also the first pattern maker. This tends to be the case in very small companies or in some specialty areas, such as children's wear. Some designers enjoy being involved in the development of their design ideas from sketches into patterns and then prototypes. Some designers find that their design ideas evolve during development and that they modify the design during the process of making the pattern and/or sewing the prototype.

The pattern maker may work with traditional paper patterns, or the pattern might be created using a computer-aided design system. There are similarities and differences between these methods, and both methods will be discussed.

Traditional Pattern Making

From the designer's sketch, the assistant designer or pattern maker begins the pattern making process, called **flat pattern** design. The pattern maker's role is critical to the accurate translation of the designer's idea. It is important that the pattern maker accurately assesses from the sketch the overall silhouette desired, the amount of ease (from very snug to very oversized), and the designer's desired proportions for the design details. An existing pattern is used to begin the new design. This pattern could be a **base pattern** (also called a **block** or a **sloper**) in the company's sample size. For example, a basic shirt block might be used as the base pattern for a new shirt style. The pattern maker creates the new pattern by adding pattern design details such as a collar, pocket, button band, back yoke, and sleeve pleats to the base pattern as indicated in the designer's sketch.

Another process frequently used by the pattern maker is to select a similar style from a previous season. For example, a shirt style for a new season might be similar to a pattern that has already been made for a previous season. Modifying an existing pattern can be the fastest way to create the pattern for the new style. Selecting the most appropriate previous style for the starting point of a new style may require some discussion between the assistant designer or pattern maker and the designer. Or the designer might make a note on the design sketch suggesting a previous style from which to begin.

The base patterns as well as stylized patterns are often made of a heavy paper called **tagboard**, *oaktag*, or *hard paper* (see Figure 7.3). (It is similar in weight to the paper used for file folders.) This heavy paper is sturdy and the edges can be traced rapidly to copy a pattern as the beginning point for the new pattern. Traditional pattern-making procedures require either that the pattern maker trace the base pattern onto pattern paper, called *soft paper* or that new patterns be made directly onto new tagboard. Style details are developed, collars can be created, new sleeves

Figure 7.3: Tagboard patterns from previous seasons are used as reference for making patterns for new styles.

designed, and pleats or gathers added in order to create the pattern pieces for the new style.

The intended fabric for the final garment is an important consideration during pattern making. For example, the amount of gathers to incorporate into a sleeve depends on the hand, or tactile qualities, of the fabric specified by the designer. The pattern maker may experiment by gathering a section of the intended fabric or a facsimile fabric to better determine the ideal quantity of gathers. To develop patterns for garments made from stretch fabrics, it is necessary to know the exact amount of stretch of the fabric in all directions. The pattern maker selects the base pattern or previous style pattern to correspond to the specific stretch factor of the intended fabric for the new style. Fabric shrinkage is another pattern making consideration. After the fabric sample has been wash tested to determine accurately its shrinkage in all directions, the pattern is made sufficiently larger to account for the shrinkage factor. All pattern pieces are expanded based on accurate length and width shrinkage ratios. The pattern maker not only needs pattern making expertise to translate a garment illustration into a pattern, but also must be knowledgeable about production aspects so the style can be made easily and cost effectively in the factories.

Pattern Making Using Computers

A computer pattern design system can be a part of an overall CAD system. Computer pattern making has been in use by some apparel companies since the early 1980s. Many apparel companies use **pattern design systems (PDS)** for some or all of the pattern making functions (see Figure 7.4). The computer pattern making process is similar to the flat-pattern process previously discussed. The base patterns and all previous style patterns are stored in the computer's memory. To begin a new style, either a base pattern, or the pattern pieces for a similar style from a previous season is pulled from the computer's memory and appears on the screen. The pattern maker uses a mouse, cursor, or stylus (which looks similar to a pen) to select specific areas to change on the pattern. Pattern making commands are either selected from a menu shown on the screen or typed on a keyboard. Once the pattern making is completed, the pattern can be plotted (drawn) in full size (see Figure 7.5).

New computer technology continues to bring remarkable advances in the ease of use, adaptability, and cost effectiveness ("CAD users report payback within one year," 1993). Some of the advantages and disadvantage of PDS are discussed below.

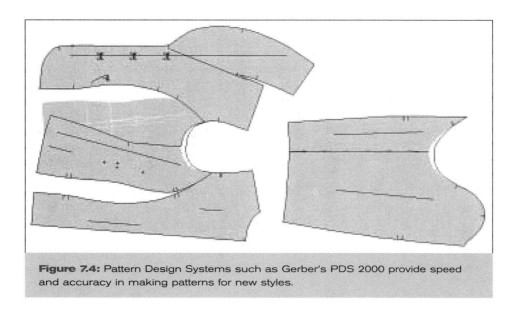

Figure 7.4: Pattern Design Systems such as Gerber's PDS 2000 provide speed and accuracy in making patterns for new styles.

Advantages of PDS

Speed.   Since the base patterns and patterns from previous styles are stored in the computer's memory and used to begin the pattern for a new style, no tracing of an existing pattern is required. Tedious pattern making tasks, such as tracing a pattern piece to make a facing, are accomplished with a fast copy command. The pattern making programs add specified seam allowances and hem allowances to selected edges very quickly. The lengths of two seam lines that need to match can be compared for accuracy with a computer command. Markings and labels such as grainlines and notches are stored in a special "library" and can be quickly added to the pattern pieces. To add gathers, the pattern maker indicates where and how much the pattern should be enlarged, and the pattern piece is spread to insert gathers instantly. A paper pattern, on the other hand, must be slashed in several

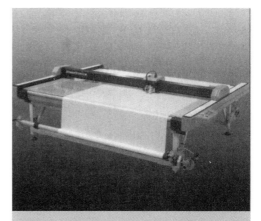

Figure 7.5: After a pattern is completed on the pattern design system, the pattern pieces are drawn full size on a plotter.

places, then spread in order to insert additional width or length for gathers. If the design is modified later in the design process, changes in the pattern can be made more quickly by PDS than they usually can with a paper pattern. Another advantage of using a PDS system that enhances the speed of pattern making is its capability to adjust other pattern pieces automatically. "On a woman's jacket, for instance, changes could be made simultaneously to the shell, lining and facings" (Staff Report, 1998, p. 78).

Accuracy. Using PDS eliminates the incremental growth that can occur when hand tracing a pattern due to the thickness of the pencil lead. Seam lengths and seam allowance widths are more exact than is possible by hand. By always using a stored pattern for the base pattern, consistency in pattern design across all styles is assured. When the pattern maker makes a modification in one pattern piece that affects other pattern pieces, some PDS software programs make an automatic change in the corresponding pattern piece(s). For example, if a change is made in the front side seam length, the back side seam length is automatically corrected. This can greatly reduce potential errors as well as increase the speed of pattern making.

Improved Ergonomics. Sitting or standing at a computer workstation can be easier on the body than bending over a pattern table. It is usually not necessary for the pattern maker to cut out soft or hard paper patterns when making a pattern by computer, saving wear and tear on the hands.

Integration with Spec Sheets. There are computer software programs that provide an interface between the pattern making process and the **garment specification sheet**. One system allows the pattern maker to write parts of the spec sheet as the pattern is being made on PDS. A file of potential sewing steps is retrieved and edited on one screen while the pattern is being made and viewed on another screen. The measurement specifications can also be written during the pattern making process. With some PDS software programs, the widths and lengths of the pattern being made in the sample size can be requested at any time during the pattern making process. This information is the basis for the completion of the measurement specifications (which are discussed in more detail in Chapter 9). The possibility of an error in the spec sheet is reduced when the pattern maker writes the spec sheet simultaneously with making the pattern.

Integration with Production. Later in the product development process, production is faster if the pattern pieces have been stored in the computer than when it is necessary to input the pattern pieces for computerized grading and marker making. These processes will be discussed in Chapter 9.

Product Information Management (PIM). The sharing of data between patterns and garment specification sheets and between patterns and production are two examples of **product information management.** The ability to share product databases electronically among all departments seamlessly integrates the business and manufacturing systems (Hill, 1999, February). All information about each style can be shared electronically by all departments. This in turn speeds the product through production and reduces the possibility of errors (see Chapter 9 for additional discussion).

Although the advantages of PDS are many, some pattern makers and company executives note that there are disadvantages.

Disadvantages of PDS

Cost. The initial cost of a PDS workstation is high, although some of the new technology systems cost less than earlier versions. Some apparel manufacturers, especially smaller companies, may not see a substantial return on their investment for a number of years. If a company produces only a limited number of new styles per season, PDS will not be utilized to its maximum. Another aspect of cost has to do with training pattern makers. Typically, pattern makers are sent to the computer software company's headquarters for a week or two of intensive training on the system. In addition to the dollar cost of the training, there is the cost of lost time while training occurs and the greater time required to make patterns while the new system is being mastered. During the transition time, some pattern styles may still be made on the table from existing patterns, while some new styles will be made on PDS and stored in the computer. Thus, both PDS and paper patterns will be used for a while, which can create complications.

Visualization Difficulties. For pattern makers who are used to working with full-size patterns, the use of PDS requires an adjustment because they are looking at reduced-size pattern parts on the computer screen. When working by hand, the pattern maker slashes the pattern for gathers and spreads the pattern the desired amount. These decisions often are based on what *looks* correct. When pattern makers use PDS, they select the quantity of gathers to add. The pattern, with the selected quantity of gathers, then appears on the screen. In other words, the pattern maker must choose the quantity before seeing how the pattern looks. However, if the quantity of gathers seems too great or too small, it takes very little time with PDS to undo the maneuver and request a different quantity of gathers. With experience it becomes easier for pattern makers to visualize scale using PDS.

User Friendliness.   One of the hurdles with learning a computer software system is memorizing the commands and the various steps needed to complete a process. Some of the early PDS systems were not user friendly. Recently, great strides have been made in the language used for commands, and in the use of "real size" pattern tables instead of smaller sensitized screen areas for pattern making. For example, the AccuMark Silhouette and PDS 2000 PDS systems by Gerber Technology allow pattern makers to work from full-scale patterns on a special sensitized pattern table. This system can reduce the time it may take pattern makers to feel comfortable with PDS.

"Down" Time.   For apparel companies located in very large cities, expert service representatives may be a quick phone call away when a computer system malfunctions or "goes down." However, for some companies, a malfunctioning workstation can cause great problems and affect the subsequent production steps. Any delays can be extremely costly to the manufacturer and retailer.

Ergonomic Problems.   There are a number of ergonomic problems with computers. Repetitive strain injuries (RSIs) such as carpal tunnel syndrome, a wrist injury, may result from long hours at the computer, certain wrist and body positions while using a keyboard or a mouse, and other factors. It is important that the keyboard, monitor, and mouse be at the correct heights for the individual and that he or she have an ergonomically designed, easily adjustable chair and good light. Frequent, short breaks can also help prevent injuries.

In the future, an increased number of apparel companies will use PDS. Cost of PDS workstations has been reduced as more price competition among CAD companies has developed and technology costs have decreased. Newer workstations operate with standard computer industry PCs, providing more price competition. Most large apparel manufacturers already rely completely on computer-generated pattern making.

Pattern Making from a Draped Design

As discussed in Chapter 6, some designers, especially in the designer and bridge wholesale price zones, create the initial garment by draping the design on a mannequin. The fabric, either expensive fashion fabric or muslin, is draped onto the sample-size mannequin. The design is developed by cutting into the fabric, molding the fabric to the desired shape, and then pinning the fabric in place. After finalizing all aspects of the design, the style lines and construction details of the drape are very carefully marked in preparation for removal from the mannequin. The fabric pieces are removed and laid flat over pattern paper. The shapes of the pattern pieces are traced onto paper, then the pattern is perfected and markings such as grainlines, notches, buttonholes, correct seam and hem allowances, and facings are added.

Regardless of the procedure by which the pattern is made—by using traditional flat pattern design, by using PDS, or from a draped design—the full-scale final pattern of the style is now ready to be cut and sewn into a prototype for style review.

MAKING THE PROTOTYPE OR SAMPLE GARMENT

The next step in the design development process is to cut and sew the prototype or sample garment.

As mentioned in Chapter 6, some apparel companies use computer software systems to create three-dimensional replicas of the styles in the line that show simulated fabrics draped on the mannequin. Rather than continuing the development process by cutting and sewing the sample, some companies use these computer-generated images to sell the styles to the retail buyers. This marketing process will be discussed later as well.

The prototype made from the first pattern for the new style may be cut and sewn by an in-house sample sewing department, or it might be made by a contractor. When patterns made by an apparel company on a PDS system are used by contractors that have compatible computer systems, the pattern can be sent electronically to the contractor.

Sample Sewing

The completed pattern is delivered to the **sample sewing department**, accompanied by a swatch of the intended fabric for the actual garment and the garment specification sheet. If the intended fabric is available (sometimes as a sample cut ordered from the textile mill), it will be used to make the prototype garment. Sometimes the intended fabric is not yet available, so a substitute or facsimile fabric, as similar as possible to the intended fabric, will be used (see Figure 7.6).

The garment spec sheet will indicate any special cutting instructions. For example, a shirt with back yoke may require that the shirt's striped fabric be cut on the lengthwise grain for the body, sleeves, and collar and on the crosswise grain for the yoke. Stretch fabrics for swimwear and body wear may require some pattern pieces to be cut with the greatest stretch in the horizontal direction and other pattern pieces to be cut with the greatest stretch in the vertical direction. The sample cutter will match plaids where specified and make other decisions about how the pattern pieces are laid on the fabric (*layout*). The sample cutter will cut all pieces needed for the prototype, including pocketing, interfacings, and linings (see Figure 7.7). The pattern is removed from the fabric after cutting, then the pattern is usually returned to the design development department rather than accompanying the fabric pieces of the prototype through the sample-sewing process.

The **sample sewer** is highly skilled in the use of a variety of sewing machines as well as in the production processes used in factories. Without an instruction sheet

Figure 7.6: A new style may be developed using a substitute fabric before a prototype is made in fashion fabric.

Figure 7.7: The sample cutter is used to cut the garment pieces for the sample or prototype.

and rarely consulting the pattern pieces, the sample sewer sews the entire prototype garment. The sample sewer moves from one piece of equipment to the next, until the garment is finished. The sample sewer may need to send a section of a prototype to another area for work. For example, it may be necessary to embroider a logo onto a shirt front after it is cut out and before the shirt is sewn. Keeping the work flowing smoothly is also part of the process. Generally, for companies that produce prototypes in-house, the prototype is completed within a few days after cutting.

If the design development department is located near the sample-sewing room, the sample sewer might consult with the pattern maker regarding a specific sewing process or technique, or they may discuss possible alternative solutions to a pattern or construction problem (see Figure 7.8). A team approach among pattern maker, cutter, and sample sewer is an advantage. After the sample sewer finishes making the prototype, it is sent back to the design development department for evaluation. Often the pattern maker reviews the prototype first to assess whether any changes need to be made before the style is reviewed by the designer and merchandiser.

Approving the Prototype

The fit of the company's products is important in achieving a competitive advantage through product differentiation. Therefore, an assessment of how each style fits can be very important to a company. A **fit model** is used to assess the fit, styling, and overall look of the new prototype. The fit model is a person selected to represent the body proportions that the apparel company feels are ideal for its target customer and that correspond to the base pattern size used to make the prototype. Some fit models, called *in-house models*, may work for the company in another capacity and are asked to try on prototypes as needed as a part of their job duties. Other companies hire a professional fit model who may work for a number of

Figure 7.8: The pattern maker and the sample sewer discuss possible alternatives for a pocket detail.

apparel companies. With professional fit models, specific appointments will be made for fit sessions, requiring both lead time to book the appointment and on-time delivery of prototypes for the fit session. Fit models can provide valuable information about the comfort and ease of the garment.

Men's wear fit models tend to have well-proportioned bodies and usually are about 5 feet, 10 inches to 6 feet tall. In missy apparel, fit models differ from runway models and photographic models. A missy fit model has body proportions that are "average," with a height of 5 feet, 5 inches to 5 feet, 8 inches, as compared to the tall and svelte runway models. Large-size, tall, and petite fit models are used for their respective size categories. In children's wear, the fit model outgrows the sample size very quickly, requiring that the apparel company search for a new fit model every few months.

In junior and missy apparel, there are wide variations among apparel companies in the body dimensions for one size (Workman, 1991). For a pant created to fit an individual with a 25-inch waist, one company may use a 36-inch hip measurement for its size standard and another company may use a 37-inch hip measurement. The pattern's crotch depth measurement may also differ among companies. Finding the "perfect" fit model for an apparel company can be a challenge, especially for swimwear and inner wear companies, which make garments that fit closely to the body. The model's cup size and bust contour are factors in selecting the fit model. Some fit models are in very high demand, especially in the more populous market centers.

When several prototypes are ready for assessment, a fit session is scheduled with the fit model. While the garment fit is a part of the assessment, much of the discussion among designer, assistant designer, and pattern maker may focus on the prototype's overall style and garment details. Sometimes production engineers are asked to provide feedback about potential difficulties in factory production of the style. If any of these aspects need revision, either the existing prototype will be redone or the pattern will be revised and a new prototype will be cut and sewn. The final design will be approved by the designer and/or the merchandiser. The style might be eliminated from the line at this point if reworking the design does not seem feasible.

After the prototype has been completed, a wash test might be performed on the finished garment using a typical washer and dryer used for home laundering. The wash test performed on garments to be sold in other countries would use the type of laundering equipment used by the customer in those countries to simulate the conditions under which the garment will be laundered. Occasionally, problems arise after laundering a garment that were not evident when the individual fabrics or trims were tested.

Of course, new fabrics under consideration are tested for such properties as colorfastness, crocking, pilling, and abrasion early in the design process. Sometimes an independent testing laboratory is used to perform specified textile tests on a new fabric being considered for adoption. Some apparel companies maintain their own testing labs that might conduct both textile testing and garment testing.

Preliminary Line Sheet

A tech drawing of each new style in the group or line will be used to develop a **preliminary line sheet** showing all the styles in the line (see Figure 7.9). Fabric swatches and other pertinent details might also be listed. The line sheet is used within the department to help all the team members keep track of the styles in the group as they are developed. The preliminary line sheet will become the basis for the development of the line brochure, or line catalog, used later to market the line.

DETERMINING THE INITIAL COST ESTIMATE

The cost to mass produce the style is an important consideration in the selection of styles for the final line. Thus, preliminary costing needs to be done prior to the decision to adopt or reject a style. An **initial cost estimate** (also called *precosting*) for the style is based primarily on material cost and labor cost.

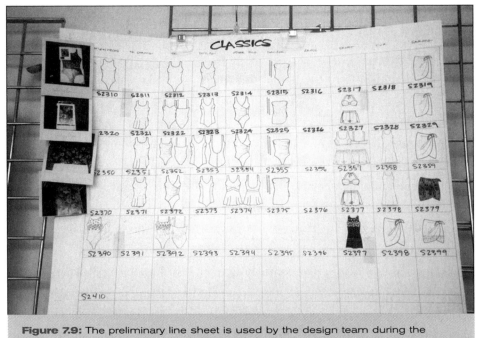

Figure 7.9: The preliminary line sheet is used by the design team during the development process of the line.

Material Cost

The cost of the materials is estimated based on the number of yards of fabric required to make the prototype. Included in the cost of materials are interfacing, pocketing, and lining needed for the prototype. To calculate the quantity of yardage required to make a new style, a layout plan of the pattern pieces called a **marker** needs to be made. The term **costing marker** refers to the layout plan for the pattern pieces that are used to determine the yardage (called **usage**) to produce one garment of the new style (see Figure 7.10). If the pattern was made using PDS, the pattern pieces for this style have been stored in the computer and can be brought into a computer program that is used

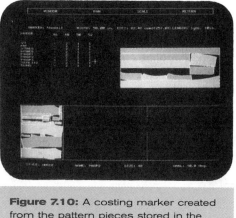

Figure 7.10: A costing marker created from the pattern pieces stored in the Pattern Design System is used to determine the quantity of material required for one garment.

to develop the costing marker. The pattern pieces are arranged by using the mouse or stylus and are viewed on the computer screen within a rectangular space representing the width and length of the intended fabric. Various layouts can be analyzed to determine the best arrangement of pattern pieces using the least quantity of fabric. This process is repeated for the lining and other materials required.

In theory, the quantity of the various fabrics needed to produce one medium-size garment multiplied by the apparel company's cost for the fabrics and trims is used to arrive at a total materials cost. If the company produces the same number of small sizes and large sizes as medium sizes, then using the size medium to average the quantity of fabrics and trims needed should provide a good estimate of the yardage. However, if the company in fact sells many more size small items than size large items, the "average" cost of materials would be higher than the actual cost. Conversely, if many more large-large size items were sold than small-small size items, then the average cost of materials would be too low. Therefore, some companies may use another size to calculate their "average" usage.

Trim and Findings Cost

The quantity of all trims and findings used for the style must be included in the initial cost estimate. Examples of trim items include braid or lace, and findings include items such as elastic, zipper, and buttons. For the initial cost estimate for the cotton pants shown in Table 7.1, one button and one zipper were needed to make this style. Note that the cost of one button is based on the cost of one item when a gross of buttons would be ordered.

TABLE 7.1

Cost to Manufacture a Pair of Cotton Pants in the U.S.

Style # 8074

	Quantity	Price	Amount	Subtotal
1. Material				
fabric	1.7 yd.	$2.90	$4.93	
interfacing	0.2 yd.	$0.55	$0.11	
ship fabric to company		$0.20/yd.	$0.34	($0.20 x 1.7 yd.)
Total Material Cost				**$5.38**
2. Trim/Findings				
buttons	1	$2.00/gross	$0.02	
zipper 7"	1	$0.13	$0.13	
Total Trim/Findings Cost				**$0.15**
3. Labor				
marking ($45)		$0.23		
grading ($70)		$0.35		
cutting ($75 for 200 units)		$0.38		
sewing labor 0.5 hour @ $10.00/hr.		$5.00		
Total Labor Cost				**$5.96**
4. Other				
packaging/hanger, hangtag, labels		$0.15		
freight		$0.35		
duty (none, U.S. production)		$0.00		
shipping agent, consolidator fees (none)		$0.00		
				$0.50
5. Cost to Manufacture			**TOTAL**	**$11.99**
■ WHOLESALE PRICE*				

*Manufacturer determines wholesale price to include overhead and profit.

Labor Cost

The other major component of the initial cost estimate is the cost of labor to cut and sew the style. The labor cost is determined by estimating the number of minutes required to cut and sew the garment multiplied by the cost per minute of labor for a specific sewing factory. For an accurate labor cost estimate, it is necessary to select a possible site for production since labor costs vary considerably around the world. In some countries, the labor cost varies month by month. One approach to estimating the labor cost for a new style is to use the known cost of labor to sew a similar garment from the previous season. However, due to economic and political conditions, it may not be feasible to use the same factory that produced a similar style for the previous season. At this point in the development process, the estimate is just an estimate. An exact cost will be calculated later. As production time nears, costs might be researched in several countries to select the source country for the best production cost (see Chapter 10). Shipping and other related costs, discussed later, need to be estimated and added to the initial cost estimate as well.

Other

When establishing the initial cost estimate, it is necessary to include other items that affect the cost. Table 7.1 details some of these items: packaging and/or hanger, hangtags, labels, and freight charges. If a style is produced offshore, other costs might include duty charges and fees to shipping agents and freight consolidators.

Target Costing

Designing a product based on **target costing** (also discussed in Chapter 6) works a little differently from the product development sequence discussed previously. Jantzen uses target costing to develop its missy and junior swimwear lines. The designer's sketch is reviewed by the *cost engineer,* called a *product technician.* The cost is carefully estimated from the designer's sketch. The design team works out fabric choices garment details, and construction factors to bring the design within the required cost for the styles in the line. The design sketch is reworked and approved, then a prototype garment is cut, sewn, and approved. Each style that is approved is added to the line, which is composed of five groups with three to four styles in each group.

The costs of material, trim, findings and labor, plus other specific costs, are totaled to determine the initial cost estimate. The cost is used as a determining factor in the next stage in the design development process.

Style Selection

Each style in the new line goes through a similar process of development and costing. When all the styles have received the approval of the designer and merchandiser, the line is ready for design review. Because of the lag time in receiving some fabrics, the review garments may have simulated textile elements in order to visualize the style in the intended fabric. For example, sometimes a print or stripe is painted onto a fabric to simulate the final textile. On occasion, these simulated prototypes are even used for promotional photos, since the difference between the mock-up and the actual garment will not be apparent in the photograph.

PRESENTING AND REVIEWING THE LINE AT THE LINE REVIEW MEETING

On the scheduled calendar date, the new line is presented for review. The merchandiser, designer, assistant designer, production engineer, and any other review team members (such as a selected sales representative) assemble for the line review meeting (see Figure 7.11). Upper management also may be included in the review session. The individual garment styles may be displayed on walls in the conference room (sometimes referred to as the war room. Or fit models may try on the garments to present the styles to the review team.

Sometimes the designer or merchandiser begins the review session with a presentation. Design presentation boards or concept boards may be included as a part of the presentation, showing fabrics, various colorways, inspirational pictures, and garment sketches. The presentation might

Figure 7.11: The design team carefully reviews each style in the line.

include information about the concept or inspiration for the line, about how the styles coordinate or work together, and about the target customer profiles for various styles within the line. It may be to the designer's advantage to "sell" the styles in the line to the company review team.

Each style in the line is reviewed, and questions are asked by the review team to determine how well the style works in areas such as the following:

- **Cost.** Will the estimated cost result in a retail price that is within the range of the target customer's expectation? Is its cost in proportion to that of other similar styles? Are there changes in design that might reduce the cost? Could less expensive buttons be substituted? For companies that do cost averaging among several similar items (see Chapter 6), is this approach feasible?

- **Production.** Are there any potential difficulties in production? Are there changes in design that could make production easier or less expensive? Could a seam be eliminated?

- **Styling.** Does the style fit the "look" of the target customer? Does the styling look too fashion forward or too conservative when compared with the rest of the line? Could pockets be added if this is important to the target customer? Does the style look sufficiently different from competitor's styles?

- **Relationship to Rest of Line.** Does the style work well with other styles in the line? Is there another style so similar that they will compete with each other? Or is the style so different from others so that it looks out of place in the line?

- **Fabric and Trims.** Are there potential problems with the fabric? If the fabric is new to the line, will it snag, pill, or wrinkle? Has the fabric been adequately tested? Are there potential problems with lengthy lead time required for a fabric or high minimum yardage requirements by the textile mill?

Each of these points, as well as others, is discussed by the review team for each of the styles in the line.

SELECTING THE STYLES FOR THE LINE AT THE FINAL ADOPTION MEETING

At the conclusion of the line review meeting, some styles will be eliminated and some changes may be required in a few styles. For styles in which changes are required, patterns are modified and new prototypes sewn and approved. The line is thus honed to develop a tight group of styles with the hope that all styles will sell well at market.

Occasionally, one or more styles are included in a line that the review team specu-
lates may not sell well to the retail buyers. This may be done for several reasons. With
some lines, a color balance is needed when showing the line to retail buyers. For example, although windbreakers that are predominantly white probably will not sell as well
as those in colors, a line without any white may not look appealing to buyers. So one
or several windbreaker styles are included in white to provide a visual balance to the
line. Or a company may want to experiment with a slightly more fashion-forward
look. The line may include one or two jackets with more updated styling than has
been shown in the past to see how the retail buyers react to these styles.

DETERMINING THE COST TO MANUFACTURE

Establishing as accurate a cost as possible is important to the successful financial
outcome of the line. A design that sells well but is underpriced can be a disaster for
the apparel company. The amount that the company calculates will be spent to
make the garment is called the **cost to manufacture**.

The cost to manufacture each of the styles to be shown in the new line must be
determined before showing the line at market. Calculating the cost requires knowledge about production techniques and facilities. Production, or cost, engineers use
known costs as well as estimated costs for unknown factors to arrive at the cost to
manufacture each of the styles. There is always the possibility that a style will actually cost more than was calculated, or perhaps less.

If an apparel company uses contractors for production, they can be asked to (1) examine a prototype garment to provide a cost figure, (2) sew a sample garment, and thus provide a cost figure, or (3) review a complete and detailed spec sheet and provide a firm cost.

The **wholesale price** is the price quoted to the buyers at market and is the amount
the retail store will pay the apparel company for the goods. The wholesale price is the
cost to manufacture the style plus the manufacturer's overhead and profit. Some
apparel companies double the manufacturing cost to arrive at the wholesale price.

Preline

Some apparel companies invite their key retail accounts (those retail buyers who place
large orders with them) to preview the line prior to its introduction at market. The preview is sometimes referred to as **preline**. The line might be composed of actual samples,

or virtual samples shown on the computer. These retail buyers provide their opinion to the apparel company about the potential success of the styles they are shown. Retailers might place orders at this time. Advantages to the apparel company of holding a preline showing include (1) knowing in advance which styles will sell well so it can be ready with an adequate quantity of anticipated successful products and avoid producing poor-selling styles and plan production needs accordingly, (2) maintaining a strong working relationship with key retail accounts, and (3) receiving feedback from retailers about styles that might sell better if changes were made. A disadvantage, though, is that since the styles have not yet been produced in the factory, unknown factors may still emerge that will require later changes in a style buyers have already ordered.

Some companies forecast sales without actual written orders from retailers. For example, black ski pants tend to be constant sellers at market. In advance of orders being placed, the skiwear company may begin production of a certain number of black ski pants to avoid the pressure on production during that industry's very short production season.

Preparation for Market

Now that the new line is ready to be shown to retail buyers, additional **samples** or **duplicates** need to be made so that sales representatives throughout the country or world can sell the line by showing samples to retail store buyers. The marketing process involved in selling the line will be discussed in detail in Chapter 8.

ORDERING AND MAKING SALES SAMPLES

Each sales representative and/or each market center showroom will require a representative group of styles from the new line to show to the retail store buyers. Because of cost limitations, not every style in every colorway will be made for sales representatives' samples, or duplicates. However, line brochures will show all colorways. As soon as the line is final, the styles that will be made as samples to sell the line at market are selected. The quantity of fabric as well as linings, buttons, zippers, and other supplies required for the samples is calculated and ordered. If the textile producer is late in delivering the ordered fabrics, complications in producing the samples on time may occur. Late arrival of fabric could result in the samples not arriving in time for the sales representatives to show at market.

Contractors or the apparel company's sewing factories cut and sew the sample garments. If any production difficulties arise during this small production run, there is an opportunity to make an adjustment to ensure a smooth run during production of the retailer's goods. Late delivery of samples from the sewing facility could also cause complications at market.

The apparel company may also produce a fashion show and visual presentation of all the company's lines at a special event for the company's sales representatives (see Figure 7.12). The purposes of this showing are to create enthusiasm for the new season's goods and to help the sales force sell the line. The line's designer (and merchandiser) may be responsible for producing the line showing. Social events might

Figure 7.12: The line might be shown in a presentation to the company's sales representatives before the line is marketed to retailers.

also be held when the representatives gather for the viewing. Events such as golf or tennis tournaments, that involve friendly competition among the sales representatives build company spirit.

LINE BROCHURE OR CATALOG

As soon as the new line has been finalized, a **line brochure** (also called a *line sheet* or *line catalog*) is prepared. This is a catalog, usually with color illustrations, of all the styles available in the line in the various colorways available for each style. Color photographs of featured styles may also be included. Charts show the sizes and colors available for each style and can serve as order sheets as well. Figure 7.13 shows a typical catalog page. The line brochure is used by sales representatives and buyers

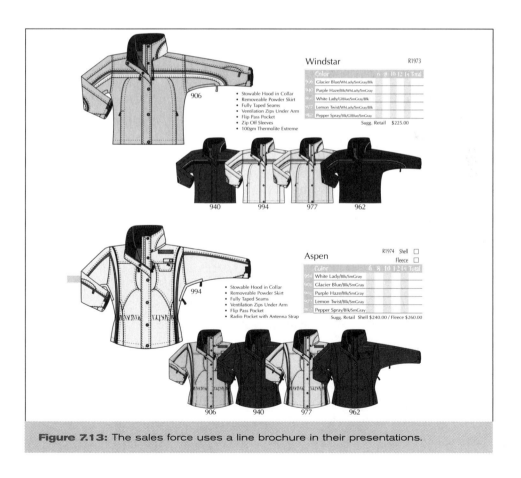

Figure 7.13: The sales force uses a line brochure in their presentations.

to augment the sample garments shown during presentations. More information about the selling process is presented in Chapter 8.

Most companies use specialized CAD or graphics software to produce the color illustrations of the garments for the line brochure. The technical details about scanning the actual fabric prints into these computer systems for the line brochure is discussed in Chapter 6. Typically, if the first sketch used in the design stage was produced using a computer system this sketch is revised as needed for use in the line brochure.

It is important that the line brochure accurately represent the colors of the actual fabrics for each style. Retail buyers expect the finished goods to match the colors depicted in the line brochure. In the early years of computer technology, color printers often made accurate color rendition difficult to achieve. Color printing technology has now improved greatly, as discussed in Chapter 6. Some apparel companies show actual fabric swatches in their line brochures, or send a set of fabric swatches with the brochures. Seeing the actual fabric texture, plaid repeat, or variety of print colorways helps sell the line to the retail buyers.

Private Label and Store Brand Product Development

In today's marketplace, there are a variety of ways in which the creation and development of an apparel line occurs. Possible design-retail relationships include the following:

1. Traditional design development in which the garment carries the brand name or designer brand of the apparel company.

2. Private label or store brand product development through one of the following arrangements:

    a. The retailer provides the garment specifications and the manufacturer or contractor sources the goods (**specification buying**).

    b. The retailer and the manufacturer collaborate in the creation of the retailer's line.

    c. The manufacturer or contractor designs the entire program for the retailer ("Regional Brands," 1996).

It is important to understand the differences between traditional design development and private label or store brand development as they affect the design, production, and pricing strategies for apparel.

We have traced the progress of a style from its creation through its development stages, using a model based on a conventional marketing channel used for brand merchandise in the apparel industry. The apparel company conceives the design, controls manufacturing (using their own factories or contractors they select), and then markets the product to the retailer. The retail buyer evaluates the sample garment and decides whether or not to purchase the style in anticipation of the retailer's target customer desiring the product. A profit is expected at each step of the marketing channel. Conventional design development, marketing, and production involves several profit-making steps, including sewing by a contractor and selling by a sales representative. The final price of the product to the ultimate consumer usually reflects the number of profit-making steps.

As the price of apparel at the retail level has escalated in recent years, retailers and apparel companies have sought ways to reduce costs and increase their share of the profit. Using offshore production in countries with lower labor costs is one solution. Another approach is to reduce the number of steps in the marketing channel. By reducing the number of profit-making steps, either the cost of the product can be reduced or the profit to companies that perform the remaining steps can be increased (or both). If a retailer works directly with an apparel company to cocreate a product or a line, the sales representative's position is no longer needed. If a retailer decides to create a product to sell in its retail stores and goes directly to a sewing contractor, the apparel company's services are not needed. These are examples of **private label product development** or **store brand product development**.

PRIVATE LABEL OR STORE BRAND PRODUCT DEVELOPMENT PROCESSES

Creating private label or store brand merchandise can be achieved in several ways. One method for developing private label or store brand goods is for the retailer to work directly with the manufacturer, sewing contractor, or their agents, providing them with garment specifications. Retailers such as Target and JCPenney that have their own product development departments tend to work directly with contractors to source and produce the goods to their very detailed specifications. Thus, the retailer assumes the responsibility of designing the product, as well as overseeing its production. One advantage to the retailer in dealing directly with the contractor for production is that the retailer has no intermediaries to deal with, thus avoiding communication pitfalls and eliminating the need to share the profits. From the contractor's viewpoint, working directly with the retailer has certain risks. Some of the risks were discussed by the president of Louie Bernard who said, "these scenarios put a lot of risk on the contractor, which serves as the bank" (Moore, 1995, p. 56). The contractor usually carries the financing for the materials during the production process. After delivery of the goods to the retailer, the contractor is paid for both labor and materials. This is different from the conventional marketing channel discussed earlier, in which the apparel company often carries the financing of the materials. As these new marketing channels expand and are modified, the advantages, disadvantages, and risks to contractor and retailer may vary as well. One future trend is that some retailers will own their production facilities.

Another of the private label or store brand development processes uses an apparel company's design and development staff to create the entire program for the retailer. NIKE, an apparel company that produces lines of apparel under its own label, also develops special lines for Foot Locker and Lady Foot Locker retail stores, carrying the retailer's label. This type of collaborative business is very common in the apparel industry. Warner's produces bras for Sears under the Sears label, and Cole of California produces Lands' End swimwear. One advantage to the retailer is that the apparel company handles all the production processes. Often the apparel company has a strong working relationship with vendors, relieving the retailer of the need to develop systems to oversee the production.

The third type of the private label or store brand development process teams a retail partner with a manufacturer in the creation of the retailer's line. In a new development for the retailer, Bloomingdale's has a joint venture with Tahari, a fashion-forward apparel company. They offer complete collections of jackets, skirts, pants, dresses, sweaters, T-shirts and outerwear ("Private label's new identity," 1999, p. 8) in place of more traditional private label merchandise based on single items. The goods produced in this type of venture are called *cobranded apparel*.

EARLY PRIVATE LABEL AND STORE BRAND PRODUCT DEVELOPMENT

The British retailer, Marks & Spencer, has been a leader in private label apparel since its merchandise development department was established. "The company's low prices were the result of trading directly with manufacturers for cash, a principle which remains unchanged to this day. Marks & Spencer's goods are immediately recognized by their

'St. Michael' trademark, which first appeared on 'pajamas and knitted articles of clothing' back in 1928" (Bressler, Newman, & Proctor, 1997, p. 68). Rather than purchasing lingerie items from apparel companies to sell in their retail stores, Marks & Spencer determined the goods it wanted to produce, then went directly to contractors who produced the goods. By eliminating the apparel company's role in the design and manufacturing process, Marks & Spencer's goods could be produced and sold at very appealing prices.

Soon, other retailers began to realize advantages of private label product development. In the 1950s, Hong Kong was well known for manufacturing knitwear, especially sweaters. The quality was good, production dependable, and prices were low. Retailers such as Frederick & Nelson (no longer in business) contracted with knitwear companies in Hong Kong to produce exclusive products such as sweaters for its retail stores. The sweater label read "Made Exclusively for Frederick & Nelson in Hong Kong." This private label product development remained a small part of the specialty and department store retail picture until the 1980s.

GROWTH OF PRIVATE LABEL AND STORE BRAND PRODUCT DEVELOPMENT

The growth of off-price stores and factory outlet mall stores in the 1980s added pressure on department and specialty store retailers to offer products at competitive prices. Added to retailers' pressures was the fact that apparel companies such as Liz Claiborne, Tommy Hilfiger, Polo Ralph Lauren, and NIKE were opening stores of their own. One solution for department store retailers was to increase the percent of private label merchandise they carried. Thus, the private label business continues to expand, both for department store and specialty retailers. According to the research firm NPD Group, "in 1998, private label accounted for 32 percent of total women's apparel sales in the U.S., or $29.3 billion" ("Private label's new identity," 1999, p. 8). Some retailers, such as Saks Fifth Avenue and Federated Department Stores reported private label sales figures accounting for 10 to 15 percent of overall apparel sales. In 1998, Nordstrom reported that private label merchandise accounted for 20 percent of the company's sales (Moriwaki, 1998, p. C4).

As department store retailers expanded their private label business in the early 1990s, most chose to produce basic garment styles such as polo shirts, shorts, casual pants, and jeans, well suited for private label manufacturing. With private label goods, all the risk in selling is in the retailer's hands. The risk to retailers is lessened by the fact that basic goods have a long-term sales potential. Another advantages is that these types of goods make differentiation between a national brand and a private label item difficult to discern. A customer could purchase a private label polo shirt for several dollars less than the national brand shirt that looked nearly identical. The price-conscious customer would eagerly select the private label polo shirt, and be well satisfied with its quality.

Most department stores strive toward a balance between national brands and their private label merchandise. For example, Macy's West offers a variety of private label lines, such as I.N.C., Charter Club, Morgan Taylor, Christopher Hayes, and Austin Grey, in addition to the national brands, such as Levi's, Quiksilver, Koret, and Pendleton (see Figure 7.14). Some retailers link their private label lines to celebrities to enhance the status of the label and the retail store. Kmart offers a Jaclyn Smith label and Wal-Mart sells a Kathie Lee apparel line (see Table 7.2).

As sales volume of private label merchandise has increased, the trend among retailers is to develop more fashion-forward private label merchandise. To do so, retailers have organized product design teams similar to the design teams at apparel companies. "With so much on the line, many retailers have put together design teams to come up with collections, rather than doing it the old way—knocking off last year's looks on the cheap and slapping any old label on the collar" (Steinhauer, 1997, D2). At Federated Department Stores, an entire department is responsible for developing advertising and marketing for its private label brands. The goal is to make the private label "brand" into a well-defined brand in the customer's mind. Mass retailers such as Target and JCPenney have had private label product development departments for years.

Figure 7.14: Private label products can enhance the status of the label and the retailer.

TABLE 7.2
Selected Private Labels

Store	Labels

May Company
    Famous-Barr,
    Meier & Frank,
    Kaufmann's, Filene's
    Foley's, L.S. Ayres,
    Lord & Taylor, ZCMI
	Karen Scott, Valerie Stevens, Claymore

Federated Department
Stores
    The Bon Marche,
    Burdines, Lazarus,
    Rich's
    Bloomingdales
    Goldsmith's
	Adirondack, Saville Row, Austin Grey,
	Charter Club, Christopher Hayes, Jennifer
	Moore, Morgan Taylor, I.N.C., Alfani,
	Style & Co.

Macy's West Macy's East	Aeropostale
Target Corporation Marshall Field's	Country Shop, Field Gear
Mervyn's	Cambridge Classics, Hillard & Hanson, Cheetah, Partners, Sprockets, High Sierra, ellemenno
Target	Greatland, Merona, Mossimo, Xhilaration
Nordstrom	Hickey Freeman, Norsport, Evergreen, Classiques Entier, Baby N, Façonnable, Halogen, Caslon, Talora
Saks Fifth Avenue	Real Clothes, The Works
JCPenney	Hunt Club, Stafford, Towncraft, St. John's Bay, Worthington, Arizona
Kmart	Jaclyn Smith, Knightsbridge, Route 66, Hunter's Glen, Kathy Ireland, Basic Editions, Martha Stewart
Sears	Carriage Court, Fieldmaster, Freeze Frame, Mainframe, Max Active, Laura Scott, Middle- brook Part, Canyon River Blues, Inner Most Intimates
Wal-Mart	Basic Equipment, Kathie Lee, No Boundaries

Chain stores, too, have been heavily stocked in private label goods for a long time. More than 40 percent of women's products are private label at chain stores (D'Innocenzio, 1998). During the 1980s and early 1990s, a number of specialty retailers opened businesses that sell 100 percent private label merchandise, or store brands (see Chapter 4). This strategy, known as *store-is-brand*, results in the retail outlet (i.e., store, catalog, Web site) and the apparel brand being one and the same in the consumer's mind. Examples of companies that employ this strategy include The Limited, Victoria's Secret, Express, Gap, Banana Republic, Old Navy, Casual Corner, Eddie Bauer, Talbot's, and Benetton. As with other retailers that offer private label merchandise, companies that offer only store brands either employ their own designers and/or product developers who turn their designs over to contractors for production or their buyers seek out full-package contractors who design, develop, and produce specified merchandise exclusively for the store. One exception is Benetton, which is a vertical operation, controlling production from fabric to finished garment. With the store-is-brand strategy, the appropriateness of the design, quality, and price of the merchandise for the target customer is imperative to the success of the retailer. Trends indicate that private label and store brand business will continue to expand, giving individuals with expertise in both merchandising management and design additional career options.

ADVANTAGES AND DISADVANTAGES OF PRIVATE LABEL AND STORE BRAND PRODUCT DEVELOPMENT

Retailers decide to offer private label merchandise, expand their private label business, or offer only store brands for many reasons. As noted earlier, one of the major advantages to private label and store brand product development is the reduction in the number of intermediaries involved, providing for increased profit (gross margin) to the retailer and/or reduced price for the consumer. Store differentiation is another reason. National brand merchandise is available at many retail and specialty stores, creating a sameness to these stores' merchandise. Once customers become familiar with retailers' private label brands or store brands, they may choose to shop at that retailer's location because the store merchandise has an appeal and is different from what other stores offer. James Coggin, president of Saks stated, "Our private label initiative is extremely important to Saks Inc. because it provides a way to differentiate ourselves from our competitors and allows us to provide quality merchandise for our customer at a greater gross margin return than normal brands" (Hye, 1999, p. 17). Presenting exclusive merchandise to the customer who wants to associate with the retailer's image is an increasingly important retail trend.

Another advantage of private label and store brand business is that the retailer can fill in voids in some product categories (D'Innocenzio, 1998, p. 14). Also, the customer is looking for value, and private label merchandise can provide that value.

Quality private label products offered at a good price can build and maintain store loyalty and private brand loyalty among customers. And "retailers want increasing control over more aspects of the product than branded manufacturers offer them. That includes at least colors, tailoring and fabrics" (Henricks, 1997, p. 40). And finally, retailers have the closest tie to the customer, to have a finger on the pulse of what the customer really is buying and what she or he wants.

The major drawback to private label and store brand business has been mentioned. The retailer takes all the risk. Since the retailer usually owns the merchandise, if it does not sell well, the retailer loses profit.

Summary

The design development stage in the progress of a new line begins with the delivery of the designer's sketch. Development of the new style includes making the first pattern using either traditional paper pattern making techniques or computerized PDS. An alternative to relying on a designer's sketch is a draped design, in which the designer creates the new style using fabric pinned directly to a mannequin. This drape is then transferred into a paper pattern.

A prototype is cut from the pattern and sewn by a sample sewer, using the intended fabric (or a substitute facsimile if the actual fabric is not yet available). The new prototype is tried on a fit model for review of the design and fit by a design team and is revised if necessary. Sometimes several prototypes of a new style are sewn in order to perfect the design. The cost for the final design is estimated. The line is reviewed again, at which time each style is scrutinized carefully by the design team. The final line consists of styles that have been approved at this stage. Additional samples of styles in the line are sewn for sales representatives, and a line brochure and other types of materials are prepared for marketing purposes.

Computer applications in design development continue to expand. Each year, more apparel companies realize the need to utilize this technology in order to survive in today's marketplace. The computer integration of design, pattern making, and production is another critical step for future survival.

The changing structure of apparel marketing channels will continue to bring changes in the relationship among apparel company, contractor, sales representative, and retailer. Trends in the apparel industry include continued expansion of private label and store brand product development.

CAREER PROFILES

Career opportunities in the development area include assistant designer/pattern maker, cutter or sample sewer or supervisor, or specification technician.

Pattern Engineer
PUBLICLY HELD SPORTSWEAR AND ATHLETIC SHOE COMPANY

Position Description
Create fit-approved and manufacturable patterns from design sketches through CAD patterns ensuring design concepts are correctly interpreted and production capabilities are considered. Manage approximately 90 to 150 styles annually from inception through distribution. Provide construction, specification, and fabric utilization expertise for the design and development of the line.

Typical Tasks and Responsibilities
- Draft prototype patterns on CAD
- Develop preliminary specifications and construction details for sewers and engineers
- Collaborate with design, development, and engineering departments to interpret sketches into cost-effective production styles
- Monitor fit sessions, review garments for measurement accuracy and construction details, revise patterns
- Calculate and provide fabric utilization information throughout the development process
- Oversee the sample making process on assigned styles
- Prepare traced patterns, specifications, construction details, usage and special grading requirements for contractor's samples

Specification Buyer
SPORTSWEAR MANUFACTURER AND RETAILER

Position Description
Responsible for assisting the product engineer in the documentation of all sample reviews and the follow-up communication to vendors relating to specification development, product evaluation, and control of specification files.

Typical Tasks and Responsibilities
- Responsible for fit reviews
- Create specification packages (bill of materials, construction, size specifications)
- Sketch front and back details of garments
- Read electronic mail from product engineer and domestic and overseas vendors
- Tag, log, and track all incoming samples
- Perform engineer's tasks when needed
- Complete counter sample reviews and preproduction reviews

Key Terms

base pattern

block

costing marker

cost to manufacturer

duplicate

fit model

flat pattern

garment specification sheet

initial cost estimate

line brochure

marker

pattern design system (PDS)

preline

preliminary line sheet

private label product development

product development department

product information management

prototype

sample

sample sewer

sample sewing department

sloper

specification buying

store brand product development

tagboard

usage

wholesale price

Discussion Questions

1. How might an apparel company interested in converting from paper pattern making to a pattern design system decide which system to purchase?

2. What are some reasons why a merchandiser for an apparel company might recommend a style be dropped from the line during a line review session?

3. What are some advantages and disadvantages to a retail buyer in viewing an apparel line as virtual samples, as compared with viewing them in a market showroom?

4. What are some advantages and disadvantages to a retailer in producing private label merchandise?

5. What are some advantages to an apparel company in producing a special private label apparel line for a retailer?

References

Bressler, Karen, Newman, Karoline, and Proctor, Gillian. (1997). *A Century of Lingerie*. Edison, NJ: Chartwell Books.

CAD users report payback within one year. (1993, September). *Apparel Industry Magazine*, pp. 76–80.

Computer center opens. (1995, May 24). *Women's Wear Daily*, pp. 22–23.

D'Innocenzio, Anne. (1998, October 7). Punching up private label. *Women's Wear Daily*, pp. 14–15.

Freedman, Linda. (1990, April). New developments in computer-aided draping. *Apparel Manufacturer*, pp. 12–14.

Gilbert, Laurel. (1995, July). CAD comes of age. *Bobbin*, pp. 48–52.

Greco, Monica. (1995, August). CAD intros accommodate multi-systems' integration. *Apparel Industry Magazine*, pp. 64–74.

Henricks, Mark. (1997, October). Convergence 2: Vertical retail. *Apparel Industry Magazine*, pp. 38–46.

Hill, Suzette. (1999, February). Product development: The next QR initiative? *Apparel Industry Magazine*, pp. 48–54, 71.

Hye, Jeanette. (1999, November 17). Saks sources technology for private label. *Women's Wear Daily*, p. 17.

Kurt Salmon Associates. (1996, January). Soft goods outlook for 1996. *Apparel Industry Magazine*, pp. 46–59.

Made to measure or mass customization: Is it for you? (1998, Vol. 18, No. 1) *Cuttings*, pp. 2–6.

Moore, Lila. (1995, April). The two-edged sword. *Apparel Industry Magazine*, pp. 54–60.

Moriwaki, Lee. (1998, August 10). Reconstructing Nordstrom. *Corvallis Gazette-Times*, p. C4.

Private label's new identity. (1999, March 11). *Women's Wear Daily*, pp. 1, 8, 20.

Regional Brands. (1996). *Kurt Salmon Associates Branding Report*.

Staff Report. (1998, November). The final round-up. *Bobbin*, pp. 74–83.

Steinhauer, Jennifer. (1997, September 27). Strutting their own stuff. *The New York Times*, pp. D1–2.

Weldon, Kristi. (1999, October). Identifying expert CAD users. *Apparel Industry Magazine*, pp. 38–44.

Workman, Jane. (1991). Body measurement specifications for fit models as a factor in clothing size variation. *Clothing and Textiles Research Journal*, 10 (1), 31–36.

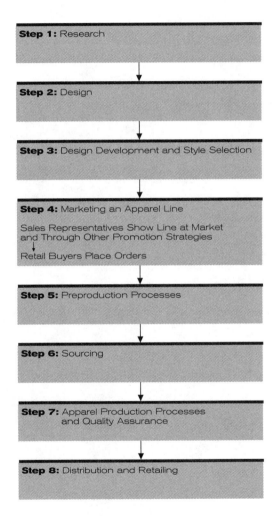

Step 1: Research

Step 2: Design

Step 3: Design Development and Style Selection

Step 4: Marketing an Apparel Line

Sales Representatives Show Line at Market
and Through Other Promotion Strategies

Retail Buyers Place Orders

Step 5: Preproduction Processes

Step 6: Sourcing

Step 7: Apparel Production Processes
and Quality Assurance

Step 8: Distribution and Retailing

CHAPTER 8

Marketing an Apparel Line

IN THIS CHAPTER YOU WILL LEARN:

■ the marketing process within apparel companies.

■ the histories, functions, and activities of U.S. apparel market centers, marts, market weeks, and trade shows.

■ the nature of the selling function of apparel companies, specifically the roles of sales representatives and showrooms.

■ the distribution and sales promotion strategies used by apparel companies.

The Role of Marketing

As discussed in Chapters 4 and 5, the term marketing is used to describe a process that includes the following components:

1. Identifying the target customer.
2. Developing the marketing mix, including the following:
   - The product or service.
   - The pricing strategy.
   - The promotion strategy.
   - The place strategy (where the products are to be sold).

Because most apparel companies approach their business from this marketing orientation, the marketing process has been a part of all stages of line development, from research through production. Using this marketing approach, successful apparel companies have accurately identified and assessed the wants and needs of their target market and produced goods that meet the needs of these consumers. Now the manufacturer must make sure the product gets to the target customer at the appropriate time and place.

Within the organizational structure of an apparel company, the area called *marketing* typically focuses on developing sales, promotion, and distribution strategies (see Chapter 4). Marketing divisions or departments in apparel companies are organized in a number of ways depending on the size and goals of the company. Figure 8.1 shows a variety of organizational structures for marketing divisions of apparel companies. Although the marketing area of an apparel company is most often asso-

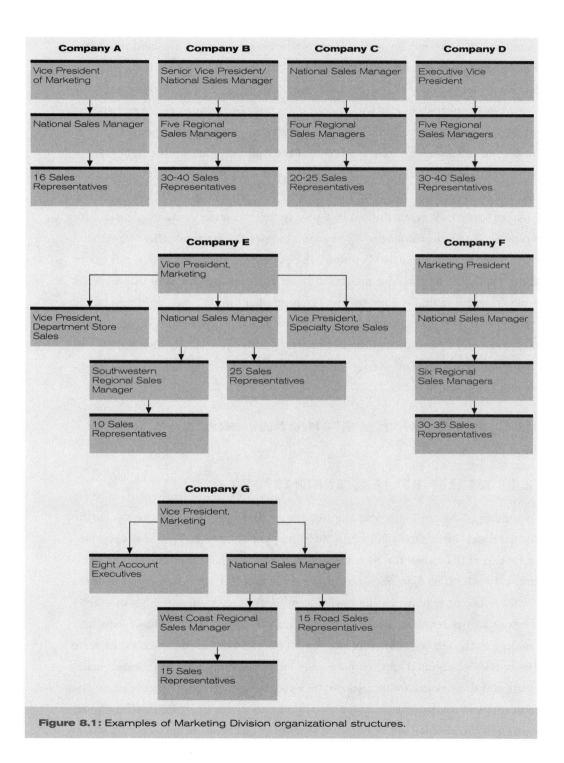

Figure 8.1: Examples of Marketing Division organizational structures.

ciated with the promotion and sales of the products, it should be noted that without an accurate understanding of the target customer and without designing and producing goods and services that meet the needs of the target customer, even the best of promotion strategies will undoubtedly fail. Thus the marketing of apparel products connects the research conducted previously with the appropriate strategies for getting the product to the consumers at the right price and in the right place.

The term **market** can be used in several ways. One may say that a particular product has a market, meaning that there is consumer demand for the product. Chapter 5 discussed research used in assessing the consumer demand or market for a product. The term *market* can also be used to refer to a location where the buying and selling of merchandise takes place. For example, retail buyers often talk about going to market to purchase merchandise for their stores. One can also market a product, meaning that the product will be promoted through the media and public relations efforts. This chapter examines apparel markets as locations where apparel companies sell their merchandise to retailers. It also explores the distribution and promotion strategies that apparel companies use in marketing their goods to retailers and consumers.

Market Centers, Marts, Market Weeks, and Trade Shows

GROWTH OF MARKET CENTERS AND MARTS

Historically, New York City was the first textile and apparel market center in the United States. Buyers from large, upscale stores would travel to New York City once or twice a year to view the new apparel lines and purchase merchandise for their stores. In addition, manufacturers' salespeople would travel from town to town within a specific region inviting buyers from local stores to see the lines in a hotel room or in the retailers' stores. With the growth of apparel manufacturing and retailing in the 1950s, regional market centers began to be established. In the early 1960s, the first regional apparel marts were built. Currently, any city where apparel marts and showrooms are located can be viewed as a market for apparel lines. The term **market center** is sometimes used to refer to those cities that not only house marts and showrooms, but also have important manufacturing and retailing industries. In the United States, these cities include New York City, Los Angeles, Dallas, Atlanta, and Chicago.

Marts

A **mart** is a building or group of buildings that house showrooms in which sales representatives show apparel lines to retail buyers. Most major cities (except for New York) have marts; some are devoted entirely to apparel, accessories, and related goods (e.g., Los Angeles' CaliforniaMart); some also house showrooms for a variety of types of products (e.g., Portland, Oregon's Montgomery Park). Figure 8.2 shows the locations and names of the major market centers and regional marts in the United States. All marts also include exhibition halls that are used during **market weeks** (primary times during the year in which seasonal lines are shown to retail buyers) as temporary showrooms for apparel companies or sales representatives without permanent showrooms at that mart. To facilitate the buyers' trips to market, apparel marts publish directories for market weeks that list the apparel lines being offered, sales representatives, and services available at the mart.

Retail Relations Programs

After experiencing growth throughout the 1980s, most apparel marts have seen business stabilize. Some even saw it decline in the 1990s. As a result, greater competition has led marts to increase efforts to attract buyers through various services designed to make the buyer's job easier. For example, in response to shorter turnaround times and faster delivery of apparel and because buyers are purchasing less merchandise more often, the larger marts are open year round; typically 5 days a week, 52 weeks a year. This allows buyers to come at any time during the year, not just during market weeks.

Most marts currently have ongoing retail relations programs, including a number of services designed to assist retail buyers. These services include educational seminars (e.g., visual merchandising, new merchandising strategies), fashion shows, trunk shows, credit and financing assistance, discounts on travel expenses, and entertainment (e.g., concerts, food fairs). In recent years, a number of marts have offered seminars focusing on international markets. Topics include how to do business in Mexico, labeling requirements for exporting goods, and other issues surrounding exporting.

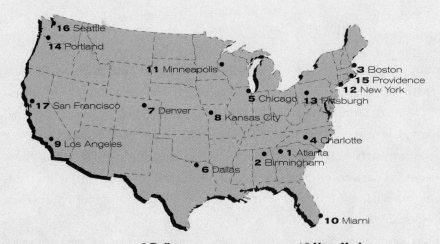

1. **Atlanta**
   Atlanta Apparel Mart
   at the AmericasMart
   250 Spring Street, NW
   Atlanta, GA 30303
   (404) 220-3000
   www.americasmart.com

2. **Birmingham**
   Birmingham Apparel Mart
   at the Birmingham Jefferson
   Civic Center
   One Civic Center Plaza
   Birmingham, AL 35203
   (203) 871-3305

3. **Boston**
   Bayside Merchandise Mart
   at the Bayside Expo Center
   150-160 Mt. Vernon Street
   Boston, MA 02125
   (617) 825-4040
   www.baysideexpo.com

4. **Charlotte**
   Charlotte Apparel Center
   2500 East Independent Boulevard
   Charlotte, NC 28202
   (704) 376-3006

5. **Chicago**
   Chicago Apparel Center
   350 North Orleans Street
   Chicago, IL 60654
   (312) 527-7777

6. **Dallas**
   International Apparel Mart
   International Menswear Mart
   2300 Stemmons Freeway
   Dallas, TX 75258
   (214) 879-8300
   www.dallasmarketcenter.com

7. **Denver**
   Denver Merchandise Mart
   451 East 58th Avenue
   Denver, CO 80216
   (303) 292-6278

8. **Kansas City**
   Kansas City Market Center
   1775 Universal Avenue
   Kansas City, MO 64120
   (816) 241-6200

9. **Los Angeles**
   CaliforniaMart
   110 East Ninth Street
   Los Angeles, CA 90079
   (213) 620-0260
   www.californiamart.com

10. **Miami**
    Miami International
    Merchandise Mart
    777 NW 72nd Avenue
    Miami, FL 33126
    (305) 261-2900
    www.mimm.com

11. **Minneapolis**
    Minneapolis Apparel Market
    Hyatt Merchandise Mart
    1300 Nicolette Mall
    Suite 4052
    Minneapolis, MN 55403
    (612) 333-5219

12. **New York**
    Fashion Center Headquarters
    249 West 39th Street
    New York, NY 10018
    (212) 764-9600
    www.fashioncenter.com

13. **Pittsburgh**
    Pittsburgh Expo Mart
    105 Mall Boulevard
    Monroeville, PA 15146
    (412) 856-8100

14. **Portland**
    Portland Apparel Mart
    Montgomery Park
    2701 NW Vaughn Street
    Portland, OR 97210
    (503) 228-7275

15. **Providence**
    Fashion Jewelry Mart
    3 Davol Square
    Providence, RI 02903
    (401) 331-7630

16. **Seattle**
    Seattle International Trade Center
    2601 Elliot Avenue
    Seattle, WA 98121
    (206) 223-6819

17. **San Francisco**
    Fashion Market San Francisco
    Golden Gate Apparel Association
    Concourse Exhibition Center
    635 Eighth Street
    San Francisco, CA 94103
    (415) 864-1561
    www.fashionsanfrancisco.com

Figure 8.2: U.S. Apparel Markets and Marts.

Although the growth of apparel marts outside of New York City was primarily due to the need for regional market centers, the larger apparel marts (e.g., CaliforniaMart in Los Angeles, International Apparel Mart in Dallas) have become more than regional centers that cater to store buyers in the local area and from surrounding states. Because of their expanded services, they are now considered national and international resources; many marts are working to attract international buyers from Mexico, Canada, Central and South America, Asia, and Europe. In fact, CaliforniaMart now offers on-site Spanish-English interpreter services free to its tenants.

Marts are sometimes viewed as self-contained in that they generally house consultants' offices, restaurants, banks, hotels, auditoriums, health clubs, and other services for retail buyers. Marts may also be involved in many aspects of the apparel industry. For example, the CaliforniaMart includes offices of major trade publications, consumer publications, buying offices, trade associations, and textile manufacturers. Thus, when buyers comes to market, the mart serves as a one-stop location for all of their needs.

MARKET WEEKS AND TRADE SHOWS

Market Weeks

Market weeks are the times of the year when retail buyers come to showrooms or exhibit halls to see the seasonal fashion lines. During market weeks, retail buyers set appointments with manufacturers' sales representatives, discover new lines, attend fashion shows, review manufacturers' lines, and purchase merchandise for their stores. They typically come to market weeks with a specific amount they can spend (referred to as their *open-to-buy*) for specific categories of merchandise. Marts generally sponsor a variety of market weeks throughout the year, each focusing on a particular product category (e.g., women's, juniors, men's, children's, bridal, swimwear, etc.) and fashion season (e.g., fall, holiday, resort, spring, summer). Market week dates are set years in advance in meetings of representatives from the various marts and New York City fashion councils. In general, market weeks for fall fashion season are held in March and April and market weeks for spring fashion season are held in October and November. Market weeks may also be sponsored in conjunction with an industry trade association. For example, the CaliforniaMart fall I market week has been held in conjunction with the International Swimwear/Activewear Market's

(ISAM) swimwear show. Through these joint efforts, buyers are exposed to a greater variety of apparel manufacturers at a single location than they would be otherwise. Table 8.1 outlines the typical months in which U.S. women's and children's ready-to-wear market weeks are held for each fashion season. Table 8.2 gives an annual calendar of typical market weeks and trade show dates.

Market weeks provide advantages for both the apparel manufacturer and the retailer. For the apparel manufacturer, sales representatives can show the new lines to a large number of retail buyers in a very short time. They can talk with the buyers and acquire information regarding retail trends. Based on buyer interest, they also can determine which pieces in the line will eventually be put into production. In addition, through such market week activities as fashion shows, apparel companies can receive publicity for their lines. For retail buyers, market weeks allow them to review a large number of apparel lines in a very short time. By attending seminars held during market weeks, they are also able to acquire information about fashion trends, advertising, visual merchandising, and a number of other topics. In addition, buyers can also become aware of new lines that they may want to purchase for their stores. Thus market weeks are important times for the apparel companies in determining the success of their lines.

Trade Shows

Some trade associations or trade show producers sponsor their own shows for the purpose of promoting lines of apparel or accessories. These trade shows, lasting anywhere from three to eight days, are typically located at large hotels or convention

TABLE 8.1

Women's and Children's RTW Market Weeks

Fashion Season	Market Weeks
Summer	NYC market: October
	All other markets: January
Fall I	NYC market: January
	All other markets: March–April
Fall II	NYC market: February
	All other markets: June
Holiday and Resort	NYC market: June
	All other markets: August
Spring	NYC market: August
	All other markets: October–November

TABLE 8.2
Market Week and Trade Show Calendar

January
United States
New York RTW Market (fall I)	NYC
RTW markets (summer)	LA, Dallas, Chicago, Atlanta, etc.
NY Accessory Market Week	NYC
NY Intimate Apparel Market weeks	NYC
International Fashion Boutique Show (RTW)	NYC
International Kids Fashion Show	NYC
Fashion Accessories Exposition	NYC
Accessories Circuit trade show	NYC
National Association of Men's Sportswear Buyers (NAFSB) Show	NYC

International
Haute Couture Collections (spring)	Paris
Paris Men's Collections	Paris
Alta Moda Roma (couture) Collections (spring)	Rome
Hong Kong Fashion Week	Hong Kong

February
United States
New York RTW market (fall II) into March	NYC
New York Premier Collections (fall I)	NYC
7th on Sixth	NYC
New York Men's Collections	NYC
Super Show (sportswear)	Atlanta
Action Sports Retailer Show	San Diego
MAGIC International	Las Vegas
WWDMAGIC	Las Vegas
MAGICKids	Las Vegas
Fashion Footwear Association of New York (FFANY)	NYC
Fashion Coterie trade show	NYC
Swimwear Association of Florida preview	Miami

International
Igedo (women's RTW, fall)	Dusselfdorf
Interstoff World	Frankfurt

March
United States
RTW markets (fall I) into April	LA, Dallas, Chicago, Atlanta, etc.
NY Accessory Market Week	NYC
NY Intimate Apparel Market Week	NYC
International Fashion Boutique Show	NYC

(continued)

TABLE 8.2 (continued)

International Kids Fashion Show	NYC
International	
Première Vision (fabrics, spring/summer)	Paris
Ideacomo (fabrics, spring/summer) or April	Lake Como
Interstoff Asia (fabrics)	Hong Kong

April
United States

Bridal Market Weeks	NYC, Chicago, Atlanta
NY Home Textile Show	NYC
NY Tabletop Market	NYC
International Swimwear/Activewear (ISAM) Market	LA
International Fashion Fabrics Exhibition (spring/summer)	NYC
New York Menswear Show (NYMS)	NYC
International Textile Show (fabrics)	LA
International	
Interstoff Season (fabrics, spring/summer)	Frankfurt
Igedo (RTW)	Dusseldorf

May
United States

NY Accessory Market Week	NYC
NY Intimate Apparel Market Week	NYC
Fashion Accessories Expo	NYC
Accessorie Circuit (accessories) trade show	NYC

June
United States

NY RTW Market (resort)	NYC
RTW markets (fall II)	LA, Dallas, Chicago, Atlanta, etc.
Fashion Footwear Association NY (FFANY)	NYC
NAMSB Show	NYC
International Fashion Boutique Show	NYC

July
United States

International Swimwear/Activewear Market (ISAM)	LA
NY Menswear Show	NYC
FFANY (shoes)	NYC
International	
Haute Couture Collections (fall/winter)	Paris
Paris Men's Collections	Paris

Alta Moda Roma (couture) collections (fall/winter)	Rome
Hong Kong Fashion Week	Hong Kong

August
United States

NY RTW market (spring)	NYC
RTW markets (resort)	LA, Dallas, Chicago, Atlanta, etc.
NY Accessory Market Week	NYC
NY Intimate Apparel Market Week	NYC
Accessorie Circuit (accessories) trade show	NYC
Fashion Accessories Expo	NYC
International Kids Fashion Show	NYC
International Fashion Boutique Show	NYC
WWDMAGIC (or September)	Las Vegas
Ladies Apparel Show Vegas	Las Vegas
MAGIC International	Las Vegas

September
United States

NY Premier Collections	NYC
Fashion Coterie	NYC
The Bobbin Show (sewn products industry)	Atlanta
Action Sports Retailer Show	San Diego

International

Interstoff World (fabrics, fall/winter)	Frankfurt
Igedo (RTW)	Dusseldorf

October
United States

NY RTW market (summer) into November	NYC
7th on Sixth Women's Shows	NYC
NY Menswear Shows	NYC
RTW markets (spring) into November	LA, Dallas, Chicago, Atlanta, etc.
NYMS (men's)	NYC
NY Tabletop Market	NYC
International Swimwear/Activewear Market (ISAM)	LA
International Fashion Boutique Show	NYC
International Kids Fashion Show	NYC
International Fashion Fabric Exhibition (fall/winter)	NYC
Los Angeles International Textile Show (fall/winter)	LA

(continued)

TABLE 8.2 (continued)

International

Première Vision (fabrics, fall/winter)	Paris
Ideacomo (fabrics, fall/winter)	Lake Como
Interstoff/Asia	Hong Kong

November

United States

NY Intimate Apparel Market Week	NYC
NY Accessory Market Week	NYC
NY Home Textile Show	NYC
Texitalia (fabrics, fall/winter)	NYC
FFANY (shoes)	NYC

International

Igedo (RTW)	Dusseldorf
Interstoff/Season (fabrics)	Frankfurt

December

No shows

Note: Months may vary slightly from year to year

centers. For example, the Accessory Circuit, National Association of Men's sportswear Buyers (NAMSB) show, New York Menswear Show (NYMS), and Fashion Coterie trade shows are often held at The Show Piers on the Hudson in New York City; the Fashion Footwear Association of New York (FFANY) shows are held at the New York Hilton Hotel; and the Ladies Apparel Show Vegas (LAS Vegas) and the Children's Trade Expo Vegas (CTE Vegas) have been held at the Sands Hotel Expo and Convention Center in Las Vegas. The Las Vegas Convention Center has been a growing hub for a number of trade shows, including the Men's Apparel Guild in California (MAGIC) International Show, which moved from Los Angeles for larger quarters, and the women's counterpart, WWDMAGIC. New York's Jacob K. Javits Convention Center is the home of trade shows such as the International Fashion Boutique Show, and the International Fashion Kids Show (see Figures 8.3 and 8.4). Some companies rely heavily on trade shows for presenting their lines; others display their lines primarily during market weeks in New York City and/or apparel marts and may attend only one or two trade shows. Retail buyers may attend both market weeks and trade shows to review lines for their stores. Web sites for trade shows include show information and registration, appointment scheduling, and show evaluations.

In recent years, trade shows have experimented with virtual trade shows through online exhibits of lines, expanding buyers' opportunities to purchase goods over the Internet. However, industry analysts are not anticipating that virtual trade shows will become more popular than face-to-face trade shows anytime in the near future. According to one retail buyer "There's something about seeing a line in person. You can judge the quality, color and texture. I might use the Web to check out T-shirt graphics. For most clothes, I would still want to see it in person" (Feitelberg, 1999, p. 15).

Figure 8.3: Retail buyers attend trade shows such as the International Fashion Boutique Show to review lines from a number of companies.

Figure 8.4: The Men's Apparel Guild in California (MAGIC) is a cosponsor of WWDMAGIC, a trade show of women's apparel and accessories.

U.S. Market Centers

NEW YORK CITY

New York City (NYC) is considered the preeminent U.S. market center for apparel and accessories. As noted in Chapter 1, NYC has a long history and tradition of being the heart of apparel manufacturing and marketing in the United States. Interestingly, NYC is the only U.S. market center that does not have an apparel mart. Instead, showrooms are located throughout a portion of Manhattan known as the *garment district*, the *garment center*, or what NYC refers to as the *fashion center*. NYC's fashion center is an area in midtown Manhattan located between Fifth Avenue and Ninth Avenue and between 35th Street and 41st Street (see Figure 8.5). The central area is between Seventh Avenue (designated *Fashion Avenue* in 1972) and Broadway. The fashion center started as a manufacturing center, but the cost of space in the city has turned it into a

Figure 8.5: New York City's fashion center, located in midtown Manhattan, is the home of thousands of showrooms.

design, marketing, and sales center. Much of the manufacturing now occurs in nearby locations outside Manhattan where costs are lower. However, even today New York State remains one of the largest apparel manufacturing centers in the United States.

Currently the fashion center includes approximately 450 buildings with more than 5,000 fashion industry tenants including showrooms and factories. It is estimated that 22,000 out-of-town buyers visit the fashion center every year. For companies that also have their design headquarters in NYC, showrooms are often in the same building—if not on the same floor—as the design area. Although NYC is the home of marketing efforts for a wide variety of companies, the NYC market is best known for women's apparel and for designer and bridge price zones. Virtually all name designers (e.g., Calvin Klein, Donna Karan, Ralph Lauren, Oscar de la Renta, etc.) have offices in New York and sponsor extravagant runway shows during NYC market weeks. In recent years many designers have held their runway shows in tents in Bryant Park as part of the "7th on Sixth" show, organized by the Council of Fashion Designers of America (see Figure 8.6). In addition to being the home of marketing efforts for a number of companies, New York City is also the home of corporate headquarters for companies such as Danskin, Nautica, Phillips-Van Heusen, Polo Ralph Lauren, Donna Karan International, and Tommy Hilfiger. Corporate headquarters for Liz Claiborne and Marisa Christina can be found in nearby North Bergen, New Jersey.

In an effort to facilitate buyers' trips to NYC, certain buildings have tried to specialize in specific apparel categories. For example, 1411 Broadway houses many swimwear manufacturers. However, despite some attempts to specialize buildings, NYC, in general, is not very convenient for retail buyers who must go from building to building to visit showrooms during their buying trips. Resources for acces-

Figure 8.6: The 7th on Sixth runway shows are a highlight of market weeks in NYC.

sories, for example, are spread throughout the garment district, adding to the inconvenience. Thus in comparing the NYC market with the "regional" apparel marts, NYC is often viewed as less personal and more overwhelming. To add greater convenience for retail buyers, the Fashion Center Business Improvement District (FCBID), funded by owners of property devoted to the garment industry, was created to provide additional services and capital improvements to enhance the fashion center. FCBID activities include administering an information kiosk on the corner of Seventh Avenue and Thirty-ninth Street, publishing the *Fashion Center Black Book* directory of fashion resources, developing a Web site (www.fashioncenter.com), distributing maps with buildings color coded according to primary industry use, and hiring sanitation and security crews to help clean up the area and provide for a safer environment.

Given the fact that the city is expensive, crowded, and inconvenient, why does NYC continue to serve as an important market center? In addition to its historic foundation as a fashion center, NYC offers companies access to buying offices, textile wholesalers, findings and trim wholesalers, consultants, advertising agencies, offices of major trade associations, and publishing companies located in the city. As a cultural center, designers can draw inspiration from the continuous influx of art, theater, dance, opera, and other cultural events. They can also view historic costume and textile collections at the Metropolitan Museum of Art and the Fashion Institute of Technology. In addition, because so many companies have showrooms in NYC, the NYC market remains a "must attend" for many buyers regardless of whether they attend market weeks elsewhere.

LOS ANGELES

Whereas NYC is considered the primary market center on the East Coast, Los Angeles is considered the primary market center on the West Coast. Los Angeles is home to the CaliforniaMart, which opened in 1964 with 700 permanent showrooms. Its 13 floors currently house more than 1,200 showrooms representing 10,000 lines of apparel, accessories, textiles, and home accessories (see Figure 8.7). The New Mart, across the street from the CaliforniaMart, provides additional space and has showrooms for many designers and brand name apparel manufacturers (currently 90 showrooms). The menswear building is home to the California International

Figure 8.7: Los Angeles is the site of the CaliforniaMart, the largest apparel mart on the West Coast.

Menswear Market (CIMM). In addition to men's and women's market weeks, the CaliforniaMart has expanded its niche shows in recent years to include contemporary design collections, the Los Angeles International Textile Show, the International Swimwear and Activewear Market, and accessories, intimate apparel, childrens' wear, and gift shows. As a result of a recent $20 million remodeling, the California-Mart has become one of the most technologically advanced of the market centers. It includes an auditorium, videoconference center, satellite broadcasting studio, and automated "faxback" system by which buyers and other retail executives can receive the most current CaliforniaMart information automatically on their own fax machines. The CaliforniaMart caters to retail buyers primarily in the western and southwestern states (e.g., Arizona, New Mexico, Nevada, Utah, Oregon, Washington, and Idaho), but is now attracting a greater number of international buyers.

Los Angeles also has a large apparel manufacturing industry with 122,500 apparel workers in 1998. This is primarily because of the availability of skilled workers, typically immigrants from Mexico. When we think of California, casual apparel and sportswear come to mind; Los Angeles is best known for sportswear and swimwear manufacturing. Companies with headquarters in the Los Angeles area include Catalina, Ocean Pacific, Guess?, Quiksilver, and BCBG Max Azria, to name a few. Top manufacturers in California in order of sales volume are Levi Strauss & Co., Guess?, Bugle Boy Industries, Hang Ten International, Koret, Byer California, Esprit de Corp, Rampage Clothing Co., Tarrant Apparel Group, and Chorus Line.

CHICAGO

The Chicago Apparel Center caters primarily to the northern and midwestern region of the United States (e.g., Illinois, North Dakota, South Dakota, Minnesota, Michigan, Indiana, Wisconsin, and Iowa). Built in 1977, the Apparel Center is located next to the Chicago Merchandise Mart. The Apparel Center has consolidated apparel showroom space to four and one-half floors allowing five and one-half floors for office space. During market weeks, the Apparel Center's 140,000-square-foot Expo Center can accommodate 500 booths from temporary vendors (see Figure 8.8). Some consider the Apparel Center's bridal market, which now consists of an entire floor with more than 60 manufacturers' showrooms, to be second only to New York's. Chicago is also home to historically significant manufacturers and retailers. The corporate headquarters for Sara Lee (owner of Hanes, Playtex, and Bali), Fruit of the Loom (owner of Fruit of the Loom and Gitano), and Hartmarx, a prominent manufacturer of men's and women's wear, are in Chicago.

Retail institutions such as Sears, Roebuck & Co. are also headquartered in Chicago. To enhance the apparel industry in the Chicago area, in 1995 the Chicago Manufacturing Center (a nonprofit consulting organization for small-to-medium size manufacturers) launched two programs specifically for apparel companies: the Sewn Products Technology Center and the Made in Chicago program. The Tech

Figure 8.8: Chicago Apparel Center.

Center provides consulting, training, and production and management services to companies. The Made in Chicago program offers networking and marketing services. In 1999 the Apparel Center Tenants of Chicago (ACT) formed the Shop Chicago International, a trade association that explores new marketing opportunities (Lee, 1999).

DALLAS

In the south, Dallas has become the key apparel market center. The International Apparel Mart and International Menswear Mart (formerly the Dallas Apparel Mart/Menswear Mart) is part of the Dallas Market Center Complex, which includes other merchandise marts (i.e., The World Trade Center, Trade Mart). The Dallas Apparel Mart opened in 1964, and the Menswear Mart opened in 1982. Currently, the International Apparel Mart and International Menswear Mart houses approximately 1,100 permanent showrooms (1.8 million square feet in the apparel mart and 400,000 square feet in the adjacent men's apparel mart). Both permanent and temporary showrooms offer retail buyers more than 14,000 manufacturers' lines. The International Apparel Mart and International Menswear Mart not only cater to retail buyers from Texas, Arkansas, Oklahoma, and Louisiana, but also attract buyers from Mexico and Central America. Dallas is sometimes viewed as a fashion barometer in that what sells at the International Apparel Mart and International Menswear Mart is typically what is going to sell across the country. In fact, some New York companies use Dallas as a test market for new lines. In an effort to attract new buyers, The Dallas market center has launched an e-commerce program including their Label Link Internet program, which guides buyers to specific types of merchandise and provides information on fashion trends (Williamson, 1999, p. 13). Dallas is also the home of the corporate headquarters of Haggar, a menswear manufacturer.

ATLANTA

The Atlanta Apparel Mart is part of the AmericasMart, which also includes the Merchandise Mart (opened in 1961) and the Gift Mart (opened in 1992). The Apparel Mart opened in 1979 with 7 floors. In 1989, the Apparel Mart expanded to 15 floors, including a large fashion theater (see Figure 8.9). It has the capacity to house 2,000 showrooms and 11,000 apparel and accessory lines, including more than 800 children's wear lines. Cross-marketing among the areas is important and the building names are being changed to AmerciasMart 1 (Merchandise Mart), AmericasMart 2 (Gift Mart), and AmericasMart 3 (Apparel Mart). Because NYC does not have a mart, the Atlanta Apparel Mart is the largest mart on the East Coast, catering primarily to states in the East and Southeast (e.g., Georgia, South Carolina, North Carolina, Florida, Alabama, Mississippi, Tennessee, Kentucky, and Virginia), although in recent years approximately one-third of the buyers attending major shows were from outside the Southeast. In the early 1990s the mart, hit hard by

Figure 8.9: The AMERICASMART 3's fashion theater in Atlanta is used for promotion events.

the recession, consolidated and reorganized the women's wear showrooms and transformed the lower floors to the International Sports Plaza, which was linked to the 1996 Olympic Games held in Atlanta. With the passage of the North American Free Trade Agreement (NAFTA), the Atlanta Mart has also seen a growth in the number of international buyers attending the mart. Corporate headquarters for Russell Corporation and Oxford Industries are also located in Atlanta.

OTHER REGIONAL MARKETS

In addition to these market centers, smaller regional marts also exist in many U.S. cities. Although these marts cater to a more localized clientele, with the increase in fast turnaround and the fact that retail buyers are buying less merchandise more often, they have grown in importance. The most prominent of these regional marts are in Miami, San Francisco, and Seattle.

Miami

The Miami International Merchandise Mart contains more than five hundred showrooms. Known for swimwear, sportswear, and children's wear, Miami's apparel industry grew as a result of Cuban immigration in the 1960s. During the 1980s, Miami saw change and increased growth in its apparel industry because of the arrival of offshore production, particularly in Caribbean Basin countries. As will be discussed in Chapter 10, in what is known as 807/9802, and *807A production* (for tarriff schedule numbers), goods cut in the United States can be sewn in other countries (to take advantage of lower wages) and tariffs are applied only to the value added to the goods. Because of Miami's proximity to many low-wage production centers in Central and South America as well as the Caribbean, Miami has attracted a number of apparel manufacturers that produce offshore.

San Francisco

In 1981 the San Francisco Apparel Mart was built to cater to northern California retailers. Although San Francisco had a thriving fashion industry, the San Francisco Apparel Mart failed because of a lack of marketing support for its tenants. Then in 1990, the Fashion Center was built in San Francisco. It catered to northern California and the Pacific Northwest, as well as to Nevada and Utah. The Fashion Center was sold in 1996. Now the Golden Gate Apparel Association presents its Fashion Market San Francisco at the Concourse Exhibition Center. San Francisco is the third largest apparel manufacturing center in the United States, after New York and Los Angeles. Many large companies have headquarters in San Francisco, including Levi Strauss & Co., Esprit de Corp, Jessica McClintock, Byer California, and Koret of California.

Seattle

The Seattle International Trade Center, which opened in 1977, is an important regional mart for buyers in Washington, Oregon, Idaho, Montana, Alaska, and British Columbia. Seattle is famous for its men's and young men's sportswear and outerwear manufacturers. In the late 1970s, Seattle was the home to Brittania Sportswear, then the largest privately owned sportswear manufacturer in the United States, with annual sales of $300 million. In Brittania's wake came a second generation of sportswear companies that achieved success in the 1980s, including Seattle Pacific Industries (Unionbay, Reunion), Generra, Code Bleu, Heet, Only Stuff, Bench, M'otto, BUM Equipment, Shah Safari, and Sahara Club. Proximity to Asian contractors is an advantage for Seattle companies that import. With the inclusion of established outdoor wear companies, such as Eddie Bauer and Recreational Equipment Incorporated (R.E.I.), and successful retailers, such as Nordstrom, Seattle has gained prominence in the fashion industry. Seattle is also known for its preline showings held prior to the Men's Apparel Guild in California (MAGIC) show. This marketing activity began when Brittania started showing lines to a few buyers prior to market weeks. Since then, the preline tradition has grown and now includes organized showings by most Seattle manufacturers (see Chapter 7 for a complete description of the preline stage of product development).

Other Marts

Marts can be found in a number of other cities, including Birmingham, Boston, Charlotte, Denver, Kansas City, Minneapolis, Pittsburgh, and Portland, Oregon. These general merchandise marts typically house permanent showrooms for a variety of merchandise, only some of which may be devoted to apparel and accessories. These marts sponsor apparel market weeks relying on traveling sales representatives who set up temporary showrooms or booths. These markets cater to buyers within a fairly small region (primarily within a 250-mile radius of the mart). For these buyers, attending a regional market is much less costly and time consuming than traveling to a larger apparel mart or to NYC. In addition, even buyers who attend other markets may attend these regional markets to supplement their stock between major market weeks.

The Selling Function

The selling function of apparel companies is handled in one of two ways: through the use of corporate selling or through the use of sales representatives and showrooms. With private label merchandise (e.g., JCPenney's Arizona brand, May Company's Valerie Stevens brand) and store brands (e.g., Gap, Eddie Bauer, The Limited) this "selling" stage is bypassed entirely. This is because merchandise is designed and produced for a particular retailer (see Chapter 7 for a description of private label and store brand product development).

Plate 1. The design process often begins with trend analysis resulting in a story board.

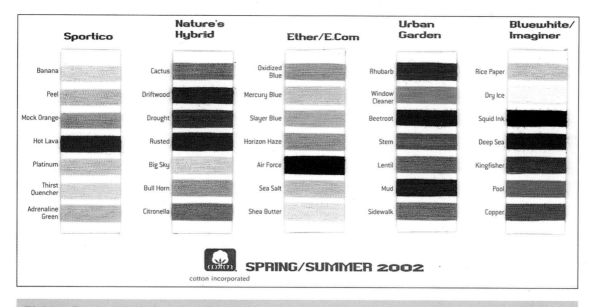

Sportico	Nature's Hybrid	Ether/E.Com	Urban Garden	Bluewhite/Imaginer
Banana	Cactus	Oxidized Blue	Rhubarb	Rice Paper
Peel	Driftwood	Mercury Blue	Window Cleaner	Dry Ice
Mock Orange	Drought	Slayer Blue	Beetroot	Squid Ink
Hot Lava	Rusted	Horizon Haze	Stem	Deep Sea
Platinum	Big Sky	Air Force	Lentil	Kingfisher
Thirst Quencher	Bull Horn	Sea Salt	Mud	Pool
Adrenaline Green	Citronella	Shea Butter	Sidewalk	Copper

SPRING/SUMMER 2002

cotton incorporated

Plate 2. Textile trade associations such as Cotton Inc. provide color forecasts to member companies approximately two years in advance.

MASTER CALENDAR FOR FOUR DEVELOPMENT SEASONS

	January	February	March	April	May	June	July	August	September	October	November	December
WEEK 1			·	-NYC Dev. Trip	-Prints in repeat	-Issue sale samples	-Final Forecast -1st Forecast	-Counter Samples approved	-Style Boards -Yarn Dye Dev. -NY line Release	-Sales Samples to DC	-NY line Release	-Yarn Dye Dev.
WEEK 2	-Concept Mtg	-Prints in repeat			-Sales samples fabric exit mills -Style Boards -Yarn Dye Dev.	-Concept Mtg	-Sales Samples to DC -Import packages exit merch. office			-Concept Mtg	-Sales samples fabric exit mills	-Issue sale samples -Prints in repeat
WEEK 3				-Import packages exit merch. office			-Issue sale samples -NYC Dev. Trip		-Final Forecast	-NYC Dev. Trip		
WEEK 4	-NYC Dev. Trip	-Style Boards -Yarn dye dev.	-Concept Mtg.	-1st Forecast			-Sales samples fabric exit mills	-Final Forecast -Prints in repeat	-1st Forecast	-Import packages exit merch. office	-Counter Samples approved -Style Boards	

■ = SPRING
■ = SUMMER
■ = FALL
■ = HOLIDAY

Concept mtg = season plan by color & style
Prints in rpt = artwork in final form from printer
Forecasts = overall unit plan to style/color level
Sales sample fabric = shipped to garment factories

Sales samples to DC = salesmen's samples arrive for salesmeeting showing
NY Line Release = sales associates show line to buyers at NY market
Ship = Final production shipped to stores

Plate 3. This 24-month master calendar shows design development for a prominent clothing company that creates for four fashion seasons.

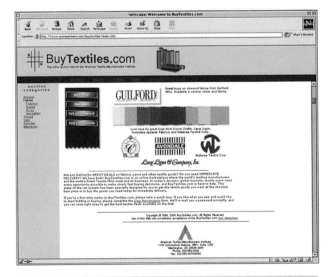

Plate 4. Web sites such as BuyTextiles.com act as an online marketplace to facilitate sourcing of fabrics, yarns, and other textile goods.

MASTER CALENDAR FOR FOUR DEVELOPMENT SEASONS (CONT'D)

	January	February	March	April	May	June	July	August	September	October	November	December
WEEK 1	Ship Spring 1		-NY line Release Ship Final Spring	Ship Summer 1		Ship Fall 1 -NY line Release Ship Final Summer		Ship Final Fall	Ship Holiday 1		Ship Final Holiday	
WEEK 2		-Sales Samples to DC	-Sales samples fabric exit mills		-Sales Samples to DC							
WEEK 3	-Final Forecast -1st Forecast		-Counter Samples approved -Issue sale samples									
WEEK 4	-Import packages exit merch. office			-Final Forecast								

▬ = SPRING	Concept mtg = season plan by color & style
▬ = SUMMER	Prints in rpt = artwork in final form from printer
▬ = FALL	Forecasts = overall unit plan to style/color level
▬ = HOLIDAY	Sales sample fabric = shipped to garment factories

Sales samples to DC = salesmen's samples arrive for salesmeeting showing
NY Line Release = sales associates show line to buyers at NY market
Ship = Final production shipped to stores

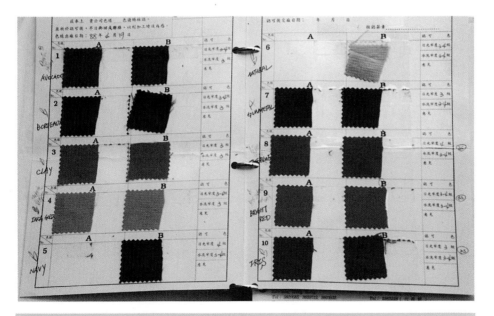

Plate 5. A lab dip includes two attempts by the vendor to match the paint chip or fabric sample provided by the apparel company. One of these two lab dips is selected, or another lab dip is requested.

Plate 6. Software such as Monarch Design Systems is used to create fabric and on-screen garment prototypes.

Plate 7. Consumer research includes an analysis of the wants and needs of targeted market segments. Just My Size® markets to a specific size category.

Plate 8. Roffe's line brochure is used to market a new line to retailers. Color technical drawings illustrate the colorways for each style in a new line.

Plate 9. Sample garments are used for Jantzen's line display to market a new line to retailers at its showrooms or at trade shows.

Plate 10. Software programs such as Artworks Studio™ provide a means to create the artwork required to design, manufacture, merchandise, and illustrate products.

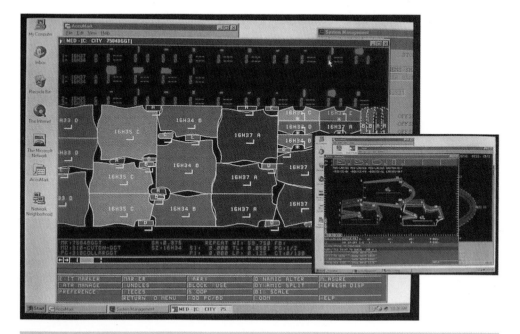

Plate 11. Computer Integrated Manufacturing (CIM) depends on automated design, grading, and marking computer software such as the Gerber AccuMark™ 100 and 200 Systems.

THE MAKING OF NIKE'S AIR TUNED MAX

1 Assigned to create the look for a crucial new running shoe, Nike Inc. designer Sean McDowell relied on a recent Florida vacation for inspiration. In particular, the image of palm trees against the tropical skyline stuck with him.

2 During a brainstorming session, colleagues persuaded McDowell to ditch his first cloud-pattern design. A co-worker quickly sketched a vertical grid pattern, a look more in keeping with the shoe's high-end technical nature.

3 McDowell designed a one-piece upper with a network of black highlights reminiscent of the palm trees. He opted for deep purple and blues, the color of the darkening Florida sky at dusk.

4 The final version featured wavy instead of straight black highlights. McDowell's boss, Dave Schenone, suggested the change to introduce "a little more motion" to the shoe. McDowell also moved the Swoosh from the back to the middle, reasoning that most of Nike's "home run shoes" have featured that look.

5 The blue and gold edition, McDowell's favorite, launched in October and swiftly sold out. Three subsequent color schemes also have sold out, including this rainbow version. But manufacturing McDowell's vision proved a challenge.

Finding a fabric that could hold McDowell's unorthodox shifting color scheme was one of the first hurdles. They settled on a polyester mesh.

The black plastic strips tended to peel off on early prototypes, demanding hours of fine-tuning.

The shoe boasted a one-piece upper – some use as many as 12 – that contributed to its minimalist look.

Almost lost amid the furor of the shoe's popularity was its innovative cushioning technology. "Tuned Air" refers to a cushion that can be customized by sport or running style.

Plate 12. Follow the steps in the design process of NIKE's Air Tuned Max.

Plate 13. In addition to using the mail or telephone, consumers can purchase goods from catalog retailer Lands' End through its Web site. My Virtual Model® enables the customer to "try on" selected merchandise by entering information on his or her measurements, coloring, and other aspects of appearance.

CORPORATE SELLING

Most apparel companies rely on sales representatives to perform the selling function, but a few rely on corporate selling. **Corporate selling** is typically used by some companies that manufacture designer price zone merchandise and sell to a limited number of retailers. For example, the designer Zoran sells to only a few high-end retailers. Corporate selling is also used by very large companies that sell moderately priced merchandise to large corporate retailers. In these cases, selling is often done through their corporate headquarters without the use of sales representatives or showrooms.

SALES REPRESENTATIVES AND SHOWROOMS

The **sales representative** or *sales rep* is the individual who serves as the intermediary between the apparel manufacturer and the retailer, selling the apparel line to retail buyers (see Figure 8.10). Other names for sales representatives are *vendor representative, account executive,* and *manufacturer's representative*. **Showrooms** are the room(s) used by sales representatives to show samples of an apparel line to retail buyers. Depending on the size of the company, showrooms can be elaborately decorated or very simple in decor. They always include display racks for the apparel

Figure 8.10: Sales representatives show seasonal lines to retail buyers.

samples and tables and chairs for the retail buyers.

Showrooms can be either permanent or temporary. Permanent showrooms are located in buildings in NYC's fashion center, in apparel marts, in buildings adjacent to marts, or as part of a company's headquarters or production facilities. During market weeks, sales representatives for companies that do not have permanent showrooms in that area use temporary showrooms or booths. Booths are visually set up and staffed by either the company's sales representative or a multiline representative. Some sales reps always use temporary showroom or booth space during market weeks. Some companies will use temporary showroom or booth space to "test the water" in a new region during a market week without having to commit to a sales rep or the mart on a permanent basis. Although using temporary space can provide companies with a feel for the mart and the sales opportunities, there are also disadvantages. Because buyers are looking for long-term customer service from sales reps, they may seek assurance of continued service from reps who do not have a permanent showroom.

Types of Sales Representatives and Showrooms.

One of the most important decisions made by apparel marketers is whether to open an exclusive corporate showroom with company sales representatives or to use established independent **multiline sales representatives**. The primary difference between the two is that company sales reps work for a particular company and are housed in corporate showrooms owned by the company; independent multiline sales reps work for themselves and typically represent lines from several different, noncompeting but related, companies. For example, a multiline sales rep may offer a variety of noncompeting children's wear lines from several companies. In addition, this sales rep may also represent lines of children's toys and nursery accessories. Both company and multiline sales reps are assigned and work in a geographic territory (**regional sales territory**), which may be quite large (e.g., the West) or quite small (e.g., northern California) depending on the company and product line.

The main criteria used by an apparel company in deciding whether to use a corporate showroom or multiline sales rep are the type of product line and the amount of business the company expects to do. The **corporate showroom** is appropriate for a company with a large sales volume in a particular region of the country. For some marts, it is recommended that the company be capable of producing at least $1 million in sales at the mart in order to support a corporate showroom. Corporate showrooms are managed by company sales representatives who represent the lines of only that company. (It should be noted that because company sales reps generally represent large companies, most are based in a showroom.) Company sales reps may work on salary plus commission or on a straight commission basis, depending on the sales philosophy of the company. If the company pays the sales rep's expenses, which is often the case for company sales reps, then commission is lower than if expenses are not paid. In addition to managing the showroom, company sales reps may travel to other mart's market weeks and trade shows and may also visit retail accounts. Road travel is most typical for lines in the moderate price zone. For this type of merchandise, apparel manufacturers can often get sample lines to the sales rep prior to market weeks, allowing the sales rep to travel to accounts and sell outside of market weeks. Because of the costs associated with producing samples of designer and bridge lines, companies that produce these lines may only have one or two sample lines per season. Thus, the sample line may travel from one city to another for their market weeks.

Corporate showrooms have advantages and disadvantages. With a corporate showroom, the staff can devote 100 percent of its time to the company's line(s) and the company's customers. In addition, the showroom can better portray the company's image and style of merchandise to retail buyers. However, a corporate showroom is an expensive investment. Space is leased from the mart; leases should be evaluated in terms of services offered (e.g., janitorial services, utilities, mart-sponsored promotion activities, directory listings), as they can vary from mart to mart.

Rather than opening a corporate showroom, many companies choose to go with an independent multiline sales representative. Multiline sales representatives typically work for small manufacturers that cannot afford or do not want to hire their own sales representatives. The multiline sales rep works on straight commission, typically 5 to 10 percent of the wholesale price of goods that are shipped by the company. This means that if the company ships $100,000 (wholesale) in goods sold by the sales rep, the sales rep would receive 5 to 10 percent of this amount ($5,000 to $10,000) as payment. Independent multiline sales reps must pay all their own expenses, including the cost of leasing and furnishing showrooms (if they have them), travel expenses to market weeks or to visit retailers, and in some cases, the purchase of manufacturers' sample lines. For smaller companies, using an independent multiline sales representative can have several advantages. The main advantage is that no initial capital investment in the showroom is needed. In addition, established sales reps are familiar with local accounts and can promote the line with buyers. Although the initial costs of using an independent rep are less than with opening a corporate showroom, additional expenses to be expected include fees for market week activities, cooperative advertising expenses, costs for hospitality service, and fashion shows. Some companies will begin with an independent rep and then, as they grow, move into their own corporate showroom.

Finding the right fit between the product line and the sales representative is important to both the apparel company and the sales rep. Companies want to find a rep who has access to the types of retailers appropriate for the product line. Independent multiline sales reps should not represent competing lines. The company must be assured that the sales rep will spend the appropriate amount of time in promoting its line(s). Another consideration is whether the sales rep is needed to travel to different retail accounts prior to market weeks. Table 8.3 compares the advantages and disadvantages of corporate showrooms and multiline sales representatives.

Sample Lines

The manufacturer provides the sales representatives with a set of samples for the line(s) being presented to retail buyers. The samples include an example of each style included in the line in one colorway. The line brochure is used in conjunction with the samples to provide information about the line to the retail buyer. Some companies require the sales rep (usually independent multiline sales reps) to purchase the samples. In these cases the sales reps are generally allowed to sell the samples at the end of the selling season. Other companies provide the samples to the sales rep (usually company sales reps).

TABLE 8.3

Comparisons between Corporate Showrooms and Multiline Sales Representatives

Type of Selling	Advantages for the Manufacturer	Disadvantages for the Manufacturer
Corporate showroom	Control over image of showroom possible	Capital investment necessary
	Staff can devote 100 percent of time to line	Lease agreements may vary from mart to mart In addition to commission, there may be other promotion expenses
Multiline sales representative	No initial capital investments needed	Determining right fit between sales rep and line may be difficult
	Established reps know local accounts	Rep may not devote adequate time to the line
	Buyers are exposed to related but noncompeting lines in the same showroom	Lack of control over image of the showroom

In these cases, the sales rep generally returns the samples at the end of the season. These companies may then allow employees to purchase samples at wholesale prices. Computer technology has made it possible for sales reps to use alternatives such as virtual samples and computer-generated buying instead of actually showing sample lines.

Virtual Samples

As was mentioned in Chapter 6, the technology is in place to show a line with **virtual samples**, which are viewed on a computer screen. The intended fabric color and print of the style will be shown, including fabric folds and shadows, so that it looks like a photograph of an actual prototype. "The fabric is draped over the form, automatically simulating an image so real that it can be used for storyboards, advertisements and catalogs. Designers and manufacturers dramatically reduce sample making costs" (Freedman, 1990, p. 12). Although these computer draping systems are expensive, the savings afforded by eliminating the cost to produce prototypes is easily justified (Freedman, 1990). It is anticipated that in the future more apparel companies will present virtual samples to buyers.

Computer-Generated Buying

Retail buyers and sales representatives can view the line and place orders without the manufacturer producing actual prototypes. Pieces of the line can be combined in a video presentation to show a variety of coordinating combinations. Video presentations can be customized for a specific customer. A photograph of the customer's site can be "dubbed" in the background. For example, "One uniform manufacturer uses its CAD system to create presentations for buyers that visualize what the uniforms actually will look like in a particular environment" (Gilbert, 1995, p. 49).

An advantage of computer-generated buying is that key buyers can "forecast" the hot-selling styles. As more aspects of design, development, and production are computerized and software programs are fully integrated, the time savings increases exponentially. The new style can be created by the designer on a three-dimensional CAD system, revised by the design team, shown to buyers (even in remote locations), and orders placed without the cost of developing a prototype.

Computer systems that are among the integrated computer-generated garment design, pattern, and material utilization functions have been developed to enhance the entire process of creating a new line. Linking the computer-aided design system to the computer integrated manufacturing system provides the maximum cost efficiency, speed, accuracy, and quality. For example, it is possible to predict the efficiency of the fabric usage for a style and to revise the garment design for a more efficient fabric utilization without going through the pattern-making process. Chapters 9 and 11 discuss computer applications in the preproduction and production processes.

Job Functions of the Sales Representative

The sales representative (whether a company sales rep or an independent multiline sales rep) performs a number of job functions, including selling activities, selling support activities, and nonselling activities (Howerton & Summers, 1988). The most obvious of the functions that sales representatives perform are the selling functions. These include the following:

- Showing lines to retail buyers and demonstrating product features,
- Negotiating terms of sale.
- Writing orders for merchandise.

In negotiating the terms of sale, the sales representative and retail buyer will focus on several areas including delivery date, cooperative advertising, and discounts (see Terms of Sale section, later in the chapter).

Order-writing software has reduced the amount of time that sales representatives spend on writing orders. For example, sales representatives for Cross Creek (a subsidiary of Russell Corporation that makes men's shirts, turtlenecks, and sweaters for department stores, specialty stores, golf pro shops, and contract accounts) use a software system called EASE (electronically automated sales entry). With this system, they can access up-to-date inventory information, enter orders for next-day shipment, and analyze information from the order database (Daniels, 1996).

Sales representatives also perform a number of activities that support and expand the selling function, including the following:

- Advising retail buyers regarding trends related to the target customer.
- Providing retailers with product and merchandising information.
- Training buyers and/or salespeople to promote and advertise the merchandise.
- Ordering and reordering merchandise for retailers to guarantee sufficient inventory.
- Dealing with complaints from retail customers regarding merchandise orders.
- Promoting customer relations.

In addition, sales representatives perform many nonselling activities including the following:

- Making travel arrangements.
- Writing reports for the company.
- Keeping books of account.
- Attending sales meetings.
- Participating in market week activities, such as fashion shows.
- Attending to showroom or trade booth management and maintenance (see Figure 8.11).

Although the career paths of sales representatives vary greatly, many sales representatives have retail buying experience before becoming a sales representative. With this background, they understand the retail buying process and can address the needs of retail buyers.

ORDERS AND CANCELED ORDERS

The sales reps work with the retail buyers in placing orders for merchandise to be produced and delivered to the retailer. It is important to keep in mind that not every style in the line that is presented to buyers will be produced. Usually only those styles that have a sufficient number of orders from retail buyers will be produced. Therefore, at the time the buyer places the order for a specific style, in specified colors and sizes, the order is tentative. Whether or not a specific style in a specific color will be produced is based on the cumulative orders from other retail buyers. The style will be produced only if the minimum number of orders for the style and color is achieved. The minimum number of items required to put a style into production is based on any of a number of factors. Sometimes a minimum order is based on the fabric manufacturer's minimum yardage requirement. Or the minimum order might be determined by the contractor who will sew the style. In some cases, a minimum of three hundred units might be required, whereas with another company, the minimum order might be 3,000 units.

Thus, retail buyers place orders without knowing for certain whether every style they order in the preferred color will be produced. In addition to insufficient orders for a particular style or color, another common reason for buyers' orders to be can-

Figure 8.11: In addition to selling merchandise to retail buyers, sales representatives also manage showrooms or trade booths (top). Temporary showrooms or booths are often set up during market weeks to show lines to retail buyers (bottom).

celed is lack of availability of the fabric from the textile manufacturer. The textile company will produce the fabric only if a sufficient number of yards has been ordered by apparel companies to meet the textile manufacturer's minimum order. As you can imagine, there is a domino effect in these related industries. Other reasons for canceled orders can include a variety of production problems, both with the textile manufacturer and with the apparel production facilities. With offshore production, natural disasters and political crises can make it impossible to meet retailers' orders.

When a retailer's order for a style cannot be filled by the apparel company, the retailer may be willing to accept a substitute style or color. Or, the retailer may cancel the order, filling in any gaps in apparel style choices on the retail floor with merchandise from other companies.

TERMS OF SALE

A number of terms of sale are negotiated between the sales representative and retail buyer including the following:

- Delivery time: how fast can the goods be delivered?
- Guarantees related to whether styles ordered will, in fact, be produced.
- Reorder capabilities and timing of the reorders. This is especially important for basic merchandise such as jeans or hosiery for which continuous inventory is essential to optimum sales.
- Cooperative advertising allowances: will the manufacturer or retailer help pay for advertising?
- Discounts if bills are paid within a certain period.
- Discounts if a certain quantity is purchased.
- Markdown allowances: is any credit given on goods that had to be marked down?
- Availability of promotion tools such as gift-with-purchase promotions or displays.

As orders are placed by the retailer for styles in the new line, delivery dates and payment terms are arranged between the apparel company and the retailer. If the apparel company does not meet the delivery date, the apparel company may be required to take a reduced payment for the shipment or the retailer may be allowed to cancel the order. Late delivery may be the result of fabric arriving late from the textile mill, production delays with the contractor, or delays in transportation. With offshore production and the resulting time needed for communication and transportation, delays can be a problem. An apparel company may have to pay the much greater cost of air shipment instead of using sea transportation to avoid a late penalty and the risk of losing the retailer's business.

The apparel company needs to be aware of financial problems facing the retailer, especially in today's business environment of mergers, takeovers, and bankruptcies. For example, on the eve of a predicted announcement of bankruptcy by a major retailer, the management of a large apparel company faced the decision of whether or not to ship a large order to the retailer. If the retailer remains in business, the late shipment penalty will cost the apparel company substantially. However, if bankruptcy occurs, the apparel company might lose far more money by shipping the goods. These are difficult management decisions.

Marketing Strategies

DISTRIBUTION POLICIES

The primary goal of a company's distribution policies is to make sure the merchandise is sold to stores that cater to the customers for whom the merchandise was designed and manufactured (the target customers). Thus it is important for apparel marketers to identify store characteristics and geographic areas that will optimize the availability of the merchandise to the target customers. For example, a manufacturer of designer price zone men's suits may identify specialty stores in areas where residents have above-average incomes as its primary retail customers. A manufacturer of moderate-priced women's sportswear, on the other hand, may identify department stores as its primary retail customer. Once these basic criteria are established, apparel marketers must next decide on the company's policy regarding merchandise distribution. In general, there are two basic distribution policies:

- **Open-Distribution Policy.** With **open-distribution policy** the apparel company will sell to any retailer that meets the basic characteristics.

- **Selected-Distribution Policy.** With **selected-distribution policy** apparel companies establish detailed criteria that stores must meet in order for them to carry the apparel company's merchandise. Typically, the criteria focus on expected sales volume, geographic area, and store image. For example, some apparel companies will only sell their merchandise to one or two retailers within a certain geographic region; others will only sell to retailers that portray an image that is consistent with the merchandise; others will only sell to retail accounts that can purchase a specified amount of merchandise.

Based on these decisions, apparel marketers focus on retail accounts that are consistent with their distribution policy. Distribution strategies will be discussed further in Chapter 12.

INTERNATIONAL MARKETING

As U.S. companies expand their businesses to include foreign markets, it is important to review the ways in which apparel is marketed internationally. There are four basic ways of marketing internationally (Ellis, 1995, p. 10):

1. *Direct Sales.* In some cases, U.S. apparel companies sell directly to foreign retailers through independent or company sales representatives.

2. *Selling through Agents.* In some cases, U.S. apparel companies prefer to use international agents to handle the selling function in other countries. These agents have expertise in market demand, import/export issues, and international currency issues. Therefore, they can facilitate the establishment and processing of international accounts.

3. *Selling through Exclusive Distribution Agreements.* In some cases, U.S. apparel companies have established agreements with specific international retailers for the exclusive distribution of the apparel line.

4. *Marketing through Foreign Licensees in a Specific Country or Region.* In some cases, U.S. apparel companies license their lines to foreign companies. These licensing arrangements with foreign companies facilitate the marketing of the goods internationally.

SALES PROMOTION STRATEGIES

Apparel companies essentially have two groups of customers that need to know about their lines: retailers and consumers. Thus sales promotion strategies developed by apparel companies will focus on both of these groups. Apparel companies use a number of promotion strategies to let retailers and consumers know about their merchandise. Decisions regarding promotion strategies are based on the company's advertising budget, characteristics of its target customer, characteristics of the product line, and area of distribution. Promotion strategies include advertising, publicity, and other promotion tools made available to retailers.

Advertising

Through paid **advertising**, apparel companies buy space or time in the print or broadcast media to promote their lines to retailers and consumers. Although some large companies may have in-house advertising departments, most companies hire advertising agencies to develop campaigns for them. Large companies that manufacture a brand name or designer merchandise (e.g., NIKE, Ralph Lauren, Calvin Klein) can spend millions of dollars per year on advertising. Companies can also share the cost of the advertisement with a retailer, trade association, or another manufacturer through **cooperative** or **"co-op" advertising**. For example, an apparel company and a retailer may share the cost of an adver-

Figure 8.12: Cooperative advertisements are often used to connect a brand name with a retailer in the consumer's mind.

tisement that features both the merchandise and the retailer (see Figure 8.12).

The specific print, broadcast, or electronic media used in advertising campaigns depend upon the advertising budget, target audience, product line, and company image. For example, a company may rely on advertisements in trade publications, such as *Women's Wear Daily* or *DNR*, when targeting retailers. When targeting consumers, designers such as Donna Karan or Calvin Klein may focus on slick print advertisements in fashion magazines; companies that manufactures national brand-name merchandise (e.g. Russell, Levi's, Fruit of the Loom, or NIKE) or store brands (e.g. Gap, Victoria's Secret) may use television ads to reach a wide audience.

Publicity

Although the effect of **publicity** is the same as advertising (to promote lines to retailers and to consumers), unlike advertising, publicity is not controlled by the marketer. With publicity, the company or the company's line is viewed as "newsworthy" and thus receives coverage in the print media or on television or radio. For example, press coverage of designers' runway shows often results in news stories and photographs or videos of the designers' collections in trade (e.g., *WWD*, *DNR*) or consumer newspapers, magazines, on television, or on the Internet. Sometimes the company will create news by sending out news releases about its company or lines. The primary advantage of publicity to the apparel company is that the company does not have to pay the media source for communicating information about the company. The primary disadvantage of publicity is that the company has little control over how the company or its merchandise will be portrayed.

Other Promotion Tools

A number of other tools are provided by apparel companies to promote their lines to retailers and to consumers.

Catalogs and line brochures or line sheets

Catalogs and line brochures or line sheets provide important information about the line to retail buyers (see Figure 8.13). They include photographs or drawings of the items in the line along with style numbers, sizing information, colors (some may even include fabric swatches), and information regarding ordering procedures and guidelines.

Press kits

Photographs, press releases, television or radio spots, and other information are sometimes provided by manufacturers for publicity purposes or for retailers to use in advertisements.

Videos

Manufacturers may provide videos for use by retailers in training their sales associates about the line or in promot-

Figure 8.13: The line brochure or catalog shows all of the styles, sizes, and colors available for a line. Sales representatives and retail buyers use the line brochure to place orders.

ing the line to consumers. For example, videos may be used to demonstrate visual displays, to demonstrate product usage, or to give fashion or styling information.

Electronic Communications

Communications technology is being used by apparel manufacturers to promote goods to retailers as well as the ultimate consumer (see Figure 8.14). Some companies, such as New Jersey–based Burlington Coat Factory are exploring the use of Web sites with virtual showrooms where retail buyers can "walk" through the showroom to view new seasonal lines. Other companies, such as Liz Claiborne, are exploring the use of private networks called *extranets* to communicate with their manufacturing and retail partners. Benefits include the ease of communication and simplification of order tracking. Liz Claiborne also has an Internet-based system that allows

Figure 8.14: Web sites are being used to market lines to both retailers and ultimate consumers.

retail buyers to place orders for merchandise online. Health-Tex's "browse to buy" Web site (www.healthtexbtob.com) allows retail buyers to view the entire Health-Tex collection, place orders and reorders, and check the status of their orders. This site has allowed small specialty store retailers not located near an apparel mart the opportunity to access the complete line (Rabon & Abend, 1999). Manufacturers and retailers have found a number of advantages in this type of technology: no appointments are necessary, paperwork is reduced, and because buyers need an ID and password to log on, security issues are resolved. Many companies also have Web sites designed as online stores for consumers to purchase goods (see additional discussion of e-commerce in Chapter 12). In addition, these sites assist manufacturers in gathering information about their target customers.

Direct Mail Inserts

As a form of cooperative advertising, manufacturers may provide promotion inserts to be included with retail store mailings (e.g., credit card bills).

Visual Merchandising Tools

A variety of visual merchandising tools may be provided by apparel companies. These can range from providing posters and signs to setting up actual in-store shops and supplying all the necessary fixtures (e.g., Ralph Lauren's in-store shops).

Trunk Shows

Typically, a retail buyer will not purchase a company's entire line for the store. Through the use of **trunk shows**, a representative from the company (or the designer himself or herself) will bring the entire line to a store. Customers invited to attend the showing can purchase or order any piece in the line, whether or not it will be carried by the store (see Figure 8.15). Designers

Figure 8.15: Trunk shows are used to promote apparel lines to prospective customers.

often make appearances at their trunk shows to promote their collections. Trunk shows can benefit manufacturers, retailers, and consumers. Manufacturers use trunk shows not only to promote their lines but also to get consumers' reactions to their merchandise. For retailers, trunk shows provide an opportunity to offer an exclusive service to their customers. They also provide feedback from their customers about their tastes and preferences. Customers benefit because they have access to the full line of merchandise. "For shoppers who love fashion and want the luxury of reviewing and trying on a designer's entire collection in an uncrowded setting, but don't mind waiting a couple of months for their goods to arrive, trunk shows are a good bet" (Agins, 2001, p. B1).

Merchandise representatives

A growing trend is the use of *specialists*, *merchandisers*, or *sales executives*, who are paid either partly by the apparel company and partly by the retailer or entirely by the apparel company, but work in the retail store(s). These individuals may be based in one store or may travel to various stores within a region. Their role is to educate the retail sales staff and consumers about the merchandise, to demonstrate display procedures, to assist retailers in maintaining appropriate stock, and to get feedback from the retailers and consumers for the apparel company.

Style Testing and Participation Promotions

Active sportswear companies often ask retail executives and athletes to test styles in a line or participate in sports activities as a way of promoting the line to retailers and ultimate consumers. For example, Columbia Sportswear invited selected retailers, sales reps, and skiers to test a new performance-oriented outerwear line on the slopes of Oregon's Mount Hood. The retailers could learn about the product and Columbia Sportswear could hear suggestions from both retailers and ultimate consumers. Nike has invited retailers to go golfing, Patagonia has sponsored kayaking trips for retailers, and Fila has taken retail executive sailing to promote their sailing apparel (Feitelberg, 1999).

Summary

The marketing of apparel products connects market research with the appropriate strategies for getting the right product to the target consumers at the right time, at the right price, and in the right place. Markets for apparel lines can be any city where apparel marts and showrooms are located. Market centers (New York City, Los Angeles, Dallas, Chicago, and Atlanta) are large markets with important manufacturing and retailing industries. All U.S. market centers, except New York City, have an apparel mart that houses showrooms and exhibition halls used during market weeks. Marts can also be found in a number of other cities throughout the United States. In New York City, showrooms are located in buildings throughout the fashion center in midtown Manhattan. During specific times of the year, known as *market weeks*, buyers come to apparel markets to purchase merchandise for their stores. They may also attend trade shows sponsored by apparel marts or trade associations.

The selling function of apparel companies is handled either through corporate selling or through sales representatives who work out of permanent or temporary showrooms. Sales representatives serve as the liaison between the manufacturer and retailer. Some sales representatives work from a corporate showroom and focus on the line(s) of one company; others are multiline sales reps, representing a number of related but noncompeting lines. The job of sales representatives includes both selling and nonselling functions.

Apparel marketers develop distribution and promotion strategies for their company. In general, there are two basic distribution policies: open distribution and selected distribution. These policies help determine which retail customers will be the focus of selling efforts. Sales promotion strategies of apparel companies are directed to both retail customers and consumers. Strategies may include advertising, publicity, and other promotion tools.

CAREER PROFILE

The marketing of apparel has career opportunities for individuals who manage apparel marts, organize market weeks and apparel trade shows, and serve as sales representatives as well as those who perform promotion work such as advertising and public relations. For these careers, an understanding of the marketing process, product knowledge, creativity, organizational skills, analytic skills, and negotiation skills are important.

Field Sales Representative

PRIVATELY OWNED DESIGNER HOSIERY COMPANY

Position Description
Sell basic stock and seasonal merchandise to the hosiery buyers for major department stores and specialty stores within a specific region; service the accounts that carry the merchandise within the sales territory.

Typical Tasks and Responsibilities
- Do six-month merchandise plans in retail and cost dollars
- Write orders
- Obtain buyers' approvals for orders
- Visit store accounts
- Talk to sales associates about the merchandise
- Entertain buyers and divisional merchandise managers
- Make sure goods are shipped as planned
- Keep in close contact with buyers and report on status of orders
- Plan and help with store promotions
- Analyze sales using spreadsheets with sell-through and stock-to-sales ratios and stock turns for each stock-keeping unit by store
- Plan model stocks (13 week supply) based on sales analysis (basic stock fill-in orders or automatic reorders are based on model stock plans)
- Hire and supervise merchandisers who also visit store accounts and conduct inventories

Key Terms

advertising

cooperative (or
  co-op) advertising

corporate selling

corporate showroom

market

market center

market week

marketing

mart

multiline sales
  representative

open-distribution policy

publicity

regional sales territory

sales representative

selected distribution policy

showroom

trunk show

virtual samples

Discussion Questions

1. Interview a retail buyer in your community. Document the type of retailer (e.g., specialty store, department store) and the type of merchandise offered (e.g., children's wear, men's wear). Ask which markets or trade shows the buyer attends and why. Compare your findings with those of your classmates. Are there any patterns in market attendance related to geographic area, type of retailer, or type of merchandise?

2. Find two examples of co-op print advertisements in either a trade publication or a consumer publication. What companies and/or associations joined forces for each advertisement? What are the advantages and disadvantages for the companies in using co-op ads as part of their promotion strategy?

3. Locate the Web site of an apparel manufacturer. What type of information is provided on the site? Would this information be useful to retailers, to the target customer, or both? Evaluate the site as to its effectiveness.

References

Agins, Teri. (2001, February 5). Trunk show chic. *The Wall Street Journal*, pp. B1, B4.

Cedrone, Lisa. (1991, December). Moving in on the marts. *Bobbin*, pp. 75–80.

Corwin, J. Blade. (1989, March). What it takes (& pays) to sell. *Bobbin*, pp. 76–82.

Daniels, Linda. (1996, March). Getting orders faster. *Apparel Industry Magazine*, pp. 46–48.

Ellis, Kristi. (1995, October). U.S. firms look overseas. *Women's Wear Daily*, p. 10.

Feitelberg, Rosemary. (1999, April 29). Retailers get a real workout. *Women's Wear Daily*, p. 12.

Feitelberg, Rosemary. (1999, December 15). Stores sticking to trade shows. *Women's Wear Daily*, p. 15.

Foxenberger, Barbara. (1994, April). West Coast harbors apparel niches. *Apparel Industry Magazine*, pp. 18–26.

Freedman, Linda. (1990, April). New developments in computer-aided draping. *Apparel Manufacturer*, pp. 12–14.

Friedman, Arthur. (1994, August 3). FCBID building a better SA. *Women's Wear Daily*, pp. 20–21.

Gilbert, Laurel. (1995, July). CAD comes of age. *Bobbin*, pp. 48–52.

Howerton, Renee, and Summers, Teresa A. (1988, Spring). Apparel sales representatives: Perceptions of their roles and functions. *FIT Review*, 4 (2), 10–18.

Lee, Georgia. (1999, December 15). Timing is everything. *Women's Wear Daily*, pp. 4–5.

Lytle, Lisa. (1990, October). The west side story. *Earnshaw's Review*, pp. 99–106.

Mart to mart. (1993, March 8). *California Apparel News*, pp. 28–34.

Rabon, Lisa C., and Abend, Jules. (1999, May). VF takes e-commerce plunge. *Bobbin*, pp. 49–52.

Smarr, Susan L. (1988, April). Seattle: Supersonic sportswear star. *Bobbin*, pp. 75–78.

Williamson, Rusty. (1999, December 15). Big plans in Big D. *Women's Wear Daily*, p. 13.

PART 3

Apparel Production and Distribution

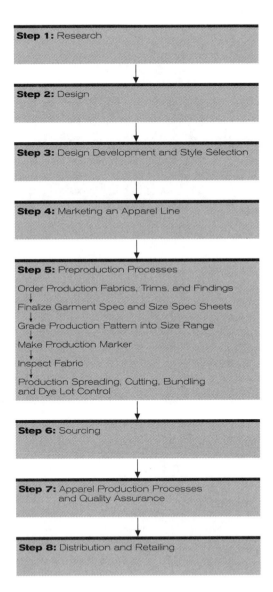

Step 1: Research

Step 2: Design

Step 3: Design Development and Style Selection

Step 4: Marketing an Apparel Line

Step 5: Preproduction Processes

Order Production Fabrics, Trims, and Findings

Finalize Garment Spec and Size Spec Sheets

Grade Production Pattern into Size Range

Make Production Marker

Inspect Fabric

Production Spreading, Cutting, Bundling and Dye Lot Control

Step 6: Sourcing

Step 7: Apparel Production Processes and Quality Assurance

Step 8: Distribution and Retailing

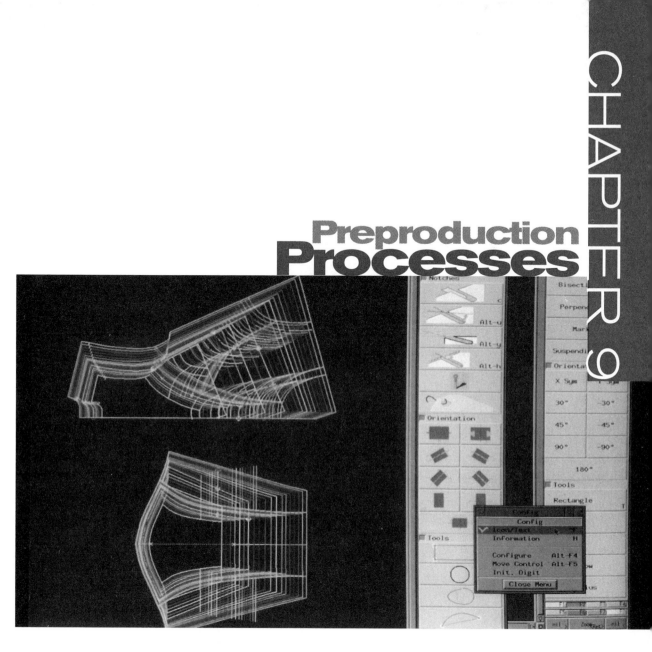

CHAPTER 9

Preproduction Processes

IN THIS CHAPTER YOU WILL LEARN:

■ the role of financial agencies called *factors* in the apparel industry.

■ the process and timing used by apparel companies to order production fabrics and trims.

■ the importance of color control in ordering production fabrics and trims.

■ the stages used to finalize a production pattern, grade the pattern, and create a production marker and to cut, spread, and bundle the fabric pieces.

■ ways in which factors such as grade rules, size range, styling cost considerations, and grading processes influence pattern grading.

■ the advantages to the apparel company of computer grading and marker making over other grading methods.

Production Orders

The sales force has shown the new line to retailers during market week, and the retail buyers have placed their orders with the apparel company. As discussed in Chapter 7, those styles in specific colors and sizes that meet the company's required minimum order will continue in the development process. Usually, styles that do not attain the minimum number of orders will be dropped from the line. Sometimes after a week or two of selling the line, a manufacturer will decide to drop a style that is not selling well. Let us imagine that, for the style we are following through the development process, a sufficient number of orders have been placed to warrant a production run.

Factoring

A company's financial credit line is an important consideration prior to the approval of any business transactions or approval of work orders. Therefore, apparel manufacturers, contractors, and retailers need to have the financial means established for a credit line or cash advance to "buy" in advance of the season in which payment will be received.

Because of the nature of retailing fashion products, there is a high level of financial risk in the textile and apparel industries. Commercial banks are used by some textile and apparel businesses for their financial backing. However, their interests rates may be high, and some commercial banks are not willing to accept the degree of risk involved with fashion related companies. Therefore, another type of financial agency called a **factor** is often used. **Factoring** is "the business of purchasing and collecting accounts receivable or of advancing cash on the basis of accounts receivable" (Young, 1996, p. 1).

Factoring agencies are the companies that provide protection against bad debt losses, manage accounts receivable, and provide credit analysis in the apparel industry. The factor's procedures include the following:

- Running a credit check on the company.
- Approving a credit line to the company.
- Approving the orders for shipping to the company.
- Receiving the invoices from the company's suppliers.
- Advancing the cash needed to pay for the invoice to the company.

The company pays interest on the money advanced until the company can repay the factor. Usually a 60-day or 90-day payment period has been arranged between the factor and the company. The length of the period is determined by the amount of time the company usually waits to be paid by its customers. For example, based on the terms of agreement, the textile producer might need to wait 90 days after shipping the fabric to the apparel manufacturer to receive payment for the fabric.

The factor's fees are similar to the interest paid on credit card debt. For example, a large apparel manufacturer might be charged the prime rate plus 1 percent of the value of each invoice.

Small apparel companies often do not qualify for financial backing by a factor because their sales volume is not acceptable. Therefore, such companies go to re-factor agencies that take smaller accounts—those apparel companies "with sales as low as $250,000 and ranging up to $5 million or more" (Rutberg, 1997, p. 12).

The financial aspects are as dynamic as the fashion industry. In 1999, the annual factoring volume was about $70 billion (Abend, 1999a). Changes in the overall economy as well as the apparel and textile industries at the end of the 1990s were reflected in the consolidation among factoring agencies. At that time, large financial institutions such as Wells Fargo & Co. and BNY Financial Corp. acquired factoring agencies.

Before production can begin, the financial arrangements must be approved by the company's factoring firm. The textile producer checks the credit of the apparel manufacturer before shipping fabric to the manufacturer, the manufacturer checks the credit of the contractor before shipping fabric or cut goods to the contractor; the contractor may check the credit of the manufacturer before deciding to accept the order; the manufacturer checks the credit of the retailer before shipping finished goods to the retailer; and the retailer may check the credit of the manufacturer before deciding to place an order. Keep in mind that the apparel manufacturer has paid the textile producer for the fabric and the contractor for the labor many months before the manufacturer is paid for the goods by the retailer. Some type of lending institution is used by all of these participants. After approval of credit, production can proceed. Some manufacturers will decide to take an account on their own, without the factor's approval. In this situation, the manufacturer carries the financial risk.

Product Information Management

In previous chapters, we have seen some of the advantages of using computer systems throughout the development process of a new style. During the early years of computer use in the apparel industry, each segment of the design, development, preproduction, and production process used different computer systems. We have witnessed vast improvements in computer software and hardware. New software provides seamless integration among all of these segments of the development process. A drawing created by the designer on a graphics program can be integrated into the garment specification sheet used by design development, preproduction, and production personnel. Data from the garment specification sheet can be integrated with the bill of materials and other forms needed for production. The first pattern created by the pattern maker using PDS is used for the production pattern. The PDS base pattern used for the new style can include the measurement dimensions and sizing rules (grade rules) coded into the base pattern, providing integration between design development and preproduction. In addition, some software programs are integrated so that a change on one form triggers that change to be made on all other forms in the data system. For example, changing the zipper length on a garment spec sheet will trigger a change on the bill of materials, the form used to order the zippers. While this system has many advantages, it can also mean that a mistake will be transmitted throughout the system too.

A term used to describe this integration of data management is *product information management (PIM)*. The software used in these systems makes it possible to store such product information as "measurement specifications, construction details, costing and bill of materials information, photographs, technical sketches, video and voice annotation files" (see Figure 9.1) (Rabon & Deaton, 1999, p. 37). To provide complete and quick access to product information for all departments, many companies use an internal company electronic network.

Companies rely more and more on computer system integration both internally (within the company) and externally (outside the company). Maintaining accurate and up-to-the-minute information about each style (and every change in each style during design development) in the line will increase the speed of work flow and increase accuracy within the system for all company personnel who need access to data.

Providing electronic access to style information to external contacts, such as vendors and contractors, speeds information exchange and increases accuracy as well. Garment specifications can be shared instantly with contractors who intend to bid on production jobs.

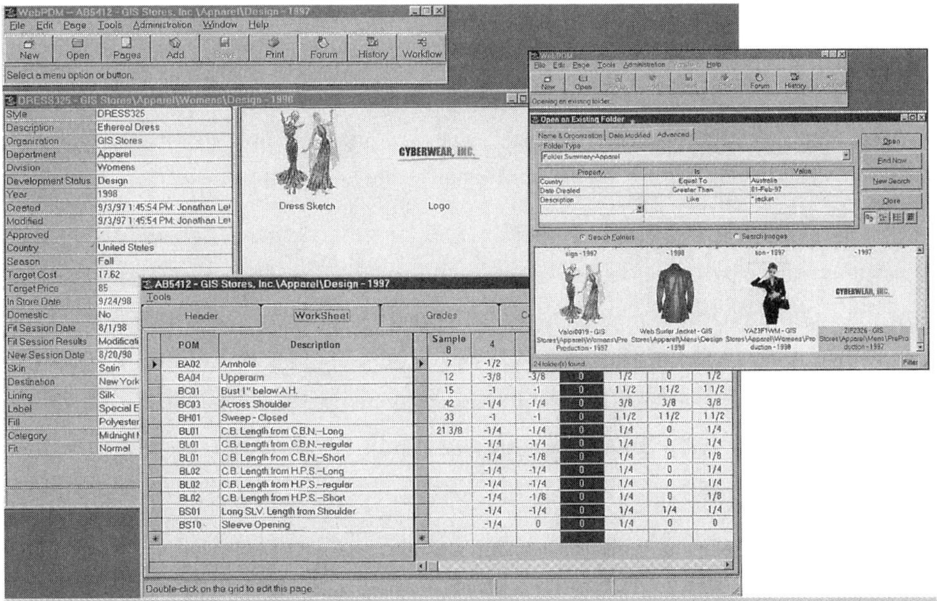

Figure 9.1: Web PDM, Gerber's Product Data Management software, operates from one system server to provide access to style information anywhere in the world by means of electronic communication.

> Product information management, as a function of the line development and sourcing processes, also is benefitting from the global reach of the Web, as CAD companies have been refining packages that facilitate global exchange of product specifications and other pertinent information within companies and throughout contractor networks. (Rabon & Deaton, 1999, p. 36)

GFT Donna is the women's wear division of Italy's largest apparel concern. This company provides an example of the benefits of using CAD and PIM systems:

> GFT Donna has made each product easily accessible to the circle of those who style, cost, order, supply and buy. Connected to that circle, a multinational network of high-end contractors does the actual cutting and sewing in Italy, Portugal, Romania, Hungary and the Far East. The new system allows complex sourcing decisions to be made at lightning speed, without losing sight of the creative function of the enterprise. (Conrad, 1999, p. 38)

With Web access to style information by vendors and contractors, the speed of receiving price quotes is greatly enhanced and the possibility for errors is greatly reduced. Sears was one of the early users of product information management, adapting the software to meet its specific needs. The director of product development stated,

> Between reducing errors by as much as 30% because of clear, detailed specs and increasing productivity by as much as 50%, the application has more than paid for itself. We've also eliminated faxes and overnight packages, which is quite a savings. And because vendors have quicker access and get digital photos and scanned documents with specs, it lessens their work as well. (Hill, 1999, p. 71)

Another advantage of product information management software is enhanced work flow management. Some of the PIM systems include calendar functions that set the dates when each phase of the new style's development needs to be completed. "As individuals complete a form or their sections of it, the application generates the next activity and sends it to the next person" (Hill, 1999, p. 54).

Cut Orders

When either (1) a targeted number of orders for a style has been placed by retailers and received by the manufacturer or (2) the apparel manufacturer decides to produce a style prior to receiving orders, a production cut order is issued. The cut order specifies the number of items in each color and each size that will be included in the production run. The cut order includes the date when the goods must be delivered to each retailer. Thus, the production schedule is calculated from end to beginning, that is, from the retailer's delivery date backward to the date when production of the goods must be finished to the date production must begin to the date when the fabrics, trims, and findings must be ordered.

Ordering Production Fabrics, Trims, and Findings

TIMING ORDERS

In an ideal situation, the apparel company would be able to wait until the majority of retail buyers had placed their orders before ordering the needed quantity of fabrics from the textile producers (a production run of one style might require 6,000 yards of fabric), as well as the trims and findings for a style in the new line. Such a situation eliminates any financial risk that results from ordering fabric that might turn out not to be needed. If apparel companies in general were to wait to order fabrics until they knew exactly how much of each fabric in their lines would be needed, textile producers, not wanting to risk manufacturing excess fabric, would also wait until the apparel companies had ordered fabric before beginning to produce the yardage to fill the manufacturers' orders. However, in this situation, the apparel company would have to wait weeks, or even months, for the production yardage to arrive at the sewing facility. Producing the apparel goods would probably take several more weeks. As you can imagine, these cumulative delays would be so lengthy that the retailers would not receive the goods at the peak selling time. Thus, the apparel company is positioned between the textile producer and the retailer, with pressures from both sides.

> In the middle of the supply chain, set against conflicting priorities, are apparel manufacturers. On one side are the retailers who ask for a variety of garments by size and color variation, delivered frequently in small lots, just in time for merchandising. On the other side, there are fabric mills that want to produce long runs and require advance commitments from manufacturers. (Gaffney, 1999, pp. 74–75)

In reality, few apparel companies can afford to wait until all or nearly all of the buyers' orders are placed before ordering production fabric for the line. Therefore, apparel companies use a variety of means to determine how much yardage to order and when to order the yardage from the textile producers. Furthermore, some companies begin production on some styles before the buyers' orders have been received. This helps maintain an even work flow during production. These methods include the following:

- Early production of proven sellers in basic colors.
- The use of preline selling.
- The use of early-season lines to predict sales.
- The use of test markets.
- The use of past sales figures.

Some companies will project production estimates of some of the more "staple" styles and colors, especially if these are carryovers from a previous season. Some colors are known to sell especially well. For example, skiwear manufacturers know that black ski pants tend to sell well every year. Therefore, they may decide to begin production early on several styles of "proven sellers" in this basic color. Early production also allows the company to maintain a constant production flow in order to avoid times when the factories are overcommitted.

Preline selling was discussed in Chapters 7 and 8. Some apparel companies invite key retail accounts to place orders prior to market weeks. Early production of these styles can be advantageous to both retailers and apparel companies.

Swimwear companies might use an early-season line to help predict which styles will sell well. An early January line of swimsuits sold at resorts in Florida could be used to help forecast production of the spring line to be introduced to northern climates in April. Some of the hot-selling styles from Florida retail sales could be put into production for the main selling season before the line is sold at market to retailers in the rest of the country.

Sometimes a specific region is targeted as a *test market* in which a small production run of the new line will be placed in key stores. Occasionally, an apparel company has its own test store(s), in which early sales help forecast production quantities.

Past sales figures and the opinions of leading sales representatives and leading retail buyers might be used to determine which styles and colors might go into early production. For styles that are carryovers, production might be started prior to buyers' orders.

SELECTION OF VENDORS

Using as much information as possible as early as possible, production yardage, trims, and findings are ordered from the various **vendors** (or **sources** or **suppliers**) of textiles, trims, and findings. Many variables influence the selection of vendors. Lead time needed to secure the goods is one consideration. Other factors include past history of on-time delivery, the quality of goods, whether the vendor uses supply chain management strategies, the minimum yardage (or quantity) requirement for an order, and the financial stability of the vendor. Some manufacturers will review bids from various vendors as part of the decision-making process. A review of the Bobbin Show in Atlanta described a computer software program, "with built-in cost analysis and international sourcing and dual language capabilities, KARAT™'s software allows a user to easily develop cost comparisons for intelligent design and sourcing decisions" ("Bobbin show review," 1995, p. 60). Clearly, many factors are important considerations in the selection of fabric and trim vendors.

PRODUCTION FABRIC CONSIDERATIONS

During the process of planning fabric production orders, constant communication occurs between the apparel company and the fabric vendors. Vigilance is required to ensure that the production fabric matches the fabric used for the samples. Some of the fabric considerations include color control, lab dips, and strike offs. Special considerations are also made when ordering printed fabrics, staple fabrics, and trims and findings.

Color Control

During preproduction processes, the apparel company needs to finalize a number of aspects regarding the fabrics that will be ordered for the new line. Chapter 7 discussed the requirement that the prototype accurately match the color of the garment style that is shown in the line brochure. It is also important that the color of the production garments match the sample that was shown to retail buyers. **Color control** is a term used to describe the color-matching procedures. Staff in the design development department might be responsible for working with the textile, trims, and findings vendors to maintain exact color matching of all components of each style and to ensure that all products in the entire production run maintain the specified color match. Color matching may begin at the prototype stage if a textile is to be dyed to match a color chip or swatch provided by the apparel company. If available, the specially dyed sample goods are used to make the prototype. Trim, findings, sample yardage, and production yardage will be ordered to match the prototype color.

It is important to the consumer, and thus to the retailer and the apparel company, that colors remain consistent throughout all the components that are used to make a garment style. First, the color of the garment style needs to match the color intended by the design team. This could require that the fabric vendor submit test samples until the "perfect" color is achieved. The trims and findings, such as buttons, zippers, and thread, must also match the garment color. If the color of the rib knit used for the sleeve band of a rugby shirt is not the same shade as the body of the shirt, the consumer will quite likely decide not to purchase the garment. Thus, when contractors supply the trims and findings for the products they make, it is important that they receive approval of the color match from the apparel company. An acceptable color match for contractor-provided matched goods is referred to as a **commercial match**.

When producing coordinates in a line, color control can be a challenge. A fabric composed of one fiber might be selected for pants and a fabric composed of another fiber or blend of fibers might be selected for the top. For example, rayon crepe pants might be planned to match a silk jersey tank. However the color of the pants may not look like an exact color match to the tank because of the different reflective qualities of the fibers and fabrics.

Lab Dip

To ensure that color matching will be as perfect as possible, the vendor will supply a sample of the product (such as fabric, rib knit trim, or button) in the color requested. The sample is called a **lab dip** because, in most cases, the fabric swatch (or trim or finding) was dipped in a specifically prepared dye bath in the "lab" to dye the sample. Vendors submit lab dips for all the individual items required in a line. Since various blends of fabrics and other materials absorb dyestuffs differently, accurate color matching of all components may require multiple attempts by vendors. The manufacturer may require that the vendor submit results of color fastness and light fastness textile tests performed by approved textile testing laboratories for each sample. These testing procedures are especially important for certain fabrics, such as nylon fabrics in neon bright colors. Each fabric, trim, and finding that is to match the line's color choice will require approval on a form supplied by the apparel company. The approval process requires time and accurate record keeping.

Printed Fabric Considerations

Not all printed fabrics are printed by the textile mills that produce the fabrics. Sometimes the fabric is printed by a textile converter to the specific textile design requested by the apparel manufacturer (see Chapters 3 and 6). Thus, many apparel companies work with textile converters as well as textile mills. The fabric might be purchased from the textile mill, then sent to a textile converter to print before it arrives at the cutting facility. For apparel companies that use textile converters, careful scheduling is required to ensure that the printed fabric is ready on time. Custom print fabrics require substantial lead time for orders; therefore, decisions about custom prints occur early in the design/production process.

Strike off

A *strike off* is a fabric sample of the textile print being developed that is printed by the textile converter (company printing the fabric) (see Figure 9.2). Chapter 6 discussed strike offs in relation to samples of textile prints submitted by textile converters. Usually a strike off consists of not more than a few yards of fabric. It shows the rendition of the textile print made from the artwork submitted to the textile converter by the apparel company (or textile company that develops the print). The strike off is examined carefully by the apparel company before approval for printing production yardage. For screen prints composed of more than one color, each color requires a separate screen. The placement of each of the screens must be exact, or the print will appear blurred. The accuracy of placement (termed *registration*) of each of the color screens is checked. The color match of each screened color is compared to color chips or fabric swatches submitted to the textile converter (see Figure 9.3). The accuracy of the pattern repeat match is checked. Sometimes it is necessary for several strike offs to be made by the textile converter before approval is given.

Staple Fabric Orders

Some staple fabrics, such as linings and interfacings, and some fashion goods, such as cotton poplin and broadcloth and wool crepe and jersey in staple colors or piece-

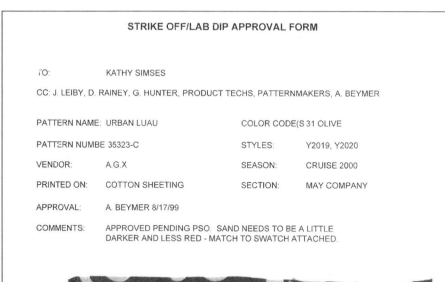

STRIKE OFF/LAB DIP APPROVAL FORM

TO: KATHY SIMSES

CC: J. LEIBY, D. RAINEY, G. HUNTER, PRODUCT TECHS, PATTERNMAKERS, A. BEYMER

PATTERN NAME: URBAN LUAU   COLOR CODE(S 31 OLIVE

PATTERN NUMBE 35323-C   STYLES: Y2019, Y2020

VENDOR: A.G.X   SEASON: CRUISE 2000

PRINTED ON: COTTON SHEETING   SECTION: MAY COMPANY

APPROVAL: A. BEYMER 8/17/99

COMMENTS: APPROVED PENDING PSO. SAND NEEDS TO BE A LITTLE
            DARKER AND LESS RED - MATCH TO SWATCH ATTACHED.

Figure 9.2: A strike off is a sample of the fabric printed by the textile vendor and sent to the apparel company for approval before the textile print is produced in large quantity.

Figure 9.3: The strike off is sent from the textile mill or converter to the apparel manufacturer for approval. Sometimes it takes several attempts to gain approval. (Left) The strike off has poor registration—the screen printing of the two colors was not properly aligned. (Right) The approved strike off—with perfect registration.

dyed textiles, can be purchased closer to production. Fabric sourcing for these types of staple goods might be very suitable for computer on-line sourcing. Textile producers are incorporating online technology using several automated sourcing services. The apparel manufacturer can view and order textiles using custom searches (Greco, 1996). For goods already produced and awaiting shipment at the textile producer, online sourcing is a viable option because it allows late-cycle ordering, which has advantages to the apparel manufacturer.

Trims and Findings

It may be necessary to order special trims very early in the planning process. For example, an elastic waistband might be ordered in a three-color stripe to match the print colors used for pants. On the other hand, elastic in a standard width and color might be ordered just in time for production. Findings such as snaps, hooks, zippers, and thread tend to be kept in stock in large quantities at the production facility. Sometimes a new fashion color requires ordering thread or other findings that are not in stock. Thus, careful planning needs to take place to ensure that all the needed trims and findings are available for production at the appropriate time.

Decisions about findings such as specifying the type of thread, may be more complex than one might imagine. For example, "in denim production, making the right thread choice is crucial because the garments typically are exposed to wash processes with harsh chemicals, enzymes and/or beds of stone" ("Thread Selection Made Simple," 1999, p. 46). Some of the issues to consider for thread selection for washed jeans include the following:

- The weight of the denim being sewn.
- The desired seam appearance or boldness of stitch.
- The wash procedures to be used.
- The desired after-wash color.
- The degradation that will occur during washing ("Thread Selection Made Simple," 1999, p. 46).

Thus, for selection of some findings, research and testing of these products will help ensure a quality finished garment.

Pattern Finalization and Written Documents

The pattern for the style that has been approved for production needs to be finalized. Every detail needs to be perfect for production to run smoothly. Sometimes, minor pattern adjustments need to be made to improve ease of production. The production pattern, which has been made in the company's sample size, is then ready for **grading**; that is, each individual piece of the pattern is remade in each of the sizes specified. Next, all the pattern pieces in all the sizes are arranged into a master cutting plan, called a **production marker**. The style is ready to move to the next stage, the production cutting and sewing operations. Each of these steps will be discussed in more detail.

FINALIZING THE PRODUCTION PATTERN

A specialist called a **production engineer** or *pattern engineer* may be part of the team that is responsible for preparing the pattern for production. Production engineers are familiar with factory production processes and types of equipment. The pattern may need some minor changes to facilitate production. The production engineer is responsible for suggesting such changes in the pattern and might also be responsible for suggesting the specific factory where production could best be accomplished.

All markings for factory production must be perfect, including notches to ensure accurate matching of one piece to its mate, drill holes to indicate dart tips (actually the drill holes are marked at a specified distance from the dart tip to avoid creating a weakness in the fabric at the dart tip), and pocket placement. One forgotten notch marking can cause production problems, especially since this notch marking would be missing on the pattern piece for the entire size range after the pattern has been graded. If the first pattern had been made on a pattern design system (PDS), any changes in the pattern needed at the preproduction stage might be accomplished very quickly because the pattern is already in the computer system (see Chapter 7).

FINALIZING THE GARMENT SPECIFICATION SHEET

At the time the designer's sketch or drape of the style is delivered to design development, a garment specification sheet (*spec sheet*) accompanies the design (see Chapter 7). The spec sheet lists all fabrics, trims, findings, and important construction details such as placement of any logo, label type and placement, and color of top-stitching thread (see Figure 9.4). Any changes that may have occurred during the development of the style must be transferred to the garment spec sheet. Not transferring any requested change to the spec sheet can cause difficulties in production. If a PIM software system is used to create and maintain the spec sheet, all changes can be made very easily as soon as they have been approved and will automatically be changed on any other necessary documents. Some computer systems include bilingual and multilingual flexibility, especially helpful when working with offshore sources.

Another component of the garment specifications is the bill of materials (see Figure 9.5). It lists the fabrics, trims, and findings requirements for each color of a style in the line.

CONSTRUCTION SPECIFICATIONS

Included with the written documentation that accompanies the style will be additional construction specifications related to the production sequence (see Figure 9.6). The production engineer or product technician often determines the sequence of steps (what will be sewn first, second, third, and so forth) required for factory production of the style. When the style is made in a factory owned by the apparel com-

Figure 9.4: (Top left) The garment specification or spec sheet includes important information for producing the style as requested. (Top right) Fabric, trim, and findings are specified on the component page of the garment spec sheet. (Bottom left) This page of the garment spec sheet details construction-related instructions. (Bottom right) The measurement page details finished garment dimensions and allowable tolerances.

pany, the production engineer is an employee of the apparel company. When the style is made by a contractor, the contractor's production engineer determines the production sequence. The sequence of production is related to the cost to manufacture the goods. Therefore, the production sequence may have been determined at the time the final cost was calculated, as discussed in Chapter 7.

Experienced production engineers can examine a finished sample garment and quickly provide a reliable estimate of the number of minutes (and thus the actual

CUSTOM/BILS1   3/28/00 15 00 03   Style Bill Of Material   *** STANDARD COST ***   PAGE   1

CO- 01   DIV-01   B-O-M TYPE-S SELLING Style B-O-M   SEA-Y YR-00 Style- NB01

SEA-Y YR-00 Style-NB01   NANCY'S WALKING SHORT   PRICE-   15.00   U/M-U   B-O-M U/M-U
Clr   Dim   SIZE   M PROCESS   Opt   PLANT   PART   LAST B-O-M MAINT. 3/28/00 STATUS-   OWNING DIV-

* C O M P O N E N T *   **** O P T I O N S ****   ******** C U R R E N T / S T A N D A R D ********
S   C   Style *** ** MANUF.***   CURR/STD   CURR/STD   STD COST OWN
     SEA T NUMBER   Clr   SX Clr   Dim SIZE PR Opt PL PA   PRICE UM CONV FACT   QUANTITY UM   COST   VARIANCE DIV S

                                 1   FOR DEMONSTRATION PURPOSES ONLY - DATA IS FICTITIOUS

D   A LF5678   001   .2500 YD   .3000 YD   .7500   01
     LINER FABRIC #5678   .2500 YD   1.0000   .3000 YD   .7500
               BLACK   STD 3/28/00 LMT 0/00/00

D   A QF1234   001   001   2.8000 YD   .4000 YD   1.1200   01
     OUTER FABRIC #1234   3.0000 YD   1.0000   .4000 YD   1.2000   .0800
               BLACK   STD 3/28/00 LMT 3/28/00

D   A QF1234   440   440   2.9000 YD   .4000 YD   1.1600   01
     OUTER FABRIC #1234   3.0000 YD   1.0000   .4000 YD   1.2000   .0400
               NAVY   STD 3/28/00 LMT 3/28/00

D   E 1/4"ELASTC 001   2.0000 YD   1.4000 YD   2.8000   01
     1/4" ELASTIC FOR LINER   2.0000 YD   1.0000   1.4000 YD   2.8000
               BLACK   STD 3/28/00 LMT 0/00/00

D   E 1"ELASTIC 100   2.0000 YD   .8000 YD   1.6000   01
     1" ELASTIC FOR WAIST   2.0000 YD   1.0000   .8000 YD   1.6000
               WHITE   STD 3/28/00 LMT 3/28/00

D   H HTNBINTL 100   .0500 EA   1.0000 EA   .0500   01
     HEAT TRANSFER NBINTL   .0500 EA   1.0000   1.0000 EA   .0500
               WHITE   STD 3/28/00 LMT 0/00/00

D   T 8X10PB   .0300 EA   1.0000 EA   .0300   01
     8 X 10 POLYBAG   .0300 EA   1.0000   1.0000 EA   .0300
                                                                                                  STD 3/28/00 LMT 0/00/00

D   W CLO0001   .0500 EA   1.0000 EA   .0500   01
     CARE LABEL #1   .0500 EA   1.0000   1.0000 EA   .0500
                                                                                                  STD 3/28/00 LMT 3/28/00

D   X WOMENSID   .1000 EA   1.0000 EA   .1000   01
     WOMEN'S ID TAG WID   .1000 EA   1.0000   1.0000 EA   .1000
                                                                                                  STD 3/28/00 LMT 0/00/00

GL& C DESCRIPTION *******   PART PROC PLNT   Opt   ***** VARIABLE *******   ******* FIXED *******

                                                          AMOUNT   PCT   AMOUNT   PCT   AMOUNT

00050 MFLAM LABOR COST CMT   2.5000   -CUR-   3/28/00
                                                          2.5000   -STD-   3/28/00

      S02 CUT/MAKE/TRIM DEVO QUICK COST
00051 MOOT OTHER INVENTORY   .2000   -CUR-   3/28/00
                                                          .2000   -STD-   3/28/00

      OVERHEAD ALLOWANCE

Style   Clr   * * * * * * * * * * Style BILL-OF-MATERIAL COST SUMMARY * * * * * * * * * * * *

Figure 9.5: The bill of material is used to order and track all components. Some garment styles require an extensive number of fabrics and trims.

Sequence Of Operations For Traditional Blue Jeans

	OPERATION NUMBER	OPERATION	RECOMMENDED MACHINE STYLE	STITCH & SEAM TYPE
PRELIMINARY				
✔	1	Hem top of hip and watch pockets	56500R18 or FS311L51-2H72	401 EFb-2 (inv.)
✔	2	Decorative stitch hip pockets	56500R18 or FS311L51-2H72	401 OSa-2
	3	Precrease hip and watch pockets	Pocket Creaser	
✔	4	Make belt loops	FS321J01-2A60Z	406 EFh-1
✔	5	Attach facings to front pockets	FS311L41-2H64CC1Z3	602 LSbj-1 (mod.)
	6	Set watch pocket to right front facing	Juki LH2178	301 LSd-2
	7	Bag pockets	Juki MO3716	516 SSa-2
✔	8	Serge left and right fly pieces	39500CRU	504 EFd-1
✔	9	Attach zipper tape (continuous) to left fly piece	56400PZ16	401 SSa-2
✔	10	Attach zipper tape to right fly piece	56300G or FS311S01-1M	401 SSa-1
FRONTS & BACKS				
	11	Set left fly piece and edgestitch	Juki DLN5410	301 SSe-2
	12	Topstitch left fly	Juki LH2178	301 EFa-2 (inv.)
	13	Set right fly piece and cord fly	Juki DLN5410	301 LSq-2b
	14	Hang front pockets	Juki LH2178	301 LSd-2
✔	15	Attach risers to backs	FS315L63-3H36CC2PA1	401 LSc-3
	16	Set hip pockets to backs	Juki LH2178	301 LSd-2
✔	17	Join backs (seat seam)	FS315L63-3H36CC2PA1	401 LSc-3

✔ *(Union Special machine available)*

Figure 9.6: Union Special, an industrial sewing machine producer, distributes this guide, which illustrates a typical production sequence for manufacturing jeans.

labor cost) required to sew a specific style. One of the reasons why production engineers are often included in the development design team (see Chapter 7) is that their engineering and costing experience is highly valuable as a factor in styling decisions. Computer software programs can be used to help analyze cost in comparing various production sequence options.

MEASUREMENT SPECIFICATIONS

The actual measurements at specific locations on the finished goods for each size specified for the style will be listed on the **measurement specification** chart. Measurement specs are part of the garment specifications. For a jacket style, for example, measurement specifications for each size to be produced might include the chest circumference, jacket hem circumference, back length from neck to hem, neck circumference, sleeve length, and waist circumference, all recorded in chart form. Since garments are measured flat, sometimes the circumferences are measured across just the front width or just the back width. These half-circumference measurements are listed as the *sweep*. This dimension information is important to maintain accurate sizes, especially if several factories will be used to produce a large order. Two jackets in the same style and size may fit differently if one factory is less accurate in sewing than another.

Some computer pattern design systems include a feature that allows the pattern maker to request the dimensions at specific points on the pattern. When this is the case, the pattern maker completes the measurement specifications on a separate computer screen during the pattern making process. This saves considerable time in comparison to measuring each of the specified locations on the pattern pieces by hand. The software can provide the measurement specs in metric measurements as well as Imperial (inches) since many offshore contractors use the metric system.

The measurement specifications also include a **tolerance**, usually listed as "+/−" a certain fraction of an inch that indicates a narrow range of acceptable dimension variations (see Figure 9.7). This means that a stated dimension on the measurement specifications may vary by the stated tolerance amount. The tolerance amount might be $1/2$ inch (1.3 cm) for larger circumferences (such as the chest) or lengths (such as back length), and $1/4$ inch (6 mm) for smaller circumferences (such as the neck). The stated dimensions, with allowable tolerance, serve as a contract between the apparel

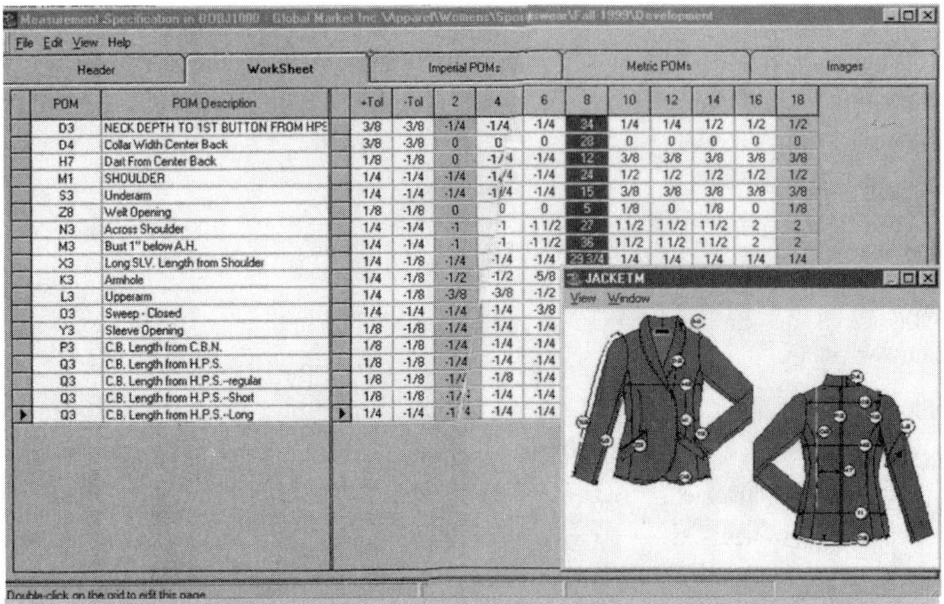

Figure 9.7: The measurement specifications include the tolerances allowed at each specified garment location.

company and the sewing facility. If dimensional accuracy is not maintained within the tolerance range, the goods can be rejected by the apparel company.

The apparel company's quality assurance department is usually responsible for checking the finished dimensions of the delivered goods. Since it would be too time consuming to measure the specified dimensions of every garment in an order, a sampling technique is used to measure a specified number of garments in specific sizes. If goods sewn by a contractor must be rejected due to size inaccuracy, the apparel company may miss the deadline for delivery of goods to the retailer. Therefore, it is important for apparel companies to select carefully the contractors with whom they do business.

Grading the Production Pattern

Pattern grading involves taking the production pattern pieces that have been made in the sample size for the new style and creating a set of pattern pieces for each of the sizes listed on the garment spec sheet. The written documents and production pattern are delivered to the pattern grading and marker making department, if the apparel company is responsible for the grading and marker making operation. As mentioned in Chapter 7, when contractors are used for production, they will be responsible for one of the following scenarios:

- Making the first pattern and production pattern, grading and making the marker, cutting and sewing.
- Making the production pattern, grading and making the marker, cutting and sewing.
- Grading and making the marker, cutting and sewing.
- Cutting and sewing (termed "CMT" for cut, make, and trim) only.

Chapter 10 discusses sourcing options in detail.

Some apparel companies that use contractors prefer to take responsibility for grading and marker making. This minimizes the risk to the apparel company of grading and marker errors that could develop at the contractor's facility and ensures that the contractor is not responsible for any errors in pattern grading or marker making. However, if anything is not correct on the pattern or marker that the apparel company has provided, the contractor can blame the manufacturer for a late delivery or other problem. For the manufacturer who provides the marker, maintaining an even work flow in grading and marker making is difficult, especially when the time frame for producing a season's line—determining that a style will be produced and having the marker ready for cutting—is very tight. Some contractors that have well-established partnerships with apparel companies communicate data such as patterns, markers, and garment specifications electronically. Although the contractor's initial investment in technology is high, the speed and accuracy provided may pay off quickly.

GRADE RULES

Grading requires different amounts of growth (for a larger size) or reduction (for a smaller size) at various points on each pattern piece. Thus, it is not possible to place a pattern piece into a photocopy machine and enlarge or reduce the pattern piece uniformly. The amounts and locations of growth/reduction are called the **grade rules**. There is no industry standard for these grade rules, and some companies guard their grade rule standards carefully.

Pattern grading is more complex than it may appear. There are different grade rules for jackets with set-in sleeves, raglan sleeves, kimono sleeves, and shirt sleeves. Style variations magnify the complexity of the different grade rules. For example, a raglan sleeve shirt could also include a front panel, so the grade rules would need to be modified for the extra style line added to the shirt front.

SIZE RANGE AND STYLING COST CONSIDERATIONS

Depending on the style and the apparel company's policy, the size range might include a large number of sizes, for example, from size 4 to size 18 for a missy dress. Another apparel company might produce garments in a size range of small, medium, large, and extra large (designated S-M-L-XL). The cost to grade a pattern with many pattern pieces into a wide range of sizes may be more than the cost to grade a pattern with only a few pattern pieces in just four sizes. These cost differences are considered from the design stage onward. Another cost variation related to styling concerns designs that are asymmetrical—that is, different pattern pieces are required for the left and right halves of the body. An asymmetrical design might also require different left and right facing and interfacing patterns. Each separate pattern piece needs to be graded, multiplied by the number of sizes in the size range. Thus, asymmetrical designs can be more costly to grade if using noncomputer grading technology.

The fabric selected may influence the size range in which the style will be produced. Some fabrics will look best in a narrow size range. Based on the scale of a plaid size and repeat, a plaid pleated skirt in missy sizes may look attractive only in certain mid-sizes, for example, sizes 8 through 16. It would be ideal to select a fabric that looks good in a wide size range, but this is not always possible. Some styles look best in certain sizes. Thus, the style may be offered in a limited size range.

GRADING PROCESSES

The pattern grading process can be accomplished by a variety of methods, and there are several approaches to these methods. Computer grading, combined with computer marker making, has gained widespread acceptance. It is the method of choice for apparel companies and contractors that can invest in a computer grading and marker making system. Other processes include hand grading and machine grading.

Hand Grading

The hand grading process requires a ruler, pencil, and paper as the minimum tools. Using the production pattern pieces for the new style, the pattern grader (person grading the pattern) traces a copy of the pattern piece, moving the pattern piece the distance designated by the grade rules at specific points throughout the tracing process. Some hand graders use special grading rulers or graph paper as aids to grading.

Machine Grading

Pattern grading machines are used by some companies to speed the grading process (see Figure 9.8). The grading machine is equipped with two dials—one for width increase/decrease and the other for length increase/decrease. The pattern piece is clamped into or taped to the grading machine, and paper is laid beneath. The pattern is traced in sequence by moving the dials on the grading machine to correspond to the grade rules at designated points on the pattern piece.

Figure 9.8: Some pattern graders use a grading machine to grade patterns into the entire size range.

Computer Grading

Whereas machine grading is faster than hand grading, computer grading is much faster than either of these methods. Computer programs for pattern grading and marker making have been in use since the 1970s. The resulting process is called **computer grading and marker making (CGMM)**, and companies that utilize computer systems to grade and make markers may refer to the department as the *computer grading and marker making department.* Many apparel companies began their shift to computerization and formed CGMM departments early on. Computer use in pattern making and design areas were developed more recently. Although the investment in hardware, software, and employee training is substantial, the cost savings is quickly evident for companies that have a substantial quantity of work. For example, Jantzen helped pay for its investment in computer equipment by running two shifts per day and serving as a CGMM facility for other apparel companies in the area, which paid for grading and marker making services provided by Jantzen.

For companies that use a computer pattern design system (PDS) for the production pattern, the pattern is ready for computer grading. Some companies, however, converted to computer grading before they began to use computers to make the patterns. For these companies, it is necessary to input the tagboard production pattern into the computer before grading can be done. The process of inputting a pattern piece into the computer can be done by tracing the pattern piece or by scanning the piece. To trace a pattern piece, a table called a **digitizer** (also called the *digitizing table*) is used. The digitizer is sensitized at very small increments in both vertical and horizontal directions. These correspond to the *x* and *y* coordinates displayed on the computer monitor. The pattern piece is laid in place on the digitizer and traced using a hand-held cursor (see Figure 9.9). The traced pattern piece appears on the computer monitor. During the tracing process, the pattern grader uses a keypad on the cursor to input the specific grade points at the desired locations. The pattern grader must plan the grade rules to be used, which may require a great deal of thought and pattern-grading experience for some complicated styles.

Scanning equipment can input the pattern piece information, including piece perimeters, grade points, and notches. Stripe lines used to match pattern motifs on the fabric and grainlines can be read from the pattern. The scanner will reorient a pattern piece as it is scanned if the pattern piece enters the scanner askew.

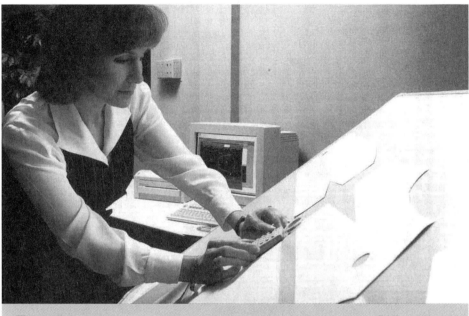

Figure 9.9: A digitizer is used to input pattern pieces directly into a CAD system if the pattern was not made using a computer system.

Patterns can be scanned from a traced drawing, from a tagboard pattern, or a plastic pattern piece.

The computer grading system not only calculates the graded dimensions for the entire size range, but also develops smooth necklines, armholes, waistlines, and other curves. Each pattern piece can be viewed on the monitor as a "nest," with all of its sizes nested together (see Figure 9.10). This helps the grader decide if a grade rule is incorrect or a curve is not adequately smoothed. By using the horizontal and vertical coordinates for a specific point, corrections can be made quickly without starting over. To check the grade, a full-size or miniature version of the graded nest can be printed or plotted.

Some PDS programs include the option to select a grading function as the pattern is being made. These systems are integrated so that the pattern blocks used to begin making the style have specific grade rules "embedded" in the pattern blocks. Once the pattern has been completed, the grading is completed automatically. A major developer of PDS, Lectra Systems, has introduced a grading package that:

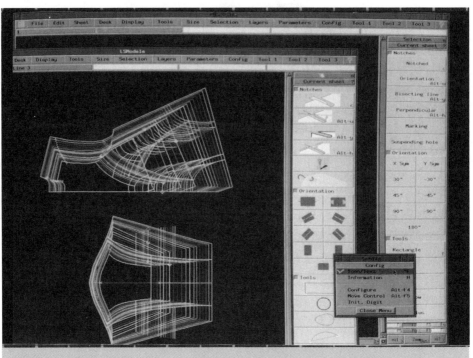

Figure 9.10: Computer screen shows a nested grade of front and sleeve pattern pieces.

enables the operator to distribute the new measurements to all affected pieces automatical-ly, without having to manually choose each pattern piece to be graded. For example, when a measurement change is made on the front shirt piece, the program automatically modi-fies the measurements of the opposite front, side and back pieces, which will save pattern makers substantial time and effort. ("Lectra demonstrates," 1995, p. 62)

Other improvements to increase speed and ease of use while reducing the possibili-ty of grading errors are in the future (see Figure 9.11).

Making the Production Marker

A costing marker, used to calculate the usage (yardage) required for one garment, was discussed in Chapter 7. At this stage in the process, another type of marker is required. The **production marker** is the full-size cutting layout of all the pattern pieces for all the sizes specified for the style. The marker is drawn on paper, showing the outline of all the pattern pieces. Arranging all the pattern pieces into an efficient layout can be a challenge. A tightly arranged layout is the goal for the marker, so that very little fabric is wasted. The waste, called **fallout**, represents fabric that cannot be used, and thus money lost to the apparel company. The efficiency of a marker's layout plan (*marker efficiency*) is measured in the percentage of fabric utilized. Thus, a high-utilization percentage represents a cost-effective marker. Highly efficient markers attain utilization with

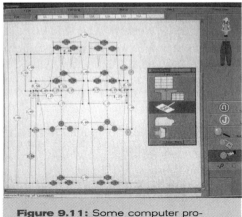

Figure 9.11: Some computer programs provide tools to allow faster grading processes, measurements of pattern dimensions, and electronic sharing of graded patterns with production facilities.

percentile figures in the high 80s and into the 90s (90 percent utilization means that there is about 10 percent fallout, or fabric waste).

If a pattern for a style requires 10 pattern pieces, and 7 sizes are produced, the marker will include 70 pattern pieces. Sometimes, a marker is planned so that the layout will have two sets of pattern pieces in the most frequently purchased sizes, those in the mid-size range. Therefore, the marker for a missy style could have two sets of sizes 10 and 12, for a total of 90 pattern pieces for the marker with 10 pattern pieces. For styles offered in the S-M-L-XL size range, it is fairly common to cut one set each of size S and size XL pattern pieces, and two sets each of size M and size L pattern pieces. The cut order specifies the sizes and number of size sets in each of these sizes needed for the marker.

MARKER MAKING BY HAND

Prior to the development of computerized marker making, markers were typically made by hand. The layout is planned on a long sheet of paper (perhaps 21 to 30 feet long), the width of the fabric to be cut. The tagboard pattern pieces are shifted into the tightest arrangement. The outlines of all the pattern pieces are traced by hand onto the paper beneath. The pattern pieces are removed, and the marker is laid onto the stacked layers of fabric. The cutter, using an industrial cutting knife, follows the drawn outlines of the pattern piece on the marker. Typically, the marker paper is of double thickness. The paper can be carbonless or have carbon between the layers, so that a copy of the original marker is made at the same time. Thus, after the original marker has been cut up, a reference copy remains. This copy can be traced again, if another production order for the same style is received. If a similar style is produced later, the marker maker can refer to the file of markers to help guide the layout plan for the new style.

OTHER HAND MARKER MAKING METHODS

Some apparel companies and contractors continue to make markers by hand. Other methods, developed years ago to increase the speed and efficiency of marker making, include: (1) the use of miniaturization of pattern pieces combined with enlargement photography to produce a full-size marker, (2) the use of light-sensitive paper in which the paper areas covered by the tagboard pattern pieces remain white while exposed areas darken to show the silhouette of pattern pieces, and (3) the use of water soluble dye sprayed over the pattern pieces while they lay on the fabric, leaving the fabric uncolored in the areas covered by the pattern pieces.

COMPUTER MARKER MAKING

While various marker making methods are in use in today's industry, computer marker making is the most efficient and effective method. With CGMM, the marker making function is tied to the pattern grading function. Thus, a company that grades by computer also makes markers by computer. The CGMM system is purchased as a package, including the plotter that draws the marker. Once the pattern pieces have been graded by computer and stored in the computer's memory, the marker maker can retrieve all of the pattern pieces needed in the size range. The fabric width is displayed on the monitor, along with markings for stripes or plaids if necessary. With the use of the mouse, each pattern piece is moved one by one into the fabric area, creating the layout plan. The computer is programmed to keep all pattern pieces aligned "on grain," to avoid skewing pattern pieces. Accidental overlapping of pattern pieces is avoided, for the pattern piece blinks as a signal to the marker maker if one piece overlaps another. After the marker is completed, the system generates a letter-size printout of the layout. The small-scale marker can be analyzed for utilization and accuracy as well as used for reference during preproduction and production.

Advantages of Computer Marker Making

As discussed earlier, the marker program calculates the fabric utilization, and this figure appears as a percentage on the monitor (see Figure 9.12). This helps the marker maker attain the highest utilization. An article in *Apparel Industry Magazine* discussed the complexity of marker making variables:

> Your greatest single cost is cloth. The management of cloth is unconditionally crucial to the successful management of your business and your profits. As you can see, finding the ideal approach to the many variables requires elaborate mathematical calculations using sophisticated computer programs. There is just no other practical way to arrive at an optimal solu-

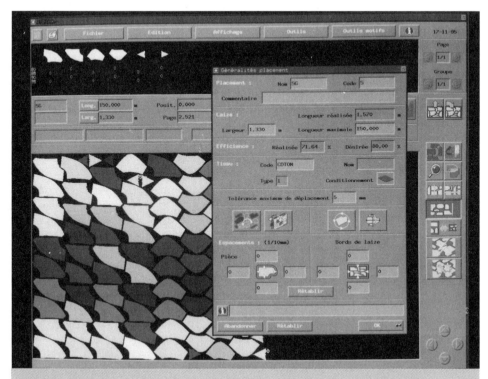

Figure 9.12: A production marker is displayed on the computer screen, showing the tight layout on the left and the utilization percentage on the right.

tion. The variety of factors make the standard approach (based on human experience) far too unreliable. (Dennison, 1993, pp. 82–84)

Some manufacturers have estimated that the cost savings in better fabric utilization has paid for the computer equipment in less than two years. According to a study conducted at Clemson Apparel Research (Hill, 1994), a computer system used for grading and marking will result in a 2 percent fabric savings per year, quickly paying for the cost of the system.

In the early years of computerized marker making, to save time, a marker from a previous similar style stored in the system might be studied by the marker maker to provide some guidance for creating a high-utilization marker on the first attempt. Some of the new marker software includes functions that will generate several possible marker layouts. Gerber's NesterServer software for its AccuMark and MicroMark CAD systems offers a processing option that "allows the system to configure several marker options based on predetermined time limits" (Rabon & Deaton, 1999, p. 36). Another computer marker making system by ScanVec has an advanced system for matching patterns on plaid and striped fabric. "This technology utilizes highly advanced mathematical algorithms along with artificial intelligence to accommodate fabric matching requirements" (Rabon & Deaton, 1999, p. 36).

Multiple copies of the marker can be plotted whenever they are needed. Accuracy is extremely high with CGMM, as each copy is exactly the same as the original. No accidental growth occurs as can happen when hand tracing markers.

Some companies that began their "computerization" with CGMM systems have integrated CGMM with other stages in design, development, and production using PIM software, as discussed earlier. Production integration will be covered in Chapter 11. Complete integration of computer systems throughout the entire process provides advantages to all parties in the fiber-textile-apparel-retail chain.

As the cost of some CGMM systems decreases and their "user friendliness" increases, more companies are purchasing these systems. Some systems are in a price range affordable to small apparel companies. Other small companies might use the CGMM service of a larger company. Many contractors in foreign production centers as well as in the United States have CGMM equipment. The apparel company's PDS can be linked electronically to the contractor's CGMM system. This saves time and increases accuracy.

Fabric Inspection

The preproduction steps include ordering production fabrics and trims. A part of this process involves approving fabric and trim colors and the quality of components (discussed earlier in this chapter). Samples are submitted by suppliers and approved by the apparel company. It is assumed by the apparel company that the production fabrics and trims will accurately match (as noted earlier, this is called a *commercial match*) the samples submitted and used for the production of the sample garments. The retailer's orders are written based on the materials, trims, and construction quality seen in the sample garment. The production fabrics are inspected to ensure that they match the samples. If the quality or color match of any part of the production goods is inferior, the retailer may reject an entire order. Fabric inspection can be the responsibility of the apparel company or the textile producer.

FABRIC INSPECTION BY THE APPAREL COMPANY

To avoid problems arising from inferior fabric quality, some apparel companies inspect fabrics on their arrival from the textile producers. Various types of machinery are used to speed this process, including computerized equipment that scans across the fabric along the entire length to note any shade variation from beginning to end of the fabric roll. Other equipment checks the density of the weave or knit. Some companies, however, rely on visual inspection. On occasion, it has been necessary to reject fabric orders because of color or quality problems. Ordering replacement fabric can delay production by weeks. At times, a textile producer may be unable to replace rejected goods. The production schedule for the contracted arrival date of the goods at the retailer can be jeopardized because of fabric problems.

If the apparel company is responsible for inspecting fabrics, the fabric goods must arrive at the cutting facility in time to allow for inspection before cutting begins. This requires a crew of workers paid by the apparel facility to inspect the goods. In addition, costs of production increase any time the fabric is in storage or in inventory and not being processed, as when the fabric is waiting to be cut and sewn. As the apparel industry moved toward faster turnaround time, it became obvious that several processes would need to change. Among them is fabric inspection by the textile producer.

FABRIC INSPECTION BY THE TEXTILE PRODUCER

Through Quick Response and supply chain management strategies, partnerships have been formed between the textile producer and the apparel manufacturer, ensuring that (a) the textile producer inspected the goods and that they were of the quality shown by the sample and (b) goods would arrive at the production facility just in time to cut and sew, as set forth by the apparel company's schedule. Therefore, the apparel company would not need to inspect fabric routinely. Instead, textile producers inspect the goods before they leave the textile facility. At the textile facility, flaws in weaving or knitting are marked along the selvage edge of the fabric, so that the apparel producer knows where the flaws are and can cut around them. Printed fabrics are inspected for color match and registration of motif placement when more than one color is printed. Once inspected, the fabric ordered for production is sent in large rolls from the textile producer or fabric wholesaler to the cutting facility.

Currently, many small apparel companies do not have the production volume to participate in this aspect of supply chain management. They continue to inspect the fabric and trims prior to sending them to cutting. Even with supply chain management participants, fabric flaws can occur. It is important for all workers to be alert to flaws, such as off-grain stripes, that could lead to the rejection of an order by the retailer.

For apparel companies that own their factories, the fabric and trims are usually sent from the supplier either directly to the company's production plant or to the apparel company's warehouse (where inspection may occur) and then on to the production facility. For companies that use contractors for the cutting and sewing operations, the fabric might be ordered, received, and inspected by the apparel company, which then sends the fabric rolls to the cutting facility. Or the fabric might be ordered by the contractor and sent directly to the production facility, in which case the contractor assumes the responsibility for the quality of the fabrics and trims. This is typically done when the fabric is manufactured offshore and the cutting and sewing also occur offshore.

Production Spreading, Cutting, Fallout Disposal, Bundling, and Dye Lot Control

SPREADING

Spreading (or *laying up*) is the process of unwinding the large rolls of fabric onto long, wide cutting tables (see Figure 9.13). The fabric is stacked, layer upon layer, depending on the size of the cut order. For **production cutting**, the fabric is laid flat across its entire width from selvage to selvage. For large cuts, thin sheets of paper may be laid between every 12 layers of fabric, in order to count quickly the stacked layers of pieces by dozens. This saves a great deal of time after cutting, when the stacks of cut pieces need to be assembled into different groups (bundles) for sewing. When a style will be produced in several colors, the fabric layers will reflect the correct number of layers for each color needed.

Fabrics that have a directional print or napped fabrics such as corduroy and velvet need to be laid so that all layers face the same direction (called *face-up*). This is

Figure 9.13: Fabric is spread carefully and stacked layer upon layer in preparation for production cutting.

a more time-consuming process than face-to-face spreading (two-directional) and is reflected in the labor cost for cutting. Fabrics such as stripes and plaids also take more time to lay up, and therefore cost more to cut. Stretch fabrics, such as fabrics used for swimwear or intimate apparel, require great care during lay-up to avoid distorting the fabric. Stretch fabrics also require time to relax on the table after laying up and before cutting.

A variety of equipment speeds the fabric laying process. **Spreading machines** guided on tracks along the side edges of the cutting table carry the large rolls of fabric, spreading the fabric smoothly. For face-up cutting, a cutting knife is sent across the fabric at the desired length (that corresponds to the length of the marker), the spreading machine is returned to its origin, and another layer is spread on top of the previous layer. Other systems utilize spreading machines that roll along the floor beside the cutting table. Some spreading machines require operators, but automatic and robotic spreaders are an option. In 1995, Saber Industries introduced the first robotic, digitally controlled spreader in the apparel business ("Saber introduces," 1995).

CUTTING

Either the apparel company or the contractor is responsible for making the production marker. The marker, whether drawn by hand or plotted by computer, is sent to the cutting facility or contractor for the cutting process. The marker made during preproduction is laid onto the top layer of fabric, serving as a cutting guide if the fabric will be cut by one of several hand processes. There are several types of specialized hand-guided electric knives and rotary cutters used for cutting the multiple thicknesses of fabric. Most electric knives look similar to a band saw, with a reciprocating blade that oscillates vertically to "saw" through the fabric layers.

Die cutting is another type of cutting process used for specific purposes. For very small pieces that will be cut repeatedly, season after season, it is more precise and more economical in the long run to use a die. The die is similar to a cookie cutter—a piece of metal with a sharp edge, tooled to the exact dimensions of the shape of the pattern piece. The die is positioned over several layers of fabric. Then, a pressurized plate is applied to the die to cut through the thicknesses of fabric. A fabric appliqué that might be used season after season is an example of a pattern piece that would be economical to cut using a die. The original cost of the die is expensive, but

Figure 9.14: A cutting protocol system interfaces with computer equipment to enhance cutting efficiency.

its continued use amortizes the initial cost and increases the cutting accuracy compared to hand cutting the same piece.

For facilities that have computerized cutting, special tables are required to accommodate the cutting equipment (see Figure 9.15). The table surface is covered with bristles that allow the cutting blade to slide between them. The fabric layers are compressed with air to provide a more compact cutting height, thereby increasing the accuracy of the cut. The table surface is designed to accommodate the required suction. The computer-generated marker is laid onto the top layer of fabric. The cutting equipment is guided by computer coordinates, not by "seeing" the pattern piece outlines on the marker. The plotted marker is used for two purposes: (1) to ensure that the marker is laid properly onto the fabric, especially when plaids or stripe notations must be aligned, and (2) to indicate the sizes of the pattern pieces and styles for the workers who will bundle the pieces after cutting. Computerized cutting is much faster and generally more accurate than hand cutting or even die cutting. Either a reciprocating knife blade or a rotary cutting blade can be used for comput-

Figure 9.15: The computerized cutter requires a special table surface to accommodate the knife blade requirements. The Dual Beam and Head GERBERcutter increases cutting productivity.

erized cutting. The rotary cutting blade is effective for cutting very stretchy fabrics, such as swimwear fabrics. The rolling action of the blade minimizes fabric stretching and thus distortion of the fabric during cutting. However, notch marking with a rotary cutter is more limited.

Laser cutting is also driven by computer. It offers many of the same advantages as knife-blade computer cutting, including high speed and accuracy. Laser cutting can be done economically with one or several layers of fabric (called *single-ply cutting* and *low-ply cutting*) compared to the many stacked layers used with computer cutting. Several low ply cutters can be purchased for about the same cost as one high ply computerized cutting system. Since low ply cutters offer the flexibility to produce small runs very quickly, there are additional benefits to consider as well. Several low ply cutters can be working on different orders at the same time. They lend themselves well to the short-cycle manufacturing environment. Single ply cutting systems are needed for individually customized cuts for the mass customization manufacturing environment (see Chapter 11).

On the other hand, if a production facility handles primarily large orders for mass production, a large-scale computerized cutter, which operates at up to 300 dozen per hour even while cutting large sizes, may be more efficient. "This higher output per machine results in an overall reduction in the number of machines required, which translates into direct labor savings" (Abend, 1999b, p. 57).

Computerized cutting and sewing facilities may be linked electronically to the apparel company's computer, so that the marker file can be downloaded by modem. This increases the speed of delivery of the marker to the cutting facility or contractor. Often sewing contractors have CGMM equipment and may be resonsible for making the marker. As mentioned earlier, the style's pattern file might be sent electronically from the apparel company to the sewing contractor, which will use CGMM equipment to make the marker and cut the style.

FALLOUT DISPOSAL

Although the marker's layout utilizes the fabric in the most efficient plan possible, there is still a substantial quantity of fallout, or waste material. In the past, the waste goods commonly were delivered to landfills. This procedure has become more expensive, in part because of the reduction in available landfill space and the increase in transportation costs. Furthermore, today's society expects responsible recycling. Textile and apparel waste recyclers provide a market for some of this waste. The payback varies among categories. For example, cotton fabric by-products are very marketable, especially if they are white. Remnants large enough to be used as wiping cloths have a good market (Kron, 1992, p. 74). While there are no official figures reflecting the size of the textile and apparel waste industry, a textile and apparel waste recycler estimated that in 1992 between 1.5 billion and 1.9 billion pounds of new fiber and fabric wastes were produced annually in the United States.

As reported in *Apparel Industry Magazine* (Kron, 1992) the Council for Textile Recycling was formed by the International Association of Wiping Cloth Manufacturers (IAWCA) with the mission of increasing the amount of waste that can be recovered. At the same time, IAWCM seeks to develop new uses, products, and markets for products derived from preconsumer and postconsumer textile waste, as well as to inform manufacturers of this industry.

BUNDLING

After cutting, the component pieces for each size and color must be grouped together in some way. **Bundling** is the process of disassembling the stacked and cut pieces and reassembling them, grouped by garment size, color dye lot, and number of units in which they will proceed through production. Bundling is done by hand, with one or more workers picking the required garment parts from the stacks and grouping them in bundles that are ready for production. The type of production process determines the number of garments included in each bundle. This varies from the cut fabric pieces for an individual unit (one garment) bundled together to bundles of a dozen units (or sometimes specified parts of a dozen garments), usually in the same size and color (including same color dye lot) for all twelve garments. For some types of production, up to three dozen units might be bundled together.

DYE LOT CONTROL

All coordinating pieces of an outfit, and those styles that are to coordinate in a line, need to be color matched exactly. Mismatching can occur if strict color control is not maintained. Even with adherence to color control, slight variations in shading can occur among dye lots of a production order. Therefore, it is important to code all fabric bolts with the dye lot number, and to maintain accuracy in matching dye lots throughout the production and distribution process.

Often an apparel company uses one sewing contractor for the suit pants production and another for the suit jacket. Each contractor receives a shipment of "matching" fabric from the textile producer. If dye lots are not matched, the suit pants might be a slightly different shade from the suit jacket. This discrepancy may not be noticed until the goods arrive at the apparel company's distribution center, the retailer's distribution center, or the retail selling floor, where the sale may be lost when the customer trying on the jacket and pants, notices that the colors do not match exactly.

Summary

Retail buyers' written orders in sufficient quantity to warrant production signal the chain of events that begins the process of producing a new style. The preproduction steps include ordering production fabrics, trims, and findings, maintaining color control, including the use of lab dips and strike offs; and finalizing the production pattern and written documents. To ensure quality production, the documents that accompany the pattern are as important as the pattern itself. These documents comprise the garment specification package. They include a tech drawing of the garment style, a list of all fabrics (with fabric swatches), trims, and findings in all colorways; construction specifications (construction details and sewing steps in sequence); and measurement specifications with stated tolerances. Accurate documentation is essential.

In company-owned production facilities, the production pattern is graded into the specified size range and a production marker is made by the apparel company. For contracted production, either the apparel company or the contractor is responsible for the grading and marking procedures. Fabric inspection may be the responsibility of the textile producer or the apparel company. Spreading can be handled by laying the fabric layers onto cutting tables by hand or by using spreading machines. Cutting can be done by hand-held cutting equipment, by computer knife blade, or by laser. After cutting, the fabric pieces are bundled into units ready for production.

Computer grading and marker making systems have gained widespread use in the apparel industry. The advantages of CGMM include increased speed and improved accuracy. Integrated computer systems provide product information management including instantaneous electronic linkage between PDS and CGMM, whether the two systems are separated by miles within a city (such as the design development department located at company offices and the grading and marking department located at the company's factory) or by an ocean (such as the design development department located in the United States and the contractor's grading and marking department located at the factory in South Korea). The future promises continued developments in a "seamless" integration of all aspects of design, development, and production.

Possible career opportunities in preproduction processes include specification writing, production pattern making, pattern and marker making, and materials management.

Purchasing Manager or Raw Materials Control Manager

PUBLICLY HELD SPORTSWEAR AND ATHLETIC SHOE COMPANY

Position Description

Manage raw materials buyers to ensure department goals are met. Manage Sales Sample Materials Buyer to ensure timelines are met and all needed materials are ordered. Develop partnerships with vendors for supply of necessary raw materials to ensure company needs are met. Develop partnerships with contractors to be sure best possible services are provided for the company. Develop, monitor, and update systems to ensure efficiency in the department and to provide necessary information exchanges with other departments and liaison offices.

Typical Tasks and Responsibilities

■Prepare annual department budget and action plans.

■Determine greige goods commitments and/or forecast company-developed styles, have contracts issued, work with offshore liaison offices to provide accurate and timely reports, updates, and information as requested to make ongoing greige goods commitments with vendors.

■Color assort and pre-order raw materials as needed, keeping excess to a minimum and maintaining a program to dispose of excess raw materials.

■Monitor lab dip and first production; submit information from the apparel lab to ensure materials will meet production timelines. Monitor deliveries to contractors. Troubleshoot quality problems.

■Generate computer reports using a variety of different systems.

■Use telephone, fax, and electronic communications to communicate with vendors, contractors, other company departments, and offshore liaison offices.

■Constant ongoing "coaching" of buyers to meet department goals.

Trim Buyer
PUBLICLY HELD SUIT AND DRESS COMPANY

Position Description
Write garment specifications, source vendors. Order trims, buttons, zippers, cording, snaps, interfacings, and lining fabrics. Work with designers and production team on trim selection. Organize shipments to contractors in the U.S. and abroad.

Typical Tasks and Responsibilities
- Make phone calls and send e-mails to vendors
- Meet with sales representatives to review lines of trim, buttons, zippers, interfacings, and linings
- Price and order trims and findings
- Organize and oversee shipments of fabrics and trims to contractors
- Meet with designers and production team to select trims
- Write the garment specifications for all styles in the line

CAREER PROFILE

Key Terms

bundling

color control

commercial match

computer grading and marker making (CGMM)

die cutting

digitizer

factor

factoring

fallout

grade rules

grading

lab dip

measurement specifications

pattern grading

production cutting

production engineer

production marker

source

spreading

spreading machines

supplier

tolerance

vendor

Discussion Questions

1. Describe orally or bring to class a product that provides an example of lack of color control, with one or more components not matching. How would you suggest that this mistake could have been avoided?

2. Give several examples of problems that may occur with fabric quality. Discuss options available to the apparel manufacturer to correct the problem, and explain how such problems—and their correction—affect production and delivery to the retailer.

3. Computer grading and marker making systems are an expensive investment. What are some ways in which a CGMM system can quickly pay for itself?

References

Abend, Jules. (1999a, May). Factors execute new strategies for apparel growth. *Bobbin*, pp. 26–30.

Abend, Jules. (1999b, October). Business is BOOMing. *Bobbin*, pp. 56–57.

Bobbin show review. (1995, November). *Bobbin*, pp. 58–60.

Conrad, Andrée. (1999, January). The industrialization of "couture" in Italy. *Apparel Industry Magazine*, pp. 36–40.

Dennison, Roger. (1993, September). Optimize cloth consumption with CAD marker making. *Apparel Industry Magazine*, pp. 82–86.

Gaffney, Gary. (1999, May). SCM: In reach for $5M to $25M firms? *Bobbin*, pp. 74–68.

Greco, Monica. (1996, February). Is on-line fabric sourcing next? *Apparel Industry Magazine*, pp. 32–34.

Hill, Suzette. (1999, February). Product development: the next QR initiative? *Apparel Industry Magazine*, pp. 48–54, 71.

Hill, Thomas. (1994, March). CAR Study: UPS, CAD provide 300%+ return on investment. *Apparel Industry Magazine*, pp. 34–40.

Kron, Penny. (1992, September). Recycle—If you can! *Apparel Industry Magazine*, pp. 74–82.

Lectra demonstrates its new CAD grading package. (1995, August). *Apparel Industry Magazine*, 62.

Rabon, Lisa and Deaton, Claudia. (1999, December). Laying the cornerstone of mass customization. *Bobbin*, pp. 35–37.

Rutberg, Sidney. (1997, October 17). Re-Factors racking up strong sales gains. *Daily News Record*, pp. 12–13.

Saber introduces first truly robotic spreader. (1995, August). *Apparel Industry Magazine*, pp. 46–48.

Thread selection made simple. (1999, April). *Bobbin*, p. 46–50.

Young, Kristin. (1996, February 2–February 8). The F word. *California Apparel News*, pp. 1, 8–9.

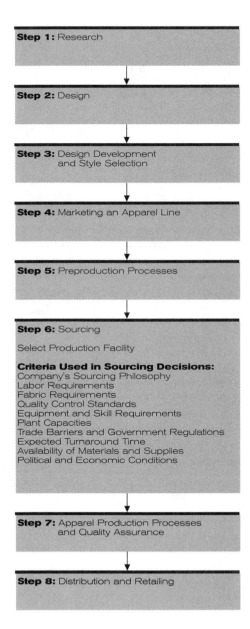

Step 1: Research

Step 2: Design

Step 3: Design Development
and Style Selection

Step 4: Marketing an Apparel Line

Step 5: Preproduction Processes

Step 6: Sourcing

Select Production Facility

Criteria Used in Sourcing Decisions:
Company's Sourcing Philosophy
Labor Requirements
Fabric Requirements
Quality Control Standards
Equipment and Skill Requirements
Plant Capacities
Trade Barriers and Government Regulations
Expected Turnaround Time
Availability of Materials and Supplies
Political and Economic Conditions

Step 7: Apparel Production Processes
and Quality Assurance

Step 8: Distribution and Retailing

Sourcing
Decisions
and Production
Centers

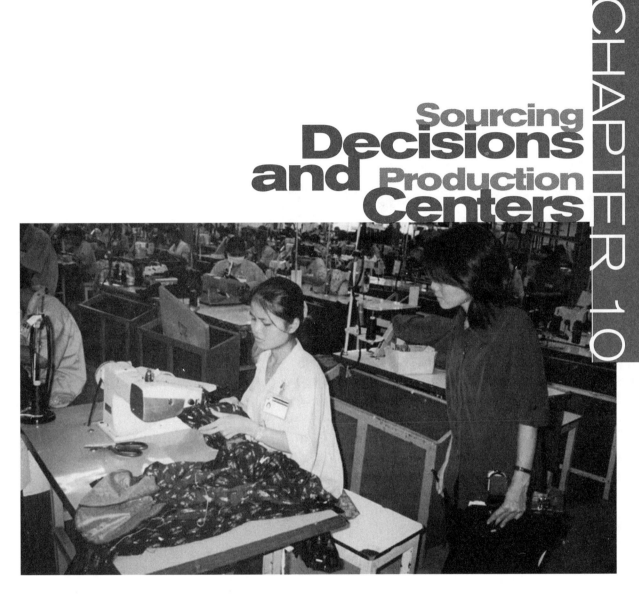

IN THIS CHAPTER YOU WILL LEARN:

■ The criteria used by apparel companies and retailers in their sourcing decisions.

■ The various sourcing options available to apparel companies and retailers.

■ The advantages and disadvantages of these sourcing options.

■ Current issues related to sourcing decisions.

■ The locations of the primary domestic and international production centers.

Sourcing Decisions

One of the most important decisions made by a company is how, when, and where to manufacture goods. This decision-making process is called **sourcing**. Sourcing decisions are important to both apparel manufacturers and retailers because they help to determine a company's competitive edge. This section outlines decision criteria, production options for companies, and issues surrounding domestic and **offshore production** (producing outside the United States using production specifications furnished by U.S. companies). On the facing page is a flowchart summarizing the sourcing process. Figure 10.1 diagrams the **sourcing options** available to apparel companies and retailers.

CRITERIA USED IN SOURCING DECISIONS

Before outlining the various sourcing options, the criteria companies use in making sourcing decisions will be examined. A number of criteria come into play when companies decide by what sources and where their products will be manufactured. The answers to a number of questions related to each criterion will help determine the best sourcing option for a company. These criteria include the company's sourcing philosophy, labor requirements and costs, fabric requirements, quality control standards, equipment requirements, plant capacities, trade barriers and government regulations, expected turnaround time, availability of materials and supplies, and political and economic conditions. "Cost has been and always will be a primary rea-

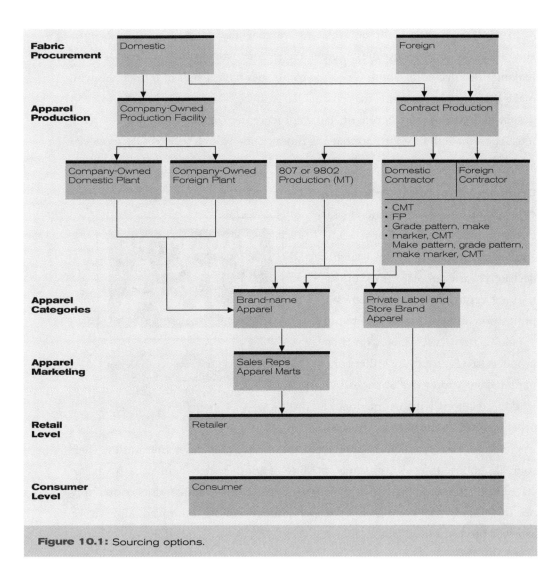

Figure 10.1: Sourcing options.

son for establishing manufacturing capacity offshore, as it is a factor of choice in country selection" (Cruz, 1995, p. 80). However, other factors must come into play when companies make sourcing decisions. These criteria are continually assessed to meet the production needs of a company. Because of the complexity of sourcing decisions, computer software programs have been developed that simulate the implications of various sourcing decisions for a company.

In small companies sourcing decisions are generally the responsibility of merchandisers. In larger companies, merchandisers may work with sourcing agents in making these decisions. Some very large companies have a staff of individuals who make the sourcing decisions for a particular product category. Those who work in design and product development, fabric procurement, and production sourcing must coordinate their efforts so that the product line will be successfully produced and distributed on time.

Company's Sourcing Philosophy

Often companies have a general philosophy toward sourcing that serves as a guideline or framework for sourcing decisions. For example, some companies are very committed to domestic production and want to be able to put "Made in the U.S.A." labels on their products (see Figure 10.2). Other companies have strong ties and positive working relations with contractors in other countries and therefore general-

Figure 10.2: For some companies the ability to put the "Made in the USA" logo on their products contributes to their sourcing decisions.

ly prefer offshore production. Some companies have guidelines that outline their sourcing philosophies. For example, because of conflicts over human rights issues stated in the sourcing guidelines, Levi Strauss & Co. pulled much of its contracting out of China in 1993 and five years later, after conditions improved, allowed for renewed production in China.

Labor Requirements and Costs

Apparel production is very labor intensive even though technological advances are increasingly automating the process. Therefore, labor costs are an important issue in sourcing decisions. Questions companies might ask include: How many workers will be required to produce the goods efficiently? What is the labor cost of domestic workers compared to workers in another country? How are the workers treated? If the company owns plants, what investments in technology and personnel training need to be made? As discussed in Chapter 1, the U.S. textile and apparel industries have always been in search of cheaper labor—first within the United States and then in other countries. Because of this, during the past 30 years, U.S. apparel companies and retailers of private label and store brand merchandise have moved a great deal of apparel production offshore where labor costs are considerably lower than in the United States. For example, in 1996 the average wage (estimates are in U.S. dollars, including fringe benefits and social charges) for apparel workers in the United States was $9.56 per hour, compared to $5.10 in Taiwan, $4.51 in Hong Kong, $2.38 in Costa Rica, $1.25 in Guatemala, $1.08 in Mexico, $.36 in India, $.32 in Vietnam, and $.28 in China. Obviously the labor costs in these other countries are much lower than in the United States. This is the primary reason why many manufacturers produce goods offshore (see Table 10.1).

TABLE 10.1

Comparisons of Apparel Manufacturing Labor Costs: Estimated Average Hourly Wages for Direct Labor Operators Including Social and Fringe Benefits, 1996 (in 1996 U.S. dollars)

NAFTA

United States	9.56
Canada	9.88
Mexico	1.08

European Union

France	15.13
Germany	18.43
Italy	14.32
Sweden	17.59
United Kingdom	9.37

Other European

Bulgaria	0.47
Russia	0.58
Turkey	1.49

Middle East and Africa

Egypt	0.63
Israel	5.65
Morocco	1.38
South Africa	1.26
Tunisia	0.98

South America

Argentina	3.45
Colombia	1.05
Peru	1.39

Asia and Southeast Asia

China	0.28
Hong Kong	4.51
India	0.36
Indonesia	0.34
Japan	16.29
Philippines	0.62
Taiwan	5.10
Vietnam	0.32

Central America

Costa Rica	2.38
Dominican Republic	1.62
Guatemala	1.25
Jamaica	1.80

Source: Werner International Inc., 1997.

To compare sourcing options according to labor cost, many companies have relied on comparisons of minimum wages. However, according to industry analysts, "direct labor comparative analyses, based on minimum wage, prove to be misleading for the following four reasons: (1) no one can sustain productive manufacturing operations on minimum wage, (2) not many significant manufacturers pay minimum wage, (3) not many employees will be attracted to work for minimum wage pay, and (4) employees typically cannot be persuaded to stay at a company when receiving minimum wage pay" (Cruz, 1995, p. 80). Instead industry-specific minimums, area-specific minimums, and plant minimums have been used for comparative purposes. When comparing labor costs, fringe benefits for workers (e.g., health benefits, retirement benefits, day care) must also be taken into account. Again, industry analysts suggest that labor cost include earned pay and that all other labor costs be included in fringe benefits (Cruz, 1995).

It is important to note that simply because the labor costs are lower in a particular country, one cannot assume that overall production costs will also be lower. Costs associated with support services and infrastructure, transportation, and shipping will vary across sourcing options and must also be taken into account when comparing costs of one option with another. Companies must examine both fixed and variable costs associated with manufacturing in the various options in order to assess accurately the financial benefits of any one option (Brooks, 1992). Table 10.2 compares the costs of manufacturing a sports jacket using offshore contract production with domestic production. Note that although the cost to purchase the jacket from an offshore contractor is less than total manufacturing costs using domestic production, transportation, credit, and administrative costs substantially raise the total buying costs. In addition, costs might not be the most important criterion for a company. According to Julia K. Hughes, chair of the U.S. Association of Importers of Textiles and Apparel, "our industry is global, but is based more on quality, availability and delivery schedules than prices" (Ostroff, 1996, p. 6).

Fabric Requirements

Whether the fabric will be procured in the United States or from a foreign supplier is also an important sourcing decision. If fabric is procured in the United States, companies may also want to manufacture the goods in the United States. If foreign fabric is used, typically the products are also produced offshore. This reduces costs

TABLE 10.2

Domestic and Offshore Contract Production per Jacket Cost for a Sports Jacket

	Production site	
Cost Element	**Domestic**	**Offshore**
Materials, including fabric, lining, and trim	$ 18.50	
Direct labor, including cut, make, trim, taxes, and fringe benefits	$ 13.40	
Factory expenses		
Supervision/indirect	$ 2.50	
Facilities	$ 2.00	$ 2.00
Insurance	$ 2.50	$ 2.50
Depreciation	$ 3.00	$ 3.00
Total cost to manufacture	**$ 41.90**	**$ 7.50**
Cost to purchase		$ 31.00
Other assignable costs		
Letters of credit (2 percent)		$ .62
Interest on higher inventory		$ .26
Transportation (5 percent)		$ 1.55
Procurement and administration		$ .31
Total transaction cost	**$ 41.90**	**$ 41.24**

by eliminating fabric shipping expenses. Another important question regarding the fabric is whether the fabric will be cut in the United States. If fabric is cut in the United States, even if the garments are sewn in another country, companies can take advantage of certain tariff allowances. This and other trade issues will be discussed later in the chapter.

Quality Control Standards

The importance of maintaining specific quality control standards is one criterion in a company's sourcing decision. Because quality is most effectively controlled in company-owned facilities, a company's response to the importance of quality control may be the primary reason for using company-owned plants for production or for selecting a contractor the company knows produces high-quality products (although they may be at a higher cost). When using either a domestic or offshore contractor, companies will expect to see sample garments and will articulate quality standards that the contractor must meet (see Figure 10.3).

Equipment and Skill Requirements

Depending on the product line, equipment and skill needs will vary. Some products require specific types of equipment or sewing skills. Therefore, companies will ask questions such as: What equipment is needed to efficiently produce the goods? How specialized are these equipment needs? What specific skills are required to produce the product line? Will different equipment be needed next season or next year to produce goods for the company? Companies will analyze the plant's equipment and the skills of sewing operators in terms of their production needs in their sourcing decisions (see Figure 10.4).

Figure 10.3: The ability to ensure that garments meet quality specifications is often a criterion in sourcing decisions.

Plant Capacities

Another criterion for sourcing decisions is what the plant capacities are relative to production needs. Companies will want to know the production capabilities of company-owned plants as well as contractors and whether these are sufficient to meet production needs. If they are found to be insufficient, the company may decide to hire (additional) contractors, expand current plants, or build new plants. Financial capacities to invest in new equipment will need to be analyzed. If plant capacities are found to be greater than needed, then downsizing strategies are in order. Facility costs will vary across countries, as will the terms of leasing. Some plants also require minimum orders. It is important for companies to read the fine print of leases to determine what is included.

Trade Barriers and Government Regulations

Under current international trade policies, textile and apparel goods imported into the United States from many countries are subject to trade barriers, such as tariffs

Figure 10.4: When specialized production equipment is required, companies work with contractors that have the needed equipment.

and quotas. **Tariffs** are taxes assessed by governments on imports; **quotas** are limits on the number of units, kilograms, or square meters equivalent (SME) in specific categories that can be imported from specific countries. Therefore, if offshore production is an option, the company must decide if and how these trade barriers may affect importing the goods they produce into the United States (or other countries). Because both tariffs and quotas add to the cost of production, companies that produce offshore must weigh these additional costs against the lower costs of labor in these countries. The North American Free Trade Agreement (NAFTA) has reduced trade barriers among the U.S., Mexico, and Canada. Therefore, a number of United States companies have moved their production to Mexico.

Other government regulations that companies consider when making sourcing decisions include country-specific laws associated with government intervention regarding industrial polution, the monitoring of air and water quality, minimum wage requirements, and child labor laws. When laws in other countries are less strict than what U.S. companies believe is appropriate, companies may establish their own codes of conduct that they require their offshore contractors to abide by. These codes of conduct will be discussed later in the chapter. Tax laws are also a consideration for companies. For example, recent changes in Mexican income tax laws may affect U.S. companies that are sourcing in Mexico ("Mexico tax reform," 1999).

Expected Turnaround Time

Other questions asked by companies are: How fast can goods be produced, shipped, and distributed to retailers? Would turnaround time be faster if production location changed? In an era when getting products to the consumer as quickly as possible is important to the success of a company, production, shipping, and distribution times need to be determined and compared. Companies should consider the distance and shipping time between the sewing factory and the company's distribution center. For example, a company with a distribution center in New York may choose a contractor in Mexico over a contractor in Thailand because of shipping time and costs. Strategies associated with Quick Response are designed to shorten the time between fiber and finished product through increased use of technology. In addition, with improved supply chain management strategies such as enhanced communication technologies (e.g., e-mail, Internet), information can be sent electronically and therefore reduce the time involved.

Turnaround time is particularly important for time-sensitive products such as swimwear. It is estimated that two-thirds of all swimwear is sold from May through July. Therefore, for reorders, swimwear companies need the fastest turnaround possible. Because of this, many swimwear companies manufacture their goods domestically. For example, Authentic Fitness, maker of Speedo swimwear, estimates that its swimwear, which can be produced in 5 weeks domestically, would take 16 weeks if produced offshore (Brown, 1995). Thus, because of the shorter turnaround time, domestic production is preferred over offshore production.

Availability of Materials and Supplies

When making sourcing decisions, companies must also analyze the availability and reliability of each country's infrastructure and support areas. Are quality trims and threads readily available? Are sewing machine technicians and parts available? Are power sources, transportation methods, and shipping options reliable? These questions are particularly important when exploring production in less-developed countries.

Political and Economic Conditions

Companies that source offshore continually monitor the political and economic conditions of countries where production is taking place. Political instability or economic problems can affect the availability of materials and the reliability of transportation and shipping alternatives. For example, the economic crisis of 1997–98 in many Asian countries led to delayed shipping of some orders or, in some cases, canceled production contracts.

Sourcing Options

Based on these factors, a number of sourcing options are available to apparel companies and retailers. In general, major sourcing decisions focus on:

1. Whether production will be
   - Domestic.
   - Offshore.
   - A combination of both.

2. Whether production will be:
   - In a company-owned facility.
   - Contracted to others.
   - A combination of both.

When using contractors, the decision must also be made about which of the following options to employ:

- **Cut, make, and trim services.** With the **cut, make, and trim (CMT)** option, the apparel company provides the designs, fabrics, and trims and the contractor provides labor and supplies.
- **Full-package services.** With the **full-package (FP)** option, the contractor provides preproduction services, fabrics, trims, supplies, and labor.

Advantages and disadvantages of each option must be weighed by companies in light of their product line, operation strategies, and organization philosophy. For some companies, the flexibility afforded by using contractors is necessary; other companies believe they have greater quality control by producing products in their own plants. Some companies produce offshore to take advantage of lower labor

TABLE 10.3

Advantages and Disadvantages of Domestic and Offshore Production

	Advantages	Disadvantages
Domestic production	Trade barriers not a concern Shipping time and costs may be lower Supported by consumers who prefer products "made in the USA"	Labor coss higher than in other countries
Offshore production	Labor costs lower than in the United States Can take advantage of 9802 production	Differences in cultural norms Language barriers Possible trade barriers

costs. However, just because labor costs are lower in another country does not necessarily mean that overall production costs are lower or that producing offshore is the right decision for a company. What follows are the basic sourcing alternatives available to apparel manufacturers and retailers. Tables 10.3 and 10.4 outline the primary advantages and disadvantages of these sourcing options.

TABLE 10.4

Advantages and Disadvantages of Company-Owned Facility Production and Contractor Production

	Advantages	Disadvantages
Company-owned facility production	Greater quality control Greater control over production timing Communication with textile suppliers and retailers optimized	Financial requirements associated with equipment and personnel Need to ensure continuous production Higher labor costs Foreign ownership creates additional financial risks
Contractor production	Greater flexibility to changing equipment or production needs No investment in factories, equipment, or training needed	Less control over quality or production timing

DOMESTIC FABRIC, DOMESTIC PRODUCTION IN COMPANY-OWNED FACILITY

In this case, fabric produced in the United States is shipped to a company-owned plant in the United States for production. This option allows for the greatest control over quality and timing of production. Communication with textile suppliers and retailers is also optimized. To be competitive, companies that own their own facilities need to (and have the control to) invest in technology to increase productivity and reduce sewing costs. Companies that choose this option typically produce similar types of goods each year so that equipment requirements do not change drastically. Companies must also invest in training personnel. It was estimated in 1994 that the cost of training new sewers could be as high as $5,000 per sewer (Ratoff, 1994). Companies must also plan to maintain consistent and continuous production so that personnel are not continually laid off during slow periods and then rehired during busy periods. To maintain continuous production, these companies will sometimes serve as contractors for other companies during times of slow production. Labor costs are generally higher for companies that own their own plants, but many companies are dedicated to making domestic production competitive through increased productivity. Generally, companies that have chosen this option are proud to put the "Made in the USA" label on their products and are committed to domestic production. The early implementation of Quick Response strategies in apparel production was common for companies that produced domestically in their own plants. Other advantages of this option are that companies do not have to worry about trade barriers and shipping costs and production time may be less than for products produced offshore. As one industry consultant stated, "owning a sewing factory requires a long-term view, commitment and deep pockets" (Ratoff, 1994, p. 7).

DOMESTIC FABRIC, DOMESTIC CONTRACTOR PRODUCTION

Under this option, fabric is procured domestically and production is contracted to a domestic company (contractor) that specializes in the type of production and services (CMT or FP) required. By using a contractor, the company may lose some control over quality and timing of production. However, with contractor production, the company does not have to invest in factories, equipment, or training personnel. This is important for small companies that may not have the financial resources to build a production plant. By using contractors, companies have increased flexibility in production methods. This is important for companies with product lines—and therefore equipment needs—that vary from year to year. Sometimes manufacturers that typically produce in their own plants choose this option when orders have outpaced their production capacity. For those that believe producing in the United States is important, companies can still put "Made in the U.S.A." on their labels when they use domestic contractors. As with the previous sourcing option, trade barriers are not a concern under this option, and shipping costs and production time may be advantageous.

An example of a successful domestic contractor is Koos Manufacturing, a Los Angeles-area jeans and pants manufacturer that has two primary customers, the Gap and Calvin Klein. Koos Manufacturing facilities includes space for fabric storage, pattern marking and grading, spreading and cutting, sewing, laundry, finishing, and shipping (Henricks, 1998).

Contractors can be located in several ways. *Sourcing fairs* are trade shows that bring contractors and companies together. At these fairs, contractors have booths with samples of their merchandise and information regarding their expertise and capacities. Sourcing fairs are also held in conjunction with other trade shows, such as the Bobbin Show or the American Apparel Contractors Association convention. Both domestic and foreign contractors use sourcing fairs to connect with companies, and companies use them to find appropriate domestic and foreign contractors. Contractors and companies also use classified advertisements in trade papers such as *Women's Wear Daily* or *Daily News Record* to advertise their need or availability. Business-to-business (B2B) electronic commerce is also being used for sourcing raw materials (fabric, trims) are well as production (see, for example, the American Apparel Producers' Network at www.usawear.org). Growth is expected in B2B electronic commerce in enhancing supply chain management (Bassuk & Skatoff, 2001), including sourcing.

DOMESTIC OR FOREIGN FABRIC WITH 807 (9802) PRODUCTION

Using fabric produced either in the United States or elsewhere, companies choosing this option combine domestic production (i.e., design and cut) with a special type of offshore production known as **807** or **9802 production**. Under the Har-

monized Tariff Schedule number 9802 (formerly number 807) of the U.S. tariff regulations, when garment pieces are cut in the United States and shipped to contractors in specified countries for assembly, tariffs are only on the "value added"
(typically the cost of assembly) to the garment. For example, hypothetically speak-
ing, suppose the value of the cut garment pieces were $50,000 when they were
shipped to Costa Rica for assembly. After assembly, the garments were worth
$150,000 when they were shipped back to the United States. Under this tariff reg-
ulation, the import tax would be calculated on $100,000, the value added to the
garment pieces.

This option provides the manufacturer with control over the design and cut of
the garments, while taking advantage of lower labor costs in other countries. Contractors that participate in this type of production offer a variation of CMT services—that is—the MT (make and trim) without the C (cut). With this option, however, companies must be concerned with any quota requirements, which are the
same as for other garments. Companies also must be able to handle possible language and cultural differences when working with contractors in other countries.
The 807(A) program, begun in 1986, furnishes duty breaks and unlimited quotas
for apparel assembled in Caribbean Basin nations using fabric produced and cut in
the United States. In some cases, fabric is cut in Texas or California and shipped to
Mexico for assembly. The term **maquiladora operations** is used to describe
"assembly plants, mostly along the U.S.-Mexico border, in which garments are
assembled from U.S.-cut parts and shipped back to the United States" (Dickerson,
1995, p. 189).

DOMESTIC OR FOREIGN FABRIC, FOREIGN CONTRACTOR PRODUCTION

This option is similar to the previous option, except that garments are not cut in the
United States. Foreign contractors can provide both CMT and FP services to companies (see Figure 10.5). The primary advantage is the lower labor costs found in other
countries. Disadvantages are similar to those for the previous option: possible trade
barriers and language and cultural differences in other countries. When using
domestic fabric, shipping time and costs may be higher than if fabrics were produced closer to the production facilities.

Nike's global operations

Nike's products are manufactured in 33 countries, touching just about every corner of the world.

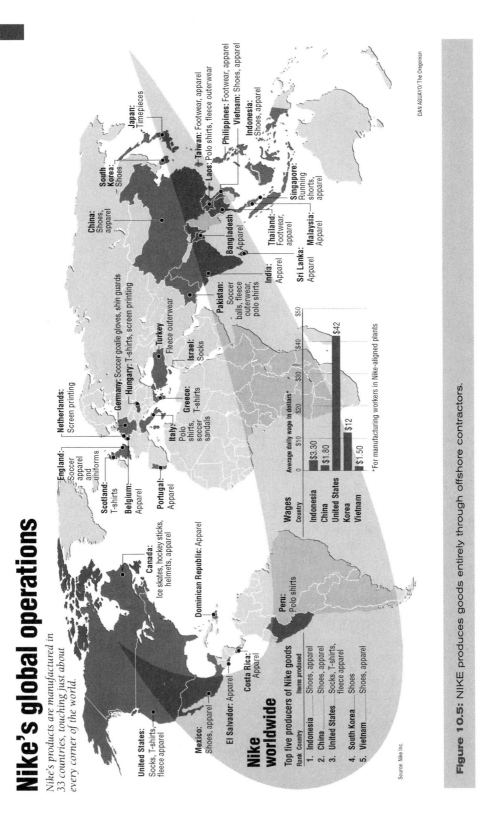

United States: Socks, T-shirts, fleece apparel

Netherlands: Screen printing

England: Soccer apparel and uniforms

Scotland: T-shirts

Belgium: Apparel

Portugal: Apparel

Germany: Soccer goalie gloves, shin guards

Hungary: T-shirts, screen printing

Turkey: Fleece outerwear

Italy: Polo shirts, soccer sandals

Greece: T-shirts

Israel: Socks

China: Shoes, apparel

South Korea: Shoes

Japan: Timepieces

Taiwan: Footwear, apparel

Laos: Polo shirts, fleece outerwear

Philippines: Footwear, apparel

Vietnam: Shoes, apparel

Indonesia: Shoes, apparel

Singapore: Running shorts, apparel

Thailand: Footwear, apparel

Malaysia: Apparel

Bangladesh: Apparel

India: Apparel

Sri Lanka: Apparel

Pakistan: Soccer balls, fleece outerwear, polo shirts

Canada: Ice skates, hockey sticks, helmets, apparel

Dominican Republic: Apparel

Mexico: Shoes, apparel

El Salvador: Apparel

Costa Rica: Apparel

Peru: Polo shirts

Nike worldwide

Top five producers of Nike goods

Rank	Country	Items produced
1.	Indonesia	Shoes, apparel
2.	China	Shoes, apparel
3.	United States	Socks, T-shirts, fleece apparel
4.	South Korea	Shoes
5.	Vietnam	Shoes, apparel

Wages

Average daily wage in dollars*

Country	
Indonesia	$3.30
China	$1.80
United States	$42
Korea	$12
Vietnam	$1.50

*For manufacturing workers in Nike-aligned plants

Source: Nike Inc.

DAN AGUAYO/ The Oregonian

Figure 10.5: NIKE produces goods entirely through offshore contractors.

FOREIGN FABRIC, FOREIGN PRODUCTION IN COMPANY-OWNED FOREIGN FACILITY

In some cases, companies may own production facilities in other countries. For example, since NAFTA there have been increased investments in production facilities by U.S. companies in Mexico. Although this option allows companies to have control over quality and timing of production while taking advantage of lower labor costs in other countries, the financial risks associated with building and running a production facility outside the United States are great. Government policies, personnel expectations, and cultural norms regarding business operations in another country may be very different from those in the United States. In fact, under some countries' policies, foreign ownership of plants is prohibited. Companies that own their production facilities must abide by the laws governing international trade regarding tariffs and quotas, just as companies that contract offshore do.

COMBINATION OF ALTERNATIVES

Many companies are diversifying their sourcing; that is, they use a combination of options depending on their production requirements at any point in time. Using a variety of sourcing options provides companies with the flexibility needed to change production in response to consumer demand, production requirements, and international relations.

Companies often combine domestic and offshore production. A company that has successfully combined domestic and offshore contractor production is Karen Kane, a manufacturer of women's better sportswear and separates. With corporate and design headquarters and distribution center located in Los Angeles, most of the cutting and all of their sewing operations are sourced to both domestic and foreign contractors that provide both CMT and full-package services. They believe these sourcing decisions allow for the greatest flexibility in meeting their production needs (Winger, 1999). Another company that successfully combines U.S. and offshore contract production is Patagonia, headquartered in Ventura Beach, California. Using 50 contractors, approximately 50 percent of their cutting and sewing operations are in the United States, 20 percent are in Asia, 20 percent are in Mexico or other countries where 807 (9802) production occurs, and 10 percent are in Europe. To ensure product quality and that the contractors abide by environmental requirements, minimum wage, and minimum age standards set by Patagonia, company representatives visit each contractor. When working with a new contractors, Patagonia orders 1,000 practice items, which may be sold later at one of their outlet stores (Welling, 1999).

TRENDS IN SOURCING

Sourcing decisions are complex and companies continually assess sourcing options to best meet their needs. In order to be competitive, production facilities, both domestic and offshore, must be responsive, flexible, efficient, and cost-effective. In the U.S. apparel industry we continue to see a trend toward offshore production. According to industry analysts:

> Much of the offshore movement has been—and is expected to continue—to areas south of the border: Mexico, the Caribbean Basin and Central America. The move south has been fueled largely by favorable trade legislation and competitive labor costs, as well as the advantages of proximity to the U.S. market: the ability to manage what are essentially nearby operations, lower shipping and transportation costs (compared to Asia) and the convenience of doing business in the same or close time zones. ("Survival of the fittest," 1998)

Reasons for the increase in offshore contract production include the number of offshore contractors that have design and/or production capabilities (full-package services), and the progress that has been made in computer compatibility, which has led to an increased use in electronic transmission of information such as garment specification sheets or patterns. Such shifts in production have contributed to declines in employment in domestic apparel production. In fact, according to the Labor Department, the number of jobs in apparel manufacturing has declined steadily since 1991.

There are numerous examples of manufacturers who once produced in the United States that have moved production offshore. Timberland, the producer of hiking boots and outerwear, contracted only 5 percent of its production in 1990. However by the end of 1995, 60 percent of its production was offshore. By 1996, virtually all of its production had been shifted to offshore contractors. In the early 1990s, 95 percent of Guess jeans manufacturing was done domestically. By 1998, 60 percent of its production was accomplished offshore (primarily in Mexico). Pendleton Woolen Mills, the all-American producer of men's and women's woolen and nonwoolen apparel, blankets, and piece goods moved some production of nonwool merchandise to Mexico to take advantage of duty-free imports under the North American Free Trade Agreement. Other companies have turned "to nearby Central American and Caribbean countries for their production needs, where labor costs are still lower than they are in the U.S., and where proximity helps improve quality control and shipping times" (Friedman, 1996, p. 6).

Production Centers

DOMESTIC PRODUCTION CENTERS

U.S. production facilities pride themselves in offering flexibility, innovation, speedy turnaround time, and efficient delivery to retailers. Employment in apparel production can be found in every state, although the states with the largest employment in apparel production are (in order) California, New York, Texas, North Carolina, Alabama, Pennsylvania, Georgia, Tennessee, New Jersey, Kentucky, and Florida (see Table 10.5). This distribution reflects the historical concentration of apparel manufacturing in the New York City and Los Angeles areas and the lower wages found in the southern states in comparison to other states. More than 120,000 people were employed in apparel production in Los Angeles in 1998, making apparel manufacturing the city's largest manufacturing sector. In New York City in 1997, nearly one-half of all manufacturing workers were in the apparel industry. New York's industry consists of approximately 4,500 companies—4,000 contractors and 500 designer/

TABLE 10.5
Top Ten States for Employment in the Apparel Industry

State	Number of Employees in the Apparel Industry
California	144,100
New York	77,800
Texas	47,200
North Carolina	41,000
Pennsylvania	35,200
Alabama	29,000
Georgia	28,100
New Jersey	23,200
Tennessee	22,900
Kentucky	20,200

Source: American Textile Manufacturers Institute. *Textile HiLights.* (2,000 September). p. 31.

manufacturers. Through the Garment Industry Development Corporation of New York City (GIDC), training and educational programs have been established to improve the skills of apparel workers.

Within the United States, Texas and California have seen the greatest growth in apparel production jobs in the past decade. Figure 10.6 shows a worker in a Levi Strauss & Co. plant. In Southern California this growth has been attributed to the pool of skilled labor, primarily from the Latino and Asian populations in the area. Growth in apparel production facilities in states that border Mexico can also be

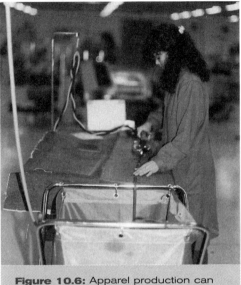

Figure 10.6: Apparel production can be found in every state, although the highest concentration is in New York and California.

attributed to the increased trade with Mexico as a result of the North American Free Trade Agreement. For example, many companies are moving production to Texas in order to be closer to Mexico, without actually moving production to Mexico. Criteria used by companies in opening or expanding production facilities include "proximity to headquarters, affordability of utilities, availability of skilled labor and an appropriate existing building" (DesMarteau, 1994, p. 80). Florida has also experienced growth in apparel production that is centered on 807 and 807(A) production, in which garments are cut in Florida and sewn in the Caribbean Basin (Moore, 1995).

FOREIGN PRODUCTION CENTERS

From a global perspective, apparel production facilities can be found in developed countries (industrialized countries) such as Canada, Japan, and countries in Western Europe; newly industrialized countries (NICs) such as Mexico, Brazil, Hong Kong, South Korea, and Taiwan; developing countries such as Bangladesh, Costa Rica, and Guatemala; and countries governed by single-party communist regimes such as

China and Vietnam. Many of the newly industrialized countries have large textile and apparel industries. For example, apparel production is Hong Kong's largest industry.

Hong Kong, Taiwan, South Korea, and China are sometimes referred to as the Big Four in textiles and apparel trade because of their importance in the global production of textiles and apparel. Worldwide, the largest apparel exporters are China, Italy, Hong Kong, Germany, and United States (see Table 10.6). The largest textile and apparel exporters to the United States are Mexico, Canada, China, Pakistan, Taiwan, and South Korea (see Table 10.7)

As with the newly industrialized countries, many developing countries rely on textile and apparel manufacturing for their economic development. Several characteristics of textile and apparel manufacturing account for this. Because textile and apparel production is highly labor intensive, the industry provides work for many people. Compared with other manufacturing industries, apparel production is fairly inexpensive to establish. Essentially, all that is needed are industrial sewing machines, pressing equipment, and a building. In addition, because of continuously changing fashion trends, there is a constant demand for textile and apparel products. Thus, the textile and apparel industry is often the first rung on the ladder of economic development for individuals as well as for countries. Therefore, developing countries in Southeast Asia, Africa, the Caribbean Basin, and South

---

TABLE 10.6

Largest Exporters of Apparel
(in billions of U.S. dollars)

Country	$Billion
China	24,049
Italy	14,036
Hong Kong	9,540
Germany	7,384
United States	6,651
Turkey	6,119
France	5,621
South Korea	4,957
United Kingdom	4,649
Thailand	4,620

Source: Verret, Raoul. (1997, September). Competitiveness and globalization: The international challenge. *Apparel Industry Magazine*, pp. 18–27.

TABLE 10.7

Textile and Apparel Exporters to U.S.
(percent share)

Country	Percent Share
Mexico	14.36%
Canada	9.90
China	7.03
Pakistan	5.18
Taiwan	4.73
South Korea	4.31
India	4.22
Hong Kong	3.80
Thailand	3.78
Indonesia	3.30
Dominican Republic	3.26
Philippines	3.22
Bangladesh	3.16
Honduras	2.20
Turkey	2.08

Sources: Jacobs, Brenda A. (1999, November). Regional pacts produce new trade patterns. *Bobbin*, p. 67; U.S. Department of Commerce, Office of Textiles and Apparel.

America greatly contribute to the global production of textiles and apparel (see Figure 10.7).

Spurred by the North American Free Trade Agreement, in 1995 Mexico surpassed China as the United States' leading supplier of imported apparel and textiles with Canada being second. In fact "between 1995 and 1998 Mexican apparel exports to the United States increased 119 percent" (Kessler, 1999, p. 54). Although analysts predict that China will again surpass Mexico once quotas are entirely phased out worldwide in 2005, Mexico has gained popularity as a sourcing option because of reduced or zero duties and shorter turnaround time as compared to Asian countries (Ostroff, 1995).

Prior to NAFTA, most of the U.S. imported apparel from Mexico had been cut in the United States and imported under 807 (9802) trade regulations. In addition, at that time, quality and communications issues kept many U.S. companies from sourcing in Mexico. Since the implementation of NAFTA, production in Mexico has become more technologically advanced, quality has improved, production has increased (particularly full-package contract production), supply chain management

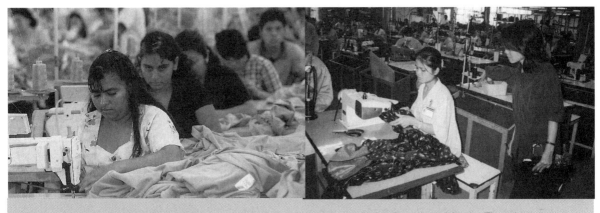

Figure 10.7: Production facilities for apparel and accessories can be found worldwide. The plant on the left produces apparel for Gap in El Salvador. The facility on the right is in Thailand.

strategies have been implemented, and U.S. apparel companies are making more long-term financial commitments in Mexico. Financial investments include capital investments in maquiladora operations, shared ownership of production facilities, and establishment of wholly owned subsidiaries in Mexico (Kessler, 1999). These new production alliances "represent a higher level of long-term organizational and transnational interfirm integration" (Kessler, 1999, p. 58) and will most likely continue to grow in the future.

Current Issues in Domestic and Foreign Production

CHANGES IN INTERNATIONAL TRADE LAWS

International trade laws are constantly changing, and it is important for apparel companies and retailers to stay on top of trade issues. Currently, one of the greatest disadvantages to foreign production is international trade restrictions, including tariffs and quotas. However, several developments in international trade laws have affected how apparel manufacturers and retailers view offshore production. The North American Free Trade Agreement, which took effect on January 1, 1994, phased in duty-free trade among Canada, Mexico, and the United States. With the success of NAFTA, a Free Trade Area of the Americas (FTAA) agreement among countries in the Western Hemisphere is now under consideration. Worldwide, other regional trade agreements have also been implemented or are under consideration. These include the European Community, the Group of Three agreement (Mexico, Venezuela, and Colombia), and other agreements among Mexico, Central American countries, and South American countries (Jacobs, 1999). In addition, the World Trade Organization (WTO) Agreement on textiles and clothing went into effect on January 1, 1995. According to the WTO, the Multi-Fiber Arrangement (MFA) and quotas on textiles and apparel will be phased out and tariffs will be reduced by the year 2005 for products of WTO member countries.

SWEATSHOPS IN DOMESTIC AND OFFSHORE PRODUCTION

What is a sweatshop? Definitions of sweatshops vary depending upon the source of the definition. According to the U.S. General Accounting Office, a **sweatshop** is an employer that violates two or more federal or state labor, occupational safety and health, workers' compensation, or other laws regulating industry. The International Labor Rights Fund defines sweatshops as "work environments that include some of the following characteristics: pay is less than a living wage, excessively long hours of work are required often without overtime pay, work is done in unsafe or inhumane conditions, and workers are systematically abused by the employer or suffer from sexual harassment, and/or workers have no ability to organize to negotiate better terms of work" (International Labor Rights Fund, 2000). As reported in the *New York Times* (Finder, 1995, p. B4), sweatshops "generally employ 20 to 50 workers, many of them illegal immigrants, willing to suffer long hours, low pay and miserable working conditions, just to have a job . . . [Owners] pay their workers in cash and often deny them the minimum wage, overtime, holidays or any other benefits." Because of the highly decentralized nature of the industry, it is difficult to estimate the number of sweatshops in the U.S. and abroad; although in the U.S., the New York City and Los Angeles areas, where there are large concentrations of immigrants, are often cited as meccas for such establishments (Malone, 2001).

Although sweatshops have been around since the turn of the twentieth century, the prevalence of sweatshops in the apparel industry has grown in recent years. A number of factors have contributed to this problem. Until the 1960s, a majority of U.S. apparel companies owned large factories where workers were usually unionized.

Federal and state agencies could easily inspect the facilities and enforce labor, health, and environmental laws. However, in a highly competitive environment, many companies moved away from owning their own facilities to using contractors for the assembly phase of production. This has resulted in a shift in apparel production from large, company-owned factories to a vast array of small, specialized contractors and subcontractors both within the U.S. and in other countries. Along with this shift, the industry has seen a growth in and proliferation of sweatshops (Bonacich & Appelbaum, 2000). At the same time, there has been a decrease in government agencies' ability to regulate working conditions. See Table 10.8 for a timeline of the sweatshop issue.

Reminiscent of the early 1900s, stories have emerged of lurid working conditions, piecework pay below minimum wage, and children working and playing alongside their mothers (see Figure 10.8) in factories (Lii, 1995) or of the notorious sweatshop in El Monte, California, where Thai immigrants were held in conditions of semi-enslavement (Bonacich & Appelbaum, 2000). In recent years, many apparel manufacturers and retailers have been admonished for using contractors in both the U.S. and abroad that violate human and labor rights by using child labor, tolerating poor working conditions, and accepting violence against union groups. Initially, the government, as well as labor, human rights, and religious groups put pressure on apparel manufacturers and retailers to refrain from using foreign suppliers that violated human and labor rights or hiring contractors in countries with political policies that violated human and labor rights. However, simply boycotting such contractors or countries was not necessarily the answer to this complex problem. In many developing countries, apparel production was found to provide much-needed jobs for thousands of workers. In many cases, the wages of working children were essential for providing basic necessities for themselves and their families. Therefore, rather than punishing these individuals by boycotting the country or contractor and leaving them without needed jobs, companies have responded by attempting to reform working conditions and make sure that workers are not abused. Manufacturers and retailers have taken greater responsibility for monitoring the working conditions of their contractors and subcontractors. Many large retailers and mass manufacturers have adopted sourcing guidelines and regularly inspect contractors' facilities to ensure that workers are not being exploited.

TABLE 10.8

A Timeline of the Sweatshop Issue

1851	Isaac Singer patents the sewing machine for factory use.
1900	International Ladies' Garment Workers Union (ILGWU) is formed to improve working conditions in the U.S. garment industry.
1911	146 garment workers die in a fire at the Triangle Shirtwaist factory in New York's garment district. The tragedy stimulates a movement to end "sweatshop" conditions.
1917	The Amalgamated Clothing Workers of America union is formed as the primary union for the men's wear industry.
1951	Employment in the apparel and knitwear industries in New York City peaks at 380,000.
1968	Minimum wage increases to $1.60 per hour.
1976	The Amalgamated Clothing Workers of America merges with the Textile Workers of America and the United Shoe Workers of America unions to form the Amalgamated Clothing and Textile Workers Union.
1984	Crafted With Pride in USA Council is formed.
1992	Levi Strauss & Co. becomes one of the first companies to establish a code of conduct for its hired contractors.
1995	The Amalgamated Clothing and Textile Workers Union and the International Ladies' Garment Workers Union merge to become the Union of Needletrades, Industrial, and Textile Employees (UNITE).
1996–April	The Kathie Lee Gifford sweatshop scandal: merchandise she endorsed, is found to have been made in sweatshops in an El Salvadoran maquiladoras.
1996–August	The White House forms the Apparel Industry Partnership (AIP), a voluntary partnership of apparel and shoe manufacturers, trade unions, consumer and human rights organizations. The Partnership's task is to develop a plan of action to end sweatshops.
1997–April	The AIP releases a code of conduct for apparel producers.
1997–Fall	Notre Dame becomes the first college or university in the country to adopt a code of conduct for companies producing licensed merchandise.
1998–July	Activists found the United Students Against Sweatshops (USAS).

1998–August	The first National Labor Committee-USAS delegation goes to Central America to speak with workers and local Non-Government Organizations (NGO). They spend one week among El Salvador, Honduras, and Nicaragua collecting data.
1998–November	The AIP creates the Fair Labor Association (FLA), backed by the U.S. Labor Department. UNITE!, the Interfaith Center for Corporate Responsibility; other NGOs drop out of the association. (www.fairlabor.org)
1999–July	The USAS National Organizing Conference is held in Washington, D.C. Some 200 students protest the FLA at the Labor Department.
1999–Fall	Anti-sweatshop activists create an alternative system to the FLA: The Workers Rights Consortium (WRC). The WRC is "a non-profit organization that supports and verifies licensee compliance with production codes of conduct." (www.workersrights.org)
1999F–2000W	Citing student demand, NIKE names 41 factory locations in 11 countries making its merchandise. Gear for Sports, Champion, Russell Athletic, Jansport, and Eastpak follow suit.
2000–Spring	A second wave of sit-ins rocks the country (U. Penn., Michigan, UW-Madison, Johns Hopkins, and Toronto). The WRC grows from 2 members to 13 (in March). U. Penn and UW-Madison are the first two schools to leave the FLA.
2000–April	Founding conference of the WRC.
2000–Spring	University of Oregon joins the WRC; Phil Knight, UO alum and institution's largest single donor, indicates he will no longer donate to the university.
2000–July	WRC successfully completes its first board meeting.
2000–November	To date, 66 colleges and universities have affiliated with the WRC.
2001–January	The FLA approves seven companies for participation in their monitoring program and accredits its first independent external monitor (Verité). To date, 149 colleges and universities have affiliated with the FLA.
2005	Quotas on textiles and apparel imported from World Trade Organization members are phased out.

Figure 10.8: Sweatshop conditions in apparel manufacturing still exist despite government and industry pressure to maintain safe and healthful working conditions.

One of the first companies to implement such guidelines was Levi Strauss & Co. In 1992, it established guidelines for its hired contractors covering issues such as the treatment of workers and the environmental impact of production (Zachary, 1994; see Tables 10.9 and 10.10). Levi Strauss & Co., which works with contractors throughout the world, regularly inspects plants and will cancel contracts with companies that breach these rules. Levi Strauss will not source in countries where conditions violate certain human rights (Haas, 1994).

In 1996, President Clinton established the Apparel Industry Partnership, a task force of apparel companies, unions, and human rights groups to focus on sweatshop and human rights issues within the global apparel industry. Member companies and groups included NIKE; Liz Claiborne; Nicole Miller; L.L.Bean; Reebok; Phillips-Van Heusen; Patagonia; Union of Needletrades, Industrial, and Textile Employees (UNITE); National Consumers League; Retail Wholesale Department Store Union; International Labor Rights Fund; and Business for Social Responsibility. In 1997 the Apparel Industry Partnership presented its agreement and plan of action to end sweatshops. The agreement outlined a Workplace Code of Conduct and Principles

Levi Strauss & Company Country Assessment Guidelines

The numerous countries where Levi Strauss & Co. has existing or future business interests present a variety of cultural, political, social and economic circumstances.

The Country Assessment Guidelines help us assess any issues that might present concern in light of the ethical principles we have set for ourselves. The Guidelines assist us in making practical and principled business decisions as we balance the potential risks and opportunities associated with conducting business in specific countries. Specifically, we assess whether the:

- Health and Safety Conditions would meet the expectations we have for employees and their families or our company representatives;
- Human Rights Environment would allow us to conduct business activities in a manner that is consistent with our Global Sourcing and Operating Guidelines and other company policies;
- Legal System would provide the necessary support to adequately protect our trademarks, investments or other commercial interests, or to implement the Global Sourcing and Operating Guidelines and other company policies; and
- Political, Economic and Social Environment would protect the company's commercial interests and brand/corporate image. We will not conduct business in countries prohibited by U.S. laws.

Source: Levi Strauss & Company

of Monitoring that companies would voluntarily adopt and would require their contractors to adopt. The Workplace Code of Conduct includes the following:

- Prohibitions against child labor, worker abuse or harassment, and discrimination.

- Recognition of workers' rights of freedom of association and collective bargaining.

- A minimum or prevailing industry wage, a maximum 60-hour work week, and a cap on mandatory overtime.

- A safe and healthful working environment.

A number of companies including NIKE, Liz Claiborne, Gap, Kellwood, Columbia Sportswear, Reebok, JCPenney, Wal-Mart, Nordstrom, and others have established their own guidelines and codes of conduct (see Table 10.11 for an example of these guidelines).

Even as companies adopted guidelines, improvement of working conditions in factories was difficult, particularly if companies did not inspect plants and enforce their codes and if governments did not enforce certain standards. In many cases,

TABLE 10.10

Levi Strauss & Company Terms of Engagement

Our Terms of Engagement help us to select business partners who follow workplace standards and business practices that are consistent with Levi Strauss & Co.'s values and policies. These requirements are applied to every contractor who manufactures or finishes products for Levi Strauss & Co. Trained assessors closely monitor compliance among our manufacturing and finishing contractors in more than 60 countries. The Terms of Engagement are as follows:

Ethical Standards

We will seek to identify and utilize business partners who aspire as individuals and in the conduct of all their businesses to a set of ethical standards not incompatible with our own.

Legal Requirements

We expect our business partners to be law abiding as individuals and to comply with legal requirements relevant to the conduct of all their businesses.

Environmental Requirements

We will only do business with partners who share our commitment to the environment and who conduct their business in a way that is consistent with Levi Strauss & Co.'s Environmental Philosophy and Guiding Principles.

Community Involvement

We will favor business partners who share our commitment to improving community conditions.

Employment Standards

We will only do business with partners who adhere to the following guidelines:

Child Labor

Use of child labor is not permissible. Workers can be no less than 15 years of age and not younger than the compulsory age to be in school. We will not utilize partners who use child labor in any of their facilities. We support the development of legitimate workplace apprenticeship programs for the educational benefit of younger people.

Prison Labor/Forced Labor

We will not utilize prison or forced labor in contracting relationships in the manufacture and finishing of our products. We will not utilize or purchase materials from a business partner utilizing prison or forced labor.

Disciplinary Practices

We will not utilize business partners who use corporal punishment or other forms of mental or physical coercion.

Working Hours

While permitting flexibility in scheduling, we will identify local legal limits on work hours and seek business partners who do not exceed them except for appropriately compensated overtime. While we favor partners who utilize less than sixty-hour work weeks, we will not use contractors who, on a regular basis, require in excess of a sixty-hour week. Employees should be allowed at least one day off in seven.

Wages and Benefits

We will only do business with partners who provide wages and benefits that comply with any applicable law and match the prevailing local manufacturing or finishing industry practices.

Freedom of Association

We respect workers' rights to form and join organizations of their choice and to bargain collectively. We expect our suppliers to respect the right to free association and the right to organize and bargain collectively without unlawful interference.

Business partners should ensure that workers who make such decisions or participate in such organizations are not the object of discrimination or punitive disciplinary actions and that the representatives of such organizations have access to their members under conditions established either by local laws or mutual agreement between the employer and the worker organizations.

Discrimination

While we recognize and respect cultural differences, we believe that workers should be employed on the basis of their ability to do the job, rather than on the basis of personal characteristics or beliefs. We will favor business partners who share this value.

Health and Safety

We will only utilize business partners who provide workers with a safe and healthy work environment. Business partners who provide residential facilities for their workers must provide safe and healthy facilities.

Source: Levi Strauss & Co.

TABLE 10.11

JCPENNEY
FOREIGN SOURCING REQUIREMENTS

SUPPLIER SELECTION.   In selecting suppliers, JCPenney attempts to identify reputable companies that are committed to compliance with legal requirements relevant to the conduct of their business.

LEGAL REQUIREMENTS.   JCPenney requires of its suppliers strict compliance with all contract provisions, as well as all applicable laws and regulations, including those of the United States and those of the countries of manufacture and exportation.

COUNTRY-OF-ORIGIN LABELING.   JCPenney will not knowingly allow the importation into the United States of merchandise that does not have accurate country-of-origin labeling.

FACTORY WORKING CONDITIONS.   JCPenney will not knowingly allow the importation into the United States of merchandise manufactured

- with convict labor, forced labor or illegally indentured labor;
- with illegal child labor; or
- in violation of any other applicable labor or workplace safety law or regulation.

MANUFACTURER'S CERTIFICATE.   JCPenney requires that its foreign suppliers and its U.S. suppliers of imported merchandise, for each shipment of foreign-produced merchandise, obtain a manufacturer's certificate that the merchandise was manufactured at a specified factory, identified by name, location and country, that neither convict labor, forced labor or illegally indentured labor, nor illegal child labor, was employed in the manufacture of the merchandise, and that the merchandise was manufactured in compliance with all other applicable labor and workplace safety laws and regulations.

FACTORY VISITS.   On visits to foreign factories, for any purpose, JCPenney associates and buying agents have been asked to be watchful for the apparent use of prison or forced labor, or illegal child labor, or apparent violations of other applicable labor or workplace safety laws or regulations, or indications of inaccurate country-of-origin labeling, to take immediate responsive action when necessary and to report questionable conduct in these areas to their management for follow-up and, when appropriate, corrective action.

CORRECTIVE ACTION.   If it is determined that a foreign factory utilized by a supplier for the manufacture of merchandise for JCPenney is in violation of these foreign sourcing requirements, JCPenney will take appropriate corrective actions, which may include cancellation of the affected order, prohibiting the supplier's subsequent use of the factory or terminating JCPenney's relationship with the supplier.

countries resisted adopting certain guidelines, which they viewed as "Western standards" of business. Large companies that may contract in more than 50 countries and work with hundreds of different contractors also found it difficult to inspect and regulate working conditions in every factory. In addition, according to some critics, some companies were interested only in the public relations appeal of sourcing guidelines, but did very little to enforce the rules (Ortega, 1995).

Increased public attention was drawn to the sweatshop issue when, in 1996, merchandise endorsed by Kathie Lee Gifford for Wal-Mart was found to have been made in sweatshops in El Salvador and the U.S. The negative publicity surrounding this scandal led many manufacturers and retailers to take human rights issues more seriously. At this same time student activists were waging protests and sit-ins on campuses throughout the U.S. asking that colleges and universities provide assurances about how merchandise bearing the college or university name and/or logo was made. In 1998, student activists founded the United Students Against Sweatshops (USAS) as a vehicle for sharing information and organizing activities ("Colleges join effort," 1999; Manning, 1999).

The need for effective enforcement of company codes of conduct resulted in the development of factory monitoring programs by companies and organizations. Many companies conduct their own factory monitoring or contract with an independent factory monitor to conduct periodic reviews of factories. In 1998 Reebok implemented a computer software system that assists them in tracking workers' salaries, hours they work, and other worker information among their contractors worldwide. Reebok also implemented a Worker Communications System by which factory workers can submit complaints through prepaid mailers, telephone, written reports placed in locked boxes within the factory, and communications with Reebok monitors (Seidman, 2001).

As an outgrowth of the Apparel Industry Partnership, in 1998 the Fair Labor Association (FLA) was established as a factory monitoring association. Members of the FLA must assure that their factories and contractors comply with an established code of conduct. In 2001, the FLA began approving company factory monitoring programs and accrediting independent external factory monitors for use by its member companies. Critics of the FLA voiced concerns over the organization's apparent industry focus. Therefore, in 1999, anti-sweatshop activists created an alternative system to the FLA, the Worker Rights Consortium, a "non-profit organization that supports and verifies licensee compliance with production codes of conduct" (Worker Rights Consortium, 2001).

In 2000, the American Apparel and Footwear Association and counterpart manufacturers' associations from Mexico, South Africa, Philippines, El Salvador, Honduras, Dominican Republic, Nicaragua, Jamaica, and Sri Lanka endorsed their own core production principles of the Worldwide Responsible Apparel Production (WRAP) program. These production principles form the basis of WRAP's factory-based certification program dedicated to the promotion of "lawful, humane and ethical manufacturing throughout the world" (American Apparel and Footwear Association, 2001). The principles address labor practices, workers' compensation, freedom of association, factory and environmental conditions, and customs compliance.

The overall goal of these factory monitoring programs and organizations and programs is to improve the working conditions in apparel factories in the U.S. and abroad. Some companies require that contractors pay the cost of any necessary improvements required to meet their codes of conduct; others help pay some of the costs. For example, Timberland has provided money for educational purposes and water treatment systems in communities in China, where its products are manufactured. When Levi Strauss & Co. discovered a group of underage workers at two contractor factories in Bangladesh, the company convinced the contractors to take the children off the production lines so they could attend school. Levi Strauss & Co. paid for the children's school fees, books, and uniforms, while the contractors agreed to continue their wages while they attended school. The contractors also agreed to stop employing child labor.

Increased media attention and customer interest has led many companies and trade associations to enhance their efforts to improve workers' conditions. However, according to former Labor Secretary Robert Reich, even though these efforts are making the situation "a bit better," sweatshops continue to exist here and abroad (Malone, 2001, p. 4).

Summary

The term *sourcing* refers to the decision-making process companies use to determine how and where the textile and apparel products or their components will be produced. In making sourcing decisions, companies take into consideration their general sourcing philosophy, labor requirements and costs, fabric requirements, quality control standards, equipment and skill requirements, plant capacities, trade barriers and government regulations, expected turnaround time, availability of materials and supplies, and political and economic conditions. Based on these criteria, a number of sourcing options are available to apparel companies and retailers. Major sourcing decisions focus on whether production will be domestic or offshore and whether production will take place in a company-owned facility or will be contracted to others. When contracting, companies also must decide whether cut, make, and trim (CMT) or full-package (FP) services will be employed.

Domestic apparel production is primarily found in New York, California, and the southern states. Foreign production is concentrated in several areas, although Hong Kong, Taiwan, South Korea, and China are primary contributors to global production. With the implementation of NAFTA, increased offshore production by U.S. apparel companies in Mexico continues. Current issues surrounding apparel production are sweatshops in the United States and abroad and changes in international trade laws that will reduce trade barriers.

CAREER PROFILE

Companies who produce goods both within the United States as well as offshore will have positions related to sourcing. An excellent knowledge of company goals, trade laws, production requirements, and available sourcing options as well as negotiation skills are important for success in these areas.

Sourcing Analyst
PUBLICLY HELD SPORTSWEAR COMPANY

Position Description
Develop sourcing plans and costing worksheets taking into consideration quotas, capacities, pricing, competitiveness, and quality of goods.

Typical Tasks and Responsibilities
- Determine source for garment production and negotiate terms of production with resources
- Determine the effect of quotas, tariffs, freight, and other miscellaneous charges on the landed cost of garments
- Determine margins analysis
- If needed, examine sample goods submitted by resource
- Communicate with other departments (marketing, product development, forecasting and scheduling, customs, cost accounting)
- Travel to inspect production facilities, examine samples, and negotiate terms

Key Terms

cut, make, and trim (CMT)

807 or 9802 production

full-package (FP)

maquiladora operations

quota

offshore production

sourcing

sourcing options

tariff

Discussion Questions

1. Many apparel companies have shifted from domestic production to offshore production (particularly in Mexico and the Caribbean Basin). Why has this shift occurred? What problems in domestic and foreign production are associated with this shift?

2. What are the advantages and disadvantages for an apparel company in its developing and implementing sourcing guidelines related to human rights and environmental issues?

References

American Apparel and Footwear Association. (2001). Industry social responsibility statement. [online] Available HTTP: http://www.apparelandfootwear.org/responsibility—info.html [April 6, 2001].

Bassuk, David and Skatoff, Ashley. (2001, February). Guidance for choosing B2B exchanges, partners. *Bobbin*, pp. 48–53.

Bonacich, Edna, and Appelbaum Richard P. (2000). *Behind the Label: Inequality in the Los Angeles Apparel Industry*. Berkeley: University of California Press.

Brooks, Gary. (1992, September). Make domestically or import: How to avoid costly mistakes. *Apparel Industry Magazine*, pp. 180–184.

Brown, Christie. (1995, September). The body-bending business. *Forbes*, pp. 196–204.

Colleges join effort to fight sweatshops. (1999, March 17). *The Oregonian*, p. B3.

Cruz, Sergio. (1995, November). Site selection: Straight talk about costs. *Bobbin*, pp. 80–84.

Dickerson, K. G. (1995). *Textiles and Apparel in the Global Economy*. (2nd ed.). Englewood Cliffs, NJ: Prentice-Hall.

Finder, Alan. (1995, February 6). Despite tough laws, sweatshops flourish. *New York Times*, pp. A1, B4.

Friedman, Arthur. (1996, March 26). Sourcing now: The proximity factor. *Women's Wear Daily*, p. 6.

Haas, Robert D. (1994, May). Ethics in the trenches. *Across the Board*, 31, 12–13.

Henricks, Mark. (1998, January). Koos Manufacturing's success is "Made in USA." *Apparel Industry Magazine*, pp. 48–50.

International Labor Rights Fund. (2000). *Definition: sweatshop*. [online]. Available: http://www.laborrights.org [July 7, 2000].

Jacobs, Brenda A. (1999, November). Regional pacts produce new trade patterns. *Bobbin*, pp. 65–68.

Kessler, Judi A. (1999, November). New NAFTA alliances reshape sourcing. *Bobbin*, pp. 54–62.

Lii, Jane H. (1995, March 12). Week in sweatshop reveals grim conspiracy of the poor. *New York Times*, pp. 1, 40.

Malone, Scott. (2001, March 22). The Triangle legacy: 90 years after fire, sweatshops persist. *Women's Wear Daily*, pp. 1, 4–5.

Manning, Jeff. (1999, March 7). Students, Nike fighting war against sweatshops. *The Oregonian*, pp. C1, C6.

Mexico tax reform exposes U.S. apparel firms to "Double Income Tax." (1999, November). *Bobbin*, pp. 56–57.

Moore, Lila. (1995, September). Home is where you sew it. *Apparel Industry Magazine*, pp. 38–54.

O'Rourke, Mary T. (1992, September). Labor costs—From Pakistan to Portugal. *Bobbin*, pp. 116–122.

Ortega, Bob. (1995, July 3). Broken rules: Conduct codes garner goodwill for retailers, but violations go on. *Wall Street Journal*, pp. 1, A4.

Ostroff, Jim. (1995, December 12). Mexico's fast trip to the top. *Women's Wear Daily*, pp. 7, 11.

Ostroff, Jim (1996, April 23). Third world sourcing: Prices are enticing, perils are numerous. *Women's Wear Daily*, pp. 1, 6–7.

Raney, Joanna. (1995, October 10). Reich: Inside the sweatshop war. *Women's Wear Daily*, p. 32.

Ratoff, Paul. (1994, May 27–June 2). To manufacture in-house—Yes or no? *California Apparel News*, p. 7.

Seideman, Tony. (2001, March). Reebok develops information system to monitor supplier human rights issues. *Stores*, pp. 102–103.

Survival of the fittest. (1998, May). *Apparel Industry Magazine*, pp. 34–36.

Welling, Holly. (1999, December). Patagonia: Small world view of big business. *Apparel Industry Magazine*, pp. AS26–AS32.

Winger, Rocio Maria. (1999, April). A marriage of style and efficiency. *Apparel Industry Magazine*, pp. 20–24.

Worker Rights Consortium. (2001). WRG Homepage [online] Available: http://www.workerrights.org [March 28, 2001].

Zachary, G. Pascal. (1994, July 28). Levi tries to make sure contract plants in Asia treat workers well. *The Wall Street Journal*, pp. A1, A9.

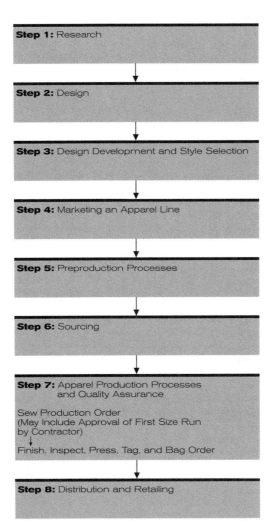

Step 1: Research

Step 2: Design

Step 3: Design Development and Style Selection

Step 4: Marketing an Apparel Line

Step 5: Preproduction Processes

Step 6: Sourcing

Step 7: Apparel Production Processes
and Quality Assurance

Sew Production Order
(May Include Approval of First Size Run
by Contractor)

Finish, Inspect, Press, Tag, and Bag Order

Step 8: Distribution and Retailing

Production Processes and Quality Assurance

CHAPTER 11

IN THIS CHAPTER YOU WILL LEARN:

- the manufacturing environments used for production.

- the production processes used in manufacturing.

- the components of quality assurance and the importance of quality assurance in delivering on-time, acceptable merchandise to the retailer.

- the role of agents who assist apparel manufacturers in bringing products produced offshore into the United States.

Production Considerations

The previous chapters discussed the development of a product line from market research, creation, design development, pattern development, and preproduction through sourcing options. The product line is now ready for production. Production is the construction process by which the cut fabric pieces, findings, and trims are incorporated into a finished apparel, accessory or home fashion product. The cost to produce the product is affected by the product design and pattern as well as by the production process used. Therefore, it is essential to the success of the company that the designer, product developer, and pattern maker be well versed in the production processes used to manufacture the product. Some of the decisions regarding the relationship among the design, pattern, and production processes occur during the planning and review meetings. Other production decisions take place as the new style proceeds through preproduction. However, if difficulties arise during the production of a new style, the designer, product developer, and pattern maker are typically consulted, along with the production engineer.

Production processes and **manufacturing environments** (which include the production facility, location of production, choice of production process, and cycle time) vary greatly depending on factors such as available technology, wholesale price zone, and geographic location of production. Computer technology has had a great impact on manufacturing environments. In turn, changes continue to occur in the entire soft goods pipeline from the fiber producer to the consumer. Continual new developments in supply chain management create great flexibility in production processes and manufacturing environments. This chapter will provide an overview of the methods of producing, assuring product quality, and importing goods within three manufacturing environments.

Manufacturing Environments

The three manufacturing environments, or strategies, as described by Peter Butenhoff, president of [TC]² (1999), include mass production, short-cycle production, and mass customization. The product type as well as the strategy used for replenishment of the product will determine which of these three environments will be used for production. Each of these three manufacturing environments is discussed below.

MASS PRODUCTION

The mass production manufacturing environment is suitable for cutting and sewing very large quantities of each product, using one of several possible mass production processes that will be discussed later in this chapter. Mass production capitalizes on economies of scale. Basic staple products such as T-shirts, jeans, underwear, socks, and hosiery fit this manufacturing environment. These products have a low fashion risk, in part because they can remain on the retail floor longer than many fashion goods. The focus of mass production is on in-store replenishment of products (see Chapter 12). Seasonal goods are staple products, such as turtlenecks, produced in seasonal colors. The selling time for seasonal goods falls between the selling time for staple goods and for fashion goods. Thus, some seasonal goods are manufactured in the mass production environment while other seasonal goods are manufactured in the short-cycle manufacturing environment, which is discussed in the next section.

The demand for staple goods and some seasonal goods tends to be easier to forecast than for fashion goods. This provides an opportunity for a slightly longer lead time for manufacturing than the other manufacturing environments offer. Longer lead time means that production can be sourced globally, providing an opportunity for lower labor costs. With the relatively high labor costs for U.S. production, production of high-volume basic products is more cost-efficient at plants in Mexico or the Caribbean Basin. Because of its longer production time and retail selling time, the cost of carrying this inventory (both to the apparel company and to the retailer) is greater than for goods that are manufactured closer to the time of their market demand. However, as long as interest rates remain fairly low, the carrying cost is offset by the lower manufacturing costs (Butenhoff, 1999).

SHORT-CYCLE PRODUCTION

A second manufacturing environment is **short-cycle production**. As the name implies, this manufacturing environment is well suited to products that are produced closer to the time of their market demand than mass-produced products. Short-cycle production is well suited to "very high-fashion products, which are placed into the market for short selling seasons (six to eight weeks), with no intention of in-store replenishment" (Butenhoff, 1999, p. SCM-4). According to Butenhoff, these high-fashion products will be manufactured predominantly in Asia because of the fabric availability and the well-established skill base there. In time, short-cycle production may migrate to Mexico and the Caribbean Basin as manufacturing capabilities become more developed in these countries and as costs in this hemisphere and those in Asia become more equal.

Due to the ever-increasing speed of the product development cycle (in part, a result of the application of computer technology to supply chain management, product information management systems, and the monitoring of consumer sales), seasonal products (such as men's slacks in seasonal colors) with a slightly longer selling season (6 to 12 weeks) are strong candidates for short-cycle production as well (Butenhoff, 1999).

MASS CUSTOMIZATION

A short-cycle manufacturing environment that is applied to an individual customer is called the **mass customization** manufacturing environment. This manufacturing environment utilizes all of the newest computer technologies, supply chain management, product information management, and some level of customization of the product for the individual customer (see Figure 11.1). "Its key technologies will include body scanning, pattern alteration software, virtual try-on, and ink jet printing" (Butenhoff, 1999, SCM-4). Each of these technologies is discussed below.

Mass customization involves the ultimate consumer in the customization of fit, design, or personalization of the product. Because the ultimate customer is involved

A sales clerk measures the customer using instructions from a computer as an aid.

The clerk enters the measurements, and adjusts the data based on the customer's reaction to samples.

The final measurements are relayed to a computerized fabric-cutting machine at the factory.

Bar codes are attached to the clothing to track it as it is assembled, washed and prepared for shipment.

Figure 11.1: Mass customization is made possible by computer technology.

with design and/or fit choices, it may appear that mass customization can best be categorized as a design variation. However, mass customization deals with products that are already designed; the customer is simply customizing the product. Thus, the topic of mass customization is well suited to a discussion of manufacturing environments (Conrad, 1999).

One key point in mass customization is that the customer selects and pays for the product before it is produced. Thus, the term *sell one, make one* is appropriate. This manufacturing environment has ramifications and advantages that will be discussed later.

Fit Customization

The more traditional approaches to developing a design for a target market have been discussed in previous chapters. The pattern is developed based on a company's target customer size standard. The "standard" size apparel fits some bodies better than others. With the development of new computer technology, product information management, and supply chain management, a type of custom apparel different from the custom-made apparel produced by personal tailors or dressmakers of the past is possible. The emergence of new technology has provided a new means to link the customer at the retail store to the apparel factory, resulting in mass customization. The cost efficiency of mass production is maintained. "It is a consumer-driven strategy that allows limited customization of a standard style, such as size, color or trim choices" ("Made to measure," 1998, p. 3). On the other hand **made-to-measure** apparel "is a fully customized process where a garment is made specifically for one individual based on his/her measurements and preferences" ("Made to measure," 1998, p. 3). The difference between made to measure and mass customization is the degree of customization offered. However, the difference is blurring as technology provides tools to blend made to measure with mass customization.

Brooks Brothers, a retailer and manufacturer of men's and women's classic professional clothing, provides an example of mass customization with which customers can build their own dress shirt. "Ordering shirts from the catalog is a simple process that gives customers basic choices, such as: neck size, sleeve length, choice of three body styles, choice of three cuff styles, and 17 top-end fabric selections. It should come as no surprise that customers love this process" ("Made to measure," 1998, p. 6). Pattern making software provides the capability to adapt the standard pattern to specific measurements, such as making one sleeve longer than the other to fit the customer's different arm lengths. Delivery takes two to three weeks.

Early ventures in made to measure using mass production at the factory included men's tailored suits. The customer is measured at the tailor's retail store. With some systems, front, back, and side view photographs of the customer standing in front of a measurement grid are also sent to the factory. The retailer's computer is linked electronically to the apparel factory's computer. The customer's measurements are input into the computer system. The body dimensions are translated into specific differences between the "standard" pattern and the customer's needed adjustments. The pattern changes are made by computer calculations, and a customized pattern is plotted. Laser cutters allow fast, single-ply computerized cutting of the garment pieces. With careful tracking through production, the cut pieces for each customized suit can be sent through the mass manufacturing process. The customer may return to the retail store for a final "fitting" for pant hemming and other minor adjustments handled by the retailer before the customer receives the finished goods.

Brooks Brothers' made-to-measure suit system is called eMeasure. Brooks Brothers formed a partnership with suit manufacturer Pietrafesa Corp. of Liverpool, NY.

> It is the culmination of four years of research and development, which began with the introduction of a manual made-to-measure process that required stores to fill out and mail to Pietrafesa order forms with alteration information. Today, eMeasure has evolved into a touch-screen kiosk system that allows customers to create and visualize 25 different made-to-measure suit silhouettes in 300 to 500 fabrics, which can be referenced through swatch books in the stores. (Rabon, 2000, p. 40)

After the selection process is complete, a sales associate enters the order into the system along with the customer's measurement information taken at the retail store. One of the challenges of made-to-measure apparel is the assessment of customer fit preferences, since some customers prefer a looser fit while others prefer a snugger fit to their suits. The system "suggests a try-on size from the store's inventory, which is an integral part of the process" (Rabon, 2000, p. 40). At the factory, patterns and markers are made automatically using a computer made-to-measure program. In the future, body scanners located at retail stores may be used to gather the measurement data for each customer. Currently, the made-to-measure cycle time is about 5 weeks. The goal is to reduce the cycle time to 2 weeks.

Mass customization options that include customizing the fit have expanded greatly with the continued development of electronically linked body measuring, pattern making, cutting, and production technology. The development of body scanning technology has greatly enhanced the capabilities of mass customization. At the retail store, body measurements of the customer are taken by a three-dimensional computerized body-imaging system that "scans" the body dimensions of the customer. With the same scanning system, the customer is provided with a close-fitting garment to wear while standing in a scanning chamber or on a platform. In just a few seconds, the scanner captures the measurements of the customer (see Figure 11.2). These data can be fed into an integrated computer pattern making system used for adapting the pattern. In addition, the data can be saved on a **Smart Card** (about the size of a credit card) that contains the customer's body measurements and that can be used again and updated by rescanning the customer if the body size changes.

Sometimes, a combination of body scanning and body measurements taken with a tape measure is used to provide sufficient body dimensions for customized manufactured apparel.

One of the benefits of using a made-to-measure pattern system is that the customer's data are saved,

Figure 11.2: Body scanners capture precise body measurement data into a manufacturer's CAD/CAM system.

ensuring accuracy and consistency for reorders. The use of the manufacturer's or retailer's Internet site for reorders becomes a fast and easy option; the selection of other colors and fabrics for a style the customer wants to reorder via the Internet is also an option.

For the manufacturer and retailer, the advantages to mass customization include the following:

- Reducing large inventories that eat up profits and floor space.
- Minimizing returns.
- Reducing distribution costs.
- Building strong customer relationships.
- Solidifying brand loyalty.
- Identifying customer preferences and buying habits ("Made to measure," 1998, p. 3).

Another product well suited to mass customization is footwear. Each person's left foot is somewhat different in size from the right foot. By scanning each foot, the shoes can be customized to fit each foot precisely. The huge inventories of shoes stocked in varying lengths and widths and styles and colors can be greatly reduced by mass customization while the customer's shoe fit can be enhanced by scanning technology.

In addition to body-scanning technology, advances in computer pattern design systems have aided the implementation of mass customization. In some cases, once the customer's measurements have been input, the software analyzes the measurements and compares them to standard profiles to recommend a best size. Some made-to-measure software systems have built-in posture adjustments, such as for round shoulders, that can be requested.

Gathering together the body scanning data of many individuals creates a large bank of information about current customer sizes. An international project, termed CAESAR (Civilian American and European Surface Anthropometry Resource) which was seeking better-fitting uniforms and gear, was launched in the late 1990s by the U.S. Air Force. It is a partnership among the military; several apparel companies such as Lee, Levi Strauss & Co., Vanity Fair, and Jantzen; and companies such as Boeing, Nissan Motor Co, and Caterpillar that build products that people need to fit into (Silverman, 1998). The project partners have exclusive rights to the database of body measurements for one year before being released to the public ("The shape of clothes to come," 2000). The bodies of thousands of men and women in the United States and Europe have been scanned to build a database of body dimensions of the current population. From this accumulated data, manufacturers may determine new size standards for their target customers. In England, a national sizing survey to body scan thousands of men, women, and children, has been funded by leading British retailers in partnership with technology vendors and universities. The intention is to use the data to manufacture made-to-measure clothing and for three-dimensional virtual shopping (Fallon, 1999).

Design Customization

Style preferences, as well as color and print choices available for each style offered can be viewed by the customer at an interactive kiosk, or even at home via e-commerce. A customer selects a style that is shown in a video catalog, then selects a preferred color, fabric print, and perhaps a choice of style features (see Figure 11.3). The customer can view his or her selection in a three-dimensional computer image. For size customization, scanned body dimensions can be used to create a three-dimensional replica of the customer's body on a computer screen by inserting the Smart Card into the system. Thus, the customer can view the appearance of the garment style he or she has selected draped on his or her own body image, as a virtual try-on, before the garment is ordered. The color, fabric print, as well as style preferences can be changed on screen, and the customer can view a range of choices before making the final selection.

Mass customization requires electronically linked, seamless integration of components throughout the entire supply chain in order to operate. It requires a manufacturing environment suited to individualization, yet with a fast turnaround time

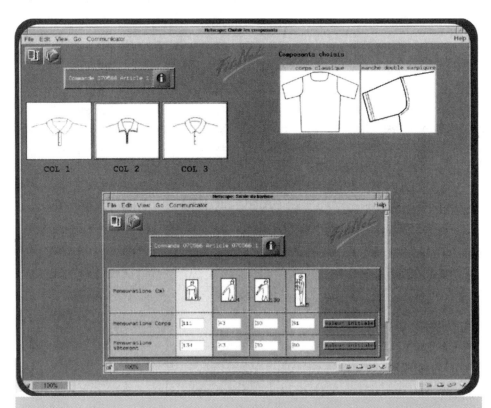

Figure 11.3: Mass customization links the customer's style preferences selected at the retail store or through the Internet to the production site.

and at a low cost. Custom tailors and dressmakers are not producing these goods; within the mass customization manufacturing environment, agile manufacturing is required. This production process will be discussed along with other production processes later in this chapter.

Levi Strauss & Co. offers customized jeans at some retail stores. Various styling options are selected by the customer at an interactive kiosk. The customer selects from three leg styles, two fly styles, and three waist styles and chooses a fabric from several fabric options. Individualization also includes having the inseam length customized for the customer. Levi's customized jeans arrive at the customer's home about two weeks later. Currently, the customized product costs more, but many customers are willing to pay an additional amount for it. A survey by Kurt Salmon Associates indicated that "more than one third (36%) of consumers said that they would be willing to pay up to 12% to 15% more for custom-made apparel and footwear" ("Doing it their way," 1998, p. 42). The customer is provided with what he or she wants, when he or she wants it. As mass customization is used more frequently as a manufacturing environment, the cost of the product to the consumer may well meet or fall below the cost to manufacture a similar style using mass production or short-cycle manufacturing environments. There is the potential for a substantial savings to manufacturers and retailers by maintaining a reduced inventory and by not producing the product until a customer-paid order has been submitted.

The future will include additional adaptations. Perhaps the pattern will be customized, the garment cut, a fabric printed with a customized print, and sewn while the customer shops at one of the megamalls, returning a few hours later to collect the finished product.

Personalization

One example of customizing a finished product, called *personalization*, is currently available at Levi's San Francisco retail store. A designated area at the retail store offers embroidery, laser etching, and fabric ornamentation while customers wait. Customers can add these personalized details to just-purchased items or to previously purchased items. This appeals greatly to customers by satisfying their desire for individuality within our mass society—with a minimum of expense and waiting time.

The three options for manufacturing environments discussed above provide the framework for examining the steps in production—from production sewing systems through delivery of finished goods. The first phase of production focuses on a discussion of the types of production sewing systems.

Production Sewing Systems

Although new production systems have been developed, older, traditional mass-manufacturing systems are still used in some facilities. It is important to understand the variety of production systems in order to make informed decisions about the production system most suitable for the garment style, price range, and sourcing option. While some apparel is still sewn one at a time in a single-hand system, most apparel is manufactured using one of several production systems of large-quantity or *mass manufacturing*. The most common categories of production systems are progressive bundle systems and flexible manufacturing systems.

SINGLE-HAND SYSTEM

As discussed in Chapter 7, the prototype product is produced by a single individual. The sample maker (also called a *sample hand*) completes all the steps required in production, moving from one type of specialized equipment to another as needed based on the garment or product style's requirements. Some apparel and accessory goods are produced in limited quantities using a system similar to that used to sew the prototype. In a **single-hand system** one individual is responsible for sewing an entire garment. The bundle for this production system would include all the garment parts for one style in one size. In today's market, the single-hand system is used for couture and for some very high-priced apparel produced in a limited quantity. This system is slower than mass production systems, and may include considerable detail or handwork during production.

PROGRESSIVE BUNDLE SYSTEM

Before the implementation of QR and supply chain management strategies, the **progressive bundle system** was the most common production system used by apparel manufacturers. With the progressive bundle system, garment parts are bundled together and put in carts that are rolled from one sewing machine operator to another. Machine operators open the bundle of the garment parts, perform one or two construction steps on each garment in the bundle, and rebundle the garment parts for transport to the next operator (see Figure 11.4). The operator's pay is calculated by the number of pieces completed per day (*piece-rate wage*).

The progressive bundle system is especially well suited to large bundles of work, usually from one dozen to three dozen units per bundle. At each operator's work station, there is one bundle in process and one or several more bundles waiting. Sometimes referred to as a *batch* or *push* system, the progressive bundle system tends to generate high levels of **work-in-process** (WIP) and often creates bottlenecks in the production line as some operators outperform others (Hill, 1992). Also, a considerable investment of inventory is tied up with the WIP.

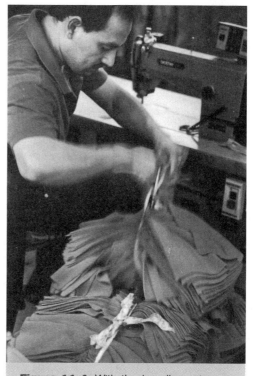

Figure 11.4: With the bundle system, a sewing operator quickly unties a bundle of garment pieces to perform one or several sewing steps on each garment in the bundle.

With the progressive bundle system, equipment is selected and sometimes customized to perform one or several functions needed for the production of the specific style. Each piece of equipment is positioned on the floor in relation to the equipment and sewing sequence required before and after each step in the production sequence. The machine operator is highly trained to perform one or several steps on specific equipment. Each sewing facility tends to specialize in certain types of products, such as backpacks or swimwear. This specialization is due in part to the fact that different types of equipment are needed for producing different categories of products.

Sometimes the facility is arranged so that the body of the jacket is assembled in one part of the facility, and the lining is assembled in another part of the facility. The two parts of each garment are united at the final assembly stage. This requires careful tagging to ensure that sizes and dye lots are matched. Due to the nature of the progressive bundle system, it can be difficult to pinpoint where a quality problem originates.

A new style ready for production may differ from previous styles in production sequence or equipment needs. Machine operators may need additional training, so it may take time to develop the expertise to run at full capacity. Equipment may have to be moved within the facility to prepare for a different production sequence.

FLEXIBLE MANUFACTURING SYSTEMS

For mass-manufactured products, the bottom line is cost containment. This is affected by (1) the length of time that is required to produce the product and (2) the length of time the product is in process (work-in-process or WIP). Reduction in one or both of these will result in a lower production cost. In the late 1980s, management at manufacturing facilities began to explore ways to improve productivity and reduce production costs. Some companies focused on developing more flexible systems for manufacturing.

Developing more flexible manufacturing systems involves some or all of the following: reorganization of existing equipment on the floor into a new systems approach, development of new equipment, reorganization of the way garments were routed through production, and reorganization of workers into teams who were cross-trained to handle a variety of operations using an assortment of equipment.

Flexible manufacturing (FM) is defined as "any departure from traditional mass production systems of apparel toward faster, smaller, more flexible production units that depend upon the coordinated efforts of minimally supervised teams of workers" (AAMA, Technical Advisory Committee, 1988, as cited in Hill, 1992). FM systems are known by many names, including modular manufacturing, self-directed work teams, compact production teams, and flexible work groups. The emphasis of the strategy is on group effort, employee involvement, and employee empowerment.

In FM systems, manufacturing management makes a shift away from high individual productivity and low cost to short manufacturing cycles, small quantity of work-in-process, and quick delivery of the finished product. Flexible manufacturing is well suited to smaller production runs compared to large production runs that are efficient with the progressive bundle system. The term **modular manufacturing** is most often used in the U.S. apparel industry to describe flexible manufacturing (Hill, 1992).

With modular manufacturing, which is often referred to as a *pull system*, the sewing facility is organized into teams of seven to ten operators each. Operators are cross-trained in all areas of garment construction. Each operator might work on two or three machines. Operators might perform several tasks at each machine, or one machine might be used for a series of assembly operations. Every team is responsible for the production of entire garments, instead of one operator being assigned a single operation, such as setting in a sleeve or a zipper. Equipment is arranged so that work can be passed from one team member to another, who may be either in a standing or sitting position. The number of units within each operation may vary from only one to as many as ten.

Within a module, operators work as a team and solve problems, thus creating a more productive environment. Flaws in production are handled as a team; if a mistake is found, the entire garment is returned to the team, where the operators decide how best to fix it. Therefore, the traditional piece-rate wage is not applicable. The team is paid not only according to the quantity it produces, but also by the quality of its work. Pay is based on a collective effort. In theory, if an apparel factory were completely "modular," it would be redesigned into modular units, with each module producing complete garments in a few hours.

A number of factors must be taken into consideration before a company decides to change to this system of manufacturing. Downtime is particularly critical with modular methods. With modular manufacturing, each minute a machine is down costs money as it can slow down the entire team's work progress.

Converting to a modular manufacturing system requires the involvement of all employees, an investment in education and training, a shift of management responsibilities from a few people to the team as a whole, and support from management (Bennett, 1988). The shift to modular manufacturing requires a cultural change within a company. To create effective teams, the way employees think and perform has to change (Abend, 1999a).

Some manufacturing facilities shifted to modular manufacturing in hopes of reducing manufacturing costs. For some companies, however, costs rose at first. Not only is there the cost involved if new equipment is purchased, cross-training employees costs money, and reduced productivity during training is an additional start-up cost. It may take months before a cost savings is realized (Abend, 1999a).

For companies that commit to modular manufacturing, its cost benefits have been realized by containing costs through inventory reduction, a reduction in work-in-process, and for some facilities, an improvement in product quality. In one plant, "It has been possible to reduce a 5 percent to 10 percent level of irregulars production to less than 1 percent in one year . . . " (Abend, 1999a, p. 51).

Productivity has increased dramatically at some facilities that shifted to modular manufacturing. Production capacity at Nygård International's "Winnipeg manufacturing headquarters jumped from 20,000 to approximately 75,000 units per week under the modular arrangement" (Winger, 1998, p. AS-16). Another advantage of modular manufacturing is that production facilities can shift from manufacturing one type of product category to another quickly. At VF Intimates, a division of VF Corporation, "they've redefined flexible manufacturing with plants that change not just styles, but entire domestic and offshore facilities that manufacture intimates, backpacks and swimwear" (Hill, 1998, p. AS-8). During a changeover, "engineers swap out the equipment as the last items in one product go through the line. Overnight the facility is ready for the new line, and then it's a matter of training operators, which can take one to three weeks to reach full capacity" (Hill, 1998, p. AS-8).

At Seams Reasonable, a contractor located in Red Boiling Springs, Tennessee, modules are composed of flexible eight-person sewing teams. Owner Toby Russell stated, "I couldn't sew the ladies' sleepwear line any other way because the production runs on certain styles are so small. We might sew four different styles out of three different fabrics in one day" (Abend, 1999a, p. 51). Russell commented that the greatest benefit of modular manufacturing is fast turnaround time on small production runs of selected goods.

Some companies that have tried modular manufacturing found it was not successful for them. Levi Strauss & Co. opened a new modular manufacturing facility in 1995. At the end of the first year, excess costs were astronomically high, attributed to exceptional start-up costs. By the end of the second year, the capacity had increased about 53 percent, but excess costs were over 31 percent. Halfway into the third year, capacity had increased 6 percent over the second year. However, the excess costs had increased to 49 percent over standard (Dunagan, 1999). In an article about Levi's modular manufacturing attempt, consulting engineer Charles

Gilbert stated, "Thirty-four months after start-up in modules, we converted the plant to the 'old' progressive bundle system" (Dunagan, 1999). Management at Levi Strauss & Co. does not have the answer regarding what went wrong with its attempt at modular manufacturing. A number of factors may have contributed to its lack of success. In some cases, companies do not completely convert to all aspects of employee training, equipment needs, and management commitment to modular manufacturing. It is clear that the choice of manufacturing method is dependent on many variables.

Unit Production Systems

To achieve efficient and effective short-cycle manufacturing, some companies have invested in new technology. One form of technology investment is a computerized overhead transport system such as the **unit production system (UPS)**. With UPS, garment parts are fed on overhead conveyors, one garment at a time, to sewing machine operators (see Figure 11.5). Garment parts are delivered directly to the

Figure 11.5: With a Unit Production System, the pieces of each garment are delivered to the sewing operator. She may not need to remove the garment from the conveyor while performing the sewing step.

operators' ergonomically designed workstations. This dramatically reduces operator handling time during production. Workstations can be moved easily to accommodate different equipment needs for various garments. Operators are cross-trained in a number of procedures in the manufacturing cycle, similar to the way they are for modular manufacturing. The transport system is designed to include bar codes to track WIP.

A study by Clemson Apparel Research (Hill, 1994) determined that UPS would provide the hypothetical apparel manufacturing plant a 329 percent return on its investment and would pay for itself in 11 months. The primary savings to the company would be in the areas of reduced direct labor costs (shorter waiting periods, less overtime, improved ergonomics) and reduced work-in-process inventory levels. Figure 11.6 shows computerized tracking of WIP. Many production facilities have shown substantial increases in production with UPS. Other companies have found UPS to be less successful. As with modular manufacturing, many variables enter into the success of UPS.

Figure 11.6: Computerized production systems permit computer tracking of work-in-process as well as increased efficiency compared with the bundle system.

Agile Manufacturing

Agile manufacturing combines a variety of technologies that together form a totally integrated, seamless exchange of information linking retailers and suppliers to the manufacturing facility ($[TC]^2$, 1993). Mass customization allows for individual changes in style, color, and fit using body measuring and modifications of a pattern based on a style developed by the apparel company. The manufacturing facility cuts an individual customized style from a PDS and marker making system linked electronically to a single-ply cutter. White fabric prepared for digital printing might be used to cut fabric pieces. Next, the cut pieces can be printed digitally (see Chapter 6) to the customer's color and print specifications. After printing, the garment is manufactured using a production system that is designed to accommodate units of one (see Figure 11.7). Rabon and Deaton (1999) contended that an overhead conveyor system for unit production (UPS) is a key to success of companies in the mass customization arena. Modular manufacturing teams of cross-trained operators sew the customized orders. Computer-based learning materials and interactive videos

Figure 11.7: Digital printing integrates design, pattern making, and production.

help provide the training sewing operators need. After completion, the order is packaged and sent directly to the customer, eliminating warehouse inventories ([TC]², 1993). It is the integration of these technologies that creates agile manufacturing.

COMBINATION OF SYSTEMS

Some production facilities utilize more than one type of production system. For example, a contractor may use UPS for certain garment styles that suit this production system, while using a progressive bundle system for other styles. As discussed earlier, the number of units to be made influences the production system. For example, modular manufacturing may be more economical for small production runs than the progressive bundle system.

PRODUCTION WORKERS' WAGE RATES

The progressive bundle system of production frequently uses a **piece-rate wage** system. Each operator's pay is based on individual productivity. The number of units the operator has completed at the end of each workday or week is the basis for the operator's pay for that time period. New developments in software provide a means to set accurate piece rates in a manufacturing environment that is constantly changing (Hill, 1998).

With modular manufacturing, some companies use a team wage calculation rate. Bonus incentives might be provided for exemplary productivity and/or a very low rate of errors or irregulars.

Some companies have decided that an hourly rate is most equitable. An hourly rate gives the flexibility to change production runs during the day, especially if a priority order has just been cut and needs to be produced immediately. Also, an hourly rate is fairer if production includes diverse products.

Developments in Apparel Production

IMPROVED EQUIPMENT

The industrial machines used in production facilities are designed to sew much faster than home sewing machines, which are driven by motors. Industrial machines have engines, with a clutch, brake, and continuous oil feed. Home sewing machines can perform many different functions (sew straight seams, zigzag, over-cast, blind hem, and make buttonholes), whereas industrial machines perform very specialized functions (sew buttonholes or sew straight seams or sew blind hems). The specialized equipment may be fitted with additional devices or guides to customize an operation further. For example, a metal plate can be added to the sewing bed to guide elastic evenly under the needle.

While many machines for production were developed so that operators sit during operation, standup sewing is another option (see Figure 11.8). It costs about $1,000 to convert a sewing machine to standup operation. The Tanner Companies LP production facility in Rutherfordton, North Carolina, utilizes equipment for eight standup sewing teams, positioned into a 100-foot loop (Welling, 1998). Ergonomic analysis indicates that there are substantial advantages to standup sewing.

A new development in production equipment has focused on reducing the puckering encountered when assembling wrinkle-resistant cotton and cotton/polyester blend dress shirts, lightweight slacks, uniforms, and other casual wear. TAL Apparel

Figure 11.8: Sewing equipment has been developed to facilitate operation by workers who are standing rather than sitting.

of Hong Kong, one of the world's largest shirt makers, spent four years developing its TAL Pucker Free process. A bonding tape is inserted into the seam between two layers of fabric. The tape containing a thermal adhesive component is melted during the manufacturing process. "The result is a strong, permanent bond along the seam that eliminates differential shrinkage between the thread and fabric, the primary cause of seam puckering" (DesMarteau, 1998). The company patented a seam sealing process in the U.S. and has licensed the technology to United States manufacturers. Licensees pay a royalty fee, a percent of the retail price of the garment, to TAL.

Equipment maintenance is a critical concern for production sewing. Any breakdown of equipment can stall production, which can be of great concern to an entire team on a production line. Maintenance personnel must be ready to troubleshoot, repair, or replace equipment rapidly. In some countries, machine parts or technicians are not immediately available, causing delays in the production schedule. New developments will alleviate some of the maintenance concerns. After two years of research and development, Atlanta Attachment Co. developed a serial bus control system designed to "simplify maintenance and repairs of automated sewing equipment" (Rabon, 1998, p. 49). All sewing stations will have the same four-wire system to distribute power and electrical information.

The noise level and airborne fiber particles in sewing facilities are concerns, especially in some offshore facilities. In the United States, workers wear protective clothing, air filtration systems are used in factories, and other environmental controls have been implemented.

High-technology systems will continue to play an increasingly important role in cost reduction efforts. Regardless of the production system used, new equipment will be developed to enhance production. These developments include new types of computerized, programmable sewing machines, robotic sewing equipment, and continued improvements in cutting equipment. Just as the cost of personal computers has declined over time, high-tech equipment costs have also declined, making it more affordable to apparel manufacturers.

COMPUTER-AIDED DESIGN/COMPUTER-AIDED MANUFACTURING

Computer-aided design, pattern making, marker making, and grading combined with computerized cutting are an important part of QR and supply chain management. These strategies, commonly referred to as **computer-aided design/computer-aided**

manufacturing (CAD/CAM), can increase the speed and accuracy of pattern making, marker making, grading patterns, cutting fabric, and sewing. In terms of supply chain management, CAD/CAM systems have a number of benefits. In a survey of 450 companies (Kosh, 1987), the main reasons reported for using computer-aided design/computer-aided manufacturing systems were: (1) improved product quality, (2) reduced sewing time, (3) reduced cutting time, (4) reduced design and sample making time, (5) reduced pattern making and grading time, (6) reduced production marking time, and (7) diversified product line. Thus, reducing the amount of time involved in the design and pattern making stages of apparel production is an important benefit of CAD/CAM.

COMPUTER-INTEGRATED MANUFACTURING

Computer-integrated manufacturing (CIM) is the integration of an apparel company's CAD/CAM systems to form a common link of information throughout the production of the product. The use of product information management enhances a smooth flow of information throughout the apparel design/manufacture process.

CIM linkages include interfaces between CAD /CAM systems and other computers for the preparation of costing models, specification sheets, and cut-order planning. Some companies also use CAD/CAM data to drive numerically controlled stitching machines. In theory, every piece of equipment that is automated or semi-automated can be part of a CIM system.

Production Sequence

An important aspect of production is planning the sequence of operations required to produce the garment style. Production includes the sewing sequence as well as other tasks performed at the sewing facility that relate to completing the product. These tasks might include fusing interfacing, applying embroidery, pressing, afixing hangtags, and folding and packaging the finished product. These steps and the time required for each step need to be determined for each garment style. This information is referred to as the *construction specifications*.

Different categories of products may require very different processes and types of equipment. For example, men's tailored suits require many more steps in production than men's casual sportswear. The types of sewing and pressing equipment are quite different for tailored apparel as compared to sportswear. Chapter 4 discussed the different sewing processes and the types of equipment required for various classifications of apparel. Boys' and girls' clothing requires similar sewing processes and equipment and could be manufactured at the same facility, whereas men's tailored clothing and men's sportswear production need to be handled by different production facilities.

As discussed in Chapter 9, the sequence of sewing operations may have been determined at the time the style's cost was calculated. The production sequence used to sew the sales representatives' samples, made to market the style to retail buyers, is frequently the same as the sequence used to sew the production orders. Any problems in production might be corrected during the production of the sales samples.

Determining the most efficient production sequence depends on many factors such as the following:

- The equipment capabilities of the specific production facility (e.g., the availability of a pocket-setting machine can greatly speed production of a style with a welt pocket).
- The labor cost of the operators (in some factories where labor is very inexpensive, more work may be done by hand than with expensive equipment).
- Whether certain steps should be subcontracted (for example, a shirt with a pleated front inset might be less expensive to produce if the fabric for the front inset were sent to a pleating contractor, then returned to the production facility for cutting and sewing into the shirt).

Some operations, such as fusing interfacing to garment sections, may be performed prior to the sewing process. The pieces to be fused are laid on conveyor belts and moved through large fusing "ovens" to adhere the interfacing. Patch pockets, such as those sewn to the back of jeans, are prepared for sewing by prepressing the raw edges to the inside. By folding the edges over a metal template of the exact size of the finished pocket, accurate dimensions can be maintained. A fusing agent might be applied to help the seam allowances adhere to the inside of the pocket. Hundreds of pockets are prepared, then delivered to the site where they will be attached to the pants. This process is most efficient for one-size pieces. Since garment pieces may be cut from dye lots with varying color, care must be taken to match pocket pieces to garment sections from an identical dye lot. If the pockets were made in small, medium, and large sizes, care must be taken to attach the prepared pockets to the correct size pant. Belt loops might be made as a long continuous strip for the entire production run. Yards of the strips are wound onto holders attached to the sewing station. The belt loops are cut to length one at a time and sewn sequentially around the pant waistband. Many processes are streamlined to provide the most labor-effective production.

Sometimes several different factories are used to produce a large order. In such cases, the production sequences may not be exactly the same at the different factories producing the same style. Each contractor submits a sample sewn at its factory to the apparel manufacturer for approval. For the samples sewn for sales representatives by contractors, the same process of submitting a sewn sample is used. The contractor's sample is called a **sew by** or a **counter sample**. After approval, this sample is used as the benchmark against which to check the sewn production goods.

Although great effort is expended to plan a smooth production run, many problems can stall production. Some problems that involve the procurement of materials have already been discussed. Production problems include complications due to delays in receiving a shipment of zippers or late arrival of subcontracted work. Troubleshooting is an integral part of production. When sourcing offshore, unexpected problems can be difficult to solve. A flood in Bangladesh, a hurricane in the Dominican Republic, or a rail workers' strike in France can cause production or delivery delays that could not be planned for or avoided. Management personnel of apparel manufacturers often travel to production facilities (whether company owned or contractor owned) to check on production or help solve production problems.

Finishing

At the end of the production line, the goods await various finishing steps. Pressing may occur only at this stage in production. Edge stitching or topstitching may be used to reduce the need to press during production, thereby reducing labor costs. Specialized pressing equipment produces excellent results on finished goods very quickly. For tailored jackets, a steam mannequin might be used to press the entire jacket while on a three-dimensional form. Other types of specialized equipment perform other functions, such as turning pant legs right side out (pants come off the production line inside out). Finishing operations include thread trimming, button and snap attachment, shoulder pad and lining tacking, pressing, and buttoning the garment.

Whereas labels placed in highly visible locations as a part of the brand identity of the goods are attached to the product during production, other labels might be attached during finishing. Providing goods with floor-ready labels and hangtags take place at this stage in production. Preparing floor-ready merchandise will be discussed later in this chapter as well as in Chapter 12.

Labels might include identifying characteristics hidden to the eye. A bar code "fingerprint" visible to a scanning device can be included in the sew-in label to identify the product's production facility or retail destination. This technology can reduce the possibility of counterfeit goods and can also be used by the retailer to verify the origin of goods returned by customers. One system uses a silicon chip tagging system. Called a **radio frequency identification chip (RFIC)**, the silicon chip is attached to an antenna made of thin, flexible silver ink that utilizes radio frequency identification technology. In addition to deterring hijacking and shoplifting, the tag can be used to sort laundry and to log the number of times a uniform has been laundered. The tag is about the size of a garment label and is coated with a plastic laminate to protect it from dry cleaning chemicals. The tag can be sewn into a seam, hidden from view to deter removal by shoplifters or counterfeiters. One of the advantages of radio frequency identification chips is that retailers can inventory the contents of an unopened box (Conrad, 1996).

Other types of finishing operations include a variety of fabric treatments. Garments might be laundered before shipping. Laundering might be performed to enhance the hand or visual appeal of the fabric. For example, stone washing has been used to soften denim fabric. Another reason for laundering is to shrink a product prior to shipping. While we are familiar with purchasing some products large enough to "shrink to fit," many consumers find it advantageous to know that the garment has been preshrunk, that the way the garment fits when it is tried on at the retail store is the way it will fit after washing at home. For garments that will be laundered after production and before shipping, the pattern pieces for the garment had to be created very carefully with the exact shrinkage factor incorporated into each pattern piece. Koos Manufacturing, located in the Los Angeles area, produces "nearly 100,000 pairs of denim and twill pants a week for Calvin Klein and the ubiq-uitous Gap chain, and produces another 80,000 garments with the help of four sub-contractors" ("A Showroom of high-tech Sewing," 1998, p. 54). These pants are laundered before shipping. The laundry section operates 24 hours a day in three shifts, processing about 200,000 units weekly.

Special finishes might be incorporated during finishing of the garments, rather than to the textile goods at the textile mill. For example, a wrinkle-resistant finish might be applied to apparel goods, such as 100 percent cotton trousers, after they are sewn. Technological developments will continue to improve garment-applied finishes.

Many apparel manufacturers purchase dyed products in color allotments based on the quantity of orders for each color. Other manufacturers produce "colorless" garments, then dye the garments during finishing. Such goods are referred to as **garment dyed**. The procedure of dyeing finished goods has several advantages. It can provide quick delivery of the goods to the retailer because production can begin on the colorless garments while the sales force is accumulating the sales totals by color. For the same reason, it represents a reduced risk to the manufac-turer. Garment dyeing can be considered one of the Quick Response strategies. Care must be taken to select buttons and other findings and trims that can accommo-date the dyeing operation.

Since concern was first raised about the environmental consequences of some finishing operations, much has been done to minimize the negative environmental impact of finishing operations. Figure 11.9 shows equip-ment designed to meet environmental standards for stonewashing, for exam-ple. New developments will continue to improve environmental protection.

Goods are prepared for shipping by being either folded or hung. At some facilities, folding might be accom-

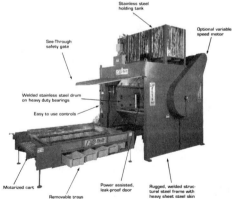

Figure 11.9: Finishing processes, such as stonewashing, require special-ized equipment that meets environ-mental safety standards.

plished by hand, with cardboard, tissue, straight pins, and plastic bags. At other facilities, machines are used to fold the goods. For garments placed on hangers, overhead conveyors bring the garment to equipment that covers each item with a plastic bag. Depending on the channel of distribution, the finished goods may be boxed and sent to the manufacturer's distribution center, to the retailer's distribution center, or directly to the retailer (see Chapter 12).

FLOOR-READY MERCHANDISE

Floor-ready merchandise (FRM) is an aspect of Quick Response and supply chain management that results from an alliance between the apparel manufacturer and the retailer. FRM shifts certain steps from the retailer to the manufacturer, where they become part of the finishing process. The FRM policies generally require that the apparel manufacturer ship the goods to the retailer's distribution center or retail store with bar coded price tickets, carton labels, shipping documents, and hanger applications. "If FRM can only remove two days of delay associated with a retailer's distribution center, and if the DC [distribution center] is typically receiving goods every two weeks, then it is possible to get 52 additional selling days per year" (Swank, 1995, p. 106). The use of floor-ready merchandise from the retailer's perspective will be discussed in Chapter 12.

Quality Assurance

As discussed in Chapter 3, **quality assurance** involves making sure the product meets the standards of acceptance set forth by the contracting party. The contracting party might be the apparel manufacturer for goods produced by a contractor. The contracting party might be a retailer for private label or store brand goods. Many of the fabrics and trims and sewing operations are specified in detail on the garment specification sheet and are an important part of quality assurance. Visual inspection after completion of production—for loose threads, for example—forms another important part of quality assurance.

The fabric inspection component of quality assurance was discussed in Chapters 3 and 9. The spreading and cutting operations include considerations such as ongrain garment parts and dye lot color matching. Quality assurance also takes place during the sewing and finishing operations. Garments are inspected during production to assure the specified quality standard. Inspectors can include machine operators, team quality auditors, plant supervisors, or quality auditors sent by the contracting party (apparel manufacturer or retailer).

Quality assurance includes the following: use of quality thread, buttons, zippers, snaps, elastic, and hem tape and other products; and the quality and accuracy of sewing operations such as stitch type and length, stitch tension, seam type, edge finish, top stitching, turned edges, buttonhole stitching, hem stitching, and plaid matching. Quality assurance personnel are well versed in evaluating all aspects of production quality and accuracy.

Another component of quality assurance is the consistency of the size specifications for all products produced in each size. All the finished products must conform to the specified tolerances (the amount the product can deviate, plus or minus, from the garment dimension) stated on the measurement spec sheet (see Chapter 9). Many apparel manufacturers check a specified number of garments in each shipment received from the contractor to determine whether the measurement specs have been met.

The difficulty lies in deciding what to do with any products that do not meet the quality standards. It may not be possible to cut and sew a replacement order of garments if a group of finished goods do not meet the specifications. The textile manufacturer may not have replacement fabric, or the time necessary to produce replacement garments may exceed the deadline established by the retailer. Some garments end up as seconds at company employee stores and outlet malls, may be purchased by jobbers, or are given to charities. In addition to the loss to apparel manufacturer and contractor, the retailer expecting the goods may suffer if an order cannot be filled. Therefore, it is to everyone's benefit to assure quality production.

In developing quality assurance programs, companies are relying less on after-the-fact inspection and more on building quality into the products during production. Through modular manufacturing methods, operators are responsible for the quality of the product throughout production. Table 11.1 compares the old way of using inspections for quality control with the new way of assuring quality products.

Current emphasis in quality assurance focuses on actively monitoring the manufacturing methods, materials, work environment and equipment to achieve the

TABLE 11.1

Comparisons of the Old Inspection-Based Quality Control Methods with More Successful Production-Based Quality Assurance Methods

Old Way 100 percent Inspect/ Quality Control	New Way Quality Assurance/ Empowerment
Acceptable quality level (AQL)	Zero defects
Inspector dominant	Associate responsibility
Attempt to *inspect* quality into the product	*Build* quality into the product
Justification for equipment investment based solely on reduction in labor content	Justification for equipment investment based on quality improvement
Need to produce volume first priority	Need to make a quality product first priority
Quality inspector given responsibility for product quality	Associate accepts ownership of quality process
Operator punishment for creating defects	Associate reward for recognizing and correcting the cause of defects
No incentive for quality production; inspector paid based on pieces processed	Incentive for quality production; associates paid based on number of first-quality products produced
Inspectors paid for finding defects (non-value-added activity)	No need for inspectors; associates paid for producing quality the first time (value-added activity)
Limited after-the-fact reporting	Causal analysis by statistical process control and other measurement tools (reporting of defects by type, quantity, area, associate)
Repair is an integral part of the process	Low or no need for repair and cost of repair not justifiable
Standards are what the supervisor says they are	Standards are based on specifications developed with consideration for process capability

Source: Continuing Education Subcommittee of the American Apparel Manufacturers Association Education Committee, reported in **Apparel Industry Magazine** (1995, December), p. 54.

expected specifications on a continual basis. One such method, statistical process control (SPC) is used by Sara International, a Miami-based company with production facilities in Pereira and Manizales, Colombia, that produces goods for Liz Claiborne. SPC "requires the in-line measurement of quality in a statistical sampling of consecutive garments—usually in small batches—as they come off a particular operation hour by hour. This is opposed to other commonly used methods, which tend to involve in-line and end-of-line inspections of large random samples" (Des-Marteau, 1999, p. 35). By in-process measurement and quality inspection, anomalies can be identified at a time when it is more likely that a correction can be made. Thus, quality assurance is a proactive rather than reactive approach to quality.

Export Agents, Freight Forwarders, and Customs Brokers

A substantial portion of the apparel and accessories industries relies on offshore factory production. Thus, it is important to discuss some of the aspects related to shipping goods out of the country where they were produced and into the United States. Many foreign countries have export regulations for shipping goods out of the country. It can be helpful for the U.S. apparel manufacturer that contracted the goods (the *importer*) to appoint an **export agent** in the exporting country to assist with exporting the products. A shipment of goods awaits clearance for off-loading in Fig. 11.10.

Figure 11.10: Container ships at the Port of Long Beach, California, unload their cargoes.

A **freight forwarding company** arranges to move a shipment of goods from the country where the goods were produced to the United States. Tariffs and quotas (regulations affecting apparel manufacturers that import apparel and textile products into the United States) were discussed in Chapters 2 and 10. The U.S. Customs Services, a part of the federal government, is the regulatory agency. A **customs broker** (licensed by the Customs Service) in the United States is an agent hired by the U.S. apparel manufacturer to assist the company in importing products. The customs broker is familiar with the complex U.S. customs regulations concerning importing textiles and apparel and will assist the apparel manufacturer to gain customs clearance. The apparel manufacturer is charged a fee by the customs broker on a transaction basis, not by the number of items in a transaction. While using a customs broker is optional, it can be very helpful to the apparel manufacturer. Sometimes, a shipment of goods is stalled by customs or sent back to the country of origin to correct the documentation. Not only does the apparel manufacturer face losing the retailer's business, but it may also face a fine by the shipping company that cannot unload the shipment. Of course, additional transportation costs are also involved. A consolidator might also be hired by the apparel manufacturer to serve as an intermediary for the freight forwarder and the customs broker.

Summary

This chapter examined some of the important aspects of production. With the background of the previous chapters, the interrelationship among research, design, pattern development, preproduction, and production should be clear. All systems must work together for production to flow smoothly. Any problem along a style's path may slow production. Delays to the contracted delivery date may cost the manufacturer not only the style's profits, but future business from retailers.

A significant portion of the cost to produce apparel is consumed by the labor required to cut and sew the goods. Reducing labor costs can help retain reasonable prices for finished goods. Specialized equipment has been developed to speed production and improve accuracy. New technology in equipment and manufacturing systems has dramatically changed apparel production and provided a more efficient use of the labor team. Workers are more actively involved in providing an efficient production system and in team responsibility for the quality of the goods produced. Even with the high cost of new, technologically advanced equipment, the increase in production efficiency rapidly pays for the cash outlay to purchase new equipment.

Changes in production sewing systems have required changes in the manner in which employee compensation is determined. Pay based on the team's performance, group incentives for high performance and quality, and straight hourly wages have replaced traditional piece rates at many facilities. Workers are cross-trained on various equipment and in a variety of skills to provide greater flexibility to the workforce.

The number of different garment styles produced per season has increased for many production facilities. This makes it more difficult for production to flow smoothly. Flexibility in production systems will continue to be an important cornerstone of increased efficiency and decreased labor costs. Concern for workers' ergonomic needs is another trend that has changed the look of production facilities. We no longer see banks of seated sewers bent over sewing machines. Workers stand, walk from point to point, and sit on stools to provide better body positioning, circulation, and muscle relaxation.

Finishing operations performed at the end of production include laundering and applying garment finishes and garment dyeing, as well as packaging products ready for distribution. Providing floor-ready merchandise for the retailer with bar coded hangtags improves the efficiency of the entire flow of goods.

Quality assurance is an integral part of the product, from its inception to arrival in the customer's hands. Quality assurance includes meeting quality standards for all aspects of the product: the textile goods, component parts such as buttons and zippers, sewing, measurement specifications, and finishing.

With the growth in offshore apparel manufacturing, it is increasingly important to understand the various processes, agencies, and personnel involved in these complex business transactions. Changes in regulations as well as in political and economic conditions and environmental considerations can affect the production of goods.

CAREER PROFILES

Careers in production include positions as production cutters, sewing operators, production supervisors, plant managers, and quality assurance coordinators. If you are considering a career in the production area, what would your position description entail, and what would some of your typical tasks and responsibilities be?

Production Manager
PRIVATE LABEL MANUFACTURER OF INTIMATE APPAREL

Position Description
Manage production of in-house sampling requirements (market, first fit, sew by, and photo samples); technical development; standards; quality control; price negotiations and place orders with suppliers and subcontractors; develop and implement production procedures and controls; and oversee production personnel. Manage contracted production in countries where garments are produced.

Typical Tasks and Responsibilities
- Serve as liaison with design, sales, and sample room as well as factories
- Visit factories for preproduction review on new styles and to check production in process as well as approve production for shipment
- Review samples from factories to check for specifications and approve fabric, trims, and color
- Organize labels and packaging
- Prepare cost sheets

Apparel Quality Analyst
PUBLICLY HELD ATHLETIC SPORTSWEAR COMPANY

Position Description
Investigate and prepare reports on all apparel quality issues working toward a resolution. Recommend action to and follow up with affected parties (development, marketing, sales, promotion). Develop and maintain a strong working relationship with related departments. Conduct meetings with departments to inform and reach a joint decision. Arrange for components, fabric, and finished product tests and inspections as necessary. Communicate with quality assurance managers in the U.S. and throughout the world. The apparel quality analyst position functions as a global position.

Typical Tasks and Responsibilities
- Communicate daily via e-mail and telephone with related departments throughout the life of the quality issue
- Prepare weekly quality logs for the QA department
- Investigate the scope, nature, probable cause, and resolution of quality issues. Samples from the field and distribution center come to this position
- Prepare reports and submit samples to the textile testing lab when the quality issue involves fabric development
- Perform inspection/audits at factories once a month. Being a field auditor is a small part of my responsibility as there are other field auditors who inspect/audit factories

Key Terms

agile manufacturing

computer-aided design/computer-aided manufacturing (CAD/CAM)

computer-integrated manufacturing (CIM)

counter sample

customs broker

export agent

flexible manufacturing (FM)

floor-ready merchandise (FRM)

freight forwarding company

garment dyed

manufacturing environment

mass customization

made-to-measure

modular manufacturing

piece-rate wage

production

progressive bundle system

radio frequency identification chip (RFIC)

sew by

short-cycle production

single-hand system

Smart Card

unit production system (UPS)

work-in-process (WIP)

Discussion Questions

1. The quality assurance department finds that the contracted goods do not meet the stated size specifications within the allowed tolerance. What are some of the problems faced by the apparel company if the shipment (or part of it) is rejected?

2. Compare and contrast the advantages and disadvantages of the progressive bundle and flexible manufacturing systems of apparel production.

3. Describe a quality defect you have encountered with an apparel product or accessory. How might quality assurance have prevented this problem?

References

Abend, Jules. (1999a, January). Modular manufacturing: The line between success and failure. *Bobbin*, pp. 48–52.

Bennett, Billy. (1988, October). It's a mod, mod, mod environment. *Bobbin*, pp. 50–55.

Butenhoff, Peter. (1999, May). Mass production, short-cyle, and mass customization: SCM's manufacturing trio. *Apparel Industry Magazine*, p. SCM-4.

Conrad, Andrée. (1996, September). "Smart" apparel. *Apparel Industry Magazine*, pp. 22–29.

Conrad, Andrée. (1999, May). Designing for demand: SCM dream or reality? *Apparel Industry Magazine*, pp. SCM-6–SCM-11.

DesMarteau, Kathleen. (1998, August). Wrinkle free now carefree. *Bobbin*, p. 188.

DesMarteau, Kathleen. (1999, July). Liz launches global quality coup. *Bobbin*, pp. 34–38.

DeWitt, John W. (1992, September). The ultimate consumer connection. *Apparel Industry Magazine*, pp. 56–62.

Doing it their way. (1998, May). *Apparel Industry Magazine*, p. 42–44.

Dunagan, Evelyn. (1999, January). Another perspective on modular manufacturing: Levi's was right. *Apparel Industry Magazine*, pp. 96–98.

Fallon, James. (1999, February 10). British retailers kick off body-scanning project. *Daily News Record*, p. 13

Hasty, Susan E. (ed). (1994, March). *The Quick Response Handbook*. Supplement to *Apparel Industry Magazine*.

Hill, Ed. (1992, February). Flexible manufacturing systems, Part 1. *Bobbin*, pp. 34–38.

Hill, Suzette. (1998, December). VF's consumerization: A "right stuff" strategy. *Apparel Industry Magazine*, pp. AS-4–AS-12.

Hill, Thomas. (1994, March). CAR study: UPS, CAD provide 300 percent return on investment. *Apparel Industry Magazine*, pp. 34–40.

Kosh, Kiki. (1987, February). Computer systems automated design function. *Bobbin*, pp. 51–64.

Made to measure or mass customization: Is it for You? (1998, vol. 18, no. 1). *Cuttings*, pp. 2–6.

Quick Response: America's Competitive Advantage [slide set program guide]. (1988). Washington, D.C.: American Textile Manufacturer's Institute.

Rabon, Lisa. (1998, November). New control system to revolutionize sewing equipment. *Bobbin*, pp. 49–52.

Rabon, Lisa. (2000, January). Mixing the elements of mass customization. *Bobbin*, pp. 38–41.

Rabon, Lisa and Deaton, Claudia. (1999, December). Pre-production: Laying the cornerstones of mass customization. *Bobbin*, pp. 35–37.

The shape of clothes to come. (2000, January). *Consumer Reports*, p. 8.

A showroom of high-tech sewing: Koos Manufacturing Inc. (1998, May). *Apparel Industry Magazine*, p. 54.

Silverman, Dick. (1998, November 11). A better fit through body scanning. *Women's Wear Daily*, p. 8.

Swank, Gary. (1995, January). QR requires floor-ready goods. *Apparel Industry Magazine*, p. 106.

[TC]² (Producer). (1993). [Video]. Agile Manufacturing: "The Vision."

Welling, Holly. (1998, December). Tanner companies: Making standup sewing stylish. *Apparel Industry Magazine*, pp. AS-34–AS-40.

Winger, Rocio Maria. (1998, December). The Nygård vanguard: The way to chargebacks. *Apparel Industry Magazine*, pp. AS-14–AS-18.

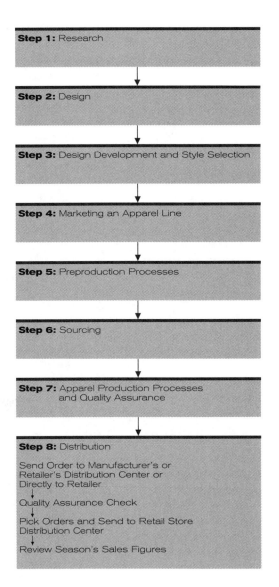

Step 1: Research

Step 2: Design

Step 3: Design Development and Style Selection

Step 4: Marketing an Apparel Line

Step 5: Preproduction Processes

Step 6: Sourcing

Step 7: Apparel Production Processes and Quality Assurance

Step 8: Distribution

Send Order to Manufacturer's or Retailer's Distribution Center or Directly to Retailer

Quality Assurance Check

Pick Orders and Send to Retail Store Distribution Center

Review Season's Sales Figures

CHAPTER 12

Distribution and Retailing

Dillard's

IN THIS CHAPTER YOU WILL LEARN:

- The strategies and processes for distributing apparel products to the ultimate consumer.

- The nature of the alliances between apparel companies and retailers in carrying out Quick Response and supply chain management activities related to distribution.

- The definitions and characteristics of the various categories of retailers.

- The primary trade publications and trade associations associated with distribution of apparel products.

Distribution Strategies

We have followed apparel products from their design through their production. The next stage is distribution to retailers and finally to the ultimate consumer. Companies must decide on the strategies they will use to distribute merchandise. Decisions regarding distribution strategies are based on the type of marketing channel to which the company belongs (these channels—direct, limited, and extended—were described in Chapter 2); the buying characteristics of the target customer; the product type; whether the product is a national, private label, or store brand; and the wholesale price zone of the merchandise. Distribution strategies can be classified as mass distribution, selective distribution, or exclusive distribution.

- **Mass Distribution.** With **mass distribution** (also called **intensive distribution**) products are made available to as many consumers as possible through a variety of retail outlets, including supermarkets, convenience stores, and mass merchandisers or discount stores. The L'eggs, Hanes, and No Nonsense hosiery brands use this method of distribution strategy.
- **Selective Distribution.** With **selective distribution**, manufacturers only allow their merchandise to be distributed through certain stores. Some manufacturers require a minimum quantity to be purchased; others limit their products' distribution to retailers in noncompeting geographic areas. Some manufacturers also set criteria as to the image and location of stores in which its merchandise can be sold.

■ **Exclusive Distribution.** With **exclusive distribution**, manufacturers limit the stores in which their merchandise is distributed in order to create an image of exclusiveness. Companies that produce merchandise in the designer wholesale price zone (e.g., Chanel, Yves Saint Laurent, Armani) often use an exclusive distribution strategy by selling goods only through a few stores or boutiques. The distribution of private label merchandise (e.g., JCPenney's Arizona brand, Kmart's Jaclyn Smith brand) and store brands (e.g., Gap, The Limited) that are specific to a particular retailer is also considered to be exclusive because the brands are available only at specific stores.

Distribution Centers

For some apparel companies, shipments of finished merchandise to their retail accounts are made directly from the production facility. For other apparel companies, the flow of goods from production facilities to retailers involves the use of **distribution centers (DCs)**. Both manufacturers and retailers utilize distribution centers as part of their distribution processes. Whether manufacturers and/or retailers use distribution centers in their distribution processes depends on the size of the company, the number of products being distributed, the number of retail stores being serviced, and the proximity between where the merchandise was produced and where the retail accounts are located. The larger the company and the more products and retailers involved, the more likely distribution centers will be used.

MANUFACTURERS' DISTRIBUTION CENTERS

Apparel manufacturers will use distribution centers when shipments to retailers consist of goods produced in more than one location (especially when contractors are used). In these cases, merchandise from the various locations is brought to a central location for quality assurance, *picking* (selecting the appropriate assortment of goods to fill a specific retailer's order), packing the merchandise, and distributing to the retail store accounts (see Figure 12.1). Technology has become important in increasing the efficiencies of distribution centers. Robotics that pick orders and conveyor systems that move orders from one area to the next have been incorporated into distribution center processes.

Figure 12.1: The distribution process includes shipping merchandise to retail accounts.

To speed up the process, some companies have reduced the use of distribution centers and are shipping to retailers directly from the production facility (Moore, 1994). Other companies are changing the purpose of their distribution centers from warehousing inventory to storing it for only short periods. Such *flow-through* facilities move merchandise from receiving to shipping with little, if any, time in storage (Nannery, 1995). For example, NIKE's 1.2 million-square-foot distribution center in Memphis, Tennessee, which opened in 1997, promotes a 12-hour turnaround from the time the product is received at the DC to the time it is shipped to the retailer. There is also a trend among apparel companies to use DCs for *adding value* (doing something to a product to make it worth more to the manufacturer, retailer, or consumer) to the merchandise by affixing hangtags, labels, and price information in order to make the goods floor ready (Moore, 1994). When manufacturers preticket merchandise, retailers do not have to spend extra time ticketing the items before the apparel hits the selling floor. This process, known as vendor marking, results in floor-ready merchandise (see also Chapter 11).

Whereas modular methods have been used primarily at production facilities (see Chapter 11), some companies have introduced systems based on the same philosophies to improve the efficiency of their distribution centers. One such company is Columbia Sportswear, headquartered in Portland, Oregon (Gilbert & Carlson, 1995), which has introduced modular methods in the customer returns and quality assurance areas of the distribution center. Similar to modular (or flexible) manufacturing practices, teams of workers move products from one operation to the next rather than one person performing the same function continually. Pay for the employees depends on overall facility performance rather than on individual performance. Columbia has found that the implementation of these systems has increased the speed for the processes and improved the quality of the work performed.

RETAILERS' DISTRIBUTION CENTERS

Retailers also use distribution centers to facilitate distribution of merchandise from a variety of apparel companies (vendors) to a number of stores. Goods are shipped from the manufacturers to a centralized retail distribution center, where merchandise for the retailer's stores are picked, combined, and shipped to the individual stores. If merchandise has not been vendor marked, then hangtags, including stock-keeping unit (SKU) codes and price information, are affixed to the merchandise at the retailer's DC. Retail distribution centers are often at geographical locations chosen to speed delivery to stores. Target has 10 distribution centers located throughout the United States; Wal-Mart has 41 distribution centers. In recent years, the productivity of distribution centers has been enhanced through warehouse management system (WMS) computer software programs. These programs assist retailers in maximizing the space within the DC, automating warehouse operations, integrating data throughout the supply chain, improving communication with vendors (manufacturers), and improving shipping accuracy (Hill, 1999).

Alliances between Manufacturers and Retailers: QR and SCM

The primary goal of Quick Response and supply chain management strategies is to increase the speed with which merchandise gets to the consumer through the sharing of data among companies throughout the production and distribution of the product. The establishment of alliances between manufacturers and retailers has been imperative for this goal to be achieved.

THE FOUNDATIONS: UPC BAR CODING, VENDOR MARKING, AND EDI

Alliances between manufacturers and retailers depend on several basic operation strategies that have been adopted by manufacturers and retailers. These include the use of UPC bar coding on products and shipping containers, vendor marking of merchandise, and electronic data interchange (EDI).

UPC Bar Coding and Vendor Marking

The **Universal Product Code (UPC)** system is one of several bar code symbologies used for the electronic identification of merchandise. The use of UPC bar coding is often seen as the foundation of many QR and SCM strategies because it is considered necessary for electronic communications between the manufacturer and retailer. A UPC is a 12-digit number that identifies manufacturer and merchandise items by stockkeeping unit (SKU): vendor, style, color, and size. It is represented by a bar code made up of a pattern of dark bars and white spaces of varying widths. A group of bars and spaces represents one character or digit. UPC bar codes are electronically scanned and "read" by scanning equipment. The scanning equipment provides a source of intense light that illuminates the symbol. The dark bars absorb the light. The scanner collects the reflected pattern of light and dark and converts it into an electrical signal that is sent to a decoder. The decoder, which may be part of the scanner unit or may be a separate device, translates the electrical signal to binary numbers for use by the point-of-sale terminal or computer. Scanners can be categorized as either: (1) contact readers that must touch or come in close proximity to the symbol, or (2) noncontact readers that can read the bar code when it is moved past a fixed beam or moving beam of light (see Figure 12.2).

UPC bar codes are attached to the merchandise by the manufacturer/vendor (**vendor marking**) or the retailer. Both vendor-marked merchandise and retailer-prepared bar codes are used to increase the speed of checkout and the accuracy of inventories. There are a number of benefits of UPC bar coding and point-of-sale (POS) scanning, including maximizing the efficiency of store personnel, speeding up the checkout process, improving the accuracy of pricing, providing accurate sales information, and providing accurate ongoing inventory counts. One of the most obvious benefits of using bar codes is the reduction in time needed to complete a transaction at the point of sale.

Figure 12.2: The Universal Product Code (UPC) or bar code (left) contains product information in electronic form. UPC bar codes on apparel hangtags (right) facilitate the collection of point-of-sale information.

An even more important benefit of scanning bar codes is that accurate SKU information is retrieved at the point of sale. This means that product sales and retail inventory are automatically tracked. With this accurate and timely sales information, retailers and manufacturers can plan inventory needs to match more closely sales or projected consumer demand. For example, with accurate sales data, retailers are able to track sales trends and thereby avoid overstocking merchandise (thus reducing markdowns). Correct point-of-sale information can also be used to reorder merchandise more efficiently and thereby reduce the possibility of a retailer being out of stock in a particular style, size, or color of merchandise. In addition, automatic reordering of merchandise (*replenishment*) is dependent upon the use of point-of-sale information provided by UPC bar codes. Replenishment strategies will be discussed later in this chapter.

In addition to using bar codes for these point-of-sale (POS) benefits, retailers also use them to scan inventory in their distribution centers and to facilitate the movement of shipping cartons in distribution centers. The bar codes identify each shipping container's contents and are used for tracking and sorting merchandise at the DCs. While the UPC bar code is made up of only numbers, two other bar code formats, code 39 or code 128, can include both numbers and letters and are often used on shipping cartons. L.L.Bean is an example of a company that successfully uses bar codes to improve the efficiency and accuracy of its merchandise distribution. L.L.Bean, headquartered in Freeport, Maine, is known for sensible, quality merchandise distributed primarily through mail order. The company has built its reputation on the fact that it can deliver virtually any item almost anywhere in the United States or Canada within 72 hours and that orders are filled correctly 99.8 percent of the time (Olive, 1988). The L.L.Bean distribution center is the core of this direct marketing effort. Incoming merchandise cases are marked with a Code 39 bar code that includes codes for the stock number and case quantity. This automatic identification information is used to improve the accuracy and speed of the processing of merchandise and inventory control.

Electronic Data Interchange.

Electronic data interchange (EDI) makes possible computer-to-computer communications between the manufacturer and retailer (see Figure 12.3). In the past, purchase orders, invoices, and any other type of written communication generated by one company were sent to another company by mail or fax. The receiving company would then enter the data into its computer. With EDI technology, business data are transmitted electronically. In other words, computers from one company "talk" directly to computers from other companies or through a third party's computer system called a *value-added network* (VAN). This eliminates the processing of

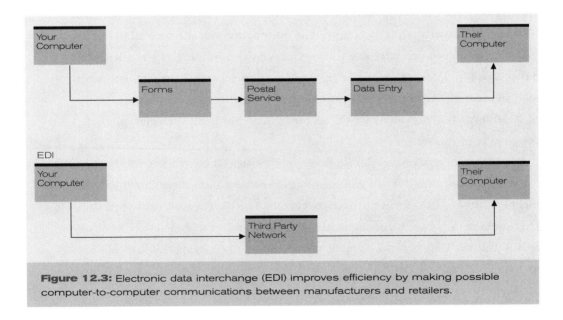

Figure 12.3: Electronic data interchange (EDI) improves efficiency by making possible computer-to-computer communications between manufacturers and retailers.

much of the paperwork and, in effect, creates a paperless office. Not only are paper documents replaced by electronic documents, but the time delays associated with using mail services and paper handling are eliminated. Currently the most common EDI transactions in the apparel industry are purchase orders, invoices, packing slips, advance shipping notices (ASN); reports of inventory counts and changes in inventory such as sales and returns data; and price/sales catalogs.

In addition, through EDI retail distribution centers can accommodate cross-dockable shipments. This means that goods are received from the manufacturer as floor-ready merchandise, so they can be sorted for store distribution without the need for additional processing (Robins, 1994). For cross-docking to happen, the retailer must request and receive advanced shipping notices from the manufacturer, and the goods must arrive floor ready. This would not be possible without EDI technology.

In the age of supply chain management, the EDI capabilities of the manufacturer have become increasingly important to both manufacturers and retailers. In many cases, EDI is the backbone of supply chain management, through which retailer POS data feeds directly into apparel companies' manufacturing systems and by which manufacturers are directly linked to the suppliers of fabric, trims, and findings. However, as Alan Brooks, president of New Generation Computing, stated, "EDI is not a technical issue as much as it is an area for management to control. We can have all the numbers and standards, but those will never bring good business judgment to the table. In the garment industry, you have to keep a feel for what is going on everywhere—especially in this electronic age" (DeWitt, 1993, p. 41).

In recent years, communities of companies, known as **eMarkets**, have moved to conducting business using the Internet.

> Fundamentally, eMarkets change the relationship dynamics between buyers and sellers from one-to-one to many-to-many. They enable trading partners to conduct business over the Internet eliminating the need for more costly paper and custom EDI methods. ("eMarkets," 2001, p. P4)

In effect, eMarkets build on the relationships established through EDI technologies and simplify the process so that each vendor and each buyer have to make only one connection—to the eMarket—rather than to each of their vendors and each of their buyers. As such, eMarkets improve buying efficiency, lower costs, and improve access to markets. Growth of the use of eMarkets in supply chain management is expected in the coming years ("eMarkets," 2001).

REPLENISHMENT STRATEGIES

In the traditional manufacturer-retailer relationship, the retail buyer would order goods from the manufacturer, and the entire order for the season would then be delivered to the retailer at the beginning of the fashion season. The retailer would hope that the correct number of each style, color, and size had been ordered and delivered. However, with this arrangement it was not uncommon for a customer to walk into a store knowing the style and size of a product he or she wanted only to find that the store did not have the size in stock. When this happened, a sale was lost. To help alleviate situations such as this, the retailer must be able to replenish merchandise in an accurate and timely manner. There are several replenishment methods used by manufacturers and retailers, including the following:

- The retailer initiates a paper order when it determines the stock level is such as to warrant a reorder.
- The retailer initiates an electronic (EDI) order when it determines the stock level is such as to warrant a reorder.
- The retailer's inventory computer system automatically reorders merchandise (through EDI) when stock reaches a certain level.
- Information about stock levels is automatically communicated to the manufacturer through EDI, and the manufacturer (vendor) automatically ships reorders when the merchandise stock at the retail store reaches a certain level.
- A specified percent of the retail buyer's order is delivered before the start of the fashion season, with the remainder of the order delivered either throughout the fashion season or as a single reorder. The mix of styles, colors, and sizes in the reorder(s) are based on POS data from the retail stores.

Replenishment strategies vary with the type of merchandise. For basic items (e.g., hosiery, jeans) replenishment may be an ongoing activity. For seasonal goods (e.g., turtleneck sweaters, outerwear), replenishment may occur only within a particular fashion season. For fashion goods, merchandise may not be replenished during the fashion season.

Manufacturers may use a variety of replenishment strategies depending upon their retail customers, and retailers may use a variety of replenishment strategies depending upon the capabilities of their vendors (manufacturers). Apparel companies often rely on electronic orders from retailers to get merchandise to the retailers in a timely manner. For example, Nygård International, a Canadian apparel manufacturer and retailer, has tied their electronic orders from retail accounts to their CAD/CAM systems. When an electronic order is received, it sets the manufacturing process into motion resulting in a 72-hour produce-and-ship time from when the electronic order was placed (Winger, 1998).

One of the strategies most beneficial to improving the efficiency in the apparel supply pipeline between the manufacturer and retailer has been to establish programs whereby sales and *stockout data* (data out-of-stock goods) are reviewed by the manufacturer and replenishments are ordered as often as required. The strategy of having the manufacturer (vendor) automatically ship merchandise to the retail store based on POS data from the retailer is known as **vendor-managed inventory (VMI)** or *vendor-managed replenishment*. In some cases, data are reviewed daily rather than monthly or bimonthly, as was done in the past (Robins, 1993). Obviously, this type of strategy would not be possible without the retailer sending POS data to the manufacturer. "While retailers early in the QR movement showed some apprehension about sharing POS data, this apprehension has all but disappeared, and the sharing of POS data is now an accepted cornerstone of QR partnerships" (Robins, 1993, p. 22).

Lingerie manufacturers generally use vendor-managed inventory strategies (see Figure 12.4). Wrangler, a subsidiary of VF Corporation that manufactures men's and women's jeans, is another example of a company that has been very successful in managing retailer inventories (Hasty, 1994). Wrangler salespeople work closely with retail buyers in determining product mix and appropriate stock levels for specific stores. Wrangler sends new orders whenever the store's stock falls below a specified minimum. Wrangler receives POS information from more than 5,000 stores either daily or weekly, and each order is customized for a specific store depending upon the store's stock levels of various SKUs. Wrangler's goal is to receive POS information in the morning and ship jeans the same day.

Duck Head Apparel, headquartered in Winder, Georgia, estimates that half of its business in men's and boy's casual wear is based on vendor-managed inventory. The retailer's POS data are directly linked to Duck Head's manufacturing and distribution systems. These systems react automatically to the retail sales data and replenishment goods are delivered to stores before stock outs happen (Aron, 1998).

Figure 12.4: Manufacturers of lingerie typically deliver preticketed, floor-ready merchandise as part of their vendor-managed retail inventory strategies.

Going the next step in vendor-managed inventory, some apparel producers are incorporating **data-mining technology** to examine sales of products by style, size, and color. Data-mining technology analyzes data information searching for selling patterns or trends in the data and identifying correlations among data characteristics. For example, one company discovered that the selling season for shorts was longer in locations with higher median incomes. According to a representative of Kurt Salmon and Associates, New York:

> A number of apparel producers are taking the data, using it to see what sizes, colors and styles are selling in a particular retail chain and then going back to the retailer, either in the next season or in replenishment, and tailoring the assortment a lot more closely to the individual outlets. It's the first level of micro-marketing, and it presents huge opportunities for improved performance. (Hill, 1998, p. 18)

The technology is also being used to justify and manage retail floor space so that the correct amount of space is being allocated to the right products. Although the technology is currently expensive, database and data-mining services will allow even small companies to take advantage of it (Hill, 1998).

Implementing Quick Response and Supply Chain Management

This book has focused on the Quick Response (QR) and supply chain management (SCM) strategies implemented throughout the textile, apparel, and retailing industries (see Table 12.1 for a summary of the most common QR strategies at each stage). The implementation of QR and SCM strategies involves a shift in a company's management style, in addition to an increased investment of a company's resources in technology, training, and evaluation. Therefore, a company typically phases in strategies that are most consistent with its strategic plans. To be competitive, companies, both large and small, have adopted these strategies. According to "The Quick Response Handbook" (Hasty, 1994, pp. 5–6), QR implementation takes place in six stages:

1. **Stage one** enables QR by installing bar coding and EDI, which provide accurate sales data and speed communications.

TABLE 12.1

Most Common QR Strategies Grouped by Manufacturing Area

Textile to Apparel
  Reduction in inventory
  Small lot fabric orders
  EDI confirmation with suppliers
  Shade sorting of fabric rolls
  Reduction of wait time
  Elimination of redundant tests

Production
  Flexible manufacturing
  Automated sewing operations
  Scan bar coding of fabric
  Overhead conveyor for handling
  Garment dyed products

Apparel to Retail
  Garment design—CAD
  Bar coding of finished garments
  Product information with customer
  EDI confirmation with customers
  Receive POS information
  Forecasting with retailer

Source: Reprinted from Kincade, D. H. (1995). Quick Response management system for the apparel industry: Definition through technologies. *Clothing and Textiles Research Journal, 13* (4), 245–251.

2. **Stage two** starts QR replenishment. Apparel firms ship reorders more frequently and faster, which increases sales by keeping stores in stock.

3. **Stage three** streamlines replenishment. Retailers and suppliers jointly review sales data, develop plans and forecasts for future demand, and reduce inventory while keeping stores fully stocked.

4. **Stage four** customizes assortments and replenishment, not only for each retailer but for each store unit in a retail chain. In many instances, apparel firms participate in or even make decisions regarding product assortment, quantities, sales floor displays and fixtures, and sales floor customer service (training and motivating associates).

5. **Stage five** adds fashion goods to the basic and seasonal goods most common in QR alliances. New products are created jointly by the manufacturer and retailer, bypassing the traditional buyer-salesperson process and shortening the time from concept to new product on the shelf. In-store testing of new products is part of this stage.

6. **Stage six** integrates all of the stages and QR capabilities with the apparel firm's total business processes in support of its strategy.

With SCM, either an order from a retailer or a retail sale electronically triggers the manufacturing process. Orders or sales data are tied to the apparel company's CAD/CAM systems and fabric and findings suppliers (Winger, 1998). At the retail level, the retailer's financial and merchandise plans are integrated. That is, the retailer's assortment plan is integrated with how much space each retail department will be allocated at each store, thus optimizing the store's merchandise mix (Hill, 1999). These processes are also phased in over time. Integrated processes include the following:

■ Integration of an apparel company's pattern-making systems (PDS) with other product information through product information management (PIM) software (see Chapter 9).

■ Integration of an apparel company's various CAD/CAM systems resulting in computer-integrated manufacturing (see Chapter 11).

■ Alliances between apparel companies and retailers, resulting in vendor-managed retail inventory.

■ Integration of retailer's merchandise assortment planning, financial planning, distribution processes, and store layout.

Apparel Retailing

By definition, **retailing** is the "business activity of selling goods or services to the final consumer," and a **retailer** is "any business establishment that directs its marketing efforts toward the final consumer for the purpose of selling goods and services" (Lewison, 1994, p. 5). Retailers range in size from small sole proprietorships that cater to a local market to large corporate store-ownership groups. Table 12.2

TABLE 12.2
Selected Major Retail Corporations

Burlington Coat Factory Warehouse Corporation (www.coat.com)
    Burlington Coat Factory Stores
    Luxury Linens
    Baby Depot
    Decelle
    COHOES Fashions

Casual Corner Group (www.casual cornergroup.com)
    Casual Corner
    Petite Sophisticate
    August Max Woman

Dillard's (www.dillards.com)

Federated Department Stores, Inc. (www.federated-fds.com)
    Macy's West
    Macy's East
    Bloomingdale's
    The Bon Marché
    Burdines
    Lazarus
    Rich's
    Goldsmith's
    Fingerhut

Foot Locker Inc. (www.venatorgroup.com)
    Champs Sports
    Foot Locker
    Lady Foot Locker
    Kids Foot Locker
    Eastbay
    Northern Elements
    Northern Getaway

Northern Reflections
Northern Traditions

Gap Inc. (www.gap.com)
    Gap
    GapKids
    babyGap
    GapBody
    Gap Outlet Stores
    Banana Republic
    Old Navy

Neiman Marcus Group (Parent Company: Harcourt General) (www.neimanmarcus.com)
    Neiman Marcus
    Bergdorf Goodman
    Neiman Marcus Direct

Kmart Corporation (www.bluelight.com)
    Kmart and Big Kmart
    SuperKmart

The Limited, Inc.
    The Limited
    Express
    Structure
    Victoria's Secret
    Lane Bryant
    Lerner New York
    Henri Bendel
    Bath & Body Works
    Intimate Brands
    The White Barn Candle Co.

(continued)

TABLE 12.2 (continued)

Selected Major Retail Corporations

May Department Stores
(www.mayco.com)
  Meier & Frank
  Robinsons-May
  Famous-Barr
  Foley's
  Kaufmann's
  Hecht's
  Lord & Taylor
  Filene's
  Stawbridge's
  The Jones Store
  ZCMI
  L.S. Ayres
  David's Bridal

Nordstrom (www.nordstrom.com)
Nordstrom
Nordstom Rack
Nordstrom.com

J.C. Penney Company, Inc.
(www.jcpenney.com)
  JCPenney
  JCPenney Catalog and Logistics

Saks Incorporated (formerly Proffitt's, Inc.)
(www.saksincorporated.com)
  Saks Fifth Avenue
  Proffitt's
  McRae's
  Younkers
  Parisian
  Herberger's
  Carson Pirie Scott
  Bergner's
  Boston Store
  Off 5th
  Saks Direct

Sears, Roebuck & Co. (www.sears.com)
  Sears
  Sears Hardware Stores
  Sears Homelife
  Sears Automotive
  Sears HomeCentral

  Sears Dealer Stores
  Western Auto Stores
  Orchard Supply Hardware Stores
  Sears Shop at Home

The Spiegel Group (www.spiegel.com)
  Spiegel
  Newport News
  (www.newport-news.com)
  Eddie Bauer
  (www.eddiebauer.com)

Target Corporation (www.targetcorp.com)
  Target
  Mervyn's California
  Marshall Field's
  Target.direct

The TJX Companies, Inc. (www.tjx.com)
  T.J. Maxx
  Marshalls
  Winners
  A.J. Wright
  HomeGoods
  T.K. Maxx

Toys "R" Us (www.toysrus.com)
  Toys "R" Us, USA
  Toys "R" Us, International
  Babies "R" Us
  Kids "R" Us

Wal-Mart Stores, Inc.
(www.wal-mart.com)
  Wal-Mart Stores
  Wal-Mart Supercenters
  SAM's Club
  Wal-Mart International

Wet Seal (www.wetseal.com)
  Contempo Casuals
  Wet Seal

Source: Jordan, C. (2001). Major Retail Corporations. Corvallis: Oregon State University.

lists of some of the primary retail corporations and the stores owned and operated by these corporations.

Retailers can be classified according to many of their characteristics, including their ownership, merchandise mix, size, location, and organizational and operational characteristics (see Figure 12.5). One typical way of classifying retailers is on the basis of their merchandising and operating strategies, which results in the following categories: department stores, specialty stores, chain stores, discount retailers, off-price retailers, supermarkets, convenience stores, contractual retailers, warehouse retailers, and nonstore retailers. Because of the diversity found among retailers, these categories are not mutually exclusive. For example, a specialty store retailer may also be a chain store operation; a department store may also engage in nonstore retailing by sending mail order catalogs. Table 12.3 lists the dollar share percentage among various apparel retail categories.

DEPARTMENT STORES

Department stores are large retailers that divide their functions and their merchandise into sections, or departments. Department stores have a fashion orientation, follow a full markup policy, and operate in stores large enough to be shopping

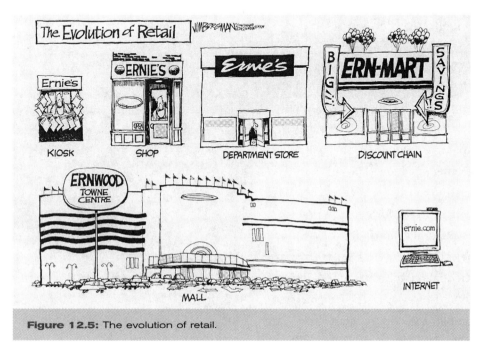

Figure 12.5: The evolution of retail.

TABLE 12.3

Apparel Distribution Channels by Dollar Share Percentage

Retail Channel	Dollar Share %
Department stores	22.5
Specialty stores	17.9
Major chain stores	14.6
Discounters/warehouse clubs	22.5
Off-price	6.7
Nontraditional*	9.9
Nonstore (direct mail, TV)	6.0

*Factory outlets, food and drug, variety, etc.

Source: NPD Group data based on dollar purchases January–June 1995. Reported in Kurt Salmon Associates. (1996, January). Soft goods outlook for 1996. *Apparel Industry Magazine*, p. 52.

center anchors (see Figure 12.6). The category includes traditional department stores such as Macy's, Marshall Field's, Dillard's, and Robinsons-May, as well as limited-line department stores such as Nordstrom, Saks Fifth Avenue, Mervyn's California, and Neiman Marcus (which were once classified as specialty stores). Table 12.4 is a list of the top ten department stores based on sales volume.

With the goal of catering to a broad range of consumers, department stores carry a wide variety of merchandise lines with a reasonably wide selection within each category. Department stores usually carry national brands and private label merchandise typically in the moderate and better wholesale price zones. Depending on their price assortment, they may also carry merchandise in the bridge and designer price zones.

Although department stores have been criticized for being boring, confusing, and "dinosaurs" of retailing, they continue to have a large share of the apparel market (Schneiderman, 1995). However, faced with increased competition, department stores are

Figure 12.6: Department stores such as Dillard's often serve as shopping center anchors.

TABLE 12.4

Top Department Stores by Sales Volume

Department Stores	Sales Volume (000)
Sears	$29,775,000
JCPenney	18,964,000
Federated	18,217,000
May	13,869,000
Dillards	8,677,000
Saks	6,423,819
Nordstrom	5,124,233
Kohl's	4,557,112
Neiman Marcus Group	2,553,421
Belks	2,200,000

Source: Stores. (2000, July). Top 100 retailers.

refocusing, with a new emphasis on presentation, customer service, and having the right products for their target market—products that are different from the products carried by other stores. This merchandising strategy, known as **relationship merchandising**, addresses the needs of individual customers. Nordstrom has been cited as the prototype of this merchandising strategy.

Many department stores also have **in-store shops** of designers and major brands. These in-store shops are merchandised according to the apparel company's specifications and carry only the merchandise of the apparel company. In men's apparel, companies with the greatest number of in-store shops are Ralph Lauren (with 1,220), Nautica (1,200), Tommy Hilfiger (1,150), Calvin Klein (1,000), Duck Head (1,000), and Jockey (650). In-store shops are less prevalent in women's wear with Ralph Lauren (with 205) and Tommy Hilfiger (100) leading the way. In-store shops benefit both the apparel company and the retailer. For the apparel company, they create awareness and make shopping easy for their customers. For the department stores, the in-store shops create a specialty store "feel" within the department store environment (Abend, 1998).

SPECIALTY STORES

A **specialty store** focuses on a specific type of merchandise, either by carrying one category of merchandise or a few closely related categories of merchandise (e.g., jewelry, shoes, eyeglasses, intimate apparel), by focusing on merchandise for a well-defined target market (e.g., men, women, bicyclists, large-size consumers), or by carrying the merchandise of one manufacturer or brand (e.g., Nine West, Ralph Lauren, Baby Guess/Guess Kids). Specialty stores carry a limited but deep assortment (i.e., excellent selection of brands, styles, sizes) of merchandise. They may carry national brands or have their own store brand (e.g., The Limited, Talbot's). Most specialty stores will carry merchandise in only one or two price zones. Two of the largest apparel specialty stores chains in the United States are The Limited and Gap (see Figure 12.7) See Table 12.5 for a listing of specialty chains. Specialty stores that concentrate on designer-price-zone merchandise or unique merchandise distributed exclusively to only a few stores are sometimes referred to as **boutiques**.

Figure 12.7: The Gap is an example of a specialty store chain that focuses on a limited number of apparel and accessory categories.

TABLE 12.5

Top Apparel Specialty Chains by Sales Volume

Apparel Chain	Sales Volume (000)
Gap	$11,635,398
Limited	9,723,334
TJX	8,795,347
Intimate Brands	4,510,836
Spiegel/Eddie Bauer	3,210,225
Ross Stores	2,468,638
Burlington Coat Factory Warehouse	2,242,500
Talbots	1,290,923
American Retail Group	1,250,000
Charming Shoppes	1,196,529
Stage Stores	1,121,567
Ann Taylor	1,084,633
Abercrombie & Fitch	1,042,056

Source: *Stores*. (2000, July). Top 100 specialty stores.

CHAIN STORES

Chain store organizations own and operate several retail store units that sell similar lines of merchandise with a standard method and function under a centralized organizational structure. Chain stores are characterized by centralized buying, no single main or flagship store (which multiunit department stores with branches typically have), centralized distribution, and standardized store decor and layout. All management and merchandising decisions and policies are made by managers at a central headquarters or home office. Chain store operations include large chains (defined as 11 or more units), which may be national or international in scope, such as JCPenney, Sears, Wal-Mart, Target, and The Limited, or they can be small chains (two to ten retail units) within a local or regional area. Although chain stores benefit from the economies of scale that comes with purchasing merchandise for a number of stores, they also carry merchandise that caters to the wants and needs of the local target markets. Private label merchandise is an important part of the merchandise mix for chain store retailers (e.g., JCPenney's Arizona, Worthington and Stafford labels).

DISCOUNT RETAILERS

A **discount store** sells brand name merchandise at below traditional retail prices and includes apparel merchandise at the mass or budget wholesale price zone. Discounters also carry private label merchandise (e.g., Kmart's Jaclyn Smith brand, Target's Mossima brand). Through mass merchandising and supply chain management strategies, discounters are able to keep prices lower than other retailers. Quantity

Figure 12.8: Wal-Mart, a national discount chain, sells a variety of merchandise including family apparel and accessories.

discounts from manufacturers and high turnover rates on products contribute to discount retailers' ability to offer lower prices to consumers. Other strategies include limiting brands and styles to only the most popular items, self-service, lower overhead costs, and promotions that cater to a broad target market. National discount chains such as Wal-Mart (Figure 12.8), Kmart, and Target buy huge quantities of merchandise from manufacturers and can operate on smaller profit margins than can department stores. Stores such as Target are sometimes referred to as *upscale discounters* because they have a department store feel and apparel accounts for 45 percent or more of total sales. Table 12.6 lists the top discount stores.

OFF-PRICE RETAILERS

Off-price retailers specialize in selling national brands, designer apparel lines, or promotional goods at discount prices. Off-price retailers are characterized by their buying of merchandise at low prices, carrying well-established (including designer) brands, and having merchandise assortments that change and may be inconsistent. The following are all types of off-price retailers:

■ **Factory Outlet Stores.** Manufacturers' outlets sell their own seconds, irregulars, or overruns (merchandise produced in excess of their orders) as well as merchandise produced specifically for the outlet stores. In some cases manufacturers will use their outlet stores as test markets for styles, colors, or sizes of merchandise. Once located primarily near production or distribution centers, factory outlet stores comprising entire shopping centers are now common throughout the United States, although they are typically located at a distance from full-price retailers that carry their goods (based on agreements with local full-price retailers).

TABLE 12.6

Top Discount/Value Stores by Sales Volume, 1999

Discount Store	Sales Volume (000)
Wal-Mart	$108,721,000
Kmart	35,925,000
Target	26,080,000
Sam's Club	24,801,000
Meijer	9,500,000
BJ's Wholesale Club	4,115,825
ShopKo	3,898,090
Dollar General	3,887,964
Ames	3,878,544
Family Dollar	2,751,181

Source: Stores. (2000, July). Top 100 retailers.

- **Independent Off-Price Retailers.** These stores buy irregulars, seconds, overruns, or leftovers from manufacturers or other retailers. Ross (Figure 12.9), T. J. Maxx, and Burlington Coat Factory are examples of off-price retailers.

- **Retailer-Owned Off-Price Retailers.** Some retailers operate their own off-price stores (e.g., Off 5th, Nordstrom Rack). In these off-price stores, retailers sell merchandise from their regular stores that had not sold within a specified time period, private label merchandise, or special orders purchased specifically for the off-price store.

Figure 12.9: Independent off-price retailers, such as Ross, sell national brands and promotional goods at discount prices.

- **Closeout Stores.** Closeout stores specialize in buying a variety of merchandise through retail liquidations, bankruptcies, and closeouts and selling it at bargain prices.

- **Sample Stores.** Sample stores specialize in selling apparel companies' sample merchandise at the end of market selling period. These stores are located near major apparel marts such as CaliforniaMart.

SUPERMARKETS

Conventional **supermarkets** are large self-service grocery stores that carry a full line of foods and related products with at least $2 million annual sales. Some supermarkets have broadened their merchandise and service offerings. **Superstores** are upgraded supermarkets with at least $8 million in annual sales and are at least 30,000 square feet in total area. Only a limited number of apparel products are distributed through either type of supermarket. Typically these products include basic items such as mass-merchandise hosiery, packaged undergarments, T-shirts, and inexpensive eyewear. These items must accommodate a self-service merchandising strategy, so visual displays that assist consumers in selecting the right style and size are common. These items are also most likely to use an extended marketing channel that facilitates the supermarkets' buying of these goods.

CONVENIENCE STORES

Convenience stores are small stores that offer fast service at a convenient location but carry only a limited assortment of food and related items. As with supermarkets, the most typical apparel products carried by convenience stores are basic items such as mass-merchandised hosiery (e.g., L'eggs, No Nonsense).

CONTRACTUAL RETAILERS

Retailers may enter into contractual agreements with manufacturers, wholesalers, or other retailers in order to integrate operations and increase market impact. Such contractual agreements include retailer-sponsored cooperatives that take the form of an organization of small independent retailers, wholesaler-sponsored voluntary chains, in which a wholesaler develops a program for small independent retailers, franchises, and leased departments. The term **contractual retailers** covers all such arrangements. Franchises and leased departments are the most typical of the contractual retailers for the distribution of apparel.

Franchises

In a **franchise** agreement, the parent company gives the franchisee the exclusive right to distribute a well-recognized brand name in a specific market area as well as assistance with organization, visual merchandising, training, and management in return for a franchise payment. The franchisee agrees to adhere to standards regarding in-store design, visual presentation, pricing, and promotions specified by the parent company. Examples of franchises include Ralph Lauren's Polo shops and Yves Saint Laurent's Rive Gauche boutiques.

Leased Departments

Some retailers will lease space within a larger retail store to a company that operates a specialty department. The larger retail store provides space, utilities, and basic in-store services. The specialty department operator provides the stock and expertise to run the department and adds to the service or product mix of the larger store. Typical **leased**

departments are beauty salons and spas, and fine jewelry, fur, and shoe shops. In each of these cases specific expertise and investment in stock are needed. With this arrangement, the primary advantage for the larger retailer is that it can offer its customers products and services that it might not be able to offer otherwise. The primary advantage for the specialty department is its association with the larger retailer.

WAREHOUSE RETAILERS

Warehouse retailers reduce operating expenses and offer goods at discount prices by combining their showroom, warehouse, and retail operations. This category includes stores such as catalog showrooms (e.g., Service Merchandise, Best Products), home centers (e.g., Home Depot, Builder's Square), hypermarkets (e.g., Wal-Mart's Hypermarket USA), and warehouse clubs (e.g., Costco, Price Club, and Sam's Club). Although apparel products are not the primary merchandise sold through warehouse retailers, one can find basic items such as underwear and casual sports clothes or manufacturer's discontinued lines at some warehouse stores. Generally, apparel is sold through self-service strategies, and there are no fitting rooms. Merchandise is obtained through an extended marketing channel in these stores.

NONSTORE RETAILERS

A **nonstore retailer** distributes products to consumers through means other than traditional bricks-and-mortar retail stores. For apparel and accessories, the three most prevalent forms of nonstore retailing are mail order/catalog, electronic/Internet, and television selling. Other forms of nonstore retailing include at-home selling and vending machines. In the past 20 years nonstore retailing, particularly mail order/catalog, electronic/Internet, and television selling, has grown tremendously. This trend is due to a number of social, economic, and lifestyle changes, including the following:

- The increased demand by consumers for convenience, product quality, and selection.
- A highly fragmented market that demands products to fulfill special needs and interests.
- The continued growth in the number of women in the workforce and dual-income families, which creates increased time pressures for shopping among household members.

■ The expanding use and promotion of credit cards, such as those offered by Visa, Mastercard, American Express, and Discover and store cards (e.g., Spiegel).

■ Increased speed of delivery by package carriers (e.g., by Federal Express, UPS, Priority Mail).

■ Technological advance in e-commerce including improved security for sending credit card numbers electronically.

In addition to selling merchandise, nonstore retailing, particularly mail order/catalog, electronic/Internet, and television retailing venues, are used by companies for a number of other purposes such as the following:

■ Educating customers about the company and its product lines.

■ Providing customers with fashion direction and style advice.

■ Obtaining information from customers regarding product preferences.

■ Building more traffic in their retail stores.

■ Providing customers with a more convenient and/or more recreational form of shopping.

■ Building relationships with customers through personalized customer service.

Retailers selling apparel via mail order/catalog, electronic/Internet, and television retailing methods are faced with a unique set of challenges. Because the customer cannot physically evaluate the product, feel the fabric, or try on the merchandise, customer service and information about sizing, fabric, styling details, and color is important. J. Crew now uses color matching software to assist customers visiting their www.jcrew.com Web site in viewing garments in their actual colors. Lands' End will send customers fabric swatches. In addition, the Pantone color specification sysem has been adapted for electronic color communication (Karas, 2001). Customers also have questions and concerns about shipping costs, timeliness of shipping, and returns. Because customers use nonstore retailing for its convenience, the ease in selecting styles, ordering, and returning merchandise is important.

Mail Order/Catalog Retailers

Mail order/catalog retailers sell to the consumer through catalogs, brochures, or advertisements, and deliver merchandise by mail or other carrier. Apparel is one of the top-selling items bought through catalogs with nearly one in five Americans buying apparel through catalogs. Customers can order by mail, phone, Internet, or fax.

All types of retailers may operate mail order/catalog businesses. Some companies focus almost entirely on the use of catalogs (e.g., L.L.Bean, Lands' End, Spiegel; see Figure 12.10). In 1975, Lands' End began its catalog. By 1985 it was distributing monthly catalogs, and in 1990, it introduced three new catalogs targeted to the home, children's wear, and men's wear markets. Spiegel also distributes specialty catalogs for specific market segments. Some companies offer merchandise through their catalogs that is not available in their stores (e.g., J. Crew, Victoria's Secret, Nordstrom). Other companies, such as Talbot's, offer the same merchandise assortment in their catalogs as in their stores. In addition to

Figure 12.10: Mail order retailers, such as Lands' End, provide a number of services to facilitate consumer purchasing of merchandise from a catalog.

paper catalogs, some companies have distributed electronic catalogs on CD-ROM disks and orders are made on forms, generated by the program, which can be phoned, mailed, or faxed to the company.

Electronic/Internet Retailers

Electronic/Internet retailers use **e-commerce**, the selling of goods over the Internet, to reach customers. Since the mid-1990s, e-commerce has grown consistently each year. With more consumers having access to the Internet and with security issues related to sending credit card numbers electronically decreasing, many apparel retailers and manufacturers have ventured into e-commerce, offering goods only over the Internet or using the Internet as an addition to their stores and/or catalog retailing business. Although online apparel sales are a small percentage of overall apparel retail sales, the number of "dot-com" Web sites devoted to apparel and accessories continues to grow. One of the first Internet sites where apparel could be purchased online was Fashionmall.com (started in 1994), which provided a central location for a number of retailers, manufacturers, and magazines to offer fashion goods and services directly to customers (see Figure 12.11). Companies that had been successful selling apparel through catalogs found they could make the transition to the Web fairly easily. In 1995, Lands' End offered fewer than 100 products online as an experiment. It is now one of the largest Internet apparel sites. Other catalog retailers that have been successful online include Spiegel, Eddie Bauer and L.L.Bean.

By the late 1990s, a number of department stores and specialty stores had added e-commerce to their businesses. Online customers gravitated to Internet sites of well-known and trusted retailers such as Gap, Wal-Mart, Target, Nordstrom, Sears and JCPenney. Store retailers have found that access to new customers can be enhanced with online services. For example, Macys.com has conducted business in

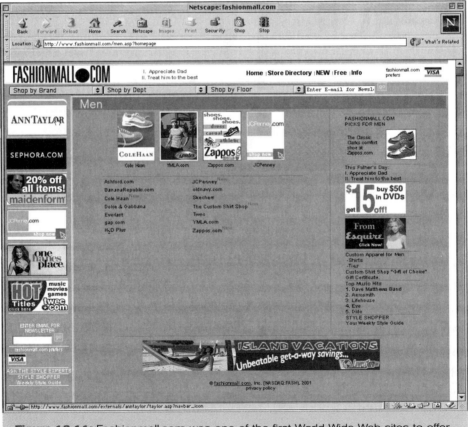

Figure 12.11: Fashionmall.com was one of the first World Wide Web sites to offer apparel to consumers over the Internet.

states where Macy's has no stores. And whereas 90 percent of Victoria's Secret's store customers are women, approximately 35 percent of their online customers are men. The success of traditional store and catalog retailers in their online operations will be based to some extent on their ability to integrate their various retail methods. For example, consumers will expect to return merchandise they purchased online to the same retailer's store (Reda, 1999).

Apparel and accessory companies also have Web sites. These sites may or may not include direct sales of merchandise to the ultimate consumer. Liz Claiborne's Web site, www.lizclaiborne.com, offers customers store information, advice, and links to Liz Claiborne lines. The North Face uses its thenorthface.com site as a vehicle to promote products, provide information about The North Face athletes and expeditions, and highlight The North Face stores and other dealers. NIKE uses its nike.com site as a way of educating the consumer about NIKE products and of soliciting information from their customers regarding product characteristics and performance in addition to selling merchandise directly to the consumer. See Table 12.7 for a listing of the top apparel Internet retailers.

TABLE 12.7

Top Apparel Internet Retailers

Retailer	URL	Online Sales to U.S. Consumers
Lands End	landsend..com	$150–175 M
The Spiegel Group	spiegel.com eddiebauer.com newport-news.com	150–175 M
JCPenney	jcpenney.com	150–175 M
Gap	gap.com oldnavy.com bananarepublic.com	125–150 M
L.L.Bean	llbean.com	125–150 M
The Limited	victoriassecret.com lanebryant.com	70–90 M
J. Crew	jcrew.com	70–90 M
Sears	sears.com	70–90 M
Wal-Mart	wal-mart.com	60–80 M
Coldwater Creek	coldwatercreek.com	40–50 M
Foot Locker Inc.	footlocker.com eastbay.com	20–30 M

Source: Stores. (September, 2000). Top 100 Internet Retailers.

Television Retailers

Some retailers use television shopping channels to sell apparel. With these formats, merchandise is presented on the television, and customers order it over the telephone (usually using a toll-free number) or on the Web. Payment is by credit card, C.O.D., or check. Merchandise is delivered through the mail or by another carrier. Home shopping has become big business. QVC (Figure 12.12), Home Shopping Network (HSN), and Shop at Home are the largest of these television shopping channels. TV shopping has expanded its merchandise assortment to include designer lines and a variety of product categories. Some retailers, such as Saks Fifth Avenue and Bergdorf Goodman, have also experimented with television shopping, although few have developed ongoing ventures in this retailing venue.

At-Home Retailers

At-home retailers use the marketing strategy of making personal contacts and sales in consumers' homes. At-home retailing includes door-to-door sales or party plan selling methods. The party plan method involves a salesperson giving a presentation of merchandise at the home of a host or hostess who has invited potential cus-

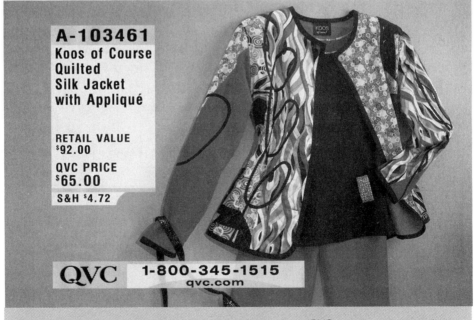

Figure 12.12: Television shopping channels, such as QVC, continue to grow in importance for apparel retailing.

tomers to a "party." The at-home retailer Doncaster also makes provision for customization of products for the customer. He or she can select style, fabric, and size, and the product is made according to his or her specifications. Accessories and lingerie are typical apparel products sold using this retail method.

Vending Machines

Vending machines are coin-operated machines used to meet the needs of consumers when other retailing formats are unavailable or when space is limited for selling merchandise. Although vending machines are seldom used for the distribution of apparel products, vending machines have been used to sell hosiery, T-shirts, and even men's dress shirts. One would most likely find such vending machines in locations such as airports or train stations.

The Future of Nonstore Retailing

Will nonstore retailing eventually put bricks-and-mortar stores out of business? Most analysts believe that many consumers still want to touch and try on garments before purchasing them. However, the growth in nonstore retailing has forced retailers to think about their retail environments in terms of better meeting customer needs. The retail store of the future will most likely merge technologies so that consumers reap the benefits of each of the retail formats. For example, malls of the future would provide Internet capability to all of their stores so that consumers could go to a kiosk at the mall entrance and search stores for the merchandise they are looking for. Retailers would stock a limited number of style samples for consumers to touch and try on, with the purchase taking place through an in-store Web-based kiosk or at the consumer's home (Welling, 2000).

Trade Associations and Trade Publications

As with other areas of textile and apparel industries, a number of trade associations and trade publications serve those involved in the distribution of apparel. Table 12.8 lists some of the primary retail trade associations. The National Retail Federation (NRF) is the largest trade association for retailers in the United States. It represents 27 national retail associations, all 50 state associations, and stores from 50 different nations. The NRF Annual Convention and Expo is held in New York each January. In coordination with the NRF, over 250 retailers (including most major retail corporations) have endorsed "The Statement of Principles on Supplier Legal Compliance," which emphasizes the importance of fair working conditions, ethical standards, and

---

TABLE 12.8

Selected Retail Trade Associations

American Management Association
1601 Broadway
New York, NY 10019
(212) 903-8389

Footwear Industries of America
1420 K Street NW
Washington, DC 20005
(202) 789-1420

National Mass Retail Association
1901 Pennsylvania Avenue NW
10th Floor
Washington, DC 20006
(202) 861-0774

National Retail Federation
325 7th St. NW, Suite 1000
Washington, DC 20006
(202) 783-7971
www.nrf.com

National Shoe Retailers Association
9861 Broken Land Parkway
#255
Columbia, MD 21046
(410) 381-8282
www.apparel.net/nsra/

Shoe Retailers League
275 Madison Avenue
New York, NY 10016
(212) 889-7920

---

legal compliance of retailers' suppliers (see Table 12.9). The NRF publishes *Stores* magazine, a monthly trade publication that addresses the interests of those in the retailing industry. A number of other trade publications cater to those involved with distribution and retailing. Table 12.10 lists some of these publications.

TABLE 12.9

National Retail Federation
Statement of Principles on Supplier Legal Compliance

1. We are committed to legal compliance and ethical business practices in all our operations.
2. We choose suppliers who we believe share that commitment.
3. In our purchase contracts, we require our suppliers to comply with all applicable laws and regulations.
4. If it is found that a factory used by a supplier for the production of our merchandise has committed legal violations, we will take appropriate action, which may range from working with the supplier to ensure that steps are taken to address the violations and prevent their reoccurrence to canceling the affected purchase contracts, terminating our relationship with the supplier, commencing legal actions against the supplier or other actions as warranted.
5. We support law enforcement and cooperate with law enforcement authorities in the proper execution of their responsibilities.
6. We support educational programs and collaborative efforts by our suppliers to enhance legal compliance on the part of their industries in the United States and abroad.

Source: National Retail Federation

TABLE 12.10

Selected Trade Publications Related to Business, Distribution, and Retailing

Advertising Age: The International Newspaper of Marketing (www.adage.com): Published by Crain Communications, this trade publication focuses on marketing and advertising news and information.

Business Week (www.businesweek.com): Published by McGraw-Hill, this weekly magazine focuses on U.S. businesses in general, covering economics, political and economic issues, and new technology. Company profiles and analyses are also included.

Chain Store Age (www.chainstoreage.com): A Lebhar-Friedman publication, this monthly news magazine focuses on information of interest to corporate executives in all major segments of retailing: home centers, supermarkets, drug chains, specialty stores, discount, convenience and department stores. Information on retailing trends and the forces behind them, with regular sections covering retail technology, merchandising, shopping center development, marketing, physical support systems, finance, legislative affairs, security, store design and visual display, strategic planning and human resources, and distribution and transportation.

Discount Store News: Retailing Today (www.dsnretailingtoday.com): Published by Lebhar-Friedman, this trade newspaper focuses on timely news related to full-line discount department stores, catalog showrooms, specialty chains, off-price retailers, membership clubs, and supercenters. Articles cover new products, licensing, visual merchandising, and industry trends.

Marketing News (www.ama.org/pubs.mn/): A publication of the American Marketing Association, this newspaper covers information and news of interest to marketing professionals including marketing strategies, retailing, market research, globalization, and technology.

Retail Merchandiser (www.discountmerchandiser.com): Published monthly by Bill Communications, this publication addresses all aspects of the mass retailing industry including management and technical issues, manufacturing, retailing, advertising, and other industry information through profiles of companies and executives.

Stores (www.stores.org): A publication of the National Retail Federation, this monthly trade magazine includes information of interest to retailers in general. Each issue reports on computer software and hardware, point-of-sale systems, credit-and-collection services, electronic commerce solutions, logistics, transportation, auditing, loss prevention, human resources, and other topics.

Supermarket Business (www.supermarketbusiness.com): Published by Bill Communications, this publication focuses on information of interest to supermarket managers such as analysis of industry trends and directions, trade relations, merchandising, operations, technology, and store development.

Supermarket News (www.supermarketnews.com): Weekly trade publication for the food distribution industry. Executives use it as their information source for industry news, trends, and product features. Published by Fairchild.

Summary

Apparel companies have a number of options with regard to the distribution of their merchandise to the ultimate consumer. Companies must decide how widely their merchandise will be distributed; some will choose mass distribution, whereas others will decide on a selective or exclusive distribution strategy. Apparel companies will distribute their goods either directly to their retail accounts or through distribution centers. Retailers with many stores may also use distribution centers as a central location for merchandise, from which it is then shipped to the various stores.

Quick Response and supply chain management strategies are important in the distribution process, and alliances between apparel companies and retailers contribute greatly to the success of these strategies. The foundations for these strategies are to use Universal Product Code bar coding on product labels and shipping cartons; to have vendors (manufacturers) assuming responsibility for affixing labels and price information on products; and to use electronic data interchange for the electronic transmission of invoices, advance shipping notices, and other information. Replenishment of goods at the retail level is built on the foundation of these operations. In some cases, programs have been established whereby the vendor (manufacturer) manages retail inventory and automatically replenishes the retailer's stock when needed. Data-mining technology makes possible even more sophisticated systems for making sure the retailer has the right stock at the right time.

The retailing level of the marketing involves the selling of merchandise to the final consumer. Retailers are often classified according to merchandising and operating strategies into the following categories, which are not mutually exclusive: department stores, specialty stores, chain stores, discount retailers, off-price retailers, supermarkets, convenience stores, contractual retailers, warehouse retailers, and nonstore retailing. Apparel manufacturers use a variety of retailers in the final distribution of their products to the ultimate consumer, although they use some (e.g., department stores, specialty stores, discount stores) more than others. Nonstore retailing including mail order/catalog and electronic/Internet retailing has experienced greater growth than traditional forms of retailing in recent years.

Careers in retailing are as varied as the stores themselves. Some of the career possibilities include store management, merchandise buying, private label product development, catalog and nonstore retailing, and promotion and advertising, just to name a few.

Retail Store Manager
WOMEN'S SPECIALTY STORE CHAIN

Position Description
Lead a management team of 3–5 assistant managers and oversee the performance of 25,000 to 30,000 square feet of store space. Identify key opportunities to increase sales, manage payroll and expenses, as well as supervise and develop assistant managers.

Typical Tasks and Responsibilities
- Ensure customer service policies and procedures are adhered to
- Oversee merchandise presentation activities on an ongoing basis
- Motivate people to reach the store's goals
- Manage payroll and operations
- Oversee the development of assistant managers

Merchandising Manager/Head Buyer
INTERNATIONAL SPECIALTY STORE

Position Description
Ensure merchandise mix, availability, distribution to all stores, inventory management, pricing, market development and trends for the future and purchase target allocation for all stores.

Typical Tasks and Responsibilities
- Select merchandise mix to be carried throughout the stores
- Work with local suppliers and negotiate terms and conditions for each line of merchandise
- Control inventory levels of merchandise (maximum three months inventory levels)
- Keep informed about the latest trends and developments (competitors, etc.)
- Set up target purchase budget on a yearly basis

CAREER PROFILES

A Look to the Future

Change has become the norm in the textile, apparel, and retailing industries. Faced with increased global competition, textile, apparel, and retailing companies have made rapid changes in order to survive. The belief has been that the strongest advantage the U.S. industries can offer in this new, global marketplace is speed. If we could produce the goods faster, we could have them at market sooner. If we could produce goods closer to the delivery date, we could predict more accurately what would sell, and we would pay less interest on borrowed money needed for inventory and business operations. If we could automatically replenish goods sold by the retailer, then consumers would be more likely to find the goods they want when they want them.

How could we increase speed without decreasing product quality? The answer was technology. It was to become our most valuable competitive edge. Though the initial cost of computer technology was high, management pushed forward. Computers invaded every aspect of the industry. It was clear that the investment paid for itself, both in speed and in accuracy. In time, integrated computer systems arrived. Now, every phase of the textile-apparel-retail complex can be linked with data interchange and data management. Ordering can be transacted online. Both Intranet and Internet computer networks form the basis for communication of images and data. A computer screen has replaced most of the paper trail. Such dramatic changes in ways of doing business have been dependent on increased alliances among companies within the textile-apparel-retailing marketing channel.

Some said that computer technology was only for the big companies. While many large companies were the first to use computer technology, small companies began to embrace technology as well. Costs have decreased and technology has improved to the point where very small apparel companies and retailers cannot afford not to use computers.

At the same time as the industry increased its emphasis on technology, the traditional assembly line approach to production was reexamined. A trend developed that centered on a team approach rather than workers functioning as individual units. Teams became responsible for work flow and were given group responsibility for the quality of the product.

Although segments of the manufacturing process continued to make advances in technology, many companies chose to manufacture offshore. For a while, labor would be cheap in certain countries. Then, as these developing countries advanced economically, labor costs would increase. New countries were selected for less-expensive labor. Many of the offshore contractors realized that they also needed computer technology for the same reasons the U.S. companies needed it a decade earlier. Contractors in the more developed countries began to utilize computers, not only for increased speed and accuracy in their facilities, but also to integrate their operations with apparel companies in the United States. Such global communication is now the norm.

A number of issues will shape the future of the U.S. textile, apparel, and retailing industries: changes in international trade laws, global competitiveness, changes in the way consumers buy goods, and changes in the way companies conduct their business. Emanuel Weintraub, president and CEO of Emanuel Weintraub Associates, and longtime apparel industry consultant, offers "ten tips for excellence in the new era":

1. Stay in constant touch with your target consumers—know their lifestyles, their wants, their needs, the limitations of their pocketbooks. Your knowledge of the marketplace is a major competitive advantage.

2. Make a desirable product. While execution of service to the customer is increasingly critical, there's no getting around the time-tested truth: "The price of admission is a merchantable product."

3. Think *strategically*. The industry's top manufacturers and retailers have been doing it for years, and a solid, consistent marketing strategy is a must for doing business with them. Latch on to the large retailers, as they will continue to call the shots and reel in the big sales via both traditional and non-traditional selling methods in the future.

4. Build trust with your clients by demonstrating fiscal stability. Strive to establish excellent bonding relationships to strengthen your ability to finance large orders, purchase piece goods and hold inventory as needed.

5. Be the low-cost value supplier in whatever you produce, whichever market you supply. "Consumers expect value for every dollar they spend, whether it's a $300 blouse or a $10 blouse."

6. Pursue excellence in product execution, from sourcing to quality assurance to logistics, warehousing and delivery. Focus on making it easy to do business with your firm. "There's no room for anything less."

7. Focus on your core competencies. For instance, if you are a private label producer, stay focused clearly on price, quality and service. If you elect to enter a new distribution channel or product category, recognize that you will need top talent and deep pockets to fuel the venture until it becomes a financial success.

8. Speed your products to market. The first garments to the selling floor have the best chance of selling at full margin price, leaving your firm at less risk for margin dilution by retailers. Continually review all internal processes that can inhibit speed.

9. Stake your claim with suppliers that are prepared to assume critical responsibilities essential to effective supply chain management. As more processes are passed from retailer to manufacturer to contractor, remember: "You may be logistically and technologically in the new millennium, but your vendors may be living in the '60s or '70s."

10. Hire the best talent your money can buy, bearing in mind that "big league" hitters—whether in information systems, marketing or other fields—often will require not only competitively high salaries but also sizeable budgets to execute their action plans. "Size of scale matters." (DesMarteau, 2000, pp. 60–62).

Thus, in the twenty-first century, the strength of the domestic textile, apparel, and retailing industries depends on our ability to change and respond to the wants and needs of consumers.

Key Terms

boutique

chain store

contractual retailer

convenience store

data-mining technology

department store

discount store

distribution center (DC)

e-commerce

electronic data interchange (EDI)

electronic/Internet retailer

eMarkets

exclusive distribution

franchise

in-store shops

intensive distribution

leased department

mail-order/catalog retailer

mass distribution

nonstore retailer

off-price retailer

relationship merchandising

retailer

retailing

selective distribution

specialty store

supermarket

superstore

Universal Product Code (UPC)

vendor-managed inventory

vendor marking

warehouse retailer

Discussion Questions

1. Describe the roles of distribution centers for apparel manufacturers and retailers. How and why have the roles changed?

2. Bring to class several apparel merchandise hangtags or packages that have UPC bar codes. What information does the bar code provide to the manufacturer? To the retailer? To the consumer? What other information is on the ticket or package that is helpful to the consumer?

3. Name and describe your three favorite stores. What type of retail store is each? What are the characteristics of the types of retail stores you named?

4. Explore three Web sites that sell apparel online. What are the common features of the sites? What strategies do these retailers use to inform customers about product characteristics?

References

Abend, Jules. (1998, September). In-store shops: Up the ante for apparel brands. *Bobbin*, pp. 32–40.

Aron, Laurie Joan. (1998, January). Duck Head: The process is the product. *Apparel Industry Magazine*, pp. 16–19.

Bailey, Thomas. (1993, August). *The Spread of Quick Response and Human Resource Innovation in the Apparel Industry*. New York: Institute on Education and the Economy, Teachers College, Columbia University.

Barnes, Mike. (1996, January). Techology's Role in the '90's. *Apparel Industry Magazine*, p. 78.

Bert, Jim. (1989, March). The EDI link. Connections. Supplement to *Apparel Industry Magazine*, pp. 4–5.

DesMarteau, Kathleen. (2000, January). 10 tips for excellence in the new era. *Bobbin*, pp. 60–62.

DeWitt, John W. (1993, June). EDI's new role: Electronic commerce. *Apparel Industry Magazine*, pp. 36–41.

Drori, Neil. (1992, February). Taking the bull out of bar codes. *Bobbin*, pp. 14–18.

eMarkets. (2001, January). *Stores*, pp. 4–8.

Gilbert, Charles, and Carlson, Dave. (1995, October). Making the modular pay in the DC. *Bobbin*, pp. 84–88.

Hasty, Susan E. (ed). (1994, March). *The Quick Response Handbook*. Supplement to *Apparel Industry Magazine*.

Hill, Suzette. (1998, May). Crystal ball gazing becomes a science. *Apparel Industry Magazine*, pp. 18–23.

Hill, Suzette. (1999, May). Sell: Demand chain tools that watch the store. *Apparel Industry Magazine*, pp. SCM-30–SCM-32.

Hill, Suzette. (1999, May). Store: A warehouse is not just a storehouse anymore. *Apparel Industry Magazine*, pp. SCM-23–SCM-26.

Karas, Jennifer. (2001, April). NRF/Pantone Partnership offers electronic color-coding system for retailers, consumers. *Stores*, pp. 124–125.

Lewison, Dale M. (1994). *Retailing*. (5th ed.). New York: Macmillan.

Mastercard International. (1996, February). Internet shopping: New competitor or new frontier? Supplement to *Stores*, MC1–MC24.

Moore, Lila. (1994, September). DCs face uncertain future. *Apparel Industry Magazine*, pp. 58–62.

Nannery, Matt. (1995, March 15). Fred Meyer bets the warehouse on QR. *Women's Wear Daily*, p. 25.

Olive, Robert. (1988, February). L.L.Bean: Rapid receiving. *Apparel Industry Magazine*, pp. 56–60.

Reda, Susan. (1999, September). Top 100 Internet retailers. Special supplement to *Stores*, pp. V–V18.

Robins, Gary. (1993, March). Quick response. *Stores*, pp. 21–22.

Robins, Gary. (1994, March). Less work, more speed. *Stores*, pp. 24–26.

Schneiderman, I. P. (1995, October 5). Lost in a maze. *Women's Wear Daily*, pp. 1, 8–10.

Welling, Holly. (2000, February). Unveiling AIM's store of the future, part I. *Apparel Industry Magazine*, pp. 24–31.

Winger, Rocio Maria. (1998, December). The Nygård vanguard: The way to no chargebacks. *Apparel Industry Magazine*, pp. AS-14–AS-18.

Organization and Operation of the Accessories and Home Fashions Industries

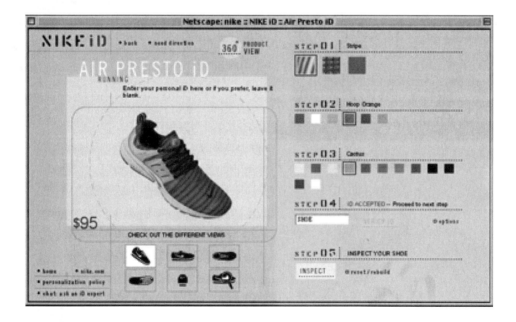

PART 4

CHAPTER 13

Accessories

IN THIS CHAPTER YOU WILL LEARN:

■ the relationship between fashion apparel and accessories.

■ the similarities and differences between the design and manufacturing of accessories and that of fashion apparel products.

■ the similarities and differences among the past, current, and future marketing and distribution strategies for fashion accessories.

Relationship of Accessories to the Apparel Industry

What would a men's suit be without the right necktie? What would a new fashion look be without the right shoe style, leg covering, or jewelry? The accessories industries comprise a vital component of the total fashion industry and is integral to the success of apparel industry. Primary accessory categories include footwear; hosiery and leg wear; hats and head wear; scarfs and neckwear; belts, handbags, and small leather goods; gloves; and jewelry. Other accessories include sunglasses, handkerchiefs, hair accessories, and umbrellas. Each season, changes occur in accessories that relate directly to the changes occurring in fashion apparel. For example, the styling, colors, textures, and scale of jewelry will correspond to the type of apparel with which it will be worn (see Figure 13.1). Fashion trends in apparel and accessories are so closely linked that one can purchase a sweater, belt, and shoes in the same "hot new fashion color" at the same time in the market. It is clear that these industries must work together.

Yet fashion apparel products and accessories are distinctly different in some respects. Some accessories can be manufactured very quickly when a new trend in apparel develops. Accessories manufacturers may respond immediately to apparel trends. In some cases, the accessories themselves are the fashion statement that can update classic apparel styles. According to the national sales manager for a hosiery company, "In developing a product mix, the hosiery industry really has to follow other market segments. We can't set the trends, but we can accessorize them" (Rabon, 1995b, p. 66).

Other accessories take much longer to produce. The footwear industry needs time to design and produce the product, including time to procure materials. The design phase for shoes may begin before the design phase for an apparel product, especially if specialty leather materials are required. Therefore, forecasters in the shoe industry must be keenly aware of market and fashion trends in order to predict accurately appropriate shoe fashions that complement and coordinate with fashion apparel. Because of the labor intensive nature of manufacturing dress gloves, longer lead times are needed in their production.

Figure 13.1: Fashion trends in apparel and accessories are closely linked.

Accessories Categories

Accessories manufacturers are grouped into categories, including the following:

- Footwear
- Hosiery and leg wear
- Hats and head wear
- Scarfs and neckwear
- Belts, handbags, and small leather goods
- Gloves
- Jewelry

Many accessory companies specialize in manufacturing only one type of product; that is, some companies manufacture only shoes; some companies produce only neckwear. Some companies prefer to diversify into more than one accessory category (see Figure 13.2). Dooney & Bourke and Coach, both traditional handbag and small leather goods manufacturers, have diversified into footwear. Other companies manufacture both accessories and apparel.

The term **cross-merchandising** refers to the strategy by both apparel companies and retailers to combine apparel and accessories in their product offerings. Some apparel manufacturers create their own accessories to coordinate with their apparel lines (e.g., Timberland, Eddie Bauer). NIKE produces a line of backpacks and sports equipment bags in conjunction with its footwear and apparel lines. Other companies form agreements to produce coordinating apparel and accessories. In skiwear, for example, Roffe Skiwear produces the outerwear apparel products and Demetre produces the coordinating knit sweaters, head wear, and hand wear. Thus, the responsibility for manufacturing each type of

Figure 13.2: Some companies, such as Kenneth Cole, produce goods in more than one accessory category.

product rests in the hands of the company with the required expertise that makes it best qualified to produce it. Retailers employ cross-merchandising through displays that create a total fashion image and show consumers how accessories can be worn.

Licensing is a very important cross-merchandising strategy for coordinating apparel and accessory looks. In the typical licensing agreements, accessory manufacturers pay a royalty to the licensor company for the use of the brand, logo, or trademark on the merchandise. As discussed in Chapter 2, licensing agreements can be beneficial to both the accessory manufacturer and the designer. For the accessory manufacturer, the designer name provides immediate brand recognition among consumers. For the designer, he or she can expand into a variety of product lines with his or her name and become a total lifestyle brand by taking advantage of the manufacturer's product and market expertise ("The spell is in the name," 1999). Some accessories companies have licensed their names for apparel lines (e.g., Hush Puppies, Kenneth Cole). Many name designers use licensing agreements with accessory manufacturers to produce the specific styles of accessory that completes the total fashion looks they desire. Designers such as Tommy Hilfiger, Ralph Lauren, Liz Claiborne, Donna Karan, and Calvin Klein have their names linked to belts, hosiery, shoes, and eyewear. Kenneth Cole has successfully licensed a broad range of merchandise including all of the company's nonfootwear products except handbags. Depending on the licensing agreement, designers vary in their involvement and approval requirements with the licensee. Some designers, such as Kenneth Cole, are involved with design and approval. Others turn over design decisions to the licensee.

Athletic footwear companies often have unique licensing agreements with professional and collegiate sports leagues (e.g., Major League Baseball) or individual teams. In these agreements, footwear companies pay the leagues or teams for the right to sell merchandise with the league or team logo. In addition, they may also purchase the right to outfit the team with athletic footwear and/or uniforms bearing the company's logo.

Consumers' purchases of accessories are often impulse buying decisions; that is, the purchases are not planned. Therefore, to facilitate these impulse purchases, accessories are often sold on the main floor of department stores, included in displays throughout stores, and positioned near the checkout locations in stores. In general, consumers favor discount stores (e.g., Wal-Mart, Kmart, Target) for their accessories purchases with nonstore (e.g., catalog, television, online) purchasing of accessories growing fast. (Accessories Council, 2000)

As with other segments of the fashion industry, the accessories industry relies on trade associations for research, education efforts, marketing, public relations, and advertising. These trade associations may focus on several categories of accessories (e.g., Accessories Council) or on a single category of accessories (e.g., Neckwear Association of America). For example, the mission statement of the Accessories Council, founded in 1995, is:

> To stimulate consumer awareness and purchase levels of fashion accessory products and serve as the advocate voice of the accessories business community—including suppliers and retailers. (Accessories Council, 1999)

Table 13.1 lists selected trade associations for accessories (see Chapter 4 for additional information). Trade publications are also essential to the dissemination of

TABLE 13.1

Selected Trade Associations for Accessories

Accessories Council
American Leather Accessory Designers (ALAD)
Fashion Footwear Association of New York (FFANY)
Fashion Jewelry Association of America
Headwear Institute of America
Jewelers of America
National Association of Fashion and Accessory Designers
National Association of Milliners, Dressmakers, and Tailors
National Fashion Accessories Association
National Glove Manufacturers Association
National Shoe Retailers Association
Neckwear Association of America
North American Hosiery Council
Sporting Goods Manufacturers Association (SPMS), and a
    sub-category, Athletic Footwear Association (AFA)
Sunglass Association of America
The Hosiery Association
Western Shoe Association (WSA)

industry news and advertising to individuals in the accessories industry. Table 13.2 lists selected trade publications related to accessories.

Although there are differences in production processes within the accessories industry, most lines are produced following procedures similar to the steps in the research, design, production, and distribution of apparel. These steps include:

- Research, including color, material, trend, and market research.
- Design, including sketching, and CAD.
- Pattern making (or creating molds in the jewelry industry).
- Developing prototypes.

TABLE 13.2

Selected Trade Publications for Accessories

DNR (published by Fairchild Publications), including information
    about textiles and vertically integrated companies.
Footwear News (published by Fairchild Publications)
Footwear Plus
Hosiery News (published monthly by The Hosiery Association)
Women's Wear Daily (published by Fairchild Publications), including
    special accessories supplements, Monday issues feature
    accessories, inner wear, and leg wear industry news.

■ Costing.

■ Marketing, including presenting a minimum of two lines per year during market weeks and at trade shows (see Table 13.3).

■ Production.

■ Distribution and retailing.

We will discuss some of the important aspects of the design, production, and marketing of accessories for each of the major categories in the following sections.

Footwear

Footwear categories include the following:

■ Athletic footwear.

■ Dress shoes and boots.

■ Casual shoes.

■ Sandals.

■ Work shoes and boots.

■ Western/casual boots.

■ Hiking, hunting, and fishing boots.

During the past few decades, the footwear industry has changed in a number of ways. First, as with apparel, footwear sold by U.S. manufacturers has shifted from domestic to global production. This is primarily because of the availability of raw materials and of rising labor costs in the United States; shoe production can be very labor intensive. Second, the production of leather footwear has been augmented by the production of footwear using a variety of manufactured materials. The types of

---

TABLE 13.3

Selected Trade Shows for Accessories

Accessorie Circuit, held in New York three times a year.
Fashion Accessory Exposition, held in New York twice a year.
Fashion Footwear Association of New York (FFANY) trade shows, held in New York four times a year.
International Hosiery Exposition (IHE).
International Shoe Fair (GDS) held in Dusseldorf, Germany, twice a year.
Shoe Fair, held in Bologna, Italy.
United Jewelry Show, held in Providence, RI, four times a year.
Western Shoe Association trade shows, held in Las Vegas twice a year.

shoes most frequently purchased have shifted as well. Athletic footwear has gained a tremendous market share of the footwear industry, with more athletic shoes sold than any of the other footwear categories (see Figure 13.3). In recent years the "brown shoe" type of footwear (i.e., rugged-looking footwear exemplified by Timberland and Wolverine) has seen market growth.

FOOTWEAR PRODUCERS

The footwear industry in the United States is sometimes referred to as an *oligopoly* (see Chapter 2) in that several large shoe manufacturers produce the vast majority of shoes. The largest shoe manufacturers in the United States are no longer fashion shoe companies. NIKE and Reebok, two companies that produce primarily athletic shoes, are the top U.S. producers of footwear. Currently NIKE controls approximately one-third of the U.S. athletic shoe market. Both NIKE and Reebok have diversified their footwear lines, with NIKE acquiring Cole-Haan and Reebok acquiring

Figure 13.3: Almost forty percent of all footwear purchased in the United States is athletic shoes.

Rockport. Several large companies also dominate the fashion footwear business. Among them are the United States Shoe Corporation and Brown Shoe Co.

From an international perspective, NIKE and Adidas are two of the world's largest footwear companies. Italy, however, has a reputation for leading fashion trends in footwear. In addition to its design reputation, Italy has for centuries produced fine leathers for apparel as well as for footwear. The handcrafting of Italian leather products has maintained a worldwide reputation for centuries as well. Salvatore Ferragamo shoes and handbags, Bruno Magli shoes, and Gucci shoes and handbags epitomize quality Italian leather materials and workmanship.

Some of the high-end footwear producers continue to utilize handstitching and other handwork. Hermès (France), Ferragamo (Italy), and Dooney & Bourke (United States) are examples of companies that feature handwork. There still exists a market for handmade shoes and boots, perhaps most evident on Savile Row in London, where custom shoemakers such as Lobb are neighbors to custom shirtmakers and tailors.

RESEARCH, DESIGN, AND PRODUCTION

The first steps in creating a footwear line and an apparel line are similar. Footwear companies begin their lines by conducting market research, including consumer research, product research, and market analysis. They examine the demographic and consumer buying trends of their target customer, explore innovations in footwear styles and technology, and analyze trends in the footwear market in general. They develop a target customer profile describing the typical customer for their various lines of footwear.

Shoe designers research fashion trends in much the same way as do apparel designers. Many shoe designers throughout the world attend the Italian leather shows as well as various shoe trade shows to view the latest developments in leather and shoe design. Shoe designers work in conjunction with the company's merchandisers and production team to develop the shoe line each season. Designers work with these shoe design components each season: the materials, trims, and styling features, and heel height and shape. It is remarkable that shoe designers create such a variety of innovative styles each season given the small surface area of footwear. The fabrication of prototype shoe styles and patterns is performed using steps similar to those discussed for apparel products.

Shoes are made by forming the raw materials around a **last**. The last is a wood, plastic, or metal mold, shaped like a foot. In the United States, lasts are sized in widths as well as lengths. Historically, the width of the last for European sizes has been different from that for American sizes. Some American footwear manufacturers produce shoes in Italy in order to take advantage of the Italian raw materials and craftsmanship. The shoes made in Italy for American manufacturers are produced using American lasts in order to fit the target customer's foot.

CAD technology has become an important part of the footwear industry. New developments in software allow the shoe design to be viewed three dimensionally on the screen. Some merchandisers for shoe companies consider computer images of the styles to be sufficient when selecting the shoes for the line. Thus, prototypes would be made only for those styles selected for production.

The sizes of pattern pieces for shoes are small compared to the sizes of most apparel pattern pieces. Accurate cutting is vitally important to the fit and craftsmanship of shoes. Therefore, cutting footwear often utilizes a die cutting process (see Chapter 9) because of its accuracy. A metal die similar to a cookie cutter is made to duplicate the shape of each of the pattern pieces. Its very sharp edge cuts through the layer or multiple layers of materials. Computerized cutting and laser cutting are other options (see Chapter 9) that provide extremely accurate cut pieces.

Leather hides are used for much of the fashion footwear produced worldwide. The hides are irregular in shape, and often have blemishes and thin areas, as is to be expected of this natural product. Thus, cutting hides for the production of shoes, handbags, belts, and other leather goods requires additional time and expertise, the waste of some material, and often single-ply cutting to avoid blemished areas. Another factor to consider is that leather hides are a commodity traded on a market with price that varies according to the supply. In this respect, the shoe industry is similar to the fur industry. Not only do prices vary based on supply, but since some of the hide sources are in other countries, the monetary exchange rate can influence the price of the raw materials.

Because shoe manufacturing involves a large number of steps that require skilled workers, labor costs tend to be high (see Figure 13.4). Adding to the production time, and thus the labor cost, is the difficulty of manipulating an awkwardly shaped product composed of many small pieces. Examine the tiny material sections of a pair of toddler's athletic or hiking shoes to imagine what it would be like to assemble the shoe sections. The development of specialized machinery has helped to keep labor costs down for those manufacturers that can afford to invest in the equipment. Most of the domestic shoe production occurs in Pennsylvania, Maine, and Missouri. As labor costs have risen in the United States, more shoes are being produced offshore. South America (especially Brazil) and Asia produce large quantities of the shoes sold in the United States. China has become a leading producer of shoes.

Figure 13.4: Shoe manufacturing involves a large number of steps that must be performed by skilled workers.

MARKETING AND DISTRIBUTION

New York City serves as the marketing center for footwear, with most companies having showrooms there. Domestic and international shoe trade shows, or markets, similar to the apparel market shows, are held two to four times a year. Fall/winter shoe lines are typically shown in January or February and spring/summer shoe lines are typically shown in August. The Fashion Footwear Association of New York (FFANY) sponsors footwear trade shows in New York City. Retail buyers, as well as manufacturers and footwear producers, attend these shows, just as the apparel trade shows are attended by people representing all aspects of the apparel industry.

The footwear industry utilizes similar promotional tools as the apparel industry in selling their lines to retail buyers. Sales representatives for footwear companies provide line sheets or brochures to their retail customers. Some companies are currently using digital images of footwear in their presentations to retail buyers, thus creating a "virtual showroom" (Thilmany, 1998). Videos, Web sites, trunk shows, and participation promotions are all used by footwear companies.

Footwear is sold in many department stores, specialty stores with footwear departments, specialty shoe stores, sporting goods and athletic footwear stores, discounters, and by nonstore retailing venues (catalog, television, Internet/Web). Some specialty shoe stores carry products from a range of manufacturers. Foot Locker and Lady Foot Locker stores, an athletic footwear chain, carry a variety of athletic footwear brands. In addition, the strategy of vertical integration is also common in the footwear industry; that is, some manufacturers own the shoe stores in which only their products are sold. Examples are Thom McAn, Redwing, and Stride Rite. Footwear companies such as Nine West, and Etienne Aigner have stores in outlet malls. Companies engaged in nonstore retailing of footwear include Lands' End, L.L.Bean, and Eddie Bauer, which offer shoes in addition to apparel products. The Nike.com Web site allows mass customization whereby customers may select colors and add monograms to the shoes ordered online (see Figure 13.5). Another type of mass customization uses body scanning equipment to individualize the size and shape of shoes to more accurately fit the intended customer (see Chapter 11).

Footwear retailing requires an immense inventory because of the large combination of shoe widths and lengths. When the range of seasonal colors is added to the

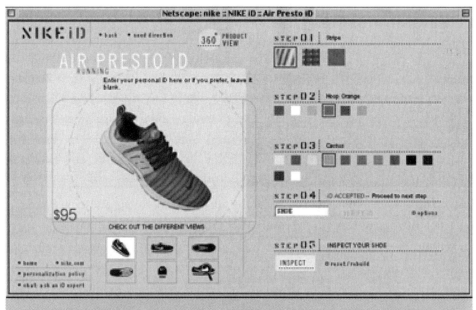

Figure 13.5: Nike.com offers customers the ability to customize their shoes by selecting the color and adding a monogram.

size inventory, it is clear that shoe retailers have a challenging task to meet the consumer's need for the right product in the specific color and size. The footwear retailer must make a significant capital outlay and have large inventory space. This is why some retailers lease their shoe departments to companies that specialize in shoe retailing (see Chapter 12).

The shift in location of footwear production from predominantly domestic, with some Western European production, to Asia and South America was discussed earlier in this chapter. The footwear industry has also shifted its customer market from domestic consumption to a global marketplace. Canadian, Mexican, and Japanese consumers have become major markets for U.S. footwear. American athletic shoes brands are sought worldwide. The reputation for quality of the casual footwear produced by U.S. manufacturers, such as Timberland, has opened European markets for these products. For survival and expansion, footwear manufacturers must continue to seek a global market for their products.

Hosiery and Legwear

The hosiery/legwear industry is composed of companies that produce men's, women's, and children's socks, stockings, pantyhose, and tights. This industry has a long and notable history in the United States. There is evidence that stocking knitting machines were in operation in New England as early as 1775. By 1875, the U.S. hosiery industry focused on the production of silk stockings, with an estimated worth of $6,000. By 1900, the industry had grown to a value of $186,413. Like textile production, hosiery production occurred primarily in the Northeast during this time. As with textile mills, however, production shifted to the South as labor costs increased in the Northeast.

The hosiery/leg wear industry underwent major developments during the twentieth century. At the beginning of the twentieth century, hosiery consisted of primarily white, "nude," and black socks and stockings in cotton, wool, and silk (and later, rayon) knits. By 1928, technological advances in knitting allowed for the production of full-fashioned men's hosiery in argyle patterns, English ribs, and cable stitches. In 1939, stockings made of DuPont's nylon fiber were introduced. Women loved their sheerness. Just as the demand for "nylons" soared, they were removed from the market. Nylon was needed for the war effort during World War II, and women wore socks that coordinated creatively with their suits. An amusing anec-dote survives regarding women's sense of loss during the war. A group of 60 women in Tulsa, Oklahoma, were asked what they missed most during the war. Twenty said they missed men the most; forty said they missed nylons the most! In 1946, when nylon stockings became available again, the crowds waiting to purchase them cre-ated a legendary sight.

Pantyhose were developed during the 1960s when very short hemline lengths required a product to replace stockings. As the name implies, the hose, or stocking, is joined to a panty, creating an all-in-one product. This eliminated the need for garters, which are used to connect the stockings to a girdle or a garter belt. Nylon is the most prevalent fiber for pantyhose. The panty portion of pantyhose may include spandex fiber to provide some figure control and a cotton knit crotch piece. Since the 1980s, blending a small percentage of spandex with nylon in the leg portion of pantyhose has gained popularity. In the 1990s, *microfiber* (smaller-than-usual fiber diameter) nylon became popular, especially for opaque pantyhose or tights. Tights are similar to pantyhose, but are made of a heavier material; they are either seam-less or seamed along the center back.

Hosiery/leg wear is a dynamic, high-fashion industry for men's, women's, and children's products. Staple hosiery goods have been replaced with socks, stockings, and pantyhose suitable for every holiday, to express one's personality, or to add extra punch to an outfit. As with apparel, hosiery/leg wear can be found in all wholesale price zones from mass/budget to designer. However, this product catego-ry has strong price appeal. The consumer can update an outfit inexpensively with accessories such as hosiery. The popularity of hosiery in today's marketplace is evi-denced by the specialty sock shops that have proliferated in retail and outlet malls.

HOSIERY AND LEGWEAR PRODUCERS

The hosiery/leg wear industry is dominated by large firms that are often part of ver-tically integrated companies that produce knitted fabrics as well as the finished hosiery and leg wear products. Most of the domestic hosiery/leg wear producers are located in the Southeast, concentrated primarily in North Carolina, Alabama, Ten-nessee, and Pennsylvania. Some of the largest U.S. hosiery manufacturers include Kayser-Roth, the parent company of which is Mexico's Grupo Synkro, one of the world's leading legwear manufacturers and distributors ("Top Mexican," 1995), Great American Knitting Mills (Gold Toe and Arrow brands), and Sara Lee Corporation (Hanes, L'eggs, and Donna Karan brands) (see Figure 13.6).

RESEARCH, DESIGN, AND PRODUCTION

Companies that produce hosiery and leg wear analyze apparel style trends and consumer buying trends to make design decisions. In addition, color forecasting plays a very important role in determining the various colors in which the hosiery and legwear will be produced. Designers also focus on new developments in textiles and knitting technology. For example, microfiber technology has provided consumers with softer and sheerer hosiery alternatives.

I AM
every size of gorgeous
under the sun.
49 million versions
of sheer beauty,
sheer style.
I AM ready to bare my soul.
Ready to bare my legs
in hosiery that looks and
fits like the skin
I AM comfortable in..

Figure 13.6: Some of the most recognized brands are in hosiery.

For centuries, stockings were knit by hand, using a circular knitting procedure so that no center back seam was required. The foot and leg shapes were produced by adding or subtracting stitches to increase or decrease the circumference of the stocking. The development of framework knitting machines (Figure 13.7) in England at the end of the sixteenth century provided a way to produce stocking blanks ("The history of hosiery," 1974). However, the material was knit flat, or **flatknit**. This meant that a seam had to be sewn along the center back to create the tubular stocking. The **full-fashioned** technique provided the shaping of the knit goods to conform to the foot and leg shapes along the seam edges. The first full-fashioned hosiery factory in the United States was established by E. E. Kilbourn in the late 1860s.

The development of circular knitting machines in the nineteenth century provided a means to produce seamless (except for the seam used to close the toe) stockings, socks, and later tights and panty-hose. Early seamless stockings did not fit as well as full-fashioned seamed stockings. When women's hemlines were shortened during the 1920s, the better fit of seamed stockings was preferred. This is reflected in the increase in production of full-fashioned stockings from 26 percent of the market in 1919 to 60 percent of production in 1929 and more than 80 percent in the 1950s ("The history of hosiery," 1974). With the development of pantyhose during the 1960s, additional changes in production occurred.

Because pantyhose are made of manufactured fibers that are heat sensitive, the foot and leg shape can be built into the product during the finishing process. A heat-setting process is used to mold the foot and leg shape by placing the hosiery over a leg-shaped board. Terms used for the application of heat to create the final shape in the finishing process are **blocking** or **boarding**.

Figure 13.7: The development of framework knitting machines provided a faster way to produce hosiery.

Socks are produced in varying lengths, including anklets, crew, mid-calf, and calf lengths. The most popular fibers for socks are cotton, wool, silk, acrylic, nylon, polypropylene, or blends of these fibers. Cotton and acrylic fibers are used frequently for ankle-length socks, while calf-length socks are often made of nylon, wool, silk, acrylic, or blends of two of these fibers. A small percentage of spandex might be added to provide some elasticity (see Figure 13.8). Sport socks or athletic socks continue to be a market growth area. These include casual sport socks as well as sport-specific socks that are designed with appropriate cushioning for various sports (Feitelberg, 1999).

The size range of hosiery varies according to the type of product. Sock and stocking sizes for men, women, and children are indicated with size numbers that correlate to shoe size. The consumer refers to a chart that shows the correct size based on the wearer's shoe size. There are fewer sock and stocking sizes than shoe sizes; each hosiery size fits a range of shoe sizes. For some products, the sock or stocking is available in only one size, which fits the majority of shoe sizes. Pantyhose generally are sized to fit women who fall within categories based on their height and weight (see Figure 13.9). Typical pantyhose sizes are *short*, *average*, and *tall*. *Queen size* and *Plus* size are size categories for the larger or taller size market. Some pantyhose producers provide a petite size as well.

In recent years several companies, including Jockey, J.G. Hook, Great American Knitting Mills (Gold Toe), Kayser-Roth (Hue), and Adams-Mills, have moved into the large-size leg wear market. The marketing manager for Adams-Mills explained,

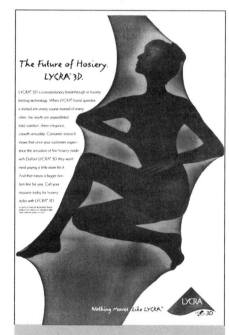

Figure 13.8: DuPont used a national advertising campaign to promote its Lycra brand spandex fiber to hosiery manufacturers.

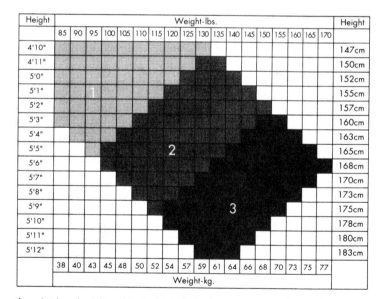

If your height and weight combination falls in the border area, you may prefer the next larger size.

Figure 13.9: Pantyhose are sized in categories based on height/weight ranges.

Just My Size socks are not simply larger versions of existing socks, but rather they are constructed with the inherent needs of tall and full-figured women in mind. Our research with plus-size women told us that fit is of paramount importance. So we made Just My Size socks with Memory Yarn, which is a combination of cotton and spandex that stretches and conforms to the individual contours of a woman's foot to ensure an unsurpassed fit and improved durability. In addition, the socks feature a knit-in arch that provides comfortable, all-day support. ("Adams-Mills launches," 1995, p. 30)

One of the strengths of the hosiery industry is the impressive variety of innovative textures, colors, and patterns available for hosiery and legwear products. New technology continues to bring an ever-increasing array of materials for hosiery. Much of the machinery required to produce hosiery is automated or computerized, and some of it operates 24 hours a day. Innovations include the development of machinery to knit a one-piece pantyhose unit ("Hosiery automation," 1995). Labor costs can be kept down by advanced technology. Thus, the hosiery industry is not threatened as much by inexpensive imports as some other industries. Another strength of the hosiery industry is that many manufacturers are vertically integrated and therefore have enhanced supply chain management opportunities.

Although the hosiery industry will face challenges in the future, it is positioning itself for continued success. Whereas the North American Free Trade Agreement has prompted more imports of hosiery into the United States, the trade balance still favors the United States. The hosiery industry relies on a close working partnership among the fiber producers, hosiery manufacturers, and retailers. By working together, the hosiery industry in the United States may be able to remain competitive with imported goods.

MARKETING AND DISTRIBUTION

Market weeks for hosiery typically coincide with those for ready-to-wear apparel, although much hosiery and leg wear are marketed and distributed through extended distribution channels. The hosiery industry is a low-margin business. This means that the dollar amount of profit per item sold that the producer earns from the sale to the retailer is small. Similarly, the dollar amount of profit the retailer "earns" from the sale to the customer is also small. Thus, the manufacturer and the retailer need high sales volume to compensate for the low margin. A number of strategies are used to create high sales volume. These strategies include vendor managed inventory systems, distribution through discount stores, enhancing ease of shopping, and licensing.

Vendor-managed inventory

To produce a large sales volume, it is important to maintain a complete stock of hosiery, in the appropriate sizes, styles, and colors. Therefore, many large hosiery manufacturers use Quick Response and supply chain management strategies, including vendor marking and vendor managed inventory. Through the sharing of sales data, stock is automatically replenished at the retail store to ensure a complete selection of products for the customer. The director of a hosiery association stated:

> Retailers are requiring new benchmarks for product development and delivery. Just-in-time and quick turnaround are realities, and it is becoming more and more pressure driven every day. The new benchmarks are for deliveries to be shipped within 48 hours of receipt of order. (Rabon, 1995a, p. 60).
>
> A casual and athletic sock manufacturer specializing in the private label business, Clayson Knitting Co. is totally computerized with full EDI capabilities, and all major customers send orders electronically. These orders are processed and shipped within 48 hours to 72 hours using back stocks that are maintained for these large customers. (Rabon, 1995b, p. 66)

Distribution through Discount Stores

Most hosiery and leg wear is sold through large discount chain stores (e.g., Wal-Mart, Target, Kmart). Brands such as L'eggs, Hanes, and No Nonsense are sold in this manner. Sid Smith, the president and CEO of the former National Association of Hosiery Manufacturers (NAHM) now the Hosiery Association, pointed out that the domination of discount store sales "means that it is extremely price competitive both at retail and at wholesale. Hosiery manufacturers have to compete very aggressively on price" (Rabon, 1995a, p. 60). To allow for a self-service retailing strategy, package marketing is used by companies that sell hosiery in supermarkets, convenience stores, and discount retailers. This includes large format sizing charts mounted on display racks, packaging that is color coded by style and size, and samples of the product available for consumers to touch and evaluate.

Ease of Shopping

Because of the number of styles, colors, and sizes, selecting hosiery can be confusing for consumers. Therefore, retail stores have adopted a number of strategies to assist the consumer in selecting the right product. Because of the self-service approach to selling hosiery and leg wear, companies have simplified packaging, improved signs, and enhanced display fixtures in an effort to assist the consumer (Feitelberg, 1998).

Fashion trends also affect the sales volume of hosiery. In the 1990s, the trend toward more casual dressing at the office may have been a stimulus for the increase seen in the sales volume of socks. Promoting hosiery as a fashion accessory rather than a staple commodity can enhance sales volume. Hosiery departments in retail stores may feature body wear in addition to the hosiery products. Many retailers have added cross-merchandising displays whereby hosiery (as well as other accessories) are displayed with coordinating apparel.

Some retailers have narrowed the number of brands or have focused on private label hosiery to simplify options for consumers. In addition, private label hosiery can provide for greater markups for the retailer. Retailers such as JCPenney, Nordstrom, and Talbots, to name just a few, distribute private label hosiery. Services for the ultimate consumer, such as automatic replenishment programs, can also increase sales volume. Both Saks Fifth Avenue and Nordstrom will send consumers a designated supply of hosiery on a regular basis (Feitelberg, 1998).

Licensing

Licensing products is another marketing strategy that has proved successful in the hosiery industry. As with footwear and other accessories, many name designers license their names for hosiery. Christian Dior, Givenchy, Ralph Lauren, Calvin Klein, Donna Karan, and Liz Claiborne are examples of designers who have licensing agreements with large hosiery companies for hosiery products.

Hats, Head Wear, Scarfs, and Neckwear

Accessories such as hats, scarfs, and neckwear typically are manufactured by a company that specializes in the specific accessory item. These accessory categories are integrally connected with apparel fashions and social norms.

HATS AND HEAD WEAR

Men's, women's, and children's dress hats comprise a much smaller segment of the *accessories* category than they did several decades ago. For women, the bouffant hairstyles of the 1960s did not lend themselves to wearing most hat styles. The pillbox hat made famous by then first lady Jacqueline Kennedy in 1961 marked the end of the hat-wearing social requirement. The custom of businessmen wearing hats began to decline during the 1960s as well. The press coverage regarding the fashion apparel and head wear of the British royal family during the 1980s renewed interest in fashion hats, but sales remain a small percent of the accessories category.

The Paris designer runway shows provide a striking contrast, though, to the lack of emphasis on fashion head wear by the masses. The hats worn during the shows to complement the designer's fashion look are highly imaginative creations (see Figure 13.10). An apparel collection shown by designer Karl Lagerfeld included a group of hats designed by a British milliner (hatmaker) created to represent French pastries—the *pâtisserie* collection. This type of millinery is an art form, with hat designers producing one-of-a-kind creations. The millinery provides strong visual interest to support the impact of the apparel collections.

Figure 13.10: Designer millinery, such as this head wear by Philip Treacy, can be highly imaginative.

Whereas the popularity of wearing dress hats has waned, the popularity of wearing casual hats, sport hats, and sport caps (especially baseball caps) has increased, providing a growth area for the industry. For sports such as skiing that require head covering for functional purposes, the demand for head wear has remained at the same level as the demand for apparel in these categories.

Many hat and head wear producers specialize in one type of product. For example, a manufacturer (sometimes referred to as an **item house**) will specialize in producing only baseball caps. Soft fabric hats and leather caps are usually sewn using construction techniques similar to those for apparel. Handwork might be required for the more-expensive hats, while less-expensive hats and head wear are machine made. Traditionally styled wool felt hats and straw hats are usually formed over a hat block, using steam to mold the hat into shape (see Figure 13.11). Men's hats are produced in sizes from $6^3/_4$ to $7^3/_4$ (in $^1/_8$-inch intervals) that correspond to head circumference, or, for less-structured hats, in sizes *small, medium, large,* and *extra large.* Caps may be produced in one size. Most women's hats are made in one size. Small children's caps and hats may be sized by age, while older children's hats may be produced in sizes *extra small, small, medium,* and *large.*

Baseball caps are used extensively as promotional items for many businesses. They can be manufactured quickly with technologically advanced equipment. A large number of baseball caps with a company logo might be ordered for a special event. Quick delivery of the product is a necessity to meet this need. The New Era Cap Co. of Derby, New York, is a business built on speedy production in large quantities through flexible manufacturing. It is a licensed official supplier of caps to Major

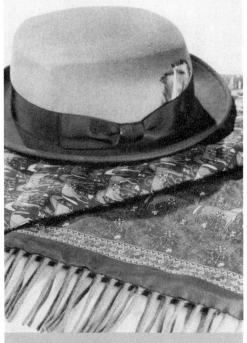

Figure 13.11: Felt hats, such as this dress hat, are molded into shape over hat blocks.

League Baseball, the National Football League, and the National Basketball Association, as well as to hundreds of Little League teams. Its two plants produce about 25,000 to 30,000 dozen caps a week (Moore, 1993).

Millinery is a term that refers specifically to women's hats and usually denotes that handwork is involved in the hat-making process. Until the late 1960s to early 1970s, most department stores had millinery departments with millinery specialists. However, very few retailers have retained such departments. The hats sold in most retail stores are machine made and moderately priced. Only a small market for fine millinery continues to exist. Most of the fine milliners are located in New York City, although milliners can be found in Los Angeles and other major metropolitan areas as well.

SCARFS AND NECKWEAR

Scarfs (preferred industry spelling) represent another product for which styles follow fashion cycles and sales rise and fall with fashion trends. At times, large square scarfs, perhaps even in shawl sizes are popular; at other times, small square scarfs or oblong scarfs might be fashionable. The scarf business is very specialized. A scarf manufacturer may specialize in only silk scarfs or only woolen (or wool-blend, acrylic, or cotton) scarfs. The printing processes used to apply the fabric design to silk are different from those for woolen materials; thus, it is common for companies to specialize in one of these materials to ensure a quality product.

Cost of producing scarfs is tied to the fabrics, designs, and printing methods used. The Italian design house of Emilio Pucci is well known for scarfs in the designer price zone. His brightly colored, geometric print silk scarfs became famous in the 1960s and have been classics ever since. Pucci-styled designs are instantly recognizable.

Many item houses in the United States produce scarfs in a wide variety of materials, from chiffon to cashmere, in an array of textures, colors, and prints. Echo is one of the best-known U.S. manufacturers in the moderate-to-bridge price zones. Echo produces scarfs, neckties, and bedding under its own label as well as producing private label goods for stores such as Saks Fifth Avenue and Ann Taylor and licensed scarfs for Ralph Lauren. In recent years, Echo has invested in CAD technology to enhance the speed and flexibility in designing scarfs and can create as many as 1,000 design patterns annually (Grudier, 1998). Many name designers, such as Ralph Lauren, Liz Claiborne, Oscar de la Renta, and Bill Blass, license their names for scarfs and neckties (see Figure 13.12).

Many scarf manufacturers use fabric manufactured in Asia and use Asian contractors for the printing as well. The material cost and labor cost related to printing may be less in Asia, thereby making it more profitable to source offshore. The actual construction process for scarfs can be very rapid, with machine-rolled hemming for moderate- and mass-priced goods, or time consuming, with hand-rolled hemming for some scarfs in the designer price zone.

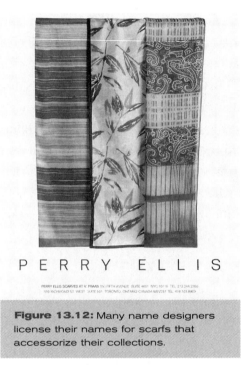

PERRY ELLIS

PERRY ELLIS SCARVES AT V. FRAAS 350 FIFTH AVENUE SUITE 4601 NYC 10118 TEL 212 244 2366
330 RICHMOND ST WEST SUITE 501 TORONTO ONTARIO CANADA M5V2B1 TEL 416 703 8901

Figure 13.12: Many name designers license their names for scarfs that accessorize their collections.

Necktie manufacturers are usually specialists, producing only neckties. Finer-quality neckties are made of silk, while lower-priced neckties are polyester. Wool, linen, cotton, leather, and other specialty materials comprise a small segment of production. Most necktie materials are woven; a small percentage of neckties are made of knit fabric. For neckties made of woven fabrics, the material is usually cut on the **bias**, or diagonal, to provide a more attractive knot and contour around the curve of the neck. Because a large amount of fabric is required to cut neckties on the bias, this practice increases the cost. The bias cut also produces the diagonal angle of the stripe seen on neckties as they are worn.

The fabric design for neckties is either a print, applied to the surface of the woven fabric, or a stripe, plaid, or motif woven into the fabric. Typical necktie stripes are called **regimental stripes** because they are derived from various historical military regiments. These stripes are spaced with wider widths for the background and narrower widths for the various stripes. Many schools (private secondary schools, military schools, colleges, and universities) have their own regimental stripes with unique combinations of colors and spacing that denotes the specific institution. The regimental stripe tie is considered a classic choice for conservative business attire.

The construction process for neckties includes machine processes; some higher-priced goods require handwork as well. The price reflects the amount of time required to produce the necktie, as well as the cost of the materials. Computer-aided textile design processes and new computer printing technologies provide additional ways to reduce the labor costs for the scarf and necktie industries in the United States.

The market for neckties reflects fashion cycles. The fashion pendulum moves from narrow ties to wide ties, from bow ties to no ties, from bright prints to subtle stripes (see Figure 13.13). With the trend toward casual business dress, neckties are no longer "required" at some offices, either on "Casual Fridays" or—especially at high-tech companies—on any other day. This change may have had some impact on the necktie business. On the other hand, specialty tie shops in retail malls are

Figure 13.13: The width of neckties, as well as the color and pattern, change with the fashion pendulum.

numerous, building consumer awareness and interest and offering convenience. *Conversational* or theme necktie prints have helped to increase sales. Whether the necktie displays one's profession or hobby or promotes a seasonal holiday, the consumer can use his necktie to "speak" to observers.

In addition to neckties, other types of neckwear include neck scarfs, or **mufflers**, often wool or silk, worn as an accompaniment to a wool overcoat for more formal occasions or worn with a casual jacket or coat to provide neck warmth. An **ascot**, a long neck scarf worn looped at the neck, is another item of men's neckwear. While neck scarfs and ascots are not purchased as frequently as neckties, retailers such as Brooks Brothers include such items as a necessary component of a well-stocked classic men's retail store.

Scarfs, neckties, and other neckwear are sold to consumers through a variety of retail venues: department stores, specialty stores, discount stores, boutiques, and nonstore retailers (e.g., catalog companies). The merchandising of scarfs and neckwear often requires instruction to consumers on how to tie the scarf or necktie effectively. Retailers often use promotion tools provided by the manufacturer to educate the consumer. These might include point-of-sale videos, booklets, and demonstrations.

Belts, Handbags, and Gloves

Some of the unique aspects of each of the accessories categories of belts, handbags, and gloves will be discussed separately in the following section.

BELTS

The belt industry is divided into two segments:
- The **cut-up trade** includes manufacturers that produce the belts that apparel manufacturers add to their pants, skirts, and dresses and supply as a component of the products they ship to retailers.
- The **rack trade** is made up of manufacturers that design, produce, and market belts to retailers.

Manufacturers in the cut-up trade specialize in low-cost, high-volume items. These garment belts might be made with less-expensive materials and processes, such as glueing, rather than stitching the backing material to the belt. Self-belts made from the same fabric as the garment might be produced by a belt contractor or the apparel manufacturer at the same time that the garment is produced.

Belts for the rack trade often provide an important component of a fashion look, therefore this part of the accessories industry works closely with the apparel segment. Belt production is centered in New York City's fashion district. Typical materials include leather as well as numerous other materials from cording to beaded fabrics. The type of material used determines the construction techniques and manufacturing processes.

For leather belts, cutting can be performed by hand or by the use of a strap-cutting machine that cuts even-width strips. Some leather belts are curved, or contoured, in which case the leather can be die-cut for speed and accuracy. A myriad of decorative effects can be used to enhance belts (see Figure 13.14). Belt designers add creativity with the use of buckles, stitching, jewels, chains, metal pieces, plastics, stones, nailheads, and other embellishments. Belt backings are attached by stitching or gluing.

GUESS
BELTS

Figure 13.14: Decorative effects using buckles, stitching, and other enhancements add a lively interest to belts.

HANDBAGS AND SMALL LEATHER GOODS

Although this category of accessories is referred to as *handbags*, a variety of products is retailed within the classification. Handbags are also called *purses*. Many of the ones produced and sold today are actually shoulder bags. Women's briefcases are included in the *handbag* category, as are wallets, coin purses, eyeglasses cases, and schedule planners. (Men's briefcases are typically sold with luggage.)

Handbags can be made from a variety of materials. Many of the handbags sold in the United States are made of leather, reptile (such as snakeskin), or eel skin. Other materials include a variety of fabrics, plastics (vinyl is the most common), and straw. Judith Leiber creates beaded and metal evening bags with retail prices beginning at approximately $500.

Structured handbags are supported by a frame that provides a distinctive shape and to which hardware, such as the closure, is attached. Soft handbags, such as pouch styles, may not use a frame. Handles or straps are attached to carry the handbag. **Clutch** bags are designed to be held in the hand (the term is derived from the fact that the bag is *clutched* in the hand) and may have a strap that can be stored inside the bag. Most handbags are lined in materials such as leather, suede, cloth, or vinyl. Structured bags may also have an interlining made from a stiff material to provide a firm shape.

Handbag styles range from large satchels to tiny clutches. While fashion trends play an important role in handbag styling, personal choice plays a role as well. Some women prefer a very functional bag, designed to hold everything, either in a roomy tote or a compartmentalized style. Other women prefer a compact style that could range from a "wallet" on a string to a decorative evening bag to hold only a few essentials. Although many European men carry bags, few American men have adopted this practice.

Designing handbags requires the same steps as many other products. Ideas are sketched and decorative trims, handles, hardware, and materials are researched. It is interesting to imagine what it would be like to be a designer for a classic handbag company such as Coach or Dooney & Bourke. How, and how much, can a designer modify a handbag? Details such as pinked edging trims a group of Dooney & Bourke bags. Colored piping in "classic," but new color combinations are added. After ideas and sketches have been generated, prototypes are made, and then the line is finalized.

Leather handbags follow manufacturing procedures similar to other leather products discussed in this chapter. Fabric handbags may use die cutting and other processes similar to garment production. For all handbags, some of the assembly processes, especially adding the hardware, require handwork. Thus labor costs are an important part of the costing structure. For leather goods, the price and availability of hides is another cost consideration. There are a number of small companies that produce many of the handbags produced in the United States. Most of these companies are centered in the mid-Manhattan area of New York City. New York City is also the primary market center for handbags and small leather goods. Since most handbags and small leather goods sold in the United States are imported, offshore production sites in Asia, Spain, Italy, and South America are important production centers.

Because many of the production processes are similar for various leather goods, shoe manufacturers might also make handbags and belts. Ferragamo produces coordinated handbags for some of its shoes, and Coach produces belts and other small leather goods as well as handbags. The handbag trade shows, generally four per year, coincide with the apparel markets.

In the 1970s, several designer names became sought after by consumers. The Louis Vuitton vinyl handbags with the "LV" logo appeared everywhere and sold at a premium price. Gucci bags became a status symbol. French fashion designer names, such as Pierre Cardin and Christian Dior, appeared on the outside of handbags. Since then, the licensing of designer and well-known brand names for handbags has become a major component of this business.

Handbags and small leather goods are sold through department stores, specialty stores, discount stores, boutiques, and nonstore venues. Some department stores have established in-store shops to feature the leather products of a specific manufacturer. Coach bags and belts often have a designated retail space, distinctively styled with shelf units and signage that the customer associates with Coach. We also see vertical integration within this industry. For example, Coach also operates its own retail stores (see Figure 13.15).

Figure 13.15: Coach handbags might be sold through in-store shops in department stores or through Coach specialty stores.

GLOVES

Gone are the days when a well-dressed man, woman, or child did not leave home without both hat and gloves. The popularity of dress gloves rises and falls with fashion trends. Functional gloves and mittens, such as those worn for cold winter weather, remain a steady part of the industry. Sport gloves are a rising segment of the glove industry, with gloves specially designed for skiing, snowboarding, bicycling, weight lifting, golf, and many other sports. Women's dress gloves are produced in a variety of lengths, from wrist-length "shorties" to shoulder-length 16-button gloves for bridal and evening wear. (The term *button* is used to designate each inch of length.)

The two primary categories of the glove industry are leather gloves and fabric gloves. The difference in the handling of these two types of materials results in substantial differences in production (see Figure 13.16 left). The majority of fabric gloves are made of knit fabric. Production is similar to that of other knit items and is located primarily in the Southeast, where many knitting mills are located. Knit gloves and mittens are produced quickly by using a circular knitting machine (see the section in this chapter on hosiery).

The production of leather gloves, however, still requires many hand operations (see Figure 13.16 right). Automating the processes is difficult, and skilled operators are required. Because of the labor-intensive nature of the industry, many glove manufacturers use offshore contractors, primarily in Asia and the Philippines, to reduce labor costs. In the United States, a large portion of glove manufacturing is located in the

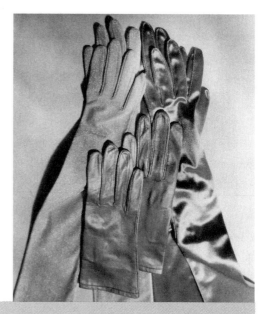

Wool Blend Gloves

A warm place for ten little fingers. Choose from a riot of colors. Soft and long-wearing 50/50 blend of wool and acrylic. Sweden.

S fits 3 to 5 years
M fits 6 to 8 years
L fits 9 to 12 years

V52001
015 Black
045 Vivid Violet
031 Magenta
051 Navy
089 Harbor Green
058 Royal
030 Red $10

Figure 13.16: Knit gloves (left) are much faster to produce than leather gloves and can be made in fewer sizes or a single size. Leather gloves (right) are produced in a variety of lengths and from many different leathers.

Gloversville, New York, area. Two of the glove industry's largest companies, Fownes Brothers and Co. and Grandoe Corporation are headquartered there.

The types of leather used for gloves need to be strong, yet thin and supple. Typical glove leathers include kidskin, lambskin (cabretta is a type of lambskin), pigskin, deerskin, and sueded leathers. Among the steps in the production of better quality gloves is a process to dampen and then stretch the leather in order to improve suppleness. Some leather glove manufacturers specialize in only one part of the production process, such as cutting. This step requires careful assessment of the hide for quality and most efficient utilization. Cutting might be accomplished entirely by hand (**table cutting**) for the top quality gloves, or by less time-consuming die cutting (**pull-down cutting**) for less-expensive gloves.

Higher-quality leather gloves include a number of separate sections that provide flexibility for hand movement. These sections include: a thumb section; a **trank** piece for the palm and another piece for the face of the hand; **fourchettes**, which are rectangular strips between the second/third, third/fourth, and fourth/fifth fingers to provide width; and three **quirks**, tiny triangular gussets at the base of the second, third, and fourth fingers. Each of these pieces requires painstaking care in construction in order to fit the pieces together properly.

Woven-fabric gloves require pattern pieces and steps similar to those for leather gloves. Less-expensive gloves may have fewer pattern pieces and therefore may not provide as much hand mobility and comfort as gloves made with more pattern pieces. The seams may be stitched so the raw edges are to the inside or may be sewn with raw edges to the outside, depending on the style of glove. Gloves can be made of a combination of leather and fabric. For example, a sport glove might have leather tranks and knit fourchettes. Some leather gloves are lined with knit fabric or fur.

Knit gloves may be manufactured in one size if the fabric stretches sufficiently to fit a wide range of hand sizes. Leather gloves usually are produced in sizes *Small*, *Medium*, *Large*, and *Extra-large*, or they are sized numerically, in $1/4$-inch intervals, corresponding to the circumference around the palm and forehand (sizes 7 to 10 for men and sizes $5^1/_2$ to 8 for women). For children, gloves and mitten sizes are related to age.

New York City is the primary market center for gloves, and most glove companies have showrooms there. Specialists called glove buyers in retail stores are of a bygone era. Today's gloves are sold in the accessory departments of department or specialty stores along with belts, scarfs, handbags, and sometimes jewelry. Gloves are also sold by specialty accessory retailers.

The competitiveness of the domestic glove industry will depend upon companies being flexible, offering high quality and fast turnaround, and having the ability to produce small lot runs. Grandoe Corporation exemplifies the type of flexibility needed by successful companies. Grandoe produces dress and casual gloves; sports gloves for skiing, snowboarding, and other outdoor activities; and private label gloves for retailers such as L.L.Bean, JCPenney, and Bloomingdale's (Rabon, 1998).

Jewelry

Jewelry is divided into three categories:

- Fine jewelry
- Bridge jewelry
- Costume jewelry

Fine jewelry is the most expensive jewelry category. This category includes pieces made from precious metals, such as silver, gold, and platinum, either alone or with precious and semiprecious gemstones (see Figure 13.17). Because gold is too soft to be used by itself, it is usually combined with other metals for jewelry. The gold content of a piece of jewelry is expressed in *karats*, or k, with 24k referring to solid gold; 18k and 14k gold are most often used in fine jewelry. Any alloy less than 10 karats cannot be labeled *karat gold*. Platinum, which is heavier and more expensive than gold, is often used for rings, particularly diamond rings. Silver is the least expensive of the precious metals. Silver is often combined with other metals (usually copper). To be labeled *sterling silver*, the metal must be at least 925 parts to 1000 parts silver.

Precious gemstones include diamonds, emeralds, sapphires, and rubies. All are measured in karats, with 1 karat

Figure 13.17: Fine jewelry often includes precious and semiprecious gemstones.

equaling 100 points. Pearls are also included in this category even though they are not a stone per se. Semiprecious stones include amethysts, garnets, opals, lapis, jade, topaz, and aquamarine. In recent years, semiprecious stones have gained popularity as consumers' preference for colored gemstones has increased. Fine jewelry companies are often vertically integrated organizations with the designer, producer, and retailer under one roof. Fine jewelry is sold through specialty jewelry stores and the fine jewelry departments of upscale department stores. Many consumers have turned to nonstore retailers, particularly television retailers such as QVC, to purchase fine jewelry.

Similar to the bridge wholesale price zone for ready-to-wear apparel, which falls between designer and better price zones, **bridge jewelry** falls between fine and costume jewelry. *Bridge jewelry* serves as an umbrella term for several types of jewelry, including ones that involve the use of silver, gold (typically of 14, 12, or 10 karats), and less expensive "stones," such as onyx, ivory, coral, or freshwater pearls. One-of-a-kind jewelry designed by artists using a variety of materials is also considered bridge jewelry. Bridge jewelry is sold in the same store or department as fine jewelry and costume jewelry.

Costume jewelry is the least expensive of the jewelry categories. Coco Chanel was the first prominent designer to accessorize her couture garments with costume jewelry, thus legitimizing the wearing of less expensive jewelry by women everywhere. This type of jewelry is mass produced using plastic, wood, brass, glass, lucite, and other less-expensive materials. Although there are large companies in the costume jewelry industry, including Monet and Trifari, the industry is dominated by small companies that produce jewelry sold through a variety of retail outlets, including nonstore retailers (see Figure 13.18).

Figure 13.18: Monet produces costume jewelry sold through department and specialty stores.

Summary

Accessories comprise vital and important segments of the fashion industry. Changes in accessories complement changes found in the ready-to-wear apparel industry. Therefore, the apparel and accessories markets work together in creating total fashion looks. Accessories are grouped into the following categories: footwear; hosiery and legwear; hats and head wear; belts, handbags, and small leather goods; gloves; and jewelry. Although production processes vary, most accessory lines are created according to the following steps: research, designer's sketches, pattern making, development of prototypes, costing, marketing, production, distribution, and retailing.

The footwear industry produces men's, women's, and children's dress shoes and boots, athletic shoes, casual shoes, and other footwear. The main raw materials used for footwear include leather, fabrics, and plastics. Shoes are produced by forming raw materials around a last or mold shaped like a foot. To reduce labor costs, shoe production has shifted from domestic to primarily offshore venues. New York City serves as the primary market center for footwear.

The hosiery/legwear industry produces men's, women's, and children's socks, stockings, and hosiery. The hosiery industry is dominated by large firms that are often part of vertically integrated companies. Most of the domestic hosiery producers are currently located in the Southeast. Production of hosiery is very automated and therefore is not threatened by imports as much as other industries are. Hosiery companies are very involved with Quick Response and supply chain management strategies, including vendor-managed retail inventory.

Although hats and head wear companies currently comprise a much smaller segment of the accessories industries than they did decades ago, they are still important. Item houses that produce specialty merchandise such as baseball caps have grown as the popularity of this type of accessory has increased. The belt industry includes the rack trade (manufacturers that design, produce, and market belts to retailers) and the cut-up trade (manufacturers that produce belts for apparel manufacturers). The handbag industry produces small leather goods as well as handbags. Leather gloves and fabric gloves are the two primary categories in the glove industry. Jewelry is divided into three categories: fine jewelry, bridge jewelry, and costume jewelry. New York City serves as the market center for virtually all accessories. Trade shows and trade associations play an important role in promoting all components of the accessories industries.

As with the ready-to-wear industry, the accessories industries include a wide variety of career possibilities, from design to production to marketing and distribution.

Color and Paint Coordinator/Assistant Designer
PUBLICLY HELD ATHLETIC SHOE COMPANY

Position Description
Create color palette for each season, decide what colors to use on each shoe taking into consideration target customer, decide on materials to use in the shoe production, paint prototype shoes.

Typical Tasks and Responsibilities
- Create different colorways for shoes
- Use freehand and streamline applications to create the colorways
- Attend meetings to communicate with others in the department and in other departments
- Render drawings for these meetings to visually communicate designer's ideas

Accessories Pattern Maker/Sample Maker
PUBLICLY HELD SPORTSWEAR AND ATHLETIC SHOE COMPANY

Position Description
Support the design prototype process for the accessories team, including drafting patterns, interpreting design and constructing prototypes, creating specifications, technical drawings, and construction details.

Typical Tasks and Responsibilities
- Draft accessories patterns from design sketches
- Construct, build, and/or sew accessories samples such as bags, hats, gloves, etc.
- Create product specifications and ensure accuracy. Create product technical drawings complete with construction details to facilitate more accurate samples from the field
- Review accessory samples for accuracy, color matching, durability, and function. Review construction details to ensure specifications are correct
- Collaborate with accessory designers, developers, and engineers to ensure the best product is produced and work out construction problems
- Calculate fabric utilization data and other costing factors in collaboration with engineers, designers, and developers. Evaluate new equipment with the Sample Room Supervisor and technology services manager
- Cut fabrics and trim. Purchase and maintain inventory of materials, supplies, and notions

CAREER PROFILES

Key Terms

ascot

bias

blocking

boarding

bridge jewelry

clutch

costume jewelry

cross-merchandising

cut-up trade

fine jewelry

flatknit

fourchette

full-fashioned

item house

last

millinery

muffler

pull-down cutting

quirk

rack trade

regimental stripe

table cutting

trank

Discussion Questions

1. Think about the accessories you are currently wearing. How do they complement the fashion apparel you are wearing? How are the design, production, and distribution of these accessories similar to and different from the fashion apparel?

2. If you were a shoe designer, before starting your next line of shoes, what sources of information would you turn to for market and trend research? Why would this information be important in your design decisions?

References

Accessories Council. (1999, April 19). Main floor magic. Advertising supplement to *Women's Wear Daily*.

Accessories Council. (2000, November 6). The accessory industry speaks. Advertising supplement to *Women's Wear Daily*.

Adams-Mills launches Just My Size socks for outsize market. (1995, September). *Hosiery News*, p. 30.

Feitelberg, Rosemary. (1998, April 6). Stores give hosiery a makeover. *Women's Wear Daily*, p. 14.

Feitelberg, Rosemary. (1999, September 13). It's not just a white sock now. *Women's Wear Daily*, p. 34.

Grudier, Alison. (1998, February). Echo on bringing CAD in and sourcing it out. *Bobbin*, pp. 36–42.

The history of hosiery: Early industry developed slowly. (1974, November 8). *Hosiery Newsletter*, pp. 3–9.

Hosiery automation advances at F.A.S.T. show. (1995, August). *Hosiery News*, pp. 32–34.

Moore, L. (1993, November). There are no caps on New Era's potential. *Apparel Industry Magazine*, pp. 16–22.

Rabon, Lisa C. (1995a, December). Makers target new benchmarks. *Bobbin*, pp. 60–63.

Rabon, Lisa C. (1995b, December). Survival of the sock. *Bobbin*, pp. 65–66.

Rabon, Lisa C. (1998, January). Gloves grip new markets to keep their hands in the industry. *Bobbin*, pp. 24–29.

The spell is in the name. (1999, April 19). Advertising Supplement to *Women's Wear Daily*.

Thilmany, Jean. (1998, December 9). Footwear digitalization. *Women's Wear Daily*, p. 26.

Top Mexican corporate executive tells American business delegation peso crisis offers his country opportunity to become export leader. (1995, April). *Hosiery News*, p. 29.

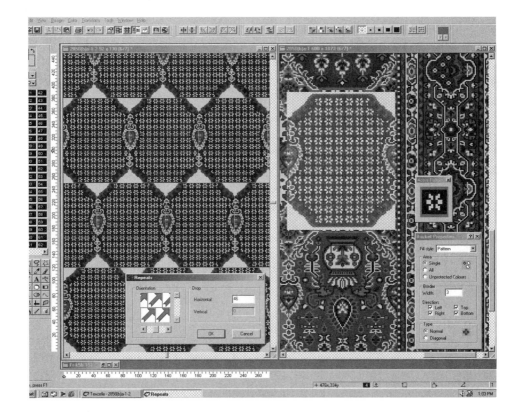

Home **Fashions**

IN THIS CHAPTER YOU WILL LEARN:

■ the similarities, differences, and relationships between the home fashions and the ready-to-wear industries.

■ the design, marketing, production, and distribution processes of textile products such as upholstery fabrics, window coverings, area floor coverings, towels, and bedding.

■ the steps the industry has taken to ensure sustainable design in home fashions.

What Are Home Fashions?

Previous chapters in this book have examined the design, marketing, and production of ready-to-wear apparel and accessories. This chapter will focus on the home fashions industry. Home fashions are textile products such as towels, bedding, upholstery fabrics, area floor coverings, draperies, and table linens for home end uses that have styles that change over time in response to changing fashion trends. Therefore, home fashions include the **home textiles**, **tabletop**, and **domestics** categories of the broader home furnishings industry. The home fashions industry consists of companies that design, produce, market, and distribute these home textile products.

This chapter will examine the similarities, differences, and relationships between the design, production, and marketing of home fashions and ready-to-wear apparel and accessories. An understanding of the organization and operation of the home fashions industry in the broader context of apparel fashions is important for several reasons. In recent years, the ready-to-wear industry and the home fashions industry have become increasingly interconnected as a growing number of apparel companies have ventured into designing, producing, marketing, and distributing home fashions.

As we examine the home fashions industry, it is important to keep in mind that the average *turn* (the frequency rate at which a product is sold and replaced at the retail store) in home fashions is less that two per year compared to the apparel industry where the average turn is four to six times a year. This difference in product turn has implications for the design, manufacture, distribution, and retail sales of home fashions.

HOME FASHIONS INDUSTRY TRENDS

Trends in the home fashions industry include the crossover between apparel and home fashions, strong consumer demand for home fashions, increased competition that creates a need for product differentiation within the industry, and the growth of private label and store brand products.

The crossover between apparel and home fashions has been a strong trend. Ralph Lauren established a home fashions division soon after initiating his apparel lines. Recent entrants from the apparel arena into the home fashions market include Tommy Hilfiger (Figure 14.1), Joe Boxer, Calvin Klein and

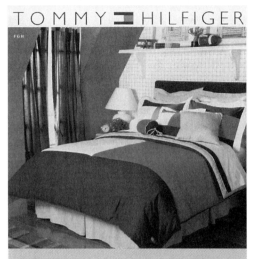

Figure 14.1: Tommy Hilfiger entered the home fashions market after attaining strong market penetration in the men's, women's, and children's apparel markets.

Donna Karan. Retailers believe that these designer names bring customers into the stores. Further expansion of new designer names into the home fashions market may be limited. Some industry analysts believe that most of the apparel designer licenses have been spoken for and have commanded so much retail space that there is a limited amount of additional shelf space available for new lines of merchandise.

Consumer demand for home fashions has been strong, and analysts predict continued strong demand. This trend can be attributed to a favorable housing industry, a growing remodeling industry, consumers' desire to spend more time at home, and the growing selection of home fashions available to consumers. "Consumers are now trading up to better quality via ensembles, collections, designer names and fashion, which are the most promising aspects of the business for all channels of distribution, especially the discounters—with Kmart in the forefront with its exclusive Martha Stewart line" ("Retailers duel," 1999, p. 20). Home fashions producers predict that retailers such as Wal-Mart, Bed Bath & Beyond, and JCPenney will remain leading retailers in home fashions.

Industry analysts predict that a few huge and powerful home fashions companies will continue to be the key players (see Table 14.1). The competition among these

TABLE 14.1

Leading Home Fashions Publicly Held Corporations

Company	1999 Net Sales (in $ Millions)
Springs Industries Inc.	2,220.4
WestPoint Stevens Inc.	1,883.3
Pillowtex Corp.	1,552.1
Dan River Inc.	628.9
Crown Crafts Inc.	362.1

Source: Based on DesMarteau, Kathleen. Home fashions leaders hone internal investment & global options. (2000, June). *Bobbin*, p. 62.

key companies is intense. For home fashions companies, product differentiation through fashion and styling is one strategy to survive the market pressures ("Retailers duel," 1999).

With intense competition among the key players, the race is on to be the lowest-cost producer. One of the strategies to lower costs is to make massive capital investments in automation, especially in production facilities. A second strategy is to capitalize on economies of scale by acquiring other firms, in some cases, complementary firms. WestPoint Stevens purchased the terry towel operation of Bibb Co. and also purchased the pillow and pad manufacturer Liebhardt Mills. West-Point Stevens expanded into the international arena by acquiring U.K.-based P. J. Flower. In another acquisition, "Pillowtex bought Fieldcrest Cannon, a company twice its size, for an estimated $700 million, and acquired towel producer Leshner Mills" ("Retailers duel," 1999, pp. 18–19). A third strategy is for home fashions manufacturers to service fewer retailers, but to work with the retail giants that own many department stores. However, other companies are focusing on the very important mass-merchandise sector and the growing specialty chain operations. In any event, the consumer is the beneficiary of low-cost manufacturing and intense competition among home fashions producers with low retail prices in relation to the quality of the merchandise.

Another trend in home fashions has been the growth of private label and store brand merchandise. This topic will be discussed later in this chapter. With this continued growth, the design, production, marketing, and distribution of home fashions encompasses a large potential market for exciting and rewarding careers for individuals who have expertise in textiles, design, and marketing.

PRIMARY END-USE CATEGORIES

In general, the home fashions industry is divided into four primary end-use categories (Yeager, 1988):

■ Upholstered furniture coverings and fillings.

■ Window and wall coverings.

■ Soft floor coverings, including area rugs, scatter rugs, and runners, and cushions (room and wall-to-wall carpeting is beyond the scope of this chapter).

■ Bed, bath, tabletop, and other textile accessories and accents.

Later in this chapter, these end-use categories will be discussed in greater detail. First, a general discussion of the organization and operation of the home fashions industry and the marketing of home fashions will provide an overall context for the design, marketing, and production of these end-use products.

Home Fashions and the Textile Industry

The textile industry forms the base for the structure of the home fashions industry. The design and performance of the textiles used in home fashions play a very important role in the success of the end-use product. For many home fashions, the design of the fabric is as important as the design of the end-use product itself. As mentioned in Chapter 3, textile companies often focus entirely on home textiles and home fashion end uses. The general organization and structure of textile companies that produce textiles primarily for the home fashions industry are the same as for those companies that produce textiles for the apparel industry (refer to Figure 3.1 for a summary of the organizational structure of the U.S. textile industry). It should be noted that many textile companies produce fabrics for both apparel and home fashions (e.g., Dan River, Milliken & Co., Burlington, Springs Industries).

The home fashions industry is dominated by vertically integrated textile companies that produce both fabrics and home fashion end-use products (see Figure 14.2). These include home fashions powerhouses such as WestPoint Stevens, Springs Industries, Pillowtex, Dan River, and Crown Crafts (Table 14.1). This is because production of home fashions is often highly automated and can be accomplished very efficiently within a vertical operation. In many cases, the fabric may not need to be cut and sewn to complete the product (e.g., towels and rugs), or minimal sewing, such as sheet hemming, is performed at the textile facility. For example, a single

Figure 14.2: Vertical integration and automation of production are typical characteristics of major producers of home fashions.

facility owned by WestPoint Stevens performs all production processes from cleaning cotton to creating the finished products (e.g., sheets and pillowcases) that are ready for distribution. Because of this vertical integration and automation of production, the home fashions industry has been somewhat less vulnerable to imports than the apparel industry, although imported fabrics are a significant competitor in certain segments of the industry, particularly high-end sheeting fabrics.

Licensing in Home Fashions

Licensing agreements involve purchasing the use of an image, design, or name by a manufacturer for use on its products (see Chapter 2 for a complete discussion of licensing). As in the apparel industry, licensing agreements have become an important component of the home fashions industry. Licensing agreements in home fashions are classified in the same categories as apparel, including designer name licensing, character licensing, corporate licensing, nostalgia licensing, and sports licensing.

Well-known ready-to-wear apparel designers have moved into the world of home fashions through licensing agreements with textile mills and home fashions manufacturers. Among the first apparel designers to license home fashions were Anne Klein, Liz Claiborne, and Laura Ashley for Burlington Domestics; Issey Miyake for Cannon; Perry Ellis for Martex; Bill Blass for Springs Industries; and Yves Saint Laurent for J. P. Stevens. Although not all of these early licenses succeeded, many of them flourished. Today some of the best known designers with home fashions licensing agreements include Ralph Lauren, Laura Ashley, Liz Claiborne, Calvin Klein (Figure 14.3), and Bill Blass.

In addition to name designers, companies with well-known brand

Figure 14.3: Calvin Klein licenses home fashions in addition to creating men's, women's, and children's apparel.

names are also entering into licensing agreements for home fashions. For example, Echo, known for scarfs, has a licensing agreement with Revman for a variety of home textiles. Eddie Bauer licenses with WestPoint Stevens for its sheets and pillowcases.

Historic reproductions and historically inspired fabrics have a strong market appeal. The Williamsburg Collection inspired by eighteenth and nineteenth century designs is produced by Waverly in a licensing agreement with Colonial Williamsburg. The "exclusive license with Williamsburg includes the fabric collection as well as wallpapers and ready-made home fashions such as bed ensembles, table covers, valances and shower curtains" (Richards, 1999, p. 20).

Licensing is also big business for home fashions geared to children. As with apparel, licensing of cartoon and movie characters (e.g., Disney, Warner Brothers), sports teams (e.g., St. Louis Rams), and toys (e.g., Barbie) have been very successful. Beatrix Potter and Winnie the Pooh are timeless and endearing character licenses for juvenile home fashions.

What makes these licensing agreements successful? As discussed in Chapter 2, a successful licensing agreement, whether in ready-to-wear or home fashions, depends on a well-recognized brand name with a distinct image and a licensed product that reflects that image. Successful licensed home fashion collections such as Ralph Lauren Home Collection and Guess Home Collection follow this strategy.

Home Fashions Design

During the design phase of developing home fashions products, textile and trim designers create exciting materials and product designers determine the form of the final end-use product. As previously discussed, some home fashion products roll out of the textile production facility as finished products. For other types of products, the product designer works with new textiles, trims, and findings to create exciting pillows, comforters, tabletop accents, and accessories. In general, designers in the home fashions industry create designs for two fashion seasons, spring/summer and fall/winter. Because fashion trends do not change as quickly for home fashions as for apparel, home fashion designs may stay on the market longer than apparel.

RESEARCH

Designers must take into account many considerations and constraints in order to develop new and exciting products successfully season after season. Inspiration can come from numerous sources when creating new shapes, textures, and color combinations. New fiber and fabric developments are also a part of the design inspiration. In addition, there are important functional needs that must be met. Performance criteria are important to the consumer. A towel must be absorbent, soft, easily laundered, and durable, as well as look attractive while displayed in the bathroom. As with apparel, fabrics used for home fashions are designed and tested for performance characteristics. Some home fashion products (e.g., rugs, fabrics for upholstered furniture) must meet specific safety standards (e.g., flammability) set by law.

The designer strives to be cognizant of emerging social, political, economic, and consumer trends. Anticipating and meeting customer needs are critical components of the design and production aspects of the industry. Two key elements of current home fashion trends are self-expression and individuality. These are evidenced by the increased customization of products to meet a consumer's individual wants and needs. The research conducted regarding home fashion products and consumer trends is similar to the research for apparel products. For example, Thinsulate, an insulative material manufactured by 3M with an established name in apparel, also has attributes suited to the bedding market. However, the fiber composition needed for bedding differs from Thinsulate's specifications for apparel products. Therefore, 3M needed to conduct research and development procedures in order to apply this fiber to a new end use in the home fashions market. "Through independent research, 3M found that consumers would be receptive to Thinsulate in bedding, and 'the consumer told us they would be willing to pay more for it'" (Rush, 1996, p. 6).

COLOR FORECASTING

As in the apparel industry, color forecasting is an important component of home fashions product development. Some of the color forecasting services mentioned in Chapters 4 and 5 provide research and trend forecasting for home fashions as well as for apparel products.

Historically, changes in the color palette for home fashions were based on a ten-year cycle. Who can forget the pink, salmon, cerise, turquoise, and gray of the 1950s; followed by avocado and orange in the 1960s; beige, yellow (harvest gold), and brown in the 1970s; mauve, forest green, slate blue, and gray, in the 1980s or the neutrals and jewel tones of the 1990s? However, that ten-year color cycle appears to be accelerating as consumers are more able and willing to change their home **decor** and companies are providing consumers with more alternatives.

Home textile sample books might be used to market home textiles for several years. Therefore, accurate color forecasting is necessary for the fashion colors to appear as up to date as possible. In addition, substantial lead time is needed to produce coordinated home fashion products. Therefore, on-target color forecasting is critical for success.

The Color Marketing Group (CMG) is an international not-for-profit association of color professionals based in Alexandria, Virginia. One of its purposes is to forecast color directions for all industries, manufactured products, and services. CMG sponsors conferences and workshops, produces color palettes, tracks existing color trends, projects colors 12 to 18 months in advance, and forecasts colors for consumer products two years in advance. CMG assembles about 700 members at its semiannual conference to analyze color and design trends. "The design workshops concentrate on outside influences that affect design, rather than the design itself. All the factors that cause design to evolve are examined, which enables members to gain insight into what the emerging colors will be" (Verlodt, 1999, p. 13). Many interrelated factors are considered during the selection process for the seasonal color palette for a new home fashions line.

The president of CMG discussed color choice as it relates to lifestyle:

> Many retailers often appeal to a specific lifestyle or age group and develop their color
> palette with that in mind. Target, Pottery Barn, Crate and Barrel, Pier One and IKEA all sell
> to a similar demographic. . . . The colors found in these stores can be very similar, rein-
> forcing the notion that design, style and price often dictate what will work on those prod-
> ucts. (Verlodt, 1999, p. 13)

TEXTILE PROCESSES

Textile Design

Textile design for home fashions includes the design of the fabric structure (e.g.,
weave pattern) as well as the surface design (e.g., printing, napping, glazing).
Although woven fabrics are more common than other fabric structures for home
fashion products, the industry has seen an increased use of knits and nonwoven fabrics, primarily for less-costly products.

Textile designers for home fashions often work with computer-aided design programs to develop their designs. Textile designers also create original painted artwork for
fabric prints that are later scanned into a CAD system. Once the textile design is in the
CAD system, details of the design are refined. The various colors used in the print
design can be separated by computer for the printing process, since each color of the
print requires a separate roller for rotary printing or a separate screen if screen printed.

CAD systems greatly speed the work pace in rug design studios (see Figure 14.4).
The textile designer creates a new rug design on a CAD system in hours or scans an
image into the system in minutes, compared to days and even weeks to create a rug
design prior to the use of computers. CAD/CAM technology provides the means to
design exclusive patterns for private label programs rapidly and easily. Design companies have "even sent a designer out with a laptop to show a customer the various
styles and let them choose exactly what they want" (Herlihy, 1999, p. 22).

Textile Printing

Prints with a larger number of colors (13–15) are more costly to produce than prints
with a few colors (1–3). The cost of developing the new print is more economical if
the print can be produced in several color combinations (colorways). Therefore, several colorways or color variations are typically created for each print design. When

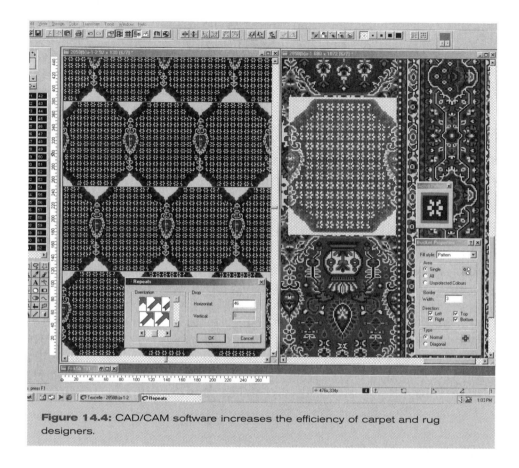

Figure 14.4: CAD/CAM software increases the efficiency of carpet and rug designers.

designing a print, textile designers must take into consideration the repeat of the print so that the design can be printed efficiently (see Chapters 3, 6 and 9 for additional discussion of textile design).

Digital printing used in the apparel industry was discussed in Chapters 3, 6, and 11. This printing technology is in use by some textile producers for home fashions. Seiren Co. is a Japan-based textile converter, dyer, printer and finisher. The company's "digital printing system is being used in Japan to create everything from custom home furnishings to apparel to auto interiors" (Rudie, 1998, p. 20).

Weaving

Weaving looms for products such as rugs are controlled by sophisticated computer-aided manufacturing programs. Computers are used in the production of woven, tufted, and printed rugs. At Shaw Rugs, the computerized looms are integrated with the CAD system.

> Once the design is ready, we e-mail it to the weaving floor, and it's converted in seconds to drive the loom. The looms are also scheduled by computer, depending on what orders have come in. It's all computerized, so we don't have to inventory all our rugs. We basically make them as quickly as they are ordered. (Herlihy, 1999, p. 22)

Converters

As in the apparel and textile industries, textile converters play an important role in the production of textiles for specific home fashion end uses. These end uses include upholstery fabrics, table linens, and other fabrics that are printed or finished to improve the performance of the end-use product. For example, soil-hiding and soil-resistant finishes are often applied to fabrics used for upholstery or table linens. As with the apparel and textile industries, most home fashions textile print converters, such as Covington, Ametex, John Wolf, Richloom, and Waverly, are based in New York and contract finishing work with a variety of finishing plants. In most cases, converters will provide original painted fabric print designs to a finishing company that will input the design into a computer system, develop fabric pigments for printing, and print and finish the fabric. For example, Waverly contracts with Cherokee Finishing Co., a division of Spartan Mills, to print and finish its upholstery fabrics.

Marketing Home Fashions

Marketing components similar to those used in the apparel industry include manufacturer's showrooms, company sales representatives, trade shows, and advertising and promotion. However, the home fashions industry relies on textile converters and jobbers to perform marketing and distribution functions more often than does the apparel industry.

As with apparel, the establishment of well-respected brand names is important in the marketing of home fashions. Consumers often rely on brand names in their decisions to purchase goods. WestPoint Stevens is well known for its Martex and Utica brands, Pillowtex for its Royal Velvet brand, Springs Industries for its Springmaid and Wamsutta brands, and Burlington for Burlington House brands.

Private label brands continue to gain market share. Federated Department Stores (such as the Bon Marché and Macy's) retail Charter Club and Home Design store brands (see Figure 14.5). Kmart is doing extremely well with the exclusive line, Martha Stewart Everyday. Martha Stewart "credits her brand's number-one status to a massive communication effort, from her retailing program at Kmart, to mail order, radio and television programs, newspaper columns, magazines, books and a Web site" (Musselman, 1999, p. 25). Store brands such as Pottery Barn, Crate and Barrel, and Pier One are also growing in importance.

MANUFACTURERS' SHOWROOMS AND SALES REPRESENTATIVES

Figure 14.5: Charter Club is one of Macy's private label store brands.

Marketing headquarters and manufacturer showrooms for many home fashions companies are located in New York City. Companies use showrooms to provide enticing visual displays of new home textiles as well as finished products for their interior design, manufacturing, and retail customers. Most companies will display new fabrics made into end-use products to show customers how the new fabrics can be used. Coordinated ensembles of products for bed and bath, kitchen, living room, and dining areas are created and presented. Companies also distribute sample books to interior design and manufacturing customers. These sample books include swatches of home textiles that are available and pictures of finished products using the textiles.

DECORATIVE FABRIC CONVERTERS AND JOBBERS

In addition to manufacturers' showrooms, textile converters and jobbers also play an important role in the marketing of home fashions. As mentioned earlier, textile converters in the home fashions industry design and sell finished textiles to jobbers, designers, and manufacturers, who use the textiles in home fashion end-use products. Some converters also produce end-use products such as bed linens and window treatments. Like manufacturers, converters create and distribute sample books and have showrooms in New York City where they display and sell their goods to jobbers as well as to interior design, manufacturing, and retailing customers.

Robert Allen, one of the largest residential woven fabric converters in the United States, serves over 60,000 accounts from its four warehouses. In each fabric category (e.g., upholstery, drapery), teams of designers work to create new fabrics for their customers. Robert Allen markets its products through showrooms and showroom boutiques, where finished products are shown using exclusive fabrics. In addition to fabrics, these showrooms have displays of wall coverings and finished products, such as bed coverings and draperies. Other well-known national converters include Fabricut, Barrow, and Kravet.

Decorative fabric jobbers are also involved in the marketing and distribution of home textile piece goods, particularly upholstery and drapery fabrics. Traditionally, jobbers have served a warehousing and distribution function within the industry. In the past, regional jobbers would visit New York twice a year, where they would buy large quantities of fabrics from a number of mills and converters. They would then sell smaller quantities to interior designers, furniture manufacturers, and retail customers. Over the years, however, the jobber market has evolved into a year-round market with a number of jobbers providing nationwide distribution. Jobbers, however, continue to select colors, designs, and fabrics that best meet their customers' needs. Like manufacturers and converters, jobbers put together sample books for their customers. In recent years, the jobber market has changed as jobbers have started providing a number of services, such as importing fabrics, creating exclusive in-house fabric designs, converting fabrics, and marketing fabrics through showrooms. "All of this has blurred the distinction between manufacturer and distributor as jobbers move into areas previously reserved for mills and converters" (Green, 1990, p. 4A). In fact, as some jobbers have turned to converting, some top converters have begun to perform jobbing functions.

MARKETING TOOLS

As in the apparel industry, companies in the home fashions industry use a variety of marketing tools to advertise and promote their products to their customers and to the ultimate consumers. These marketing tools include sample books (for home textiles), catalogs, print advertisements in trade and popular press publications, and television advertisements. Co-op advertising (see Chapter 8) helps to provide the links in consumers' minds between brand names, end-use products, and retailers. Electronic information interchange and the use of Web technology will continue to expand, opening new marketing possibilities for the entire soft goods pipeline. Business-to-business communication and Web-based commerce have opened new opportunities for marketing home fashions.

TRADE ASSOCIATIONS, TRADE SHOWS, AND TRADE PUBLICATIONS

Trade Associations

In both the ready-to-wear and the home fashions industries, there are trade associations for various textiles, general categories of merchandise, and specific aspects of the industry. Textile trade associations for home fashions are the same as those for fashion apparel. These include the American Textile Manufacturers Institute (ATMI), Cotton Incorporated, and the Wool Council (see Chapter 3 for a description of these trade associations). For example, Cotton Incorporated has been developing and promoting the use of cotton in home fashion products (see Figure 14.6). Cotton Incorporated's research department develops new products that are then adopted and produced by textile mills.

Sheets. Towels. Jeans. Underwear. When it comes to comfort, consumers everywhere look for cotton. Cotton. The fabric of our lives! www.cottoninc.com

Figure 14.6: Cotton Incorporated, a trade association, promotes the use of cotton fiber for the home fashions industry.

Cotton Incorporated also has developed cotton fabrics that can be used for upholstery, window treatments, wall coverings, table linens, and area rugs (Stapleton, 1994).

Some trade associations promote home furnishings or home fashions in general. Other trade associations focus on specific aspects of the industry. These trade associations, such as the Carpet and Rug Institute (CRI) and the Decorative Fabrics Association (DFA), assist in conducting market research and in promoting specific end uses or areas of the industry. Table 14.2 lists selected trade associations in the home fashions industry.

TABLE 14.2

Selected Trade Associations for the Home Fashions Industry

American Furniture Manufacturers
Association (AFMA)
P.O. Box HP-7
High Point, NC 27261
(336) 884-5000
Fax: (336) 884-5303
www.afmahp.org

Carpet and Rug Institute (CRI)
P.O. Box 2048
Dalton, GA 30722-2048
(706) 278-3176
(800) 882-8846
www.carpet-rug.com

International Furnishings and
Design Association (IFDA)
204 E Street, NE
Washington DC 20002
(202) 547-1588
Fax: (202) 547-6348
www.ifda.com

International Home Furnishings
Representatives Association
(IHFRA)
209 South Main, M-1215
P.O. Box 670
High Point, NC 27261
(336) 889-3920
(336) 883-8245
www.ihfra.org

National Association of Decorative
Fabrics Distributors (NADFD)
3008 Millwood Avenue

Columbia, SC 29205
(800) 445-8629
Fax: (803) 765-0860
www.nadfd.com

National Association of Floor
Covering Distributors (NAFCD)
410 North Michigan Avenue
Chicago, IL 60611-4267
(312) 321-6836
Fax: (312) 245-1085
www.nafcd.com

National Home Furnishings
Association (NHFA)
P.O. Box 2396
High Point, NC 27261
(800) 888-9590
Fax: (336) 883-1195
www.homefurnish.com/NHFA/
home.htm

Upholstered Furniture Action
Council (UFAC)
Box 2436
High Point, NC 97261
(336) 885-5065
Fax: (336) 885-5072
www.homefurnish.com/UFAC/

Window Coverings Association of
America (WCAA)
2339 Meadow Part Court
Maryland Heights, MO 63043-1518
(888) 298-WCAA
www.wcaa.org

Trade Shows

Trade shows that showcase products from the home fashions industry often cover a variety of other related markets as well. In addition, home fashions may be displayed in trade shows that focus primarily on other industries. For example, gift markets include some home fashions products. The Atlanta International Gift and Home Furnishings Market includes home accents, fine linens, and area rugs in addition to tabletop accessories, fine furnishings, and fine gifts. Design trade shows are attended by interior designers and architects as well as some professionals in the home fashions industry. One example is the Chicago Design Show, which is geared toward furniture, lighting, kitchen cabinets, and wall coverings as well as textiles, carpets, and bath products. Other trade shows focus on decorator fabrics, such as Heimtextil in Frankfurt, Germany. In addition to housing most manufacturer showrooms for home fashions, New York City is also the home of the New York Home Textiles Show. During market weeks, companies show samples of home textiles to jobbers, designers, manufacturers, and retailers.

Some of the home fashions markets are held in the same merchandise marts that house the apparel trade shows (such as the Chicago Merchandise Mart where the Chicago Design Show is held) and Dallas Market Center (where the Dallas National Gift and Home Accessories Show is held) (see Figure 14.7). On the other hand, the

Figure 14.7: Textiles are marketed to home fashions manufacturers at trade shows (left). The New York Home Textiles Show, held twice a year, is advertised as America's premier bed, bath, and linen show (right).

International Home Furnishings Market, held in High Point, North Carolina, is the largest home furnishings market in the United States and shows upholstery fabrics as well as furniture. Most of the markets for the home fashions industry are held twice a year. Table 14.3 lists selected trade shows for the home fashions industry.

Textile trade shows, such as the International Fashion Fabric Exhibition (IFFE) held in New York, include some suppliers of decorative fabrics used for home fashions, although most of the exhibitors are for fabrics used in apparel and accessory production.

TABLE 14.3

Selected Trade Shows for the Home Fashions Industry

***Trade Shows in the United States* (most of these markets occur twice a year, in the fall and spring)**

Atlanta International Gift and Home Furnishings Market, AmericasMart, Atlanta
   home accents, fine linens, fine furnishings, tabletop, fine gifts, area rugs

Chicago Design Show, Merchandise Mart, Chicago
   furniture, lighting, textiles, wall coverings, carpets, kitchen cabinets, bath products

Dallas National Gift and Home Accessories Show At Home section, Dallas Market Center, Dallas (January, March, June, and September)
   occasional furniture; lighting and lamps; home accessories such as vases, candlesticks, throw pillows, wall art; textiles and floor coverings; and related products

Decorex USA, Chicago
   residential design show

International Home Furnishings Market (Also called High Point Market), High Point, NC (October and April)
   largest home furnishings market in the U.S.

New York Home Textiles Show, Jacob K. Javits Convention Center, New York City
   bed and bath fashions, kitchen textiles, area rugs

New York International Gift Fair, At-Home division, Jacob K. Javits Convention Center, New York
   pillows, floor coverings, home furnishings, lighting and lamps, decorative accessories

New York Tabletop Market, New York Merchandise Mart or other locations, New York

San Francisco Home Furnishings Market Center, San Francisco
Showtime Fabric Fair, market buildings, High Point, NC
   decorator fabrics

(continued)

TABLE 14.3 (continued)

Selected Trade Shows for the Home Fashions Industry

International Trade Shows

Decorex International, various locations, London
   decorator fabrics

Decosit International Trade Fair, Expo Brussels, Brussels
   decorator fabrics

Focus, Chelsea Harbour Design Centre, London
   interior design, including decorator fabrics

Heimtextil, Frankfurt
   decorator fabrics

Heimtextil Americas, Miami Beach Convention Center, Miami, Florida
   contract and residential fabrics and finished products; caters mostly
   to Latin American audience

Heimtextil Asia, Hong Kong Convention and Exhibition Centre, Hong
Kong (November)
   decorator fabrics

Pitti Immagine Casa, Florence, Italy (September)
   linens for table, bath, bed, and kitchen; decorator fabrics; designer
   home collections; soft at-home wear

Maison et Objet, Paris, France (held twice a year)
   furniture, rugs, decorative lighting, home textiles

Salon Indigo: International Exhibiton of Design and Textile Production,
Parc des Expositions, Paris
   upholstery fabrics, home textiles

Trade Publications

Trade publications are an important source of information for professionals in the home fashions industry (see Figure 14.8). As with the apparel industry, some trade publications cover the entire industry, whereas others focus on specific aspects of the industry. See Table 14.4 for a listing of selected trade publications in the home fashions industry.

Production of Home Fashions

Price, value, and quality are key features sought by home fashions consumers. These features are related to the production of the product. Fast, efficient production can help to control costs. Chapter 11 discussed how quality must be built into the prod-

Figure 14.8: Trade publications provide important information to industry professionals.

TABLE 14.4

Selected Trade Publications for the Home Fashions Industry

BEDtimes: published monthly by the International Sleep Products Association, geared toward the mattress-manufacturing industry, its suppliers, and other sleep products trades.

Decorative Home: published monthly by Fairchild; retailers' guide to decorative accessories and home gifts.

FDM–Furniture Design and Manufacturing: published monthly by Chartwell Communication; articles on the furniture, bedding, and upholstering industries.

Floor Covering Weekly: published weekly by Hearst Business Publishing; geared to the flooring and interior surfacing product industry; reports news to floor covering retailers, contract dealers, distributors, and manufacturers.

(continued)

TABLE 14.4 (continued)

Selected Trade Publications for the Home Fashions Industry

Flooring: The Magazine of Interior Surfaces: published monthly by Douglas Publications; contains in-depth feature stories; the latest industry news; and information on all the latest products and services in areas such as wood flooring, ceramic tile, carpet, vinyl flooring, and accessories.

Home Accents Today: published monthly by Cahners Business Newspapers; merchandising and fashion news for the home accent industry; aimed at decorative accessory, specialty home accent, and major gift buyers shopping the major furniture markets in High Point, Dallas, Atlanta, and San Francisco and gift markets in New York, Los Angeles, Atlanta, Dallas, and Chicago.

HFN: (previously named *Home Furnishings News*) published weekly by Fairchild; news of the home fashions industry for retailers, wholesales, manufacturers, and suppliers; covers furniture, bedding, floor coverings, giftware, and housewares.

Home Fashions Magazine: published monthly by Fairchild; for the home textiles retailer.

Home Furnishings Executive: published monthly by National Home Furnishings Association; for the home furnishings retail trade.

Home Furnishings Review: published monthly by the Home Furnishings International Association; home furnishings industry information written by industry experts.

Home Textiles Today: published weekly by Cahners Business Information; covers the marketing, merchandising, and retailing of home textile products.

HomeMarket Trends: published bi-monthly by Lebhar-Friedman; covers the home fashions industry; includes furniture, bed and bath, table top and window treatments.

Interior Design: published monthly by Cahners Business Information; for professionals who design office, commercial, and residential interiors.

Upholstery Design & Manufacturing (UDM): published monthly by Chartwell Communications; covers information related to the design trends, fabrics, and manufacturing innovations of upholstery textiles and upholstered seating for the home, office, institutions, hospitality, and transportation industries.

Wall and Window Trends: published monthly by Cygnus Publishing.

Source: Ulrich's International Periodicals Directory, 2000.

uct throughout the production processes in the apparel industry. This is also true for home fashions. Quality assurance programs are an integral part of home fashions production facilities.

As indicated earlier, the home fashions industry includes a number of vertically integrated companies that produce not only the fabric but also the end-use product. To avoid increasing costs, some vertically integrated companies have ceased production of their own yarns. For example, a mill might save money by outsourcing yarn production rather than investing in new yarn facilities (Frinton, 1996). Some domestic apparel manufacturers turned to offshore production as a cost-saving procedure years ago. This trend has repeated itself in the home fashions industry. In recent years, some home fashions manufacturers have elected to cease domestic production, sourcing production in other parts of the world.

Quick Response strategies and supply chain management, which were discussed in previous chapters, are applicable to the home fashions industry as well. Home fashions companies will continue to upgrade their operations with product information management and computer integrated manufacturing. Building new information-processing systems has strained the resources of many companies, but these systems are crucial to remaining competitive in the home fashions industry (Page, 1999). Internet communication provides immediate access for fiber, fabric, trim, and findings suppliers; manufacturers and contractors; retailers; and consumers.

As in the apparel industry, fast delivery of raw goods from suppliers and quick turnaround time on production help speed the product to the retailer and ultimate consumer. Continued reduction in the lead time needed to produce goods will provide additional cost savings. Increased partnerships among segments of the industry, UPC bar coding, and floor-ready merchandise have allowed for faster delivery of products.

For example, Oriental Weavers, a rug supplier in the area rug business, has developed a quick-ship program called "10 Days to Success," which provides for 10-day delivery to retailers of the company's 20 best-selling machine-made rugs. Another rug supplier, Capel, has implemented a program known as "Zip Ship," which promises that if an order is received by 10 A.M., any rugs in stock will be shipped out the next business day. For custom rugs, Masland, a Mobile, Alabama, area rug supplier has implemented "ZAP," a quick-delivery program that promises delivery of custom area rugs in two weeks.

End-Use Categories

As stated earlier, the home fashions industry is divided into four general end-use categories: upholstered furniture coverings and fillings; window and wall coverings; soft floor coverings, including area rugs, scatter rugs, and runners; and bed, bath, tabletop, and other textile accessories and accents. Coordinated ensembles among categories have become popular. The same or coordinated textiles produced by one textile manufacturer might be used for the upholstered furniture, window treatments, bedding, and wall coverings for an entire room. Waverly has been at the forefront of providing consumers with a coordinated, total home look by producing coordinated bed linens, bath rugs, shower curtains, laminated fabrics, lamp shades, and other products. Coordinated prints, stripes, plaids, and monochrome cotton fabrics are produced by Laura Ashley, in addition to coordinating wallpaper, lamp shades, ceramic tile, and tableware. For children's nurseries, Daisy Kingdom in Portland, Oregon, manufacturers complete lines of coordinated cotton and cotton/polyester fabrics for window treatments, bedding, and apparel.

UPHOLSTERED FURNITURE COVERINGS AND FILLINGS

Upholstery fabrics for home fashions are used primarily for sofas, love seats, chairs, and ottomans (see Figure 14.9). Textiles used for upholstery fabrics are made from many natural and manufactured fibers. Before the development of manufactured fibers, wool, cotton, and linen were the most prevalent fibers used in upholstered home fashions. Silk has been used less frequently for upholstery, due to its cost, care requirements, and delicate structure. Manufactured fibers, particularly nylon, are commonly used in today's market. Fiber companies in the United States known for producing fibers for upholstery fabrics include BASF, Cytec, DuPont, Hoechst Celanese, and Monsanto. In recent years, olefin (also known as polypropylene or polyolefin) has made gains in the upholstery market, and cotton has regained some of its importance. Rayon blends for upholstery fabrics are experiencing growth in sales.

The performance characteristics of wool and cotton fibers are highly valued for some types of upholstered home fashions. The rising cost of these natural fibers lowered their market share in comparison to the less-expensive manufactured fibers. Currently, the high-end market uses a higher percentage of natural fibers than the moderate and mass markets.

Figure 14.9: Upholstery fabrics create an important part of the atmosphere for the home.

Fabric structure is another important consideration for upholstery. The durability of a fabric is affected by its fabric structure. For example, twill weaves are very durable. While both pile and nonpile fabrics are used for upholstery, nonpile fabrics are preferred for heavy-use upholstered items, such as family room sofas.

Some upholstery fabrics are coated with a backing substance to enhance end-use properties such as durability. Protective finishes are often provided for upholstery fabrics. One of the protective finishes most recognized among consumers is Visa by Milliken, a soil release finish (see Figure 14.10). DuPont developed "Teflon Hydrophyllic Stain Release that protects fabrics by combining stain-release properties with moisture transport" (Rothstein, 1999, p. 8). In this way, stains can be absorbed into the fabric, rather than beading up on the fabric surface.

The price range for upholstery fabrics is broad. Some upholstery fabrics are created and sold to the high-end market segment. Striking high-end fabrics created under the Jack Lenor Larsen name are innovative in color and texture.

Over-the-counter upholstery fabrics (sold at fabric stores) provide a source for individuals who wish to create their own home fashions. Consumers enjoy the opportunity to coordinate their home fashions from the broad choice of materials offered over the counter. Textile converters such as Waverly sell decorator fabrics over the counter to individuals as well as to manufacturers. Thus, individuals who wish to create their own home fash-

Figure 14.10: Soil resistant finishes are often applied to fabrics used for upholstery or table linen fabrics.

ions have access to some of the same fabrics used in manufactured home fashions.

WINDOW AND WALL COVERINGS

Window treatments consist of draperies, curtains, and fabric shades as well as decorative treatments such as valances, cornices, and swags. Curtains are typically described as "sheer, lightweight coverings that are hung without linings" (Yeager & Teter-Justice, 2000, p. 261), whereas draperies are described as "heavy, often opaque and highly patterned coverings usually hung with linings" (Yeager & Teter-Justice, 2000, p. 261). Curtains might be combined with draperies for home use, providing both decorative and functional purposes. During the day, sheer curtains allow diffused light into a room while providing some privacy. At night, opaque draperies can be drawn for total privacy and increased warmth. In recent years, fabric valances, cornices, and swags have seen a resurgence as popular window treatments.

Customers feel more confident about changing window treatments than about changing more expensive items of home decor. Thus, the category of window treatments is a very popular segment of home fashions. However, the display of window treatments in retail stores is a challenge because window treatments require substantial floor space. In addition, the presentation of the window treatment at retail greatly influences its sales success (Abend, 1997).

The fibers and fabrics used for curtains and draperies must withstand more exposure to heat and sunlight than many other textile products. Some manufactured fibers, such as nylon and polyester, withstand environmental exposure better than natural fibers, such as silk and cotton. Linen and wool, at one time quite commonly used for window coverings, are now used only occasionally. Manufactured fibers such as rayon, acrylic, nylon, and polyester fibers are typically used in blends with other fibers for window treatments. The ease of care of manufactured fibers and blends that combine natural with manufactured fibers is another important consideration for many consumers. Figure 14.11 gives a sense of the wide variety of fabrics available for home fashions.

There are many similarities in the design, development, and production processes of apparel products and home fashions. However, one of the differences is the length of time the home fashion producers want fabric lines to be available for reorders compared to the time wanted by apparel producers. Home fashions producers want the fabric lines to be available for several seasons, whereas many of the fabric lines used by apparel producers change every season. For those home fashions producers, such as window treatment companies, who use some of the same fabrics used by the apparel industry, this presents a problem.

Figure 14.11: A variety of colors and textures adds an inviting fashion appeal to bedding and window coverings.

Therefore, selection of fabric lines that will remain in production for several seasons is critical to the window treatment producers.

A variety of textiles is used for **wall coverings** and vertical panels and partitions. Fabric used as a wall covering can provide a room with a cozy ambiance or an elegant distinctiveness. There are various techniques for applying fabrics to wall surfaces. A tightly woven material with a sturdy fabric structure will withstand the tension needed to provide a smooth fabric surface. Cotton is one of the easiest and most versatile fabrics for use as a wall covering. Luxurious visual statements can be made with velvet or moiré fabrics; however these fabrics are more challenging to mount. Silk fabrics function best as wall coverings if they are first quilted or laminated to a backing fabric to stabilize them.

SOFT FLOOR COVERINGS

Soft floor coverings include wall-to-wall carpeting, area rugs, runners, and scatter rugs. This discussion of the end-use category will focus on area floor coverings (area rugs, runners, and scatter rugs). Area floor coverings are produced in a wide variety of fibers and blends. For kitchens and bathrooms, cotton, polyester, and nylon fibers are most typical. Ease of cleaning is an important consideration to the consumer for bath and kitchen area rugs. Bedroom area floor coverings might consist of natural fibers, including wool and cotton, manufactured fibers, or blends of fibers.

For other areas of the home, such as the living room, family room, and dining room, a wide variety of fibers is available. Fibers used for area floor coverings include nylon, polyester, olefin, wool, and cotton, as well as sisal, jute, and other natural plant materials. Companies in the United States that produce manufactured fibers used in carpets and rugs include DuPont Nylon Furnishings, BASF, and Hoechst Celanese.

Area floor coverings might be laid atop a hardwood floor or carpeting. A variety of sizes for area rugs and runners provide many home fashions options (see Figure 14.12). Scatter rugs are usually small, for example 2 by 3 feet or 3 by 5 feet. Area rugs tend to be larger, in sizes such as 8 by 11 feet or 11 by 14 feet. Runners are long and narrow because they are designed for hallways or entries.

Some area floor coverings are made by machine, in a process similar to that used for carpet manufacturing. The design and texture of an area rug is often determined during the production stage by varying the colors and types of yarns used or by varying the weaving or fabrication techniques. Multicolor effects can be achieved by applying the same

Figure 14.12: A golf rug includes textured sand traps, serving as a source of entertainment as well as an area floor covering.

dye color to a yarn composed of different fibers, producing a heather effect. Continual improvements in technology in carpet and rug production have increased the variety of patterns and textures available to the consumer. For example, Regal Rugs has 25-yarn systems that allow the company to create different multilevel surfaces, colors, and textures in rugs ranging from basic bath rugs to high-fashion accent rugs (Johnson, 1996).

Several other production methods are used to create hand-woven, braided, hooked, crocheted, knotted, or embroidered area floor coverings. Many ethnic floor coverings are produced by hand processes. Both the ethnic design and hand processes add an exotic flavor to home fashions.

BED, BATH, TABLE, AND OTHER TEXTILE ACCESSORIES AND ACCENTS

Textile accessories and accents include the following:

- Textile bedding products, including sheets and pillowcases, blankets, bedspreads, quilts, comforters, and pillows (see Figure 14.13).
- Textile products for the bath, including towels, bath rugs and mats, and shower curtains.

- Textile accessories for tabletops, including tablecloths, napkins, table runners, and place mats.
- Textile products for the kitchen, including towels, dishcloths, hot pads, and aprons.
- Textile accents, such as textile wall hangings, tapestries, quilts, needle-work accents, and lace accents.

The term **linens** refers to towels, sheets, tablecloths, napkins, and other home textiles once made almost exclusively from linen. Although these products are rarely made from linen anymore, they are commonly still referred to as linens.

Figure 14.13: Bedding includes sheets as well as mattress covers and top-of-the-bed items such as comforters, duvet covers, blankets, bedspreads, dust ruffles, pillow shams, and throws.

Bedding and Bath

Cotton fiber has an estimated 60 percent share of the sheet industry. Most sheets are made from a blend of cotton and polyester (often 50 percent of each fiber). A number of companies also offer 100 percent cotton sheets. In recent years, wrinkle-free, all-cotton sheets have become popular. Several luxury producers offer linen and silk sheets.

Percale and flannel are the most typical fabric structures for sheets. Satin, sateen, and jacquard weaves are available for the specialty market. Knit fabric, especially cotton jersey knit, is another option for sheets. Eyelet trims, contrast piping, and scalloped edging are used as embellishments.

Besides fiber content and fabric structure, woven sheets are distinguished by their **thread count** and their size. Thread count refers to the total number of *threads* or yarns in one square inch of fabric. The most typical thread counts range from 200 to 300. A higher thread count tends to signify a softer fabric. Sheets are available in crib, twin, double, queen, and king sizes corresponding to standard bed sizes.

The **top-of-the-bed** category includes comforters, duvet covers, blankets, bedspreads, dust ruffles, pillow shams, and throws. This category has been growing in recent years as consumers strive for a coordinated look in bed and bath decoration. Bedspreads are made from a variety of fabrics and in a variety of styles, including quilted fabrics. Quilts and comforters typically are made from multicomponent fabrics and filled with down, feathers, fiberfill, or other materials.

The infant-and-juvenile bedding category has grown in recent years. Licensed printed goods are spurring the market. Disney products, featuring characters such as Mickey and Minnie Mouse, and Looney Tunes products with characters such as Bugs Bunny are examples. Mary-Kate and Ashley Olsen, twin television stars, have licensed their name to West Point Stevens to produce a line of bedding for the young teen segment of this market (see Figure 14.14). There are specialty trade shows and associations for the juvenile market. The International Juvenile Products Show at Dallas' International Apparel Mart is the largest trade event for specialty baby-to-teen retailers. The show includes furniture, bedding, and decorative accessories. One of the leading trade associations for this segment of the market is The Juvenile Products Manufacturers Association.

In the bath market, cotton is by far the dominant fiber with an estimated 95 percent share (see Figure 14.15). Terry cloth is by far the most popular fabrication for towels. The yarns forming the loops of terry cloth are generally all cotton to enhance moisture absorbency for drying purposes. The warp and weft yarns that form the base weave structure that holds the loops in place might consist of a blend of cotton with a small percentage of polyester for increased durability. When sheared on one side, the terry cloth fabric is called *velour*.

Figure 14.14: Licensed products, such as the Mary-Kate and Ashley Olsen line of bed linens, licensed to West Point Stevens, are a part of the business for home fashions geared to the young teen segment of the juvenile market.

Towel size is a product feature that can provide market appeal. For years, towel sizes were standardized. Then, longer towels became popular at luxury hotels and spas. Soon manufacturers began to offer a variety of towel lengths at various price points for the retail market.

Market research on customer preferences contributes valuable information to both producers and retailers. What are the factors customers consider to be the most important for their towel-purchasing decisions? A survey conducted by *Home Furnishings News* asked respondents to rank the importance of specified factors in their bath towel buying decisions. Respondents felt that absorbency was the most important factor, rating it

Figure 14.15: In the bath market, cotton is by far the dominant fiber.

slightly more important than softness (see Table 14.5). Brand name ranked as a relatively unimportant factor (seventh) in the buying decision. While the bath towel's absorbency was rated as the most important buying factor, the towel's ability to dry quickly was ranked as eighth in importance ("Get back to basics," 1999). The vice president of advertising and sales from Fieldcrest Cannon was quite surprised by the results of this survey. "In all my 31 years in home textiles, I've never seen a consumer survey on towels in which color was not number one" ("Get back to basics," 1999, p. 7). This underscores the importance of market research.

A wide variety of coordinating bath mats contributes to an increase in sales in the bath category. The surge in the bath market coincided with a similar increase in popularity of coordinated kitchen towels, dishcloths, oven mitts, pot holders, and aprons.

TABLE 14.5

Most Important Factors in Buying Bath Towels

Buying factor	Percent of respondents
Absorbency	26.0
Softness	23.8
Fiber content (cotton, polyester)	12.8
Price	11.8
Style (pattern/design/color)	9.3
Size	9.3
Brand name	2.5
Quick dry	1.3
Other	9.3

*Multiple responses resulted in percentages totaling more than 100.

Source: Get back to basics with bath towels. (1999, September 27). ***HFN***, p. 7.

Textile Accessories for Tabletop and Kitchen

Textile accessories for the tabletop include tablecloths, napkins, place mats, and table runners. The terms **napery** and **table linens** are both used to refer to tablecloths and napkins. Tabletop accessories can protect the finish of fine wood tables and can enhance the warmth and visual theme of a dining room (see Figure 14.16). Therefore, many fibers and fabrics that provide visual appeal are used in tabletop accessories. One especially important feature for tabletop accessories is that they be easy to care for. For example, Milliken applies a soil-release finish to table linens to increase their performance. Tabletop accessories are available in a variety of sizes to fit a wide range of table shapes and sizes.

Figure 14.16: Table linens provide visual appeal as well as protection for table surfaces.

Labeling laws require that the "cut size" given on labels on tablecloths must be the dimensions of the finished product.

Textile accessories for the kitchen include towels, dishcloths, pot holders, oven mitts, and aprons. As with other textile accessories, both appearance and performance characteristics are important determinants for fiber and fabric choices.

Distribution and Retailing of Home Fashions

Home fashions constitute an important segment of the retail industry. Discount retail stores, such as Wal-Mart, Target, and Kmart, are the dominant players in the retailing of home fashions. Sears has expanded its efforts to capture a larger market share in home furnishing by creating its Home Solutions stores, the first of which opened in Denver, Colorado. These stores are stocked with floor coverings, window, bed and bath fashions, and products for kitchens, bathrooms, and home entertainment (Abend, 1997, p. 44).

Bed, bath, window and wall coverings, floor coverings, and upholstered furniture provide substantial sales for department stores. Specialty stores, including chains such as Eddie Bauer Home and Strouds, are an expanding retail segment. Three of the largest specialty home retailers are Bed Bath & Beyond, Linens 'n Things, and the Home Place.

Direct marketing companies such as Lands' End Coming Home, Spiegel, Pottery Barn, Domestications, The Linen Source, The Company Store, Garnet Hill, and Crate and Barrel fill another market niche. Some direct marketing companies also operate retail stores. Electronic and television retailing are other distribution venues.

Consumers are currently updating the decor of their home environments more frequently by changing the decorative fabrics used in their homes. In light of this trend, the retailing of home fabrics has grown in recent years. Some stores, such as Calico Corners, headquartered in Kennett Square, Pennsylvania, focus entirely on home fabrics. For other fabric stores, an increasing percentage of their business comes from home fabrics. In response to this growing demand for over-the-counter home fabrics, a number of home furnishing fabric suppliers, such as Waverly, Regal, Dan River, Concord Fabrics, and Springs Industries, have increased their attention to the over-the-counter home textiles business.

Jo-Ann Stores, based in Hudson, Ohio, is the largest fabric and craft retailer in the United States. The Martha Stewart Home decorator fabric produced by P/Kaufmann is sold at Jo-Ann Stores as well as Calico Corners (see Figure 14.17).

Social and Environmental Responsibility

The soft goods industry thrives on change at a fast pace. This can lead to a public perception that it is an industry that encourages waste. As a society, we discard many products long before their full potential for use is exhausted. In recent years, the industry has focused on social and environmental responsibility in all phases of the product use cycle. The home fashions industry has been a leader in efforts to promote **sustainable design** (also called *green design*), a term used to designate the "awareness of the full short- and long-term consequences of any transformation of the environment" (DesignTex, 1995, p. 53). Sustainable design encompasses the concept that the creation, use, and discarding of a product should not cause harm to the ecosystem (see Figure 14.18). Sustainable design efforts include the following examples from the fiber stage through the discard stage:

Figure 14.17: Jo-Ann Stores, one of the largest fabric and craft retailers in the United States, markets Martha Stewart Home decorator fabrics.

- Naturally grown fibers, such as cotton and ramie.
- Humanely sheared, free-range sheep.
- Yarn blended for user comfort and compostability.
- Environmentally compatible dyes and chemicals.
- Elimination of pollutants used in textile manufacturing.
- Use of recycled components (e.g., fibers) in textile manufacturing.
- Elimination of toxic vapors emitted during production or product use (such as formaldehyde on fabric wall coverings).
- Biodegradability or reuse of postconsumer products.

Several years ago DesignTex, based in New York City, created an environmentally responsible line of textiles that meets the sustainability guidelines (DesignTex, 1995). William McDonough and Michael Braungart designed a fabric collection for upholstered furniture. Their first collections utilized fabrics made from a blend of wool and ramie, both natural fibers. "This guaranteed that the fabric would be compostable and so operate in a closed loop organic life-cycle" (DesignTex, 1995, p. 62). Working with an independent environmental research institute in Germany and an environmental chemist, DesignTex selected dyes that used no toxins. The textile mill selected to manufacture the fabric improved its manufacturing processes to conform to McDonough's design principles and criteria. McDonough

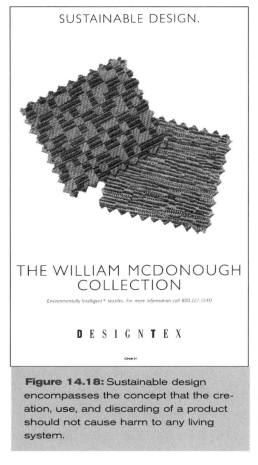

SUSTAINABLE DESIGN.

THE WILLIAM MCDONOUGH COLLECTION

Environmentally Intelligent™ textiles. For more information call 800.221.1540

D E S I G N T E X

Circle 31

Figure 14.18: Sustainable design encompasses the concept that the creation, use, and discarding of a product should not cause harm to any living system.

calls this "the Second Industrial Revolution. What we're now saying is that environmental quality must be an integral part of the design of every product" (DesigntTex, 1995, p. 65). The fabric is named Climatex Lifecycle, and is priced similarly to other high-end wool fabrics.

Another company, Park B. Smith, headquartered in New York City, produces an Eco-ordinates line of bedding, bath, window, rugs, table linens, and kitchen products (see Figure 14.19). This line is advertised as:

■ Using color extracted from plants, flowers, barks, seeds, and vegetables using authentic, centuries old dyeing techniques.

■ Containing all natural, vegetable dyed 100 percent cotton home fashions that protect the beauty of the earth.

■ Making an ecological statement.

Their fabric lines are named to reflect their ecological philosophy as well, for example, a plaid pattern is named Eco-Horizons.

Another approach is to recycle postconsumer materials into new products, rather than creating a new fabric. Wellman has been the world's largest recycler of plastic bottles, particularly soft drink bottles, since 1979. Plastic bottles are transformed into a fiber, Fortrel EcoSpun. This fiber is used for carpets and filling for pillows and comforters. Wellman teamed up with Carlee Corporation, a premier producer of polyester fiberfill, and create EcoFil, made from recycled material ("Fiberfill that is recycled," 1993). Some users of EcoFil claim that it is superior to virgin fiberfill.

Figure 14.19: The Eco-ordinates line features fabrics for bedding, bath, window, rug, table linens, and kitchen products that reflect the company's ecological philosophy.

The home fashions industry provides many other examples of sustainable design. Local, regional, and national network directories offer databases of references to locate product manufacturers that utilize recycled materials.

The retailer may play an additional part in a product's life cycle. Some retailers offer convenient home pickup and recycle options for the discarded product consumers who have purchased a new product. At the time a new mattress is delivered to the consumer, the old mattress might be picked up by the retailer's delivery crew and recycled.

Life cycle evaluation of products from the producer's, the retailer's, and the consumer's points of view will continue to be an important component in the home fashions industry. It may add complexity and cost to the design-manufacture-market-consume process, but sustainable design is important to future success in business.

Other forms of socially responsible behavior in the industry include community development efforts by local and national companies. For example, Atlanta-based Home Depot was commended for its willingness to help out after natural disasters. The

80,000-employee home improvement chain deploys teams of volunteers to help repair homes damaged by hurricanes, floods, earthquakes, and other disasters. It also donates supplies, conducts on-site, do-it-yourself clinics, and declines to raise prices on supplies needed during such emergencies ("Home Depot wins community award," 1995, p. 8). This is just one example of a company that is committed to donating goods and fostering community volunteer involvement by its employees.

Our global marketplace provides opportunities to support economies throughout the world. New York-based Tufenkian Tibetan Carpets sells carpets made by Tibetan weavers using Tibetan wool and weaving techniques. The carpets are produced in Nepal, which neighbors Tibet, because political conditions make it impossible to export carpets from Tibet. By providing a marketing outlet for these beautiful products, the company helps ensure that traditional Tibetan carpets can continue to be produced. The weavers, both Nepalese and expatriate Tibetans, earn a livelihood with satisfactory working and living conditions, and Tufenkian provides a Montessori school for children at the factory site. To avoid pollution of the environment, the carpet washing is not done in Nepal, since pollution controls there are inadequate. This collaboration of producer/weaver, product, and marketer provides an example of social, economic, political, and environmental responsibility.

Summary

This chapter has focused on the home fashions industry, which includes four end-use categories: upholstered furniture coverings and fillings; window and wall coverings; soft floor coverings; and bed, bath, tabletop, and other textile accessories and accents. The design and performance of the textiles used for home fashions play a very important role in the success of the end use. That being the case, the textile industry is the base for the home fashions industry, which is dominated by vertically integrated textile companies that produce both fabrics and home fashion products. Production of home fashions is often highly automated and can be accomplished very efficiently within a vertical operation. Some home fashions, such as towels and rugs, come off the production line as finished goods, not needing further cutting and sewing to complete the product.

An understanding of the organization and operation of the home fashions industry in the broader context of apparel fashions is important for several reasons. In recent years, the apparel and home fashions industries have become more interrelated. Apparel companies such as Tommy Hilfiger, Joe Boxer, and Donna Karan have entered the home fashions market. Some well-known apparel designers have moved into home fashions through licensing agreements with textile mills and home fashions manufacturers. Other licensing agreements for children's home fashions include ones for cartoon and movie characters, sports teams, and toys.

Consumer demand for home fashions has been strong. Home fashions constitute an important segment of the retail industry. Discount retailers such as Wal-Mart, Target, and Kmart are dominant competitors in the retailing of home fashions. Other important home fashions merchants include department stores, specialty stores, direct marketing companies, off-price retailers, and television retailers such as QVC. Sales of over-the-counter fabrics for the home sewing industry are on an upswing.

Market research and color forecasting are conducted prior to developing the seasonal collections. The textile and trim designers who create innovative materials and the product designers who determine the form of the final end-use product consider many factors and work within many constraints. Important functional needs and performance criteria must be met. Some products must also meet safety standards set by law. Converters that print or finish fabrics to improve their performance play an important role in the production of textiles for home fashions. Often the converter contracts for specific finishing work with a variety of finishing plants.

The marketing process for home fashions is similar to the process used in the apparel industry that includes the use of manufacturers' showrooms, company sales representatives, trade shows, and advertising and promotion. However, the home fashion industry relies on converters and jobbers to perform marketing and distribution functions more frequently than does the apparel industry. The establishment of well-respected brand names such as Royal Velvet, Martex, and Burlington House is important in the marketing of home fashions. Trade associations, trade shows, and trade publications form an important network for promoting the home fashions industry.

In recent years, the industry has focused on social and environmental responsibility for all phases of the product use cycle. The home fashions industry has been a leader in efforts to promote sustainable design, encompassing the concept that the creation, use, and discard of a product not cause harm to the ecosystem. Efforts to practice sustainable design include procedures from the fiber stage through discarding of the product. In addition, some retailers have entered the arena by providing consumers with recycling services when new products are delivered to their homes.

As with the ready-to-wear and accessories industries, the home fashions industry includes a wide variety of career possibilities, from design to production to marketing and distribution.

Design Manager, Woven Bedding
HOME FASHIONS PRODUCTS COMPANY

Position Description
Supervise woven bedding design team in product development, color direction, and finished product for all retail channels of distribution.

Typical Tasks and Responsibilities
- Coordinate with design, sales, product development and outside resources to achieve goals and meet deadlines
- Responsible for maintaining a flow of woven and heat transfer prints for use in top of the bed and sheeting
- Provide leadership in color direction, design, and product development for top of the bed and sheeting products

Stylist, Sourced Product Development
HOME FASHIONS PRODUCTS COMPANY

Position Description
Responsible for assisting the design manager in the development of concepts, finished art, colorings, concept boards and vendor specification packages for sourced bed and bath products.

Typical Tasks and Responsibilities
- Assist design manager to develop concept boards
- Utilize CAD and graphics software to create finished art for textile prints
- Responsible for providing vendor specification packages for bed and bath products

CAREER PROFILES

Key Terms

decor

decorative fabric jobbers

home fashions

linen

napery

soft floor coverings

sustainable design

table linens

textile accessories and accents

thread count

top of the bed

upholstery fabrics

wall coverings

window treatments

Discussion Questions

1. What are three aspects of the home fashions industry that are similar to the ready-to-wear apparel industry and three aspects that are different? Why do these similarities and differences exist?

2. Select a home fashion product (e.g., towel, rug, sheets). Outline the process used in the design, production, marketing, and distribution of the product.

3. Select a home fashion product in your home that will need replacement sometime in the future. Discuss sustainable design criteria that might be used in the selection of the replacement product and the disposal of the used textile product.

References

Abend, Jules. (1997, October). Window treatments: Here's to sheers! *Bobbin*, pp. 37–44.

Blackwood, Francy. (1995, April 10). Name dropping. *HFN*, p. 25, 74.

DesignTex, Inc. (1995). *Environmentally Intelligent Textiles*. (2nd ed.). (#DT052495). Charlottesville, VA: Author.

Fiberfill that is recycled. (1993, May/June). *What's New in Home Economics*, p. 40.

Frinton, Sandra. (1995, November 20). Strength in baby bedding. *HFN*, pp. 19, 21.

Frinton, Sandra. (1996, February 22). The good news and the bad news. *HFN*, pp. 25, 30, 31.

Get back to basics with bath towels. (1999, September 27). *HFN*, p. 7–10.

Green, John. (1990, October 1). Call them decorative fabric distributors. *HFD*, p. 4A.

Herlihy, Janet. (1999, September 27). CAD/CAM advances fuel rug industry. *Home Furnishings' News*, pp. 19, 22.

Home Depot wins community award. (1995, December 4). *HFN*, p. 8.

The home fashions leader board. (1999, June). *Bobbin*, p. 52.

Johnson, Sarah. (1996, March 18). Regal develops new rug yarn. *HFN*, p. 23.

Musselman, Faye. (1999, September 20). Familiar textile brands provide sense of security. *HFN*, pp. 20–25.

Page, Melinda. (1999, October 18). Technology woes hurt 3 textile makers. *HFN*, pp. 10, 15.

Retailers duel for consumer dollars. (1999, January). *Bobbin*, pp. 18–22.

Richards, Kristen. (1999, October 18). Waverly Lifestyle 2000. *HFN*, p. 20.

Rothstein, Shari Lynn. (1999, August 23). Teflon for home textiles. *HFN*, p. 8.

Rudie, Raye. (1998, September). Seiren's new take on digital printing. *Bobbin*, pp. 20–30.

Rush, Amy J. (1996, February 19). 3M's Thinsulate coming to bedding. *HFN*, p. 6.

Stapleton, Maureen A. (1994, June 20). Cotton Inc. develops new home products. *HFD*, p. 32.

Verlodt, Patricia. (1999, August 30). Color trends: Technology, nostalgia are equal influences. *HFN*, p. 13.

Yeager, Jan, and Teter-Justice, Lara. (2000). *Textiles for Residential and Commercial Interiors*. (2nd ed.). New York: Fairchild Publications.

Yeager, Jan. (1988). *Textiles for Residential and Commercial Interiors*. New York: HarperCollins.

Glossary of Terms

advertising Strategy by which companies buy space or time in print, broadcast, or electronic media to promote their lines to retailers and consumers.

agile manufacturing Use of a combination of technologies that form an integrated, seamless exchange of information linking retailers and suppliers to the manufacturing facility. ([TC]^2, 1993; see Chapter 11)

ascot A long neck scarf worn looped at the neck.

atelier de couture Workrooms of haute couture designers and staff.

base pattern, block, or **sloper** Basic pattern in the company's sample size, without any style features, used as the starting point for creating a pattern for a new style.

bespoke Custom made apparel, especially men's tailored apparel.

bias The diagonal cut of fabric, or 45 degrees to the length or width of the fabric, used to produce better shaping of the fabric than a straight-grain cut.

block see **base pattern**.

blocking or **boarding** The application of heat to create the final shape in the finishing process for knit goods.

board of directors Chief governing body of a corporation; elected by the corporation's stockholders.

boarding see **blocking**.

boutique Specialty store that concentrates on designer price zone merchandise or unique merchandise distributed to only a few stores.

brand name Merchandise with a company label that is well-recognized by the public.

brand-name fiber Fiber sold under a specific trade name, e.g., *Lycra*® spandex.

brand position Strategy by which products are developed in alignment with the company's target customer and position in the market.

brand tier Strategy by which an apparel company offers brands in two or more price zones with each brand focusing on a specific price zone.

bridge jewelry Umbrella term for several types of jewelry including those make from silver, gold (14K, 12K, 10K), and less expensive stones; jewelry designed by artists using a variety of materials.

bundling The process of disassembling stacked cut fabric pieces and re-assembling them grouped by garment size, color dye lot, and quantity of units ready for production.

carryover A garment style repeated in a line from one season to the next.

chain store Retail organization that owns and operates several retail outlets that sell similar lines of merchandise in a standardized method and function under a centralized form of organizational structure.

classification Apparel may be categorized (classified) by the type of merchandise produced, by the wholesale prices of the products or brands, or by an industry classification system for government tracking.

clutch Handbags designed to be held (clutched) in the hand, but may have a strap that can be stored inside the bag.

collection A group of apparel items presented together to the buying public, usually by high fashion designers.

color control Color matching requirement for all like garments in a line and all their components such as knit collars and cuffs, buttons, thread, and zippers.

color forecasting Predictions of consumers' future color preferences and trends in textiles and apparel. Predictions are based on research conducted by color forecasters for companies and trade associations.

color stories Color palettes identified for each fashion season that represent the predictions of consumers' future color preferences.

colorway The variety of three or four seasonal color choices for the same solid or print fabric available for each garment style.

commercial match Contractor-provided acceptable match of color for fabric, trim, or finding to a control color chip or fabric provided by the apparel company.

computer-aided design (CAD) Both the hardware and software computer systems used to assist with the design phase of the fabric design or garment design.

computer aided design/computer aided manufacturing (CAD/CAM) The combination of computer systems that link pattern design, grading, marker making, cutting, and sometimes sewing operations.

computer grading and marker making (CGMM) The computer hardware and software systems that process the pattern grading and marker making segments of the pattern for production.

computer integrated manufacturing (CIM) The integration of an apparel company's CAD/CAM systems to form a common link of information throughout production to produce a finished product.

concept garment End-use garment created by a textile company to promote its new fibers to textile mills.

conglomerate Diversified company involved with significantly different lines of business.

consolidation The combining of two companies with the result being a new company.

consumer research Information gathered about consumer characteristics and consumer behavior including broad trends in the marketplace as well as more specific information about a target group of consumers.

contractor Company that specializes in the sewing and finishing of goods.

contractual retailer Retailer that has entered into a contractual agreement with a manufacturer, wholesaler, or other retailers in order to integrate operations and increase market impact.

controlled brand-name program or **licensed brand-name program** Marketing strategy whereby minimum standards of fabric performance for trademarked fibers are determined and promoted.

convenience store Retailer that offers fast service and convenient location.

conventional manufacturer A company that performs all functions of creating, marketing, and distributing an apparel line on a continual basis.

conventional marketing channel Independent companies that separately perform the manufacturing, distribution, and retailing functions.

converted goods or **finished goods** Fabrics that have been dyed, printed, or finished.

converter or **textile converter** Company that specializes in finishing fabrics.

co-op advertising A type of advertising strategy whereby companies share the cost of the advertisement that features all of the companies.

copyright The exclusive right of the copyright holder to use, perform, or reproduce written, pictorial, and performed work.

corporate selling Strategy by which apparel companies sell their merchandise directly to retailers without the use of sales representatives.

corporate show room Show room owned and operated by a single company to market its apparel lines; generally managed by company sales representatives.

corporation Company established by a legal charter that outlines the scope and activity of the company. Corporations are legal entities regardless of who owns stock in the company.

cost, wholesale cost, or cost to manufacture The total cost to manufacture a style, including materials, findings, labor, and auxiliary costs such as freight, duty, and packaging.

cost to manufacture see **cost**.

costing marker The layout of the pattern pieces for the prototype used to determine the yardage required for the new style (yardage is one of the factors required to calculate the cost).

costume jewelry Mass produced jewelry made from plastic, wood, brass, glass, lucite, and other less expensive materials.

cotton gin Machine that cleans cotton seed from the cotton fibers; invented in 1794 by Eli Whitney.

counter sample or **sew by** A sample garment sewn by a contractor and submitted to the apparel manufacturer for approval. This sample is then used as a benchmark to compare the sewn production goods.

counterfeit goods Products that incorporate unauthorized use of registered tradenames or trademarks.

couture A French term that literally means "high sewing," it refers to the highest priced apparel produced in small quantities, made of high quality fabrics utilizing considerable hand sewing techniques, and sized to fit individual clients' bodies.

couturier(ière) Designer of haute couture (couturier = masculine; couturiere = feminine).

Crafted With Pride in U.S.A. Council Trade association formed in 1984 to promote U.S.-made textiles and apparel.

croquis or **lay figure** A French term that refers to a figure outline used as a basis to sketch garment design ideas.

cross-merchandising Strategy by which apparel companies and retailers combine apparel and accessories in their product offerings.

customs broker A person in the United States, licensed by the Customs Office, to assist apparel manufacturers in gaining customs clearance to import goods produced offshore.

cut, make, and trim (CMT) Apparel contractors who cut, make, and trim the garments for the apparel manufacturer.

cut-up trade Belt manufacturers who produce belts for apparel manufacturers to add to their pants, skirts, and dresses.

data-mining technology Technology used by companies to analyze purchasing data to determine selling patterns or trends and identify correlations among data characteristics.

décor The interior decoration that creates a room's ambiance.

decorative fabric converters Companies that design and sell finished textiles to jobbers, designers, and manufacturers who use the textiles in home fashion end-use products.

decorative fabric jobbers Companies involved in the marketing and distribution of home textile piece goods, particularly upholstery and drapery fabrics.

demographics Information about consumers that focuses on understanding characteristics of consumer groups such as age, sex, marital status, income, occupation, ethnicity, and geographic location.

department store Large retailer that departmentalizes its functions and merchandise.

design development The process by which a new style moves from concept sketch to prototype.

die cutting A piece of metal with a sharp edge similar to a cookie cutter tooled to the exact dimensions of the shape of the pattern piece (the die). The die is positioned over the fabric to be cut; then a pressurized plate is applied to the die to cut through the fabric layers.

diffusion line A designer's less expensive line (e.g., Armani A/X, DKNY)

digitizer A table embedded with sensors that relate to the X and Y coordinates (horizontal and vertical directions) that allow the shape of the pattern piece to be traced and converted to a drawing of the pattern in the computer.

direct market or **store brand** Brand name on merchandise that is also the name of the retail store, e.g., Gap, L.L.Bean.

direct marketing channel Marketing channel by which manufacturers sell directly to the ultimate consumer.

discount store Retailer who sells brand name merchandise at below traditional retail prices including apparel at the budget/mass wholesale price zone.

distribution centers Centralized locations used by apparel companies and retailers for quality assurance, picking, packing of merchandise, and distribution to retail stores.

distribution strategy Business strategy to assure that merchandise is sold in stores who cater to the target market for whom the merchandise was designed and manufactured.

dividend Corporate profits paid to its stockholders; dividends are taxed as personal income.

draping A process of creating the initial garment style by molding, cutting, and pinning fabric to a mannequin.

dual distribution or **multichannel distribution** Distribution strategy whereby manufacturers sell their merchandise through their own stores as well as through other retailers.

duplicate or **sales sample** A copy of the prototype or sample style used by the sales representatives to show and sell styles in the line to retail buyers.

e-commerce Buying and selling of goods and services conducted via the Internet.

e-market Companies that "enable trading partners to conduct business over the Internet eliminating the need for more costly paper and custom EDI methods" (eMarkets, 2001, p. 4; see Chapter 12).

electronic data interchange (EDI) Computer-to-computer communications between companies.

electronic/Internet retailer Company that offers goods and/or services over the Internet or uses the Internet in addition to its stores and/or catalog retailing business.

Empire A dress with a raised waistline and a tubular silhouette, named for Napoleon's empire.

exclusive distribution Strategy whereby manufacturers limit the stores in which their merchandise is distributed in order to create an image of exclusiveness.

export agent A person located in the country that produced the goods who assists the (U.S.) apparel manufacturer with exportation of the products.

extended marketing channel Marketing channel in which wholesalers acquire products from manufacturers and sell them to retailers or jobbers buy products from wholesalers and sell them to retailers.

Fabric and Suppliers Linkage Council (FASLINC) Organization formed in 1987 to establish voluntary electronic data interchange standards between textile producers and their suppliers; disbanded in 1991.

fabric construction Methods used to make fabrics from solutions, directly from fibers, and from yarns; weaving and knitting are the most common methods.

factor An agency that provides protection against bad debt losses, manages accounts receivable, and provides credit analysis in the apparel industry.

factoring The business of purchasing and collecting accounts receivable or of advancing cash on the basis of accounts receivable ("The F Word," 1996, p. 1; see Chapter 9)

fallout The fabric that remains in the spaces between pattern pieces on the marker, representing the amount of fabric that is wasted.

fashion colors Colors used in a seasonal line that reflect the current color trends, determined by the apparel company for the target customer.

fashion forecasting service A company that predicts consumers' future style preferences and trends in textiles and apparel. Predictions are based on research conducted by its staff and other associations.

fashion magazines Magazines sold over-the-counter as well as by subscription whose primary focus is on the latest fashion trends.

fashion season Name given to lines or collections that correspond to seasons of the year when consumers would most likely wear the merchandise; e.g. spring, summer, fall, holiday, and resort.

fiber The basic unit in making textile yarns and fabrics.

filament yarns Yarns created by the spinning together long continuous fibers.

fine jewelry Jewelry made from precious metals alone and with precious and semi-precious stones.

finish "Anything that is done to fiber, yarn, or fabric either before or after weaving or knitting to change the appearance (what you see), the hand (what you feel), and the performance (what the fabric does)" (Hollen, Sadler, Langford, & Kadolph, 1988, p. 300; see Chapter 3).

finished goods see **converted goods**.

first adoption meeting Gathering when a new line is presented (often as sketches and fabric swatches) and each style in the line is reviewed by the design team.

fit model The live model whose body dimensions match the company's sample size and who is used to assess the fit, styling, and overall look of new prototypes.

flat or **flat sketch** Also called a tech drawing, this technical sketch of a garment style represents how the garment would look lying flat, as on a table. Garment details are clearly depicted.

flatknit Goods that are knit flat, as compared to goods knit in a tube (tubular knit).

flat pattern The pattern making process used to make a pattern for a new style from the base pattern (or block or sloper).

flat sketch see **flat**.

flexible manufacturing system (FMS) "Any departure from traditional mass production systems of apparel toward faster, smaller, more flexible production units that depend upon the coordinated efforts of minimally supervised teams of workers" (AAMA Technical Advisory Committee, 1988, as cited in Hill, 1992, p. 34; see Chapter 11).

floor ready merchandise (FRM) Merchandise shipped by the manufacturer or distribution center affixed with hangtags, labels, and price information so that the retailer can place the goods immediately on the selling floor.

fourchettes Strips for gloves used between the second/third, third/fourth, and fourth/baby fingers to provide depth for the thickness of the finger.

franchise A type of contractual retail organization whereby the parent company provides the franchisee with the exclusive distribution of a well-recognized brand name in a specific market area as well as assistance in running the business in return for a franchise payment.

freight forwarding company A company that moves a shipment of goods from the country where the goods were produced to the U.S.

full-fashioned Goods knit with shaping along the edges to conform to the body contour.

full-package Apparel contractor that provides a full package of service options including fabrics, trims, supplies, and labor.

garment dyed Apparel produced as white or colorless goods, then dyed during the finishing process.

garment specification sheet or **garment spec sheet** A listing of vital information for the garment style including garment sketch, fabric swatches and/or specifications, and specifications for findings, sizes, construction, and finished garment measurements.

general partnership Form of ownership in which co-owners of a company share in the liability as well as the profits of the company according to the conditions of the partnership contract.

generic family Classification of fibers according to chemical composition and characteristics.

grading or **pattern grading** Taking the production pattern pieces made in the sample size for a style and creating a set of pattern pieces for each of the sizes listed on the garment spec sheet.

grade rules The amounts and locations of growth or reduction for pattern pieces to create the various sizes.

greige goods Fabrics that have not received finishing treatments such as bleaching, shearing, brushing, embossing, or dyeing; unfinished fabrics.

group Coordinated apparel items using a few colors and fabrics within an apparel line.

hand How a fabric feels to the touch.

haute couture Also sometimes referred to as couture, apparel in the highest price zone. This apparel is produced in small quantities, utilizes hand sewing techniques, is sized to fit an individual's body dimensions, and uses very expensive fabrics and trims.

hide An animal pelt weighing more than 25 pounds when shipped to the tannery.

home fashions Textile products for home end uses such as towels, bedding, upholstery fabrics, area floor coverings, draperies, and table linens.

horizontally integrated Business strategy whereby a company focuses on a single stage of production/distribution but with varying products or services.

importer/packager Company that develops full lines of apparel with contractors in other countries and sells them to retailers as complete packages for use as private label merchandise.

initial cost estimate The preliminary estimate of the cost of a new style based on materials, trims, findings, labor, and other components such as duty and freight.

in-store shops Areas within department stores that are merchandised according to manufacturers' specifications and carry only the merchandise of the manufacturer.

intensive or **mass distribution** Strategy whereby products are made available to as many consumers as possible through a variety of retail venues.

International Ladies Garment Workers Union Formed in 1900, the primary union of garment workers in the women's apparel industry until 1995 when it combined with the Amalgamated Clothing and Textile Workers Union to form the Union of Needletrades, Industrial, and Textile Employees (UNITE).

item house Contractor that specializes in the production of one type of product such as baseball caps.

jobber An intermediary in the apparel industry who carries inventories of apparel for ready shipment to retailers.

kip Animal pelt weighing 15 to 25 pounds when shipped to the tannery.

knockoff A facsimile of an existing garment that sells at a lower price than the original. The copy might be made in a less expensive fabric and might have some design details modified or eliminated.

lab dip The vendor-supplied sample of the dyed-to-match product such as fabric, zipper, button, knit collar or cuff, or thread.

last A wood, plastic or metal mold, shaped like a foot and used to form shoes.

lay figure see **croquis**.

leased department Contractual retail agreement whereby a retailer leases space within a large department store to run a specialty department. Typical leased departments are fine jewelry, furs, and shoes.

leveraged buyout Purchase of a public corporation's stock by a group of investors who borrow money from an investment firm using the corporation's assets as collateral.

licensed brand-name program see **controlled brand-name program**.

licensing An agreement whereby the owner (licensor) of a particular image or design sells the right to use the image or design to another party, typically a manufacturer (licensee), for payment of royalties to the licensor.

licensor Company that has developed a well-known image (property) and sells the right to use the image to manufacturers to put on merchandise.

limited liability Arrangement whereby owners of a company are liable only for the amount of capital they invested in the company but are not personally liable beyond that for debts incurred by the business.

limited marketing channel Marketing channel in which manufacturers sell their merchandise to consumers through retailers.

limited partnership A specialized type of partnership in which a partner is liable only for the amount of capital invested in the business and any profits are shared according to the conditions of the limited partnership contract.

line One large group or several small groups of apparel items developed with a theme that links the items together.

line brochure or **line catalog** or **line sheet** A brochure or catalog of all the styles and colorways available in the line, used to market the line to retail buyers.

line catalog see **line brochure**.

line sheet see **line brochure**.

line-for-line copy A garment made as an exact replica of an existing garment style, produced in a similar fabric.

linens Towels, sheets, tablecloths, napkins, and other home textiles once made almost exclusively from linen, even though these products are rarely made from linen anymore.

long-range forecasting Research focusing on general economic and social trends related to consumer spending patterns and the business climate.

mail-order/catalog retailer Retail company that sells merchandise to consumers through catalogs, brochures, or advertisements, and delivers the merchandise by mail or other carrier.

manufacturing environment Production circumstances including choice of production facility, location of production, production process, and cycle time to produce goods.

maquiladora operations "Assembly plants, mostly along the U.S.-Mexico border, in which garments are assembled from U.S.-cut parts and shipped back to the United States (Dickerson, 1995, p. 189; see Chapter 10)."

marker A master cutting plan for all the pattern pieces in the sizes specified on the cut order to manufacture the style.

market 1) consumer demand for a product or service; 2) location where the buying and selling of merchandise takes place; 3) promote a product or service through media or public relations efforts.

market analysis Information about general market trends.

market center Name given to cities that not only house marts and showrooms but also have important manufacturing and retailing industries, e.g., New York, Los Angeles, Dallas, Atlanta, Chicago.

market niche Specific segment of the retail trade determined by a combination of product type and target customer.

market research Process of providing information to determine what the customer will need and want and when and where the customer will want to make purchases.

market week Time of the year in which retail buyers come to showrooms or exhibit halls to see the seasonal fashion lines offered by apparel companies.

marketing Process of identifying a target market and developing appropriate strategies for product development, pricing, promotion, and distribution.

marketing channel Sequence of companies that perform the manufacturing, wholesaling, and retailing functions to get merchandise to the ultimate consumer.

mart Building or group of buildings that house showrooms in which sales representatives show apparel lines to retail buyers.

mass customization The use of computer technology to customize a garment style for the individual customer, by individualizing the fit to the customer's measurements, by offering individualized combinations of fabric, garment style and size options, or by personalization of a finished product.

mass distribution see **intensive distribution**.

mass production Type of production in which identical apparel is made in large quantities using machines for production.

measurement specification The actual garment measurements at specific locations on the finished goods for each of the sizes specified for a style.

merchandiser 1) An apparel company employee who is responsible for planning and overseeing that the company's needs for a line are met. This person often coordinates several lines presented by the company, 2) one who visually displays merchandise within a retail store (visual merchandiser).

merchandising 1) The process of buying and selling goods and services, 2) area of an apparel company that develops strategies to have the right merchandise, at the right price, at the right time, at the right locations to meet the wants and needs of the target customer.

merger Blending of one company into another company.

millinery Women's hats, and especially hat making that requires hand work.

modular manufacturing A term often used in the U.S. apparel industry to describe flexible manufacturing (Hill, 1992, p. 34; see Chapter 11).

monopolistic competition Competitive situation in which many companies compete in terms of product type, but the specific products of any one company are perceived as unique by consumers.

monopoly Competitive situation when there is typically one company that dominates the market and can thus price its goods and/or services at whatever scale its management wishes.

mufflers Long oblong scarves, often wool or silk, worn as an accompaniment to an overcoat.

multichannel distribution see **dual distribution**.

multiline sales representative Individual who sells lines from several, non-competing but related companies to retail buyers.

muslin An inexpensive fabric, usually unbleached cotton, often used to develop the first trial of a new garment style.

napery or **table linens** Home fashions products that include tablecloths and napkins.

national/designer brand Brand name that is distributed nationally and to which consumers attach a specific image, quality level, and price.

nonstore retailer Distributor of products to consumers through means other than traditional retail stores.

North American Industry Classification System (NAICS) U. S. Department of Commerce categories and subcategories based on the company's chief industrial activity.

off-price retailer Retailer who specializes in selling national brands or designer apparel lines at discount prices.

offshore production Production outside the United States using production specifications provided by U.S. companies.

oligopoly Competitive situation in which a few companies dominate and essentially have control of the market, making it very difficult for other companies to enter.

open distribution policy Policy by which a company will sell to any retailer who meets basic characteristics.

ownership flow or **title flow** Transfer of ownership or title of merchandise from one company to the next.

partnership Company owned by two or more persons; operation of partnerships are outlined in a written contract or "articles of partnership."

patent "Publicly given, exclusive right to an idea, product, or process" (Fisher & Jennings, 1991, p. 595; see Chapter 2).

pattern design system (PDS) A computer hardware and software system that is used by the pattern maker to create and store new garment (pattern) styles.

pattern grading see **grading**.

payment flow Transfer of monies among companies as payment for merchandise or services rendered.

pelt The unshorn skin of an animal used in making leather and fur.

personalization The process of customizing a finished product.

physical flow Movement of merchandise from the manufacturer to the ultimate consumer.

piece-rate wage Method of compensation whereby each production operator's pay is based on individual productivity, that is, specified task completed by the operator on the total number of units in a given time period.

power loom Automated machine used to weave cloth. Francis Cabot Lowell invented the power loom in 1813.

preliminary line sheet Catalog of styles in a line used internally by a company in the process of line development.

preline A preview of the line shown to key retail buyers prior to its introduction at market. These accounts may place orders in advance of market.

price averaging A price strategy whereby one style will be priced to sell for less than the company's typical profit margin while another style in the same line will be priced to sell for more than the typical profit margin. The margin's gain and loss of the two styles are averaged.

private corporation Type of corporation whereby there is not a public market for the stock in the corporation and stock has not been issued for public purchase.

private label   Merchandise that includes a retailer's label on a product in which the retailer has some or full control of the manufacturing operation.

private label brand   Brand name that is owned and marketed by a specific retailer for use in its stores.

private label production development or **store brand product development**   Development of new styles by retailers to sell in their retail stores under a store brand label or private label.

product development department   Team of employees that 1) works from the concept stage through preparing the new style package ready for production or 2) develops the product after the designer and merchandiser have approved the new style for development.

product information management (PIM)   Electronic access to style information throughout the design, development, and manufacturing processes within a company and by external contacts such as vendors and contractors.

product research   Information gathered by a company regarding preferred product design and product characteristics desired by a specific customer group.

product type   the specific category or categories of apparel the company specializes in producing.

production   The construction process by which the materials, trims, findings, and garment pieces are merged into a finished apparel product, accessory, or home fashion.

production cutting   Process in which the production fabric, laid open across its entire width and many feet in length, is stacked in multiple layers with the marker resting on the top, and cut by computer or by using hand cutting machines.

production engineer   A specialist who is responsible for the production pattern and/or for planning the production process, facilities, and final costing.

production marker   The full size master cutting layout for all the pattern pieces for a specific style, for all the sizes specified for production.

progressive bundle system   Groups of a dozen (usually) garment pieces placed in bundles and moved from one sewing operator to the next. Each operator performs one or several construction steps on each garment in the bundle, then passes the bundle on to the next operator.

promotion flow   Flow of communication to promote merchandise either to other companies or to consumers in order to influence sales.

prototype or **sample**   The sample garment for a new style in the company base size made in the intended fashion fabric or a facsimile fabric. If made in muslin, the prototype is usually called a toile.

psychographics   Information gathered about a target group's buying habits, attitudes, values, motives, preferences, personality, and leisure activities.

publicly held corporation   Type of corporation whereby stock has been issued for public purchase and at least some of the shares of stock are owned by the general public.

publicity Promotional strategy whereby the company's activities are viewed as newsworthy and thus are featured or are mentioned in print, television, or other news media.

pull-down cutting The process of cutting gloves by die cutting the pieces.

pure competition Competitive situation in which there are many producers and consumers of similar products, so that price is determined by market demand.

quality assurance Area of a company that focuses on quality control issues but also takes into consideration satisfaction of consumer needs for a specific end use; standards of acceptance set forth by the contracting party (the apparel manufacturer, for example) for the product being produced.

quality control Area of a company that focuses on inspecting finished products and making sure they adhere to specific quality standards.

Quick Response Comprehensive business strategy that promotes responsiveness to consumer demand, encourages business partnerships, and shortens the business cycle from raw materials to the consumer.

quirk Tiny triangular gusset in gloves at the base of the second, third, and fourth fingers.

quotas Limits on the number of units, kilograms, or square meters equivalent in specific categories that can be imported from specific countries.

rack trade Belt manufacturers who design, produce, and market belts to retailers.

radio-frequency identification chip (RFIC) A silicon chip attached to an antenna that utilizes radio frequency identification technology. The chip is incorporated into a garment label and used for purposes such as to sort laundry, log number of times a uniform has been laundered, or to deter hijacking and shoplifting.

ready-to-wear (RTW) Apparel made with mass production techniques using standardized sizing; sometimes referred to as "off-the-rack."

regimental stripe Fabric used for men's ties with wide and narrow stripes that were used originally to signify the various historical military regiments.

regional sales territory Geographic area assigned to be covered by a corporate or multiline sales representative.

regular tannery Tannery that buys skins and hides, performs tanning methods, and sells finished leather.

relationship merchandising A refocusing of department stores with an emphasis on presentation, customer service, and having the right products for their target market that are different from the products carried by other stores.

retailer "Any business establishment that directs its marketing efforts toward the final consumer for the purpose of selling goods and services" (Lewison, 1994, p. 5; see Chapter 12).

Retro The return to the fashion look of recent decades (abbreviated use of the word retrospective).

sales representative Individual who serves as the intermediary between the apparel manufacturer and the retailer, selling the apparel line to retail buyers.

sales sample see **duplicate**.

sales volume The actual level of sales, expressed as either the total number of units of a style that sold at retail or the total number of dollars consumers spent on the style.

salon de couture Haute couture designer's showroom.

sample see **prototype**.

sample cut A three-to-five yard length of fabric ordered from a textile mill by the apparel manufacturer to use for making a prototype garment.

sample sewer A highly skilled technician who sews the entire prototype (sample) garment using a variety of sewing equipment and production processes similar to those used in factories.

sample sewing department The team of highly skilled technicians who cut and sew new style samples.

selected distribution policy Policy by which a company establishes detailed criteria that stores must meet in order for them to carry the company's merchandise.

selective distribution Strategy whereby manufacturers allow their merchandise to be distributed only through certain stores.

sell through The percentage computed by the number of items sold at retail compared to the number of items in the line the retailer purchased from the manufacturer.

sew by see **counter sample**.

sewing machine Through inventions of Walter Hunt (1832), Elias Howe (1845), and Isaac Singer (1846), this machine made it possible for apparel to be made quickly and in factory settings.

shopping the market Looking for new fashion trends in the retail markets that may influence the direction of an upcoming line.

short-cycle production Mass production of goods that can be produced quickly. It is especially suited to high fashion products that are produced close to their market demand.

short-range forecasting Researching specific fashion trends and new styles for an upcoming season and determining the level of demand and timing for these styles (also referred to as what, when, and how much to manufacture).

show room Room(s) used by sales representatives to show samples of a line to retail buyers; may be permanent or temporary.

single-hand system A garment production method in which an individual sewer is responsible for sewing an entire garment. It is used primarily for couture or very high-priced, limited production apparel and for sewing prototypes.

size standards Proportional increase or decrease in garment measurements for sizes produced by a ready-to-wear apparel company.

skin Animal pelt weighing 15 pounds or less when shipped to the tannery.

sloper see **base pattern**.

Smart Card Personal data, such as a customer's body measurements, stored on a computer-read card, about the size of a credit card, that is used for mass customization orders.

soft floor coverings Area rugs, runners, and scatter rugs, as well as wall-to-wall carpeting.

sole proprietorship Company owned by a single individual.

source or **supplier** or **vendor** Company from which textile producers, apparel manufacturers or retailers purchase components or products necessary in their production and distribution operations (e.g. fiber sources, fabric sources, apparel product sources).

sourcing Decision process of determining how and where a company's products or their components will be produced.

specialty store Retailer who focuses on a specific type of merchandise.

specification buying Retailer-initiated design and manufacturing of apparel goods in which the retailer may work directly with the sewing contractors (or their agents) to produce store brand or private label goods. Sometimes the retailer works with an apparel manufacturer to produce store brand or private label goods.

spinning mill Company that specializes in the spinning of yarn. The first spinning mill in the U.S. opened in 1791 by Samuel Slater.

spreading The process of unwinding the large rolls of fabric onto long, wide cutting tables, stacked layer-upon-layer, in preparation for cutting.

spreading machines Equipment designed to carry the large rolls of fabric, guided on tracks along the side edges of the cutting table, to spread the fabric smoothly, and quickly.

spun yarns Yarns created by the spinning together short staple fibers.

staple colors Colors such as black, navy, white, gray, and tan, that are used in a line that appear constantly or frequently, season after season.

stockholder Owner of stock or shares in a corporation; each share of stock owned by a stockholder represents a percentage of the company.

store brand see **direct market brand**.

store brand product development see **private label product development**.

strike off A length of sample yardage of a printed fabric, used to proof the colors and quality of the print.

style number A number (usually 4 to 6 digits) assigned to each garment style that is coded to indicate the season/year for the style and other style information.

Sundries and Apparel Findings Linkage Council (SAFLINC) Formed in 1987 to establish voluntary electronic data interchange standards between apparel manufacturers and their non-textile suppliers. In 1994 it was integrated into the Quick Response Committee of the American Apparel Manufacturers Association.

supermarket Retailer who carries a full line of foods and related products using a self-service strategy.

superstore Up-graded large supermarkets.

supplier see **source**.

supply chain management "Collection of actions required to coordinate and manage all activities necessary to bring a product to market, including procuring raw materials, producing goods, transporting and distributing those goods and managing the selling process" (Abend, 1998, p.48; see Chapter 1).

sustainable design A term used to designate the "awareness of the full short- and long-term consequences of a transformation of the environment" (DesignTex, 1995, p. 53; see Chapter 14).

swatch A small sample of the fabric intended to be used for a garment style.

table linens see **napery**.

table cutting The process of cutting gloves entirely by hand, on a work table.

tagboard A heavy weight paper (also called oaktag or hard paper) used for pattern pieces instead of pattern paper.

takeover The result of one company or individual gaining control of another company by buying a large enough portion of the company's shares; can be either a merger or consolidation.

tannery see **regular tannery.**

tanning The process of finishing leather, making the skins and hides pliable and water resistant.

target costing A pricing strategy in which the fabric cost and styling features are manipulated in order to provide a new style for a pre-determined cost.

target customer Description of the gender, age range, lifestyle, geographic location, and price zone for the majority of the company's customers for a specific line.

tariffs Taxes assessed by governments on imports.

tawning The process of finishing furs making the pelts pliable and water resistant.

tech drawing A drawing of the garment style as viewed flat rather than depicted three-dimensionally on a fashion figure (an abbreviation of the term technical drawing). It could include drawings of close-up details of the garment. A tech drawing might also be called a flat or a flat sketch.

textile "Any product made from fibers" (Joseph, 1988, p. 347; see Chapter 3).

textile accessories and accents Includes a wide variety of textile products for bedding, bath, tabletop accessories, kitchen, and textile accents such as wall hangings, tapestries, quilts, needlework, and lace accents.

Textile/Apparel Linkage Council (TALC) Organization formed in 1986 to establish voluntary electronic data interchange standards between apparel manufacturers and textile companies. In 1994 it was integrated into the Quick Response Committee of the American Apparel Manufacturers Association.

Textile/Clothing Technology Corporation [TC][2] Non-profit corporation that develops, tests, and teaches advanced apparel technology.

textile converter see **converter.**

textile jobber Company that buys fabrics from textile mills, converters, and large manufacturers and then sells to smaller manufacturers and retailers.

textile mill Company that specializes in the fabric construction stage of production (e.g., weaving, knitting).

textile testing "Process of inspecting, measuring and evaluating characteristics and properties of textile materials" (Cohen, 1989, p. 165; see Chapter 3).

thread count Total number of yarns (warp plus weft) in one square inch of fabric.

throwsters Companies that modify filament yarns for specific end uses.

title flow see **ownership flow.**

toile A French term whose literal translation means cloth, it refers to the muslin trial or sample garment.

tolerance The stated range of acceptable dimensional measurements as a (+) or (-) in inches (or metric dimensions) from the size specifications.

top of the bed Home fashions products that includes comforters, duvet covers, blankets, bedspreads, dust ruffles, pillow shams, and throws.

trade association Non-profit association made up of member companies designed to research, promote, or provide educational services regarding an industry or a specific aspect of an industry.

trade dress Subset of trademark law, it protects the overall look or image of a product or the packaging of a product.

trade show Event sponsored by trade associations, apparel marts, and/or promotional companies, to allow companies to promote their newest products to prospective buyers who have the opportunity of reviewing new products of a number of companies under one roof.

trademark "Distinctive name, word, mark, design, or picture used by a company to identify its product" (Fisher & Jennings, 1991, p. 595; see Chapter 2).

trank The section of a glove that covers the palm and the face of the hand.

trend research Information on future directions of consumer behavior, color, fabrics, and fashion styling obtained by reading trade publications and/or fashion magazines, making observations, or other data collection methods.

trunk show Marketing strategy by which a company will bring an entire line to a retail store as a special event to show and sell to customers.

unit production system (UPS) Production system whereby the parts for each garment are transported on conveyors, one garment at a time, to the sewing operators who perform one or several sewing operations, then release the garment for transport to the next work station.

Universal Product Code (UPC) One of several bar-code symbologies used for electronic identification of merchandise. A UPC is a twelve-digit number that identifies the manufacturer and merchandise item by stock-keeping unit.

unlimited liability Situation in which owners of a company are personally liable for debts incurred by the business; often the case in sole proprietorships and in some partnerships.

upholstery fabrics Textile goods used primarily for sofas, love seats, chairs, and ottomans.

usage The number of yards (yardage) of fabric(s) required to make the garment style. It usually denotes the most economical layout to use the least amount of fabric.

vendor see **source**.

vendor-managed retail inventory Programs whereby retail sales/stockout data are reviewed by the manufacturer and replenishments are ordered as often as required.

vendor marking Affixing hangtags, labels, and price information to merchandise by the vendor (manufacturer).

vertical integration or **vertical marketing channel** Business strategy whereby a company handles several steps in production and/or distribution.

vertical marketing channel see **vertical integration**.

virtual draping Computer created simulation of a fabric draped three-dimensionally over an image of a garment as shown on a body or mannequin.

virtual samples Digital images of merchandise samples which are viewed on the computer screen.

Voluntary Interindustry Commerce Standards Association (VICS) Formed in 1986 as the Voluntary Interindustry Communication Standards Committee. It initially focused on Voluntary standards

for product and shipping container marking. The association has now expanded into standards for floor-ready merchandise and Internet commerce.

wall coverings Products such as textiles used to cover walls, vertical panels, and partitions.

warehouse retailer Retailer who reduces operating expenses and offers goods at discount prices by combining showroom, warehouse, and retail operations.

window treatments Draperies, curtains, and fabric shades as well as decorative treatments such as valances, cornices, and swags.

wholesale cost see **cost**.

wholesale price The price of the style that the retailer will pay the apparel manufacturer for the goods. The price is based on the manufacturer's cost to produce the style plus the manufacturer's profit.

wholesale price zone Designates a price range for the approximate wholesale cost of the merchandise produced by a manufacturer.

work-in-process (WIP) The quantity of goods in the process of assembly in the sewing factory at a given time.

yarn Collection of fibers or filaments laid or twisted together to form a continuous strand strong enough for use in fabrics.

zeitgeist The social spirit of the time of a popular culture during a specific time frame.

Index